PATTERNS OF GOVERNMENT

PATTERNS OF GOVERNMENT

The Major Political Systems of Europe

by SAMUEL H. BEER

ADAM B. ULAM

HARRY H. ECKSTEIN

HERBERT J. SPIRO

NICHOLAS WAHL

all of Harvard University

under the editorship of
Samuel H. Beer *and* Adam B. Ulam

RANDOM HOUSE   NEW YORK

CONTENTS

v

Contents

LIST OF TABLES

PREFACE

This is a time of great ferment in political science. The old search for a more scientific basis for the study of politics is being shaped by new ideas. The authors of this book are convinced that these new ideas should not be confined to the learned journal and the graduate seminar, but should be shared with undergraduates and indeed with students just beginning the study of politics.

In this book, therefore, we have tried to state and to use an explicit method of analysis. The essence of this method is that we look at the politics of each of the four countries as a system. A system—whether in political science or any other science—we take to be a set of interdependent variables. The basic variables, or patterns, in terms of which we have sought to identify, classify, and analyze political phenomena are four: political culture, power, interests, and policy. The task of Part One is to explain these terms and to illustrate briefly how they can be used. In each of the following sections, dealing respectively with Great Britain, France, Germany, and the Soviet Union, the method has been put to work. The test of any method of political analysis must be: Can it be used in the concrete tasks of inquiry? Does it provide a framework for comparing the politics of different countries—particularly those with radically different institutions? Does it suggest interesting problems? Does it direct attention to the basic elements in terms of which these problems may be solved? Does it suggest the possibilities of future development?

But if we have stressed a certain scientific method, we have by no means disdained the conventional virtues of the introductory textbook. If one is to describe a political system, one must generalize. The authors have sought to clarify and support their generalizations with as much concrete illustration as space permits. They have made a liberal use of history. They have described, sometimes in detail, elements of formal structure, such as laws and constitutional conventions. They have also devoted a great deal of space to the social and economic forces impinging on the given political system. Not only the facts of the constitutional and political structure but also their interplay with the economy and the general social structure are considered.

While factual, however, each account is selective in its use of facts. Each is concerned with a certain problem and evidence is mustered only insofar as it is relevant to a problem. This, we believe, is good scientific procedure. It means, however, that some practices and institutions that would normally be discussed in a textbook are passed over, while others are given relatively more attention.

What are these problems around which the authors have organized their analyses? Is there a single problem common to all? While each author has been free to choose the focus he believes will bring to light the questions of greatest importance to him, a common concern can, we believe, be traced through the whole book. Each author is centrally concerned with the problem of stability and instability. How well has the system stood the test of time? What are the forces that keep it working? What are those that tend to paralyze or disrupt it? And while the authors have not tried to predict, they have permitted themselves to raise the further question: Can the system last?

This book grew out of discussions among colleagues, all engaged in teaching political science at Harvard. We asked whether it might not be possible to write a textbook that not only had the "facts," but also presented them with a degree of scientific sophistication. So we talked, we argued, we wrote memoranda. Together we considered both the general approach of the book and how it might be worked out in the analysis of particular systems. These analyses were guided by our common outlook; in turn this outlook was developed in the light of the particular country accounts. We trust that the result of our experiment has merit. What we especially hope, however, is that it will communicate to the beginning student something of the spirit, the promise, and the excitement of the study of politics undertaken as a scientific discipline.

For this as for any textbook, acknowledgments due are legion. While all the authors have done original research in their respective fields, in this work they have been obliged, in the nature of the case, to rely very largely on the work of others. In the bibliographies, we have tried to acknowledge these large debts.

SAMUEL H. BEER

ADAM B. ULAM

PART ONE

THE ANALYSIS
OF POLITICAL
SYSTEMS

by Samuel H. Beer

CHAPTER 1

How Scientific Is
Political Science?

The study of government and politics is called political science. This may seem a little pretentious. Think of the other subjects that come to mind when we speak of "science"—physics, chemistry, biology and so on. Just what claim can our subject make to belong in this company? Is political science—or can it hope to be—really "scientific"?

When you start your first-year college course in chemistry, you are introduced fairly early to certain basic "laws." For example, your textbook will state and discuss the law of conservation of mass, i.e., that in a complete system, the total weight of substances undergoing change is constant. It will also explain the other laws stating weight relations in chemical reactions, such as the laws of definite composition, multiple proportion, and so on. These laws are broad generalizations based upon experiment and close observation of the facts in the laboratory and in nature. And we all recognize that one mark of a science is the effort by observation and, if possible, by experiment to arrive at such empirical generalizations. The political scientist may not expect to achieve the degree of precision and high probability of the laws of chemistry. But if he is truly scientific, he will do more than merely describe particular events. He will not be content with merely writing history. He will also look for uniformities of behavior and recurrent relationships and will try to generalize from this empirical basis.

But your chemistry textbook will not stop at the statement of empirical generalizations—even those as broad as the laws we have referred to above. From time to time it will also introduce theories—for instance, the atomic theory or the kinetic theory of gases. Of what use is a theory? One major use is that it *explains*. According to the atomic theory, for example, all elements are composed of atoms—minute, indivisible particles, all atoms

3

of the same element having identical properties and mass. Starting from this theory we can reason as follows: In a chemical process no atoms are created or destroyed; moreover no change in the mass of individual atoms can occur. Hence, there will be no change in the total weight of the system—a conclusion confirmed by the evidence summarized in the law of conservation of mass. And similarly from the theory we can reason to conclusions that are confirmed by the other basic laws. The atomic theory, by giving us a model or picture of the nature of matter, explains why substances have the properties described in the basic laws. Very briefly put, the law or empirical generalization states *what* happens; the theory explains *why*.

No less important is the power of theory to suggest questions for further research. From a theory we may be able to deduce certain conclusions about how things ought to behave. These hypotheses we then check against the facts by further observation and experiment. Fruitful research in science often proceeds in this way. The scientist working from the implications of a theory—or perhaps only from an educated hunch—so organizes his research as to confirm or disconfirm a hypothesis. He does not plunge blindly into the facts, hoping that random observation and experiment will thrust significant generalizations on him—although occasionally they do. The mere collection of facts is not science. And one of the criticisms of much political science today is that it is "hyper-factual": masses of data are collected, studies are made of this or that election or legislative decision, but rarely is an effort made so to organize the data as to check some important hypothesis or fill out a promising theory. In physics, chemistry, and biology, nature is interrogated; questions are put to the facts. The political scientist should do likewise with his material.

These then are some of the leading traits of a science: the checking of all statements directly or indirectly against the facts; generalization from observation and, if possible, experiment; a search for theories that will explain empirical generalizations and suggest hypotheses for further research.

What chance is there that political science can fruitfully use this method? What hope that it can become a science in this sense of the word?

The first thing that needs to be said is that, quite apart from what we may hope to get done in the future, our present accomplishments are far from negligible. Political science is not, nor should we try to make it, an exact image of physics or chemistry. We need not expect that the propositions of political science are ever likely to achieve the precision and probability of the laws of chemistry and physics. (Parenthetically we may note that many of these laws are no longer regarded as having the exactitude and invariability they were once considered to have.) Indeed, in the subject matter of politics there seems to be an element of "pure history"—of the unique, the non-recurrent, the purely individual—that cannot be reduced to general law. Yet at the same time, politics, like other fields of social behavior, reveals important uniformities and recurrent patterns—as any elementary textbook in political science will show.

As has often been pointed out, for instance, the prediction that there will be a presidential election in the United States every four years has a degree of probability that compares not at all badly with the probability of natural scientists' predictions. We know that if the British Cabinet is defeated on a vote of confidence, it will either resign or dissolve Parliament—and again we can refer to a multitude of cases that confirm this generalization. Like the periodicity of presidential elections, this uniformity depends on a rule of a constitution; both are matters of law, or of convention approaching the force of law. Much of political science has always been, and must be, concerned with such formal structure. Political behavior can rarely be described or understood without reference to these formal elements. But, of course, political science is also concerned with patterns of behavior not directly dictated by law or convention. The instability of French cabinets, for instance, while not depending upon a rule of formal structure, is a central uniformity of French republican government. And the prediction that a given cabinet in that country will not last more than six months is hardly more of a gamble than, say, the forecasts of the weatherman. Indeed textbooks on government and politics, such as the present volume, could not be written unless political scientists had built up a very considerable body of generalized knowledge about various political systems. There are patterns of government; therefore, we can generalize.

So it appears that we need not be excessively humble about what political science has achieved. Yet the present is a time of sharp self-criticism among political scientists. It is widely felt that much could be done to make our subject a still more scientific discipline. This is not a new desire. It goes back at least to Francis Bacon, who was as much interested in applying scientific method to the study of politics as to the study of nature. Perhaps indeed it goes back to Aristotle. But recent thinking has brought out new and promising ways of looking at old problems.

Two principal criticisms that have been stressed are, first, that political scientists have not made clear what their subject matter is, and, second, that they have not given enough attention to theory. One purpose of this book is to raise these questions and to suggest how they might be dealt with—and to do this not merely in an abstract discussion, but in the course of the study of four systems of government. That is half the battle:

not merely to state a more fruitful method of analysis, but actually to put it to work in empirical study.

To say that we ought to make clear the nature of our subject matter may seem to raise an idle problem of definition. What is politics? What is government? What is a political system? Surely, we can waste a good deal of time on these questions that might be better spent on the study of political behavior and actual systems of government. Yet writing a book on comparative government, such as the present one, can hardly fail to force these basic questions on us. We say that we are studying the political system of Soviet Russia, as well as those of Britain, France, and West Germany. But what does Communist Russia have in common with the other three countries that justifies our saying that each has a political system? We find "politics" and "government" in all four countries: in all of them there is something the same that makes them comparable and justifies their being studied in one book. Only if there are elements of sameness can we go on to show significant differences. What are these elements of sameness? What are the main features of any political system?

Political scientists, as we claimed above, have built up a large body of generalized knowledge about particular political systems. But they have tended to be uncritical of the terms in which they conduct their inquiries —of the headings under which they order their material. Suppose, for instance, that the present volume were concerned only with the three democratic countries—Britain, France, and West Germany. We might then be content to examine them under such headings as the system of parties, the representative legislature, the responsible executive, and so on. And certainly analysis along these lines would tell us a good deal worth knowing. But of what use are these terms, these headings, when we come to Russia? There is no system of parties in Russia. And while there is an organization—the Communist Party—that calls itself a "party," it could well be argued that this organization is essentially a weapon of control for the dictatorship—more like a police department than what the West calls a party. Likewise, do we find a legislature and an executive in Russia? The Supreme Soviet is called the legislature, but surely it would be misleading and a waste of time to compare this body with, say, the House of Commons or the French National Assembly and to give it the kind of attention we give these truly legislative bodies. In short, the headings under which we have classified our knowledge of the three democratic countries would, if followed in the study of Russia, direct our attention to nothing at all or to bodies virtually without power.

Perhaps that last word "power" is the key. We study the House of Commons and the French National Assembly because they have power. If we follow this clue in our study of Russia, we shall brush past the

Supreme Soviet and track down the source of effective power, which lies almost entirely outside such bodies and within certain higher organs of the Communist Party and of the military and civil bureaucracy. Here we find a set of persons and organs that regularly make the major decisions of Russian policy. Here is the heart of the pattern of power in the Soviet Union. And power to make decisions on policy is something we find in all four countries.

Now, one could argue—and some political scientists do—that power is the central concept of political science and that the pattern of effective power is the main, and indeed the sole, heading under which we should classify our material. In this book each writer is greatly concerned with the process by which policy decisions are made and tries to describe in general terms *the pattern of power* displayed by this process in each case. Yet by a political system they mean something more than a pattern of power. For they are interested not only in *how* decisions are made, but also in *what* decisions are made. Putting the matter very broadly, they are interested in purpose as well as power. And this concern directs attention to two other facets of a political system: *the pattern of interests* and *the pattern of policy*.

The content of policy decisions will depend upon the aims pursued by individuals and groups with power. A political system, such as the Russian, may not have a system of parties, but it is bound to include individuals and groups that are seeking to promote or prevent the adoption of certain policies. We think of the peasant's desperate resistance to collectivization or of the recent struggle in the party Presidium over the production of more or fewer consumers' goods. Whether a system is democratic or dictatorial, one aspect of it will be such a pattern of interests. It is from the interplay of these two patterns—of interests and power—that policy emerges. And by policy we mean not simply the basic decisions themselves —the laws, cabinet decrees, and so on—but also their impact. The pattern of policy includes the content of particular policies—collectivization in Russia, the farm program in Britain, industrial regulation in Germany, the Monnet Plan in France—and their consequences for the society and, above all, for the political system itself.

Power, interests, and policy—these are three broad headings under which we can order our material. A fourth heading to which we attach particular importance is *political culture*. Precisely what we mean by political culture and the role it plays in a political system we shall try to explain below. Here it may be worthwhile to put our point briefly and in general terms. For in developing this conception we have tried to do something to meet the criticism that political science has neglected theory.

We stress political culture because we are concerned with the context of values and beliefs within which political conflict takes place. Politics within a nation, as between nations, is conflict, struggle, sometimes war. This, to be honest, is one reason that politics is exciting: both to those who study it and to those who take part. Every day in our own country we witness—and perhaps share in—these struggles. We see the immediate questions at issue: taxes, pensions, property rights, civil liberties and so on. We see something of the means by which an individual, group, or party seeks victory: the clever use of publicity, the mustering of voters, the organizing of campaigns of pressure. As students of politics, we seek also to penetrate behind immediate events and trace these conflicting interests and different bases of power to underlying causes. And often we can find an explanation in the economy or social structure—in the distribution of wealth, the massive organization of a labor movement, the impact of depression on industry. Such factors in the environment of political conflict can tell us a great deal about the everyday conflicts of politics: why a new interest has arisen, why one group rather than another has a greater influence on policy.

The factor that we call political culture will also be of the first importance. For the political values and beliefs of a people are also a part of the context in which the immediate political struggle takes place. And the character of these values and beliefs will have great bearing upon the fortunes of the political system as a whole: whether it is stable or unstable; whether it is capable of gradual and orderly development or is caught in a paralyzing stalemate; whether the political struggle is kept within bounds or bursts forth in self-destroying excess.

2

The Balance of Power Theory

We can see the cutting edge of this approach, this theory, if we contrast it with an opposing view—the "balance of power" theory. Briefly stated, this is the notion that we can explain the actions of groups and their interrelations simply in terms of a balancing of power and an adjusting of interests. While this approach can be followed in the study of politics within a nation, it is most familiar as a way of looking at international relations. A stable international order, it is sometimes said, depends upon a balance of power among nations, such as that existing in Europe in the nineteenth century after the Napoleonic Wars. In this kind of situation, each nation possesses territory, arms, wealth, and other elements of power in such relation to other nations as to lead it to believe that any attempt to increase its power will be met by a superior combination among the others. As a result each accepts its place in the international pattern of power. And in accord with this balance the various conflicting interests of the nations are adjusted, those with greater power realizing their goals more fully, but not so far as to throw the balance out of line. Such a model presupposes no common ethical standards restraining the means that nations will use to get their way, or defining the ends that they may pursue. Why not approach in the same way the relations of contending groups within a nation and so explain the decision-making process and the general stability or instability of the system?

Right off we must emphasize—and we shall come back to this point— that the balance of power theory does indeed explain a great deal about both international relations and the relations of groups within a nation. The trouble with it is that it is grossly one-sided. It directs attention to only one aspect of the facts. For it is a matter of fact that during periods of international stability nations normally do share important political values and beliefs. Among the nations of nineteenth-century Europe there was substantial, if not complete, consensus on the means and ends of international politics. Certain methods of settling disputes were deemed effective and right—for example, established diplomatic procedures, frequent meetings of great powers, the use of arbitration, the making and keeping of treaties. And even when violence did break out there were laws and conventions of war that enjoyed some respect. But perhaps more important was the consensus on ends. The nation-state, for example, was widely accepted as the proper unit of government, and while wars often led to annexations, they did not normally involve the destruction of the defeated nation or its absorption by the conqueror. Conflict was sharp; differences were real. But in the background powerful ties of community undergirded the international order. Precisely because these massive forces in the political culture of Europe did their silent work so well, thinkers of the time could sometimes forget them and imagine that the peace rested solely upon a balance of power.

Today we see all the more clearly these forces and appreciate their role in the nineteenth-century world because they are lacking in our own. Peace between the Communist bloc and the West depends upon a balance of power and on little else. Accordingly we have not peace, but at the best "cold war." The contrast with Victorian Europe could hardly be more striking. Then a defeat in war meant an indemnity, the loss of a border province, a lessened influence among the Great Powers. Today it may mean the total extinction of the conquered nation. Where there is no cultural community, peace is as tenuous as the prospect of defeat for either side is unbearable.

In the politics of a nation as in politics between nations, the patterns of power and interest will be conditioned by political values and beliefs. For stability in a political system we can rely neither upon a mere balance of power nor upon a natural harmony of interests. Some degree of consensus is indispensable. Indeed, the deeper and wider the consensus, the less likely are its values and beliefs to be explicitly stated. In politics, as in other spheres, people concentrate their attention on the immediate, practical questions precisely when they are agreed on the great issues. A pragmatic "interest"-oriented politics bespeaks a political system founded on consensus.

Revolutionary forces may, however, disrupt a political order. To stress the role of political culture is by no means to imply that in every system consensus will reign. Any political culture will be strained by some internal inconsistencies and from them will flow consequences for behavior. Radical dissensus, like the division of the world in the cold war, will continually menace the stability of the system. Where political values are radically opposed to one another, the legal framework of government, far from reflecting a common ideal, will be more in the nature of a treaty between enemy nations. Interests will be so conditioned by opposing cultural currents as to make their adjustment difficult or impossible. To the observer from a country blessed with consensus, such conflicts may seem very foolish indeed. "Objectively" the same interests are in conflict as in his own system. But there, adjustment and reasonable compromise are accepted by groups in conflict, while in a system divided on basic ideals, compromise appears only as injustice to be again attacked after a brief armistice.

Political culture is by no means the sole determinant of group behavior or of the various patterns of power, interest, and policy in a political system. We have suggested that other elements are also important by noting that the balance of power model is a useful concept in political analysis. The authors do not approach their task from the premises of cultural determinism or idealist sociology. They do insist, however, that the integrating—or disintegrating—effects of political values and beliefs are a major problem for the political scientist.

CHAPTER 3

Political Culture

In political science, as in any social science, we begin with individuals—actual men and women going about the business of politics. The unit that is the individual is unique. There is something about it making it unlike any other. In human beings this distinctive something may be so striking and powerful that we call it genius; or it may be one of the amiable peculiarities that enable us to tell one friend from another. If we are to understand politics, we cannot rule out individuality, whether it expresses itself in the works of great men or in the sum of effects produced by the eccentricity and originality of many ordinary people. But for all their individuality, people also have much in common. They share a common human nature—certain emotional drives, intellectual capacities, and moral tendencies. As we find it in any particular society, however, this common human nature expresses itself in certain values, beliefs, and emotional attitudes, which, with greater or lesser modification, are passed on by instruction or imitation from one generation to the next. These we call the culture of the society.

Certain aspects of the general culture of a society are especially concerned with *how* government ought to be conducted and *what* it should try to do. This sector of culture we call political culture. As with the general culture of a society, the principal components of the political culture are *values*, *beliefs*, and *emotional attitudes*. In turn, within each of these we can distinguish between elements that emphasize means and those that emphasize ends—between *conceptions of authority* and *conceptions of purpose*.

Political Values: Conceptions of Authority

What do we mean by a conception of authority? There is nothing abstruse or difficult about the idea and we can readily illustrate it from our everyday knowledge of our own country. In the United States certain

12

general notions of how our government ought to be conducted are spread fairly widely throughout society. This does not mean that most people have retained from their high school civics course an exact idea of the constitutional powers and relations of Federal and State governments, or of Congress, the Presidency, and the Supreme Court. But the great bulk of Americans do share certain political ideals: that there should be elections at stated intervals for legislative and various executive offices, that elected officials should have the determining voice in making laws and public policy, that power should be divided between states and nation and at each level among various branches. We say that in general people believe that our system ought to be democratic, federal, and constitutional —although many might not use these words or be able to define them. These words, however, refer to elements of the American political tradition. With notable exceptions—such as the Civil War—this tradition has been shared by most people in this country. And in the light of it, the analyst of our political system today can explain much of the behavior of voters, officeholders, parties, and other groups. Thinking of this tradition as a present and living influence on our political behavior, we refer to it as the political culture of the American system.

Looking more closely at this tradition, we see that one major part consists of certain standards, certain norms, of *how* decisions ought to be made and carried out. It is concerned with means, rather than ends; with the methods and procedures by which decisions are made rather than the contents or purposes of decisions. These norms define, for instance, how officeholders should be chosen and the procedures they should follow in making policy. The decisions of an officeholder chosen in a rigged election or of a legislature bought up by bribery may be obeyed, but—so far as the public knows the facts—these decisions will tend to lack the moral sanction attaching to decisions that have been properly made by properly chosen officials. Quite apart from whether the policy is good or bad, people want also to know whether it was made in the right—the authoritative— way. Such procedural norms comprise our conception of authority and because we believe that by and large these norms are followed when policy decisions are made we accept these decisions as having authority.

It is of the essence that these norms have moral force. Authority is a moral quality making commands issued in accord with its norms morally binding upon those accepting these norms. It is one reason for obedience. Authority, however, is only one of various factors that may account for obedience. Physical force cannot be wholly left out of account. Indeed, in some political systems—for example, Russian-occupied Hungary—obedience is rendered primarily out of fear of physical violence and other forms of coercion. But even in these cases we may well find that the ruling group itself—such as the elite of the Communist Party—is bound together by an ideology that includes a conception of how this group itself is to be governed. In his account of the Soviet system, Dr. Ulam examines this problem, showing how the Leninist doctrine of the role of the Communist Party and its governing bodies has developed into a conception of authority accepted by wide sectors of the Soviet elite. Whatever we may say about the relations of the Soviet ruling classes with the rest of the nation, we cannot credit force alone with the acceptance of decisions within these ruling classes themselves. They accept the dictatorship in some measure because they hold it to be legitimate.

Sheer habit and unthinking custom will normally also be a powerful support of a regime. So also will the dictates of self-interest: to find your own welfare bound up with a certain system of government is a reason for supporting that system, although it is hardly sufficient alone to explain why men endure all the burdens that government commonly inflicts on them. But beyond such further supporting factors—force, custom, self-interest—a widely shared conception of authority will enhance the stability of a political system.

Common knowledge of our own country illustrates what we mean by the term. The Soviet example reminds us how radically other people's ideals of authority may differ from our own. The primitive tribe, the Greek *polis*, the Roman Empire, the medieval *regnum*, the modern nation-state, the totalitarian dictatorship, suggest the enormous variety we may find in political cultures and in people's ways of conceiving the rights and duties of rulers and ruled. In some systems authority is highly personal and traditionalist, legitimate power being vested in certain families and rigidly restricted in its manner of exercise by unchangeable custom. In contrast, our own and most modern Western systems vest authority in an impersonal structure of bodies and procedures, defined in general terms and distinguishing sharply between the person and the office he holds. Sometimes we find consensus within a system. But the values embodied in a political culture and expressed in its norms are not always harmonious with one another: we think, for instance, of the unsolved conflict of the Middle Ages over the respective authority of the temporal and spiritual powers.

In the study of these various ideals of authority and the conflicts within political cultures, the history of political philosophy may be a great help: Plato for Greece, Cicero for Rome, Hooker for Tudor England, John Locke for early America, Lenin for Soviet Russia, and so on. But as these illustrations immediately suggest, political philosophers are often not entirely accurate guides to the really operative ideal or ideals of authority in a political system. The noblest speculations may be of little use to our inquiry. For what we are concerned with are the cultural forces that actually guide and shape the choices of people in everyday political life.

Our inquiry is into operative ideals. It follows that we cannot be satisfied with merely legal definitions. The constitutional laws and conventions of a system will often be a helpful guide to the conception (or conceptions) of authority of that system. But what we are interested in, so to speak, lies behind these laws and conventions. It may go beyond them; it may even be in conflict with them. As we shall have occasion to point out from time to time in the course of this book, constitutional law—the law laying down the frame of government—does not have the same status and function in each system. In any particular case we cannot presume without inquiry that it faithfully portrays the dominant conception of authority.

The American example itself shows how far the norms of authority may go beyond the requirements formally imposed by law. Our democratic ideal, for instance, requires that major decisions be made only after opportunity for wide discussion and criticism. If, therefore, a legislative majority uses its power to stifle debate and prevent adequate discussion in the assembly, we feel that it has acted improperly, even though legally. We like to think that electoral contests are determined in some degree by rational discussion of candidates and issues—we speak of them as "debates." Hence, we feel that the influence of money on elections may at some point become excessive. Indeed, it is because we first believe this influence to be improper that we take up the question of making a law to restrict it. Putting the matter briefly, we may say that the American ideal of authority requires that, on the whole, decisions should be made only after free and rational debate by people sincerely aiming at the common good. This ideal is expressed partly—but only partly—in law. Much of it is a matter of political ethics, externally sanctioned only by the diffuse rewards and penalties of public esteem.

Conceptions of authority differ not only from place to place, but also from time to time within the history of the same community. We speak of *the* American conception of authority, and no doubt in some respects that conception is the same today as in 1776. Yet in others it has profoundly changed. In the beginning we were not, as a people, committed to democracy. The extent of the suffrage was for long an issue of our politics—and with regard to the right of Negroes to vote in the Deep South it is still an issue today. Or to take a matter of lesser importance: we know that the founders of this country regarded political parties with suspicion and hostility. Madison spoke of them as "factions" and while he did not think they could be eliminated from politics, he sought means to nullify their effects. In time Americans came to take a more tolerant view and today they regard political parties as legitimate and valuable parts of the governmental process. British attitudes have gone through a similar evolution. Indeed, the common view in Britain today gives to parties far greater importance than they enjoy in the United States. We still entertain a certain suspicion of party—"independence" in a voter or in a Congressman is to be praised—and would regard as "bossism" the centralized control and discipline that the British tolerate and expect. To them two tightly knit and strongly led parties are indispensable to meaningful elections and the proper conduct of government. In these contrasting attitudes toward party we find an important difference in the ideals of authority of the two countries—a contrast, it hardly need be said, that makes a great difference to the ways the two political systems actually work.

Political Values: Conceptions of Purpose

Rarely, if ever, will people accept a conception of authority without also entertaining some idea of what that authority is to be used for. Our ordinary use of the term "constitution" suggests this fact: a constitution is taken to mean, on the one hand, the structure by which authoritative decisions are made and executed and, on the other, an indication of what purposes these decisions are to serve. In our own political tradition, these purposes include such objects as the preservation of private property, freedom of speech, defense against external enemies—the preamble to the Federal constitution gives a familiar enumeration.

To put the matter broadly, we may say that the political culture of the United States includes both procedural and substantive values. It includes standards setting out the broad procedures that are to govern the way policy is made and executed—our ideal of authority. At the same time it includes certain notions of the common good with which the substance of public policy should be in accord. Like our conception of authority, these ideals of common purpose have moral force. Policy that we believe to be in accord with these ideals will receive support for this reason as well as for reasons of self-interest and custom; and government action cannot for long radically violate these values without endangering the stability of our system. This does not mean that all Americans are perfectly agreed upon the proper scope and subject of government action. The stakes for which parties and politicians contend in "the great game of politics" are often high. Still the figure of speech is apt: American politics is not war, but a game, hedged in and moderated by massive consensus on means and ends.

Like conceptions of authority, the common purposes of political systems range through many different possibilities. The drive for booty of warrior kingdoms; the traditional social values of the *ancien régime*; the mission of empire of Victorian Britain; the millenary hopes of revolutionary governments—these too were purposes that the members of these political systems accepted in greater or lesser degree and that the actions of governments—tribal, royal, aristocratic or popular—were expected to serve.

Finally, we must stress that the presence of consensus on common purpose at any time in the history of a political system by no means excludes the possibility of change and development of such conceptions of common purpose as of authority. Our own history illustrates the point. Like our ideas of the proper extent of the suffrage, our ideas of the proper objects of government policy have altered. We have decided, through civil war, that we no longer would accept the maintenance of Negro slavery as an element in our national purpose. Other changes have been less violent. The general expectation today that government is responsible for maintaining a high level of employment marks a substantial change in our notion of the proper goals of public policy. The consensus on *laissez faire* of a few decades ago has shifted to a new consensus that includes a limited acceptance of the welfare state. In Britain, as Dr. Eckstein shows, a more radical shift in this direction has taken place. In both cases, the development in political culture, while avoiding violence, passed through a state of sharp conflict before reaching a new consensus.

In describing the conceptions of authority and purpose of a system, how far should we go toward including particular institutions and policies? How abstract or generalized will such conceptions be? To this there can be no single answer. The values of the traditionalist system are highly particular. In both procedure and substance they lean on the past for standards of what is proper and legitimate. And these standards form not a generalized, but an exact, particular image of the past. The reigning values are embedded in rigid and specific practice; hence, to change even what we might regard as a detail is to threaten a violation of common ideals. On the other hand, in rationalist systems, values are more general, admitting different interpretations and divergent applications to specific cases. This is an important fact when we examine the conditions that permit political conflict to take place without danger to the survival of a system. Where values take a more generalized form, different interpretations will legitimately and indeed inevitably arise. Yet the conflicts that result need not disrupt consensus on the fundamentals of the system.

By and large such a generalizing and rationalizing of political values is a necessary condition for the emergence of modern democratic parties. Because American political values, for instance, are of this sort, two parties can differ over such questions as the powers of the President or the level of farm price supports while agreeing on the fundamentals of American constitutional democracy. Even in times of far sharper political strife—as during the New Deal period—a plane on which consensus prevailed could be found in the American system. Dr. Eckstein maintains that the same has been true in Britain, even when we find "capitalism" and "socialism" in conflict.

Perhaps in some systems the distinction between conceptions of authority and conceptions of purpose is hardly worth making. In the traditionalist system, for instance, the very idea that laws can be deliberately "made" is alien. Laws rather are "declared" on the basis of what has always been done and accepted in the past. The ideal of procedure itself rigidly restricts the substance of law. But in the more rationalist system, there is a greater likelihood that procedural standards may be satisfied only at the cost of substantive ones—or vice versa. In constitutional governments during wartime, for instance, there may be a strain between the need for rapid and forceful government action and the expectation that the authoritative but slow-moving procedures of the system will be respected. A similar problem may arise in peacetime, as Dr. Eckstein brings out in his discussion of British policy since World War II. New policies were adopted, but old and accepted modes of procedure made it difficult to devise new machinery of government appropriate to the new policies.

Problems such as these are likely to arise in the strongly "constitutionalist" systems in which the dominant political values give high priority to established procedures. Other political cultures may develop so great a stress upon purpose that the norms of procedure cannot stand against the needs of policy. Something of the sort has happened in Soviet Russia. Lenin's notion of "democratic centralism," while providing a foundation for dictatorship, did retain some vestiges of democratic control within the Communist Party. But, perhaps from the very start of the Soviet regime, the drive to industrialize and to banish Russian backwardness has had a far higher priority, as a national purpose, than "democratic centralism." Thus the pre-eminence of the economic drive contributed to the erosion of the remnants of democratic control that Lenin's doctrine had allowed.

Belief Systems

So far we have spoken of conceptions of authority and purpose as if they included only values, i.e., standards of right and wrong in political conduct and definitions of good and bad in the goals of public policy. But as the discussion must have suggested, these conceptions include not only values about what "ought" to be, but also beliefs about what "is"; not only normative propositions, but also existential propositions. Closely linked with the values of authority and purpose we find beliefs about the actual behavior of men and societies.

We can illustrate the distinction and the connection by looking at the democratic ideal as it is conceived in America and Western Europe. This ideal includes certain norms, such as that the adult population of a country has the right and duty to take part in political discussion and electoral decisions. But this ideal also includes the *belief* that ordinary people, on the whole, have the capacity to take part in politics with some degree of rationality. To say that most men are rational is not the same as saying that they ought to have the vote. Yet both are essentials of the democratic conception of authority. And if, for instance, it became widely believed that most voters were not rational, adherence to the democratic norm would be severely shaken. The democratic ideal includes both the norm of wide popular participation and the belief in the rationality of the common man.

Similarly, conceptions of purpose have a normative and an existential side. The ideal of *laissez faire,* for instance, was supported by an elaborate ethical theory inhibiting governments from interfering with private property and freedom of contract. John Locke gave this ethical theory a classic statement that was echoed by other writers in the eighteenth and nineteenth centuries. But support for *laissez faire* also derived from the economic theory that we think of as originating with Adam Smith. In its own terms this economic theory was primarily descriptive and analytical, not ethical. Yet as a demonstration that the wealth of the nation would be increased by a hands-off policy, it lent powerful support to the prohibitions of the Lockean ethic. Again, in the decline of the ideal of *laissez faire* we may distinguish these two aspects. As Dr. Eckstein shows, the welfare state in Britain has been advocated and justified on the grounds of ethical theories that broke with the rugged individualism of the nineteenth century. But its growth and acceptance was also immensely forwarded by the Keynesian "revolution" in economics. Today in Britain government intervention to maintain employment is accepted not only on ethical grounds, but also on the grounds of the new, Keynesian economic beliefs that have spread widely through British society.

Of what use is this distinction to political analysis? One use is that it often helps us to see what is at issue in political conflicts. What at first sight looks like a clash of values may turn out on closer inspection to be mainly a disagreement over the facts. In the debates over the extension of the franchise in America and Europe in the early nineteenth century, for instance, both sides often agreed that in principle all men subject to a government ought to have the right to participate in it. Some of those who accepted this principle, however, rejected manhood suffrage and defended a property qualification for voting on practical grounds. They contended that in practice men without property could not be trusted to respect the property of others, or, what might be still worse, would be overly subject to the influence of wealth. Macaulay argued much along these lines in opposition to a democratic suffrage in Britain, although he granted that his argument did not apply with the same force in America. Apart from unspoken reasons that participants in the controversy may have entertained, the dispute was essentially a matter of fact: What is your view of human nature, and especially your view of the tendencies of unpropertied men in Britain or America at a particular time? Similarly, the controversies today over more or less government intervention in the economy are only in part conflicts between opposing ethical principles—such as "human rights" versus "property rights." Much of the difference lies in differing views of the long-run effects of government intervention. The controversy is not so much over the "rights" of property as over the question whether government control is actually "the road to serfdom."

Where political conflict is essentially one of values, a reconciliation by rational argument is far more difficult. However, if the issue is a question of fact, there is hope that an appeal to the evidence and to the reasoned outcome of factual inquiry may bring together the parties in conflict. Such a conciliating function is not a primary role of the political scientist, but the distinction between value and belief suggests a hypothesis that may help him understand change and development. Without trying to state the proposition as a general rule, we may say that in modern Western societies belief systems seem to be more easily subject to change than do value systems. Not only science in the technical sense, but also systematic thought and research in general have become widespread activities, highly institutionalized and continually producing and spreading new knowledge. Moreover, the members of these societies have grown accustomed to accept and act on such new knowledge—consider, for example, the swift impact new medical discoveries such as polio vaccine have had on behavior. At times, of course, new knowledge may affect important values in the political culture. It may undermine old beliefs on which old values depend, causing severe tensions as individuals and groups accept the new beliefs, yet cling to old values. Ultimately, the force of the new beliefs may compel an adaptation of values. Racial discrimination, for instance, has depended in part upon a belief that certain races were inferior. Since biology has exploded this belief, people accustomed to accepting new knowledge validated by science can no longer entertain it. In time we may hope the old norms of racial discrimination will be altered by the new beliefs.

Distinguishing beliefs from values also helps the student of politics to identify ways in which the political culture of a system is related to the general culture of the society. Ideas that do not appear at first glance to have relevance to politics may be intimately connected with it through the belief systems of the political culture. Christian theology is not primarily concerned with political man. Yet its various forms, within both the Catholic and Protestant traditions, have frequently provided the foundation for political beliefs. We think, for instance, of the role of Calvinism in the contending political theories and civil wars of Europe in the sixteenth and seventeenth centuries. Likewise, the democratic ideal, especially in the form in which it spread throughout Europe in the late eighteenth and early nineteenth centuries, appeared as the political expression of the large and complex system of thought elaborated by the philosophers of the Enlightenment and was intimately associated with beliefs in progress, science, and human perfectibility. In general, the beliefs and values of a political culture are aspects of a world-outlook in the development of which we may find the origins of changes in the patterns of the political system.

While it is right to make the distinction, it is hardly less important to recognize how hard it may be to separate values from beliefs in the actual course of inquiry. In some elements of political culture the two may seem inextricably intertwined. *Laissez-faire* economics—to return to a former example—was on its face a "value-free" analysis of how an economy actually would operate. Yet no one can read the classical economists of the nineteenth century without sensing the potent judgments of what was right in conduct and what was desirable as goals of policy. The very overriding concern with the increase in national wealth reflected such a judgment of value. A different concern—say, with non-economic goals and conditions—would have led to a quite different social analysis.

Often sociologists use the term "ideology" to refer to belief systems that have such a bias derived from value-judgments. One of the most striking examples of ideology in this sense is Marxism-Leninism. This system of thought purports to be an objective, indeed a scientific, description and analysis of the development of society. Yet, obviously, the whole corpus of these writings is loaded with moral exhortation. Hence, the political culture of the ruling classes of Soviet Russia has a dual aspect. On the one hand, it is Marxism-Leninism as a system of belief that interprets the course of world history, specifically laying down as a matter of fact that Russian society will be led through the present stage of socialism by the Communist Party acting as the vanguard of the proletariat. In itself this belief does not state what "ought" to happen or what anyone "ought" to do. Yet in fact Marxist-Leninist ideology in Soviet Russia today embraces political values endowing the Communist leaders with authority and their policies with the sanction of common purpose.

Emotional Attitudes and Symbolism

One of Edmund Burke's lasting insights was his perception that a purely intellectual and ethical commitment to a theory of government is not enough to ensure political stability. He condemned the "barbarous philosophy" of the French Revolution because in it "nothing is left which engages the affections on the part of the commonwealth." Yet, he contended, without such a basis in emotion, the laws of a country are weakly founded, being "supported only by their own terrors, and by the concern which each individual may find in them from his own private speculation or can spare to them from his own private interests." Sharply aware of the role of emotional forces in politics, political scientists today would agree with Burke's emphasis and would stress the symbols and symbolic acts by which emotions favorable or hostile to a system are excited and by which leaders seek to manipulate the behavior of the masses. These symbols we may call *expressive symbols* in order to indicate the fact that they refer to emotional attitudes and feelings. Symbols may also, of course, refer to political values and beliefs—they may be evaluative and cognitive as well as expressive. But what we are interested in here is the symbolism that gets at the emotional side of politics. The role of the political emotions in the stability of a system can hardly be exaggerated: we think of the deep, unreasoning ties of patriotism and the support they lend to the common values and beliefs of a polity.

Underlying this subject is a general problem of social psychology—the problem of motivation. In particular there is the question of how values are geared into motives—how ideas of what is worthwhile as an object of individual achievement as well as ideas of moral rights and duties can themselves become needs enlisting the energies of the human organism. Sociologists and social psychologists discuss this problem as part of the complex process of "socialization" through which in earliest childhood the basic values of a culture are transferred to the motivation of individuals. We are concerned here, however, not with this, but with a related process by which political values are strengthened and reinforced by expressive symbolism.

Obvious examples of expressive symbols in politics are flags, anthems, national monuments, and the like. Persons too may become symbols. The British monarch is the key figure in the ceremonial institutions of Britain, symbolizing and keeping alive those pre-democratic attitudes that Dr. Eckstein finds to be of central importance in British government. Party leaders—totalitarian or democratic—may perform similar functions, like the legends of a people's history, speaking to the emotions and continually re-creating the attitudes from which political action flows.

The particular things or persons that become symbolic, however, need to be seen in the context of action in which they are used. We recognize the function of public ceremony in strengthening political solidarity— occasions such as the Fourth of July in the United States, Bastille Day in France, a coronation or opening of Parliament in Britain, as well as the mass demonstrations of the Soviet May Day, or the Nuremberg rallies under the Nazis. On such occasions emotional commitment to a regime may be, so to speak, acted out and at the same time revived and rein- forced. While external objects, such as flags and monuments, will be used symbolically, the essential symbolism lies in the collective action of the people as they take part in the ceremony. Such action will not, of course, always be favorable to the regime. Parties as well as regimes have their particular symbolisms and if they are revolutionary, their gatherings and acts of symbolism will express this fact—we think, for instance, of the clenched fist salute of the Communists.

Such special occasions when action is wholly or largely ceremonial are normally only a small part of the expressive symbolism of a political sys- tem. Throughout the whole vast process of everyday politics, action has an expressive as well as an instrumental aspect and we need to consider this emotional side of political action and discourse if we are to under- stand the forces making for the stability or development of a system. When, for instance, a member rises in his place in the House of Commons and puts his question to a Minister at Question Time, he is seeking, say, to bring out some error of administration or to show the superiority of his party's position or to demonstrate his own dialectical ability. This is the instrumental aspect of his action. At the same time, however, this act of participation expresses an attitude toward the House, an attitude of ac- ceptance and identification. Apart from its instrumental effects, the daily participation of members expresses and heightens their emotional com- mitment to the system, strengthening their trust in one another and also the hold of the system over them.

It is essential, of course, that these acts conform to "the House of Com- mons manner." Speakers must be at least ostensibly courteous, the tone of discourse conversational, not oratorical, and the whole style of behavior and speech conforming not only to the rules of procedure of the House, but also to a complex and largely unspoken set of conventions producing the "tone and temper" of the proceedings which Dr. Eckstein emphasizes. This style is no insignificant aspect of the political process. Unspoken though its criteria may be, they constitute a rigorous discipline and perform an important function. It is a rule of rhetoric that style must fit content if there is to be effective communication. The same holds for political speech. How can you, for instance, call for a revolution and echo the cries of a distressed proletariat when standing in a back row without a table to pound or a tribunal to orate from and bound to speak of your class-enemy as "the Right Honorable gentleman"—and all in the tone of drawing-room conversation? You could, of course, say the words of such a message, but restricted by such a style, how could you make it reach the emotions of your audience in Parliament or outside? It is no wonder that, as Aneurin Bevan remarked, the House of Commons "softens the acerbities of class feeling."

If political action is to be effective, if it is to get results among those to whom it is directed, it must arouse emotions appropriate to the conduct it aims to produce. But the style of British politics, not only in the House of Commons, but also generally, is not likely to touch off revolutionary zeal. On the contrary, it is a style conforming to the sedate and tolerant gradualism affirmed in the values and beliefs of British political culture. This does not mean that the style of British politics prevents an appeal to the emotions, but rather that it severely limits the range of emotions that can be effectively reached, restricting them to attitudes that support the generally accepted frame of authority and purpose. This limitation, effected through the system of expressive symbolism, thus protects the emotional foundations of the political system and is one source of its great strength.

Another way of making the same general point is to look at expressive symbolism from the point of view of political propaganda. In Britain, as in any other country, a political leader may manipulate the behavior and opinions of people by an appeal to certain emotions, inducing them to take actions which they would not have taken if they had merely considered the sober meaning of his words. Yet the common symbolism of British politics sets severe limits on what propaganda can accomplish by such an appeal. Some other systems are less fortunate. The revolutionary tradition in France, for instance, has perpetuated among many Frenchmen a certain predisposition to respond to the appeal of the political extremist. And not only a receptive audience but also a personal manner, a style of discourse, even certain key words are provided by that tradition, ready at hand for a Thorez or a Poujade. The division in French political culture that Dr. Wahl analyzes is not only a conflict between two sets of ideas and beliefs; it is also a conflict on the plane of emotions—and for that reason, all the more serious.

Nor will we always find that dominant emotions are perfectly matched with the explicit values and beliefs of a political system. Attitudes inherited from a long authoritarian past may impede the operation of a democratic system, even though most of its members sincerely accept the democratic ideal. If so, the manner and style of politics in the system may tell us more about the emotional forces at work than the explicit declarations of politicians and people. Germany under the Weimar Republic would provide interesting material for an analysis along these lines. Even today, in the democratic and liberal Bonn regime, the style of German politics, as Dr. Spiro portrays it, suggests an emotional preference for judicial and administrative methods of settling disputes and an aversion to the informal and pragmatic methods common in the older democracies. In these attitudes we may find the lingering effects of the practices and values of the *Rechtsstaat* of the old bureaucratic days of the Bismarckian Empire.

We have previously speculated on whether values or beliefs are more easily changed. How would we answer the same question with regard to the political emotions? Clearly, there is no brief and general answer. But the question is worth raising, since it is plausible to think that ideas, values, and emotions do not necessarily change at the same rate. In some circumstances, an appeal for action can be so directed to certain emotions that people will act contrary to the settled dictates of their own good sense and moral principles. Mob action provides many examples. And again and again the history of the totalitarian demagogues of this century illustrates how the political action of masses of people can be controlled by "the deliberate manipulation of sub-conscious, non-rational inference," to use Graham Wallas's phrase. We can well believe that many Germans who became Nazis took the decisive step in becoming followers of Hitler under the compulsion of powerful emotions whose intellectual and moral meaning they did not understand, and that only afterward and in time they adapted their beliefs and values to the Nazi system. Such cases as these—mob action and totalitarian self-surrender—are close to pathological. Rather more common and understandable would be the sequence in which ideas change first, then values, and finally and last, basic emotions. People often become intellectually and even morally convinced of the desirability of new institutions or new policies, and yet find that they can only gradually conquer their emotional attachment to the old ways. This is the order of change we might well expect if we started from Burkean premises. And we might draw from it the Burkean lesson that if a reform of institutions or policies is to succeed and endure, it should be no more rapid than the slow-moving emotions of the people permit.

CHAPTER 4

The Pattern of Power

How are political decisions really made? What influences actually determine the choice of leaders, the making of policy, and the way it is carried out? What interests motivate the various groups attempting to win power? What actually are the goals that they are trying to reach through government? Political culture does not tell the whole story. The political scientist may have a good grasp of the dominant values and beliefs of a system and yet be unable to answer such questions. Conceptions of authority and purpose will condition the pattern of power and the pattern of interests, but other influences will also play a part. If we want to get at political realities—"who gets what, when, and how"—we must examine these influences and their relations to political ideals. Complex as this task is, it is one of the most exciting the political scientist can engage in.

Let us look at the question of power. First a definition: One person exercises power over another when he intentionally acts in such a manner as to affect in a predictable way the action of the other. This definition may appear either too narrow or too broad. It might be thought too narrow since it excludes cases in which persons affect others without realizing or intending the effects of their action. Continually the acts of an individual set in motion trains of consequence of which he is not aware. Around the everyday behavior of any of us there is such a penumbra of "unconscious power," lying outside the focus of our attention. Quite unwittingly we may make a friend or an enemy, bestow a benefit or frustrate a hope. Indeed, such influences may not only lie outside the focus of our attention; they may be so complex and devious as to escape our comprehension, even if we tried to understand them. Yet in a sense such influence is a kind of power that the individual might come to recognize and use. Continually our knowledge of social relations is telling us more about such unanticipated consequences of individual and group behavior—in the relations of parent and child, of participants in economic life, of speakers and

26

listeners in opinion formation. And frequently such knowledge reveals power relations that had not been suspected before and new forms of power that may be exercised for good or ill in the future. As we shall see later, this whole sphere of unanticipated consequences is of major concern to the political scientist.

It is more likely, however, that our definition will appear to be too broad. It states that there is power where a person—or a group—by an intended act brings about an intended result in the action of another. He may do this by the use of some sort of sanction—by an inducement, such as a bribe or other favor, or by the threat of a deprivation, such as a blow or withdrawal of esteem. Some might prefer to restrict the definition of power to influence supported by sanctions. This would exclude compliance resulting from manipulation or "mere" influence—as when, for instance, a newspaper or political orator sways public opinion by rational persuasion or an appeal to the emotions. If you wish to stress this distinction, you will say that what we call "the pattern of power" ought to be called "the pattern of power and influence." We have chosen the shorter phrase. And in actual political life, the two kinds of operation usually go together. Candidates mingle promises of benefits with "glad-handing"; pressure groups work on legislators both by threats of electoral retaliation and by appeals to sentiment.

Power in society takes many forms. An obvious one is wealth—every day each of us exercises this form of power by paying money in return for goods and services. Other familiar forms are physical strength, social status, education, moral character, personal magnetism, military, legal, or managerial skill. Often we may be able to trace the power of an individual over others to one or more such factors, his "power base." And similarly with groups: Dr. Eckstein, for instance, points out the principal power base of each of various groups within the Labour Party—in the case of the Fabians, brains; in the case of the constituency parties, political activism; in the case of the trade unions, money; and so on. Naturally, the power base of a group will normally be a complex of several factors.

To speak thus of the power base does not mean that power is something that the individual or group simply "has." Power is relational. The influence that one person has over another depends not only on the power-holder, but also on the person he influences. The situation of the person influenced will certainly make a difference. The poor man will probably be more subject to the influence of money than the rich; the unarmed man more subject to the influence of force than the armed. Moreover, the interests and general psychological equipment of the person to be influenced will affect the outcome. The martyr will not be swayed by threats of violence, the dunce by appeals to reason, nor the atheist by promises of heavenly bliss. While these are examples of special individual traits, they also suggest how the culture of society will profoundly condition the forms of power that may arise within it.

Authority is a form of power. To have won office according to the approved procedures of the political culture gives the officeholder a certain power—that is, it enables him by acting in a certain way to affect predictably the behavior of others. The American legislator, for example, makes laws, with the majority of his colleagues in both houses and with executive approval. Apart from other reasons, these laws meet with compliance because the bulk of the people accept the ideal of authority according to whose norms the officeholders have been chosen and the laws enacted. Indeed, in a democratic system, each of the people also has his minuscule ration of authority—above all, the vote—through which he too may exercise influence. When, in speaking of democratic systems, we say that size is one element in the power of a group, we are referring primarily to power based on this form of authority—the right to vote.

It hardly need be said that the holders of such power (i.e., authority) can profoundly affect the distribution of other forms of power in the society—as, for instance, by the redistribution of wealth or by schemes for public education. Conversely, the possibility is raised that the holders of other forms of power may use them to influence or win authority. It is because in any political system this possibility will in some degree be realized, that in political analysis we must distinguish the pattern of power. One general factor determining that pattern will be the power—other than authority—of groups in the political arena. Where we find that a group has considerable influence, we shall want to see how far this is explained by such reasons as the quality of its organization and leadership, and the level of wealth, social status, and relevant skills of its members. In American politics, for instance, we should expect that, other things being equal, a relatively poor group would be at a disadvantage in competition with a more wealthy. On the other hand, greater skill in organization may be able to offset this disadvantage. The pattern of power will be determined by the distribution of such forms of power as well as by the distribution of authority.

Asking such questions may help us particularly when we try to identify and explain changes in the pattern of political power. Take, for instance, the increase in wealth of the industrial middle classes in Europe in the nineteenth century or the rise of trade union organization in recent generations. Such changes in the balance of "non-authoritative" power will almost certainly affect the pattern of political power. On occasion this balance of power may come into radical conflict with the dominant ideal of authority and the legal institutions expressing it—as in France before the Revolution of 1789 or in Britain before the Reform Act of 1832. The balance of power in this sense cannot be left out of account when we seek to explain the stability or instability of a pattern of political power.

What is the function of conceptions of authority? This depends on the extent to which a political culture is divided or united. So far as there is consensus, the conception of authority will have a stabilizing effect, guiding and integrating the relations of groups in their struggle for political power. In the first place, we must remember that a conception of authority in some degree confers effective power. Therefore, despite the shift in the balance of other forms of power, certain constants remain in the pattern of political power. Although a group in a democratic system may suffer a decline in some elements of its power (wealth, for example), its various political rights, particularly the right to vote, limit the extent to which its effective political power may fall. Similarly, in an aristocratic system, a rise in the level of wealth and education of the non-aristocratic classes is almost certain to affect the pattern of political power. Yet the aristocratic classes—quite apart from other foundations of power—will retain some significant influence because of their position as the repositories of authority.

Equally important, the way in which groups use their non-authoritative power will be shaped and limited by the conception of authority. One reason decisions are accepted is that they are believed to have been made in the prescribed way. If a group is itself to enjoy the benefits of authoritative decisions, it can hardly afford to undermine the basis on which the power of such decisions rests. Hence, in influencing decisions it must conform—or at least appear to conform—to the norms of authority. Nor should we think of this conformity as merely external and "insincere." Political values are operative ideals precisely because they become "internalized," as the sociologists say. To the extent that they do, the norms of authority will be self-enforcing. For instance, when groups in a democratic polity do not resort to bribery, the reasons certainly include not only fear of consequences, but also the self-imposed ethical restraints of the democratic ideal itself.

In general, then, the conception of authority provides a framework of decision-making that defines within broad limits what power various participants shall have and how they shall proceed in making decisions. Not its least important function is to determine when a result—i.e., a decision—has been reached. Consider, for instance, the function of the norm of majority rule. According to this norm, when the majority of the people— or of the legislature or council—has declared for a certain outcome, a decision has been made. Without some such common norm, the struggle to influence government action could go on indefinitely without a decision being reached. In this sense, a conception of authority has an integrating effect upon the struggle for power.

But what if we find not consensus but dissensus on authority? The differing status of public law will illustrate the effects of political culture in the two cases. Where there is consensus, a principal expression of the common ideal of authority will be the basic legal framework of government. By this we mean the laws of its constitution and possibly also certain other important rules, such as those embodying the fundamentals of the electoral system and of parliamentary procedure. This aspect of a political system, although sometimes called "formal," is no insignificant force in the shaping of the pattern of political power. In the American system, our right to vote depends in the first instance upon the law. Whatever we may find out about the other sources of the power of a group and about the informal procedures by which it influences government, the actual power it wields in political struggle normally depends in very great degree upon this right. And this right—the law defining and establishing the power to vote—in turn is supported not only by special legal sanctions but also by a massive consensus throughout the society. According to Dr. Eckstein the same is true of the British system.

When we turn to France, however, we find a divided culture and an entirely different status for public law. An old and sound interpretation identifies two main opposing currents in the French tradition of authority, one representative, the other authoritarian. Following Dr. Wahl's account, we can carry further this familiar view of *les deux Frances*—the Red and the Black—and show how these two clusters of political values have become identified respectively with the legislature and the administration. From time to time, different classes and groups have tended toward one or the other of the traditions and accordingly have viewed one governmental structure with favor, the other with hostility. As a result of this fissure in political culture, Frenchmen for generations have found it virtually impossible to establish a basic legal framework—a constitution—that enjoys the whole-hearted support of the major segments of the people. The basic institutions of self-government of the Third and Fourth Republics have rested not on consensus, but rather on a compromise among dissident groups, none of which has been strong enough to get the constitution it really wants.

Compromise, of course, is a feature of all constitution-making, and not even the British or American consensus extends to all details. But in the French case, the differences go much deeper than details or matters of mere degree. As a result the basic legal framework of the French polity has not that direct and congruent relation with a single, unified conception of authority enjoyed by the British constitution. Indeed, the constitutional laws governing the relations between executive and parliament in France resemble the terms of a treaty between opposing nations rather than the expression of a common view of government. As the seventy years of the Third Republic demonstrated, such a system can survive—although deeply afflicted by immobilism, weak and short-lived ministries, and, from time to time, ominous threats from Left or Right.

What of the Soviet "constitution"? Its status and function are very different indeed from the status and function of the constitutions of the three other systems. To call it a "constitution" is an extreme of Pickwickian language. Its rules are not laws in any ordinary sense of the word. Of course, they cannot be enforced by legal procedures and sanctions—such as an appeal to the courts—but that is often true of constitutional laws in the free countries. But when legal sanctions are lacking in free countries, constitutional rules are supported by other sanctions. Attempts to change radically the "rules of the game" would be resisted by an exercise of power, of which economic power—such as the power to strike—is only one of the more obvious examples. In comparison, the Russian constitution is simply so many words, having no relevance to the actual pattern of power.

Yet, as Dr. Ulam argues, the case is not quite so simple. Without these words the actual pattern of power would not be exactly the same. To some Soviet leaders and some indeterminate number of Soviet citizens, their system really is democratic. The words of the Soviet constitution state these values and thereby strengthen the effective power of the dictatorship. The proceedings of such bodies as the Supreme Soviet are functional as a kind of ceremony. Instrumentally insignificant, they express the belief, not entirely extinguished among Russians, that their system should and does express the "real" will of the masses.

The Supreme Soviet is controlled from outside, real power resting principally with the higher organs of the Communist Party. Yet the Communist leaders can secure compliance with their decisions on policy in some degree because they operate this "dumb show" of the Supreme Soviet from time to time. Some shred of authority attaches to its proceedings. As Dr. Ulam suggests, this raises an interesting, if distant, possibility. In a crisis, the "balance" upon which the power of the present leaders depends might shift in favor of other groups among the Soviet elites—the army or the managers, for example. In such a case, the Supreme Soviet might become a significant focus of decision-making—as at the overthrow of Mussolini the Grand Council of Fascist Italy, until then a "paper" body like the Supreme Soviet, sprang into life. This does not mean that the Supreme Soviet would become genuinely democratic. It might become, however, a body in which the representatives of various elites seal the bargains in which they agreed to tolerate one another and according to which they would rule the country. All this, of course, is highly speculative. But it suggests what would have to happen before the present constitution could become a major determinant of the actual pattern of political power in Russia.

CHAPTER 5

The Pattern of Interests

The analysis of the relations of political groups cannot be conducted solely in terms of power. We must also examine their interests—what they are trying to use power for. On the plane of political culture, we have distinguished authority from purpose. Similarly, on the plane of political action we must consider not only the pattern of power, but also the pattern of interests. Very broadly, the distinction between power and interest is the distinction between means and ends. The power of an individual or group consists of its means of influencing others; its interests are the goals—the ends-in-view—it uses power to achieve. As means and ends affect one another in any human act, so in political action power and interest are mutually conditioning. Obviously, the pattern of power itself —say, the alliances and hostilities among groups—cannot be understood unless we look into the interests entertained by participants. Nor, as we have seen, can we understand the power base of a group or individual without taking into account the interests of those influenced.

Interest is a slippery term and we need at the start to clear up certain ambiguities. One is the tendency to take "interest" as meaning "self-interest." For instance, when people talk about the activities of "interest groups" in politics, it is often with an overtone of disapproval, as if the goals of these groups were necessarily in conflict with the common good or with moral standards. That is not the meaning attached to the term in the present discussion. By interest we mean here simply a disposition to act to achieve some goal. Such a disposition has two sides. One is emotional— the felt need that gives the push or drive leading to action. But rarely is such a need entirely blind and undirected: associated with it is a cognitive aspect—some notion of the object or state of affairs that answers to the felt need. Even in an infant, the brute feeling of hunger soon becomes connected with some understanding of the object that will satisfy hunger; accordingly the infant tries to control his acts in such a way as to achieve

33

this object. In the case of adults this cognitive side will be involved with a fairly complicated set of ideas about the nature of the thing desired and how it can be reached.

It is true, of course, that for child or adult, for the individual alone or in a group, achieving the desired state means satisfying the underlying emotional need and thus enjoying a feeling of psychological satisfaction. Looking at the emotional side of interests, therefore, we may say that in this limited sense all interests are "selfish"—and that there is a grain of truth in the Utilitarians' "law of universal selfishness." However, when we look at the cognitive side of interests—the goals to which they are directed —we see the distinction that common sense makes by means of the terms "selfish" and "unselfish." One interest aims at a benefit to the actor. Another aims at a benefit to others. This, as we shall see, is an important distinction in political behavior. Yet each kind of motive is called an interest, as we have defined the term here. An interest, defined as such, includes a disposition to promote the relief of the poor as well as a disposition to pursue success, profits, or material luxury for oneself.

Perhaps it should also be noted that an interest may be positive or negative. As we use the term here, an interest may be a disposition to bring about a certain state of affairs; or it may be a disposition to prevent or do away with a certain state of affairs. We think of everyday efforts to acquire some useful object or to avoid or relieve pain. And certainly we need to make our definition of interest broad enough to include the fact that the groups active in politics are as often concerned with blocking some act of government or eliminating some existing condition as they are with promoting government action or setting up a government service helpful to themselves.

What in general are the factors that create and shape interests? Certain ones, obviously, are founded upon needs inherent in the human organism— the need for food, for example. No doubt there are others that have a psychological rather than a biological nature. The whole question of "inherent needs" is, and long has been, surrounded by controversy; it is essentially the problem of the "instincts." Fortunately we need not solve the problem to carry on political and social inquiry. For we do at least know that the interests we find in society and in politics have been profoundly shaped and directed by social experience. And we can with some success track down the contribution that society has made to forming these interests.

The very situation in which an individual finds himself will play no small part in directing his interests to one set of goals rather than another. A people's tastes in food will be shaped by the products available in the environment. The ambitions of politicians will be molded by the opportunities and barriers that confront them—by the existence of few or many elective offices, a parliamentary or presidential form of government, a multiparty or two-party system. Likewise in economic life, the profit "motive" itself is not an inherent psychological drive, but rather an interest shaped by the opportunities of a free enterprise system.

Along with the social situation, the general culture of a society will condition interests. Among the most important of these cultural influences will be the prevailing belief systems—in the sense in which we have used this term above. Interests are directed toward certain goals, but what people believe about the way they can most efficiently achieve their goals will have a real effect in shaping the goals themselves. When we think of the various things we wish to achieve—or avoid—we do not think of them apart from one another. Hunger leads us to eat, but what particular food we eat will be affected by our beliefs about the kinds of food that promote health. In this way, our goals tend to be interdependent. We may reject something we desire because we believe it to be incompatible with something we desire even more. Thus our beliefs about the relationships of goals will affect what goals we embody in our interests.

The role of belief systems is particularly striking when we consider the complex interests that groups pursue in modern politics. In the case of labor, farm, and employers groups, for instance, beliefs about how the economic system actually works will profoundly affect the interests the groups press for through political action. The American farmer's interest in high price-supports depends upon certain beliefs about the effects government action will have on farm income and on the general health of the economy. If most farmers believed—as probably a few do—that such intervention menaces the farmer's freedom and will ultimately hurt his pocketbook, the interests that farmers pursue in American politics would be very different from what they currently are. There is in this sense a strong element of "theory" in the interests of even the most hard-headed and practical pressure groups.

Hardly separable is the conditioning influence of values. Some values—sometimes called "appreciative" values—define the goals that are worthwhile achieving for oneself. A moment ago we mentioned the "profit motive." Generally in Western society in modern times the achievement of pecuniary success in a free market has been a goal of intense interest for many people. This interest depends not only upon the economic situation, but also upon an "ethic" that leads us to attach prestige to such success and to take gratification in achieving it. This goal has had far less importance in other times and other places where entirely different values have directed self-interest—in Western civilization saintly discipline and the chivalric virtues once far outranked pecuniary or professional success as models for personal ambition. Political power itself has a value and prestige that vary from one political culture to another. As compared with the businessman, the politician has a higher standing in Britain than in the United States. The essential trait of appreciative values is that they shape our notions of self-interest. They have an important function in relating self-interest to another class of values that we may call moral values.

As distinguished from appreciative values, the characteristic of moral values is that they lay down the rights and duties of individuals and groups toward one another. Typically the function of moral standards is to define not objects of self-interest, but rather an order of relationships to which self-interest must be subject. The contents of moral codes vary as widely as do other elements of culture. Some lay a heavy burden of obligation on members of the community in relation to one another, erecting an elaborate system of rights and duties around various classes and ranks, each with its special responsibilities and legitimate demands toward the rest. Others conceive of society as composed of equal individuals, each with the same limited rights and duties.

Could a society survive without a moral code, the motives of its members being guided solely by self-interest? Some philosophers have thought so. Indeed, this would seem to be a major premise of the Utilitarian school. Their argument in brief was that although all men are creatures of self-interest, they can live together in peace and good order, if they will only take a sufficiently intelligent view of their long-run advantage. Hence a stable society and political system could be founded upon enlightened self-interest. As has often been pointed out, however, the Utilitarians made an important assumption, namely that the character of the various goals that are pursued are such as to make possible a natural harmony of interests. This, we hardly need say, is a very dubious assumption. Empirically, it appears that social and political stability cannot be explained as a result of any such natural harmony: in a stable order we find some common moral code in terms of which the conflicts inevitable in any society can be harmonized to some degree.

Yet, much as we need to stress the function of a common moral code, we must also recognize the importance of the particular goals that are pursued as objects of self-interest. Here the function of appreciative values is crucial. The point can be illustrated from British experience in recent years. Along with the development of the welfare state has gone a certain reshaping of moral values. In general there has been a redefinition of the rights and duties of individuals and groups—particularly in relation to private property—and of the role of government as an instrument of these new moral standards. At the same time appreciative values have moved away from the standards of the era of vigorous capitalism and the goals of self-interest have been accordingly modified. The profit motive is under such a cloud as would be inconceivable in the United States. And while capitalistic acquisitiveness has declined, the evaluation of and interest in economic security has risen. Such a change in the goals of self-interest is complementary to the new moral and political values of the welfare state. For the sake of the stability of the political system, this is fortunate. Otherwise, the strain between new moral values and old interests might be excessive.

Common Purpose and Interests

We have been considering the relation of interests to the social situation and to culture in general. Let us look more closely at the role of political culture. The values and beliefs that are relevant are principally those of common purpose. Common purpose values are a class of moral values, since they are concerned with the rights and duties of individuals and groups. Their special character, however, comes from the fact that they define the role of government in relation to these rights and duties. They are the standards we follow when we decide that a certain condition is a problem *for* government—that government ought to do something to help one group or to hinder certain kinds of action or to direct some sphere of social action along certain lines. The problems that government tries to solve are not simply "given," confronting the political system, so to speak, from outside. There was a time, for instance, when unemployment was not a problem for government because interference with the economy lay outside commonly accepted notions of national purpose. Whether a condition is held to be a problem will depend, in part, at least, on a conception of common purpose in the light of which it is judged that government action should be taken to change this condition. The resulting policy is required and justified by the rights and duties of individuals and groups toward one another or toward the community as a whole.

The principal point to be made here is simple. It is that *interests are normally asserted as demands for policy only when they are felt to be justified by some conception of common purpose.* This is fairly easy to see when we consider interest groups that advocate some benefit for others. Such groups normally justify their demands by an appeal to the obligation of government to protect or enforce certain rights and duties, an appeal that more or less explicitly involves a view of common purpose. Advocates of legislation to restrict child labor, for example, pointed out the benefits to the community that would flow from protecting the health of growing children. But we must observe that groups urging action primarily favorable to themselves also press with greater or lesser sincerity some justification of their demand in terms of a view of the common good. When American farmers demand action to protect farm prices, they argue that this policy is based on the government's obligation to protect certain groups against undue economic hardship. Moreover, they contend that it will promote the health of the economy in general by maintaining the purchasing power of an important group of buyers. The demand for a benefit for themselves is intimately linked with a view of the whole American economy.

Such views of common purpose can be highly instrumental in bringing into the political arena interests that, without these views, might remain non-political. A broad example will illustrate the point. We all recognize how economic development may reshape the pattern of interests of a political system. Consider the rise of socialism and social reform in Europe during the past three quarters of a century. We cannot understand these changes in the pattern of interests in European political systems unless we look at the new wants that sprang from the growth of an industrial economy. But, as the history of the nineteenth century shows, such wants may be felt, and felt acutely, and yet not be asserted as demands on government, unless they are also believed to be justified by some conception of common purpose. People may endure the deprivations of unemployment, poor housing, and inadequate medical care, and yet make no significant demand for government action because they consider such intervention neither proper nor efficacious. Those affected may, of course, try to improve their lot in other ways. But in the absence of some view of common purpose legitimizing government action, they will remain aloof from politics. To a considerable extent this was the case in many European countries during the heyday of *laissez faire*. In mid-Victorian Britain, for instance, even the trade unions accepted the orthodoxy of Liberalism and made remarkably few demands on government, stressing instead their function as "friendly societies" in relieving the ills of their working-class members.

It follows that if we are to understand how the wants industrialization created eventually developed into the swelling demands for the welfare state, we must look beyond economic development alone. We must also consider the new views of the responsibility of the state and of the nature of the economy that provided ready justifications for new political demands. Not only economic conditions, but also—as Dr. Eckstein shows—the break with the political values of rugged individualism, prepared the way for the massive government intervention that has taken place in recent decades.

In the example just mentioned economic development is seen as the source of new wants. We must recognize, of course, that there may be other sources. New ideas of the standard of living that a man can and should enjoy—such as those that are sweeping over Asia and Africa today —can have as revolutionary an impact on the pattern of interests as an industrial revolution. Moreover, if these new ideas are bringing a revolution in political demands, it is because they have been introduced in the context of new political values and beliefs. The idea of a higher standard of living, for instance, has not spread to these continents as part of the doctrine of *laissez faire*. On the contrary, it has been spread in the context of theories of the welfare state, socialism, and communism—all of which, however much they differ on certain vital issues, make the satisfaction of this interest a primary duty of government. Conceptions of common purpose have given a fierce, political impetus to the new interests rising out of a cultural revolution.

This impressive role for political values and beliefs is not confined to systems that enjoy consensus. When new ideas of the proper goals of policy arise in or are imported into a political culture, they may deeply divide it and put severe, even revolutionary, strains on the system. Consensus on common purpose, on the other hand, like consensus on authority, will be a force making for political stability. Such general agreement on the broad objectives of government and its role in society is, as Dr. Eckstein points out, a principal reason for the fruitful and pragmatic politics of the British system. The principal interests asserted in British politics are shaped by the same basic view of government's role and responsibility and of the general scheme of priorities in the light of which conflicts should be settled. Given these common premises, interests can be adjusted and differences compromised without deep offense to the sense of justice of contending parties.

Special-Interest and General-Interest Groups

Common sense, as we noted above, suggests that some groups may be more, some less, concerned with the common good—that in terms of the goals they pursue, some are more selfish, some less. Is this distinction of importance to political analysis? Psychology distinguishes between ego and superego functions; sociology between self-oriented and collectivity-oriented action. Political science should also be encouraged to examine the surmise of common sense.

The distinction that we wish to follow up is sometimes stated as that between special-interest groups and general-interest groups. The goal of the special-interest group is primarily a benefit to itself; that of the general-interest group primarily a benefit to others. This is a familiar distinction of everyday experience. But in the light of our previous discussion one qualification immediately springs to mind. The special-interest group, while putting primary stress on a benefit to itself, will also in the normal case be motivated by a view of common purpose—a theory of justification for its demand. This expression of political values may set the group in conflict with other groups. Or it may provide common premises that help it reconcile its goals with those of others. In either case, this operative ideal —the view of the common good in terms of which the group justifies its demand for benefits—is geared into the motivation of the members of the group, and so, strictly speaking, is part of its interest. In short, the criterion of the special-interest group is not exclusive, but only relatively greater, concern with benefits for itself as compared with others. Similarly, the general-interest group, while concerned primarily with others, will also normally think of its action as benefiting itself. Pure altruism, like pure egoism, may occur, but neither seems to provide a model that often fits the interest groups we know.

How can the political scientist use the distinction between the two types of groups? How does this difference in motive make a difference to the structure and behavior of groups? Several possibilities come to mind. One is that the general-interest group is likely to be more "permeable" than the special-interest group. To belong to it you need not be someone who will benefit particularly from its activities, but rather a person concerned with certain values. For this reason such groups are sometimes called "open-ended." The special-interest group, on the other hand, in seeking to build up its membership will have, so to speak, a "ready-made" clientele, its potential membership being more clearly delimited and more easily identifiable than that of the general-interest group.

Another possibility is that the special-interest group will show greater perseverance and intensity than the general-interest group. We can readily think of examples of general-interest groups—those passionately committed to an "ideology" or a "crusade"—that have shown perseverance and intensity far greater than the ordinary special-interest group. Still, it is a common experience for the "reform" group, after a burst of idealistic activity, to subside, lose members, and break up, while the group based solidly on a program of self-interested benefits continues to maintain its membership and press its demands. In municipal politics this is often the fate of the "do-gooders" as compared with the "machine."

While the different emphases in motivation will tend to have consequences for the structure and behavior of groups, it is clear that these consequences will also depend upon other factors in the situation. The degree of dissensus will be one such factor. Where a political culture is radically divided, these divergencies in values provide foci for the formation of opposing general-interest groups. If that happens, there is real danger that such groups will tend to exacerbate further the conflicts of goals among self-oriented groups. It is quite true that self-oriented groups will already in some degree reflect the divisions in the culture. Dr. Wahl takes this fact into account by classifying pressure groups as well as parties under the main ideological divisions of French politics. This peculiar cultural context is one reason why pressure groups in France and Britain, with similar economic bases, have different political goals. The self-interest of such groups, as we have seen, will be shaped by the political values to which they are committed. Moreover—and this is the main point being emphasized here—the stress on ideology by some French parties—which in terms of our present discussion are general-interest groups—still further intensifies the conflicts among self-oriented groups.

In a context of consensus, there may well be an opposite tendency. So far as the general-interest group puts its emphasis on values that are part of a generally accepted culture, its function will be to lessen the conflicts of self-oriented groups. British political parties perform some such function. Between them there are significant disagreements on values and beliefs. But the many basic views and sentiments they share make them a powerful force for cohesion in the polity. Frequently, self-oriented groups in British society find themselves in sharp conflict over opposing goals. When one of the major parties intervenes in such a situation, it is in a position to promote a solution reflecting generally shared premises and priorities.

CHAPTER 6

The Pattern of Policy

Two aspects of any human act are the end being pursued and the means adopted to reach it. A third aspect is the consequence—the product of this process of problem-solving. Similarly, in a political system we may distinguish, as the outcome of the interplay of interests and power, the pattern of policy. This analogy, we hasten to add, cannot be strict. The state, as has often been shown, is not a person. Yet in important respects a political system is like a personality system. In the language of sociology both are "action systems." In both a pattern of values and beliefs interprets the situation and sets broad goals and norms that guide action. In both ends are pursued and results achieved.

These results in the political system we have called policy. This means, in the first place, the authoritative decisions of the system. We think, for instance, of the laws passed by a legislature or the decisions on foreign policy made by an executive. Decisions of this sort, however, need to be carried out—the pension law needs to be applied to particular cases, the appropriations for defense or conservation to be spent. Such acts of administration will also be performed by persons endowed with authority —civil servants, officers of the armed services, judges—and political groups may be as much concerned with influencing these decisions as with influencing major acts of the legislature or executive. When we speak of the pattern of policy, then, we mean all such acts and decisions of authority— in modern governments, a vast complex of activities and programs.

To study the pattern of policy will normally mean giving considerable attention to the bureaucracy. But this is not to say that bureaucrats can automatically be excluded from the patterns of power and interest. In each of the four systems we deal with, bureaucrats, especially those in the higher positions, have some measure of effective power in the decision process. This power may arise from the degree of discretion that has been left them by the broad decisions of the legislature or other chief policy-

42

making organ. It may consist in the influence that their expert knowledge gives them when they advise their superiors. Whatever its source, to say that the bureaucrat has power is to say that we cannot draw a line between those persons who make decisions and those who merely carry them out; that the distinction between "policy-making" and "administration" is only relative.

This is surely the common sense of the matter. We try to make our system a "government of laws, not of men" and to frame laws that will dictate as precisely as possible their application to particular cases. Yet we know that even the cop on the beat often "makes policy": he may turn a blind eye on the bookies, give the "bad boy" another chance, bear down on those whom he personally dislikes. Nor can we assume that the bureaucrat is wholly disinterested and neutral. In actual fact, of course, civil servants—and judges, policemen, generals, and so on—will have views of what is good for society, especially in their particular fields, as well as the usual human motives of ambition and self-interest. Since such ideas and sentiments are often related to the social class from which bureaucrats are drawn, it may well be important to look into their social origins as well as the other forces that shape their political outlook. Decision-making—the interplay of power and interests—penetrates the whole of a bureaucracy.

When studying the pattern of policy, we ask first, "What was decided?" We ask further, "What are the consequences of the decision?" The latter question will usually lead our inquiry beyond the bounds of the political system. Our concern, however, is still primarily political. Recent agricultural policy in Britain will serve for illustration. This policy has committed the government to providing "guaranteed prices and assured markets" for various farm products. Originating during World War II when the government took steps to increase home farm production, it has been carried out by means of a program of subsidies annually negotiated by the government with representatives of the farmers. One immediate economic effect has been to bring unprecedented prosperity to British farms. Of course, the cost to the taxpayer has been high. Some economists argue that the present system is wasteful and that its main goals could be achieved at much less expense. Such questions are crucial in a country as heavily taxed as Britain and as much in need of a scrupulous use of national resources.

Now, to raise the question of the economic consequences of policy may seem to lead the political scientist outside his field and into that of the economist. This is quite true and there is no way to avoid it. Certainly we do not need to argue the point that what happens in the economic system may have great impact upon the political system. This does not mean, however, that the concern of the political scientist with the economy is the same as that of the economist. The political scientist is interested in tracing out the economic effects of policy only insofar as they have further effects on the political system. For example, the main pressure group among British farmers—the National Farmers Union—has more than doubled its membership since prewar days, and one modest, but not insignificant, reason for this increase has been the simple fact that in recent years farmers have had far more money. Being richer, the Union can now afford a large staff of experts and publicity men and, not least important, a full-time, paid president—all instruments that have made it a more formidable power in British politics.

The example is very simple and by no means exhausts the indirect political effects of British farm policy. It serves to illustrate, however, how government policy itself, through its effect on the economy, can bring about a shift in the balance of power in the political system. As Dr. Eckstein shows, the whole vast set of programs of the welfare state through its economic and social effects is reshaping the pattern of power in Britain.

But such indirect effects of policy will affect the pattern of interests as well as power. In the history of a political interest group, for instance, we often find that its demands are weak and confused until a relevant government program has been set up. The existence of such a program gives sharper definition to the interests it favors and in turn intensifies and clarifies the demands of the favored group. Before World War II—to turn again to the British farmers—the National Farmers Union included only about half the farmers of Britain and was concerned mainly with keeping up the price of home-grown products by means of producer-controlled marketing boards. During and after the war, as we have seen, government policy took a radically new direction and the farmers were given a position of importance in the administration of policy. From its new role in the annual negotiation of the subsidy, the Union has gained in power and prestige. Equally important, the new policy has given the Union a new definition of its goals. Hence, in recent years the Union's principal effort has been to maintain, and if possible increase, the government guarantees for the various farm products.

The pattern of policy, we have said, refers primarily to the impact of policy. We have illustrated the point by referring to the effect of various programs on the economy. Policy may, of course, affect other non-political aspects of society—religion, social class, family life—in such a way as to have indirect effects on the political system. But the impact of policy may also be directly felt by the political system. Consider Dr. Eckstein's analysis of the effect of the welfare state on the traditional machinery of government in Britain. These new programs of social security, farm subsidies, the health service, housing, and so on, have immensely expanded the scope and complexity of policy. Far more major decisions and far more decisions involving intricate consequences and technical knowledge must be made than ever before. As a result, Ministers have not been able to maintain the same degree of control over the whole apparatus that they once had, so that some power has shifted from Ministers to civil servants. At the same time, representatives of interest groups—such as the farmers—have become more closely associated with government departments in the administration of the new programs, thereby gaining considerable influence over the course of policy. Hence as compared with Ministers, the bureaucrats—whether the public bureaucrats of government departments or the private bureaucrats of interest-group organizations—have gained in the pattern of effective power.

In most Western political systems changes of this sort in patterns of policy in recent decades have had similar effects on patterns of power. Even in Russia, where power is highly centralized, it has been hard to establish effective control over the vast activities of government. In consequence, as Dr. Ulam shows, there has at times been a shift of some degree of power from the central elites to lower levels of the bureaucracy—only to be followed by an attempt to reassert strict central control.

Thus within the political system policy may affect power. But the flow of consequences may also be in the other direction. If Britain has carried out a more massive program of government intervention than France or Germany, one reason surely lies in the fact that it has cabinet government based on a tight two party system. These elements in the British pattern of power provide the foundations for the coherent policy-making and coordinated control of administration without which large-scale government intervention will be self-defeating and ineffective. Indeed, one might argue that the British system of strict party government under "programmatic" parties encourages the assertion of demands for more services and more active intervention. Government is an effective way of getting things done; hence, groups readily turn to it for the satisfaction of their interests. Conversely, weak and incoherent government discourages demands. Thus the pattern of power may affect the pattern of interests.

One general point in conclusion: That the various aspects or patterns of a political system will affect one another follows from the fact that the concept of a "political system" can be taken seriously. To say that a set of entities form a system is to say that they are interdependent. The present discussion has tried to show that it is a fruitful approach to the study of politics to consider political culture, power, interests, and policy as forming a system. If the political scientist will order his material under these four headings and will look for interdependence among the patterns he is likely to find interesting relationships. What he finds, of course, depends on his own insight—and the facts.

CHAPTER 7

Intention and Situation

The stress given to values and beliefs in this Introduction may seem to commit the authors to a kind of cultural determinism. We do indeed mean to say that the political culture—and of course the general culture— of a society will have great effect on the behavior of individuals and groups and on the way the political system works. The basic values and beliefs of a people will tend to shape their institutions, so that when we find a change in their institutions it is plausible to look for the reason in a preceding change in political culture—just as when an individual acts differently it is plausible to seek the reason in a preceding change of intention. But this is not the only direction in which the inquirer should look. When trying to understand a change in behavior or institutions, we must make an analysis not only of intentions, but also of the situation. In tracing out the lines of cause and effect, we find that some are intentional, while others are situational.

Broadly speaking there are two ways of explaining human action. One is to ask what the person set out to do—what was his intention or end-in-view. The other is to ask what the situation "forced" him to do—what circumstances he was obliged to adapt to and how this affected what he did. Rarely will the way be so smooth that a man need not adapt his intentions to the situation. The same holds of a society. We presume that the broad purposes of a community, as embodied in its religious and ethical values, make a deep imprint on its history. But we also recognize the influence—sometimes almost amounting to compulsion—that is exerted by physical environment. And a familiar theme of history is how climate, geography, and resources have shaped the development of institutions.

Physical environment is not the only compelling circumstance. The social environment itself—man-made institutions and patterns of action— may as powerfully condition behavior as geography or climate. Economic

46

institutions are perhaps the most familiar example. We need not accept the extreme view that the mode of production wholly determines the shape of social action in all other spheres, but we can hardly deny that it will greatly affect the form taken by family life, the class system, government, and even religious and artistic activity. An underdeveloped economy in which the mass of the people are sunk in poverty, while a small minority enjoy great wealth, will be a poor foundation for a genuinely democratic regime. A primitive system of communications alone will tend to limit severely the area within which there can be general and active participation in government. This consequence is not intentional. It does not flow from a deliberate design to sabotage a democratic regime; we may even presume that people are doing their best to make their communications system as efficient as possible. The effect, nevertheless, is to limit and shape the possibilities in the political sphere.

Within the political system, as we have seen, the patterns of power, interest, and policy will condition one another in a similar way. When in Britain, for instance, the expansion of the scope of policy shifted some power from Ministers to civil servants, this was not an intended consequence of the welfare state. It was not one of the aims of the reformers, nor can it be regarded as a direct reflection of the values of British political culture. Quite the contrary. But in spite of their preferences, Ministers were faced with conditions that made it impossible to maintain the close and effective control they had exercised in the past. Given the fact that the new programs were being carried out, the shift of power resulted from the situation, not from anyone's intention. It was, so to speak, an unplanned consequence of planning.

Not only between the basic patterns of a political system, but also within one pattern, the action of individuals or groups will be conditioned by the situation. The pattern of power in Britain, including as it does cabinet government and a tight two-party system, will shape pressure-group activity along quite different lines from those prevailing in the United States. Hence, although a British and an American pressure group may have much the same goals of public policy, they will adopt different tactics. Along with the group's ends-in-view, the compulsions of the situation shape its pattern of action.

That politicians, pressure groups, and parties must adapt their conduct to circumstances is a commonplace—indeed it is part of what is meant by the maxim that "politics is the art of the possible." Yet it needs to be stressed in order to guard against the easy temptation to explain political action solely in terms of the immediate intentions or long-run values and beliefs of the actors. Within the arena of the day-to-day struggle of groups; among the basic patterns of the political system; between the political system itself and other spheres of social action, the lines of unintended consequence may lead to results far different from anything hoped for or expected by individuals or groups.

International as well as domestic politics illustrates the point. In trying to explain a war between two nations, we may set out to discover which had designs of aggression. This line of inquiry may be fruitful, as Nazi and Soviet behavior have shown. The revolutionary character of their values and beliefs is a major explanation of their respective imperialisms. Yet we also know—and if we do not, Hobbes can teach us—that war may occur even though both parties to it are sincerely seeking only to defend themselves. One nation, knowing that wars do occur and that national defense is a necessity, strengthens its armaments and alliances. The other, alarmed by these steps, takes similar ones—which confirm the initial fears of the first nation and lead to further preparation. Finally, although each nation has sought only security, the logic of the classic armaments race leads to war. It is the situation—in particular, the existence of separate, sovereign states—as much as the intentions of the nations, that has determined the course of events.

A look at the French system will help clarify what we mean by situational analysis and why it is important. Consider two uniformities in the pattern of power of that system: that elections to the legislature are held about every four or five years; and that ministries fall on the average about every six months. The first of these results from the explicit provisions of a law which, in broad outline, is understood and approved by the bulk of the French people. In short, it is intentional. To say this, of course, does not end the analysis, but it is a sound, if obvious, first step. In explaining Government instability, however, we cannot start from such a generally accepted intention among the French people or French politicians. No one planned the instability of Governments during the Third and Fourth Republics. Deputies and party groups did not have as a set purpose that Governments should frequently fall. Yet each party group in pursuing quite other purposes brought about that result. The reason, we say, is to be looked for in the French multiparty system. Given such a system, instability will follow: it is an unintended consequence of the party situation.

Normally, in France, Governments must be based on coalitions and no group joining a Government will be able to realize all or even most of its program. At the same time it is confronted with the fact that there are other party groups outside the coalition that are competing for similar electoral support but that are unimpeded by the frustrations of coalition government. Hence, some groups in the Government will be strongly tempted to break away and restore their competitive position by reasserting the whole of their demands—that is, in the French phrase, to resort to a *cure d'opposition*. The intentions of the groups are the "normal" ones of a political party: to win a share of power, put their men in office, enact their programs, maintain and expand their electoral support, and so on. But when these intentions are followed in the situation we have described, certain groups find it necessary to withdraw their support. Conceivably, in some cases, they do not know they will bring down the Government; that, at any rate, is not the end they are seeking. The end they do seek, however—the maintenance of electoral support—cannot be achieved if they remain in frustrating coalition with other party groups. Over a period of time, since the same party situation prevails, similar compulsions will operate and similar decisions will be made; hence, a characteristic uniformity of the French pattern of power—the frequent fall of Governments.

The analysis of intentions—whether the basic values and beliefs of political culture or the immediate aims and interests of groups—cannot suffice. The institutions that men deliberately create, like the tactics they pursue in political battle, may produce patterns and consequences that no person or group has intended or perhaps even foreseen. Sometimes institutions turn upon their creators with impersonal coercions that defeat the very purposes they were designed to serve. Then men, the creators, are driven along by the things they created in a course they never planned, and that may not only frustrate their original intentions, but also reshape these intentions to fit the new model of action. Thus, unplanned and unintended development may remake political style, tactics, ambitions, and ideals, reaching perhaps to the deepest levels of political culture. We have stressed the role of values and beliefs in shaping political behavior. Here we stress that unplanned and unintended patterns of behavior may themselves sometimes remake values and beliefs.

Consider again the case of France. If there was one purpose on which the bulk of Frenchmen were united at the Liberation, it was that the political patterns of the Third Republic should not be restored. Dr. Wahl describes these patterns—multipartism, instability of Governments, immobilism, and so on. While at the birth of the Fourth Republic, the French soon found that they could not agree on a radical remodeling of their system, they created some new institutions and parties and there was certainly a new spirit—"the spirit of the Resistance." Yet, in spite of the wishes of most of the actors on the scene, as Dr. Wahl goes on to show, the old system soon reappeared and along with it much of the old and despised spirit of the declining days of the Third Republic. The crusading, reformist politicians of the Liberation gradually adapted themselves, taking on the attitudes and traits of the politicians of prewar days. As the French themselves remarked, *"Le système bouffe les hommes,"* "The system gobbles up the men."

In no sense does the sociological principle expressed in this maxim apply only to democracies. Its irony is only heightened when we turn to Soviet Russia. Surely it would seem that in this mighty dictatorship, where political power is total and wholly centralized, the men in command could avert or control the compulsions of circumstance. Yet they are equally the creatures of their system. A principal theme of Dr. Ulam's analysis is that the success of the dictatorship in performing its major task, the industrialization of Russia, has created conditions and attitudes that make difficult, if not impossible, the continuance of a dictatorship of the Stalinist variety. But if the present dictators cannot go backward, neither can they safely go forward: to relax their coercions at home or in the satellite countries is to raise demands and strengthen forces that threaten the whole basis of their power. They are all-powerful, yet at the same time pressed relentlessly by circumstances that their system itself created.

Nor have their personal characters and motivations been untouched by these compulsions. The system, so to speak, selects the types of personality that can rise to power, as Dr. Ulam points out in his discussion of the prominence of the *apparatchik*. Moreover, by the kinds of action that the system continually involves, it leads men to accept and indeed to prefer these kinds of action. The personalities of the dictators are in no small part creations of the system they presumably command.

Cases such as these, where values and beliefs are remade by the development of unintended patterns, bring home the need to consider both situational and intentional factors. Having made the point, we may strike a more hopeful note. For, of course, the two sorts of factors may also work in harmony. As Dr. Eckstein points out, it is central to the British conception of authority that government is bipolar; that is, that a predominant authority of initiative and decision shall be in the hands of a central body, nowadays the Government, which conducts its business subject to the constant criticism and influence of an opposing body, nowadays principally the Opposition. In the British system, this ancient principle can be more easily realized because there are two major, disciplined parties. And if somehow many parties were to arise, the familiar and approved pattern of politics in terms of Government versus Opposition could be maintained only with great difficulty. As the British system now operates, however, any maverick group or individual tempted to follow the ways of multipartism is massively discouraged by the near monopoly of political power possessed by the two major parties. The compulsions of the party situation work in the same direction as basic political values and beliefs.

Of course, we must add, in Britain as in other countries, "the system" has its inevitable effects on the personalities and styles of its members. The new M.P. may at first find it distasteful invariably to troop into the division lobby at a signal from his chiefs and regardless of his personal opinions. In time, however, he comes not only to accept this odd division of opinion on all questions into only two sides, but even to feel that it is right and natural. Daily behavior, as well as parliamentary tradition, gently but firmly makes him a "House of Commons man"—and proud to be one.

Finally we should point out that though the need for situational analysis results from the fact that the control men exercise over their institutions is only partial, such analysis may, if successful, broaden the extent of that control. A familiar example from American experience will illustrate. The fathers of this country quite deliberately used the separation of powers to build into our system certain side-effects favorable to their cherished values. Recognizing that separate, but co-equal, powers will inevitably tend to look on one another with some suspicion, they divided federal authority among several bodies. They explicitly intended this result as a means of checking excessive power and protecting liberty; and experience has shown their "institutional engineering"—to use Dr. Spiro's phrase—to have been eminently successful. We today, on the whole, accept their values and approve the results of their design. So also do the legislators, executives, and judges who directly exercise authority within the system. Officeholders find themselves forced by the situation to adopt attitudes of watchfulness toward the other bodies in the great triumvirate. Yet, at the same time, they are aware of the institutional reasons for this tension, and as believers in the American system, approve them. What is compulsive on one level of analysis proves to be intentional on another.

Patterns of government may arise from situational or from intentional factors—usually, indeed, from both. The authors of this book are centrally concerned with the way in which intention and situation may interact to create patterns of political action. Environment shapes man and man shapes his environment. This is true of political man in his political environment, as of man in general.

PART TWO

THE BRITISH
POLITICAL SYSTEM

by Harry H. Eckstein

I suppose there are some folk who enjoy speaking in the House of Commons, and rise without a doubt or tremor. It is impossible to tell: for everyone must leap to his feet with the same alacrity if he is to catch [the Speaker's] eye. . . .

There is, of course, almost every possible ingredient of unease in that place. An after-dinner speaker or a platform speaker may reasonably expect to have the attention of most of his audience. They are in front of him, and they cannot easily get away. He has a table, or desk, for his notes and papers. Even the "front-bencher" commands the length of the House and can use the Dispatch Box for his notes and papers—and thumping fist, if necessary. The back-bencher, clutching his notes, is like a lonely man standing up in the middle of a public meeting. His audience is all round him, some in front, some behind, some above him, some below—. . . . An interruption, a sneer, an ironical laugh, may hit him from any quarter. And, if he rounds upon the interruptor to the south-west, or the sneerer to the east, he may be reminded that he must address his remarks to the Chair, which lies north.

More, unless he is very good, or fairly important—and even if he is—his audience is moving and changing all the time. Members, good friends, it may be, receive urgent telephone messages or "green cards," bow to the Speaker, and march out as he approaches his principal, or only, joke. The Minister whom he hopes to convert, or intends to shatter with a deadly jest, is relieved by another Minister and goes out for a cup of tea, just before the unanswerable argument or the crushing quip is reached. The Front Opposition Bench, in the same way, are constantly coming and going. There is a procession of Members to the Table, putting down Questions and getting advice from the Clerks. Others go up to the Speaker and engage him in conversation. There is movement everywhere. It is like making a speech in a beehive. And those who remain motionless are not necessarily attentive, or even silent. Ministers and Whips must confer upon the course of the debate, check facts and figures, read documents about something quite different. A Member will come in with a resolution or an amendment to another Bill, to which he is seeking signatures. He goes from friend to friend, and there is a whispered colloquy with each. . . . Behind the orator may be one of those Members who have the

55

habit of muttering a running commentary—"Quite right, too"—"Not with this Government"—"They're *Afraid*"—quite friendly, maybe, but maddening. Then there are the professional interruptors, who, if they do not like the speaker or the speech, make it their business to snap at him from time to time—"Nonsense!" "Rubbish!" . . . and so on . . .

Here is perhaps the fundamental cause of alarm. Whatever jokes may be made about it, the House of Commons is a formidable body, drawn from every class and corner. They may not all be philosophers or senior wranglers, which is just as well; but you could mention hardly any subject, they say, without some Member shyly coming forward and confessing that he knows all about it.

——A. P. HERBERT, *Independent Member**

* Copyright, 1950, by A. P. Herbert. Reprinted by permission of the author, Double-day and Company, A. P. Watt and Son, and Methuen and Company.

CHAPTER 8

Leadership and Democracy in Britain

The Effectiveness of British Government

British government, as a comparison with the other systems treated in this book will indicate, is unique. Britain alone, of all these countries, lacks a written constitution. Only in Britain has there existed an enduring and genuine political consensus, that is, a broad and spontaneous agreement on what is authoritative in government: how the rulers are to be selected, laws made, and the scope of law limited—a fact that may itself explain why the British have not found it necessary to codify their constitutional views in a formal constitution. Again, only Britain has a government that can trace its pedigree through centuries of gradual development, even beyond the serious constitutional conflicts of the seventeenth century. Nowhere else, in consequence, have so many aspects of premodern government survived in political offices, procedures and attitudes. But it is not the old alone that is unique in the British political system: only Britain, for example, has a party system consisting of two tightly disciplined parties, and such political parties are very modern phenomena indeed.

But most important of all, Britain alone of all the countries dealt with here has managed to maintain, over a long period of time, effective democratic government, if by this we mean a great capacity for constructive action on the part of responsible political leaders. British Governments have suffered neither the acute instability nor the near-paralysis that characterized the Weimar Republic and the Third and Fourth Republics in France. Their capacity for action has been great enough to let them carry through a large-scale remodeling of British social and economic structure in this century, chiefly in a brief space of five years after World War II. This remodeling, moreover, was accomplished strictly within the limits of the traditional constitution and by a set of leaders who, far from being

Stalins or Bonapartes, were rather mild and colorless even by British standards. It follows that the capacity for action of British Governments is not derived solely from the abilities of British leaders to use the political system effectively: from their charisma or iron control over great party machines. Where a Clement Attlee or a Neville Chamberlain exercises quite as much power as a Winston Churchill or a Lloyd George the power exercised must be an attribute of the political system rather than of the individual wielding power. This *inherent* capacity for effective action is the truly distinctive characteristic of British government, one it shares with practically no other important democratic system.

To what can this inherent capacity for action be attributed? The question is important not merely as a puzzle in political sociology but also because the tendency to attribute the effectiveness of British government to the wrong causes has done real damage in other countries. It has sometimes been assumed that if one wants a government as stable and active as the British, one need simply imitate the more important characteristics of the British machinery of government. Wherever this was done, unintended consequences at best, disaster at worst, followed. For example, the power of the British executive to dissolve Parliament was written into the organic laws of the French Third Republic only to fall into total disuse for peculiarly French reasons.[1] And while this did not happen in the Weimar Republic it might have been much better if the power of dissolution had atrophied there too, considering the unfortunate uses to which it was sometimes put.

This does not mean, of course, that the machinery of British government is irrelevant to the way the system works, but only that machinery alone cannot explain its effectiveness. What makes British government so uniquely effective is not only its organization but the peculiar environment (including the political culture) in which the organization of government functions.

The Party System and Political Deference

British government would not be as effective as it is if it were not for two factors, one cultural, the other structural. The cultural factor is the British conception of authority, which attributes to leadership a far larger scope of legitimate independent action than that of any other democratic country—"independent" action meaning action taken on the leaders' own initiative rather than as an expression of popular or parliamentary will. The structural factor is the disciplined two-party system, which almost

[1] See below, pp. 224, 282.

always provides a united leadership backed by a marvelously obedient majority of legislators: "solid masses of steady votes." [2] These two factors may be considered the immediate causes of effective parliamentary government in Britain. How do they operate?

The principal advantage enjoyed by British government over most other parliamentary systems is the stability of its cabinets. Since the turn of the century Britain has had one cabinet for every five or six in France, despite the fact that British governments, no less than French, can be deposed by adverse votes of confidence in the legislature or simply by defeats on policy. This stability has a great many desirable results. It enables ministers to learn the ropes of governing (no easy task in this age of highly technical legislation); it prevents excessively abrupt changes in policy; it allows governments to plan their legislative activities far in advance and to introduce long-range projects without fear of interruption in mid-implementation, so to speak. The crucial reason why the British have such cabinet stability and the French not is of course that the British have a disciplined two-party system and the French an undisciplined multiparty system. In a multiparty system, cabinets are necessarily based on party coalitions—unless, as has happened in a very few countries, including postwar Germany, a single party can get an absolute parliamentary majority—and coalitions, in the nature of things, are bound to be less stable than one-party governments. A two-party system alone, however, will not inevitably produce stable governments, for the parties themselves may be coalitions, united only for certain particular (e.g., electoral) advantages, as they are in the United States. In Britain, however, the two major parties are not mere electoral coalitions parading under a common label. They are "solid masses" because they almost always vote as unified bodies on parliamentary issues in accordance with instructions by the party leaders or caucuses. Occasionally, to be sure—very occasionally—British parties split. Sometimes also there are "free votes" in Parliament (votes on which M.P.s may, with their leaders' permission, vote as their consciences, not their leaders or party caucuses, direct). On such occasions there will be a certain amount of cross-voting in Parliament. But this is very unusual; the reports of "divisions" in the British Parliamentary Reports (*Hansard*) almost always show a steady mass of Labourites in one column and a solid phalanx of Conservatives in the other. The system works with such marvelous consistency that it is not unusual for an M.P. to criticize his party in a parliamentary debate and later to vote with it in the actual

[2] The phrase is that of Walter Bagehot, author of a classic account of British government, *The English Constitution*, published in 1867. Bagehot thought that parliamentary government could not be made to work without such obedient and reliable majorities.

"division," although party discipline, rigidly applied, demands not only a member's vote but also his silence, or, indeed, sometimes his public support of policies with which he privately disagrees.

This, by almost any standard, is a remarkable state of affairs and goes a long way toward explaining the unique effectiveness of British government. But it does not fully explain it. For it is not only cabinet stability and the consistent ability of the British legislature to make constructive decisions that makes the British system effective, but also the great leeway it offers for independent leadership. The plain fact is that in both parties —although perhaps more in the Conservative than in the Labour Party— it is the party leaders rather than the party caucuses who determine how their disciplined supporters are to vote. Nor is this fact grudgingly conceded by the supporters simply as one of the hard facts of party life. On the contrary, it is regarded as being somehow natural and right, the way things should be: "legitimate." Voluntary submission to leadership is, even today, in the age of mass democracy, a vital part of British political culture.

The habit of deference to political leaders and in general social behavior, which Bagehot made the keystone of his analysis of British politics almost a century ago, is generally glossed over in more modern commentaries. The tendency in these commentaries is to stress what we have come to regard as modern democratic attitudes, and not without reason. The British do profoundly believe in basic civil and political liberties; they insist that public authority be exercised in conformity with "the rule of law"; they believe in the binding force of the popular mandate. But the first two of these principles, however congenial to modern democrats, originated in much older (especially medieval) notions of constitutional government, and are wholly reconcilable with non-democratic forms of government. Only the principle of the mandate is truly modern and distinctively democratic, and that, significantly, is subscribed to by the British in a very ambivalent and peculiar way.

In most democratic countries the idea of representative government, if not its practice, involves a simple set of principles: ultimate authority lies in popular will, which is expressed in the election of candidates whose chief function is to enact the policies for which they campaigned and to represent the interests of their constituents. In Britain the matter is much more complicated. British ideas of representative government stress not only the derivative character of political authority (i.e., that authority lies *in* popular will) but also its independent character (i.e., that authority is exercised *over*, or *regardless of*, popular will). These two ideas are of course inconsistent, but the British believe in both nevertheless; indeed this very want of logic explains why their conception of authority, democratic though it is, leaves such inordinately great room for leadership.

[It is probably correct to state, as a general rule, that the British expect their rulers to *govern* more than to *represent* them.] The people who govern Britain are, of course, representatives in the sense of being popularly elected. But once they get into Parliament they are not expected to act as mere delegates of those who elected them. This means, first, that their constituency is supposed to be the nation as a whole; hence the curious fact (curious, at any rate, to Americans) that members of Parliament are not required to reside in the constituencies they represent. Undoubtedly, British M.P.s perform certain of the representative functions familiar in our own country, such as going to bat for their constituents in the administrative departments, but [it would be thought improper for a member of Parliament to make himself a mere middleman between his constituents and Westminster.] Even more important, [the representatives of the British people are presumed to have a certain legitimate independence even from the public opinion of the nation.] The ultrademocratic idea that Parliament is, so to speak, an assembly of the nation in miniature and that it is consequently the will of the nation, not the will of Parliament as such, that makes parliamentary decisions legitimate, never took as deep root in Britain as elsewhere.

This emphasis on government over representation comes out even more clearly in the fact that the British do not even expect Parliament as such to govern them. [They not only permit, they even expect, a particular section of Parliament—the Cabinet—to govern, pretty much independently of the private will of the ordinary member of Parliament.] In fact they would be very surprised if a large number of ordinary M.P.s ("backbenchers") had independent political wills and insisted on voting their private convictions. [The relationships of the Cabinet to Parliament are very much, in gist, like the relationships of Parliament to the nation. The Cabinet is expected to represent the majority in Parliament, in the sense of being chosen from the majority; but once it is chosen it is expected to be more than a mere mouthpiece for the "public opinion" among its supporters.]

In a brilliant essay, L. S. Amery has expounded the dual nature of the British conception of authority.[3] This conception he distinguishes from the Continental view of representative government which derives from the French Revolution and which makes political power a delegation from the individual citizen through the legislature to an executive dependent on the legislature. In contrast, [the British constitution, today as in the distant

[3] L. S. Amery, *Thoughts on the Constitution* (Second ed.; London, 1953).

past, has two basic elements: an initiating, directing, energizing element —nowadays the Cabinet—and a checking, criticizing element—nowadays the House of Commons and especially the Opposition. Given this notion of authority, it follows that "Parliament is not, and never has been, a legislature, in the sense of a body specially and primarily empowered to make laws." The function of legislation is mainly exercised by the Cabinet, while the principal task of Parliament is to secure full discussion and ventilation of all matters as a condition of giving its assent to what the Government does. "Our system," he concludes, "is one of democracy, but of democracy by consent and not by delegation, of government of the people, for the people, with, but not by, the people."

The bi-polar structure that Amery traces back to the Middle Ages and makes the central feature of the British constitution does not mean that Britain is not democratic. It means rather that British democracy has grown up within a certain framework of authority to which it has been obliged—perhaps at the sacrifice of some consistency—to accommodate itself. The idea of the mandate expresses the belief that Governments are responsible to the people for their major acts and policies. As the suffrage has been broadened and particularly since the Reform Act of 1867 this idea has been taken more and more seriously. In 1903, for example, Chamberlain raised the tariff question so that at the next general election the public might give a "mandate" on it. In 1923 Baldwin dissolved Parliament, not because of an adverse vote of confidence or a defeat on policy, but solely because he felt he could not undertake tariff reform (then a very important issue) without obtaining an expression of popular will on the matter. The principle of the mandate is certainly a part of British political culture, and, what is more, is frequently acted upon.

But mandate theory has never fully replaced the idea of independent authority. Even when it is invoked it is frequently little more than normal political cant, a convenient stick with which to beat one's opponents when better arguments are lacking. Some very important policy decisions have been made, even in the heyday of mandate theory, for which no mandate has existed, without in the least outraging anyone's constitutional feelings; thus Baldwin, who felt he could not reform the tariff without a specific mandate, gave women the suffrage without the slightest suspicion of one. Much more important, it seems to be generally recognized that the Government ought sometimes to ignore its lack of a mandate, or even to act counter to a mandate, if doing so would be definitely in the national interest—a loose principle which may cover a multitude of independent actions. The case most frequently cited to make this point is the famous "Baldwin Confession" about Britain's failure to rearm against the Nazi threat before 1935. Baldwin argued that until 1935 every government had been given a mandate for disarmament and collective security under the League of Nations, and that the country's mind on the issue had been revealed emphatically at general elections and by-elections; hence he felt rearmament could not legitimately be undertaken until 1935, when some sort of mandate for it was given.[4] The position taken against this argument by Baldwin's opponents was simply that the Government—having, as it claimed, a clear apprehension of the military danger and the futility of the League of Nations—should have acted in the best interests of the nation anyway; that in fact it was its *duty*, as the Government of the country and His Majesty's ministers, to do so, regardless of any electoral consequences. We need not determine which of these views has greater merit. It is enough to note the fact that both could seriously be advanced in the first place. It may be true that one or the other conception of the authority of government is invoked only when it is politically convenient to invoke it, but the great point is that both conceptions can be used for political convenience, i.e., to make an impression on the public. Both conceptions, however inconsistent, have solid roots in British political culture.

The British party system and the most basic British conceptions of authority are marvelously complementary in their effects. Both tend to produce strong and stable leadership and a great capacity for positive action. What is more, the practical working of the disciplined two-party system in a sense reconciles the illogical inconsistencies of the ideas of authority, or at least keeps the British unaware that these inconsistencies exist. For what is in fact an independent exercise of power can always be made to appear derivative by the solid masses of steady votes in Parliament. And just as the party system supports the ideas of legitimacy, so these in turn support the party system, for the meek submissiveness to leadership by ordinary M.P.s itself reflects the habit of deference in British society. But while political deference and the two-party system reinforce and support one another they do not cause one another. To find why they exist at all we must probe more deeply.

The Bases of Political Deference

Gradual Political Development

What accounts for the ready acceptance of independent leadership by the British? The very nature of their ideas of authority suggests the

---

[4] A very vague mandate, it should be noted. The Tories merely inserted an ambiguous reference to rearmament into their election program.

answer. The important thing to note is that these ideas represent the dominant strains in Western ideas of authority since the Middle Ages. ✳ [The idea of limited government in accordance with a somehow transcendental (superhuman) law is the cornerstone of medieval constitutionalism. The idea of the independent authority of the sovereign is the contribution of the age of absolutism, in England the Tudor and Stuart periods. The idea of the mandate is the basis of modern representative government. Can we not infer that the British permit such great scope to leadership because modern ideas of derivative authority have been merely superadded to older ideas of independent authority? And if that inference is correct, is not the ultimate cause of political deference in Britain to be found in the gradual, almost entirely peaceful, development of British political institutions, a process in which each new age has established its characteristic political attitudes without ever fully replacing those of preceding ages?]

[Historically this makes sense. Both British democracy and British absolutism developed less abruptly and less violently from their antecedents than, for example, French democracy and absolutism.] So-called Tudor absolutism was nothing like Continental absolutism chiefly because the great institutions of medieval constitutionalism—Parliament and the common law courts—continued to operate alongside the instruments of royal absolutism, the king's personal Council and courts. The Stuarts did aspire to a kind of Bourbon absolutism, but succeeded only in precipitating the one major revolution in British political history: a revolution, moreover, that (unlike the French) ended, to all intents and purposes, in a restoration of the old constitution. The English constitution thus grew by a kind of prescription, a heaping up of strata of belief, where those of the French and Germans grew out of a succession of sudden, even violent, upheavals. True, in France and Germany also old political beliefs are still very much alive. But where in these countries the incidence of new upon old beliefs produced profound social fissures, in Britain, as a result of the slow tempo and piecemeal character of constitutional change, the various ideas of authority are combined in a single, generally shared, political culture.

This does not mean, however, that British political ideas have remained rooted in tradition while British society and government have become modernized. It is difficult to conceive of the survival of the ideas of authority without a concomitant survival of institutions to express them, or of deferential attitudes in politics that have no basis in other forms of social behavior. [And indeed both the institutions of British government and British social structure contain ancient elements similar to those of British ideas of authority, which provide the ideas with a solid social basis]

Ceremonial Institutions

In the case of governmental institutions there is of course the vast paraphernalia of titles, offices, rules, apparatus and procedures which have survived from previous eras: the peers, the Lord Chancellor, the common law, the Speaker's Mace, the "calling for candles," and a thousand similar things. No other country has discarded so few of its offices and processes in the course of its political development; seeing a Lord Mayor's parade in London is like seeing a pageant of all British history. Few of the ancient offices and processes, of course, perform any longer the functions they once performed. Like the monarchy, they have become transformed from "efficient" into ceremonial institutions, into mere ritual, the chief purpose of which is just to be formal and dignified and to edify the eyes and heart. No other democratic system, in consequence, provides such a feast for the sentiments as the British. However, the ceremonial trappings of British government, from the monarchy down to the barristers' wigs, are not to be dismissed as mere theatrical scenery simply because they are now chiefly adornment upon more prosaic but more effective institutions and processes. They too are part of the pattern of effective power in Great Britain because they affect, however indirectly, the way authority is exercised.

Merely by existing, the ceremonial institutions keep the past concretely alive in the present, and thus obscure the radical changes that have certainly occurred in British government, in however piecemeal a fashion, since the Middle Ages. Even in the short space of the last century tremendous changes in British government took place: the relationships between the Parliament and the people were radically altered by the Reform Acts and the rise of popular, nationally organized parties; parliamentary procedure was overhauled; the role of the Cabinet and the methods by which it is formed were changed; so were the organization of public administration and a multitude of less important things. But the important point to grasp is that at the end of the century the government did not visibly appear to have changed very much. The Monarch was still there; so were the Lords; so was the Privy Council; so was the Chancellor of the Duchy of Lancaster. Thus, however much the structure of government had changed, it had not *manifestly* changed, a fact which helped to keep intact the old ideas of authority as well.

What is significant about the ceremonial institutions, therefore, is first and foremost that they expressively symbolize the predemocratic conceptions of authority and thus keep them vividly alive in the popular mind. One cannot sit through the most ordinary session of the House of Commons without becoming aware that one is not only in a democratic as-

sembly but also, and more palpably, in the presence of awful and superior
majesty. There it is in the great golden mace on the table, the dignified
Georgian figure in the Speaker's chair, the obsequious bows in his direction by even the most radical members—indeed, some members of Parliament after bravely going upon the hustings have been rendered speechless
by the mere sight of the Speaker's wig. And if the impression of an
ordinary session in the Commons is majestic, how much more so is a
session in the Lords or an extraordinary session like the Opening of Parliament, when the Commons dutifully trudge to "the other place" on
gracious invitation and dutifully listen, while standing, to the gracious
Address from the Throne. The same thing applies to the Courts; the wigs
are important because they symbolize an attitude, and therefore also, even
if in a roundabout way, a practical fact; they are not simply scenery.

Indeed, the predemocratic institutions—the monarchy, the Lords, the
Lord Mayor, etc.—have an almost complete monopoly on the expressive
symbolism of British politics. There simply is nothing of democratic
vintage to compete against them except dry and abstract slogans. This
helps to inject into British political culture a pervasive set of non-democratic attitudes, and it also gives Britain something that few other democracies possess: a set of intelligible symbols of government and authority
that fully enlist the fancies and emotions of her people. Bagehot once said
that monarchy is the only form of government fully intelligible to ordinary
people and the only kind of government in which they will take a sustained personal interest:

> To state the matter shortly, Royalty is a government in which the atten-
> tions of the nation are concentrated on one person doing interesting
> actions. A Republic is a government in which that attention is divided
> between many, who are all doing uninteresting actions.[5]

Certainly there is a tenable point here. Constitutional government and
party government are hard things to be clearly conceived by ordinary
minds; they are too legally abstract and too complex in practice to be fully
intelligible to anyone but professionals, if indeed they are fully intelligible
even to them. Hence, the popular mind affixes loyalty to symbols (the
flag, the constitution), and the most effective of all such symbols are real-
life persons who can be cheered, speculated upon, gossiped about and
idolized. It is not insignificant in this connection that the British royal
house, despite the fact that it is composed mainly of very ordinary people,
should be as newsworthy in America as it is in Britain.

The ceremonial institutions therefore make for strong government in
two ways: by symbolizing and preserving predemocratic attitudes and by
endowing public service with a dignity, hence prestige, it possesses in few

[5] W. Bagehot, *The English Constitution.*

other democratic societies. "I wrote books," one Englishman is reputed to have said, "for twenty years, and I was nobody; I got into parliament, and before I had taken my seat I had become somebody." "English politicians," says Bagehot, "are the men who fill the thoughts of the English public . . . and it is hard for the ordinary spectators not to believe that the admired actor is greater than themselves."

Class Structure and Class Consciousness

Deference in politics is paralleled, indeed perhaps maintained, by deference in general social behavior. [Even in this age of the welfare state the British lower classes are still surprisingly deferential in their attitudes towards the British upper classes, a fact which helps to explain both why politics and administration (at least on the higher levels) are still very much in the hands of upper-class people and why they can wield such strong authority.] Indeed, the most substantial remains of the past in present British behavior are to be found not in government but in ordinary social life. The social ideologies associated with the rise of democracy, especially egalitarianism, have probably had a less substantial effect on British life than democratic theory itself, although the class relations which result have themselves modified the impact of democratic theory.

There is a vivid description of the British class system in the first chapter of H. G. Wells's *Tono-Bungay:*

> In that English countryside of my boyhood every human being had a "place." It belonged to you from birth like the colour of your eyes, it was inextricably your destiny. Above you were your betters, below you were your inferiors, and there were even an unstable questionable few cases so disputable that you might for the rough purposes of every day at least, regard them as your equals. Head and centre of our system was Lady Drew, her "leddyship," and . . . Miss Somerville, her cousin and companion. When I was a boy I used always to think of these two poor old creatures as superior beings living, like God, somewhere through the ceiling.
>
> Then there came and went on these floors over our respectful heads, the Company. . . . on the lowest fringe of these real Olympians being the vicarage people, and next to them came those ambiguous beings who are neither quality nor subjects. The doctor in Bladesover ranked below the vicar but above the "vet," artists and summer visitors squeezed in above or below this point according to their appearance and expenditure, and then in a carefully arranged scale came the tenantry, the butler and housekeeper, the village shopkeeper, the head keeper, the cook, the publican, and second keeper, the blacksmith (whose status was complicated by his daughter's keeping the post-office), and so forth. Dominating all these memories is the figure of my mother who knew with inflexible decision her place and the place of everyone in the world.

This is a description of rural society in the late nineteenth century, when the English caste system was rigid. Much has altered since, but nothing has changed so fundamentally as to make Wells entirely inapplicable to the present. Consider what another Englishman wrote at the height of World War II:

> The classes that in a crisis trust each other cannot in fact speak to each other. Even if their language is mutually intelligible (as it is not always), they have little or nothing to say to each other. The resident foreigner takes many years to learn the truth that you never come to the end of the English class structure, that new castes and sub-castes are forever being discovered. In despair, the observer may come to the conclusion that the English class structure consists of forty-odd million classes and that the one thing those classes have in common is Englishness, which may be nothing more (or less) than an unconscious acceptance of this odd state of affairs as right and natural for Englishmen. In no Western country is class-consciousness so widely spread, so much taken for granted.[6]

The war itself has undoubtedly made the system less rigid than it used to be; but even the war has not altered things in gist. It may be easier nowadays to engage an English stranger in conversation over a drink than it was once, but the pubs are still divided into public, private and saloon bars, and there are still great distinctions among the types that frequent them, in what they drink, and in how they amuse themselves. The "Bladesover" system, as Wells called it, still exists, even after a half-century of progressive Education Acts, democratization and socialization, and it is probably the key to everything that is distinctively British and perplexing to the foreign inquirer.

> Grasp firmly—said Wells—that all England was Bladesover two hundred years ago; that it has had Reform Acts indeed, and such-like changes of formula, but no *essential revolution* since then; that all that is modern and different has come in as a thing intruded or as a gloss upon this predominant formula; and you will perceive at once the reasonableness, the the necessity, of that snobbishness which is the distinctive quality of British thought.

That this snobbishness is itself a residue from premodern times, and therefore a result of Britain's lack of "essential revolutions," can be seen in the factors which determine one's place on the social stratification scale. These factors express typically aristocratic values. In a nutshell, *what* one is matters less in determining one's "place" than *who* one is: as the sociologists say, achievement is less important than ascription. Achievement matters, of course. If it cannot make one really "U" in Nancy Mitford's rather exotic sense it can at least make one near-U, and, indeed, British society has always been characterized by considerable social mobility. But the achievements valued most are themselves reflections of aristocratic values. The right education matters perhaps most of all. Next to that come the things which the right educational institutions—the

---

[6] D. Brogan, *The English People* (1943).

better "public" schools and Oxford and Cambridge—inculcate (and which can perhaps be learned nowhere else), the right manners and tastes: correctly accented speech, the right vocabulary, wit, certain kinds of dress, the right religion (High Church is upper class, Low Church is not), the right preferences in sport (cricket, rugby football, rowing, not soccer, dog racing or darts), in food and drink and entertainment. Least important perhaps is unmitigated wealth. Affluence helps one up the social ladder, but chiefly by making it relatively easy to acquire the right education and to indulge the right tastes: to become a "gentleman." British class stratification is therefore a matter of social rather than economic stratification and in this sense reflects the hierarchical ideas of aristocratic days.

Deferring to one's betters does not, however, imply being callously exploited or abjectly submissive. The extent to which deference is rendered is highly limited, especially nowadays. An immaculate accent will not buy precedence in a queue, or an extra allowance on the ration book, or an extra vote (a university degree did buy one up to 1950). Moreover, deference can be a matter of mere formality rather than outright submissiveness, and much of the deferential behavior of the British no doubt is ceremony pure and simple; thus, the fact that the British secretary habitually addresses her boss as "sir" does not mean *ipso facto* that she feels differently toward him from the American secretary who habitually calls her boss by his first name. British politics are certainly more democratic than a bald description of British class structure might lead one to expect.

Nevertheless, so deeply ingrained a set of behavior patterns as support the British class system are bound to affect political life. The upper classes are still today, despite democratization and economic leveling, ascendant: in the Cabinet, in Parliament and in the civil service; and, what is more important, their ascendance is almost beyond dispute. No doubt the composition of the upper classes has changed since the nineteenth century and no doubt there are more people of dubious social standing in positions of power today than there used to be, but the intrusion of lower strata into the higher circles of public life is less remarkable than the persistence of upper class domination. Democratization has put their reign upon another footing, party politics and the popular mandate, but the idea of the ruling class has been able to survive the broadening of the franchise simply because it has a solid foundation in public attitudes and behavior.

Bases of the Party System

However great the readiness of the British to accept strong leadership may be, this fact would not be important if the political system did not so constantly provide strong leaders. The reason it does is, of course, the disciplined two-party system; but what accounts for that?

It is very difficult to give a full explanation of the British party system, but one necessary element of it can be stated very simply. This is the extraordinarily pragmatic approach of the British to politics. There could be no two-party system and no party discipline—no meek marching into the division lobbies, no ready sublimation of private political beliefs—if the British were not so remarkably willing to compromise their political convictions. People are not likely to split into merely two camps on any single issue and certainly not on combinations of issues over protracted periods; hence the two-party system—unless indeed it is a multiparty system in disguise—presupposes a persistent willingness to compromise opinions. But under what conditions will people habitually compromise political opinions? Clearly, they are unlikely to do so if they profoundly and passionately believe in them, or if their convictions are derived not from isolated appraisals of isolated cases but from some general, all-inclusive ideology. There is no compromise with dogma. The fundamental secret of party discipline and the two-party system in Britain, therefore, is that British politicians, as a general rule, are not warm partisans, and, as someone has said, are "hard to work up to the dogmatic level." The prevalent political atmosphere is "empirical," "pragmatic," "unideological"—however one should put it. Few politicians seem to have a deep emotional or a profound philosophical stake in their positions and there exists a remarkable willingness to treat issues on their individual merits rather than on the basis of general political theories. Extremism is as hard to find on the Left as on the Right; the British have no deep doctrinal attachments to socialism or free enterprise, or indeed to any other set of dogmas. Closely related to this is the fact that the atmosphere of parliamentary debates is unusually courteous and rational.

But why are the British so calm and pragmatic in their approach to politics? Why are they never moved to rioting in the House of Commons and what keeps their disagreements so consistently out of the realm of metaphysics? Here it may be tempting to invoke the mysteries of the Anglo-Saxon soul, i.e., to say that the British are simply tepid and prosaic people. It is difficult to believe this. The crowds that cheer the royal outings are certainly not tepid crowds and the British have produced (but rarely followed in action) their fair share of political "philosophies." Nor is it necessary to be as mysterious about the phenomenon as this. Indeed, one may find a less obscurantist explanation for the sober atmosphere of British parliamentary politics in the very intoxication of the crowds that cheer the queen. This needs to be explained in a somewhat roundabout way.

Once upon a time an M.P., accused by an opponent of making an anomalous statement, replied that he was delighted to hear it because the British are a people who like anomalies; and that moreover they had been able to operate democratic institutions so effectively precisely because they were an "illogical" people. The point was made facetiously but, in a curious way, it is both true and important. The British are "illogical," first, because of their profound emotional attachment to persons and institutions that are, from a superficial practical standpoint, mere glitter and gloss and probably unjustifiable in terms of the Briton's own conscious political values. They are illogical, second, because they leave such a vast range of their political behavior to usage rather than to rationally devised rules and processes. But these, one may argue, are the very things that account for their extraordinary pragmatism in politics and therefore also, indirectly, for the effectiveness of their parliamentary system.

First of all this means that the British, although they probably have as much need for emotional behavior as any other people, can act with sober pragmatism in parliamentary politics because their political passions are channeled toward and satisfied by other aspects of their political system: their ceremonial institutions—above all, of course, the monarchy. Party politics, that is to say, are insulated against excessive emotional behavior simply because the political passions of the British have other outlets in a set of generally accepted and politically innocuous (if not irrelevant) institutions. Where the political emotions do not readily find such outlets they tend to fix themselves on other objects, frequently political ideologies. Such ideologies, more often than not, are held for emotional rather than rational reasons and, above all, have the function of enlisting the passions of people who want at least to appear "reasonable" in their political behavior.

The emotional value of political ideologies, however, is not their only *raison d'être*; they have an even more important function. By providing comprehensive theories of politics (or indeed life in general) they make it unnecessary to deal with individual issues on their individual merits; in short, they make it unnecessary for people to think and to deliberate. Ideologies are like theoretical sausage machines; one feeds in problematic meat at one end and out comes a string of policy sausages at the other, beautifully integrated and consistent. And because they obviate real thought on individual issues they can become terribly necessary under certain conditions, particularly when the political system presents an unusually large number of unresolved issues, or, putting the same point another way, when an unusually large area of behavior is subject to political decision-making. This point can perhaps be clarified best by an analogy with individual behavior. We know that individual men tend to break down—frequently, indeed, as the French sociologist Durkheim found, to commit suicide—when they are confronted with the need of making a vast range of decisions. The human personality seems capable of handling only a limited range of problematic choices and when the range becomes too large, when too much action becomes subject to rational deliberation rather than to authority and conditioning, *anomie* (as Durkheim called it) is likely to result. But suicide, or some other obvious derangement, need not be the inevitable result of *anomie*. Indeed, it may be more normal to respond to the situation by compulsively seeking out and subscribing to some comprehensive ideology that makes thought superfluous. This does not mean that human beings are incapable of making rational decisions on problematic choices; it does mean that the smaller the demands on their reasoning faculties the more likely they are to use reasoning, and not some pseudo-reasoning.

The British, then, are highly immune to ideologies—pragmatic in outlook—not only because their passions are channeled out of ordinary politics but also because the political system confronts them, comparatively speaking, with a narrow range of unresolved issues. And this in turn is due to two factors. First, it is due to the very weight attached to usage in British political ideas. Questions that are highly explosive issues in other societies—for example, the basic question of the proper organization of government and proper procedure—are left in Britain, to a very large extent, to be settled by custom. Second, it is due to a factor mentioned at the very beginning of the chapter: the existence of broad political agreement on questions not settled by habit—broad agreement not only on the constitution but even on policy. This agreement is seen most clearly in three things: the absence of any important extremist groups, Right or Left; the lack of constitutional issues among the major parties; and the reconciliation of the Conservative Party to the welfare state largely instituted by the Labour Government of 1945. It is a very old axiom of political science and of common sense that people are more likely to reconcile their political differences by rational discussion if they have a large range of views in common. But, even more important, a large area of political agreement simply limits the range of problematic choices and thereby enables men to approach the issues in a more sober and open, i.e., rational, frame of mind.

If political pragmatism does not sufficiently explain why the British *do* have a disciplined two-party system, it does at least explain why it is *possible* for them to have such a system. A full and sufficient explanation would no doubt take into account also the habit of deference to political leaders, the fixed idea, derived from the very mechanics of parliamentary government (the constant alternation of Government and Opposition), that government is somehow naturally conducted on a bi-polar basis, the special need for large-scale party organization created by the single-member constituency electoral system[7]—perhaps even the peculiar seating arrangements of the House of Commons.[8] But none of these things could be of the slightest significance if it were not for the spirit of British politics; that is indispensable and fundamental.

Democracy in Britain

We have dwelt at length upon the extraordinary capacity of the British political system to produce strong leadership—even when the leaders are not commanding personalities—partly because it *is* so very unusual for a democratic system to produce such leadership so consistently. But is Britain really a democracy?

Ultimately this is a semantic issue and no more. But no one will deny that British government and politics have at least some of the more important characteristics generally considered democratic. If mandates are not the only source of authority, a clear mandate, once given, is considered absolutely binding. Ordinary people have considerable opportunities to participate in the political process, not only in elections but through parties, interest organizations and ideological associations. The channels through which they participate are highly regularized and institutionalized. They are regularly presented with choices among competitive sets of rulers and the essential civil liberties which alone make political liberty effective are scrupulously preserved. Thus, if the cabinet—as some writers have alleged—is practically a dictatorship, it is a dictatorship strongly tempered by democratic processes that are not mere façade.

Even more important, British Governments are powerfully restrained by some of the very factors that account for their great power in the first place. That the British constitution has very ancient foundations, that it has developed by accretion rather than upheaval, means that it contains not only authoritarian elements but also the restraining values of pre-absolutist constitutionalism. The idea of a binding law not subject to human will, the ideas of due process and limited government, the ideas of parliamentary authority over finance and its rights as a committee of grievances—all of which are medieval—have survived in British political culture quite as much as the absolutist notions added later. There is, then, in Britain a powerful "constitutional morality" that does quite as much to tame the leaders' power as democratic processes. The authority of the leaders is accepted as something independent, but it is also *contingent*

[7] For a discussion of this point, see below, pp. 132-135.

[8] See p. 93.

upon their adherence to rules that tradition and the sense of the nation prescribe and the restriction of public action to areas that, in the constitutional sense of the nation, are subject to public action. No leadership would be considered authoritative if it suspended elections (except in war), imposed censorship upon the press, kept Parliament in dissolution, quarreled openly within itself, or even perhaps merely violated those niceties of parliamentary procedure that the British sense of ceremony insists upon. And by far the most important of the rules on which constitutional morality insists are rules guaranteeing the parliamentary opposition full rights of debate and criticism on measures introduced by the Government, the chance to ask questions about the conduct of administration, and the chance to air grievances in special debates—in short, rules especially useful in imposing discipline upon the rulers themselves. "To discipline Parliament ministers must first discipline themselves" because they operate "within a framework of established expectations"—these phrases by H. J. Laski put the point exactly.

This framework of established expectations is all the more constraining because it is so widely agreed upon and puts such a high value on usage. Consensus on policy and process may set in motion a chain of effects that ultimately produce strong leadership, but consensus in its very nature limits the exercise of such leadership to what is consented to. That the British are so widely agreed upon the essential outlines of the postwar welfare state may give British leaders great power to institute certain social and economic measures, but it puts an equally powerful limit on their ability to institute others. So, even more, does the attachment to usage. Thus, the Labour Government of 1945 was able to enact a program of social and economic legislation unparalleled in scope among democratic societies; but when it tried to reform certain aspects of the cumbersome, time-wasting, traditional processes for enacting financial legislation in the House of Commons it had to settle, in the face of powerful opposition, for only one small and very insignificant change.

In short, whether Britain is a democracy or not, British government is at least supremely constitutional in character. Indeed, British political culture contains within itself a sort of check-and-balance system, in that it makes simultaneously for active and limited leadership, the twin purposes of any separation of powers. And this is the case because British conceptions of legitimacy are a unique combination of democratic and predemocratic notions, expressed in a set of governmental processes that daily revive and re-enact the past, in a society where ideas of equality and hierarchy coexist in easy inconsistency.

CHAPTER 9

The Cabinet

Cabinet and Parliament

[The central structure in the pattern of power of the British political system is the Cabinet.] It does not, of course, act in a vacuum. Its freedom of choice is hemmed in by the influence of many other centers of power—in the parties, in the civil service, in groups among the electorate. We can conceive of a political situation in which such a body would be in effect powerless in the face of such influences, obliged merely to record the decisions already made elsewhere. The electoral college in the United States is in this position, in fact able only to register the results of the presidential contest in the various states. So also is the Supreme Soviet in relation to the higher organs of the Communist Party of the U.S.S.R. While not by any means without limits, the wide freedom of choice normally enjoyed by the Cabinet makes it the natural place to begin a study of the distribution of power in the British system.

Bagehot, in a classic and still useful formula, said that the Cabinet is "a combining committee—a hyphen which joins, a buckle which fastens, the legislative part of the state to the executive part of the state." [It is not, however, merely a glorified liaison committee mediating between the legislature and the executive; nor will it do to describe it, as it has often been described, as the executive committee of the majority party in the House of Commons.] This formula suggests too much dependence on Parliament, too much "democracy." To be sure, [Cabinets are almost invariably composed of the leaders of the majority party in Parliament and Parliament can unmake them as well as make them, so that, in a sense, the Cabinet exercises only those powers that Parliament suffers it to exercise.] But when one penetrates behind appearances the Cabinet turns out to be a very curious legislative committee indeed. In the first place, [it may include men who are not members of Parliament at all. Much more seriously, it possesses certain powers that make it not the creature

75

but the master of Parliament. For example, as Parliament can unmake the Cabinet, so the Cabinet can unmake Parliament, by dissolving it and calling new elections. Again, Parliament is not entitled to be informed of Cabinet proceedings, and many things done in Cabinet are in fact withheld from it. In addition, the Cabinet possesses a kind of veto over certain kinds of measures—specifically those involving expenditures of money (i.e., most important bills)—even if they are wanted by an overwhelming majority of Parliament, because constitutional usage provides that such measures must be initiated by a Minister of the Crown. Not long ago, for example, the House of Commons, in a lopsided vote, came out for an increase in M.P.s' salaries; but so unsupreme is Parliament in matters having a financial aspect that the Cabinet's refusal to introduce legislation killed the project more effectively than any presidential veto in the United States.

Undoubtedly, the Cabinet can dictate to Parliament chiefly because of the brute political facts that make for party discipline in Great Britain, but that is not the only source of its authority. It also derives power, both directly and indirectly, from the fact that it has taken over the powers historically lodged in the Crown, powers that are not directly dependent either on parliamentary grant or sufferance. "Powers of the Crown" of course means powers considered to inhere in the sovereign: the queen's "prerogatives." In the distant past these were quite considerable but in the course of centuries more and more inroads into them were made. Some were signed away by "contracts" between king and "people" (e.g., Magna Charta); some were taken away by prohibitive legislation (e.g., the prohibition of the early royal privileges of pre-emption and purveyance); many simply disappeared through long disuse. But the residue is not negligible. It is a prerogative of the Crown to make peers and create other titles of honor, to appoint a large number of public officials, to pardon criminals, to perform all acts of an "international character" (declaring war, making treaties, carrying on diplomatic relations) and to summon, prorogue and dissolve Parliament. It is not, of course, the queen herself who does these things. The sovereign, as the classic formula goes, has only "the right to be consulted, the right to encourage and the right to warn": in short, to influence her ministers. It is the ministers who in fact exercise the "prerogatives." Nevertheless, this does not mean that the powers of the Crown are, indirectly, "parliamentary" powers after all. It means simply that the Cabinet is the repository, at one and the same time, of powers flowing from Parliament and from the monarchy, of derivative and independent powers. The Cabinet has, therefore, a dual character. On one hand it is the leadership of Parliament; on the other, it is also the institution that it was the historic function of Parliament to limit and control, the Crown; and as the latter it is something more than the former, something more powerful, more mysterious, and more august.]

Is it any wonder that there has been a great deal of talk in recent decades about "cabinet dictatorship" in Britain? Certainly even the barest outlines of its functions make it appear suspiciously omnipotent. The Cabinet defines the lines of national policy; it controls and co-ordinates administration; it arranges parliamentary business and introduces the vast majority of bills; it is responsible for all expenditures and taxes; it controls appointments to great offices of state. This does not mean, of course, that the Cabinet is a "dictatorship" in any serious sense. But certainly when the British refer to the Cabinet as *"the* Government" they do not do so as a mere matter of form. How then is the Cabinet constituted and how does it discharge its tremendous responsibilities?

How a Cabinet Is Constituted

Selection of the Prime Minister

[The first step in the constitution of a Cabinet is the appointment of a Prime Minister, who in turn appoints the other Cabinet members and non-Cabinet ministers (or rather "advises" the queen that they be appointed although her action is mere formality)] The appointment of the Prime Minister is one of the few remaining functions of the sovereign that are of any importance, although this power too is so limited by convention as to be almost an empty formality. The general rule is that the queen must appoint whatever leader is capable of commanding the support of a majority in Parliament.

[In the vast majority of instances the need to select a new Prime Minister arises under conditions that pose no problems at all and leave the monarch no free choice among various candidates.] Nowadays elections generally culminate in an outright majority in the House of Commons for one of the two major parties and each party almost invariably has a recognized leader. The queen's function after a national election therefore is simply to ask the known leader of the successful party to form a Government. [When a Government suffers a parliamentary defeat—a rare occurrence in this day of tight party discipline—it has two courses open to it. It may dissolve Parliament and appeal to the electorate by means of a new election, or it may resign—in which case the queen will call on the recognized leader of the opposition party (and he is always known because he draws a government salary) to form a new Government.] If a Prime Minister dies or resigns there usually is a recognized second-in-command to take his place[Difficulties arise only when the majority party has no recognized leader or no recognized second-in-command, when there is no clear majority, or when the majority party is torn by dissension.]

In 1931, Ramsay MacDonald, then Prime Minister of a Labour Government, felt obliged to offer his resignation because of serious dissension in his Cabinet. In opposition at the time were not only the Conservatives, but also a substantial group of Liberals. If MacDonald had simply resigned without tendering advice, the king might have had some freedom of choice of a successor. As was his right, however, MacDonald, advised that the king confer with the Conservative and Liberal leaders, both of whom recommended that the king ask MacDonald to continue as Prime Minister, but at the head of a coalition Government. While this undoubtedly was the king's personal preference also, it gave him no opportunity to act independently and on his own. Similarly, the resignation of Neville Chamberlain in 1940, although taking place in an unusual parliamentary situation, did not result in any significant exercise of power by the king. Chamberlain, the head of what was essentially a Conservative Government, lost the support of a large block of his normal supporters in the House, although he did not suffer an outright defeat. He concluded that since Britain was at war, it would be necessary to form a coalition Government including all parties. Finding that Labour would not serve under him, he consulted with two leading Conservatives, Winston Churchill and Lord Halifax, on the question of whom he should advise the king to summon. Halifax having bowed out, it was clear that the duty would fall on Churchill, who proceeded to form his famous wartime Government.

When Harold Macmillan became Prime Minister after Sir Anthony Eden resigned early in 1957, it looked to many observers as if the queen had passed over the obvious and proper choice. This was R. A. Butler, former Chancellor of the Exchequer, who was generally regarded as the second-in-command to Eden and who had presided over the Cabinet during Eden's long absence from the country before his resignation. We do not yet know the inside story of this surprise. We do know that the queen acted on the advice of certain elder statesmen of the Conservative Party. It has also been said that behind this advice lay the fact that during the Suez crisis Butler had aroused the strong hostility of certain sections of the party. In consequence, as soundings in the party showed, the supporters of Butler would serve under Macmillan, but those who preferred Macmillan would refuse office under Butler. Again, however, as in the other cases mentioned above, the sovereign in fact had no real freedom of choice.

[Before the middle of the nineteenth century the monarch often had a real choice among rival candidates for the Prime Ministership, but in recent generations the mechanics of the two-party system have generally ground out the man for the job, without difficulty.]

Selection of the Cabinet and Ministry

[The first task of the Prime Minister is to appoint his Cabinet and Ministry. While all Cabinet members are Ministers, not all Ministers are Cabinet members] Nowadays, a Prime Minister has nearly one hundred political appointments to make upon taking office and the vast majority of these appointments are to offices having ministerial status. There are, first of all, about two dozen administrative departments (such as the Treasury, the Admiralty, the Ministry of Health, the Home Office, the Colonial Office) to which Ministers—"Departmental Ministers"—must be appointed. Then there are a small handful of ministerial positions which involve no departmental duties and to which the Prime Minister generally names important politicians whom he wants to serve him as general advisers; e.g., the Lord President of the Council, the Lord Privy Seal, the Chancellor of the Duchy of Lancaster, the Paymaster General, and whatever "Ministers without Portfolio" the Prime Minister wishes to create— usually none, since the ceremonial ministries enumerated provide ample scope for the appointment of general advisers. Then,[since 1941, a number of ministers called "Ministers of State" have been in existence; their purpose has been to assist the Departmental Ministers of important and overworked departments while having a higher status than the parliamentary Secretaries of the Ministries] The latter are also Ministers, but a lowlier variety[Technically they are not "Ministers of the Crown," since they are not appointed by the queen] their main purpose is to assist the Ministers, especially in their parliamentary duties, and most of them are young men who are being trained for bigger and better things. Finally, there are still a few other persons who have ministerial status, most notably the[Government Whips, whose chief function is to help the Prime Minister ride herd on his supporters in the House of Commons and who are generally made Lords of the Treasury or given appointments in the Royal Household, all ceremonial positions we need not worry about.]

Not even the British, with all their gift for committee work, could operate a Cabinet composed of all these people, or even of the Departmental Ministers alone. Hence[it is up to the Prime Minister to determine which of them shall sit in the Cabinet,] and the Cabinets of the present century have in fact had memberships varying from an even half dozen to close to two dozen, the size lately having been between sixteen and eighteen. The great and old Departments of State—the Treasury, the Foreign Ministry, the Home Office, etc.—almost invariably rate Cabinet seats; the less important Ministries sometimes manage to get representation, e.g., when they are headed by a Minister who has a relatively high status in his party or when they deal with a subject that for the moment looms large in the public eye. Thus, when Aneurin Bevan was Minister of Health during the years when the National Health Service was brought into operation, the Ministry of Health rated a Cabinet seat. But when the important Mr. Bevan was replaced by the relatively less important Mr. Marquand the Ministry was dropped from the Cabinet. One cannot therefore be absolutely sure, from one Ministry to the next, what Ministers will have Cabinet status.[1]

Constitutional convention gives the Prime Minister complete authority to decide who will be members of his Cabinet. His actual power, however, is greatly circumscribed by political realities. Every Prime Minister has certain eminent and powerful colleagues whose appointment to the Cabinet is a foregone conclusion. Every party, in the nature of the two-party system, has wings of opinion whose leaders must, in the interest of harmony, be included. Hence, a certain number of Ministers *known* to have been objectionable to their chiefs (e.g., Joseph Chamberlain, Sir William Harcourt, probably also Aneurin Bevan) have found their way into the Cabinet. Again, every Ministry (and indeed every Cabinet, including the Socialist Cabinets) contains some peers to represent the Government in the House of Lords.[2] There is a certain amount of geographical selection—a Scot and a Welshman are almost invariably

---

[1] Compare, for example, the Labour Government of 1949 and the Conservative Government of 1955. Ministers included in both were the following:
　　(1) Prime Minister and First Lord of the Treasury (it has long been customary for the Prime Minister to assume the title "First Lord of the Treasury")
　　(2) Lord President of the Council (Leader of the House of Commons under Labour)
　　(3) Lord Privy Seal (Leader of the House of Commons under the Conservatives)
　　(4) Secretary of State for Foreign Affairs
　　(5) Chancellor of the Exchequer
　　(6) Lord Chancellor
　　(7) Secretary of State for the Home Department
　　(8) Minister of Defence
　　(9) Chancellor of the Duchy of Lancaster (also Minister of Materials in the Conservative Government)
　　(10) Secretary of State for the Colonies
　　(11) Secretary of State for Commonwealth Relations
　　(12) Secretary of State for Scotland
　　(13) Minister of Labour and National Service
　　(14) President of the Board of Trade
　　(15) Minister of Education
　　(16) Minister of Agriculture and Fisheries (also Minister of Food under the Conservatives)
　　The Minister of Health was included in 1949 but not in 1955, the Minister of Pensions and National Insurance was included in 1955 but the two Ministers responsible for these things in 1949 (before the Ministries were combined) were left out. Thirteen Departmental Ministers were left out in 1949, eight in 1955.

[2] The appointment of a certain number of peers to ministerial positions is required by law.

included. Certain men come in because a powerful and therefore indispensable man espouses their cause; in fact "combinations"—by which one man refuses to enter the Government unless certain others are also chosen —are known. A good many men are selected almost on the basis of seniority, for having served long parliamentary apprenticeships as faithful party wheel-horses; a few have the influence—e.g., family connections—to force their way into prominent positions; and Junior Ministers are usually selected on the recommendations of their seniors. Indeed, even the division of Cabinet offices is not freely up to the Prime Minister. Powerful and eminent politicians are frequently in a position to pick their places. And it should not be forgotten that when a party is out of power it forms a "shadow Cabinet," certain of its leaders being charged with leading the opposition in specific areas of policy. These men consequently have a powerful claim to the Ministries of their special areas.

None of this means, however, that the Prime Minister merely recognizes a series of *faits accomplis* on taking office. Much is still left to his discretion and the days when he sees his colleagues to discuss appointments are days of great suspense outside No. 10 Downing Street and, one gathers, no little excitement inside. "It is like the Zoo at feeding time," said Lord Salisbury. Ramsay MacDonald, in 1929, remarked to Hugh Dalton, then a promising young man being offered an undersecretaryship: "It's been terrible: I have had people in here weeping and fainting." The Prime Minister can keep, and has kept, out the most eminent of politicians and, as he can appoint a man, so also he can dismiss him. While dismissals of Ministers have been few and far between they have occurred, and so have forcible transfers of Ministers from one job to another. The Cabinet is the Prime Minister's Cabinet and the Ministry is the Prime Minister's Ministry, just as much as it is a party Cabinet and Ministry.[3]

How the Cabinet Works

Collective Responsibility: Secrecy

Much of the Cabinet's procedure is shaped by two of the most basic constitutional conventions applying to its operation, the rule of collective responsibility and the rule of secrecy in regard to Cabinet business. One former Prime Minister stated the rule of collective responsibility thus: "For all that passes in the Cabinet each member of it who does not resign is absolutely and irretrievably responsible, and has no right afterwards to say that he agreed in one case to a compromise, while in another he was persuaded by his colleagues." "This means," explained Lord

[3] But it is worth noting that dismissals of Ministers were far more common in the nineteenth than in the twentieth century, because, no doubt, of differences in the importance of party.

Morley, "that the Chancellor of the Exchequer may be driven from office by a bad dispatch from the Foreign Office, and an excellent Home Secretary may suffer for the blunders of a stupid Minister of War." The British Cabinet, in short, is a truly collective leadership: the acts of each member are the acts of all, and all stand or fall together. This does not mean that all Cabinet decisions must be taken unanimously; majority decisions are enough. What the rule does require is that if a Minister (Cabinet or non-Cabinet) wants to take his dissensions into the public light he must resign his office, as Aneurin Bevan did in 1951 after it was decided to put charges on National Health Service dentures and spectacles, or as Anthony Eden did in 1938 because he disagreed with Neville Chamberlain's appeasement of Hitler. If he does not want to resign, he must refrain from opposing the Cabinet's decision in public and indeed must support it in Parliament, before the party and before the public, not only by obediently voting for the Cabinet's decision but even by speaking for it. Lord Melbourne once said after a Cabinet meeting in the early nineteenth century: "By the bye . . . what are we to say? Is it to make our corn dearer, or cheaper, or to make the price steady? I don't care *which*: but we had better all be in the same story."

Collective responsibility no doubt imposes strains on the Cabinet as a whole and on individual Ministers. Even on the most unimportant level of Cabinet mechanics it creates certain difficulties, which a looser, more American, conception of the Cabinet's operation might obviate. For example, there is a great reluctance to take votes in the Cabinet, and consequently a tendency to spin out discussion, since the Cabinet tries to conceal its divisions even from itself. When votes are taken, all sorts of subterfuges are used to prevent the exact divisions from becoming known; and, as we shall see below, the doctrine of collective responsibility used to make for a very inadequate system of Cabinet records. How then did the doctrine originate and what purpose does it serve in the current operation of British government? Why is it one of the fundamental rules of the constitution?

The notion of collective responsibility first developed in the eighteenth century—when Ministers were still the King's Ministers in a real sense—as a protective device used by the Cabinet against the king. As long as Ministers stood or fell individually it was relatively easy for the sovereign to dominate them, since someone could always be found to replace an individual Minister. But to replace a whole Ministry was another matter. Subsequently, the rule proved as useful a protective device against Parliament and party as against the Sovereign. The opposition is deprived of the opportunity to set Ministers against one another and embarrass the Government. Likewise, factions within the majority party itself are prevented from promoting the political fortunes of this or that minister at the expense of his rivals in the Government. The notion of collective responsibility, therefore, has a curiously paradoxical historical significance. In its infancy it played a role in the development of parliamentary government; subsequently, as the dominance of Parliament over Crown and of the majority party in Parliament was established, it served as a disciplinary device over the parliamentary hordes and thus helped to preserve that degree of executive independence that is the hallmark of the British parliamentary system. In either case the rule served to increase the power of the Cabinet.

There are exceptions to the rule of collective responsibility, and there need to be, since it is manifestly impossible to take all administrative and policy decisions, even the most important, in Cabinet. In fact, the Cabinet as a group transacts only a small proportion of ministerial business. The vast majority of decisions are taken by individual Ministers, the rule being, in gist, that nothing is to be brought before the Cabinet unless it is the subject of serious political controversy or unless serious disagreements between different departments exist—and woe to the Minister who imposes on his frantically busy colleagues by repeatedly bringing unnecessary business before them. Hence, the notion of collective responsibility is not so overdone as to become a manifest fiction: there is such a thing as individual responsibility as well. If, for example, a particular Minister is seriously unpopular, the Government may improve its public relations by dismissing him (forcing him to "resign") or by reshuffling offices. It is even possible for the Government to force an individual Minister to take responsibility for what was really a Cabinet decision in order to save its own skin, although this, admittedly, is very exceptional. The case usually cited is that of Sir Samuel Hoare's resignation over the so-called Hoare-Laval Plan in 1935. With the Cabinet's knowledge and approval, Hoare, the Foreign Secretary, had made an agreement with Laval, then French Prime Minister, approving a partition of Ethiopia as a means of appeasing Mussolini. When word of the agreement was "leaked," a storm of wrathful protest swept Britain. The Cabinet bowed, repudiated the agreement and dropped Hoare from office.

On the other hand, it is not quite so unusual for the Cabinet to leave questions "open," so that Ministers may publicly say what they please about them. One Government, the National Government of 1932, composed of Conservatives, Liberals, and a few Labourites, took the unprecedented step of engaging in a public "agreement to differ" over extremely important points of policy, for the sake of preserving if not true unity then at least a semblance of it in the face of the great depression.

Just as there are exceptions to the rule of collective responsibility, so are there chinks in the Cabinet secrecy it helps to preserve. When responsibility is publicly fixed on some individual Minister, Cabinet secrets tend to tumble out. Even more, when individual Ministers feel constrained to shed the chains of collective responsibility by resigning, revelations usually are made, the rule being that any resigning Minister may explain his reasons to the House and, if given permission to do so by the Crown (and permission is usually given), may then reveal Cabinet transactions.

[The rule of secrecy is enforced by an oath taken by all Cabinet members as Privy Councillors and by the Official Secrets Acts, which forbid the publication of Cabinet documents] But it is not really law that makes British Cabinet members so very secretive; as usual, the law takes second place to practical considerations.[Cabinet secrecy, like collective responsibility, is a defensive device against outsiders] indeed the two concepts developed together, the latter presupposing the former and both being directed against the same "enemies." Even more important, perhaps, secrecy makes for free expression by Cabinet Ministers and for speed in the transaction of business. If Ministers were aware that their remarks in Cabinet would be made public, their Cabinet behavior would certainly be different from what it is. They would probably suppress a good many facts and their statements would lose that frankness and brevity that make plural decision-making possible under modern conditions.

Organization and Process

[But however useful the rule of secrecy may be from a practical standpoint, there was a time when it drastically interfered with the efficiency of the Cabinet. Before the first World War the rule was taken so seriously that no Cabinet records were kept and no Minister was even allowed to take notes of Cabinet discussions. The only exception was the Prime Minister, who was permitted to take cursory notes of decisions to enable him to report accurately to the sovereign. The results, as government became a constantly more pressing affair after the leisurely days of Peel, can be imagined.] They are vividly suggested in a famous note from Lord Hartington's private secretary to Gladstone's secretary in 1882: "Harcourt and Chamberlain have both been here this morning, and *at* my Chief about yesterday's Cabinet proceedings. They cannot agree about what occurred. There must have been some decision, as Bright's resignation shows. My Chief has told me to ask you what the devil *was* decided, for he be damned if he knows." Nevertheless, it was not until 1916 that someone (Lloyd George) did something about the situation, and then of course it was the stress of war that helped to break down the old convention, both by showing the need for displacing it and by creating an atmosphere of urgency in which the change could be made.

Since then a set of records (the Cabinet "Conclusions" or, as they are more generally known, "minutes") has been kept and the Cabinet has been provided with a Secretariat to keep them and in other ways to facilitate Cabinet business. Something of the old rule, however, lives on in the brevity and anonymity of the records kept by the Secretariat. Nothing like a stenographic record is taken. A Cabinet "minute" usually summarizes the documents on which the Cabinet has had to make a decision, sets out the gist of any pertinent statement of *fact* made in discussion and of the general arguments urged by a member, and then gives a full statement of the decision taken. The notes on which the "minute" is based are taken by a member of the Secretariat. The Cabinet tries to preserve its privacy at all costs and tolerates only as few outsiders as absolutely necessary, even from its own staff. This also is a convention with a purpose. Herbert Morrison, an important member of the postwar Labour Government, has pointed out that when "strangers" are present in the Cabinet a certain constraint is likely to fall upon discussions, and certain things that would certainly be talked out in a conference of party colleagues, particularly items of political strategy and tactics, are likely to be suppressed.[4]

The Cabinet Secretariat itself was taken over lock, stock, and barrel during World War I from the Committee of Imperial Defence[5] and today consists of a Permanent Secretary, two Deputy Secretaries, an Under-Secretary, a Senior Assistant Secretary and five Assistant Secretaries, a rather intimate group of extremely high-powered and privileged officials. The original purpose of the Secretariat was to keep records of Cabinet decisions, but by the end of the war it was clear that it could facilitate Cabinet business in a great many other ways as well and its duties have therefore gradually increased, as has its staff. Guided by the Prime Minister, it prepares the Cabinet agenda; it sees to it that all items of Cabinet business are properly supported by memoranda and that the memoranda are properly circulated to the proper people at the proper time; it makes sure that non-Cabinet Ministers involved in an item of Cabinet business are present at the relevant discussions. At times the Secretariat has also

[4] Meetings on "political" subjects are in fact held without the presence of a member of the Secretariat and, of course, no records of such meetings are kept.

[5] The Committee of Imperial Defence was created shortly after the turn of the century, for the purpose of co-ordinating defense measures and basing military policy, both in peace and war, on consistent plans. It had only one permanent member, the Prime Minister, but the persons usually attending, besides the Prime Minister, included the political heads of the military departments and the Commander in Chief, with the heads of the military Intelligence Departments as joint Secretaries and a clerk from the Foreign Office to keep minutes. As the Committee's work grew, and as it proliferated, as Committees will, into a large number of subcommittees, it gradually acquired a sizable Secretariat to prepare the agenda, keep minutes and perform liaison work with other departments (notably the Foreign Office) interested in defense policy.

included special advisory and fact-finding bodies; for example, during World War II and for some time after it included an Economic Section and a Central Statistical Office, which, in fact, did most of the fact-finding and thinking on which central economic planning was based.

No doubt the work of the Secretariat has made modern Cabinets somewhat more efficient than their Victorian counterparts, but even so it may be difficult to see how the Cabinet can be an efficient instrument of government. First, there is its size. It is notoriously difficult for large groups to transact business jointly and the Cabinet, nowadays, is certainly a large group. In the nineteenth century, Cabinets rarely had more than a dozen members and after the first World War a special committee—the Machinery of Government Committee of the Ministry of Reconstruction —decided that this was just about the ideal size. Between the wars, however, Cabinets grew to as many as twenty-two members, and the usual size nowadays is sixteen to eighteen. But even this figure includes only Ministers of *regular* Cabinet status and does not give an accurate idea of the number of persons who participate in Cabinet discussions, since non-Cabinet Ministers interested in items of policy before the Cabinet are almost invariably called in for its conferences. The *real* size of the Cabinet makes it verge upon a public meeting.

Since there is general agreement on the desirability of smaller Cabinets —and since in times of urgency, especially war, Cabinets have been greatly reduced in size[6]—it seems clear that forces beyond the control of Prime Ministers are pushing the Cabinet's size in an undesirable direction. One of these forces is obvious: the growth in scope and complexity of the pattern of policy. This expansion of government business has led to a proliferation of administrative departments and every administrative department, by custom, has at least a claim to Cabinet representation. But this is not the whole story. The custom of excluding the less important administrative departments has long been established and from an administrative standpoint it is surely enough to allow the Ministers of the excluded departments to sit in on Cabinet meetings dealing with matters falling within their jurisdiction. Hence, it seems reasonable to assume that certain other factors are of greater importance than the proliferation of Departments. One perhaps is sheer habit: the custom of including departments in the Cabinet if at all possible, a legacy of the more intimate administrative days of the nineteenth century. Another is a matter of politics: Cabinet membership is the greatest political prize short of the Prime Ministership. The more powerful party men are rewarded with it the less gnashing of teeth and intriguing there is likely to

[6] Lloyd George's War Cabinet had five members; Sir Winston Churchill's Inner Cabinets during the second World War consisted first of eight, then seven, members.

be in the Prime Minister's party; and the larger the number of Cabinet members the less onerous the burden of selection upon the Prime Minister. The rules of political calculation in this instance simply outweigh the rules of administrative calculation, as indeed they usually do in a democracy.

Closely related to the size of the Cabinet as a factor making difficult its efficient operation is the great pressure of business it must discharge nowadays. The good old days when a Prime Minister could keep a personal check on all the administrative departments, acquaint himself with all problems of policy and express informed opinions on them, ended with Peel.[7] Gladstone tried to emulate his great predecessor for some time but as he grew in age and wisdom he gave up the attempt—and government in Gladstone's day was ridiculously simple compared to what it is today. A Cabinet that tried to keep its fingers on all the hundreds of pulses of modern public life could hardly manage with a mere twenty-four hours in the day. Yet the Cabinet scarcely meets more often today than in the days of Peel himself; it usually has two meetings a week lasting about two hours each. Nor could it be otherwise. Cabinet members have far too many non-Cabinet duties to spend a very large proportion of their time in No. 10 Downing Street. They are parliamentarians and must spend a good deal of time in the House; they are the high command of a political party with electoral purposes to achieve; they are ceremonial figures who must often preside at public functions; they are the heads of administrative departments, which they are supposed to supervise. How then does the Cabinet economize its business so as to make ministerial life bearable? How can it perform its plethora of functions in a mere four hours a week?

The first labor-saving device it uses, as we already know, is to leave as much as possible to the decision of individual Ministers. Another is full interdepartmental discussion of business involving more than one administrative jurisdiction. But undoubtedly the most important of all the devices that help the Cabinet do its work are the Cabinet Committees, usually composed of a small number of Cabinet members but sometimes also of non-Cabinet Ministers and distinguished non-parliamentary experts. These committees perform what amount to Cabinet functions in certain specific areas of policy. Like individual Ministers they may refer questions to the Cabinet for decision or decide them themselves (any Minister being allowed to appeal a committee decision to the Cabinet). But since their function is to relieve the Cabinet of work most questions are nowadays decided in committee rather than in full Cabinet session.

The use of Cabinet committees can be traced back to the nineteenth century, but they began playing a prominent part in the machinery of

[7] Sir Robert Peel was Prime Minister from 1834 to 1835 and 1841 to 1846.

government only in the twentieth, as the pressure of Cabinet business continually grew. A vivid conception of the quantitative changes that have occurred in the process of government in the last few decades can be gathered from a brief glance at the development of the Cabinet Committee system during the last generation. In 1929, apart from the Committee of Imperial Defence and a small number of *ad hoc* committees formed from time to time for special purposes, only one Standing (i.e., permanent) Committee was in operation—the Home Affairs Committee. This, moreover, performed a technical rather than deliberative function, its duties being confined to the examination of Bills about to be presented to Parliament. Most business was transacted by the full Cabinet. In contrast, the post-World War II Labour Government used no fewer than seventeen Standing Committees. The most important were: (1) the *Defence Committee*, presided over by the Prime Minister, and including among its members the Foreign Secretary, the Minister of Defence (as Deputy Chairman), the three military Service Ministers (the First Lord of the Admiralty and the Secretaries of State for War and Air), the Minister of Labour and the Minister of Supply—with the Chiefs of Staff usually present at meetings; (2) the *Lord President's Committee*, a kind of general purposes Committee on domestic policy; (3) the *Economic Policy Committee*, again presided over by the Prime Minister himself, and responsible for high economic policy and the supervision of economic planning; and (4) the *Legislation Committee*, which consisted of the Lord Chancellor (the presiding officer of the House of Lords and the head of the whole judicial system, but appointed by the Prime Minister), the Law Officers (Attorney General and Solicitor General) and the Chief Whip, the function of this Committee being to examine the drafts of Parliamentary Bills, important delegated legislation, and to keep an eye on the general progress of the Government's legislative program. Alongside these Standing Committees there also existed a great many *ad hoc* Committees (e.g., the Committee on the National Health Service, the Committee on the Distribution and Marketing of Meat, Fruit and Vegetables) while the Standing Committees themselves frequently proliferated into large numbers of subcommittees. Finally, there were undoubtedly also certain informal groups of the sort that generally develop in a large Cabinet but are not dignified by the term "Committee," the most important being the small clique of trusted cronies and high-powered politicians that generally clusters around the Prime Minister, constituting a sort of inner Cabinet, where, in all likelihood, most great decisions are made.

The Prime Minister

One writer on the British Constitution has put the position of the Prime Minister in a nutshell: "The Government is the master of the country; and he is the master of the Government." It follows, in the curious logic of British government, that the Prime Minister's status should be as "conventional," i.e., non-legal, as that of the Cabinet he heads, and the law knows him only as a man who draws down £10,000 a year[8] through the Ministers of the Crown Act 1937. Yet the British constitution vests him with wide authority and his actual political power is surely as great as that of any of the Presidents or Prime Ministers of other democratic countries. The Prime Minister is the "first" of the Ministers, in the sense that he has powers they do not possess, that he is frequently in a position to get his way over powerful opposition, and that even the weakest of Prime Ministers have been, in one sense or another, dominating figures. As Hopkins once wrote to Roosevelt during World War II: "Churchill is *the government* in every sense of the word." But, there is also another side to the matter. The Prime Minister, even during a war and even if he is an overwhelming figure like Churchill, functions within certain boundaries that, in view of their historical origins, it is not far-fetched to call a framework of ministerial equality. If one were asked to compare him with the American President one might do it thus: the Prime Minister, because of the concentration of responsibility in the Cabinet and the discipline of British parties, has, as a general rule, far greater powers than the President, whose freedom of action is severely limited by the separation of powers, but the President can usually exercise his powers far more independently as an individual than can the Prime Minister. The British executive is a plural executive, in spite of the predominance of the Prime Minister.

The Prime Minister's indubitable "firstness" over his colleagues is the result of a large number of causes, some constitutional, some party-political, some psychological. Constitutionally, he acquires special eminence from the fact that all ministerial offices derive from him and depend on him, that it is he who makes and unmakes Ministers. Legally, ministerial offices are conferred by the sovereign and are a private matter between her and the Minister concerned. Constitutionally, however, all offices are at the Prime Minister's disposal. Apart from his powers of appointment, he may dismiss a Minister simply by notifying him and the sovereign that he desires to replace him with someone else; and he may cause the utter dissolution of his Government simply by resigning, something, certainly, that no mere Minister is able to do. A second constitutional factor that gives him an especially august position is that he alone, of all the Ministers, may make great decisions without the approval of the full Cabinet. It is generally accepted as constitutional for the Prime Minister to act in the name of the Cabinet, if the matter at issue urgently requires decision and it is not feasible to decide it in Cabinet in proper time. In actual fact,

[8] Reduced by the Churchill Government to £7,000.

the Prime Minister frequently acts on his own initiative even when the urgency of a situation does not require it, but in these cases he can assert himself not so much for constitutional as for party-political reasons. He is the "Leader" of his party and this, particularly if he is a Conservative, gives him great powers over party policy, both in form and practice. The relevant forms vary between the two major parties,[9] but in practice the powers of Conservative and Labour Prime Ministers are not greatly dissimilar. In both cases the ultimate sanction behind the Prime Minister's powers to assert himself, to make independent policy statements and to commit his party to them, is the omnipresent fear of a split in the party if his statements are publicly repudiated. To split a party in Britain is to deliver the Government into the hands of the enemy; hence, even when certain members of a party are deeply out of sympathy with its leader they treat him in very gingerly fashion. They may resign from office and criticize, but they rarely launch a direct attack on the leader and in public they usually swallow their disagreements altogether. There are in consequence few resignations over policy disagreements.

Closely related is another party-political factor that contributes to the Prime Minister's power: the fact that general elections in Great Britain are fought, to a large extent, between two rival candidates for the Prime Ministership. These two are more in the limelight than any other candidates. They lead what Gladstone called the "popular agitation" in the nation, while others stick to their constituencies. It is usually their voices that issue from the B.B.C. and their faces that smile down from the hoardings. And a great many elections, since Gladstone and Disraeli set the fashion, have been, to all intents and purposes, popularity contests between rival party leaders.

Here we come to the third group of factors that set the Prime Minister apart from his colleagues, the psychological factors. The Cabinet is always thought of as *his* Cabinet; the Government as *his* Government; he is, in popular imagery, something apart from the minor stars in the Cabinet galaxy. This popular conception is reinforced by the fact that of all the important "efficient" officers of government he comes closest to having also an important ceremonial function. He frequently represents the nation on ceremonial occasions; he is second only to royalty itself as a national symbol. And if he has a colorful personality, a caricaturable face, and is the master of certain kinds of stage business (like Churchill's V sign and Baldwin's amazingly convincing impersonation of an ordinary country squire) he may even rival the monarch as a symbol.

What factors then circumscribe his powers vis-à-vis his colleagues? For his position *is* severely circumscribed, even in the cases of the most color-

[9] See Chapter 12.

ful Prime Ministers under the most auspicious circumstances. A most striking example occurred during World War II, when Prime Minister Churchill and President Roosevelt met on H.M.S. *Prince of Wales* to work out the Atlantic Charter. Harry Hopkins, who had earlier reported that Churchill was *the government*, was struck by the fact that while Roosevelt seemed to be completely on his own, willing and able to commit the American people to anything that might be agreed upon on his personal authority, Churchill seemed unable to take a step without getting in touch with his War Cabinet in London and especially his second-in-command, Clement Attlee. In three days, more than thirty communications passed between the *Prince of Wales* and Whitehall. Churchill obviously operated within a restraining framework of "collective leadership" to which the American President, under similar circumstances, was not subject.

The factors guaranteeing this collectivity of leadership are, primarily, two. One is that the idea of ministerial equality is deeply ingrained in British constitutional morality and that the idea of the committee rather than the individual boss as a decision-making agency is deeply ingrained in every Englishman's experience. The British use committees for managing practically everything, from lawn-tennis and social clubs to the Cabinet itself, from the kindergarten to the geriatric home. Discussions, consultations, negotiations, are a matter of almost everyone's daily experience, and this accounts both for the fact that the British so often make collective decision-making work and for the fact that they insist upon it even under the most difficult circumstances. But there is also a practical consideration that enforces collective decision-making in the Cabinet: the fact that British Ministers are, as a general rule, men of some political standing, whose views it is never quite politic to ignore, and also, as a general rule, men of more than ordinary capacities, whose views it is never quite wise to ignore. In the first respect, if not the second, they differ markedly from American Cabinet members, many of whom frequently have no political experience, let alone important political standing. But even in the second respect they probably outstrip other species, if only because British ministers must usually spend long apprenticeships and pass a series of difficult tests before they can qualify for high office. Certainly a man who is a bad parliamentarian—who cannot convincingly marshal a set of facts and arguments, hold his own in the cut and thrust of debate, turn a phrase and think coherently on his feet—has no chance of achieving high office, and people who *can* do these things well are not likely to be mere yes men for any Prime Minister.

CHAPTER **10**

Parliament

The Symbolism of the House of Commons

[The British monarchy and Cabinet pose a striking paradox: one is dignified by the most solemnly formal constitutional ritual, but has only the most peripheral relevance to the actual conduct of British government.] The other is dignified by neither legal forms nor constitutional ritual, but is of the most crucial significance from a practical standpoint. If we elevate this curious circumstance into a general law—the more "dignified" a British political institution the less its practical significance—Parliament immediately confronts us with a serious ambivalence. It is a curious mixture of ceremony and improvisation, of ancient usage and modern invention, and this perhaps is explanation enough for the many learned disputes about its role in British government. In any case, the mixture of old and new, formal and informal, is the most palpable thing about the House of Commons the moment one enters it. It is the essence of its atmosphere, and the atmosphere of the House is a matter of practical no less than aesthetic significance. To understand fully what Parliament is and does one must experience it, even if only vicariously.

Let us imagine that the reader is sitting in the visitors' gallery of the House for the first time. No doubt his first impression will be of the physical appearance of the House. This, even if he does not find it attractive, he will almost certainly find surprising. In particular, if the visitor has seen other legislative chambers, he will be surprised by the unique size and seating arrangements. [From the standpoint of size it is little more than a glorified Town Hall. It seats fewer than two thirds of its members, despite the fact that it makes no space-consuming concessions to members' comforts (such as desks and individual chairs) but seats them all on long benches, with the august representative lap the only support for papers.] The chamber measures roughly three thousand square feet, while the American House of Representatives, despite a much smaller member-

92

ship, commands more than four times that much space. The prevailing atmosphere of the House of Commons can, therefore, only be described as intimate—except on great occasions (e.g., before an important "division") when, with over six hundred odd members crowding into a space designed for 346, the chief impression is one of excitement and expectancy.

The feeling of excitement at such times is further increased by the seating arrangements. In most of the world's legislative chambers members sit in semicircular or straight rows, all facing a rostrum from which members address the chamber and from which its presiding officer conducts the proceedings. The impression is of an auditorium facing a stage on which individual legislators play the star turn. In the House of Commons, however, members sit on two sets of long benches, graded upward and *facing each other*, one at the left, the other at the right of the Speaker, who sits at the head of and between the rows of benches. To the right of the Speaker sit the Government and its supporters, Ministers on the front bench (or Treasury Bench, as it is sometimes called), ordinary members ("backbenchers") grouped behind them like obedient and anonymous soldiery. On the other side sit the Opposition, the "Shadow Cabinet" on the front bench and its own soldiery arrayed on the benches behind. The two groups face each other like football teams in a scrimmage, and when members make their verbal cuts and thrusts, they inevitably appear as the members of a team, not as individuals temporarily elevated, in splendid individuality, to the national tribune.

Since the present House of Commons is only a few years old (the old House having been destroyed by German incendiary bombs in 1941) neither its layout nor its small size are accidental. Despite certain obvious discomforts, it was decided to make the new House of Commons almost exactly like the old, not alone because of attachment to the past but because it was widely felt that the physical character of the House somehow affected the character of its proceedings. For example, Mr. Churchill, the most insistent spokesman for the small Chamber, felt that the whole style of debate in the House would be changed for the worse if the House were enlarged; that the effects of meeting in a large and half-empty hall (and the House is rarely full even now) would be depressing; that the old sense of crowding urgency on great occasions would go; and even that the clean-cut two-party system would be endangered if the seating arrangements were altered.

The next thing the visitor to the House will notice is the general tone of its proceedings. It is here that he will be impressed most by the curious mixture of formality and informality. In some ways the House of Commons is the most formal of all legislative chambers. Its deliberations are governed by procedures most of which are hoary with age and many of which are pure ceremony of the quaintest sort, procedures that either no longer serve a useful function or have long since been adapted to new uses while maintaining their old form. The visitor may, for example, be in the House when it is getting dark. Suddenly the cry goes up: "Mr. Speaker, I call for candles." True, candles have not been used to illuminate the House for decades but if a member were to say, "Mr. Speaker, how about putting the electric lights on," he might, with the same effectiveness, make his request in Swahili. The rules of parliamentary procedure include a multitude of precedents set by rulings of the Speakers over the centuries. Until the late nineteenth century, in fact, almost all the business of the House was covered by usage, there being only a small handful of Standing Orders, as the rules deliberately adopted by the House to regulate its proceedings are called. Since then the S.O.s have grown by leaps and bounds, but by far the greater part are still a matter of custom.

[For such a solemn and ceremonious set of rules a solemn and ceremonious presiding officer is appropriate, and the House of Commons does not fail to provide him.] If any physical evidence of the continuity of British parliamentary institutions were needed, Mr. Speaker would furnish it. There he sits in his chair (his "throne" one should perhaps say), looking like nothing so much as the frontispiece from a biography of Handel, with his flowing wig, his black satin knee breeches, his buckled shoes and long black gown; a figure straight out of the age of squirearchy. He is an arresting figure, and not only does he look much prettier than his French counterpart, who sits in the bourgeois drabness of modern evening dress, but he is far more authoritative. To cite a simple example: if the French National Assembly gets out of hand the President of the Assembly rings a bell, an act which often merely augments the prevailing din. But if the House of Commons becomes disorderly (as it rarely does) the Speaker almost always manages to restore order without recourse to mechanical devices merely by rising from his chair, the rule being that when Mr. Speaker is on his feet all members must be off theirs. And only at times of riotous turmoil does he resort to the ultimate, almost unfailing, method of getting order: putting on his hat. His powers over debate, the putting of motions and questions, and over members' conduct, are vast and to some extent arbitrary.

[But even more important than his formal powers is the readiness with which his rulings are obeyed. No doubt his effectiveness as a presiding officer is, in large measure, due to the same factor to which the monarchy largely owes its popularity, the fact that his political impartiality is completely established and unquestioned. He is the very embodiment of the rules of procedure and, like the rules, neutral. This neutrality is guaranteed in numerous ways. [The Speaker is elected for the life of a whole Parliament, not, as in France, for a single session, and will be re-elected, by a convention dating back to the early eighteenth century, as long as he wishes. Speakers, like monarchs, thus are generally in office for long periods and acquire the usual venerability of age and experience. Although elections to the Speakership may be contested by the parties, only men who have not been violent partisans are put up and the aim is always to secure a unanimous election. Finally, once a man has become Speaker, he is divested of his political personality, so to speak, in a number of ways. Although he continues to be a member of Parliament his constituency chores are taken care of by another member. He may vote only if there is a draw in a decision and then only to preserve the status quo; he never takes part in a debate (absolutely never); and his seat is never contested by the other party ("never," in this case, in the Gilbertian sense; there have been four contests for the Speaker's seat since 1714).

But whatever the sources of the Speaker's power, he has it—and does not greatly need it. The normal tone of the House is orderly and polite; it is a chamber with an aristocratic past and with palpably aristocratic habits. True, the prevalent politeness is to some extent backed by rules. For example, in referring to another member a member speaking in the House must never use his name but refer to him by a ceremonious title: "the Honorable member for ———" (if he is an ordinary M.P.), "the Right Honorable member" (if he is a Privy Councillor), "the honorable and learned member" (if he is a lawyer), "the honorable and gallant member" (if he is a former officer in one of the armed services) or "the noble Lord" (if he is an Irish or Scottish peer not entitled to sit in the House of Lords, or the son of a great nobleman, in possession of a courtesy title). These ceremonious titles are not conducive to belligerence, however much venom certain members manage to inject into them. Again, the Speaker is empowered to see to it that members use only decorous language and may have obstreperous members removed by the Sergeant-at-Arms and, indeed, suspended from the House altogether. A brief but representative list of expressions ruled unparliamentary in the late nineteenth century includes: "cowardly," "a poltroon," "of remarkably fragile honour," "a bigoted, malevolent young puppy," "the reverse of the truth," "bloodthirsty," "mendacious."

But it would be mistaken to suppose that the *politesse* of the House is merely a matter of rules. The rules and precedents are often overlooked, particularly when they are picayune, and Messrs. Churchill and Bevan, among others, have unburdened themselves of expressions that would have astounded the fastidious Speaker Denison in the nineteenth century. The courtesy and good humor of the House are rather a part of its spirit. They come out most clearly and under least compulsion when a member has made a "maiden speech," his first essay in the House of Commons. No matter how miserable the speech, the next speaker, whether friend or foe, will congratulate him on an eloquent and informative performance, express the pleasure of the House in hearing it and the hope that the member will be heard from frequently on other occasions.

This courtesy toward the maiden speaker is also a rule, even if it exists merely in the intangible spirit of the House. It is part of the ritual by which the House never lets one forget that it is both an ancient and a solemn institution. The House, no less than the monarchy, appeals to the form-worshipper, the pomp-worshipper, that dwells in most of us. Yet, for all its formality, it is, as the visitor will immediately sense, basically an intimate and informal place. Here, of course, is where its size plays an important part. It is, for example, not unusual for the great table which supports the golden Mace to support also the gangling legs of some elongated front-bencher. Members present in the House of Commons sit in almost every conceivable posture: some, like Balfour, on their shoulder blades; others reclining on their sides. And there is an almost constant coming and going, bowing in and bowing out, and conferring behind the Speaker's Chair. But the prevalent informality is most notable in the speeches. British parliamentarians need suffer neither the academic pompousness of German legislators nor the incessant Fourth-of-July oratory of the Americans. The tone of the House of Commons is conversational rather than declamatory, witty rather than learned, and it could hardly be otherwise. In so small a chamber, lectures and orations invariably sound ludicrous—except on the greatest of occasions or when delivered by semi-legendary figures like Sir Winston Churchill. Moreover, it cramps the orator's style to be compelled to speak in his place, in the midst of a multitude, rather than from a special tribune. It equally cramps his style to have no desk to put things upon, nor even a rail on which to lean. It cramps his style not to be allowed to use a prepared speech or even special notes.[1] And, not least, since all remarks in the House are to be addressed not to other members but to Mr. Speaker, a man can sound ridiculous haranguing a crowd of one. Speeches, therefore, tend to be calm. They also tend to be concise, partly because that is the tradition of the House, partly because the Speaker may immediately suppress all irrelevant remarks and tedious repetitions, but partly also no doubt because the crush of modern business demands dispatch.[2]

[1] The House permits only Ministers making important announcements of policy, where every word counts, to read their speeches.

[2] In more leisurely days, conciseness was not one of the virtues of the House of Commons. In 1797, for example, Lord Colchester made the following note in his diary: "In the House Mr. Grey moved a vote of censure on Mr. Pitt for his conduct. . . . Only Mr. Grey, Mr. Pitt, and Mr. Fox spoke. The debate began at half-past six, and lasted till one in the morning."

But informality is not all. The House can be a mercilessly discourteous audience, particularly if a member departs from its mores, and it is always a tough audience. A. P. Herbert, never one to tremble before a crowd, called it the "Torture Chamber," and with good reason. In almost any circumstances, members, unless they are completely bored, will keep up a running fire of interjections. But if the speeches offend the House, a merciless cacophony may break loose. The would-be orator, for example, will almost certainly be engulfed in a tumultuous rustling of papers, stamping of feet, coughing and sneezing, or, as has happened once or twice, such a continuous chorus of "hear, hear" that he cannot be heard. The House is (generally) courteous and calm; but it is never easy on speakers in the sense that it will tolerate nonsense or lack of decorum or blatant unconventionality.

Class Composition of the House

The right word for the atmosphere of the House of Commons is, if not aristocratic, at least gentlemanly, and no doubt it is so gentlemanly because it is predominantly filled with "Gentlemen." True, the House is not as homogeneously composed of Gentlemen as it was in the eighteenth century, when it was controlled by the aristocracy (younger sons) and gentry, the true and original Gentlemen. Nor is it even as uniformly "gentlemanly" as it was in the nineteenth, after the influx of the new upper and upper-middle classes. Universal suffrage and the rise of the Labour Party have inevitably injected into the House a previously alien strain, so that one cannot today draw up an occupational chart of the members without using such categories as "Railway Clerks," "Commerce: clerical," "Skilled Workers," even "Unskilled Workers." As classes and groups, previously excluded from politics, have risen in political power in the country, their representatives have made their way into the House of Commons. From this some observers have concluded that the character of the House has profoundly changed. But has it?

There can be no doubt that the House of Commons, as a *whole*, is still predominantly upper-class and middle-class in composition. About one half of all the members in recent Parliaments had attended universities, nearly a third of them Oxford and Cambridge, and, as for secondary schooling, about one out of every six had been to Eton. In the Parliament of 1951-55 there sat 95 lawyers (most of them barristers, the higher echelon of the British legal profession) and 74 professional writers; and, on the Conservative side alone, about 100 company directors, 30 "farmers" [3] and 24 bankers and business executives. But one scarcely needs statistical docu-

[3] Mainly owners of estates.

mentation for this. The visitor to the House can immediately experience its dominantly higher-class character simply by listening to the members' voices, examining their dress, observing their table manners in the House of Commons restaurant, and so on.

It must be admitted of course that the Labour benches are less solidly "respectable" than the Tory benches. "They look like a bunch of damned constituents," as a Tory M.P. was heard to mutter when the new Labour hordes flocked into the House after the landslide of 1945. But it would be difficult today to tell a Labourite from a Tory as easily as all that. One reason is that the House of Commons, by virtue of its well-defined character and style, tends to make people over in its own image, and its style is pronouncedly upper class. If new members are not yet domesticated to the upper strata when they enter it the House will almost invariably carry their training a long way. Aneurin Bevan, a devotee of class conflict, has realized this as well as anyone else, and chafed under the fact:

> The atmosphere of Parliament, its physical arrangements, its procedure, its semi-ecclesiastical ritual, are . . . all profoundly intimidating for the products of a board school system who are the bearers of a fiery message from the great industrial constituencies. . . . To preserve the keen edge of [their] critical judgment [they] will find that [they] must adopt an attitude of scepticism amounting almost to cynicism, for Parliamentary procedure neglects nothing which might soften the acerbities of [their] class feelings. In one sense the House is the most unrepresentative of representative assemblies. . . . It is a social shock absorber placed between privilege and the pressure of popular discontent.

But there is another reason for the pronounced degree of surface homogeneity in the House and a much weightier one, namely that Labour members are themselves surprisingly higher class and do not, as a general rule, need to be House-broken. Here two points are particularly worth noting. First, as Labour representation in the House of Commons has increased in the course of the twentieth century, the number *and proportion* of upper-class Labour members has also risen. To cite only one example: in 1936 the formal education of 49 per cent of Labour members had been limited to elementary school and only 17 per cent had been to a university; in 1951 the figures were 24 per cent and 33 per cent respectively. In a decade and a half, the proportion of lower-class membership was halved and that of higher-class membership doubled. It is almost as if the ruling classes had begun seriously to infiltrate the new party once it showed signs of becoming politically important.

Secondly, it seems fairly clear that, just as the Liberal Party was the chief means of entrance into politics of the new upper classes of the nineteenth century, so the Labour Party has become the chief means of entry of the latest additions to the upper strata. The social composition of the House has undoubtedly changed in the last century, but so has the content of the social stratification scale. The expansion of higher education, particularly the scholarship system, has channeled into the higher strata people effectively excluded before, and one sizable chunk of society in particular has become "respectable": the members of certain professions. Only a half century ago—certainly not more than a century ago—doctors, solicitors (the lower echelon of the legal profession), journalists and schoolteachers were still frowned upon as artisans rather than gentlemanly professional men.[4] Today they are almost, if not quite, as respectable as gentlemen "farmers," military officers, and those who live off private means. Once this is realized the figures on the social composition of the present House of Commons become very suggestive. More than half the Labour members belong to what we generally consider the professions, and among these the largest chunk consists of schoolteachers, the second largest of journalists, and another sizable chunk of solicitors. There are 30 journalists on the Labour side and 19 on the Conservative; fourteen Labourites are solicitors against eleven Conservatives; and—most striking of all—59 Labourites are schoolteachers as against a mere two Conservatives. The actual number of "professionals" on the two sides is about even, but the Conservatives draw the vast majority of theirs from the old professions, the first to become "respectable": barristers (66 to 21 for Labour) and military officers (47 to 2!).

The Work of Parliament

What precisely is it that all these proper people do in their solemn habitat? What is the role of the House of Commons in the actual conduct of British government? What is its power in the whole scheme of decision-making? What are the specific functions through which this power is exercised?

These are crucial questions about British government and, needless to say, they are not easy to answer. There are, however, two extreme positions that we can dismiss. One is that the power of Parliament is "transcendent and absolute," in fact as well as in theory. The simple truth is that the House of Commons is dominated by the Cabinet, primarily by means of the stern weapons of party discipline. But from this it does not follow that the other extreme view is correct: that Parliament is merely, as Ramsay MacDonald once said, an electoral college, a body that dutifully registers the people's will in electing an executive and then deserts the field to the men of its choice. Unlike the American electoral college, it remains in

---

[4] Note, for example, Dickens' treatment of them in *Bleak House, Nicholas Nickleby* and the *Pickwick Papers*.

session after performing its electoral functions, and it is certain that what it does in session is of some consequence, though of less consequence than the transcendental absolutists make out. To determine how much less we need to examine its work in some detail.

Legislation

"The chief function of Parliament," said the famous lawyer Maitland, "is to make statutes." On the surface, of course, he is right. [The House of Commons spends more time discussing bills than doing anything else.] It is the principal house of the British legislature, and no statute can have the force of law unless enacted by it. Neither, however, would any statute have the force of law without the royal assent, yet no one thinks of the queen as having any real legislative function. The problem to solve is to what extent the time Parliament spends discussing bills is of practical consequence.

Any legislative process may be dissected, for analytical purposes, into three stages. Registering Yeas and Nays is only the last of these stages. [The first is the initiation of bills,] including not only the conception and drafting of legislative projects but also the business of introducing them in the legislature and deciding which projects the legislature is to discuss. Under modern conditions no legislature can allow all of its members indiscriminately to introduce legislation and then thoroughly discuss all the projects. Some method is required to decide what the legislature is to consider, when, and at what length. And whoever is empowered to decide this has great powers over legislation—something like a veto in fact. [The second stage of the legislative process is, of course, "deliberation,"] i.e., debate to determine the pros and cons of a legislative project by means of discussion among open-minded men. Such deliberation the classic philosophers of popular government (e.g., Bentham) considered to be the very heart and soul of "legislating." The purpose of the legislative process, they felt, is to give expression to popular will; this is done by debate among the people's representatives, from which emerges a decision registered in a vote.

Who then determines what legislative business is to come before the House? To what extent do its discussions conform to the classical model? And when the members troop into the Division Lobbies[5] do they really decide whether the Bill before them is to become law or has that already been decided?

So far as initiation is concerned, Parliament as such clearly does not

---

[5] Translation: vote. The method of voting is for members to walk through two special rooms, one *for* the Bill (or motion), one *against*, where a count is made and the names are registered. It is a time-consuming method of voting but, as Herbert Morrison has pointed out, a socially pleasant one.

legislate, since the business of introducing legislation is almost completely monopolized by the Government. The legislative projects of "private members" (i.e., backbenchers, ordinary M.P.s) hardly ever obtain even a hearing. As the table below shows, bills are conceived and promoted by all sorts of different agencies, in and out of the Government. But very, very few can ever be more than a gleam in someone's eye unless the Cabinet agrees to act as parliamentary midwife. Ministers must "introduce" them, however they "originate."

There are both constitutional and practical reasons for this. One constitutional reason is the rule that all legislation involving financial expenditure must have the consent of the Crown; and much, if not most, important legislation involves the expenditure of money. But more important than this definite rule is a sort of general constitutional prejudice, not

TABLE 1   **Sources of British Legislative Projects**
(*Session 1936-37*)

Cabinet	9
Administrative Departments	27
Voluntary Associations (i.e., pressure groups)	9
Government Policy, under known outside pressure	3
Administrative Departments, after consultation with "voluntary associations"	7
Local Government Associations	2
Private Members (on own initiative)	2

shared by other democratic societies, that introducing legislation is somehow rightfully the business first and foremost of the Government. There is, as usual, a democratic rationalization for this attitude. Parties contest elections on platforms and once a party has won a majority, it is argued, democratic principles demand that its program should have priority in the legislature. This, however, is probably little more than a rationalization. Few parties assume office with mandates for such a vast amount of legislation as did the Labour Party in 1945 and in an average session legislation for which a mandate has been given occupies only a tiny fraction of the time spent on bills. In the session dealt with in the table above, for example, only one project (out of seventy) was derived from the election program and the vast majority of the rest had only the loosest connection, if any, with a mandate. British Ministers enjoy their legislative privileges because of the widespread belief that it is the business of the Government to govern and because party discipline puts them in a position to monopolize the parliamentary timetable. This conclusion is reinforced by the fact that the practical considerations making for ministerial monopoly of the legislative agenda—e.g., the pressure of important business—also exist in other countries, without producing similarly cavalier attitudes toward the legislative rights of private members.

If a private member wants to introduce legislation he can do so only on certain days predetermined by parliamentary usage and the generosity of the Government in power.[6] By long usage, Wednesdays and Fridays are private members' days, Fridays for Bills and Wednesdays for motions.[7] Since the beginning of the war, however, no Wednesdays and fewer than the traditional number of Fridays have been available to private members, so that the old tradition seems in process of being superseded by a new one even less kindly to the backbencher. During the war, of course, the Government had abundantly good reason for taking away all private members' time, and after the war the Labour Government, with a vast mandate to fulfill, had an equally good reason for monopolizing the timetable. Thus, for almost a decade no "private members' Bills" were dealt with in the House of Commons.

The Government, then, practically monopolizes the initiation function. But what of the other two stages of the legislative process? Is the decision to enact or reject a bill the result of "deliberation" among the members of Parliament or not?

This question may seem foolish since the House of Commons undoubtedly debates legislative projects at great length and with great seriousness. In fact, it debates prospective statutes more frequently, if not more thoroughly, than almost any other legislature. Before a bill can become an Act it must pass through five (sometimes six) stages. The first stage, after drafting, is called the First Reading and is largely perfunctory. The Minister in charge of the Bill to be introduced, being called upon by the Speaker, rises and bows to the Chair; the Clerk of the House of Commons reads out the title of the bill from a "dummy" which has been laid upon the Table (so seriously does the House take its ritual make-believe); and the Minister then names the date on which the next stage in the passage of the bill, Second Reading, is to take place. The bill is

[6] And under the Ten Minutes Rule. This is so complicated and insignificant that it is better ignored.

[7] "Motions" here refers to non-legislative motions. It is necessary in the House of Commons to hinge every debate on a specific motion. Hence, if a member simply wants to criticize some particular ministerial act or aspects of a policy, he must put down a motion. This may or may not be debated, depending on whether it is allowed to go on the actual agenda.

now printed and distributed to members and, on the appointed day, the Second Reading takes place. This involves a debate, sometimes very long, in which the main principles of the bill are discussed, but the main principles only. This means, among other things, that amendments to the bill may not be moved. If the bill is approved after the debate it goes to Committee—usually one of the Standing Committees,[8] sometimes a Committee of the whole House. Here only the details of the bill are discussed, the fundamental principles having been accepted on Second Reading. This is the stage, consequently, at which amendments to the bill may be moved, provided only that they do not conflict with the previously adopted general principles of the bill. When the Committee has finished its deliberations it reports the bill back to the House (Report Stage), whereupon another debate on the details generally takes place. Then comes the final stage of the process, Third Reading, when there may be still another debate on general principles; and while by this time the House usually has little left to say, on some occasions Third Reading debates have been as tense and thorough as debates on Second Reading.

Thus there are plenty of opportunities to debate both the principles and details of bills. But it is doubtful whether the House really deliberates when it debates, if by "deliberation" we mean the formation of opinion through discussion or if we imply that the debates have significant effects on the contents of Bills. A. P. Herbert liked to refer to the House of Commons as the "Gas Chamber" and, so far as the effects of its debates on the contents and success of legislative projects are concerned, that, to all intents and purposes, is all it is. Normally it is certain that any Bill introduced by the Government will pass, substantially in the form in which first submitted, whatever splendid oratory, indisputable facts, and tight logic may be advanced against it in the Chamber. The reason, of course, is party discipline. As long as discipline holds, the Government need not really convince anyone of the soundness of its proposals. It need only send out a three-line Whip to its supporters, a letter "urgently requesting" each member's presence in the House at such and such a time when a division is expected to take place, and the troops will obediently march in and do their job, regardless of what is said in the debate.

The House, then, is not a deliberative body, and, this being the case, we need not consider its role in the third stage of the legislative process at any length. Except for an occasional "Free Vote" private members vote not upon conscience or conviction but upon compulsion. The real deliberative agency in Britain, then, seems to be the Cabinet, and not only because it can make its supporters troop into the Division Lobbies. It can

[8] To be discussed below.

also—together with the leaders of the Opposition—dominate the parliamentary debates themselves by arranging with the Speaker who is to be allowed to speak.[9] And it possesses one other great advantage, compared to the Governments of other countries: it can always see to it that the House votes on a Government bill in the form submitted, by preventing distortion through important amendments, since amendment is not permitted until the principles of a bill have been approved.

However, as the table on the Sources of Legislative Projects will suggest, the Cabinet does not fully monopolize the deliberative function. It is, in essence, merely the decisive apex of a very complex structure of decision-making, involving all sorts of forces (the party in and outside Parliament, the civil service, pressure groups) that press upon the Cabinet and, by constant intervention, help shape the principles and details of legislation. It is this constellation of forces, rather than any single body, that "deliberates" on legislation, in the sense we have used the term. But in this constellation of forces Parliament itself undoubtedly plays a role. Like the parties, the press, the bureaucracy, and the pressure groups, it can exert influence on the Cabinet's decisions, sometimes important influence. Its debates frequently reveal flaws in bills and lead to the acceptance by the Government of technical changes. More important, on at least a few occasions Parliament has caused the Government either to withdraw unpopular legislation or to introduce popular measures it had not intended to introduce. The Education Act of 1936, for example, was withdrawn after heavy criticism in the House. A few years ago the House persuaded the Government to raise old-age pensions against its previous will. And it was the Labour rank and file that persuaded the Government to nationalize Civil Aviation and to reduce compulsory military service from eighteen to twelve months. The list of such cases is impressively short; but it covers only the *publicly* known cases, not the considerable influence exerted by members of Parliament behind the scenes, through the Parties, the committees of the Parliamentary Parties,[10] and informal consultation, both before and after the formal introduction of bills. The fact is that British Governments, for all their great powers, go to very great lengths to ascertain and accommodate the views of the parliamentary rank and file. The power of the House of Commons to kick out a Government may not be a very real threat in this day and age, but it is always there as a silent reserve, a sword of Damocles hanging over the Government. Nor can a

---

[9] Formally, the Speaker decides who is to participate in a debate. If members wish to speak they must rise in their places upon the conclusion of the previous speech, and the first one to "catch the Speaker's eye" will be named to speak. In practice, however, the leaders of the Government and Opposition pretty much arrange the order of speaking to suit themselves. Lists of the principal speakers are submitted to the Chair and the Speaker generally calls out the prearranged order.

[10] See below, p. 146.

Government afford for very long to be consistently criticized by its own supporters, even if they obediently vote for it in the divisions.

[Among the sources of influence on legislation and policy is the other house of Parliament, the House of Lords.] There was a time when the Lords was truly the upper house, the more powerful as well as the more dignified of the two. But with the rise of democracy, and especially in this century, its real powers have been in continuous and rapid decline, making it today a body of only minor importance. Its composition makes clear why this must be so. [Nearly all its members are noblemen—dukes, marquesses, earls, viscounts and barons—who have inherited their titles and their right to sit in the Lords or who have been elevated to the peerage by the sovereign. In addition to these more than eight hundred hereditary noblemen, are twenty-four bishops and two archbishops of the Church of England; sixteen peers chosen to represent the peers of Scotland; and the survivors of the twenty-eight Irish representative peers who held their seats in 1922 at the time of the recognition of the Irish Free State. There are also nine lords of appeal in ordinary, who are peers only for life. These last are appointed because [the Lords, as well as being a legislative body, is also the highest court of appeal in the United Kingdom.] When sitting as a court, however, only the law lords, the Lord Chancellor and other lords with judicial experience actually take part in the proceedings.]

Some Ministers, as we have seen, will be peers, responsible for answering questions and conducting Government business in the Lords. [The Government, however, is responsible only to the House of Commons,] in the sense that only a defeat there can bring it down. Moreover, while normally all bills are passed by the Lords as well as the Commons and the forms of procedure are broadly similar in both houses, the legislative power of the Lords has been whittled down to the vanishing point. Today the [Lords can legally delay public bills only for one year, except for those public bills that are money bills, which it can delay only for one month.]

Unrepresentative in a democratic age and constitutionally far inferior to the House of Commons, the Lords yet manages to exercise a modest influence. Some of its members are men who previously have won distinction in public life, the professions, business, even trade union activity. Among the Anglican prelates, leaders of force and character are often found. When therefore the Lords debate the large questions of modern politics—the subject of one impressive debate a few years ago was nothing less than the "Reorganization of Human Society"—the public and possibly even members of the Government may pay heed. Perhaps even more important, however, is the work of the Lords in examining and revising the details of legislation. Given the pressure under which much complicated legislation goes through Commons, the presence of a chamber of revision is useful. The Lords can also exercise a somewhat similar function by means of their powers to reject or withhold consent from statutory instruments.

Control over Administration

This deflationary appraisal of the legislative function of Parliament will not surprise anyone acquainted with its history. [The primal function of Parliament was neither to legislate nor to govern but to advise and control those who did govern] Even in the heyday of Whig parliamentarianism this notion of the function of Parliament persisted. Burke, for example, explicitly says that Parliament is primarily a "controul" over the Government on behalf of the people. And just as it is fashionable today to argue that Parliament does not really make the laws, so also it is fashionable to maintain that its real function—the work it does really well—is to control the administration of the laws. To determine whether this is so or not we need to examine first the means by which Parliament exerts such control: the Question Period, debates on motions to adjourn and motions of censure, and the machinery for supervising delegated legislation.

[The first hour of every sitting day (except Fridays) is set aside for questions to Ministers about matters for which they are responsible] Any member of Parliament may ask up to three "starred questions" a day (i.e., questions for which an oral answer is to be given by the Minister in the House)[11] and these questions may and do cover the whole range of governmental activity and the nation's life. [By prearrangement, different Ministers appear on different days and answer questions put to them as they appear on the Order Paper.] Members may add oral supplementary questions if a reply given by the Minister seems unsatisfactory. And the usual impression given by Question Time is of rapid-fire give and take that puts the Minister to a severe test. Nothing the House of Commons does is more surely calculated to expose weaknesses in a Minister; nothing the Minister does is more likely to impress or disenchant the House. No doubt most of the Minister's prepared answers are fed him by his civil servants, but no permanent official can fully protect the Minister against the supplementary questions that members may ask after an answer has been given to the original question. Ministers and bureaucrats dread the Question Period, religiously prepare their answers, and anxiously try to anticipate Supplementaries.

By usage, [Ministers are always required to make some answer to questions, while a member may ask about anything he likes, provided he observes certain specific rules.] If these are transgressed, the Clerks of the

---

[11] Unstarred questions are answered in writing, but since most questions are meant not only to elicit information but also to publicize a subject, to put a Minister on the spot, or to provoke a debate, starred questions predominate.

House may change his question or throw it out altogether. Questions must be short and framed so as to elicit facts and not opinions. The subject matter must be one for which the Government and the specific Minister questioned are responsible (e.g., questions about the private lives and transactions of citizens are clearly out of order). A question already answered cannot be put again in the same session. Questions must not repeat rumors or gossip. Their language must not be ironical or hypothetical or argumentative, and must in general be such as would be admissible at other times in debate. (Thus, "Whether the Foreign Secretary agrees that it would not be obvious to anyone but a complete ass that the rearmament of Germany, which he proposes, will prevent the reunification of that country," is out on almost every conceivable ground; while the question, "Whether the Home Secretary is not a well-meaning but inflated solicitor" would be admitted only after removal of the adjectives.) These rules are designed to prevent loose and abusive questions. But they do little to take the bite out of Question Time.

If an answer given by a Minister is considered unsatisfactory, even after Supplementaries, members have several methods available to prevent the matter from being buried. If, for example, the matter urgently requires debate, it may, under Standing Order 9 of the rules of procedure, be brought to debate on the very same day. The member who wants such a debate must rise and say, "Mr. Speaker, I beg leave to move the adjournment of the House on a definite matter of urgent public importance, namely that . . ." The Speaker must then decide whether the matter is really definite,[12] urgent[13] and public;[14] and if he finds that it satisfies all three criteria (and forty members of the House agree to the debate) then all prearranged business comes to an end at seven o'clock that day and a debate on the adjournment motion begins. Again, a motion to adjourn is usually made at the end of each daily sitting, and debate on this motion can also be used to go into a subject raised during Question Time. The House automatically adjourns at 10:30, but at ten the regular business of the day is almost always interrupted. A motion to adjourn is then made and this motion leads to debate until 10:30 on a subject raised by a member, usually to air an individual or local grievance, sometimes to air a subject of the most general importance. Similar debates, obviously useful to expose acts of administration, take place on the eves of periodical holidays, e.g. Christmas, Easter, Whitsuntide and the Summer Recess.

[12] The motion must not deal with more than one subject; it must deal with a particular case rather than being couched in general terms; it must not be hypothetical; official information must be available.

[13] The matter must have happened recently and require immediate attention.

[14] The matter must raise a "larger issue" and not merely involve an individual or local grievance.

[Debates on motions of censure may be used in extreme cases to air matters a government wants to hush up] Such motions, like motions of confidence, involve a solemn and direct challenge to the Government by the leaders of the Opposition. But unlike motions of confidence, which are concerned with general policy, they are concerned with specific ministerial actions and are thus used especially to attack administrative behavior.

[Finally, there is the machinery for the control of delegated legislation] This is important, if only because so much legislative power is now delegated by Parliament to Ministers and the Cabinet. Parliament simply lacks the time and technical knowledge for certain kinds of legislation, while others require a flexibility in rule-making that would be impossible to achieve if Parliament laid down specific provisions. Delegated legislation —to be precise, rules with the force of law made by the executive under a broad authorization of Parliament—now accounts for around a thousand "statutory instruments" (the technical legal term) a year, some of very great length and complexity. It far overshadows regular Parliamentary legislation, at least in quantity, and it has multiplied five-fold in half a century. Needless to say, this is a matter that worries a great many people, and much has been written about what Chief Justice Hewart called "the new despotism"—the despotism of the bureaucrats who in fact not only administer but also make most of the rules under which people in Great Britain live.

[The obvious means for controlling the rule-making powers of the bureaucrats is to require parliamentary approval of the rules they make] The requirement may take two forms: "affirmative resolution" (i.e., a specific vote of approval without which the statutory instrument cannot acquire legal force) or "nullifying prayer" (a negative vote that prevents an instrument from going into force). In examining statutory instruments laid before it for approval or disapproval the House gets help from a special committee of its own members, the Select Committee on Statutory Instruments, created in 1944 to examine all pieces of subordinate legislation and to call to the attention of Parliament any which seem to require special examination. The Committee is assisted by Speaker's Counsel, an expert lawyer and parliamentarian. It is not permitted to register opinions but only to call the attention of Parliament to certain instruments.

How effective is all this machinery? Does the House really "control" the executive in any more meaningful sense of the term than it "legislates"? That it has a great many opportunities to go into matters of administration there can be no doubt. It has perhaps more such opportunities than Congress, and certainly enjoys one incalculable advantage over it: the fact that Ministers are actually present in the House, where they may be challenged, interrogated and embarrassed. The formal doctrine is that, as a general rule, for every administrative action some Minister is liable to answer in the House of Commons, and not only to answer but even to resign, if a grave error of judgment, a serious transgression of law, or abuse of power is involved. British Ministers enjoy none of the comfortable protections of the separation of powers. But is this stern doctrine more than theory? When the House discusses matters of administration is it doing anything more than going through the motions?

Unfortunately, again, there is probably more to be said on the negative than the affirmative side. For example, despite the doctrine of ministerial responsibility for acts of administration, a vast range of public activities nowadays is practically exempt from parliamentary control, i.e., the activities of independent authorities, like the public corporations that administer the industries nationalized by the Labour Government, and those of certain semi-independent authorities created for the specific purpose of exemption from normal political supervision. The number of these agencies is large and they deal with a vast area of activities. Indeed, next to the growth of delegated legislation, their development is probably the most significant constitutional development of the last three decades.[15] But the difficulty is not only that much administration is exempted from parliamentary control. Much more serious is the fact that the means for supervising the activities subject to parliamentary supervision are not as effective as they are sometimes made out to be.

Consider, for example, the case of delegated legislation. Parliament is so spendthrift with its legislative powers because it does not have the time or knowledge for certain kinds of legislation, and if these factors keep it from legislating in the first place they also prevent the effective supervision of administrative lawmaking. Nor is the Select Committee on Statutory Instruments of great help. It is better than nothing. But it is, after all, composed of ordinary M.P.s, it has an enormous amount of work to do, and, in fact, it has called to the attention of Parliament an average of only a dozen statutory instruments a year (out of a thousand) since its inception. In addition, much delegated legislation is not even made subject to parliamentary approval or disapproval, but need only be laid before the House for a certain period or, indeed, sometimes not even that. Most important of all, of what use are resolutions and prayers against statutory instruments if the Government calls out its majority to back them? And this point applies equally to all the other means of controlling administration.

In gist, the House of Commons is no more a controlling body than it is a legislating body—and no less. The same considerations apply to both

---

[15] They already existed in the nineteenth century, but in nothing like the present quantity.

activities. [Party discipline not only gives ministers an effective monopoly over legislation but also immunity from parliamentary control,] if they choose to press it to its ultimate extremes. But they rarely choose to do so. Annoying adjournment debates are rarely, if ever, forestalled, even if they could be. Questions are generally answered scrupulously. Occasionally a master of evasion appears (like Gladstone, who used to wrap his answers to Questions in such a cloud of abstract metaphysics and cumbersome technicalities as to leave his listeners numb). But most Ministers make an effort to give an honest accounting to the House; and the fact is that the departments do take immense pains over Questions.[16] Similarly, while nothing absolutely needs to be done about uncovered grievances, something usually is done about them. The House of Commons, then, does at least affect the course of administration, and it affects it for much the same reasons it can affect legislation. But, also as in the case of legislation, the controls the House of Commons exercises over administration are exerted jointly with other bodies, not least again the House of Lords. The House of Commons is simply one part in a complex framework of control. The airing of a grievance or exposure of an administrative error in the press may be as effective as a debate in Parliament, and so also may direct representations to the Minister.

Publicity

In essence, then, the position in the case of both legislation and control is that the Government is vastly more independent of Parliament than the transcendental absolutists suggest, and yet far more willing to listen to Parliament—to take its advice, redress its grievances, cater to its preferences—than would a true Cabinet dictatorship, indiscriminately wielding the Whip over its disciplined supporters. In part, this self-effacement of the Government is certainly a matter of "constitutional discipline." But there are important practical sanctions as well; above all, the fear that certain kinds of ministerial behavior may lead to dissension in the majority party, and fear of the repercussions actions in Parliament may have in the electorate. The first of these practical considerations is easy enough to grasp. Insofar as the Government's position rests on party discipline it would be suicidal to alienate a sizable chunk of its supporters. [Party dissension is now the main factor that compels an occasional Government to resign] Precisely for this reason, however, the fear of dissen-

[16] Indeed, it has been frequently alleged that this is not an altogether unmixed blessing. As Hugh Gaitskell has said: "Anybody who has ever worked in a Civil Service Department would agree with me that if there is one major thing which leads civil servants to be extremely cautious, timid and careful and to keep records which outside the Civil Service would be considered unnecessary, it is the fear of the Parliamentary question."

sion is perhaps less of a limitation on the Government than might appear.
If a party split occurs, everyone in the party suffers, leaders and led alike.
The Opposition comes in and they are usually "worse" than the leaders
of one's own party; the party goes into the wilderness and the streams of
normal political advancement may dry up for a protracted period. In
short, the specter of dissension keeps the rank and file in line no less than
it restrains the leaders. The Government's fear of repercussions in the
electorate at large is therefore, in all likelihood, a more powerful constraining factor than fear of intraparty disagreements.

Apart from democratic morals, the chief reason for the Government's
scruples about opinion in the electorate is, of course, that it is compelled
periodically to put its fortunes to the electoral test. While exercising
power it is always preparing for the next general election. But even this
would not be a sufficient explanation for its generally scrupulous sensitivity to pressure and criticism were it not for another fact: that Parliament
—much more than the American Congress, for example—is in the public
limelight to a really extraordinary extent. For example, the sales of the
daily *Hansard*—which, like the Congressional Record, records verbatim
the parliamentary proceedings—have been as high as 12,000 copies and
those of the *Weekly Hansard* as high as 16,000 copies. Ordinarily, a publisher who sells that many copies of a light novel considers himself fortunate, and *Hansard* is not light, however much fiction goes into it. In addition, the British press gives remarkably extensive coverage to Parliament.
The *Times* and the *Manchester Guardian* carry nearly verbatim reports of
the debates; even the yellow journals have their special Parliamentary
Correspondents; the British Broadcasting Corporation gives a nightly
fifteen-minute report on Parliament (usually delivered by an M.P.). Even
the humor magazine *Punch* has a sizable and usually serious section on
Parliament in every issue, while, in contrast, the *New Yorker* restricts itself
to an occasional brief report of a ridiculous extract from a Congressman's
speech. Parliament, by the standards of many other countries, gets a great
deal of publicity, and one may suspect that this publicity makes a particular impact on that small proportion of the population—the floating vote—
that actually determines the outcome of elections.

In a sense, therefore, the proceedings of Parliament are of consequence
because a sufficiently large number of people *believe* they are of consequence, although it is not only misconceptions of Parliament's proper
role that cause people to take an interest in the parliamentary proceedings.
Most important, perhaps, the House of Commons provides a thrilling
arena for political conflict, an arena of a sort no legislature in a separation-
of-powers systems can match. The floor of the House of Commons is the
place where all the leaders of the great parties constantly confront each

other in face-to-face conflict—questioning, prodding, debating. The reader need only imagine a political forum in which, almost daily, President Eisenhower, Mr. Stevenson, Mr. Nixon, Senator Kefauver, Mr. Dewey and Mr. Truman have at each other. Such a forum would be bound to be more in the public eye than Congress, even if it exerted less practical weight. But we have nothing to rival the House where Gladstone and Disraeli faced each other, year in and out, in constant, direct conflict.

All this may explain why Parliament spends so much time debating Bills and exposing acts of administration, even if the results of its proceedings are so frequently a foregone conclusion. Parliament, in short, has still a third function, additional to legislation and control of the executive. It is, as John Stuart Mill said, the nation's Congress of Opinion no less than its Legislature and Committee of Grievances. It has what Bagehot called a "lyrical" as well as a legislative and controlling function. How well does it perform *this* function?

On this question, at least this much must be said in favor of Parliament: its debates are generally conducted on a surprisingly high intellectual level, and it provides an unusually large number of opportunities for general policy debates and wastes little time on technical and provincial matters, which are not likely to be of great import to anyone except experts and a few interested parties. This is due in the first place, to the very fact that the substantive powers of members over legislation and administration are so severely limited. If parliamentary debates are unlikely to lead to many changes in a Bill—if no concessions are to be won for Little Wopping or the Brotherhood of Turf Accountants on the floor of the House—there is simply no point in meddling with detail and all the reason in the world for general analysis. Hence, parliamentary debates tend to be rather more interesting and informative than the proceedings of other legislatures. Then too, there are special debates, held every year, designed specifically to be general policy debates, i.e., to inform more than to decide. Every session of Parliament, for example, begins with about a week of such debate, the Debate on the Queen's Speech. The tradition is that when Parliament begins a session the sovereign addresses it in the House of Lords, outlining—in a speech written, of course, by the Cabinet —the main business to be transacted that year. Then a debate takes place that covers the whole range of the speech itself. An equally important vehicle for general policy debates is afforded by the Debates in Committee of Supply (which are discussed in Chapter 14) and by debates on motions phrased in very general terms.

All this is to the good; but even here entries must be made on the negative side of the ledger. The chief one is the severe lack of time for adequate parliamentary discussion. Parliament nowadays has so much business to transact that everything must run according to a strict time-table and debates are almost always severely limited by Governments that have the necessary support to limit them. Three devices may be used for this purpose: closure, "guillotine" and "kangaroo." Closure may be moved by any member after debate has gone on for some time. The Speaker must then decide whether the Opposition has had a fair day in court on the subject under discussion and, if he decides that this is the case, the question is immediately put to the vote. If carried with the support of at least 100 members the debate is finished. Needless to say, Governments have little trouble stopping debate when they want to by this means. The "guillotine" (or Closure by Compartments) is an even more drastic weapon: it can be used to limit debate before it has ever begun. In essence, a guillotine motion is a Government motion that sets out at what precise time the various stages of a parliamentary proceeding are to end, e.g., so much time for Second Reading, so much in Committee, so much time for the Report Stage, and so on. When the appointed time comes the ax falls on the debate and the next item of business follows, whatever important people are still to speak, however many aspects of the question have not yet been discussed. Finally, as a further limitation on discussion, the Speaker, in putting amendments to debate, has the power to skip over any he does not consider important or representative of significant sections of opinion. This power is called the "kangaroo."

In limiting debate (and, as we shall see below, in devising the parliamentary timetable) the most scrupulous regard is given to the wishes of the Opposition, which, in fact, directly controls a great deal of Parliament's time. This point is of very great importance, for insofar as publicity is one of the chief functions of Parliament it is correct to say that the Opposition is more important than the Government in the House of Commons. After all, it is chiefly the Opposition that prods, probes, criticizes and exposes those in power.

It should not be supposed, however, that in publicity we have finally found *the* function of Parliament—its particular and peculiar task in the British scheme of government. Again, it is a function that it shares with many other agencies: the press, radio and television, the soapbox orator in Hyde Park, party meetings and conventions, party publications, ethical societies, and so forth. But the dignity and solemnity of the House, the excitement that pervades its debates, and the decisiveness the public attributes to its proceedings undoubtedly make it the most powerful among all the various agencies of political expression.

The Transcendence of the Government

"The government of a nation by a large assembly of its elected representatives," says Walter Bagehot in *The English Constitution*, "is nothing less than a miracle." The government of Great Britain at least does not refute this proposition, for it is certain that Parliament does not govern Britain. Far from being transcendent and absolute, it is at most one force in a great complex of forces that press upon and limit those who do govern. And this conception of the role of Parliament applies not only to the functions discussed so far but even to its role as an "electoral college." Parliament does not exclusively determine who is to govern. The electorate, the parties, and, to a lesser extent, the chosen Prime Minister, do that, although Parliament certainly plays a crucial part in the education, testing and weeding out of prospective Ministers.

But it is the Government that is transcendent, however much it is forced to operate in a framework of pressure and control. And, in all likelihood, that is why the miracle of effective parliamentary government has come to pass in Britain. Parliament leaves ample scope for leadership and *expertise*, leaving to others the functions for which popular assemblies of popular politicians are generally unsuited: the definition of coherent national policy, the elaboration of technical detail in legislation, the superintendence of departmental administration. It provides its leaders with the means necessary to enact their policies: reliable majorities in the House of Commons and guaranteed priorities in the allocation of parliamentary time. But it does all this without becoming a mere rubber stamp imprinting legitimacy on the dictatorial actions of the Government, a mere ceremonial institution like the monarchy.

The true relationship between Government and Parliament can be seen most clearly perhaps in two crucially important activities of Government. One of these—the planning and control of parliamentary time—has already been dealt with to some extent in this chapter. The other, which has not yet been touched upon at all, is financial legislation and control of expenditure. But since both of these subjects are of particular importance in the functioning of the contemporary welfare state, they will be discussed not here but in Chapter 13, where the relationships between the policies and processes of British government are analyzed.

CHAPTER **11**

Administration

Ministers and Civil Servants

A hundred years ago it would have been perfectly possible to analyze British government adequately with little more than a passing reference to the bureaucracy. Today this would be like doing *Hamlet* without the Prince of Denmark. The civil service has grown, in Britain as elsewhere, at a phenomenal rate: from about 20,000 in 1832 to 100,000 at the turn of the century to 700,000 in 1950. Needless to say, it has a far greater range of functions to perform. And its character has changed profoundly because of professionalization. What was once a field entirely for patronage, a safe haven for those who had failed elsewhere or wanted an easy life, has become, since Gladstone, in 1872, acted on the famous Northcote-Trevelyan Report, a career service for which the Firsts of Oxford and Cambridge grimly compete. Indeed the intellectual level of the British civil service is unusually high even by the standards of other contemporary civil services, because of the way in which its members are recruited. And not only has the intellectual level risen: the service has acquired an *esprit*, a style, a corporate consciousness and a tradition as well. All this makes of it an effective instrument of government, one without which the administration of modern policies could hardly be imagined.

But is it not perhaps too effective: so effective as to undermine the power of those whose instrument it is supposed to be? Undoubtedly certain factors tending to decrease the power of private members of Parliament—the pressure and technicality of much modern business—tend also to erode the power of their leaders and to shift power to the permanent officials in the administrative departments. To some observers it appears that the Cabinet occupies the "central" position in the pattern of power only in the sense that it is a focus for two decisive streams of pressure that tend to coalesce into policy through its mediation: political pressure from the electorate, bureaucratic pressure from the departments. That, at any rate, is what a noted writer on British government, Sir Ivor Jennings, thinks. ['The civil service *governs;* the Ministers *control* the process of government']; and he quotes approvingly Sir William Harcourt's aphorism that Ministers exist to tell the civil servants what the public will not stand.

Whether this is really so or not, and to what extent, is a point difficult to settle, because we have even less inside information about the Civil Service than we have about the Cabinet, and we have perhaps least information of all about the actual relationships between Ministers and their permanent officials. Almost nothing ever leaks out about these relationships from either side. [The Minister is a wonderfully effective buffer between the Civil Service and the public:] it is always he who gets the praise, and it is always he who takes the blame, even to the point of resigning for the errors of his officials. There is undoubtedly much to be said for this arrangement. Above all, [by keeping politics out of the Civil Service, it helps to keep the Civil Service out of politics,] and the undesirable evils of the Congressional fishing expedition are spared the British Civil Service. But it also tends to keep the British public as well as political scientists in the dark about one of the most crucial aspects of the governmental process. Nor do the memoirs of Ministers illuminate the subject very much. No Minister likes to admit being a puppet for his permanent officials; all have a stake in preserving the fiction of the constitutional myths on the subject. Hence, as K. B. Smellie[1] has said, in the biographies of statesmen the few references to their official collaborators are as complimentary but also as uninformative as tombstones.

[On the civil servants' side the darkness is just as impenetrable, if not more so. They are prohibited, under the Official Secrets Acts, from publicly divulging information, on pain of criminal penalties.] They write regrettably few memoirs and when they do write them they are invariably and frustratingly discreet. Lord Beveridge has said that the Civil Service works under a sort of modern version of the Franciscan monastic rule: "poverty, anonymity, and obedience"; and there can certainly be no question about the anonymity aspect of the matter, nor the poverty. Do they keep the vow of obedience as strictly as the other two?

Constitutional theory is unequivocal on the subject. Policy-making, as we usually understand that term, is supposed to be the province of the political chiefs. [The permanent official is expected to advise, suggest and warn, but beyond that he is supposed to keep his hands clean by seeing to it that whatever the Minister orders is done.] This insistence upon neutrality is reflected in a number of formal rules governing official behavior. For example, [civil servants are not themselves permitted to be candidates for Parliament.] If they work in departments that have administrative rela-

[1] K. B. Smellie, *A Hundred Years of English Government* (1937).

tionships with local governments, they are not allowed to stand for local office. Similarly, they are not allowed to speak or canvass for political candidates and are not supposed to comment on public affairs in books or articles, even on affairs not handled by their own departments. In the 1930's, for example, an official in the Ministry of Health was dismissed for writing an article, under a pseudonym, commenting on British policy in the Italo-Ethiopian war.

It is inevitable, however, that the Civil Service should not be as submissive or self-effacing vis-à-vis the political officials as the constitutional myths require. Ministers, after all, are usually amateurs in their fields, while their permanent officials are professionals, with years of *expertise* to draw upon. Ministers tend to be men skilled in the art of swaying opinions, "expressive" minds; civil servants tend to be men skilled in the art of analyzing problems, "analytical" minds; and the two kinds of minds rarely coexist in the same person. Every department, moreover, is a storehouse of traditions and precedents, of routines that make the whole machinery run smoothly; in every department, therefore, there is bound to be a certain amount of intractable administrative inertia that even the most dynamic Ministers will not be able to move. Not least, of course, the Minister is heavily dependent on his permanent officials for his own advancement. That impressive mastery of detail, those subtle, well-organized arguments that mark him out as a man to watch, presuppose conscientious briefings and coachings by the anonymous mendicants in his department. Indeed, it is perhaps the most ambitious Ministers, those most eager to make a splash in Parliament, that tend most easily to become puppets in the hands of officials.

Undoubtedly, enough is known to make it certain that civil servants sometimes dominate their Ministers, even if the Minister is "strong" and the subject a matter of great importance. Ernest Bevin, for example, was anything but a weakling, but, in contravention of his party's publicly expressed policy, he entirely swallowed the Foreign Office line on Palestine, imposing on Palestine a fiercely repressive pro-Arab policy of the sort the Foreign Office had promoted ever since the Balfour Declaration of 1916. Yet, there are things to be said on the Ministers' side too. Compared, for example, with French Ministers, British Ministers have a very long life expectancy in office and, in consequence, far greater opportunity for acquiring *expertise*; and those who attain office are, on the whole, men of very considerable ability. Secondly, it is clear that when a party has a clear mandate, the Civil Service is generally powerless to impose its own will, at any rate without revealing that it is doing so. And, in fact, it would be difficult to find any instances of a clear mandate that the bureaucracy has sabotaged. Similarly, if a Minister is a man with settled convictions and some force of character, he will generally have no trouble getting his own way in his department, as did Arthur Henderson at the Foreign Office, Sir Kingsley Wood at the Post Office, or Lloyd George at the Ministry of Munitions in the first World War.

[But more important than either the clarity of a party's mandate or the forcefulness of a Minister's personality is the simple fact that civil servants are also to a really remarkable extent constitutionally disciplined and will not sabotage policies politically decided upon or otherwise go beyond the boundaries of official propriety. Cases of administrative corruption are amazingly few in Great Britain, particularly in view of the low salaries paid and the very great opportunities for augmenting them. From this standpoint, the Civil Service has indeed a kind of monastic quality. But whatever the forces that make for its incorruptibility, they also make for its political reliability, for a certain deference to Ministers in no sense warranted by objective considerations. Sir Robert Morant, for example, did his "very best and utmost" to make the Education Bill of 1906 a workable measure, even though it reversed a great deal of the Education Bill of 1902, which he had fathered. And there was the famous case of the official in the Colonial Office who, when informed that his Minister intended to bring up the question of salaries in West Africa, replied that, as soon as he had learned whether the Minister wanted to raise them or to lower them, he would prepare, "in either event, a perfect case."

It was widely felt however—not least by the British socialists themselves in the early days of the Labour Party—that the political neutrality of the service would break down if a socialist Government ever came to power. But many of the Ministers in the Labour Government of the 1920's have paid tribute to the co-operative attitude of their officials, and not a single one has complained. This, however, was not considered decisive evidence of the political reliability of the Service by some commentators, since MacDonald's Labour Governments were never in a sufficiently strong parliamentary position to undertake major social reforms. The real sabotage was to come when and if Labour ever won a really workable majority. It did win such a majority in 1945, it promptly embarked upon the most sweeping program of social reform in British history—and it carried the program through without a jot of visible sabotage or obstruction by the bureaucracy.]

But why had the loyalty of civil servants toward a socialist Government been doubted in the first place? What interests could conceivably impel them to use their power to thwart the policies of their ministerial chiefs? To understand the reason, it is necessary above all to understand that the internal structure of the Service faithfully reflects the class structure, and, to a lesser but still important extent, the economic inequalities, in British society. This is due mainly to the fact that the recruitment system is closely geared to the educational system, which, as pointed out previously, is the chief determinant of British class differentiations. Except for certain "industrial" employees (e.g., men performing certain mechanical tasks in the Post Office), certain purely departmental officers (e.g., inspectors of various kinds), and certain professional men (doctors, lawyers, engineers), the Civil Service is divided into five "classes" (the so-called Treasury Classes), for each of which a different examining and recruiting method is used.

At the top of the pyramid is the *Administrative Class,* numbering altogether about 4,000 men and women. About 100 new members, between the ages of 20 and 24, are recruited to the class annually, chiefly by means of stiff written examinations, which test general intelligence and academic competence,[2] and the preponderant majority are graduates of the better public schools and the ancient universities, i.e., higher-class people. Those who are not higher class become higher class soon enough upon entering the Administrative Class. The members of this Class monopolize the higher grades of the Civil Service and recruits to it assume important duties not long after their brief probationary period. They are the elite of the Service. Just below them is the *Executive Class*, numbering about 60,000 members and engaged mainly in responsible but routine jobs for which "policy" is established by political officers and members of the Administrative Class. Members of the Executive Class are recruited at various levels, but many between 17½ and 18½ years, i.e., among those just completing secondary school and not going on to universities. Next comes the *Clerical Class*, composed of people who do most of the actual routine work of the departments (correspondence, record-keeping, etc.), and recruited mainly between the ages of 16½ and 17½. Finally, there are two very lowly classes, specially reserved, in characteristic British disdain for the weaker sex, to women: *Clerical Assistance*, recruited between the ages of 15 and 16 and requiring only an elementary education, and the *Typist Class*, which speaks for itself.

It should be noted that each of these classes is practically a self-con-

----

[2] Two methods of examination are, in fact, used. Method I involves two written examinations, one in subjects testing general intelligence, "culture," and information, another on academic subjects varying from Arabic to zoology, among which the candidates have free choice; in addition there is an interview by a Board selected by the Civil Service Commissioners designed to test the candidate's "personal" as distinguished from his more academic qualities. The aim is not to discover special skills so much as general ability. Method II, instituted experimentally after the War, involves an adaptation of procedures developed during the War for the selection of Army officers. It also involves written examinations, but more stress is put on the close observation of candidates over a two- or three-day period under a variety of conditions. At one time candidates were assembled for weekends at a country estate for the purpose but at present the Civil Service Selection Board conducts its observations in London.

tained unit, in the sense that there is little mobility between the classes. There is more mobility today than there was twenty years ago; but in the normal case, once one is, say, in the Clerical Class one is in the Clerical Class for life, with little chance for crashing through to the Executive Class and certainly none whatever of getting into the Administrative Class.

With few exceptions, therefore, the higher rungs in the Civil Service are the private preserve of the able sons of the upper classes, although a gradual increase in members of lower-class origin has been taking place. A recently published study of members of the administrative class above the rank of assistant secretary showed that in 1929 only 7 per cent were children of manual workers or domestic servants; while in 1939 and 1950 the percentages were 10 and 17—an increase, but not a sizable one when it is considered that these categories account for the large majority of the whole population. Only 5 per cent in Britain live off private means or belong to the main professions or are owners and managers of important businesses, but 32 per cent of the higher civil service are sons of such people. Twenty-eight per cent of adult males are in unskilled or partly skilled occupations; but only 3 per cent of the higher civil service come from such backgrounds. And these 3 per cent are not "lower-class." By their achievements in the service, and no doubt also by their educational backgrounds they are absorbed into the upper classes.

[It was widely believed that people so linked with the upper classes would not take kindly to a powerful socialist Government. In fact, whether they did or not, they carried out the tremendously ambitious reforms of the Labour Government of 1945 without a murmur] This may not be absolutely conclusive, but it certainly suggests that Sir Warren Fisher's classic formulation of the role of the Civil Service is substantially correct:

> Determination of policy is the function of ministers, and once a policy is determined it is the unquestioned and unquestionable business of the civil servant to strive to carry out that policy with precisely the same good will whether he agrees with it or not. That is axiomatic and will never be in dispute. At the same time it is the traditional duty of civil servants, while decisions are being formulated, to make available to their chiefs all the information and experience at their disposal and to do this without fear or favor, irrespective of whether the advice thus tendered may accord or not with the Minister's initial view.[3]

In the final analysis, British Ministers and officials have something vitally important in common that may account for the easy surmountability of the differences between them better than anything else: a shared agreement on the forms and procedures of government—a constitutional

[3] Evidence before the Royal Commission on the Civil Service, 1929-1931.

consensus that seems to be quite independent of class position and political interest. Indeed, nothing perhaps illustrates more clearly the significance of British constitutional morality than the wide difference between the latent powers and actual role of the Civil Service under *any* Government.

The Departments

Ministers and Civil Servants come face to face in the administrative Departments. It is here that the foreigner would find himself most at home, since the British administrative Departments are not greatly different from those of other countries, a fact which happily makes it unnecessary to embark on lengthy and tedious recitals of technical administrative detail here. But even the Departments have a few peculiarly British characteristics.

One feature which sharply distinguishes the British from American departments, for example, is the extent to which the higher administrative positions in the former are filled by career officials—civil servants. Except for the Ministers themselves and two or three Junior Ministers in each Department, no political appointments to executive positions are made. Even the Junior Ministers are in a rather different position from, say, the politically appointed American Under Secretary. They cannot, for example, overrule, on their own initiative, decisions or suggestions made by the career officials in the Department; only the Minister himself can do that. They are there merely to help the Minister and to learn the departmental ropes, but they are in a sense outside the real departmental hierarchy. This runs from the Minister directly to the Permanent Secretary (who is the highest of the career officials, the general manager of the Department and the chief adviser to the Minister on both matters of policy and administration) and from the Permanent Secretary to one or two deputy secretaries, a small number of assistant secretaries, and, below these, the principals and assistant principals of the Department, the lowliest members of the Administrative Class.

The fact that career officials have all the higher departmental positions makes the smooth change to a powerful socialist Government all the more remarkable, of course. When there is a change of administration in the United States problems of administrative loyalty simply do not arise, at any rate on the higher levels, since the new administration is in a position to replace the higher officials with its own politically reliable appointees. It is still assumed in America that not only the heads of the departments but also their higher assistants ought to be in political tune with the President. Not so in Great Britain. A change in Government involves changing only about a hundred officials, some seventy of whom are little more than water boys for the Ministers.

[Another aspect of the departmental system an American would find rather curious is the very large number of Departments—about thirty altogether.] Perhaps nothing conveys more vividly how very much the functions and powers of Government (if not the constitutional myths and processes) have changed in the last two centuries. In the middle of the eighteenth century, the departmental structure was very simple and concerned with little but "basic" governmental activities. There was a Treasury (the most ancient of all the Departments, because the first to be separated from the royal household), concerned, of course, with financial administration; a Secretary of State, dealing with domestic and overseas matters in general; an Admiralty; and the offices of the Lord Chancellor, the Lord President, the Lord Privy Seal and the Chancellor of the Duchy of Lancaster, then rather less purely ceremonial in function than they are today. The whole structure was concerned with collecting and expending revenues, keeping the domestic peace, carrying on war and diplomacy, and little else. Almost the whole of the complex modern departmental structure has grown, by a series of convulsive cellular splits, from this exceedingly primitive structure. The Secretary of State, for example, has become a very large number of Secretaries of State, all in charge of their own departments, but all considered constitutionally a single entity, since they all derive from a single entity. In 1782, foreign and domestic affairs were separated for the first time, by the creation of special Secretaries of State (the Foreign Secretary and Home Secretary); in 1794 they were joined by a Secretary of State for War; in 1854, by a Secretary of State for the Colonies. And there matters rested until the twentieth century, when a rash of new Secretaries of State broke out: one for Commonwealth Relations, another for Scotland, and, in the last Churchill Government, one for the Co-ordination of Transport, Fuel and Power.

[A similarly large number of Departments has grown out of the Privy Council] the Board of Trade, the Ministry of Education (via the Board of Education), and the Ministry of Agriculture and Fisheries (via the Veterinary Department under the Privy Council). These offspring of the Council have, in turn, sired further Departments: for example, the Ministries of Labour, Transport, Food, and Fuel and Power, all of which issued from the loins of the Board of Trade in the present century. Still other Departments grew out of the authorities supervising the poor relief, sanitation and health activities of local authorities in the nineteenth century, e.g. the Ministries of Health and Housing. Significantly, only a few of the most modern departments were directly created by legislation.[4] The rest can, in characteristic British fashion, trace their ancestry back to the days of the Plantagenets.

The multiplication of Departments has caused a great deal of anxiety, since it has brought a host of administrative problems into being, particularly problems of co-ordinating the necessarily related activities of the various Departments, so as to prevent duplication and inconsistency. The famous Machinery of Government Committee (the Haldane Committee), which sat after the first World War, recommended, for example, a sweeping reorganization of Departments into a small number of divisions —for finance, national defense, foreign affairs, research and information, production, employment, supplies, education, health, and justice—rather on the American model. This has not been done, and the chief reason is to be found in another aspect of British departmental administration that is far more peculiarly British than those mentioned so far: the tendency of British administrators to set up co-ordinating committees, large and small, formal and informal, solemn and frivolous. It has been said that when two or three Englishmen get together they form a club; it might also be said that when two or three English officials get together, they form a Committee. "We are," said Sir Winston Churchill, "overrun by them, like the Australians were by rabbits." But the compulsion for committees at least saves the British from the need to create formally streamlined, rigidly co-ordinated administrative machinery. Even if such machinery were created it is doubtful that it would replace the present wealth of committees, since service on committees is part of the everyday experience and training of almost every Englishman, and thus built into his social and political reflexes, so to speak.

More will be said about the methods used to co-ordinate administrative activities in Chapter 14 but we should mention here a Department that itself bears much of the responsibility for co-ordination, and, in addition, is by far the most important of all the administrative Departments. This is the Treasury. Its unquestioned pre-eminence among the administrative departments is due to a number of factors. There is, in the first instance, its position as the most ancient of the Departments, a rather intangible factor that, in a country like Great Britain, has very tangible effects. Like Parliament itself, the Treasury is in possession of ancient ceremonies and ritual, solemn forms that no upstart department can match. Equally significant, the Treasury is invested with importance by public attitudes, i.e., by the fact that it is *believed* to be the greatest of the Departments. It gets prestige from the fact that its head, the Chancellor of the Exchequer, is a prominent politician and, often, the next in line to the

[4] E.g., the Ministries of Pensions, Defence, Supply, Works, and Civil Aviation.

Prime Minister; that he holds forth in Number 11, Downing Street, next
to the Prime Minister's residence; and that the Prime Minister himself
dignifies the Treasury by taking the title of First Lord of the Treasury.
But by far the most important reason for its pre-eminence is that it dis-
charges a number of functions that affect the work of all the other Departments and thus exercises a great amount of control over them and the
power to co-ordinate their activities.

[Treasury control, like Cabinet government itself, is one of the vital facts
of the British Constitution] It involves, above all, the following activities:
financial control, economic planning, supervision of the Civil Service, and
supervision of the internal organization and methods of the Departments.
Financial control is exercised in three ways: by control over the departmental Estimates (i.e. requests for annual appropriations); by the power
of *virement*, i.e., the power to authorize departments to shift funds from
one expenditure subhead in the appropriation to another; and by the
power of prior approval, based on the rule that all departmental innovations involving finance must be cleared with the Treasury before being
undertaken, or discussed with it before being taken higher up to the
Cabinet level. More will be said about these means of control when we
discuss the administrative problems raised by the modern welfare state
in Chapter 14, which is also the appropriate place for discussing the
Treasury's planning activities. But it should be evident, even from this
bare enumeration of financial functions, that the Departments can take
almost no actions having financial implications, save routine actions,
without the intervention of the Treasury.

[The Treasury's control over the Civil Service gives it equally pervasive
powers.] Actually, there is no law giving it power to control the civil
servants in other Departments; but for a number of reasons it has acquired
the power, and it exercises it today almost without question. Because it
is desired to have a unified national Civil Service rather than a number of
different departmental services, central supervision of the Service has to
be vested in a single body and this power has irresistibly gravitated into
Treasury hands: partly because of the Treasury's power of the purse, partly
because it is the Prime Minister's own Department, partly because its
special co-ordinating and controlling functions have long been recognized.
One of the two Permanent Secretaries of the Treasury is therefore known
as the Head of the Home Civil Service, and its Establishment Division
trains the Assistant Principals on entry into the Service, and, in general,
supervises the other Departments' personnel administration by the distribution of circulars on the subject. Strictly speaking, these circulars do
not require compliance; theoretically each Department may run its own
personnel affairs and has an Establishment Division for the purpose. But

this freedom is much more formal than real, because of usage and, perhaps more important, the Treasury's power to punish financially any failure to comply. Finally, in view of these pervasive powers over finance and personnel, it was altogether natural that, when it was decided to create a special agency to keep an eye on the Departments' internal organization, and their methods of administration—in short, to create a sort of board of efficiency experts for the Departments in general—it was decided to lodge this function too in the Treasury. It is now performed by its Organization and Methods Division.

Thus, the Treasury supplements the broad co-ordinating functions of the Cabinet itself. There can be no doubt that, next to the Cabinet, it is the principal center of power in British government, so important in fact that it has been argued that the Treasury is no less than a "balance" against the ministerial structure as a whole, almost a kind of permanent Third Chamber, rather than a mere cog in the administrative machine. However this may be, the Treasury is clearly so important that the efficiency of the general administrative structure, and especially, the degree of its suitability to modern purposes of administration, depend, above all, on the Treasury's own organization and methods.

CHAPTER **12**

The Party System
and Interest Groups

[The British governmental process presupposes a tightly disciplined two-party system.[1] In Chapter 8 several reasons, centering on certain features of British political culture, were invoked as explanations of this system. This is not by any means the only line of analysis taken by writers on the subject. In contrast some writers have stressed the homogeneity of the British people and—a related point—the absence of pressure groups from British political life. Others have given much weight to legal structure, especially the electoral system and the power of dissolution. The tight internal organization of the parties themselves has also been considered as a reason for their discipline and strong leadership. None of these approaches gets at the underlying factors, but all touch on such important matters that they are worth discussing at some length.

---

[1] The Labour and Conservative Parties are not the only parties, of course. The Liberal Party is still a live force in the country, however much a spent force in Parliament. In both 1945 and 1950 it polled about 9 per cent of the vote although it ran candidates in only some of the constituencies (304 candidates in 1945, 475 in 1950, and only 109 in 1951 when its popular vote shrank to 2.6 per cent). The Communists, while never amounting to much, have elected M.P.s (one in 1922, 1924 and 1935 and two in 1945) and other parties successful in parliamentary elections have been the Independent Labour Party (which broke with the Labour Party itself in 1932 and has most of its support in Scotland), the Commonwealth Party and the Scottish Nationalists. Independents have also sat in Parliament from time to time. But the size of the vote polled by minority parties and independents has been so small—save for a transitional period when the place of the Liberal Party was being taken by Labour—and their representation in Parliament so very inconsiderable, that we may properly call the British party system a two-party system. It comes as close to it, in form and actual party behavior, as any party system ever has.

126

Interest Groups

That the British party system is a reflection of the homogeneity of the British people is not true simply because the British people are not particularly homogeneous. Anyone who asserts they are does not know them. Ethnically they are no more alike than the people of most countries, and a good deal less than many. From the standpoint of speech, manners, and consumption patterns, they are far less alike than the people of the United States; just compare the voices of the Cockney and the inhabitant of Mayfair, a short bus ride away. Religion?—there are very great differences indeed. If there is any homogeneity in Britain it is to be found in the dominance of urban life, and this has little more than statistical significance. The truth, one suspects, lies somewhere between Disraeli, who thought Britain was two nations, and Dennis Brogan, who thinks the number is closer to 44,000,000. The kindest view to take perhaps is that writers who emphasize British homogeneity confuse homogeneity with agreement, or suppose that any coherent culture is necessarily "homogeneous." France, with a far more chaotic party system, is not manifestly less homogeneous, and neither is the United States. We can dismiss this argument out of hand.

A related and more serious point concerns the role of interest groups in British politics. It is sometimes suggested that the pattern of interests in British society is far more simple than that of the United States or Continental countries and that accordingly pressure groups—organizations advocating these interests in the political arena—are of negligible importance. Where pressure groups do thrive—as in the United States—they prevent the tight integration of opinion and leadership in large political parties. On rare occasions, such as presidential elections, the various groups in each party pull together, but this unity is ephemeral and effective for very limited purposes. Britain in contrast—the argument concludes—can have two large integrated parties because interest groups are relatively few and pressure groups do not divide political opinion into a myriad of jostling factions.

Undoubtedly the pattern of power among political parties is conditioned by the pattern of interests in the society. But in Britain, as in any modern industrial society, the pattern of interests is complex and diverse and in the British political system pressure groups are correspondingly numerous and active. True, political science has discovered the existence of British pressure politics only recently, but this has not been due to their insignificance. In the words of one of the discoverers, they are at once "numerous, massive, well-organized and highly effective"—indeed perhaps more massive, organized and effective than the pressure groups of the United States. That it took so long to stumble upon them may be blamed on the adhesiveness of old political theories and also on the fact that British pressure groups work through channels far more inconspicuous and difficult to detect than those used by American pressure groups. [The distinctive traits of interest group politics in Britain may be examined in terms of the patterns of power, policy and political culture.] More specifically we need to look at certain aspects of governmental structure, of government activities and programs, and of political attitudes in the British system to understand how British pressure groups operate and why they operate differently from those in other countries, especially the United States.

It is a general rule that where there is power, pressure will be applied. The distribution of power in the American system practically compels interest groups to concentrate a very great deal of their activity on Congress, which, for many reasons—the separation of powers, lack of party discipline, the role of its committees, its powers over the budget, etc.—is a highly useful instrument for interest-group purposes. [Power in Britain is concentrated in the parliamentary leaders. It follows that pressure groups, to promote their interests, must influence the leaders, and this they can do effectively only by putting pressure on them directly or by acting through agencies that can, above all the parties and civil servants.] Parliament, of course, also has some influence with its leaders, hence it is not entirely useless for British pressure groups to try to influence M.P.s. But compared to the pressures exerted through parties and civil servants their parliamentary activities are secondary.

[The need to focus pressure on the bureaucrats is reinforced by the activities of British government. First, the vast scope and technical character of decision-making required by welfare-state policies has led to the devolution of more and more decision-making authority to the bureaucracy, so that there is in Britain a vast amount of executive legislation.] Equally important, the decision-making powers delegated to the Departments are likely to be of special concern to interest groups. General policy, of course, is still predominantly made by the Government, but technical details, especially the sort needing fairly frequent revisions (e.g., how much money is to be paid to doctors in the British Health Service; what prices to guarantee to the farmers; on what basis to grant or withhold licenses to build, import, issue securities or acquire raw materials), are taken care of by the Departments—and such details are likely to be of as great concern to interest groups as policy in its broad sense.

Finally, [the tendency to focus pressure on administration is reinforced by British attitudes toward politics. In this connection we must first realize that the British, compared to Americans at any rate, tend to be rather unsuspicious of group politics.] Their political tradition is far less individualistic than the American and the intervention of "corporations" between the individual will and public policy is considered nothing reprehensible. Indeed the medieval corporatistic conception of society may still be said to have a stronger hold on British attitudes than more modern individualistic notions, however much British philosophers may have developed individualistic political theories influential in other countries. The importance of these attitudes is that they encourage institutionalized contacts between "lobbyists" and decision-makers and tend to remove inhibitions on the part of civil servants against regular relations with interest-group representatives. Hence there is very close and continuous collaboration between pressure groups and civil servants: so close that in some instances groups affected by departmental activities have been almost directly assimilated into the Departments without anyone's seeming to think this remarkable.[And the tendency of pressure groups to focus their activities on the Departments is reinforced by a second factor: the consensus on broad policies in Britain today.] Parliament is mainly concerned with such broad policies. The filling out of this framework, however, is the work almost exclusively of the executive. This means that disagreements and conflicts of interest are often more acute in the sphere of executive decisions than in that of parliamentary decisions. Again the effect is to shift the focus of politics from Westminster to Whitehall.

[It is therefore on the departmental level, where everything is less "visible," less exposed to public scrutiny, than on the parliamentary level, that the bulk of British pressure-group politics takes place.] Interest groups do not make nearly so much use of Parliament as they did in the eighteenth and nineteenth centuries when it was a much more important place. But Parliament, as we have seen, is not yet totally in eclipse and the fact that interest groups still find it worthwhile to exert some pressure on it is itself evidence of this. Many British associations, for example, make use of Parliamentary Agents: law firms specializing in parliamentary business and hired by interest groups to scrutinize bills and Regulations, to draft bills and amendments for submission to Ministers and private members, and, in general, to keep an eye out for the group in the House. The National Farmers Union, the National Federation of Property Owners, and the Institute of British Launderers, among many others, are known to have such Agents under permanent retainer. They are, it should be noted, perhaps the closest thing to our professional lobbyists the British have.

[Again, Parliament is full of people who are themselves members of interest groups and act as their spokesmen in Parliament: "interested M.P.s," as they are generally called.]There are large numbers of honorary officers or former officers of interest organizations on both sides of the House and they may represent their associations as much as their constituencies. Indeed, it has been argued that there are more "lobbyists" in America than in Britain simply because pressure groups are far less comprehensively represented right in Congress than in Parliament, and statistically speaking this sounds sensible enough, the majority of Senators and Congressmen being lawyers, i.e., representative of only a single interest group. Finally, and most curiously from an American standpoint, many members of Parliament are paid a regular salary and/or their election expenses to represent the views of certain groups in Parliament. It is difficult to say just how many of these "retained M.P.s" there are, but over a hundred receive payments from trade unions alone and we know that many other organizations (e.g., the National Union of Teachers and the National Association of Local Government Officers) hire parliamentary spokesmen.

There is absolutely no secrecy or subterfuge about all this. It is all widely known and nowhere deplored, simply because the British are not afflicted with our extreme individualist biases. Indeed, only two formal rules restrict the interest-group representative in Parliament. Any M.P. having a personal financial interest in any subject before Parliament is expected to declare his interest before taking part in the debate, although this does not apply to an M.P. who is "merely" retained by an interest group; he must have a direct personal pecuniary interest, e.g., be an importer arguing in favor of the lifting of import controls and not merely in the pay of an importers organization. Secondly, no threats may be used, no bribes offered (retainers are not bribes), no money payments or "social privileges" (e.g., membership in a club) withheld or withdrawn to induce a member to take a specific stand on a specific issue. That is a "breach of privilege" and punishable by the House sitting as a High Court. The M.P. after all is a member of Parliament before he is a representative of anything, constituency or interest group.

But what precisely can all these people do to make it worthwhile to hire them in the first place? They can of course raise questions. They can put down motions for debate and see to it that their associations' views are stated when Parliament performs its lyrical function. They can move amendments or try to influence ministerial decisions by personal interviews or by representations before the special committees of the parliamentary parties. These are not altogether useless powers. But the fact remains that as parliamentary powers have been shifted more and more to the parties and departments of state, so also, logically enough, have the activities of the interest groups.

The Labour Party is in large degree an association of pressure groups.

While the structure of the Conservative Party is not formally corporate in character, it is nevertheless true that most business organizations—from small trade associations to large organizations like the Federation of British Industries, the National Union of Manufacturers, the Economic League and Aims of Industry—are aligned, although not openly affiliated, with the party. There is, for example, a great deal of overlapping of membership between the committees of the Conservative and Unionists Associations and the committees of trade associations. And we know that on a number of occasions Conservative policy has been made by negotiations between the Tory political leaders on one hand and employers' organizations on the other. The exertion of group pressure through the parties, however, has important drawbacks that keep the parties from totally absorbing and transmitting such pressures. Since parties exist chiefly to win elections, only groups having large numbers of members or great economic power are likely to be consistently influential in party councils. For the same reason, no party can afford to become too narrowly identified with any limited set of interests. After all elections are won by winning over the floating voters. It is also unwise for interest groups to become too openly affiliated with any one party, if only because that party is not likely to be constantly in power and therefore in a position to promote the group's interests. And not least, parties rarely make more than very general policies, i.e., the sort of policies on which there is substantial agreement among all sections of society. From every standpoint, then, we are driven toward administration as the chief area of interest-group activity.

Contacts between administrative officials and interest-group representatives are almost too numerous and variable to describe, but for the sake of simplicity they may be divided into four categories. First, there are formal interest-group deputations and negotiating committees either sent out by the pressure groups themselves or invited to enter into consultation by the government Departments. For example, when the National Health Service was being drafted between 1945 and 1946 constant meetings took place between the Minister of Health, his officials, and a formally constituted British Medical Association Negotiating Committee. Again, annual agricultural production plans and prices are worked out by negotiations between the Minister and representatives of the National Farmers Union. Secondly, there is a great deal of informal contact between the officers of private associations and their opposite numbers in the bureaucracy—contact by telephone, via social gatherings, luncheon, teas, in the pub and at Lords (the Yankee Stadium of cricket), perhaps even in the tube on the way to the suburbs. One cannot describe the whole variety of such contacts, but no doubt almost all minor and routine problems are handled in such informal ways. Third, private associations are directly represented on government committees. The Federation of British Industries, for example, has representatives on some seventy government committees, the Trades Union Council on sixty. The National Union of Manufacturers in 1950 was represented on, among *many* other committees, the Dollar Exports Council, the Dollar Exports Advisory Executive, the Anglo-Canadian Trade Committee, the Consultative Committee for Industry, the Trade Negotiations Committee, and the Customs and Excise Committee. Finally, pressure groups are used directly in the administrative process, not only to help the Departments formulate policy but even to help them carry it out when it has been made. Thus, the Ministry of Food (which was in existence during the war and much of the postwar period, but is now defunct) operated almost entirely through various Food Distributors' Associations, to the point that the Ministry's policies were actually carried out by the trade associations to which they applied. Similarly, the Ministry of Supply for a long time controlled the iron and steel industry through the Iron and Steel Federation, a private trade association.

That private pressure groups should not only have ready access to the bureaucracy but even help it administer and formulate government policy in a formal way would be objectionable in a society in which more individualistic ideas prevailed, but the British not only take this sort of thing for granted; they positively encourage it. Indeed, the very fact that the British consider "corporatistic" politics so normal may account for the fact that their political scientists for so long ignored British pressure groups. There just was nothing unusual to take note of. However this may be it is clear that we cannot explain the British party system in a simple way by merely conveniently denying the existence of British interest groups.

The Electoral System

That Britain has a two-party system is frequently attributed to the British electoral system, specifically the fact that the British have a simple-plurality, single-vote, single-member, constituency system. This means: (a) that Britain is divided into a number of constituencies of roughly equal size; (b) that each constituency elects a single member of Parliament; (c) that the candidate polling the highest vote in any constituency is elected for that constituency regardless of the size of his vote; and (d) that voters may vote for only one candidate, and are denied what is technically known as the "alternative vote." [2] Such a system, so the argument goes, inhibits

---

[2] I.e., a vote for a second, third, etc., choice. In some electoral systems, if all candidates fail to get an absolute majority, second choices are added to the original totals,

the development of small parties because if a party is not large enough to win pluralities in a sizable number of constituencies it cannot gain any sizable parliamentary representation. Hence, since it would be wasting its time to try to work through Parliament, it is more likely to attempt influencing the public by other means, including working through one of the major parties. What discourages the activists in minor political groups also discourages their passive supporters. To vote for a minor party is generally tantamount to "wasting one's vote" hence minor political groups can rarely count on receiving electoral support equal to the amount of sympathy they command in the country. Finally, small political groups in Britain take a financial risk in contesting elections: the Representation of the People Act (1918) provides that every candidate must deposit £150 at the time of nomination, the deposit being forfeited to the Treasury if he fails to obtain one-eighth of the total vote.

It is true, of course, that these considerations do not prevent the British party system from changing: note the decline of the Liberal Party and the rise of Labour in this century. But the decline of the Liberals in a sense confirms more than refutes the argument, since it indicates that the electoral system tends to preserve the two-party system in form even while its "content" is changing. It does this in two ways. First, the Labour Party managed to establish itself, even as a minor force, only by its affiliation and co-operation with the Liberal Party in its early years. "Lib-Lab" collaboration early in the twentieth century meant co-operation by Labour and Liberal ministers not only in Parliament but also in the elections, i.e., undertakings by one or the other party not to contest certain seats in order to prevent three-cornered contests from splitting the vote in favor of the Conservatives. Thus, in the early years of the century, Britain had what amounted to a two-party system, despite the existence of three parties, the moral being that only groups that can adjust themselves to the two-party system can hope to establish themselves as important political forces. And once Labour, having established itself, cut the umbilical cord to the Liberal Party, the parliamentary decline of the latter was swift and comprehensive, as the table below indicates. It is usually argued that this swift disintegration of a party that in 1906 had won one of the greatest majorities in British history is incomprehensible if one does not take into account the intolerances of the electoral system for more than two important parties. Once Labour had become a significant electoral force it was increasingly difficult for the Liberals to win pluralities, hence parliamentary representation in any fair proportion to their popular support. And once this had happened, the electorate increasingly shifted away from

---

and so on until some candidate does poll an absolute majority. The aim is to prevent the election of representatives who are strongly opposed by most of their constituents.

TABLE 2 Results of British General Elections

	CONSERVATIVES		LABOUR		LIBERALS	
YEAR	SEATS	PER CENT OF VOTE	SEATS	PER CENT OF VOTE	SEATS	PER CENT OF VOTE
1922	346	38	142	29.5	115	29
1923	258	38	191	30.5	159	30
1924	419	48	151	33	40	18
1929	260	38	288	37	59	23
1935	431	54	154	31	21	7
1945	212	40	394	48	12	9
1950	298	43.5	315	46	9	9
1951	321	48	295	49	6	3
1955	345	50	277	46	6	3

the Liberals, even in cases where Liberal sympathies had not been lost.

Yet electoral systems like the British have not always produced party systems like the British; indeed, in some cases (for example, pre-fascist Italy) such systems have produced almost diametrically opposite results: very chaotic multi-party systems. This surely means, at least, that the single-member constituency system alone is not sufficient explanation for the British two-party system. Nor was it reasonable to expect that it would be sufficient. After all, if it is advantageous under the single-member constituency system to form large parties capable of insuring pluralities in large numbers of constituencies, it is similarly desirable to form large parties under other electoral systems for other purposes, above all the ultimate purpose of winning power. The larger, more inclusive and cohesive a party is, the greater its chance of success in *any* context and under any electoral system. Hence, it seems reasonable to infer that if a country has a very large number of small parties, its party system must be the result of considerations which override mere electoral calculations. But electoral systems clearly can influence party structure and behavior only via electoral calculations. In Great Britain such calculations are exceedingly important but that is because of the broad range of political agreement in British society and the moderate, pragmatic attitudes of British politicians. It is this that makes it possible for voters to shift from one party to another just for the sake of casting a useful ballot, and for politicians to compromise with one another for the mere purpose of jointly achieving power. Thus, the British electoral system tends to compress British parties into the two-party mold because it functions under the specific conditions outlined in the first chapter. Explaining the British two-party system by means of the electoral system does not, therefore, refute the argument in Chapter 8; it presupposes it.

The Power of Dissolution

The fact that British Governments enjoy an unlimited power to dissolve Parliament is frequently invoked to account for the extreme docility of M.P.s vis-à-vis their leaders. Here again it is easy to see the sense in the argument. When the supporters of a Government desert their leaders they may face a dissolution and new elections in which the recalcitrant M.P.s may lose their seats. Or, even if this does not happen, the other side may win a majority in Parliament. And in any case, elections cost money and consume time, in short, are nuisances better avoided. Hence, if there is a disagreement between leaders and supporters on one hand and, on the other, a three-line whip demanding compliance with the leaders,[3] British M.P.s usually swallow their convictions and comply.

But this argument too is refuted by brute fact. The power of dissolving Parliament has existed in many countries—France, Germany, Italy—without leading to any pronounced docility on the part of M P.s, and it is not difficult to find reasons why, under certain conditions, dissolution provisions should be useless as disciplinary devices. First, the power to dissolve Parliament can be used by leaders to exact compliance only if in fact they are willing to use it; but what guarantee is there of that? In the French Third Republic they were not willing to use it, because of the widespread association, after 1877, of the power of dissolution with authoritarianism.[4] An even more instructive case is postwar Italy. Here an unlimited power of dissolution exists, there are no popular prejudices to inhibit using it, and on several occasions since 1950 Governments have fallen that might legitimately have appealed their case to the electorate. But not a single dissolution has occurred, chiefly because of justified fears that elections

---

[3] Individual M.P.s are notified weekly, in writing, about impending parliamentary business by the party Whips. Under each day's business it is standard operating procedure to state: "Your attendance is [particularly] requested." When this is underlined once, it means, "Come if you like but don't put yourself out by any means"; underlined twice it means, "Stay away if necessary but it really would be much better if you were present"; underlined thrice, it means, "You had better have a first-rate excuse for being absent, or else it is highly likely that we will do something terrible to your political career." What this "something terrible" is will be clearer below.

[4] See below, pp. 223-227.

would lead to gains for the extremist parties—Communists, Monarchists and neo-Fascists—and the belief that surrendering power to a new set of moderate leaders was preferable to taking a chance on that.

Conversely the power of dissolution can have a disciplinary effect only if members of Parliament are in fact generally unwilling to incur the risks and discomforts of new elections. But again, they may not be. Where politicians tend to be very dogmatic it may simply be impossible for them to compromise their *Weltanschauungen* for electoral convenience. Where they represent constituents whose predominant interests run counter to the proposals of the leaders (and where the relationship between representative and constituents is very close) it may be far more risky for the representative to defy his constituents than to defy his party leaders. In Britain, Governments are ready to dissolve Parliament when they are defeated and M.P.s highly reluctant to have dissolutions occur; but to understand why this is so—why, in short, the power of dissolution in Britain *does* produce party discipline—we must know more than that the power exists.

Apart from the fact that the power of dissolution is recognized as a legitimate prerogative of leadership, the willingness to use it on the part of British Governments is due to the fact that they are not excessively reluctant to risk having their opponents come to power. And this attitude, in turn, reflects the fact that their own outlook is highly pragmatic and that of their opponents sufficiently like their own. Again, we are driven back to consensus and moderation in politics as the decisive factors. As for the general unwillingness of M.P.s to risk elections, a slightly more complicated explanation is required. The decisive fact probably is that ties between representatives and constituents are extraordinarily loose in Britain. Very few, if any, M.P.s owe their position primarily to their close relationships with their constituents and the M.P.'s function, in popular attitudes, is not so much to represent a district as to help constitute a majority. This implies that his relationships to his party are more important than his relations with the constituency, and party organizations are massive and national, not provincial, in character. For these reasons, among others, the British vote for the party label rather than individual candidates, so that to be deprived of the party label (i.e., to refuse to stand as a regular Labourite or Conservative, or to be refused permission to do so) usually means to be doomed, politically speaking.

The postwar Labour Government offers two instructive examples. In 1948, 37 Labour M.P.s, including a gentleman named Platts-Mills, sent a telegram of good wishes to the Italian pro-Communist Socialist Nenni. When called upon by the Labour leadership to withdraw the telegram all but Platts-Mills complied; whereupon Platts-Mills was deprived of the right to stand as a regular Labour candidate at the next General Election and dropped by his local Constituency Party (Shoreditch and Finsbury, a very leftist district). At the next election he polled only 18 per cent of the vote as against the official Labour candidate's 53 per cent. Not long after, another Labour M.P., Konni Zilliacus, was deprived of the party label by the leaders. Unlike Platts-Mills, however, Zilliacus was retained as a candidate by his local Labour Party; but despite this, when the national party sent in a national candidate to contest the election, Zilliacus polled only 15 per cent of the vote, against an official Labour vote of 45 per cent.

The power of dissolution, therefore, works as it does in Great Britain because of the overwhelming importance of the official party label to the voters. But why is the label so important? It is not enough to say: "Because in parliamentary systems one is really choosing a Government when choosing a representative," for the simple reason that the party label is not nearly so important in other parliamentary systems. It is important in Britain, first, because ideologies are not, and second, because of the very existence of a highly disciplined two-party system, which makes voting for independents tantamount to wasting one's vote. But that leaves us enmeshed in a hopelessly circular argument and takes us back again to the point from which we started.

One possibility remains: that party discipline, if not the two-party system, is the result of certain aspects of British party organization itself. This argument we cannot dismiss quite so briefly as the others. We must first examine in detail the organization of the major parties and the distribution of power within them.

Party Organization

The organization of the political parties represents the truly new in British government, superimposed upon the old because of the constant extension and reform of the franchise since the Reform Act of 1832. Mass democracy (or should one simply say mass suffrage?) has produced mass parties profoundly different from the intimate, informal factions of pre-Reform days. One can discern four phases in their development. The first comes after the Reform Act of 1832 itself. At this stage British electoral organization was still extremely primitive by modern standards, largely because the Reform Act itself was not a very revolutionary innovation. Before 1832 almost no party organization existed outside Parliament, local electoral affairs being managed by local "notables" while national parties were in fact merely ephemeral factions of individual and independent M.P.s. The Reform Act changed this in two respects. To make sure that voters entered their names on the electoral registers local registration associations were formed, still chiefly under the control of local notables—and never for the purpose of nominating candidates. At the same time, embryonic national political organization emerged in two political clubs (the Carlton Club, founded by the Conservatives, and the Reform Club, founded by the Liberals, both in the 1830's), both composed of M.P.s, candidates for seats, and provincial notables, and acting as primitive co-ordinating bodies for the local associations and liaison committees between local and parliamentary politicians. [The second stage in party development consists of the union of the local registration societies in formal national organizations,] the Liberal Registration Association (founded in 1861) and the National Union of Conservative and Constitutional Associations (1867); this, of course, was the crucial step in the transition from informal local to formal national electoral organization.

[Stage three then elaborated what stage two merely foreshadowed. The local associations became fully open to membership and "representative" in form;] the national associations acquired stable organization (national councils and executive committees, with formally determined membership, meetings and functions); and a party bureaucracy (professional election officials) made its appearance. But even at this stage, following the Reform Act of 1867, the party system as we know it was not yet fully developed, chiefly because the parties in Parliament still vastly overshadowed the party machinery outside. In fact, both the National Liberal Federation (founded in 1877) and the Conservative National Union were used chiefly as vehicles for arousing popular enthusiasm and endorsing the policies of the parliamentary leaders. Thus, at this stage of their development the national electoral associations had a democratic structure but not yet a democratic policy-making process. [Stage four then consists of the gradual emergence of a more democratic kind of decision-making in the national party organizations, a gradual shift of some power from the notables in Parliament to the representative and bureaucratic party organizations outside of Parliament.]

But it is vastly important to note that this process has not gone so far as to make the parliamentary politicians mere puppets of the party organizations. [The parliamentary leaders still tend to dominate the party machines,] however much the development of the organized mass parties has cut into their former independence. And they dominate the machine not because they are "bosses" in the American sense but just because they *are* parliamentary notables. This indicates that even the present party system, however much the product of democratization, has its roots firmly in the pre-democratic past. And this is true not only of the Conservative Party, which has a very long history, but even of the Labour Party, which came into being just at the turn of the century. Appropriately enough, the dominance of the parliamentarians over party conventions and officials is greater in the former than the latter, but the similarities between them are perhaps even more important than the differences.

Membership Organization

All the members of the Conservative Party belong to the party as individuals rather than as members of other organizations. The Labour Party also has individual members, but most of its membership—over five out of six million—consists of members affiliated with the party as groups, making the Labour Party very largely a federation of politically minded but primarily non-political organizations. Most important among these affiliated groups are the trades unions, since they supply almost the whole of the affiliated membership—although only about 60 per cent of all trade unionists belong to the Labour Party.[5] Affiliation is by individual unions rather than by the national organization of the British trade union movement, the Trades Union Council (T.U.C.), and under the Trades Disputes Act of 1946 members of affiliated unions may "contract out" of Labour Party membership by signing forms to that effect. This, however, does not mean that 60 per cent of the trade union movement consists of active supporters of the Labour Party; it means only that 60 per cent have not signed the contracting-out forms. One can get a more accurate idea of the number of "active" Labour supporters in the trades unions by considering pre-1946 figures. Before that year members of affiliated unions had to sign a form stating their positive willingness to contribute before they could be charged a political levy, and while this was the rule no more than 30 to 45 per cent of trades union members were affiliated with the Labour Party. Hence, it seems proper to infer that nearly half of the presently affiliated trades union members are in the party out of inertia or forgetfulness rather than positive conviction.

Among other affiliated organizations are a co-operative society[6] and certain socialist and professional societies: the very important Fabian Society, the Haldane Society (a society of socialist lawyers), and the Socialist Medical Association, none having more than a few thousand members.[7] Almost all the non-union members, therefore, are individual members, as are the more activist union members themselves.

[5] This figure is for 1953, when total trades union membership was 8,088,450, of whom 5,071,935 were dues-paying members of the Labour Party.

[6] The Royal Arsenal Co-operative Society.

[7] In 1955, trades unions accounted for 5.5 million members, co-operative societies for 28,000, individual members for nearly a million and socialist societies for a mere 9,000, about 6,000 of whom were members of the Fabian Society.

In both the Labour and Conservative parties, individual members are organized in local associations that correspond to the parliamentary constituencies and are therefore generally called "constituency parties." These associations are, in the case of both parties, organized in a "representative" manner[8] and have three principal functions. First and foremost, their task is to electioneer and recruit members to the parties. In this they have the assistance of professional election agents: men with special skills in electoral propaganda and special knowledge of election laws and local political conditions, usually trained in the national headquarters of the parties and always subject to the approval of the national organization. (The Labour Party, it might be noted, has fewer such agents and pays them less than the Conservative Party, for the simple reason that the Tories have more money.) Secondly, the constituency parties choose candidates for the parliamentary seats, and third, they send representatives to the national conventions of the parties.

The Selection of Candidates

Choosing a parliamentary candidate is not, however, a purely local affair (as it tends to be in the United States). In both parties the local choice is inoperative until centrally approved and often the real choice is made by the national leaders. The need for central approval is quite explicit in the case of the Labour Party. Its constitution provides that selection of a candidate "shall not be regarded as completed until the name of the person has been placed before a meeting of the National Executive Committee,[9] and his or her selection has been duly endorsed," endorsement being conditional on acceptance and conformity to "the Constitution, Programme, Principles and Policy of the Party" and an undertaking by the candidate to "act in harmony with the Standing Orders of the Parliamentary Labour Party." The penalties for non-compliance are severe: the party label will be withdrawn and so will financial support from the national organization, the Leader of the party will refuse to send to the voters the usual formal letter of endorsement of the candidate during the election campaign and no parliamentary bigwigs will be sent into the constituency on his behalf. The result is almost certain defeat. While exercising a veto over local nominations the national party leadership may also recommend to the local party consideration of a particular

[8] For example, in the Labour Party individual members are grouped in wards and all may attend ward meetings. The constituency parties themselves are governed by General Management Committees, consisting of delegates from the ward committees, special women's sections, and organizations affiliated with the local party (e.g., trades union branches). Constituency organization in the Conservative Party is not significantly different.

[9] For a description of this committee, see below, p. 142.

candidate, usually a bright young man or a worthy member of the party bureaucracy, who will often be adopted by the local party.[10]

It has been said that control over the selection of candidates is much stricter in the Labour Party than in the Conservative Party, but while no doubt it is more explicit, the actual processes by which Conservative candidates are selected are, in practice, very similar. Again, the local party does the choosing. But a special national committee (the Standing Advisory Committee on Parliamentary Candidates) and a Vice-Chairman of the Party Organization frequently suggest candidates from a specially prepared file and keep an eye on candidates adopted. Approval from the center is necessary before selection of a candidate and the adoption of a *persona non grata* will have the same consequences as in the Labour Party, with very much the same ultimate effect.

National Party Organization

The national organization of the Labour Party is simply the national instrument of the local and affiliated organizations. That of the Conservative Party is more complex because it is composed simultaneously of bodies representing the constituency associations and bodies that act as agencies for the parliamentary notables, especially the Leader. This structural difference is, as we shall see, symptomatic of certain more important differences between the two parties.

The official national organ of the Labour Party membership is the annual party Conference, attended by representatives of local parties or affiliated organizations, plus representatives of regional party organizations and certain members sitting ex officio (e.g., members of Parliament, prospective Labour candidates, and delegates of the Labour League of Youth). The total number of members qualified to attend was 2,604 in 1950. The Conference spends its time debating reports from the party leaders in and out of Parliament, important statements of policy (e.g., the party program), and resolutions submitted by affiliated organizations. For purposes of voting each affiliated organization is permitted as many votes as it has members, so that about five million votes are cast by trades unions, one million by the constituency parties, and only 60,000 by the socialist societies and the Royal Arsenal Co-operative combined, all usually in "blocks." [11]

The Conservative Party has not one but two large conventions every

[10] But not always. After the split in the Party of 1931, for example, the constituency parties commonly passed over the names of ex-ministers recommended for adoption by the national leaders.

[11] The figures are for 1950. The Labour Party constitution does not require block voting, but it is customary and delegations rarely split.

year: the meeting of its Central Council and that of the party Conference. These two bodies do not seem very different. True, one meets in the spring, the other in the autumn; one (the Conference) has a truly gargantuan membership of 5,000,[12] the other numbers a more modest 3,600; but both are composed of the same people: chiefly representatives of the constituency organizations,[13] Conservative M.P.s and peers, prospective candidates and important party bureaucrats. Nevertheless, the two bodies are not in theory duplicates of one another. The Council is the governing body of the National Union of Conservative and Unionist Associations, i.e., of the members. The Conference is the annual meeting of the *party*— and party and party members are *not* considered identical by the Conservatives. *The party*, to be sure, includes the party members and their associations, but it also includes something more: the parliamentary notables and their Leader. It goes without saying, of course, that these notables are themselves members of the party, but—and this is the crucial point—their role as party members is something separate from their role as the party's parliamentary notables; so that it is proper to say that the Conference is composed of party members and parliamentary notables in their role as notables, while the General Council is composed of party members, including the parliamentary notables. The same people, by and large, are involved. Nevertheless, the distinction is not mere hairsplitting, because it represents an attitude within the Conservative Party—i.e., the independence of parliamentary notables from party—that is of great constitutional significance and has important practical consequences.

Both parties have special bodies to manage their affairs while the annual meetings are not in session. That of the Labour Party is called the National Executive Committee and has 28 members: 20 elected by affiliated organizations (12 by the trades unions, 7 by the constituency parties, and 1 by the rest), 6 elected by the Conference as a whole (5 women and the Party Treasurer, who is a person of importance precisely because he is the only male chosen by the whole Conference), and 2—the Leader of the parliamentary party and his deputy—sitting ex officio. The NEC meets monthly and is, according to the party constitution, "subject to the control and directions of the Party Conference, the Administrative Authority of the Party." Its powers over party organization are, however, impressive and it has, besides, a special voice in policy-making. It is the NEC that controls the party bureaucracy, which in turn takes care of routine administration; and, above all, it is the NEC that has the power to enforce party discipline by expelling individual members or disaffiliating

---

[12] The actual attendance, as in the Labour Party, is usually not much more than half this total.

[13] Four in the case of the Council, seven in the case of the Conference.

organizations. Its disciplinary actions, to be sure, are subject to review by the Conference, but the Conference almost always overwhelmingly endorses the NEC's decisions. In regard to policy, the NEC, together with the parliamentary leaders, makes up the party's election manifesto, its reports and resolutions set off many of the most important Conference debates, and its members are accorded certain special privileges in these debates.

The Conservative Party also has an Executive Committee, a mammoth organization, having approximately 150 members.[14] But the Conservative Executive Committee is not quite in the same position as that of the Labour Party. Like the Central Council, the Executive Committee is merely an organ of the constituency associations and is chiefly concerned with routine organizational matters and the preparation of the meetings of the Central Council. And unlike Labour's Executive Committee it shares control over national party work with a very complicated series of other bodies that are not representative of the constituent organizations and most of which have far more important work to do.

One of the most important of these other organizations is the Central Office, the permanent party headquarters where the party bureaucrats do their work under the guidance of the party Chairman. There is a remote equivalent of the Central Office in the Labour Party, the Head Office in Transport House. But the Labour bureaucracy is directly under the National Executive Committee, and the party Secretary (who heads the Head Office) is its creature and that of the National Conference—thus making the Labour bureaucracy a tool if not an offshoot of the membership organization. Over the Conservative Central Office, on the other hand, the members of the party have virtually no control. Its Chairman and two Vice-Chairmen are appointed by the party Leader in his capacity as leader and its function, to put it succinctly, is to help the constituency associations, but to act on behalf of the parliamentary notables.

Alongside the Central Office is another party organ chiefly composed of party functionaries, the Research Department. This is, in a sense, the Tories' answer to the Fabian Society: a body of expert research-workers who advise the party leaders on policy and who brief Conservative M.P.s on issues before Parliament and help them, if necessary, to work up their speeches. The importance attached to the Department may be inferred from the fact that its chairman, a direct appointee of the party Leader, in the postwar period was R. A. Butler. Finally, there exist on the national

[14] Hence it does most of its work through a General Purposes Sub-Committee; but even that is twice as large as the NEC of the Labour Party. The membership of the Executive Committee consists of area representatives of the constituency parties and principal officers of the Party, both in Parliament and the party bureaucracy. It is assisted by a very large number of Advisory Committees.

level a number of important National Advisory Committees, which, while including some representatives of the National Union, are certainly less the instruments of the Union than of the notables. By far the most important is the Advisory Committee on Policy; its chairman and deputy chairman are both appointed by the party Leader, while Parliament and the Executive Committee of the National Union contribute seven members each. There are also two Advisory Committees on party finance, both having representation from Parliament, the National Union and the party bureaucracy, but both also effectually under control of the Leader. Finally, there is the Standing Advisory Committee on Parliamentary Candidates previously mentioned; 5 of its 8 members coming from the membership organization and 2 from the Central Office. In practice, however, the main responsibility for party candidates is vested in the Vice-Chairman of the Party Organization—an appointee of the Leader, and not even a member of the Advisory Committee.

It will be seen that while in the Labour Party there is a straight flow of authority from the grass-roots organizations to the Conference, from the Conference to the National Executive Committee, and from the NEC to the party Secretary and bureaucracy, in the Conservative Party authority flows in two channels: from constituency associations to Central Council to Executive Committee, and from the Leader to the Central Office and the Research Department; whereupon the two streams of authority become amalgamated in a series of bodies deriving authority from both: the party Conference and the advisory Committees. But all the important bodies—those dealing with policy, finance, parliamentary candidates, research and party administration—are either under the direct jurisdiction of the Leader or headed by officials he appoints.

From what source, then, does the Leader of the Conservative Party derive his immense authority? The official selecting committee, until 1937, consisted simply of the Conservative members of the two Houses of Parliament and the party's prospective candidates—in short, the actual and potential parliamentary notables. In 1937, however, a sop was thrown to the rank and file (and the democratic principle) by the addition of the Executive Committee of the National Union to the group. But since this only involved adding some 100 votes to the 1,000 votes already qualified, it did not produce any significant shift in power from parliamentarians to the rank and file. The one-thousand-odd Conservative members of the House of Commons and the House of Lords still far outweigh the nearly three million dues-paying members of the party in selecting the man to lead them in Parliament, to govern the country when the party is in power, and to control the party's most important extra-parliamentary organizations. Moreover, it would be wrong to suppose that even these one thousand really determine who the Leader is to be in every case. Often they merely ratify a decision already made, usually by very few people. This is especially likely to happen when a Conservative Prime Minister dies or resigns and is succeeded by another Conservative leader. In that case, the sovereign, advised by whom she selects to advise her, names the succeeding Prime Minister, who is then elected Leader of the party. Thus, upon Churchill's resignation in 1955, Eden was named Prime Minister and subsequently Leader of the party.

Nothing suggests more unequivocally that British parties too have roots in the past than the Conservative Leader's authority and the method by which he is elected. It is not only that parliamentarians play such an important role in choosing him but that even they refrain from wielding their formal powers when a Conservative has already been named First Minister of the Crown. And it is not only that the Leader can control the party bureaucracy; he has a host of other independent powers as well that give him a position of power unrivaled in other democratic parties. It is he who appoints the party's Chief Whip; it is he who appoints the party's Shadow Cabinet when it is in opposition; most striking of all, he alone can authoritatively commit the party to policy or present an election program. In 1945, for example, the Conservative Party had no party program at all; there was merely "Mr. Churchill's Declaration of Policy to the Electors."

The Labour Party Leader enjoys nothing like the same explicit authority. Indeed, in terms of the party constitution, no Labour Party Leader exists at all. The Parliamentary Labour Party (i.e., the Labour M.P.s) does, to be sure, elect a leader, but the words of the party constitution make him only the Leader of the parliamentary party, not the Leader of the Labour Party. While this distinction is of little practical importance the fact remains that the post lacks many of the formal powers explicitly given the Conservative Leader. Not the Leader but the parliamentary party appoints the Chief Whip; nor does he appoint the members of the Shadow Cabinet—again, the parliamentary party does—or the head of the party bureaucracy. He does not autocratically pronounce policy; on the contrary, final authority over the formulation of policy, as over all other party concerns, is vested by the party constitution in the party Conference, its "sovereign" authority. Not least, when the Labour Party is out of power its Leader is elected annually, unlike the Conservative Leader who holds his position as long as he likes, until he dies or resigns, presumably as a symbol of his "independence" from the party machine.

In the Labour Party, therefore, the formal powers of the Conservative Leader are assigned partly to the organization of the party outside Parliament and partly to the Parliamentary Labour Party. The latter differs rather strikingly from its Conservative counterpart precisely by the fact that it is assigned powers that the Conservatives commit to their Leader. Strictly speaking, indeed, the Conservative Party has no parliamentary party in the Labour sense at all. It does have a series of committees composed of Conservative backbenchers that advise the Leader on policy (if he wants their advice) and help him to gauge rank-and-file feelings. There are about twenty "functional" committees, the principal officers of which form a Business Committee that has ready access to the Leader, and in addition there is the more amorphous "1922 Committee," composed of all the backbench Conservative members, the function of which is simply to elicit rank-and-file views to be communicated to the Leader, the Chief Whip, and other "notables." But it is not even pretended that these backbench organizations can make decisions binding on the leaders.

[In the Labour Party, on the other hand, the parliamentary party has much greater formal power—at least when the party is in opposition. It is the governing organ of the party in Parliament.] Its policy decisions are binding on all Labour members and, as we already know, its "Parliamentary Committee" (elected by the Labour members of the House of Commons) is the Labour Shadow Cabinet. The Whips are its own instruments, not the Leader's, and the Leader himself is its annually elected creature. [When the party is in office, however, all this abruptly changes. Although its Leader is invariably named Prime Minister, the parliamentary party does not choose the Cabinet, that being the Prime Minister's prerogative. At the same time it ceases to make decisions binding on all the members of the party, including the leaders.] It becomes in fact rather like what the Conservative parliamentary party is all the time: a series of "Study Groups," headed by a "Liaison Committee" that, like the Conservative Business Committee and the officers of the "1922 Committee," keeps the leaders in touch with sentiment on the benches behind. This dual character of the Parliamentary Labour Party is, as we shall see in the next section, indicative of something very important.

Power Relationships in the Parties

So far we have discussed only formal organization; but this is mere skin and bones. What are the vital organs of the two parties? Where does power to make binding decisions really reside? We know where it is formally lodged: [in the Labour Party the Conference is sovereign, in the Conservative Party it is the Leader.] But one must never accept such formal provisions at face value. When one inquires further into the matter, even as sketchily as we shall here, the two parties turn out to be not so very different from one another after all, one being far less democratic, the other far more, than they pretend to be. Let us consider the Labour Party first, that being the more complicated case.

[It has often been asserted that the Labour Party is not in fact a democratic organization because it is dominated by the leaders of the more powerful trades unions.] Statistically the point is well taken. Not only are five out of every six votes at the Conference cast by the trade unions but of the eighty unions affiliated with the party six account for more than half the membership.[15] Financially the point is well taken too; most of Labour's money comes from political dues collected by the unions. And the fact is that the Party and the unions have only rarely been seriously at odds. But none of this means necessarily that the Labour party is "undemocratic," even if we concede that the trades unions themselves are not in every case models of democracy and have been, on the whole, like-minded on important questions of policy.[16] For money and voting strength at the Conference are not the only determinants of power in the Labour Party.

[A considerable amount of money certainly is needed by the party, but money alone will not make it successful. To achieve its purpose—i.e., to win elections—the party also needs "activists":] people to run the constituency parties, to canvass for members, to get out the vote and to whip up enthusiasm, and this the agents cannot do alone. But the party activists are to be found almost entirely in the constituency parties; even the activist trades unionists generally join constituency parties and act through these rather than the unions. For this reason alone the unions cannot consistently bully the Conference against the opposition of the individual members. After all, what good would it do to sweep Conference after Conference only to find that the constituency parties will not energetically work for the program during a campaign? The socialist societies and the Parliamentary Party have special weapons too with which to assert themselves. The Fabian Society is still the brains of the movement: the party research organization and its chief source of ideas—not nearly so much as it was in the heyday of the Webbs and Shaw and H. G. Wells but still

[15] The Transport and General Workers Union (830,000 members), the National Union of Mineworkers (651,000), the Amalgamated Engineering Union (595,000), the General and Municipal Workers (400,000), the National Union of Railwaymen (366,000) and the Union of Shop Distributive and Allied Workers (317,000).

[16] "Like-minded on important questions of policy" does not mean unanimous on all questions of policy. There are, in fact, important political splits among the six largest unions. Three (the Transport and General Workers Union, the Mineworkers, and the General and Municipal) have been consistently conservative in the past, while the Railwaymen, Engineers and the Distributive and Allied Workers have been consistently left-wing. These divisions are not of course fixed. Under their new leader, Frank Cousins, the Transport and General Workers have been veering hesitantly left while, after the death of James Figgins, the Railwaymen were practically bound to veer right. On the whole, however, the bulk of the trades unions have been considerably to the right of the constituency parties.

enough to give it influence. And the Parliamentary Party gains power
from the very fact that it is the party's arm in Parliament. It is required
to enact into law the party program; it has the special prestige that all
British parliamentarians possess; and its leaders are the party members
most in the public eye, not least during election campaigns.

[The Labour Party, then, consists of a series of countervailing powers—
trades unions, constituency party activists, socialist intellectuals, and members of Parliament—each of which is useful if not indispensable to the
others] Intraparty decision-making involves the interplay of all these forces,
and this explains why Labour policy has been consistently neither as left-
wing as that of its "left-wing enthusiasts" nor as right-wing as that of the
"dull-witted and conservative trades union officials." (The epithets are
Beatrice Webb's.)

[The quantitative power of the trades unions, moreover, is greater in the
Conference than on the National Executive Committee and greater on
the NEC than in the Parliamentary Party.] And it is not as great among
the parliamentary leaders as among the parliamentary rank and file.
But the NEC undoubtedly has greater power than the Conference as a
whole; the party in Parliament frequently dominates the party outside,
and the parliamentary leaders (especially the Leader) can usually control
the parliamentary party. This is important both to appraise correctly the
power of the unions and to understand the party's actual decision-making
processes.

[The annual Conference neither is nor could be, in practice, what it is
supposed to be in theory: the party's sovereign decision-making body.]
Two thousand people, meeting for four and a half days in some crowded
seaside resort to consider some three to four hundred resolutions, to debate
the voluminous reports of their leaders and to hear their addresses, cannot
make policy as a truly deliberative assembly. They can and do raise an
occasional row, and sometimes—very infrequently—they win out in a
conflict with the leaders. They played a decisive role in 1918, again in
1935, and still a third time in 1954. But each time, it should be noted, the
"leaders" were divided among themselves.[17] They sometimes, by the tone
of the discussions, stiffen the attitudes of the leaders[18] or soften them.

[17] In 1918, the Parliamentary Party wanted to remain in the Lloyd George Coalition
but a special party Conference demanded withdrawal; the NEC, however, was in favor
of withdrawal as against the parliamentary leaders. In 1935 the Conference in effect
dictated to a divided parliamentary party on the sanctions issue. And in 1954 the
Conference decided the party's attitude on German rearmament, again because of deep
divisions among the parliamentary leaders and on the NEC.

[18] As in 1936, on the issue of the party's attitude toward the Spanish Civil War, and
in 1945 when the Conference wrote into the party program a clear commitment to
public ownership of land, heavy industry, banking, etc., against an NEC resolution
recommending more ambiguously the transfer to the state of "power to direct the
policy" of various sectors of the economy.

But for the Conference to carry a point against a united NEC or, even more unlikely, an NEC united with all the parliamentary luminaries, is exceptional indeed, and when it does it is usually ignored. No doubt this means that the NEC is adroit at adjusting itself to any strong sentiment among the rank and file. But it means much more clearly that the NEC simply tends to dominate the Conference—that the Conference is a rally, a chance for the activists to become acquainted, a chance for the leaders and would-be leaders to show their paces, a chance for the people at the top to feel out sentiment at the bottom, but little more.

Again, the parliamentary party holds a specially privileged position vis-à-vis the party outside, especially when the party is in power. It holds such a position, above all, because British constitutional practice does not tolerate government by party caucuses. The Government is supposed to be carried on by Her Majesty's Ministers, not by a party's bigwigs. Her Majesty's Ministers have access to information not available to ordinary people. Their duty is (according to Mr. Churchill) first to the country, then to their constituents, and only then to their party. They alone understand the problems and are in control of the parliamentary time-table.[19] Hence, how could ordinary people presume to dictate to them?

That this is no empty constitutional theory may be illustrated by an incident that occurred in 1945 while the wartime Coalition Government was still in office. Mr. Attlee, a member of the Coalition, was to accompany Mr. Churchill to the projected Potsdam Conference. The then chairman of the Party, Professor Harold Laski, declared shortly before the meeting of the Conference that the party could not be committed to any decisions that had not been debated by the NEC or the Parliamentary Labour Party. Churchill seized on this with enthusiastic indignation. Would a Labour Government really be a dictatorship of the National Executive—a body "unknown to the British Constitution"? Would government secrets communicated to Labour Ministers as His Majesty's Privy Councillors be communicated to members of the Executive who were not subject to the Privy Councillor's oath of secrecy? Mr. Attlee answered with a statement that may be taken as definitive. The Parliamentary Labour Party consults with the NEC before the opening of every parliamentary session and at any other time it wants to consult with it, but "at no times and in no circumstances has the National Executive Committee ever sought to give instructions to the Parliamentary Labour Party arising out of the consultation. Indeed . . . it has no power to do so."

There can be little doubt that Parliamentary Party here means first and foremost the parliamentary leaders, although their powers are undoubtedly

---

[19] See below, p. 179.

much greater when Labour is in office than when it is not. Consider the following comment by R. T. McKenzie on the fate of the party's "Study Group" under the Government of 1945:

> Those Members of Parliament who expected that the Groups would give them a chance to take part actively in policy-making have had their hopes rudely dashed. From the start the Ministers made it clear that they did not look on the Groups in this light. The Ministers' reasons for taking this position were twofold: They felt that constitutionally they could not reveal proposed legislation to a few Members before presenting it to the whole House; and they believed that as a practical matter it would be risky to discuss legislative proposals with Backbenchers because the latter might speak for only a narrow minority of the Party, or they might "leak" to the press, or they might try to obstruct or alter Cabinet proposals. Some Backbenchers have come to feel that the group meetings are a waste of time, or, even worse, that they are a means of keeping the rank-and-file occupied with trivial tasks so that their influence would be minimized.[20]

And it has been argued that Clement Attlee emerged as a strong figure after becoming Leader not only because he was much more than he appeared to be on the surface—"a sheep in sheep's clothing," Winston Churchill once called him—but because his position carried with it certain inherent powers and prestige, which it communicates even to the meekest occupant. Very few Prime Ministers indeed have failed to make use of these powers. The plain fact is, as a writer on British government recently said, that "in spite of . . . Labour's tradition of back-bench participation in policy-making, the parliamentary leaders have maintained a sphere of independent action probably as wide as that of the Conservatives' leadership *when in power*." But we have reason to think that the privileges bestowed upon the leaders in power also enhance their influence in opposition.

We should realize, however, that the Labour leaders' sphere of independent action rivals that of the Conservative leaders not only because the Labour leaders have more power than formal party theory suggests but also because the Conservative leaders have less. Certainly, the Leader of of the Conservative Party does not wield in practice the comprehensive powers assigned to him by theory, at least not single-handedly and arbitrarily. Backbenchers, the "ardent partisans" (as Churchill put it) outside Parliament, the research members of the party—all wield influence as in the Labour Party, and for similar reasons. These reasons are that winning elections is the overriding purpose of the party—among the Conservatives even more than the Labourites—and that the Leader cannot win elections by himself. That point was made unmistakable by the General Election

[20] R. T. McKenzie, *British Political Parties* (1955).

of 1945. The Conservatives then had a Leader as popular personally as any democratic Leader is likely to be. They waged a campaign which did little but exploit Churchill's popularity. They let him arbitrarily declare policy and manage the electioneering. And they were crushingly defeated by the Labour Party.

That this experience had important effects can be seen in the way party policy has been evolved since 1945. Before that the normal practice had been for the party to put forward men and for the men to propound measures, more or less as they went along. After 1945 a clamor arose, particularly among the younger members of the party, for concrete statements of *party* policy with which to counter Labour actions and propaganda. By 1950 two very lengthy documents setting forth such policy, the *Industrial Charter* (1947) and *The Right Road for Britain* (1950) had been published. To be sure, the parliamentary leaders played the dominant role in the preparation of these documents. *The Right Road,* for example, was worked out under the supervision of a committee of the Shadow Cabinet and clearly made subject to the Leader's veto. Material for the deliberations was prepared by members of the Research Department, a draft was prepared by the special Committee, which was submitted to the Leader and other prominent Conservatives for approval, published, and then approved almost unanimously at the Conference. But the fact that the parliamentary notables took the lead in the preparation of the document is not as important as the very fact that such a statement of policy was prepared at all. For although it was not formally accorded the status of an election program—that would have been much too abrupt a break with usage—and although Churchill truculently announced to the Conference that he still intended to make "personal" policy, a declaration of policy so overwhelmingly supported by the party and so widely distributed in the country could not fail to affect Conservative policy in Parliament.

The Right Road was made at the top and acclaimed at the bottom; but this is not different from what happens in the Labour Party. And as in the case of the Labour Party, the rank and file, usually docile, more anxious to cheer than to carp, has on occasion forced its point of view on the leaders. The best recent example is the housing debate at the 1950 Conference. The Conference was debating a routine motion condemning Labour's housing policies. In the course of the debate a speaker mentioned that 300,000 houses should be built annually. The figure caught on like "a prairie fire"; speaker after speaker repeated it amidst the constantly growing enthusiasm of the delegates. There can be no doubt that the leaders would have preferred a nice ambivalent resolution, leaving them a free hand to build as many houses as they felt proper in the course of developments, but the delegates were not to be denied. At last, Lord Woolton, the chairman of the party, arose and accepted the figure on behalf of the leadership, "to bloodcurdling yells of triumph from the floor," according to the *Observer*. Nor was the incident ignored. The Conservative Government of 1951 did proceed to build 300,000 houses, and the Minister in charge of the housing program, Mr. Macmillan, promptly became a celebrated figure in the party. The prairie fire of 1950 was certainly exceptional, but none the less significant for that. It suggests that in the Conservative Party, as in the Labour Party, the leaders are not unconditionally independent of the pressures arising from the rank and file in and out of Parliament.

Thus, one of the most striking characteristics of the two major British parties is that despite having utterly different formal structures their actual decision-making powers are strikingly similar. Labour has avoided "caucus government," the Tories autocracy; both are in fact oligarchies tempered by a sense of dependence on mass support. Is it not reasonable to infer that this is so because both parties function under conditions that forcefully push them in the same direction?

The first of these conditions is the prevalence of certain political conventions and attitudes throughout British society, especially those that have their roots in predemocratic times. These explain better than anything else the dominance of the Leader in each party. There is, first of all, the long tradition of personal leadership by parliamentary notables, dating to the time when parliamentary parties were really personal factions and when the concept of the mandate was practically unknown. Inevitably this tradition of commitment to a leader plays a greater role in the Conservative than in the Labour party, but it has probably affected the latter too by being a parliamentary tradition—part of the style of the House. More important, Parliament has always been regarded as something other than a convention of delegates, either of parties or of constituencies; its legitimate function, in short, is "to govern the country," not (in the first instance at any rate) to legitimize local or party interests. This applies most forcibly of all, of course, to the members of the Government. To be one of Her Majesty's Ministers, a member of the Cabinet and of the Privy Council, is to be set aside from mere party, not only in the sense of being given a special responsibility for the *national* welfare but in the sense of being given a special right to make policy toward this end. The actual (not formal) distribution of power in British parties, therefore, even in the case of the Labour Party, is deeply affected by the more ancient and nondemocratic aspects of the Constitution. This emerges most strikingly from the fact that when Labour is in power its Parliamentary Party acquires a structure very similar to that of the Conservative Party while its leaders formally cut themselves off from the party organization in Parliament and cease to be bound by its decisions.

But just as the structure of action in the Labour Party is affected by the non-democratic aspects of British political life so that of the Conservative Party is affected by its democratic aspects. Whatever Conservative Party theory may say on the subject, it is a violation of British political sensibilities, including Conservative sensibilities, to ride roughshod over popular sentiment. To ignore such sentiment is barely legitimate, but to defy it is clearly not. Outside of their Constitution the Conservatives do pretend that they are a democratic group. Equally important is the much more tangible fact that the Conservatives no less than Labour must seek to win power by means of universal suffrage, and that mass democracy imposes certain inescapable institutional conditions on a mass party; that was the great lesson of 1945. Mass democracy in its very nature requires ardent enthusiasts, party bureaucrats, party research offices and mass finances, as well as popular leaders. Hence, just as it gives to the socialist intellectuals and local Labour Party activists powers to balance off against the trades unions, so it gives to the enthusiasts of the National Union and the intellectuals and bureaucrats of the Conservative Central Office and Research Department countervailing powers against the parliamentary notables. Party democracy may be accepted only truculently by the Tory Leader, but it is, in some degree at least, a necessary consequence of electoral democracy, however much modified, in both parties, by more ancient traditions.

Party Organization and Party Discipline

To what aspects of party organization, then, can party discipline be attributed? One obvious possibility is the screening of parliamentary candidates by the national headquarters of both parties. Such screening no doubt helps to eliminate some blatant heretics, but whether it does more than that is doubtful. There is, in strict point of fact, little cautious screening of potential M.P.s by the party oligarchs, chiefly because blatant heresy is itself unusual among British politicians. And attributing party discipline to central screening begs the question of why the local party organizations so meekly submit (as a general rule) to central control, and why there is a kind of party discipline outside Parliament that helps to make possible party discipline inside Parliament. After all, effective central screening of local parliamentary candidates is not simply a technical device that can be used in any country as people please. It may itself be a consequence of the same factors that make for party discipline in Parliament; but, in any case, it presupposes conditions that are far from universal.

The most important of these conditions in Britain is the importance of the party label to successful political candidacy. But is the party label successful qua party label, as we supposed in a previous part of the chapter, or because of the concrete penalties that follow its withdrawal? The chief penalty it entails is of course withdrawal of central financial support, but that, while certainly annoying, is not so severe a handicap to the constituency parties as might appear. In the Conservative Party the constituency associations are very well able to fend for themselves financially. In fact, the chief financial function of the Central Office seems to be merely to redistribute funds from the more to the less well-to-do constituencies.[21] This is not of course the case in the Labour Party, at least not to the same extent. But British elections are in any case relatively inexpensive and financial considerations in consequence not so pressing as might be thought. Few candidates spend more than £1,000 in a campaign and most considerably less, since there is much less general hullabaloo in a British election and time on radio and television are furnished free by the B.B.C. This sum is hardly out of reach of most constituency parties, particularly since the trades unions often directly support the campaigns of Labour candidates.[22] Thus, financial support from the center, while always welcome, is not so vitally necessary in either party as to account for their extraordinary obedience to central advice on candidacies.

There are two other important objections against theories attributing party discipline in Parliament to the power of the party organizations outside. One is that the party organizations of both parties are themselves much more under the control of members of Parliament than M.P.s are under the control of the party organizations and that the high cohesion of external party machinery, like discipline in Parliament, is due to the dominance of the parliamentary leaders. Hence, while their domination over external party machinery reinforces the dominance of the leaders over the parliamentary parties, it is more plausible to attribute both to the same basic causes than to make one the determinant of the other. Finally, if the power of external party organization (including financial power) were the decisive determinant of party discipline in Parliament we should expect to find more solid discipline on the Labour than on the Conservative benches; yet, if anything, the opposite is the case.

This fact itself suggests that the explanation of the British party system

[21] Two-fifths of the Conservative associations are helped by the national party organization with money collected from other local associations.

[22] 140 in 1950 and 138 in 1951. Trades unions may contribute up to £300 annually to constituency parties and pay up to 80 per cent of a candidate's election expenses.

developed in Chapter 8—that it is a result, essentially, of the British political "spirit"—is correct. Although the outlook of the Labour Party, like that of the Conservative Party, is predominantly pragmatic, attachment to "principles," dogma, even ideology is considerably more common among Labourites (especially the extreme left wing) than Tories, though still uncommon enough. Hence it is the Labour Party—and before Labour it was, for similar reasons, the Liberal Party—that always seems in danger of suffering party splits as the result of irreconcilable opinions, and it seems always to be the extreme left wing whose opinions are intractable. The Conservatives, even when divided (as over Suez in 1956-57), never seem in great danger of splitting. The decisive factor inducing the disciplined two-party system then is the British "genius for political compromise," and this is not so much the result of the political disadvantages always entailed in severe internal party disagreements—these disadvantages after all exist also where parties are not disciplined—as of the peculiarly British conditions earlier discussed.

CHAPTER **13**

The British Welfare State

[Since the end of World War II Great Britain has acquired a very highly developed welfare state. This means simply that the state has assumed a high degree of responsibility for the condition of the British economy and for the economic welfare of every member of British society.] It tries, by public direction, to assure an economy that is highly productive, financially stable, and capable of selling the exports that Britain must sell to survive. At the same time it tries, by public policy, to assure full employment and guarantees to all members of society, even those who cannot be employed, a certain minimum standard of subsistence. [The principal means employed to achieve these ends are three: nationalization measures (i.e., measures transferring certain privately owned business concerns to public authority), economic planning and control measures, and redistribution of wealth measures (i.e., measures designed to transfer wealth from the well-off to the not-so-well-off).]

These developments have changed the British political system in several important respects. Not only the pattern of policy itself, but also the pattern of power has changed. The sum total of government activities has grown immensely. Moreover, the government is now engaged on a large scale in unprecedented *kinds* of activities, especially the direct provision by the state of goods and services to the members of society (medical care and drugs, all sorts of insurance, coal, transportation, electricity, gas, and entertainment, in addition to the more traditional public goods and services, education and postal services), and the direct assumption by the state of certain decision-making functions in areas previously subject solely to private decision-making, e.g., by means of price controls, rationing, or the allocation of capital goods.

[Contemporary British government, then, is something novel, both in scope and kind.] But the machinery of government that has to perform the new functions developed in times when government was a more leisurely activity and much less directly concerned with the direction of social and economic affairs. Hence, a host of serious problems arise about the interplay of the new activities with the old machinery. More generally, this is the question of the interrelations of the pattern of policy and the pattern of power. To what extent is the structure of government, as developed in the past, appropriate to the efficient performance of the tasks of the welfare state? To what extent has it been possible to make the necessary adaptations and adjustments? And to what extent are these adjustments compatible with the values and structural requirements of democratic, responsible, parliamentary government?

Before we attempt to deal with these questions let us analyze in some detail the policies that give rise to them and why they were adopted. We need to examine the changing pattern of interests—the rise of new interest groups and the developing views of political parties. We need also to look at the changing economic conditions and the changing values and beliefs that gave rise to those new interests that are reflected in the policies of the welfare state today.

The Origins of the British Welfare State

The British welfare state is certainly not exclusively a development of the postwar period. Long before the Labour landslide of 1945 Great Britain had a certain amount of public enterprise (most of it, incidentally, the creation of Conservative Governments), at least a little public economic planning, and a good deal of public economic control and social security legislation. The development of the welfare state is a long and continuing story and to find its origins one must go back at least to the middle of the nineteenth century, when the first public health measures were enacted. But this unfolding of the welfare state has been tremendously accelerated in the postwar period, and in this period occurred also the culmination of the more important trends in socio-economic legislation that can be traced to earlier times. What forces, then, induced the British to create a highly developed welfare state in this period?

No doubt much of the explanation may be found, as usual, in attitudes —in subjectively conceived social values and objectives. The postwar British welfare state crowned with success half a century of political agitation by trades union Labourites and Fabian socialists. But it is mistaken to think of the British welfare state purely in these terms. To a considerable extent, its development was a matter of need no less than choice. Certain objective forces ("objective" in the sense that they were given in the environment of policy and not subject to anyone's choice) did as much to impel Britain in the socio-economic direction she has taken since the war as any political agitation, a fact reflected in the startlingly close agree-

ment among the parties on social and economic issues. To some extent
this consensus on policy may be due to the remarkable ability of the
Tories to trim their program to any prevailing wind of doctrine, but the
kindlier and perhaps more accurate construction to put on the matter is
that choice among policies in postwar Britain has been severely limited by
given conditions that party politics cannot wish away.

The most serious and intractable of these conditions is the British international economic position. Everyone knows that international trade is
a matter of life or death for Great Britain; that she is heavily dependent
on imports of foodstuffs and raw materials to support her population and
keep her factories running; and that, as a corollary, she must have large
and reliable export markets for her manufactured goods in areas that can
supply her needs for primary materials.[1] Unfortunately, the international
economic outlook for Britain has been bleak and growing steadily bleaker
for a very long time, and World War II came very close to delivering the
economic *coup de grâce* after a long history of deterioration.

Although British war losses, in cold statistical terms, were not as serious
as those sustained by Germany and Russia, or, for that matter, France, in
a relative sense, particularly in view of her desperate dependence on
international trade, they were perhaps the most devastating, because the
least easily replaceable of all. A few statistics will vividly tell the tale.
Between 1939 and 1945, more than one billion pounds of Britain's overseas investments (chiefly "dollar" investments) had to be liquidated in
order to raise foreign currencies with which to buy war equipment and
supplies. In the same period, Britain's external debt rose from £760,000,000
to £3,355,000,000, leading to vastly increased pressure on her foreign currency resources in both principal and interest payments. And, again during
the same period, "reserves" (meaning actual holdings of gold and United
States dollars) dwindled from £864,000,000 to £453,000,000, while shipping, a reliable earner of "invisibles" before the war, dwindled from
22,100,000 to 15,900,000 tons. In short, on V-J Day victorious Britain was
bankrupt, with no long-run relief in sight; and this situation was con-
founded still further by certain postwar events, particularly the loss of
Eastern European markets as a result of the cold war, and the loss of India,
Ceylon and Burma, which had previously been more or less exclusive
British trading areas.

[1] Francis Williams, in *Socialist Britain* (1948), points out that before the war,
"nearly three-quarters of all the food [Great Britain] ate came from abroad, 55 per
cent of her meat, 75 per cent of her wheat, 85 per cent of her butter, all her tea,
cocoa, and coffee, three-quarters of her sugar. . . . Moreover, with the single exception of coal, the raw materials upon which her major industries depended were largely
or wholly imported; all the cotton, all the rubber, five-sixths of the wool, practically
all the petroleum, two-thirds of the iron ore, most of the timber." About a quarter of
the national income went in payment for imports of various sorts.

The American loan and ECA aid provided short-run relief but could hardly be a permanent solution of Britain's economic problems. What was needed first and foremost was a vastly expanded volume of exports and an import bill kept down to the minimum. Exports were needed to fill the hiatus left by the vanished invisible earnings from British overseas investments and the supply of services (e.g., shipping).[2] But how was the necessary surplus of exports to be achieved? Clearly, postwar Britain had to export much more than prewar Britain. But, objectively, postwar Britain was hardly in a position to produce as much as prewar Britain, because the war had done a serious amount of property damage, not least to productive facilities. Hence, the required volume of exports could be achieved only by the severe curtailment of domestic consumption. But this also was no easy task. The war had created a large unrequited demand for consumer goods in Great Britain just as it did elsewhere. Personal possessions had deteriorated no less than capital equipment. Nearly half a million houses had been destroyed or damaged beyond repair. Another three and a half million needed repairs, major and minor. No hospitals had been built since 1938, nor any schools, or other public buildings.

The danger therefore was that Britain would consume herself into destruction rather than export her way to recovery, particularly since manufacturers could make fortunes almost without effort in the starved home market or in other easy markets in soft currency areas, instead of going into the highly competitive and sales-resistant hard-currency markets, especially the North American markets. Under those conditions no postwar Government could have taken a chance on an undirected economy. The Labourite socialists therefore had a high degree of public planning and control thrust upon them, however much they might have been predisposed to central economic controls in the first place.

The need for a great deal of public intervention in economic affairs was further accentuated by the internal condition of the British economy. It goes without saying that the seriousness of the international economic problems was inversely proportional to the internal efficiency of British industry, which, quite apart from the results of war damage, was (and is) quite low. A single figure will suffice to illustrate the point: a study done in identical years in 32 manufacturing trades showed that the ratio of productivity between the United States and Britain has been at a level of 216 to 100 in favor of the United States, and countless visiting productivity teams on both sides have confirmed the impression conveyed by this ratio. To some extent, the internal difficulties of the British economy may be the result of the very factor one might expect would have given

---

[2] Before the war, invisibles paid for one-fifth of all British imports; after the war for only one-fiftieth.

it the greatest advantage over those of other countries: Britain's head start in the industrial revolution. There is perhaps such a thing as an overdeveloped economy no less than an underdeveloped economy, and Britain is the chief case in point. For example, the older capital equipment is, the more it consumes in maintenance and repair. From this standpoint it is extremely suggestive to note that Britain has, since the war, devoted on the average 20 per cent of her national income to capital formation rather than consumption expenditure—a strikingly large proportion—and yet has managed to increase her total capital resources only very slightly. To some extent this no doubt is due to the capital investment devoured by war damage and war neglect, but it also reflects the relatively great age of much of Britain's industrial plant. Again, once a country has acquired a highly developed industrial apparatus—once it has committed a large proportion of its capital resources—it is extremely difficult, for psychological as well as physical reasons, to scrap and totally renew sizable portions of it, thus keeping up with the technical level of more recently industrialized societies.

To make a long and very complicated story short, [there has existed in the postwar period a sort of permanent economic crisis in Britain, partly as a result of changes in her position wrought by the war, partly as the result of the continuation of long-range international economic tendencies in her disfavor, and partly as the result of a long series of provisional circumstances so strung together as to constitute almost a permanent emergency.] Invisible earnings have not been recovered to prewar level; the terms of trade, despite some bright periods (e.g., during the Korean War), have been steadily worsening; tariff walls impede exports; and German and Japanese competition has revived to a dangerous degree. The cold war has demanded the diversion of goods desperately needed for export or home consumption to defense, and colonial crises have put a similar drain on equipment and manpower. Not least, there has been considerable inflationary pressure on the domestic market.

[Given all these handicaps, the economic recovery made by the British in the postwar period has been astonishing: a large postwar deficit in invisible payments and receipts had been turned into a small surplus by June 1948.] The current accounts balance of payments was changed from a deficit of £630,000,000 in 1947 to a surplus of £30,000,000 a year later (though it soon went into the red again). And exports were enormously increased, especially to the Western Hemisphere, in the midst of severe domestic shortages (in 1948 they were 60 per cent greater than in 1938). But these achievements have not been sufficient to remove the pressures pushing Britain in the direction of the welfare state, at least in its economic planning and control aspects. The volume and severity of controls have been relaxed by both Labour and Conservative Governments in the course of the postwar period, but Britain has not been able to achieve a position in which she can take a real chance on the risky and wasteful luxuries of free enterprise.

But it would be a gross distortion to suggest that the British were dragged kicking and screaming into the postwar social policy by blind and irresistible economic forces. Most of the postwar social policy certainly was the product of a startlingly broad "ideological" consensus in British society. To understand the origins of the British welfare state we need consequently to grasp the reasons for this general agreement on its desirability in British society. Why the overwhelming Labour Party victory in 1945 and, even more important, why so little disagreement among the parties, of the sort that raged in America, on how to proceed in the postwar world? After all, objective economic conditions cannot explain the broad agreement on comprehensive social insurance and state responsibility for a national minimum. On the contrary, strict economic calculation would have tended to justify much less generous public policies toward individuals in favor of social welfare as such.

In this connection it is vitally important to note that Britain has little, if any, doctrinal laissez-faire tradition of the sort to be found both on the Continent and in the United States, so that it was relatively easy for the idea of the social service state to entrench itself in all sections of opinion. The official British social philosophy of most of the nineteenth century— if any social philosophy may be so described—was Benthamite utilitarianism, and this is sometimes thought of as liberal and in the classic laissez-faire tradition. But erroneously so. The utilitarians were never committed to—indeed, they explicitly attacked—the grandiose social metaphysics, the providential apparatus of natural law, by which classical laissez-faire liberalism was justified. They were in favor of laissez-faire only because the loosening of legal restraints on economic activity seemed to them conducive to their sole categorical imperative, "the greatest good of the greatest number." Hence, their laissez-faire opinions were always pragmatic and conditional and, above all, coupled with a very considerable tendency toward public manipulation, both to reform rationally the existing exercise of public authority and—more important—to exert public authority in areas where it had not been exercised before. Benthamite utilitarianism tended toward the negative state or the positive state, without any consistency of doctrine, depending solely upon whether public authority or private liberty seemed most conducive to public welfare. It was, in short, a typically British sort of creed. Before the middle of the

nineteenth century it was still predominantly laissez-faire in its preferences; after that it was gradually transformed, particularly by John Stuart
Mill, into a near-socialist creed.

[Apart from utilitarianism, the most influential intellectual movements
in the last century or so (politically speaking) have been Oxford Idealism
and Fabian Socialism, both of which preached doctrines anything but
laissez-faire in character.] Fabianism may be regarded, for all practical
purposes, as manipulative utilitarianism taken to its logical conclusion,
leavened with a tender-minded humanitarianism and ornamented with a
few ill-digested concepts and theories from the Continental socialist
ideologies. Idealism, a philosophy elaborated chiefly from German antecedents by an impressive succession of influential Oxford professors—
T. H. Green, F. H. Bradley, Bernard Bosanquet—also justified the social-
service state, although on far less pragmatic grounds than either post-
Benthamite utilitarianism or Fabianism.

[All these movements were, of course, largely "intellectual" movements
rather than popular ideologies] however much more influence they wielded
than the usual American intellectual movement. But they reflected an
altogether different movement which had perhaps greater influence on
modern British society than any other: the Evangelical movement. The
importance of Evangelicalism in molding both private and political
morality in Great Britain can hardly be exaggerated. One famous historian
has attributed the fact that England escaped without lower-class revolution in the nineteenth century largely to its influence, and if this means
that Evangelicalism induced attitudes among the upper classes that helped
to take the curse off the Industrial Revolution and the callousness from
bourgeois liberalism the theory is substantially correct. Out of it grew a
number of complementary political and economic strands. In the working
class it induced both a certain resignation to the condition of being a
worker and a commitment to an essentially ethical, fundamentalist socialism; at any rate, the non-conformist chapel, for a long time, was the chief
center of British trade unionism and socialism. Among the upper classes
it induced chiefly a crusading private humanitarianism, an almost incredible amount of philanthropy, of which the names of Edwin Chadwick
and Lord Shaftesbury have become symbolic. The movement was not
restricted to non-conformists but gradually won adherents also among the
Anglicans, if only as a defense against the rapid strides of the non-conformist sects. As a result, [Britain was well on the way toward acquiring a
welfare state by private philanthropy long before she acquired one by
government legislation, and when the postwar welfare state came into
being much of it simply involved taking over facilities previously provided
by voluntary (mainly charitable) associations: hospitals, ambulances, cer-

tain insurance services, and so on. But the important point to note here is that the Evangelical influence, as much as and more than the British tradition of pragmatism, blocked the way for the entrenchment of the harsher laissez-faire doctrines as well as the harsher reactions to those doctrines.

Inevitably, these currents of thought were reflected in party politics. It is almost useless to search British party history for a free-enterprise party.[3] It may be easy enough to find parties looking out for business interests but this is not the same thing as ideological commitment—pronounced mental predisposition—to a free-enterprise system. The Conservatives, for example, engaged in a downright indecent wooing of the lower classes in the nineteenth century, trying, like Bismarck in Germany, to steal the thunder of the social reformers and thus to preserve the submissive loyalty of the lower classes to the aristocracy. Thus, Disraeli's Tory Democracy envisaged an alliance between "the cottage and the throne"—the lower classes and the aristocracy—by which the latter undertook to enact broad social and economic reforms in return for the political support of the former—and it should not be forgotten that the most crucial extension of the franchise in the nineteenth century, the Reform Act of 1867, was made by Disraeli's Conservative Government. When Harold Macmillan wrote his book *Reconstruction* in 1934 he showed that the tradition of Tory democracy was then still very much alive in Tory ranks. His book was a staunch defense of capitalism, but a capitalism conceived as a sort of super-New Deal, involving a high degree of public planning, cartel-like controlling councils over various sectors of industry jointly operated by management and trade-union leaders, guaranteed annual wages to employees, and an extensive range of public social services, among other things in kind. This Conservative tendency toward economic radicalism is no doubt the result, in part at least, of political opportunism, but it also reflects the aristocratic foundations of the Conservative party, particularly the aristocratic tradition of paternalism and social service, which powerfully reinforced the Christian motivations of great nineteenth-century reformers like Lord Shaftesbury.

The Labour Party's welfare state was less a radical innovation than an extension of and compromise between all these currents of ideas, powerfully reinforced by "circumstances": the constantly more serious and more perceptible deterioration of Britain's economy from neglect and old age, the traumatic impact of the Great Depression, and, most important of all, the impact of the second World War. The war pushed Britain into the present welfare state not only by its effect on the British economy, but even more by its impact on social thought. The worst problems of

[3] Only certain wings of the nineteenth-century Liberal Party qualify.

prewar society vanished in the war. Unemployment disappeared and a major effort was made to share the resources of the country fairly among all by rationing, price controls and subsidies, the net result being, strangely enough, a greatly increased standard of living for most of the British population. The chief condition of this desirable state of affairs seemed to be collective effort and a deep community consciousness in the whole nation—a feeling of neighborliness and fraternity unprecedented in British history. The War therefore strongly consolidated opinion behind the idea of dealing with the problems of peace as with those of war: by public planning, collective controls, and social guarantees to every individual of a "fair share" of the national wealth. It is no exaggeration to say that Göring's Blitz was the force that coalesced all the converging strands of Christian humanitarianism, utilitarian pragmatism, Idealistic statism, Fabian socialism, and aristocratic paternalism into the social program pursued since the War. In outline, at any rate, the whole program was sketched in the two Beveridge Reports that appeared in the course of war—one on Social Insurance, the other on means to ensure full employment by public policy—and that all parties were pledged to implement as soon as circumstances would permit.

[In view of all this it is not surprising that most of the social policies resorted to by the postwar Labour Governments actually originated outside the party and the Fabian Society; that they were subscribed to by almost all sections of political opinion; and that they seem now to be accepted, in essence, almost as a natural feature in the social landscape.

We must now examine these policies in some detail. The discussion will be confined chiefly to the welfare state as it existed under the Labour Governments of 1945 to 1951, for two reasons: we know more about what was going on then than about what is going on now, and, in any event, the Conservatives have not changed much that was absolutely vital in Labour's socio-economic program.[4]

The Welfare State in Operation

Nationalization

When Labour set about nationalizing a number of important industries the step was widely represented in America as revolutionary in character, and, except perhaps for the socialized medical services (which also involved nationalization of a sort), the nationalized industries have received more publicity abroad than any other aspect of the welfare state. It is not difficult to understand this foreign emphasis on socialization measures, but it is nevertheless misplaced. [There certainly was no wholesale ex-

---

[4] For a list of changes made by the Conservatives, see p. 177.

propriation of private property of any revolutionary sort; all that happened was the transfer, at generous (perhaps overgenerous) rates, of the stock of a few enterprises from private to public hands. Most of the British economy is still privately owned and, indeed, Labour seems committed even now to nationalizing no more than about one-fifth of the economy. The only industries and businesses nationalized were the Bank of England, coal, electricity and gas, inland transport (railways, canals, road haulage), iron and steel, air transport and cable and wireless— strategically important sectors of the economy all, but still only a fraction of the sum total of the economic establishment. It follows that nationalization has been approached as a means rather than an end in itself and that greater weight is attached to other aspects of the welfare state, a deduction confirmed by the fact that much of the Labour Party, especially the important trades union section, seems to have become increasingly disenchanted with nationalization as something unnecessary to its really major objectives.

Moreover, the ground for the postwar nationalization measures had been prepared by the Liberals and Conservatives at least as much as by Labour. It was the Liberal Party that began the whole trend toward public enterprise by the creation of the Port of London Authority (which owns and operates docks and harbor facilities on the lower Thames) in 1908, and the Conservatives powerfully pushed the trend along by the creation of the Central Electricity Board in 1926, the chartering of the British Broadcasting Corporation as a public corporation in 1927, and the creation of the London Passenger Transport Board in 1933 (by a Conservative-dominated National Government). Equally important, almost all the postwar nationalization measures (iron and steel being the sole exception) were undertaken as the result of the findings and recommendations of Conservative-dominated investigating committees: the Bank of England measure, for example, as a result of the Macmillan Report, coal because of the Reid Report, gas because of the Heyworth Report, and electricity because of the McGowan Report. And not least, nationalization, as carried out by Labour, had much less effect on the structure of the industries nationalized than might be supposed. There was no revolutionary upheaval in management, or in the organization of the industries, or in labor relations, or even in commercial practices. The change from private to national enterprise, as the more radical Labourites learned to their displeasure, involved changes in form much more than in substance. Nevertheless, one should not deflate the nationalization program too much. It is noteworthy because it provides an excellent insight into the attitudes that gave rise to the British welfare state and because it has raised, despite its modesty, serious institutional problems.

A great deal can be learned about the character of modern British socialism by an examination of the reasons that induced the nationalization measures. [Nationalization may be the result of two very different kinds of reasons, one essentially "ethical" (or doctrinaire, ideological, philosophical, theoretical—whichever term is preferred), the other essentially "pragmatic-economic."] The older socialist arguments for nationalization were overwhelmingly of the ethical variety, even in the case of the Fabians. For all their managerialism, the Fabians' distaste for "unearned increment," their distrust of large private power concentrations, and their ethical preferences for industrial democracy were as decisive in shaping their views as their criticisms of the wastefulness of private enterprise. But throughout the twentieth century the case for public enterprise was shifted more and more onto pragmatic-economic grounds. [Thus, in *Let Us Face the Future*, the Labour Party's election manifesto of 1945, it was stated that only industries "ripe or overripe" for public ownership should be nationalized. And a pamphlet issued in 1948 to clarify this rather ambiguous formula (*Public Ownership, The Next Step*) pointed out that this meant industries having one or preferably more than one of the following characteristics: that the industry be (1) a *basic supplier of raw materials*; (2) *monopolized* by a large trust; (3) *inefficient*, because unable to find finance for capital investment, or split into units too small for economical operation, or burdened with a very low standard of management; (4) an investor of capital on a very large scale; (5) suffering from very *bad industrial relations*. Except for the neglect of the fourth consideration, the postwar program of nationalization faithfully followed these highly pragmatic criteria.]

The Bank of England,[5] for example, was nationalized for the following reasons. [First, because the Bank already had such close relations with the Treasury that nationalization was essentially only a formality. As Chancellor of the Exchequer Dalton put it, "the Old Man of the Treasury and the Old Lady of Threadneedle Street should be legally married to avoid any further danger of their living in sin." But these close relations rested mainly on an informal basis and, it was feared, depended on a community of outlook and interests between the Bank's directors and the people in the Treasury that would cease to exist once a socialist Government

---

[5] Since American readers can hardly be expected to be familiar with so strange a foreign phenomenon as the Bank of England, a brief description is probably in order. The Bank is a sort of cross between an ordinary bank, a Federal Reserve Bank and the Treasury itself. It was a private bank until 1945 but handled all government funds, all foreign transactions, made loans, set interest rates, etc. It acted in close alliance with the Treasury, but its directors could and sometimes did act independently. It was owned by private investors but actually run by a Court of Directors that was not elected but was a sort of self-perpetuating oligarchy.

achieved full power. This fear was the result particularly of beliefs that financial policy between the wars had been made less by the Treasury than by Mr. Montagu Norman (later Lord Norman), the Governor of the Bank from 1920 to 1944, and that, on a number of occasions, the Bank had actually used its position to sabotage government policies. Hence, the second reason for nationalization: to make the Bank a reliable and obedient tool for economic planning, and particularly an instrument with which to control the activities of the private banking system for public ends. At one time, indeed, Labour Party theoreticians had argued the necessity of wholesale nationalization of the banking system for purposes of financial planning to maintain full employment, but this more ambitious proposal was dropped in favor of nationalizing the Bank of England only and giving it general powers of direction over the private banking sector.

The case for nationalizing the coal industry was even more strikingly pragmatic. Coal is a raw material of absolute vital importance in the British economy. It is the only raw material found in anything like abundance domestically and, in fact, practically the only source of fuel and power available, there being no alternative domestic fuels to speak of. But this industry, on which the whole of Britain's industrial life depended, was in desperately bad condition in 1945 and had been for some decades before. It had given no evidence of being able to straighten out its difficulties and absolutely none of being able to command the capital investment necessary to expand and improve to the level required by the planned postwar expansion of production. Hence, what, other than transferring the industry to public ownership, could be done? Almost everything that could have been wrong with the industry was wrong with it. It suffered from all sorts of geological disadvantages. It was technologically hidebound and backward, and organized in a wasteful way. It was afflicted with bad working conditions: rates of accidents and occupational sickness were shockingly high and getting worse almost yearly.

Needless to say, labor relations in the industry were not cordial. The miners hated management with an implacable hatred and quit the industry at every opportunity, sometimes at the greatest hardships, even during the Great Depression, thus slowly robbing it of precious manpower, the more precious because of its inadequate technological condition. Management, in turn, behaved according to the worst stereotypes of the capitalist. For all the faults of the industry it never missed returning a profit, not only because the owners skimped on wages, but also because they economized on maintenance, reserves and replacements, taking out everything possible in dividends and fixing prices by cartel-like arrange-

ments that allowed even the most marginal of mines to return a profit at
the worst of times. A number of investigating commissions had found
these facts out between the wars and a number of schemes to correct the
situation had been tried, none with any significantly good effects. The
last straw came when, during the war, a government controller had to
take charge of the industry. No government could possibly have avoided
nationalizing the industry after the war.

The reasons underlying Labour's other nationalization measures (electricity, gas, railways, road transport, civil aviation, and iron and steel)
confirm the point suggested by the cases we have examined. Labour did
not nationalize because it was doctrinally convinced of the superiority of
public over private enterprise (although some Labourites undoubtedly
were so convinced) but either to rescue vital industries from decay or bring
under public control sectors of industry vitally important to effective
planning. This conservative character of postwar nationalization can also
be seen in the fact that nationalization was not used to achieve any real
copartnership between labor and management in the direction of the
industries, much less to achieve industrial democracy in the old and usual
sense of the term. And this is particularly worth noting since industrial
democracy, in one sense or another, was, once upon a time, the whole
raison d'être of nationalization. In 1919, for example, the Annual Conference of the Labour Party instructed its Executive Committee to work
out a scheme for the actual control of industry by workers in which the
only problematic point seems to have been whether workers in general or
only workers employed in the specific industries concerned should control
nationalized enterprises. By the end of World War II, the last spark of
syndicalism had apparently gone out of the Labour movement. In the
nationalized industries, either no arrangements for workers' participation
in management were made, or they were made only for the very lowest
management levels (e.g., at pit level in the coal industry), or given such
nominal advisory functions, shared with so many other interests (as in
the case of the Transport Consultative Committees) as to make them
almost valueless. In short, as if to emphasize the non-doctrinaire, almost
involuntary, character of its nationalization program, the Labour Government saw to it that, except for the rationalization of industrial organization and similar purely utilitarian considerations, things after nationalization would be very much as they had been before. In view of this, it is
not surprising that nationalization appears to have had no exhilarating
effects on the workers in the nationalized industries and to have increasingly disillusioned the trades unions, which seem now to be staunchly
opposed to further nationalization.

Central Economic Planning and Control

[The idea that it is the responsibility of government to direct the economy into socially desirable channels and that the market cannot be relied upon to produce spontaneously an optimum of social welfare is now deeply entrenched in Britain, and central planning is accepted as normal rather than extraordinary procedure.] But even in their approach to economic planning and control the British are essentially pragmatic. This is most evident in their preference for certain kinds of planning over others, particularly in their preference for certain "loose" kinds of planning requiring a minimum of direct interference in private decision-making. British postwar planning has been "open-ended" and predominantly Keynesian in character—"open-ended," in the sense that it has not aimed at specific distant goals in the manner of the Russian Five-Year Plans but relied mainly upon short-term adjustments to changing economic conditions in light of certain broad criteria (to increase production, reduce the import-export gap, prevent unemployment, and so on); Keynesian, in the sense that British planners have tended to rely far more on indirect, financial methods of steering the economy (budget policy, control of the interest rate, etc.) rather than on direct physical controls to achieve their objectives. That is not to say that direct physical controls—like price controls, rationing, allocation of scarce materials, special licensing requirements—have not been used; in the nature of Britain's postwar situation they had to be used to a very large extent. But the tendency has been to use a minimum of such controls and, to whatever degree possible, to scrap them in favor of more indirect methods.

[A brief word on Keynesianism is in order here, since, together with Fabianism, it provides the chief theoretical foundation of the British welfare state and has probably replaced classical Fabianism as the orthodoxy of the Labour Party] This of course is not the place for even a sketchy exposition of Keynesian theory, but at least the basic attitude of the Keynesians should be understood. Like the laissez-faire theorists, [the Keynesians believe that the economic system operates in accordance with determinate laws—in predictable patterns—and that it is not chaotic. Unlike laissez-faire theorists, however, they do not believe that spontaneous market activity (free enterprise) necessarily and mechanically leads to the most desirable social results] But unlike the socialists, Keynesians do not believe that to solve the economic problems created by free capitalism, capitalist society must be remade in an entirely new image. On the contrary, they want to save capitalism by using the mechanics of the market] —after these mechanics are properly understood—to guide the system into desirable directions, avoiding cyclical economic movements, unemployment, inflation, etc. And this they feel can be done with a minimum of bureaucracy and little limitation of entrepreneurial freedom, by purely fiscal methods (e.g., by public spending, taxation policies, or control of interest rates)—methods that would sacrifice few of the virtues of economic individualism while preventing its more unfortunate effects.

These ideas—and Keynesian methods as well—have been the very essence of British postwar planning. The first objective of such planning has been the maintenance of a high and stable level of employment; never again was there to be unemployment of the sort that had existed in the nineteen-thirties. [The chief means used to ensure full employment have been two: (1) the maintenance by the government of a level of expenditure considered adequate to provide full employment (i.e., the main proposal of the Beveridge Report on Full Employment) and (2) control of the location of industry.] The latter was considered necessary to maintain full employment for the simple reason that adequate total "outlay" alone could not assure jobs for everyone if demand for labor were "misdirected," i.e., if it arose in communities having a scarcity of labor rather than in communities having a surplus. And demand for labor, in the absence of proper policy, is always likely to be to some extent "misdirected" if labor is less mobile than inanimate resources, which it is everywhere, but especially perhaps in Britain. To solve unemployment problems due to low mobility of labor it was decided to bring work to the workers by persuading or compelling new industries to build in specially designated areas. This was done partly by the Distribution of Industry Act 1945, which compels any manufacturer intending to build establishments above a certain size to notify the Board of Trade, which might then presumably plead with him not to go (like everyone else) to London, but to a so-called "Development Area." Even more was accomplished by the requirement that licenses for new construction had to be obtained from the Ministry of Works, which could of course issue such licenses only on condition of construction taking place in the Development Areas.

[The economic situation prevailing after the war made it crystal clear that full employment, however important, could be neither the sole nor even perhaps the overriding purpose of planning.] Even more important—because, in the long run, the availability of sufficient employment itself depended on it—was [the need to maintain a decent balance of payments, particularly with the dollar area.] The chief means used to achieve this objective fell into two categories: means used to control and reduce imports, and means used to assure an adequate level of exports. For the first purpose, the most obvious device—import licensing—was employed. For the second, both direct and indirect methods were used. Certain manufacturers were "induced" to sell a certain proportion of their production abroad by certain government sanctions, and necessarily so since extremely easy profits were available in home markets compared to very uncertain ones in areas to which Britain had to export. And, in addition, especially high "purchase taxes" were put on certain items, to discourage excessive domestic demand for them no less than to achieve a certain leveling of incomes.

Closely related to this second objective of British planning are two others, which are both, in a sense, ends in themselves and subsidiary to other purposes of planning: [the need to maintain "adequate balance" in production and the need to guard the economy against inflation] "Adequate balance" in production simply means that scarce capital goods and materials are not squandered frivolously, but used in the most economical way, in accordance with national priorities, where most needed. This objective, of course, required a vast machinery for deciding the allocation of materials, channeling investments, and issuing licenses, which, in a sense, constituted the very heart of the planning process. Inflation was feared, as it was everywhere, for its effects on the domestic economy, particularly on certain income groups whose money incomes are not highly adjustable, but equally for its possible effects on the export program, since rises in domestic prices would, of course, lead to increases in export prices or to currency devaluation, which has its own disadvantages. The chief means used to prevent it were what one would expect: a high level of income taxation to siphon off purchasing power, appeals for wage restraints and dividend limitation, profits taxes, and, in some cases, direct government subsidies to producers and distributors to limit the prices of certain specific goods.

[To achieve all these objectives and to exert general control, direct or indirect, over the economy the government acquired control in one way or another over the following things: foreign exchange, domestic credit, capital issues (securities), prices, incomes, the allocation of materials, and the distribution of labor] In addition to these specific powers, the general condition of the economy could be influenced by direct government expenditures (which grew from about 6 per cent of national income in 1907 08 to about 40 per cent in 1949-50); direct government investments (which, in 1949, accounted for about one-third of all investments, while another third was made by industries and services in which the government plays a large role); by direct public employment of a vast labor force (one-third of all the employed); and by informal influence exerted over both trade unions and employers, especially, of course, trade unions under the Labour Governments.

But we have not yet discussed what was and is perhaps the most crucial objective of all postwar British economic policy—most crucial because all other objectives involve it in one way or another. This was [to stimulate productivity, not only in absolute terms, but, even more important, relative to other countries.] That is to say, what was needed was not merely a statistical rise in productivity—that was something easy to achieve in most industries as a result merely of technological advances. What was needed, even more, was a rise in productivity, if not to the American level then at least to that of the more efficient competitive European countries, since, in the final analysis, Britain's economic welfare depended upon her ability to keep step with or outstrip the economies of her competitors. But here too, despite the urgency of the matter, the Labour Government was surprisingly circumspect about maintaining the system of private enterprise. Essentially, its approach was the following: first, it established a number of Working Parties, composed of employers' representatives, trade union representatives and independent specialists,[6] to study conditions in the more important industries and to report on means to improve their productivity, based on maintaining the system of private enterprise. Then, it established a series of Development Councils, constituted after the tripartite pattern of the Working Parties, the chief task of which is to do joint research for the industries concerned (by means of funds compulsorily levied on the industry) and to make recommendations, which various parts of the industry may or may not choose to accept; the whole matter being put on a purely voluntary basis, except for the use of certain special financial inducements to "persuade" certain industries to use their Development Councils. Given British industrial conditions, nothing more solicitous of the privacy of private enterprise could be imagined.

[In central economic planning, then, the approach of both parties has been to rely on fiscal policy as much as possible] in stimulating productivity, the emphasis has been on "industrial self-government," a friendly synonym for what, in other countries, would be called monopoly. Only in respect to one sector of the economy, agriculture, was a sterner approach adopted, and this more on the statute books than in practice.

Agriculture was already a major problem area in the British economy long before the war, but it became an even more serious problem during and after the war. Because of Britain's international economic position, it was clearly necessary for her farmers to produce as much as possible of her requirements in foodstuffs, although obviously self-sufficiency was out of the question. Increases in agricultural production were particularly required since one of the basic axioms of the "fair shares" policy was to

---

[6] Seventeen such Working Parties were established, for the following industries: cotton, boots and shoes, carpets, china clay, heavy clothing, light clothing, waterproof clothing, cutlery, furniture, glassware, hosiery, jewelry, lace, linoleum, pottery, wool, jute. Their reports are gold mines of information on British industrial conditions.

raise average nutritional standards, which, prior to the war, were, for one of the more highly developed and civilized countries, appallingly low. But British agriculture was poorly equipped to meet the task required of it. In the words of an American observer:

> On the eve of the Second World War *virtually everything* was wrong with British agriculture. Farming methods were badly out of date, the land was deteriorating, and all classes of the farming population . . . were becoming impoverished.[7]

In the 1930's, the reaction of the predominantly Conservative Government of the period was characteristically Tory: to establish a number of agricultural cartels (Marketing Boards, to use the technical term) controlled by the major domestic producers, to give these cartels legal power to regulate the sale of commodities at any stage between producer and consumer, and to supplement their authority with periodical grants of special aids and subsidies to the Boards. Seventeen such semi-official monopolies were created, and British agriculture, which previously had been ruggedly, though almost disastrously, individualistic, was to a very large extent brought up to the industrial level of corporatization.

On the whole, postwar policy has been not to undo the policies of the nineteen-thirties but to supplement them with new legislation, the Agriculture Act of 1947. This was essentially a bargain between government and farmers by which the government obligated itself to find assured markets at guaranteed prices for most of the British farmer's produce, in return for an undertaking on the part of the farmer to manage his land efficiently, in accordance with certain rules of good estate management and husbandry. Under the Act, the Minister, through negotiations with representatives of the farmers (the National Farmers' Union), works out annual agreements on the commodities to be produced and the prices to be paid for them, the N.F.U., representing as it does some 80 per cent of all the British farmers, undertaking to see to it that production is oriented toward certain annual, mutually agreed targets. In return, the farmers are obligated, under the Act, to cultivate their lands efficiently, on penalty of being dispossessed by the Minister of Agriculture.

These are the harsher measures referred to above. The Agriculture Act of 1947, in fact, came very close to being a nationalization measure, in the sense that all land privately held is now held only conditionally, the conditions being set by the government. But, as might have been expected, the bark of the legislation has been much worse than its bite. There has been no wholesale confiscation of farm land, nor is there likely to be, even in cases permitting a legal case for dispossession to be made. Farmers who do not live up to the required standards are given every opportunity to

[7] R. A. Brady, *Crisis in Britain* (1950).

remedy their ways before the ax falls and to see to it that the ax does not fall without sound reason. In addition, supervision of the practices of farmers is exercised through County Agricultural Committees, composed of local farmers, who tend, not incomprehensibly, to be rather soft on the farming practices of their neighbors. And perhaps most important of all, there seems to be genuine reluctance on the part of the authorities to use the harsher provisions of the Act. In fact, almost no confiscations at all have taken place, even in glaringly bad cases.

Redistribution of Wealth

The purpose of both nationalization and economic planning has been to increase the efficiency of the British economy. The purpose of redistribution-of-wealth measures is to distribute its benefits more equally by means of public services financed by heavily discriminatory taxation. These measures fall into four categories.

First, the state provides a large range of compulsory social insurance services, based on the recommendations of the Beveridge Report on Social Insurance and Allied Services of 1942. The Beveridge Report's proposal that the state should assume responsibility for providing all Britons with security "from cradle to grave" by means of compulsory public insurance was approved almost unanimously in Britain, both parties being pledged to implement it in the postwar period—a fact which indicates the impact of the war on British opinion. As a result the British now have a remarkable series of social-security measures providing for income during sickness, disability, unemployment, maternity, widowhood, and old age, while special grants are provided for maternity and burial expenses. In short, almost every conceivable exigency of life is covered. These measures are, of course, insurance measures, but they also involve some redistribution of wealth since they are financed only partly from the contributions of the insured, their employers being forced to make sizable contributions to the insurance funds.

Secondly, there are certain "public assistance" measures, financed entirely out of taxation. The purpose of the public insurance measures was, of course, to make "relief" to the poor unnecessary: to replace public charity with enforced voluntary thrift. But it was impossible, even with the greatest foresight, to provide for all conceivable contingencies by means of insurance. Moreover, it was decided, for reasons stated in the Beveridge Report, to base the insurance services on flat-rate contributions and flat-rate benefits, i.e., to have everyone covered by the system pay the same contribution into the national insurance fund and receive the same benefits for various contingencies. But the same contingencies can create different degrees of need under different circumstances: hence, provision was made for special "assistance" in special cases.

Third, certain public services and payments, paid for out of taxation, are provided directly to the public. All British families receive a weekly "family allowance" of eight to ten shillings for every child (after the first). For a long time after the war the local authorities also provided certain foods: e.g., orange juice, cod liver oil and bananas, to families with children, partly for hygienic reasons and partly to see to it that very scarce foods were devoted to the most urgent uses. But most important under this category—indeed perhaps the most ambitious project undertaken by the Labour Government—is the National Health Service. Since 1948, all people in Great Britain have been entitled to receive either free of charge or for payment of very small charges all medical services (including general practitioner, specialist and hospital services) and a large number of auxiliary services: dentistry, ophthalmic care, drugs, health visiting, aftercare, convalescent care and home nursing. One can get some idea of the importance of the project from the fact that it consumes annually some £400 million, which is the largest item of civil expenditure in the budget and some 4 per cent of the total national income. The Health Service also involves employment of over 300,000 persons, which makes it one of the largest consumers of man power and physical resources as well. And not least, it is the only aspect of Labour policy that reflects the basic value of classical socialism (to each according to his needs) and that displaced a pre-welfare state system of services with an almost completely new one.[8]

Fourth, certain measures used by the Labour Government were intended to make available to the public goods considered basic necessities of life, at prices everyone could afford to pay. In certain cases, for example, direct subsidies were paid to producers in order to keep their prices down; in others the government itself bought goods in bulk (e.g., meat) and sold them to distributors at a loss. These devices were coupled with retail price fixing and, in cases where special shortages existed, rationing. The items chiefly affected were clothing, food and housing—although not all clothing, food and housing. In the case of clothing, for example, the government subsidized and fixed the prices of certain kinds of cloth and ready-made garments ("utility" clothing) to make them easily purchasable, while putting special purchase taxes on other, especially high quality, expensive cloth, the idea being to make available to everyone adequate

---

[8] "Almost" completely new because some remnants of the old system of medical services still exist. Some hospitals—for example, "private" hospitals (i.e., those run for profit), some denominational hospitals and trade-union hostels—were not taken over by the Ministry of Health. There is also still some private medical practice, since neither doctors nor patients were compelled to go into the Health Service. But over 95 per cent of both are in it.

clothing at low prices, at least partly by penalizing those who insisted on being fashionable. A similar system was used in the case of foods. Not all foods were subsidized, but only "basic" foods not naturally available in such abundance that market mechanics could be relied upon to keep their prices down. Even in the days of the most rigid austerity one could live a gourmet's life in Britain, but only at a considerable price, since the prices of non-subsidized and non-rationed foods were raised by the very fact that others were both subsidized and rationed.

All this necessarily involved a considerable leveling of economic differences in society. It is impossible to say just how much in absolutely precise terms, but a few figures will convey at least a general idea of the shift in income distribution. During the postwar period about 40 per cent of total national income in Britain was disposed of by public authorities (compared to approximately 20 per cent in the United States). Not all this 40 per cent, of course, was redistributed income. About half of it went into "running the government," some of it was "redistributed" to the upper and middle classes themselves, and some of it came from taxes paid by the lower classes. Making these allowances, it is generally estimated that some 10 per cent of national income was actually given to people as "free income" in the form of gifts, via the state, from the well-to-do. This is reflected in the fact that real income in the working class (even before "free income") was up 16 per cent over 1938 while the real incomes of salary earners were down 19 per cent and those of dividend earners down 4 per cent. Again, while in 1938, 7,000 people had reported incomes of over £6,000 (then worth $30,000), in 1948 only 70 people had such incomes (then worth $17,000); but at the same time the number of people living in comfortable circumstances, i.e., earning a good but not spectacular living, increased immensely.

But even in the case of economic leveling by means of "fair shares" policies, one can find more than a trace of characteristic British caution. The leveling process was not carried as far as it might have been; certainly postwar Britain was not made into an egalitarian society. The social distances between rich and poor were reduced but the rich were not abolished. But how could one become rich, or even merely stay rich, under Labour policies? The answer is: by living off wealth amassed before the war, or by making large "capital gains" (these, incongruously, were never taxed by Labour), but chiefly by "diddling" the tax collector. It is safe to say that a good many of the larger British incomes are the result mainly of unreported earnings, rigged expense accounts and similar devices. This does not mean that postwar Britain is a plutocrat's paradise, but only that the welfare state has left at least some room for acquisitive activity, conspicuous consumption, and for savings and investment.

One can also see the cautiousness of Labour's approach toward leveling in the fact that it made no innovations whatever in the field of education— and education, as we have seen, is an important source of social differences in Britain, certainly more important than unadorned wealth. It is true that a comprehensive Education Act was enacted by the coalition in 1944 and that its provisions made it easier for gifted lower-class children to make their way into the better secondary schools and universities. But the Education Act of 1944, while opening the educational system more than in the past, did not alter the system in any significant sense. The fact that the sweeping program of the Labour Government of 1945 made no provision for education can therefore only mean one of two things: either that Labourites were unaware of the role of education in determining British social stratification, or, much more likely, that they were not prepared to carry the Cautious Revolution to the deepest roots of the British social system.[9]

[9] It was earlier indicated that the Conservatives, while not dismantling the Labour Government's policies, did change some of them. We should briefly sketch the more important of these changes. First, a small part of Labour's nationalization program— iron and steel and a part of road transport—was denationalized. Second, most *physical* controls over the economy (price fixing, rationing, import licenses, etc.) were suspended. Third, there was some de-leveling too: the utility clothing scheme was abolished, purchase taxes on luxury goods somewhat reduced, food subsidies severely reduced, government bulk-buying discontinued, and certain minor charges put on dental, optical and pharmaceutical services. The first two were scarcely radical departures. Physical economic controls had already been greatly relaxed when the Conservatives came into power in 1951 and Labour's intention was to relax them even further. Health Services charges too were introduced by the Labour Government. It was undoubtedly in leveling policies that the important difference between Conservatives and Labourites (if there is any at all) is to be found.

One important aspect of the postwar welfare state, at once a nationalization, planning, and social welfare measure, has not been discussed here. This is Town and Country Planning, designed to achieve general control over land use in Britain. This legislation is so intricate, however, that even a superficial account would consume more space than a general work such as this permits.

CHAPTER 14

The Changing Pattern
of Power

It goes without saying that the innovations in social and economic policy described in the preceding chapter have brought about changes also in the machinery of government. The problem is how to assess the significance of these changes. It is possible that structural innovations made with no more revolutionary intention than to achieve efficient administration may create changes on the most fundamental level of the governmental process: in the distribution of effective power. On the other hand, the extent and nature of structural innovations for welfare-state purposes have themselves been limited by ancient usage and contemporary values, simply because Britain is a country where usage counts for a great deal and where welfare-state values do not have a monopoly on the political sentiments. The impact of the welfare state on the British machinery of government involves, in fact, an interplay between the exigencies of effective administration on one hand and the injunctions of constitutional values on the other.

Thus, when we ask whether welfare-state socialism is compatible with British democracy we are really asking two questions. One is whether a form of government developed in another era can survive the institution of socialist policies. The other, equally important but raised much less frequently, is whether such policies can be effectively administered within the obstinate limits of a constitutional system evolved for altogether different purposes.

Parliament in the Welfare State

The eclipse of Parliament—that is, the shift of decision-making powers from the House of Commons to its leaders and to the administrative De-

178

partments—is not solely or even primarily a result of the welfare state. The process was already well under way before 1945. Parliament never possessed "sovereignty" in the sense that French Assemblies have possessed it; and what drained away its powers in the twentieth century was the development of a highly disciplined, national two-party system, much more than welfare-state policy. Nevertheless, the welfare state undoubtedly has acted as a catalyst on the process, because of its demands for special technical knowledge in decision-making (which an assembly of politicians, in the nature of things, can hardly be expected to possess) and because of the tremendous volume of business Parliament would have to transact if it tried to preserve the old balance between its own decision-making powers and those of other agencies.

The Parliamentary Timetable

The unavoidable impact of the welfare state on British political institutions can certainly be seen most clearly in the effects the sheer quantitative pressure of business has had on parliamentary transactions. Almost every decade in the last century the number of days spent in session has increased: from 111 "sitting-days" in 1865-74, to 127 in 1895-1904, to 149 in 1925-34, to an enormous 172 in 1954; and that, one may suppose, is just about the maximum.[1] But even this brutal extension of the session has not sufficed to arrest certain regrettable tendencies discussed in an earlier chapter: the vast increase in the amount of executive legislation, the severe curtailment of parliamentary debates, and the decline in the powers and status of private members. Even if no tremendous constitutional issues are raised by the pressure of business and its consequences the matter raises such great practical difficulties in the conduct of government that we ought to take a closer look at how parliamentary time is allocated.

The timetable (agenda) governing parliamentary business is announced weekly by the Leader of the House of Commons, whose chief function is to control the allocation of parliamentary time and who is usually a very high-ranking Cabinet officer, on a par with the Chancellor of the Exchequer and the Foreign Secretary in the upper echelons of the Cabinet. The announcement is usually made on a Thursday, in response to a "private notice question"[2] by the leader of the Opposition. It is frequently followed by a row, as private members protest against the omission of pet subjects. But these rows almost never achieve their object

[1] Parliament cannot, of course, spend 365 days a year in session. One must subtract from the total: week ends (130 days per year, counting Fridays as half-days) and time for holidays (perhaps another 45 days, including a summer holiday of civilized length).

[2] Such questions are not printed on the Order Paper and are therefore used whenever it is desirable to secure an answer to a question without delay.

against the hordes of automatic supporters of the Government. This does not mean, of course, that the parliamentary agenda is arbitrarily determined by the Government and forced on the Opposition. On the contrary, it is invariably the product of close consultations between Government leaders and Opposition leaders, Government Whips and Opposition Whips, and while it is the Government that decides, it almost invariably does so with scrupulous regard for the reasonable requests of the Opposition. Indeed, as we shall see, the Opposition not only has influence with the Government in regard to the parliamentary timetable but directly controls a very sizable chunk of it.

While the parliamentary agenda is announced weekly it is in fact planned, in broad outline if not in narrow detail, for a much longer period: a whole session or, indeed, the whole five-year tenure of a Government. Such long-range planning is supremely necessary for a Government with a sizable mandate (like the Labour Government of 1945) since without it the sheer pressure of parliamentary business could prevent enactment of its program. Hence, it is scarcely surprising that the institution of long-range planning of the parliamentary agenda was one of the first innovations brought about by the postwar welfare state. The whole process in fact was begun by the Labour Government of 1945.

When Labour came to power in that year it was confronted by a very nasty problem in regard to parliamentary time. It had an unusually large mandate to fulfill as a result of its victory in the General Election. It had to pass through Parliament certain absolutely urgent bills not a part of its program (for example, the annual Army and Air Force Bills). It was confronted by volumes upon volumes of bills wanted by individual administrative Departments and advocated, at Cabinet level, by various Ministers. And there was the usual clamor for the usual masses of legislation by interest groups. Clearly, there was no chance whatever of submitting all the legislative projects involved to Parliament. But how was it to decide which projects to introduce and in what order?

The first task was to calculate the amount of time available for legislation. This could be done by taking the total number of sitting-days in the session and subtracting from it time for the following things:

(1) *Private members' time*, i.e., time set aside for backbenchers to put down motions for debate or introduce legislative projects.

(2) *Opposed private Bills*,[3] which are debated evenings after 7 P.M.

---

[3] Private bills are not to be confused with private members' bills. The latter are simply "public bills" introduced by private members. Public bills lay down legal provisions pertaining to the whole community or general classes of the community (doctors, drivers, pedestrians, etc.). Private bills deal only with specific local, corporate or individual interests. Such bills must be passed whenever, for example, a local authority wants to introduce some new service (say a bus service) or whenever an organization

at the discretion of the Chairman of Ways and Means,[4] time being taken for such business out of Government, not Opposition or private members', time.

(3) *Debates on Urgency Adjournment motions,* the time required for this again coming out of Government time, at the virtual discretion of the Speaker.

(4) *Debates on motions of censure,* the tradition here being that whenever the leaders of the Opposition put down such a motion the Government is required to make available out of its own time at least one whole day for debate.

(5) *Debates on subjects on which very large numbers of members want debates,* especially non-party or foreign policy subjects, for which, provided public demand in Parliament is large and vociferous enough, permission to use the Government's time is hardly ever refused.

(6) *Annual financial business,* to be described below. The time devoted to financial business, much of it under the direct control of the Opposition, accounts for by far the largest chunk of time not under Government control (approximately 45 days every year).

(7) *Other kinds of routine or recurrent debates,* such as the Debate on the Address (6 or 7 days per session), debates on the eves of periodical holidays, and on the reports of the nationalized industries (although these are not yet a firm fixture in parliamentary usage). Here again, much time is actually at the disposal of the Opposition.

(8) *Debates on Statutory Instruments.*

(9) *Government motions,* i.e., motions designed to obtain endorsement of some Government action, or proposed Government action, where no formal parliamentary motion is really required, or motions to obtain an expression of parliamentary opinion for any purpose.

After subtracting time for all of these purposes from the probable total of the session, something in the neighborhood of 70 days was found to remain for the Government's legislative business. This, however, was only the first, and the easiest, of the calculations that had to be made. In addition, a fairly elaborate scheme of priorities for projects had to be devised. Then, it was necessary to calculate how much time each Bill to be submitted would require in the House. Finally, all these calculations had to be converted into a schedule for the five-years' legislative business and the schedule itself adjusted and modified as unforeseen circumstances arose. Herbert Morrison, who was Mr. Attlee's Leader of the House, has described the whole process, accurately enough, as the "slaughter of the

created by Act of Parliament (e.g., a railroad) wants to do something that its parliamentary charter does not authorize. Parliament transacts a vast amount of such private business, most of it routine, only disputed projects coming before it for debate.

[4] One of the presiding officers of the House.

innocents," the knife being wielded by a special Cabinet Committee (the Future Legislation Committee, headed by Morrison himself) in close consultation with Ministers, whose chief contribution to the process seems to have been endless and impassioned pleading for their own pet projects.

All this illustrates two important points, apart from the sense in which the welfare state has affected the governmental process. One is the amazingly tight control British Governments have over parliamentary time.[5] It is this, of course, that made it possible for the Labour Party to enact such a thoroughgoing program of reform. Secondly, the process by which parliamentary time is allocated illustrates that the considerable powers of British governments are exercised in a disciplined and constitutionally "moral" way, with due respect for parliamentary usage and in close collaboration with the Opposition. But "Opposition" here, it should be noted, means the leaders of the Opposition, not any mere backbencher. When negotiations regarding parliamentary time take place through what the British call "the usual channels," it is the actual and potential leaders of Parliament (or their Whips) who do the negotiating, while private members can exercise influence on the agenda only through their spokesmen. Indeed, the item of traditional parliamentary business that is usually encroached upon by Governments to eke out the meager ration of time is Private Members' Time. The sanctity attaching to Opposition time does not at all attach to backbenchers' time, and that is important.

Because of the negligible role played by private members in the planning of the agenda, the close collaboration between Government and Opposition leaders is all the more important to prevent arbitrary control of parliamentary business by the Cabinet. And because of this perhaps the most regrettable consequence of the constriction of parliamentary time has been to subject the easy collaboration between Government and Opposition on the agenda to severe strains which indeed may ultimately have important constitutional consequences. There is some evidence that, because of acute pressure of business, Governments are becoming rather less tolerant of Opposition demands for time than they used to be; note, for example, the great increase in the number of guillotine motions (almost always opposed by the Opposition). On the other hand, the Opposition seems to be discovering that it can use the pressure of time in the House as a political weapon, as did the Conservatives in 1951 when they tried to break the Labour Government by subjecting it to a long series of all-night sessions debating delegated legislation.[6] Thus pressure of business, however

[5] Compare the power of British Cabinets over the parliamentary agenda with that of French Cabinets. Nothing illustrates more strikingly the differences between the two systems.

[6] Motions on delegated legislation are not subject to the Hour of Interruption at 10 P.M. and therefore are ideal instruments for obstructing other parliamentary business or breaking overworked Ministers.

prosaic and merely quantitative a change, has not only produced difficulties in calculation and procedural adaptations (like the increased use
of the guillotine or of parliamentary committees), but may even produce
changes on the far more fundamental constitutional level, i.e., in the
relations between Government and Opposition.

Could anything be done to relieve the pressure of business? Writers on
British government have made a great many minor suggestions[7] and one
major one: a drastic change in the parliamentary committee system. The
House of Commons has been frequently criticized for taking too much
legislative business in Committee of the Whole House.[8] This, it is argued,
is unwise, since the purpose of the Committee Stage in legislation is to save
time for the whole House and to get the sort of free, easy, intimate and
technically informed debate one is unlikely to have in a large assembly.
But the consideration of legislative business in Committee of the Whole
House is a deeply ingrained tradition that, despite constant attempts at
reform, has tenaciously persisted. Governments have rarely let "great measures" get off the floor of the House of Commons at any phase of their
passage and at present it is generally agreed that Bills of "first-class constitutional importance" should be considered by Committee of the Whole
House rather than one of the smaller Standing Committees.

More seriously, there has been much criticism of the Standing Committees of the House themselves, chiefly on three grounds. One is that they
are not specialized committees—like those in France and the United
States, which deal with special functional categories of legislation (Agriculture, Finance, Foreign Affairs, etc.)—but general purpose committees
which deal with any legislation brought before them, regardless of subject.
Secondly, the British committees have been criticized for their enormous
size. Each consists of around sixty members (selected so as to duplicate
the proportions of Government and Opposition supporters in the House
itself). That means they are really miniature Parliaments, each almost as
large as the American Senate, and hardly the sort of place where business
can be transacted expeditiously. Finally, it has been alleged that the committees are too few—in fact there are only five, called Committees A, B,
C, D and Scottish, although other countries seem unable to do with fewer
than a dozen or two, not counting subcommittees.

There can be no doubt that a committee system consisting of a large
number of small specialized committees would be more powerful than
one consisting of a small number of large general-purpose committees. If

---

[7] E.g., omission of the Financial Resolution Stage in the discussion of Bills, reducing
the number of debates on financial legislation, reducing the amount taken for private
Bills, omitting certain forms of parliamentary ritual, etc.

[8] A Committee of the Whole House is simply the whole House of Commons with
the Speaker not in the chair.

any confirmation is wanted, it is surely provided by the French system. But that does not necessarily mean that the former is preferable to the latter. Committees of the French and American variety tend, more often than not, to produce an alternative leadership, frequently in open conflict with Cabinet ministers, so that although the system might save time, it might also impair the coherence of policy. Again, in small committees— even if they do not develop the compulsive oppositional tendencies of French committees—Governments can scarcely have as much control over their majority as in large ones and are therefore far more likely to be defeated, or embarrassed by undesirable amendments. The defection of one or two supporters may indeed mean complete loss of control over a legislative project on such committees; hence Governments are likely to be even more reluctant to let important Bills off the floor of the whole House than they already are. Thus the institution of a committee system designed to dispatch parliamentary business might, paradoxically, succeed only in slowing it down.

There is no easy way to adapt Parliament to conditions created by the welfare state without severely altering its role in British government. And if the choice is between an expeditious Parliament and one from which coherent and consistent policies emerge then surely welfare-state values themselves require that expedition be foregone.

Financial Business

Because of the emphasis put on financial planning and control in the British welfare state it is particularly necessary for the Government to have control over financial legislation in the House of Commons. Planning by means of fiscal methods can be successfully done only under certain institutional conditions. At a minimum, it presupposes that the planners have some sort of effective control over public spending and taxation, a requirement rarely met in democratic countries. But in Britain the Government's control over finance is, if anything, even greater than its control over the parliamentary agenda, so great in fact that it may be misleading to attribute to Parliament any practical role in budget-making at all. When Parliament debates financial legislation, for example, it almost never actually debates financial policy—how much money is to be spent, for what purposes, on the basis of what sort of revenues—but uses the debates for purposes of airing grievances against administration or for criticizing policy. Even more striking, British Governments are so absolutely sure that their financial proposals will be adopted by the House that they begin contracting for expenditures even before the annual Appropriation Act is passed; and the House is so sure that it will adopt the Government's financial policies that it gives legal sanction to the tax proposals even before it has had a chance to discuss them. Nothing is more puzzling to the foreign observer than the fact that the House debates financial proposals after it has, in effect, adopted them, and nothing should be more instructive. It makes it clear that the House, whatever it may be, is not a deliberative assembly, deciding policy by exchange of views.

British financial policy is made in two overlapping phases, one concerned with appropriations and culminating in the annual Appropriation Act, the other with taxation and culminating in the annual Finance Act. The process of appropriation begins every year sometime in February when the Estimates are introduced in the House. These are departmental requests for money needed in the impending financial year, collated and reviewed by the Treasury and presented to Parliament in the case of the armed services by the appropriate departmental minister and in the case of other services by the Financial Secretary to the Treasury. Ultimately the estimates are embodied in the annual Appropriation Act, which is usually not passed until some time late in July or early in August. Since the financial year starts on April 1, provision needs to be made for departmental expenditure pending passage of the Appropriation Act. This the House does by voting before April 1 part of the total sum for which departments have asked. Before that date also the House will vote various Supplementary Estimates requested to cover departmental expenditure in excess of the amounts appropriated for the current year.

For all this business the House has set aside a total of twenty-six days— the Supply Days —which are fitted into its work at various times from February until the middle of the summer. On most of these days the House, sitting as Committee of Supply, concerns itself with the estimates of a particular Department. These debates, however, are not normally on financial matters, such as how much money should be provided for a Department or for one of its services. They center rather on Department policies and programs. Thus a grant to the Ministry of Housing and Local Government might be the peg on which is hung a debate over whether the Government in its public housing program is making an efficient use of manpower. The estimate for the Post Office has afforded an opportunity for debate on increased telephone charges—in Britain, it will be remembered, the Post Office owns and operates all tele-communications— and the Foreign Office estimate has been used to set in motion a wideranging debate on the foreign policy of the Government.

In essence, then, debates on expenditure provide convenient pretexts for airing grievances and propagandizing the electorate; hence, also, it is entirely appropriate that the twenty-six Supply Days should be Opposition time, that is, days on which the leaders of the Opposition may determine what subjects the House is to discuss.

The situation in regard to taxation is little different. As in the case of expenditure, tax policies are decided by the Treasury and the Cabinet long in advance of April I. They are submitted to Parliament sometime in April on what is called "Budget Night," when the Chancellor of the Exchequer appears before the House of Commons to deliver a long speech explaining not only the Government's proposed tax policies but also its financial policy in general for the year. In recent years, indeed, the Budget Speech has almost invariably been a high-level exercise in applied Keynesian economics, particularly so when Hugh Gaitskell, a former teacher of economics at London University, was Chancellor. Needless to say, Budget Speeches are not, and have never been, intrinsically enjoyable affairs, except perhaps in the hands of such a great Budget speaker as Gladstone, who "was the only man who could lead his hearers over the arid desert, and yet keep them cheerful and lively and interested without flagging." Nevertheless, Budget Night is a great state occasion, when the House is crammed to capacity, when Extras are published and almost everyone in Britain is in a state of excitement; the reason being, of course, that the Chancellor's announcement of policy is much more than a mere announcement; it *is* policy and therefore affects everyone where he is likely to be interested most. After the Budget Speech, which is likely to last some hours, the House immediately passes all the tax resolutions (except one which does not actually affect the level or limits of taxation), so as to allow the Government to collect all the new taxes immediately. Then, having approved the tax proposals, the House proceeds to debate them (*sic*), basing its debates on the one unapproved resolution. The debates, first on the Chancellor's budget proposals, then on the Finance Bill brought in to give them effect, last in sum about two and a half weeks, and are distributed, like the debates on expenditure, throughout a period of some months, while the Government acts on the safe assumption that the outcome will be favorable.

From the standpoint of welfare-state values, this is almost an ideal system. At least it means that the British Parliament is no barrier to effective fiscal planning, unlike the more powerful Parliaments of other countries with their chronic propensities to increase proposed expenditures and reduce taxation and to turn out budgets less by means of any considered economic planning than by haggling among ministers, committees and private members.

If the system has flaws they are that financial business is profligate with parliamentary time and that the system operates, as in other countries, on an annual basis. Of all the activities of Parliament, financial business is by far the most time-consuming. There is, moreover, a great deal of repetition in the financial debates, one general policy debate seemingly following another, with roughly the same speakers saying roughly similar things time and time again. More seriously, objections can be lodged against the whole idea of annual budgets, as inappropriate to the activities of the social-service state. The periods for which funds are given and the intervals at which financial policies are reviewed do affect the efficiency of administration, simply because economic conditions do not conveniently change to coincide with the beginning of new financial years. A certain sum designed to buy so many airplanes or hospital beds may, because of changes in price levels, turn out to be wholly inadequate for the purpose, while a certain fiscal policy may be made obsolete by the outbreak of a war, or an American tariff change, or a shift in the terms of trade.

These problems are not, of course, insoluble within the framework of annual budgets. It is always possible, if a Department's funds run unexpectedly low, to submit Supplementary Estimates for additional appropriations, and it is always possible to introduce new Budgets in face of unexpected circumstances. The real problem, however, is posed by services requiring appropriations for periods longer than a single year, and many of the new state services require precisely that. The clearest case, perhaps, is the hospital part of the National Health Service. The function of the new hospital authorities, the Regional Hospital Boards, is to plan the general character of the hospital system: its organization and distribution, the conversion of facilities for purposes of optimum utility, the expansion of facilities, the building of new facilities, the hiring and firing of higher personnel, etc. None of this can be done without money and little of it within the space of a year; it just takes longer to build new hospitals, or nurses' annexes, or to convert a maternity hospital into a tuberculosis sanatorium. But funds are voted on a yearly basis and experience has shown that plans made on the basis of one year's expenditure may be nullified, even when implementation has already started, by appropriations made in light of the following year's own peculiar exigencies. There has, consequently, been some agitation for breaking the single annual budget into a number of different budgets, running for different periods—a social-service budget perhaps, an armed-forces budget, and a routine departmental budget—or for annual budgets from which certain services, like the hospital service, are exempt. But it is easy to see the flaw in this. Granted that special budgets would be fine for special services, what becomes of the over-all financial planning function of the Government? In the final analysis, the difficulty is that welfare-state policies have not only introduced new institutional demands, but a large set of different and *contradictory* ones, the administrative requirements of different kinds of welfare-state policies not always being conveniently the same.

Administration

The Problem of Co-ordination

Inevitably, the most conspicuous adjustments to the welfare state have been made in the administrative system, (the most visible change of all being a very considerable growth in the number of public employees and administrative agencies). This in itself is not perhaps very important. But the growth in the number of civil servants and administrative departments since the advent of the "positive" state has given rise, indirectly, to at least one serious problem: (how to co-ordinate their activities) (Co-ordination is required both in policy-making and in the administration of policy.) In the case of policy the most obvious reason is the desirability of pursuing a consistent line toward a single set of goals. But equally important is the fact that the policies of one Department almost always impinge on others, even when they are not directly related, and even if only in the sense that new policies frequently involve new charges, so that the adoption of one Department's policies almost always means the frustration of another's. The purpose of co-ordination in policy-making, therefore, is not only to achieve consistency but, perhaps above all, to assure that precious commodities (money, materials, parliamentary time, certain types of manpower) are distributed so as to do the most good, by a kind of marginal utility calculation, rather than being allocated by the blind forces of competition between Departments and Ministers. In the case of the execution of policy, co-ordination is necessary simply because the work of Departments can never be entirely self-contained, and it is especially unlikely to be so when the number of Departments is very large and specialization very narrow.

[The need for administrative co-ordination is not, of course, something peculiar to the welfare state, but the welfare state has accentuated it by making the machinery of government more cumbersome and complex and by extending government activity to areas in which faulty co-ordination is particularly annoying and wasteful. A good example is housing. Under the Labour Government it was necessary for five major Departments to collaborate before any house could be built in Britain. The Town and Country Planning Ministry had to clear the site, the Board of Trade had to provide certain raw materials, the Ministry of Labour manpower, and the Ministry of Works building licenses, while the Ministry of Health was responsible for housing policy as such. Faulty co-ordination among these Departments could have physically ruined the housing program: sites might have been cleared where no houses were ever built, building materials allocated where no sites were made available, labor assigned where no permission to build had been given. And what applies to housing applies, with a vengeance, to over-all economic policy. That frightful muddles rarely occur (they do sometimes occur) attests to the effectiveness of British co-ordinating machinery.

This machinery works on many levels of British government. At its apex is, of course, the Cabinet, concerned almost exclusively with the co-ordination of policy in the broadest sense. The Cabinet is, in theory, responsible for settling all departmental disputes and smoothing out all friction, but its actual role as an instrument of co-ordination must not be exaggerated. In fact, it acts largely as a high court of appeal settling such disputes as are brought to it (and under modern conditions Ministers are always reluctant to bring even serious disputes before it) and as a body making "high policy," which simply cannot be bothered with all the petty details of co-ordination. Much more is done by Cabinet Committees, although these again are concerned chiefly with very general problems or very notable disputes. The bulk of the work, here as always, is done not by Ministers but by officials, and by the Treasury, the traditional co-ordinating Department.

On the official level co-ordination is achieved in a variety of ways. A great deal is accomplished by multiple appointments, i.e., appointing the same person to related jobs in different ministries. The Chief Medical Officer of the Ministry of Health, for example, has for a long time also been Chief Medical Officer in the Ministry of Education, under whose jurisdiction falls the School Medical Service. Another co-ordinating device is the joint Advisory Committee, i.e., a committee advising a particular Department (or the Cabinet) on which representatives of various other Departments are invited to sit. More important than either of these are the ubiquitous interdepartmental committees, referred to in a previous chapter; more than anything else—even party discipline—these committees are the distinctive hallmarks of British government. They exist for all sorts of purposes, from the broadest to the narrowest. There is, for example, an interdepartmental committee for housing and, on the other extreme, there was formed, shortly after World War II, a "Committee on the Spontaneous Manifestation of Personal Gratification on the Cessation of Hostilities." There is also a famous story about a Foreign Office official whose job was to do nothing but make the rounds of Committees the Office was represented upon, and who spent all his time riding about in a taxi, looking in on a committee, smoking a pipe, then taking off again for the next committee.

All this may sound ludicrous, but it is effective chiefly because the British civil service is imbued with a tradition of co-operation like that of no other country. Indeed the most effective method of administrative

co-ordination in Britain is simple informal contact among members of the
higher civil service, of which the more ephemeral kind of interdepartmental committee is merely the least informal instance. Members of the
Administrative Class have, generally speaking, similar backgrounds, tastes
and manners. A good many of them know one another very well, indeed
are related to one another. All become, upon entering the Class, members
of a very close-knit in-group, having a tradition, a common speaking voice,
a common education and common manners. This sort of thing helps to
"cement" the executive structure.

But this informal network is concerned more with the co-ordination of
administration than of "policy." The co-ordination of the latter is accomplished, in the sense of consistency, mainly by ministerial committees, and,
in the sense of deciding the marginal utility of projects, chiefly by the
Treasury. The latter is a particularly suitable agency for balancing departmental proposals against one another since it has "control" over both
finance and establishments (i.e., staff), both of which are likely to be
immediately affected by important innovations, and both of which are
likely to raise the issue of "balance" (the utility and disutility of various
projects relative to one another) in its starkest and most easily compre-
hensible form. It is moreover a particularly effective agency for balancing
departmental proposals since in fact no successful appeal against its
decisions is possible in Parliament, once they have appropriate ministerial
support. The only way to challenge the Treasury's decisions is to take the
issue before the Cabinet itself. But there appeals on anything but the
most urgent and notorious matters are likely to be resented, while, in any
case, the Chancellor of the Exchequer is almost invariably one of the most
powerful members of the Cabinet itself. Disputes between the Treasury
and other Departments do arise and are sometimes taken all the way up-
stairs, but more often than not the Treasury seems to get its way. But
how precisely does the Treasury balance departmental projects?

The review of departmental estimates prior to their submission to
Parliament is only one of a number of such means, and while it affords
an excellent chance to examine departmental outlays as a whole, weighing
them against one another, it is perhaps less important than another means
of Treasury control: day-to-day or week-to-week control. This involves, in
essence, an obligation on Departments to obtain Treasury approval for
any changes in departmental activities having a financial aspect, a rule
which, typically, has no statutory basis but arises out of long tradition. In
practice, this rule makes the Treasury an omnipresent partner in almost all
departmental planning. The Treasury therefore "controls" departmental
projects not only by its power to make trouble by disapproving but also
through the tendency of Departments to bring the Treasury in on their

plans at an early stage. Once it has been called in, the Treasury of course brings to bear the Treasury view on the Departments' planning, that is, a government-wide view that is, ideally at least, thoroughly informed on general economic policy, general policy priorities, means likely to be available to staff and finance new projects, and the plans of other Departments to draw on these means. (Co-ordination by the Treasury, therefore, is not something done once a year when the Budget is prepared, but a continuous process.)

Since control of economic planning of the British sort is essentially a matter of co-ordinating economic policies, and since the British prefer financial to other kinds of planning, it is not surprising that the chief responsibility for it is lodged in the Treasury. But the Treasury merely plays the pivotal role in a rather complicated set of planning arrangements, which, due to the importance of economic planning and its unprecedented character among government activities, we will look at in some detail.

The Organization of Economic Planning

It is perhaps significant that the organization of planning and the process by which it has been carried out have been so very much in the established British administrative tradition. (The burden of work has fallen on the inevitable committees, ministerial, official and joint advisory, and what these committees do is, in essence, not so much to pursue rationally predefined quantitative goals as to adjust and reconcile conflicts (achieving "balance") in light of broad criteria.) Perhaps this is due to the fact that the British have a genuine preference for a type of planning so loose as to be hardly planning at all, but little more than surveying, forecasting and compromising. Yet the essentials of postwar planning organization came into being *in reaction against* economic planning machinery considered too loose to be effective. It is therefore plausible to infer that the "traditionalistic" organization and process of planning result from an inability to adjust administrative usage to the new functions of the state.

(Until 1947 the Labour Government tried to carry out economic planning solely by means of the time-honored methods of plural authority, shared by a number of Departments, ministerial committees and interdepartmental committees, with the Cabinet the nominal unifying agency.) Chief responsibility for economic planning was vested in a special ministerial committee, the Lord President's (Mr. Morrison's) Committee, except for the export drive and fiscal policy, which were managed by the Board of Trade and Treasury respectively. Under those three focal points of responsibility, at the official level, worked a number of interdepartmental committees, headed by a committee of the permanent heads of the main economic Departments, "the central economic team," which did the important work of gathering data, preparing forecasts, framing plans and supervising their execution. This entirely catholic mode of organization, working in the traditional way (by constant adjustment and compromise), was discredited by the severe economic crisis of 1947 and scrapped for the sake of "tighter" machinery; but precisely of what sort? The "logical" step would perhaps have been to institute some rigidly centralized form of planning organization: perhaps a super-Minister of economic affairs, in direct control of all subordinate economic departments; perhaps an economic general staff drawn from the various Departments but in a position, unlike the usual interdepartmental committee, to issue orders from its central vantage point. These, or similar "centralist solutions," seem almost corollaries of the prevalent desire for more positive and more coherent economic planning. But in fact little more was done than to shift the chief responsibility for planning from a Cabinet Committee to the Treasury, a change that did not, and could not, change the essential character of planning organization and process. It did simplify things by placing the co-ordination of economic policy in the same Department as that of fiscal policy, but that is all. That planning organization and process, even after the metamorphosis of 1947, still followed the loosest traditions of British administration will be seen from even the sketchiest description.

The planning machinery that emerged from the crisis of 1947 must be dealt with on two levels, ministerial and official.[9] On the ministerial level the planning function was vested in the Chancellor of the Exchequer as the head of the Treasury and, at Cabinet level, a small Economic Policy Committee chaired by the Prime Minister and consisting of the Ministers of the chief economic Departments. On the official level, the work was done by the Economic Section of the Cabinet, the Central Economic Planning Staff, and a large number of special interdepartmental committees. The Economic Section, manned by professional economists, was chiefly responsible for gathering comprehensive economic data. These data became the raw material for the work of the Central Economic Planning Staff, which was now, as the committee of permanent heads of economic Departments had been before, the "thinking part" of the whole structure, its function being, in essence, to make decisions to be ratified by Ministers.

[9] There is also what one might call a consultative level, consisting of bodies on which business and labor as well as government are represented. These consultative bodies are of great importance since they furnish information of actual field conditions, provide expert advice, and help to "sell" government decisions to the people who must make them work.

⌊Despite this centralization of planning organization, interdepartmental committees of the orthodox kind continued to operate, two of particular importance: the Investment Programmes Committee and the Import Programmes Committee.⌋ But in view of this, one may ask what purpose was served by the transfer of planning "responsibilities" from a ministerial committee to a single department? What was the function of the Economic Affairs Division of the Treasury, other than to provide chairmen to the various interdepartmental committees concerned with economic policy? Herbert Morrison has supplied the answer.[10] "It was the duty of the [Central Economic] Planning Staff and the Economic Section *to see that the consequences of taking action in one field were considered in relation to our problems as a whole.*" ⌈The activities this implies are very much in the tradition of Treasury control and British administration in general.⌋ The function of the CEPS was to determine, on the basis of data supplied by the Economic Section, what the common economic problems were and to publish the findings, together with the general policy proposals, in the annual *Economic Survey*. The *Survey* was not to be an operational plan but merely a broad analysis of the situation and a modifiable statement of policy. Planning was to remain open-ended in the sense of not aiming at rigid quantitative goals, but it was to be systematic nevertheless, in the sense of being carried on under conscious, suitable and informative criteria. The *Survey*, in short, was a sort of Platonic ideal, not a working blueprint for planning. Nor could it have been anything else, in view of the methods by which planning decisions were actually made. Two aspects of this method are especially important. One is that the initiative for action in economic as in financial matters was allowed to remain entirely in the hands of the operating Departments. It was they who initiated requests for materials or suggestions for their allocations; it was they who developed capital schemes and proposed import quotas. The Treasury, as in the case of departmental Estimates, simply brought to bear on these departmental proposals the "Government view," as defined by the work of its corps of economic planners, especially in the *Survey*. Moreover, bringing the Government view to bear on proposals did not mean exercising an arbitrary veto or peremptorily altering departmental schemes. The method of bringing it to bear was in almost all cases negotiation and the end of negotiation was to achieve "agreement" on general Government policy. ⌈The Treasury, in short, for all the centralization of planning functions after 1947, never made itself more than a specially important party in the interdepartmental economic team.⌋ Considering the severity of the economic crisis of 1947, the economic adjustments made were certainly impressively mild. Why? Is not the obvious answer that

[10] *Government and Parliament.*

the tough solutions that might have been adopted are alien to some of the deepest traditions of British politics and administration? The British have a firm tradition of collective responsibility, a system of leadership in which no single Minister can order other Ministers about but in which decisions are made collectively by the heads of Departments. This is "Cabinet democracy." Inevitably, this method of high-level decision-making has affected the character of lower-level decision-making. Since departmental decisions, if important enough, may ultimately come up against the collective give and take of the plural executive, even the lowest-level decisions are often the result of interdepartmental consultations, designed to prevent higher-level squabbles. Hence the absence in British administration of those clean lines of command that are the joy of American and German professors of administration. The Treasury style of co-ordination, in which commands are not given but interdepartmental consultation is highly institutionalized, fits the system perfectly. A super-economic department, able to give direct orders to other Departments, would have been profoundly out of tune with it.

But this not only explains the mildness of the reforms made in the planning machinery after 1947. It also helps to explain why British planning has been so mild and limited in scope, so consistently wary of explicit direction toward predetermined quantitative goals. Planning by consultation and compromise, in the style of Treasury co-ordination, clearly lends itself only to open-ended planning, and best of all to planning by financial methods. No doubt British liberalism has something to do with the cautiousness of British economic planning, but so also has the intolerance of the British administrative system for an activity unsuited to the traditions of the plural executive.

The Public Corporation

The welfare state has altered the structure of British administration chiefly by the great multiplication of administrative bodies standing outside the regular departmental system. Of these, the Public Corporations that operate the nationalized industries are of course the most prominent, although other "autonomous" or near-autonomous agencies have been created to operate the National Assistance Program, to distribute financial grants to the universities, to supervise government-sponsored scientific research, to manage the National Parks, and to administer the Agriculture, the National Health Service, and the Industrial Development Acts.

There are many differences among the various public corporations, but all have at least one thing in common: a high degree of administrative independence, and this in four senses: first, in the sense of political autonomy, i.e., the relative absence of ministerial control over the corporation and of ministerial accountability to Parliament for the corporation's affairs; second, financial autonomy, i.e., freedom from ordinary government budgeting and therefore Treasury Control;[11] third, autonomy in regard to personnel, i.e., exemption from normal civil-service procedures in regard to the recruitment of staff, promotion, pay and pensions; and fourth, freedom from administrative procedures that are standardized among the Departments. It should not be difficult to see why administrative bodies having these characteristics should have been chosen for the purpose of supplying goods and services to the public. One need only consider what the operation of the nationalized industries by the ordinary Departments would have meant: questions in the House of Commons on any aspect of their activities, the scrutiny of their work by parliamentary select committees, and Treasury control over their finances and personnel. As a result administrators in charge of the nationalized enterprises would have become reluctant, under the constant threat of parliamentary criticism, to take quick and risky (that is, "businesslike") decisions, and procedure would have become rigidified into the usual civil-service routine. There might have been outright interference for political purposes in the day-to-day affairs of the enterprises as well, quite apart from parliamentary criticism. The public corporations might not have been able to attract adequate personnel, because the low level of civil-service salaries and the limited opportunities for ambitious young men in a civil-service system. And there would have been excessive centralization of administration, under a Minister responsible to Parliament.

For all of these reasons, public corporations were considered appropriate instruments to use wherever businesslike administration was especially desirable. The prewar public corporations—the British Broadcasting Corporation, the London Passenger Transport Board, the Port of London Authority and the Central Electricity Board—were therefore given a remarkable degree of autonomy, ordinary political control over them amounting to little more than the appointment of board members by the Minister and, in the case of the B.B.C., a periodical review of its charter. Since the war, however, the British have had something of a change of heart about such very independent corporations and, in fact, the public corporations created since 1945 are not nearly so autonomous as their predecessors. Why not?

In the first place, it was widely felt that the old arguments about the incompatibility between politically responsible and businesslike, efficient management were much exaggerated. Some people indeed felt that making

[11] Most public corporations in Great Britain are financed, like any private business establishment, by selling goods and services to the public and by borrowing funds from the public or the Treasury.

the managers of the nationalized enterprises politically responsible would stimulate effort and initiative rather than the opposite. After all, the public corporations were, in effect, public monopolies; and without either competition or political criticism to prod their managers, what, save an inherent "sense of workmanship," was to keep them from becoming lazy and slovenly? In addition, certain ordinary government Departments were in fact already engaged in providing goods and services to the public, some with notable efficiency. The British Post Office, for example, is big enterprise in the most exacting sense. It deals not only with letters and parcels but also telegrams, cables and telephones, certain technical aspects of sound broadcasting, runs the largest savings bank in the country, and pays government pensions and allowances. And there are relatively few complaints about it.

Secondly, many of the postwar public enterprises were nationalized at least partly to facilitate national economic planning; consequently, it would have been absurd to give these enterprises independence from the control of the planning authorities. But whether public enterprises were nationalized for planning purposes or not, there was in any case to be central economic planning, and this made it clearly undesirable to create a series of public monopolies, all in basic industries, that might pull in entirely different economic directions. Prewar Governments were not committed to central economic planning; hence they could afford to give the public corporations much more autonomy than could postwar Governments.

It will be evident from this that the public corporation poses a serious dilemma. On one hand, it seems advisable to prevent the more regrettable consequences that might follow from ordinary departmental administration; on the other it is equally necessary to prevent excessive administrative autonomy; yet any step to prevent the one is always likely to lead to the other. Is there a golden mean?

If there is one it is safe to say that the British have not yet found it, although their solution of the problem may superficially seem very convincing. This solution rests on a distinction between the "general policies" of the nationalized industries and their "day-to-day management," the theory being that the latter is properly the private function of the corporations while the former is the sphere in which political control may be constructively exercised. But, however sound this solution may be in principle, it immediately raises some uncomfortable problems in practice: one, the classic problem of how precisely to distinguish between policymaking and administration; another, by what specific arrangements to prevent political control of routine management while assuring political control over policy. Confronted by these problems the British have simply taken refuge in muddle.

The powers of Ministers over the nationalized industries fall into three main categories. First, they may appoint and remove members of their governing Boards—a traditional but not therefore a negligible power. Second, they possess what are generally called "specific powers," varying a great deal from one case to another, although some of the powers involved are exercised over all the corporations. For example, all the corporations must furnish statistics and other kinds of information on request; in all cases, also, the Minister must approve large-scale capital outlays. Finally, Ministers have in all cases been granted power to issue "general directions" to the Boards of the industries. It will be seen at once that these powers are both extensive and, in the last case, vague. One cannot therefore get a clear idea of the scope of Ministers' powers by reading the statutes, since everything depends on how they interpret their functions vis-à-vis the Boards.

Just how they have done this is very difficult to determine, but from the shaky evidence available two points emerge. One is that, on the whole, the Ministers appear to have been reluctant to interfere in the affairs of the public corporations. Between 1946 and 1951, for example, not a single "direction" was issued by any Minister to a Board. Secondly, Minister–Board relationships, despite common tendencies, vary a good deal from one case to another, not so much because of differences among the statutes as because of the vagueness of their terms and differences in how they are interpreted. For example, under the Labour Government of 1945, the Minister of Fuel and Power seems to have interfered a good deal in the public corporations under his jurisdiction, the Minister of Transport hardly at all, for no immediately discernible reason other than temperament and, to some extent perhaps, the public notoriety of the industries under their jurisdictions.

Relationships between the Minister and Parliament (specifically, the extent to which Ministers are answerable in the House for the activities of the public corporations) are, if anything, even more muddled. The subject, in fact, is so much in flux that it may be misleading to say anything definite about it at all. Parliamentary questions are both the clearest and most contentious case in point. In principle, once again, the matter is simple: Ministers must answer questions on subjects for which they are responsible and may refuse to answer all others. But this straightforward formula tells us almost nothing at all since we do not know precisely how to determine the extent of a Minister's responsibilities. And, in fact, a host of uncomfortable problems, contradictory procedures and absurd formulations have emerged within the boundaries of the formula. At one time it was held by the Speaker that Ministers were liable to answer only those questions about the postwar public corporations that they were liable to answer about the prewar corporations—a patent absurdity since the role of the postwar corporations was altogether different. [A great deal of squabbling has revolved around whether questions resembling questions a Minister has previously refused to answer should simply be thrown out by the Clerks or whether the Minister should in every case decide whether to answer the specific question or not.] Still more squabbling has taken place about whether Ministers were answerable to Parliament only for those actions they actually take in regard to the Boards or also for Board activities they *might* arrogate to themselves. Most of all there has been quarreling about what constitutes policy and what administration— whether the lateness of a train is a matter of policy, whether the lateness of fifty trains is, whether a power cut that ruins thousands of Sunday dinners is not something more than a matter of administration, and so on.

But this muddle is not accidental, any more than the looseness of British economic planning. It is, indeed, inevitable and suggests an important lesson about the institutional significance of the welfare state, namely that the adjustment of institutions to the requirements of the welfare state has been difficult simply because these requirements are so different and contradictory. In this case, the main contradiction is between the management of public enterprises and the commitment to central economic planning: the one requiring a great deal of administrative autonomy, the other demanding very little. The British have dealt with this contradiction only by evolving seductive generalizations while muddling along from power cut to power cut, cheap railway fare to cheap railway fare, in an eclectic, experimental spirit from which a proper solution of the general problem may or may not emerge. It is difficult to see that anything else could have been done.

The Impact on Politics

[Apart perhaps from the conversion of the Conservative Party to "socialism," the chief impact of the welfare state on politics has been in the area of interest-group activity] In essence, the welfare state has had three effects on such activity: it has accelerated the tendency of interest groups to concentrate pressure on the Administration, intensified their efforts and made them more powerful. Concentration on the Administration is simply the result of the further shift of decision-making powers to the Administration, especially the growth of executive legislation. And it is not just the large volume of delegated legislation that is relevant here but the fact that administrative Departments rather than Parliament make most of the decisions in which interest groups are particularly interested. The National Farmers Union is certainly interested in broad agricultural policy, the sort made presumably by "political" processes; but it is safe to say that it is more interested in the production targets and minimum price arrangements that are worked out each year, principally at the administrative level, under existing legislation. The British Medical Association is undoubtedly interested in broad medical and sanitary policy, but it is far more intensely and immediately interested in the terms of service under which Health Service doctors work, and that is a matter left almost entirely to executive decision-making. The welfare state has made pressure group activity more intense simply because private associations have more to gain or lose from government decisions than in the past. The Committee on Intermediaries, reporting in 1950, found that the public then annually made some 19,000,000 applications for licenses, permits, and similar things to government Departments—and this on the basis of an incomplete survey and without reckoning certain routine and simple applications, like applications for food ration books. To give the reader a more concrete idea of what this involved, the Ministry of Supply had to deal annually with some 1,500 applications for licenses to manufacture, 54,000 to acquire steel, 20,000 to acquire cotton, 400,000 for stockholders' licenses for acquisition of iron and steel products—and a host of other applications for similar purposes. It will be seen at once that for many individuals and firms the success or failure of applications can be a vital matter, the result being a vastly increased use of "intermediaries" (people with influence, special knowledge, legal skills) to push along individual applications and intensified interest-group activity to influence the grounds on which administrative decisions are made.

All this is simple enough. But why should the welfare state have increased the *power* of interest-group activity? This question will be easier to answer if we first understand what factors tend in general to make pressure groups powerful. Three such factors seem particularly relevant: the size of the group, its ability to supply *expertise*, and the extent to which its co-operation with government is required. Size is important for obvious electoral reasons, so important in fact that certain large groups in society—particularly if the political loyalties of its members are not fixed, or not known to be fixed—can achieve their objectives even without bringing direct pressure to bear on the government. The case of old-age pensioners in Great Britain is a good example. Their number is constantly growing both in absolute terms and relative to other social groups. Hence, there has developed in recent years a kind of competition for the old-age vote in the form of promised increases in old-age benefits. Before the general election of 1955, for example, both parties committed them-selves to raising old-age pensions and the Conservatives opportunely raised the pension shortly before the election actually took place. Very similar things also apply to other relatively uncommitted groups, such as schoolteachers and farmers.

A group's possession of *expertise* can make it politically effective for two reasons. First, because laymen always tend to feel a certain deference toward professionals; and the more a mastery over a subject presupposes *expertise* (rigorous training, like professional training) the more likely this is to be the case. The civil servant or the politician is always likely to feel that farmers know farming, architects building, and doctors medicine, and therefore also policies appertaining to farming, building and medicine. Secondly, and more concretely, Departments, in making decisions, may genuinely need skills that only members of the interest group can provide. Finally, the power of a pressure group depends on the *extent to which its co-operation is required.* One simply cannot, for example, carry out an agricultural policy without getting farmers to co-operate, as the Soviets have had opportunity to discover on innumerable occasions. While the need for a group's co-operation does not of course guarantee that it will achieve its political objectives it does limit the extent to which these objec-tives can be frustrated, even in totalitarian countries, and limiting the extent of undesired policies is merely the obverse of winning legitimation for desired policies.

British interest groups tend to be more effective now than in the past, first, because welfare-state policies have in a curious way increased the size of interest groups. Size here should not be understood in the usual sense but as something one might more appropriately call "politically effective size." In determining the political effectiveness of a group what matters is not only its absolute size (e.g., the number of people who are farmers, or doctors, or veterans) but also how many of the members of the group are actually organized for political action, on the general principle that even in democratic politics the cohesive battalions are more effective than the disorganized ones. In this connection it is noteworthy that as the state has expanded the scope of its activities over British agriculture the number of farmers belonging to the National Farmers' Union has also increased, until today the N.F.U. includes almost all the farmers in Great Britain.[12] And this is not only because organization pays, but also because govern-ment policies have deliberately encouraged the formation of comprehen-

---

[12] Membership growth of the N.F.U. has been as follows:
    1919— 88,889
    1929—111,500
    1940—132,401
    1948—194,000

sive voluntary associations, particularly by making such associations official negotiating bodies, giving them permanent membership on advisory committees and even assigning them roles in the administration of policy. Thus, under the Agriculture Act negotiations are carried on not with "farmers" but the National Farmers' Union. Under the National Health Service Act it is not, in practice, the "profession" that deals with the Ministry of Health and furnishes members to advisory, disciplinary and administrative committees, but professional organizations, especially the British Medical Association and its local branches.

Perhaps the clearest example of how the other two factors (*expertise* and the need for a group's co-operation) have increased the power of interest-groups in the welfare state, is medicine. First of all, medicine is a field in which the gulf between professional and layman is particularly deep, partly because of the very demanding training required of a doctor, partly because of deeply rooted popular attitudes toward medicine. The doctor is always something more than the professor of an arduously acquired skill; he is more a magician, an initiate into a particularly subtle mystery, than a mere graduate of a difficult course of technical training. Secondly, a great many of the decisions that officials in the Ministry of Health must make require professional knowledge or touch intimately upon clinical practice: for example, a decision as to how to distinguish a "medicine" from a "food" for the purpose of setting limits on what general practitioners may or may not prescribe, or decisions on the conversion of hospitals, the purchasing of medical equipment, types of medical report forms, the organization of the maternity services, and so on. Finally, it is obvious that a socialized medical service requires, above all else, a co-operative medical profession—for example, the service must be able to attract and hold the better specialists, especially for purposes of full-time service, since the majority of doctors are always likely to enter a service used by a majority of patients. In view of all this it should surprise no one that the British Medical Association has been a wonderfully effective pressure group from the outset of the Service. It is constantly consulted by the Ministry and it rarely fails to get anything it wants very badly. The B.M.A. badly wanted an Amending Act to the National Health Service Act guaranteeing that the profession could never be paid salaries (the Minister had already given a verbal promise to this effect); it got it. When a large number of Registrars (young doctors training in specialties) were to be dismissed from the hospitals and diverted into general practice the B.M.A. violently objected; only a few were in fact dismissed. No single recommendation of the National Health Service Council (a professional advisory committee on the Health Service) has ever been suppressed or even just turned down by the Ministry of Health. One of the chief reasons for the remarkably general acceptance of the Health Service in the British medical profession—and it is almost universal—may in fact be that, having dreaded bureaucratic enslavement, the profession has now realized that bureaucrats tend to be very reasonable, malleable and accommodating people, at least where doctors are concerned.

The Cabinet Today

From what has been said it follows that the contemporary distribution of effective power in British government is different from what it was in Bagehot's day or even just a generation or two ago. But how different? Parliament certainly debates less thoroughly and controls less comprehensively than it used to; autonomous and semi-autonomous administrative organizations do much more than they used to; an increasing proportion of government decisions are made neither in Parliament, nor the Parties, nor the Cabinet, nor the Departments, but in non-official associations. But has the essential organizational principle of British government been significantly affected by welfare-state pressures, i.e., what Bagehot called the real secret of the British Constitution, the concentration of responsibility ("fusion of powers") in the hands of the Cabinet? The distinctive product of eighteenth- and nineteenth-century politics in Great Britain undoubtedly was Cabinet Government; and Cabinet Government was the proper institutional expression of the constitutional attitudes discussed in Chapter 8. But has the welfare state had any significant impact on the Cabinet and its role in the machinery of government?

One can argue with some force that it is precisely here, where one would perhaps least expect it, that the welfare state has had its most revolutionary impact. We may indeed be in the midst of one of those crucial metamorphoses that are the very essence of British constitutional development and seem to recur with a startling regularity: the conversion of an "efficient" institution (in this case the Cabinet) into a ceremonial institution, by a draining off of its practical functions until little more than empty formalities remain. The transformation is certainly not yet complete and has not, of course, gone nearly as far as the conversion of the Privy Council into a ceremonial body. "It is just possible," as a British journal recently said, "that the British Cabinet is still an important body." But it is certainly a very different body from what it was once and we have good reason to think a less important one.

The Cabinet has changed, in the first place, from a small and intimate discussion group into a large and complicated piece of administrative machinery. It has become as large as it is at least partly because of the growth of state activities and the consequent multiplication of administrative Departments, particularly if we take its size to be determined not by the number of Ministers having official Cabinet status but the number who actually participate in Cabinet deliberations. The Cabinet has become a complicated machine, because of its size, and also because of the character of the decisions it has to make and the activities it has to supervise and co-ordinate. The Cabinet, after all, is, like Parliament, composed primarily of professional politicians and is, if anything, even more pressed for time than the legislature. For all of these reasons it cannot possibly be what it was when Bagehot discovered that the fusion of powers in the Cabinet was the secret of the British Constitution.

The position of the Cabinet in the British machinery of government has changed in two ways under the pressure of welfare-state policies and of the modern party system, and both involve a draining off of its powers. On one hand, some of the former functions have become concentrated in fewer hands. The making of high policy, in particular, seems to be increasingly concentrated in the hands of the Prime Minister and a small group around him, sometimes composed of great Ministers, sometimes merely of the Prime Minister's intimates. Some of the greatest decisions of state seem in recent times to have been made by such special juntas and presented to the Cabinet almost as *faits accomplis,* over the known disagreement of certain Cabinet members. This diversion of effective power from a whole body, functioning collectively, to a special segment of it is also what happened to the Cabinet's historic predecessors: the House of Lords, the King's Council, the Privy Council and the Cabinet Council. Concomitantly, other Cabinet functions have become dispersed to an almost unfathomably complex administrative and deliberative machinery. Decisions once made collectively in the Cabinet are now made by Cabinet committees, by individual Ministers, bureaucrats, the Treasury, official committees, party machinery, and even private associations; and, most often, by interaction among all of these bodies. If power is concentrated anywhere in the British machinery of government it is concentrated not in the Cabinet but in this complex framework of decision-making, the Cabinet itself—i.e., the body that meets three or four hours a week in the Cabinet Room of No. 10 Downing Street—being no more than a part of the framework. But what precise role it plays as a collective entity is far from clear. It has been suggested that its real function is to act as a court of appeal when disputes arise within the normal decision-making machinery; but if the analysis here is correct the change in its functions is even greater than that.

Conclusion

We may now answer in a general way the general questions raised at the beginning of the chapter: whether a form of government developed in another era can survive the institution of socialist policies, and whether such policies can be effectively administered within the limits imposed by a constitutional system evolved for different purposes, however much altered for the sake of the policies. The answers are rather complicated but can be stated briefly thus:

Perhaps the most basic institutional requirement that must be satisfied if welfare-state policies are to be successful is strong democratic leadership: a high degree of executive control over the legislature (e.g., the allocation of time, financial policy-making, and probing into the affairs of public enterprise) and the administrative machinery; a high degree of co-ordination in policy-making and administration; and considerable continuity and stability of leadership. This is clearest of all in the case of economic planning, where everything depends on the concentration of decision-making powers in the hands of an agency pursuing consistent objectives by coherent means. Now British Cabinet government, as we saw particularly in the case of the budgetary process, seems to satisfy this requirement nearly to perfection, because of its stability and because its very essence is the integration of decision-making powers. It appears to be, compared to other parliamentary systems, and compared also to presidential systems, a marvelously appropriate instrument for the purposes of the social-service state, despite the fact that it has not been perfectly suitable in detail to all particular welfare-state objectives.

But Cabinet government seems, chiefly under the impact of the social-service state, to be itself undergoing a fundamental transformation, the essence of which is the scattering of decision-making powers and thus the loosening of leadership. Resting as it did on a beautifully simple idea— that the same leaders should initiate policy, supervise its execution, and co-ordinate administration, being accountable for all they did to the people's representatives—it worked effectively in the beautifully simple nineteenth century, but seems to be dissolving into something hideously complex under the complexities of twentieth-century politics and policies. But if this is indeed the case, what becomes of the suitability of the British machinery of government to welfare-state purposes? Is not the answer to our problems an ironic one: that welfare-state socialism would function best under an institutional framework that Britain once provided but that welfare-state socialism itself is transforming into something much less suitable to its own aims?

CHAPTER 15

Prospects

When one reviews the character of contemporary British government and politics, and, even more, when one reflects upon British political history, one is immediately struck by a number of remarkable things. [Britain has long been blessed by a high degree of political integration, of which the broad consensus on the Constitution and on policies is only the most remarkable instance.] The British conception of authority highly corresponds to the British pattern of effective power, in the sense that political decisions are in fact made largely as they are ideally supposed to be made. The result of these two things is a minimum of tension in the political system and therefore a very high degree of political stability—[stability both in the sense of stable Governments and the even more important sense of a stable constitution.] Moreover, stability in the first sense is reinforced by the character of the British party system, while stability in the second sense is supported by the fact that British political processes are effective enough to satisfy a large volume of political demands, so that no important group need be alienated from the system because of its inherent inability to effect the group's political aims. Is such a system likely to undergo any important changes in the foreseeable future?

[Even if "Cabinet government" is being transformed into something different from its classic form under the situational pressures of welfare-state policies, this does not imply any vitally important change in the British political system.] How important, after all, is the redistribution of certain Cabinet functions compared to the persistence of a disciplined two-party system, or the continued existence of broad political agreement, a "ruling class" and the deferential attitudes it elicits, or indeed even the very tone of British government? True, these things are themselves undergoing changes. But so far only in content, not in form. Thus, what the British are agreed upon today is not what they agreed upon fifty or even twenty years ago, but the existence of broad agreement itself has not changed. Recruitment into the ruling class, its composition, the depth of the sentiment of deference—all these have changed, but deference to leaders and to the social strata expected to supply leaders still exists. And it is these things—party discipline, consensus, deference, and the survival of the past in the symbols and ceremonies of government—that make Britain what it uniquely is: an unusually effective democratic system, resting on a remarkable political culture in which a host of logically irreconcilable attitudes (democratic and non-democratic, autocratic and responsible, liberal and collectivist, hierarchical and egalitarian) are smoothly integrated.

However, we cannot simply assume that these things will not change, if we proceed from the conviction that British politics is not the result of British genes, but of determinate historical forces and, indeed, a certain amount of luck. But from what sources might such basic changes come? One possible source is the welfare state—not as much in its impact on governmental institutions as in its impact on political attitudes. There are no violent antagonisms between socialists and anti-socialists, as we have seen, but welfare-state socialism has created psychological tensions in other senses. Curiously, it has produced much unrest among its most ardent supporters, the radical Left. One reason for this unrest is that the Tories have so smoothly adapted themselves to the welfare state that many people in the Labour Party have felt bereft of a program. The result has been much compulsive seeking after policies with which to counter the political appeal of the Conservatives—one sometimes feels almost any policies. It is altogether possible that such policies will ultimately come from that section of the party that has become disillusioned with the achievements of post-war policy and feels it is imperative to go far beyond it. There is certainly much feeling among the more radical Labourites that the objectives of 1945 have not been achieved despite the enactment of the Labour program. Post-welfare-state Britain, after all, is not so vastly different from pre-welfare-state Britain in certain—to the left-wing Labourites, important —respects. What has become of industrial democracy in the nationalized industries? What has happened to economic planning under the Treasury? Granted that economic leveling has been considerable, has there been enough of it, and what has become of social leveling? Does the educational system not still maintain all the old, deplored social distinctions? People who deplore the cautiousness of the cautious revolution are not of course in control of the Labour Party. On the contrary; there has been a right-wing as well as a left-wing reaction against the disappointments of the welfare state in the party, and at present the right-wing is in control. But we cannot be sure that in Labour's frantic groping for new ideas it will retain control.

Among Conservatives there is also some disgruntlement. The Conservative Party has made the best of the new order, but not all of its supporters have adapted themselves smoothly to it. It must be remembered that many people have had to make major readjustments to the new condition of things: especially people with fixed incomes, the salariat, and indeed the whole middle class—the class that has been truly leveled down. We must remember also that many avenues of achievement have been narrowed for the ambitious and that it has been made difficult if not impossible for many members of the upper classes to sustain a way of life they had come to regard as natural: taking periodic trips abroad, unencumbered by the annoyances of tourist allowances, sending their children to boarding schools, having more than one servant, and so on. Not all have adjusted gracefully and there are certainly pockets of deep resentment, even of despair, in British society. It would be wrong to suggest that all British suburbia is seething with discontent, but undoubtedly more than a lunatic fringe is alienated from postwar policy.

The welfare state, in short, is resented on one extreme as having done too much and on the other as having done too little. That perhaps is only natural and, since only extremes are involved, not very serious. There is, however, another source of potential tension in British society that may have far weightier consequences. It is not the result of British purposes but of the British situation in the postwar world: specifically, the need for the British to adjust themselves to being a second-rank international force.

In the immediate postwar period the British faced the task of reconstruction and their other immense economic problems with equanimity, even enthusiasm. Sir Stafford Cripps's austerity measures were received with resolution. People endured the queues and the shortages with great good nature. Even the miners occasionally worked on Saturdays. But all this was in the flush of victory, when it was not clear, as it certainly is now, that Britain would never recover her prewar eminence. Had the outlook seemed less hopeful one wonders whether such trials would have been endured so good-humoredly. It is one thing to feel that one is reconstructing one's society and quite another to feel that one is barely keeping it afloat. A magnanimous gift of sovereignty to a former dependency flatters the ego; forcible dislodgment even from a mere sphere of influence does not. Recent events, of course, have made it clear, even to the most die-hard chauvinists perhaps, that Britain is no longer top dog. But for a number of reasons we cannot yet be sure that the necessary psychological readjustments to the new "situation" will be made as successfully and smoothly as have the economic adjustments.

It is certainly not inconceivable that the international decline of Britain will create disruptions in her internal political culture. Most seriously of all, it may endanger the survival of that broad consensus that has for so

long characterized British politics and given Britain such great stability.
This agreement was due at least partly to the acceptance by the lower
classes of upper class leadership and the satisfaction by the upper classes
of demands for important political, social and economic reforms; in short,
deference on one hand and moderate reformism on the other. But neither
of these is unconditionally a part of British political culture. Submission
to leaders, although having a solid basis in British social structure, may
have been predicated upon their success in governing, and that success
has never, since the eighteenth century, seemed as questionable as it does
today. But on what ground other than its inherent fitness to govern, as
measured by success, can a political class retain its hold upon the popular
imagination? By expressive symbolism perhaps; the sheer theatrical pomp
and show and the fairy-tale romance of ceremonial institutions. But between symbolism that exalts and symbolism that seems empty burlesque
the dividing line is thin. Even the most ancient and solemn ceremonial
needs a basis of belief, and that, in Britain, one suspects, was always
supplied by a universal British conviction of the rightness of British institutions—the Anglo-Saxon genius for self-government, as the Anglo-Saxons
used to call it. Can it survive national relegation to the second rank?

Conversely, upper-class (especially Conservative) moderation, the second condition of consensus, also shows signs of cracking. Certainly the
Suez affair was not a result of good pragmatic sense. This, of course,
should not be taken as conclusive evidence that the British Conservatives
have finally lost their genius for sensible adjustment. Upper-class (and
indeed also lower-class) jingoism is nothing new in Britain. Nor is im-
moderation in foreign relations. Indeed, one of the more curious aspects
of British political behavior has always been the abrupt metamorphosis
Britons seem to undergo when dealing with non-Britons, especially colo-
nials. And, not least, if there have been significant divisions among the
British they have been, even in the past, most acute in the case of foreign
and imperial, not domestic, affairs. But if international frustrations continue to produce the bitter animosities among the parties generated by
Suez it is not unlikely that these animosities will be reflected also in
intransigence on domestic issues.

The most somber possibility therefore is that the two sources of tension
in British society, domestic and international, may reinforce and deepen
each other. That they can do this is clear. After all, did not the Bevanites
transfer their domestic socialist frustrations into a championing of international neutralism? What then would happen if the Conservatives, in a
mistaken diagnosis of Britain's international problems, unmade the welfare
state in a really serious way—or if Labour, in search of issues, made international relations a greater bone of contention than it has?

That a society has achieved remarkable stability; that its political culture is highly integrated; that its concept of authority closely corresponds to its structure of effective power; that its decision-making processes are effective enough to satisfy a large volume of political demands—all this means that it is relatively safe from instability as a result of its internal dynamics, but not that it is absolutely immune to major change. For, first, no society has absolute control over its situation, and culture and situation obviously are related. And, second, the purposes on which a society is agreed may themselves, in operation, have deeply problematic and divisive consequences.

PART THREE

THE FRENCH
POLITICAL SYSTEM

by Nicholas Wahl

Third Legislature—1956-1957 Session
Verbatim Record—Twenty-third Meeting
Second Sitting of Tuesday, November 6, 1956

Homage to the Hungarian People

THE PRESIDENT*: My dear colleagues, I believe I am expressing the profound emotion . . . [*On all benches, at the left, at the center and on the right and extreme right, the deputies rise. Several members in the center and on the right addressing themselves to the extreme left shout:* On your feet, on your feet!] . . . the emotion of the men and women of heart in the French National Assembly when I assure the Hungarian people of the friendship and homage their courage and sacrifice merit. [*Strong applause on the left, the center, the right and the extreme right.*] The martyrdom they are still undergoing by heroically resisting the odious aggression of a foreign army . . . [*From several benches on the extreme left:* Suez! Port Saïd! *From several voices on the right and in the center.* Assassins! Keep quiet!] . . . this aggression wins for them the admiration of all those who remain faithful to the purest French revolutionary tradition [*Interruptions on the extreme left.*] of total solidarity with peoples who fight for the defense of the rights of man and their liberties. [*Strong applause on the left, center, right and extreme right—protestations on the extreme left.*]

M. PINEAU, *Minister of Foreign Affairs:* I would like the floor.

THE PRESIDENT: Monsieur the Foreign Minister has the floor.

M. PINEAU: Monsieur the President, the French Government would like to associate itself with the words you have uttered. [*From the extreme left:* Suez!] It bows respectfully before the workers, the peasants, the students . . . [*From the extreme left:* Down with the counterrevolution!] . . . the Hungarian patriots . . .

M. LIANTE (Communist): Victims of fascism!

M. PINEAU: . . . who died for the cause of liberty. The Government requests that in their honor the National Assembly observe a minute of silence. May history judge those who do not associate themselves with this homage! [*Applause on the left, center, right and extreme right.*]

M. DENIS (Communist): Yes, liberty for the murders of Communists and the people!

* Of the National Assembly.

THE PRESIDENT: The minute of silence is begun. I will discipline those who interrupt now.

M. DENIS: The fascist assassins!

. . . .

THE PRESIDENT: M. Daniel Mayer has the floor.

M. MAYER (Socialist): Monsieur the President, I would appreciate it if you would ask the National Assembly to adjourn this sitting . . . in respect to the freedom fighters, whose heroic groups, reminiscent of the Paris Commune . . . [*Loud interruptions from the extreme left—Applause on the left, center, right and on several benches on the extreme right.*]

MME. VERMEERSCH (Communist): Look who is applauding you!

M. MALLERET-JOINVILLE (Communist): The V*ersaillais!**

M. PRONTEAU (Communist): They are collaborators† and V*ersaillais!*

M. DENIS: Does or does not war rage in Egypt and North Africa? Why don't you talk about that? [*Exclamations on the right and center. From numerous benches on the right*: Murderers! Murderers! *Loud interruptions from the extreme left.*]

THE PRESIDENT: Monsieur Denis, I call you to order once again.

M. ROCLORE (Conservative): Friends of Ribbentrop, keep quiet!‡

M. MAYER: . . . heroic groups reminiscent of the Paris Commune . . . [*From the extreme left*: No! No!]

M. CACHIN (Communist): That's grotesque!

M. MAYER: . . . these groups are still carrying on an apparently hopeless battle . . . but they are thus inscribing their names in the long martyrology of working class history. [*Applause on the left, center, and on several benches at the right—Loud interruptions from the extreme left.*]

M. PIERRARD (Communist): Hitlerites! [*Exclamations on numerous benches.*]

M. PRONTEAU: They like the working class bloody—like roast beef!

M. JACQUET (Conservative): We certainly defend the working class more than you do. Keep quiet!

M. GRENIER (Communist): You represent the "proletariat" of the boards of directors!

M. JACQUET: And you a "trade union" of murderers!

M. MAYER: The ultimate sentiment and perhaps the noblest upon which the Assembly's unanimity should be formed is pity for the victims and the dead. [*Loud applause on the left, center, right—on these benches, then on the benches of the extreme right, the deputies rise. At this moment the deputies sitting on the extreme left rise in turn and chant*: Fascism shall not pass! *From the center and right*: Murderers! Murderers! Back to Moscow, back to Moscow! *Noise of desk tops being opened and shut.*]

* The regular army corps that crushed the Paris Commune in 1871 came from Versailles.
   † Frenchmen who cooperated with the Germans during World War II are called "collaborators."
   ‡ Ribbentrop was the Foreign Minister of Nazi Germany who signed a treaty of non-aggression with the Soviet Union on the eve of World War II.

M. GUYOT (Communist): Fascists! Down with war! [*From the extreme left:* Down with fascism, down with war!]

THE PRESIDENT: Judging by the reception given M. Mayer's proposal, I am going to adjourn the sitting. [*Loud interruptions from the extreme left— Noises.*]

—Excerpts from the *Official Journal of the French Republic, Parliamentary Debates, November 7, 1956.*

CHAPTER 16

Conflicting Ideals
of Authority

The Two Historic Traditions

[The uniqueness of French political institutions lies not in their instability or lack of effectiveness but rather in the length of time they have remained unstable and ineffective] Today as during the nineteenth century, observers of French politics are struck by three characteristic traits: First, the frequent, apparently capricious, changes in government. Second, the inability of short-lived Governments to resolve the outstanding problems of French society.* Third, the seemingly chaotic turbulence of French political competition and the continuing existence of large groups of citizens permanently hostile to the constitution. Long before the Great Revolution, British writers of the eighteenth century were already noting the vagaries of French political life and, of course, attributed this to shortcomings in the flighty French character. Indeed, these three traits were as prevalent under monarchies as under republics, under dictatorship as under parliamentary democracy—and France has tried all of these since 1789.

One could argue, however, that in one respect French politics and government have been quite stable: unlike German, British and Russian government, which have changed continually, [French government retains its outstanding characteristics notwithstanding new constitutions and new political personnel] It is, for this reason, essentially unreformed government, in which changes that have occurred have not replaced pre-existing institutions but rather have simply been grafted onto existing customs and laws. Thus the restored monarchy in 1814 retained much of the revolutionary and Napoleonic regimes; the restored Napoleonic Em-

---

* It should be noted that in European politics the word "Government" frequently refers to the administration alone, and in particular to the political executive or cabinet. To distinguish this usage from the more general meaning, the word is capitalized when reference is being made to the Cabinet or the executive branch.

pire of the mid-nineteenth century retained much of the monarchic experience; the restored Republic of 1870 retained much of both the monarchy and the Empire; and after World War II the new Fourth Republic retained much of the old Third Republic of prewar days.

As a consequence, there exists a great legacy of the past in French political institutions. For instead of an integration of the past with the present, there has been a piling-up of different and often incompatible political institutions that has made French government a cumbersome patchwork, vulnerable to instability, lacking effectiveness, and generally ill-adapted to modern problems. The situation may be compared, hypothetically, to one that would have prevailed in the United States had the institutions created by the Articles of Confederation been largely preserved after the adoption of the Constitution. But in France the situation was further complicated by the fact that on the plane of political culture the area of agreement over political institutions had been narrowing steadily since early in the eighteenth century. France has long been known as the nation of the Great Revolution, the cradle of democracy and reason, the mother of innovations in style and ideas. But it is often forgotten—and particularly by Americans—that France was also the nation that perfected political absolutism and that has epitomized reverence for the traditional, above all in economic and social customs. In political ideas, therefore, France has developed a split personality that has been perpetuated by the historical experience of the nineteenth-century revolutions and by the peculiar resistance of French society to social and economic change. Thus, for example, partisans of authoritarian government have had, since the Revolution, four chances to create regimes that ultimately paid homage to principles of the *ancien régime*—the last one being as late as 1940-44 in the Vichy Government of Marshal Pétain.

Nor has France undergone the rapid industrialization and soaring urban population growth that constituted the potent material force in favor of democratic government in Great Britain. Unlike the latter, whose society became predominantly urban as a result of industrialization, French society became more complex, with her industrial sector simply added on to an agricultural and commercial sector that hardly gave way to the new economic forces. Politically this meant that parties and interests committed to old France were not obliged to transform themselves in order to represent new France. The increasing social complexity was therefore mirrored in the accretion of political factions, each fighting for its class, interest, or historical "layer." It was then natural for the more conservative among them to look to the administrative and elitist institutions of government to protect them, while the "new" classes looked increasingly to suffrage and parliament as their protectors. Divided already for genera-

tions, the French political process was permanently cast into two competing and hostile institutional patterns, rendering its neutrality—and therefore a true constitutional settlement—impossible.

[Today, the open advocates of authoritarian government are relatively
few in France, yet her government is still shot full of institutions that en-
shrine the purely administrative tradition of government by an elite, operating through a powerful centralized bureaucracy—independent of a representative assembly and much as it existed in Napoleonic times] And ranged
against these institutions, of course, is the powerful parliament that continually attempts to impose its will upon the bureaucrats by totally controlling the intermediate agent, the Cabinet. This dualism in political
institutions is reflected in a dualism in French law and jurisprudence.
The rights of the state and its administration are dealt with by "public
law" while the rights of individuals form "private law." Although since the
Revolution the state has been equated with the collectivity or the will of
the people, nonetheless the ancient dualism exists and Frenchmen still are
tried for crimes against the state under a jurisdiction different from that
relating to crimes against their fellow citizens. There has developed, therefore, a coexistence of two primitive patterns of politics, the state-minded
administrative pattern and the individual-oriented representative pattern.
Unintegrated and unreformed, they remain competitive and mutually
hostile because they are supported by hostile groups in society. For it is a
sad fact that there still exist in French opinion groups that believe that
these primitive models can each produce effective government independent of the other. [In brief, the principle of mixed government has
not been realized in modern France.]

Modern governments such as the British or German have powerful
bureaucracies and potent executives as well as alert and effective representative assemblies. What distinguishes them from French government
is that a decision has been made and respected as to the proper relations
between institutions of administration and execution and those of representation and criticism. In the case of Great Britain the decision was
made by a gradual constitutional settlement in which the proper relations
between Crown, Cabinet, and Commons were regulated by custom and
law. In the case of Bonn Germany a balance was created by the deliberate
decision of a constituent assembly, to which all parties have adhered. In
the Soviet Union the decision in favor of government by an elite—the
Communist Party—was made by a revolutionary act to which subsequent
generations have been obliged to adhere.

[Although France has often settled the relationship between legislative
and executive branches in theory, in practice neither in the Third nor in
the present Fourth Republic has there been a true constitutional settle-

ment, expressed in an effective division of powers. French government alternates between periods of "immobilism" in which little is done because the executive has been deprived by the legislative of the ability to act, and short periods of frantic activity when a temporarily empowered executive suddenly "liquidates" pending affairs while parliament waits in a self-imposed abdication. And of course behind the scenes is pursued the permanent struggle between the bureaucracy, eager to exploit periods of governmental paralysis in order quietly to impose its expert will, and the parliament, constantly on guard against usurpation by the state and its agents. It would not be an error to say that for part of the time France is ruled by civil servants, whose vocation usually is to preserve the status quo, and another part of the time it is ruled by parliamentary leaders who seek to undo the work of the bureaucrats rather than effect new policy. When France does have short periods of effective government, the head of the executive, the Premier, manages to become independent of parliament and, supported by public opinion, obliges the bureaucracy to do his will.

The dualism of conceptions of authority in French political culture has often been stressed. According to the familiar interpretation France has been divided into two irreconcilable camps since at least 1789. On the one hand are the popular forces of progress, fighting under the ensign of the revolutionary motto: *Liberté, Egalité, Fraternité*. On the other hand are the aristocratic forces of reaction, committed to a restoration of the past and supported by the Catholic Church.

Such an essentially ideological analysis is inadequate, for the conflict between the two Frances during the past century and a half has been far more complex. The alignment of forces at first was not that of the aristocracy versus the people, but rather part of the aristocracy versus the middle class. While the original cleavage may have indeed occurred along ideological lines of traditionalism versus liberalism, by the middle of the nineteenth century economic and social interests became the sources of conflict. By that time, moreover, the middle class had allied itself with the aristocracy to oppose the rising working class. The two Frances were no longer those of the late eighteenth century, yet the basic cleavage remained, and, what is most important for our analysis, so did the opposed political institutions around which the original conflicting ideologies had been formed. And in their exclusive faith in either the administration or the representative assembly, Frenchmen have perpetuated the dualism of conceptions of authority that continues to provide the cultural framework within which political forces carry on their struggles.

This dualism is, of course, the malady of French politics, principally responsible for preventing the emergence of a parliamentarism in which institutions of leadership and democracy are suitably combined. A brief recapitulation of French political and constitutional history may help to indicate the causes for this inability to jettison the past, integrate the two historic patterns of government, and produce a political system adapted to modern needs.

A Century of Constitutional Instability

The reasons for France's failure to develop satisfactory parliamentary government during the Third Republic lie in the period 1789-1870. During this time four developments appeared that have had critical influence on the evolution of her political institutions. First, there occurred the Great Revolution, which precluded the continuity of a natural evolution toward limited, or constitutional, government. Second, under Napoleon there was created a bureaucratized dictatorship whose institutions became permanent. Third, there followed the introduction of a defective parliamentary regime in which a multiparty system and constantly changing Governments were encouraged by monarchs who continued to seek unfettered personal power. Fourth, under Napoleon III there emerged a corrupt economic liberalism that, unlike its British counterpart, refused to nurture true parliamentarism, but opted for authoritarian government.

In his study of the French Revolution, Alexis de Tocqueville shows that rather than the extreme harshness of conditions in eighteenth-century France, it was, in fact, the increasing liberalism of the monarchy that encouraged the taking of the Bastille. There is, indeed, much to indicate that the years just prior to the Revolution were producing at least a de facto limited monarchy. Louis XVI had hardly the unlimited authority of Louis XIV and he repeatedly found himself bowing to the wishes of the rising middle class, as expressed in the Parlements of Paris—the quasi-legislative law courts. Even after July 14, 1789, there was still the possibility of preserving the continuity of legitimate government, for superficially the king seemed willing to accept constitutionalism. But unlike his British counterpart, the French king lacked the realism to understand the permanence of the middle class's demand for power. While paying lip service to the first revolutionary assembly, he plotted secretly to restore absolutism—and this time, that of the seventeenth century! On the side of the revolutionaries, too, the moderates lost power and in 1792 the First Republic was proclaimed, thereby ending the monarchy and rejecting the British alternative of constitutionalism within the framework of legitimacy. This act proved that a decision as to the form of government could be taken by a handful of mortal men. The king and his administration were replaced by the sovereign assembly and its administration, ostensibly representing the will of the people. Thus was born the revolutionary myth of popular sovereignty and its institutional form—the all-powerful representative assembly. At the same time, of course, the remnants of feudalism were eliminated and a nominally democratic society was decreed.

Naturally the great mass of the French people remained aloof from these changes and judged proceedings in Paris against simple human standards. When wartime conditions as well as imprudent policies created a disorder that went beyond any that existed under the *ancien régime*, the time was ripe for reaction. Napoleon seized the opportunity and restored order and authority—but not the royal order and authority, for this the Revolution had seemingly exiled forever. At this point the legitimacy of hereditary government was joined in limbo by the new legitimacy of popular government, the supporters of the two forms of government often going into at least a spiritual exile. There thus began the process of division in French society that has been one of the sources of political instability. Because no one emerged the clear winner in the Revolution, the battle was fought over and over again during the nineteenth century. Each crisis became a revolution because each side hoped, this time, to win the final victory.

Napoleon both achieved and undid the Revolution. His creation of a military order in society, thanks to highly centralized bureaucratic government, forcibly established the national unity and equality of treatment that the Revolution had sought. But it accomplished these ends by the constraint of absolute monarchy rather than the consent of democracy. He accepted the Revolution's destruction of feudal privileges and the rise of the commercial middle class, but he promptly created a new aristocracy based largely on this middle class and committed henceforth to his person for its status. There was thus established still another political faction, one made up of Frenchmen whose status depended not on the existence of a hereditary king, nor on the creation of a democratic republic, but on the existence of a military dictatorship to which they paid allegiance in return for social peace.

The fall of Napoleon ushered in the Restoration of the Bourbon monarchy (1814-30) and the July Monarchy (1830-48). But the return to legitimate monarchic rule in 1814 did not bring back the *ancien régime*. Louis XVIII introduced a form of parliamentary government, having spent his years of exile in England where he had been impressed by the prevailing governmental system. The peculiar hybrid of parliamentarism that emerged between 1814 and 1848 differed considerably from its British model. Responsible for this was the king himself, who, unlike his British counterpart, sought to retain a maximum of his personal prerogative behind the form of a largely advisory parliament. The king was in fact assured of predominance over parliament by three factors: First, the Governments he named were rarely homogeneous, thus making it difficult to hold any one party accountable. Second, Governments were responsible to the king alone, who could name them and dismiss them at will. Third, unlike the British king during this period, the French monarch made no effort at organizing solid Government majorities in Parliament against which the rest of parliament could organize a similarly solid opposition. As a result, [parliament was divided from the start among many small, competing groups] This the king welcomed, for it allowed him to rule un-fettered by the responsible criticism of a single and powerful parliamentary opposition.

Moreover, [while in England there was a constant effort to increase the suffrage, in France succeeding monarchs made the suffrage more, not less, limited] Parliamentary government therefore was not allowed to develop healthily in France at the time it was being successfully adopted in Great Britain. France's two constitutional monarchies, however, did maintain the principle of elected assemblies and the centralized bureaucracy, the former to retain the loyalty of the rising middle class, the latter to assure more effectively the monarch's ultimate control. Representative institu-tions were used as means, not ends, and no effort was made to educate the population for a more responsible political role.

As a consequence, when another revolution established the Second Republic in 1848, French society was not much more democratic than it had been in 1789. The new Republic was declared in a predominantly agricultural country that was naturally conservative and monarchist. [As the First Republic had been, the Second was the work of Parisians—a coalition of the Parisian "people" and the middle class, chafing under the king's repressive policies. But unlike the earlier experience, 1848 was char-acterized by the participation of people who called themselves socialists] The threat to private property thus appeared and the revolutionary coali-tion foundered upon it when the fearful middle class leaders abandoned their pressure for universal suffrage and representative government. Again a Napoleon—the great one's nephew—came to restore order, instituting a plebiscitary dictatorship which exploited the conservative majority in public opinion to give a democratic sanction to his regime.

[Now parliament was reduced to even greater impotence than under the Restoration and the July Monarchy. The administrative pattern of gov-ernment prevailed, civil and political rights were severely curtailed, and the emperor continued his uncle's policy of winning a large degree of consent for his rule—from business to peasantry and even the city workers —by means of a paternalistic economic and social program.] The result of this was that the opposition to his tyranny was reduced to its smallest expression, in a group of doctrinaire intellectuals. Bonapartism again struck a lethal blow at liberalism and its political form, parliamentarism. Yet under Napoleon III the middle class ultimately came to hold great power and the mass of the people developed a superficial feeling of participation without the aid of representative institutions. Indeed, Napoleon III successfully identified limited suffrage and parliament with the memory of the oppressive constitutional monarchies, hence for a time thoroughly discrediting parliamentarism as a conservative invention in the minds of the urban population. Thus was born the latent bias for Caesarism that time and again was to threaten constitutionalism in France in the years to come.

The Second Empire survived military defeat no better than had the First. The victory of Prussia in 1870 left France in the throes of another revolutionary convulsion, Paris being in the hands of a socialist "Commune" while in Bordeaux a moderate republican government set about making peace with the victor. For the second time in French history—the first had been in 1848—the French people were called to the polls in a free election. Reacting against both the extremist democratic Commune in Paris and the military adventure of the latest Bonaparte, they returned a conservative majority to the National Assembly that was dedicated to constitutional monarchy. The constitution drafted in 1875 reflected this renewed desire to escape the alternation between extremes that had dogged France since the Great Revolution. But this does not mean that the bulk of either the people or the National Assembly were finally united on basic political values. The constitution on which they finally agreed was like an armistice between opposing armies, in which supporters of the two rival traditions of authority agreed to a momentary compromise without surrendering their hopes for a "pure" system to be established in the future. There was thus created a parliamentary government, again patterned on the British, and studiously poised halfway between the assembly regime of 1792, which provided for an all-powerful, unicameral legislature, and the one-man rule of the Bonapartes.

The Third Republic: 1870-1940

The constitutional laws of the Third Republic created a system of government that seemed excellent—at least in theory. Their vital innovation was a real separation of powers that appeared to provide a safeguard against the extreme of a demagogic legislature in the hands of a revolutionary elite as well as the danger of a dictatorial chief of state in the Bonapartist tradition. The lower house, the Chamber of Deputies, was invested with broad legislative powers and assured by the constitution of a fixed period every year for its deliberations, as well as various other prerogatives] It shared with an upper house, the Senate, the duty of electing the head of the executive branch of government, the President of the Republic—who also served as chief of state] The latter chose his Ministers, had the right to propose legislation, and could dissolve the Chamber, with the approval of the Senate, and call new elections. Although personally he was invulnerable to the Chamber's hostility, his Ministers were declared collectively responsible to parliament.

On the face of it, the constitution seemed to provide France at long last with true "mixed" government] Although separation of powers and ministerial responsibility were provided for, it soon became apparent that the drafters of the constitution had left the executive in a potentially predominant position. In particular, there was no mention in the laws of 1875 of the office of Prime Minister, that is, the truly responsible head of the executive. It was assumed that the President of the Republic would exercise all executive duties, just as the king had been, in effect, head of government under the constitutional monarchies. Since the President of the Republic was elected for a seven-year term and was not responsible to parliament, abuse of the executive power of dissolving parliament appeared possible. And indeed this is not surprising when it is remembered that the drafters were monarchists who actively hoped for the day when the contending pretenders to the French throne would come to an agreement and the monarchy would again be restored.

But the intention of this royalist majority was never realized and a conservative republic became, in the words of its first President, Adolphe Thiers, "the regime that divides us least." As the years went by without a decision as to which branch of the French royal family would rule, conservative opinion became reconciled to the only available guarantees against the "risks" of universal suffrage: the powerful surrogate for a king, the President of the Republic, and centralized administration, which the Republic retained in its full Bonapartist form.

The crisis came on May 16, 1877, when Marshal MacMahon, the royalist who had been elected second President of the Republic, decided to dissolve the Chamber of Deputies. While this was within his constitutional rights, it was interpreted by growing democratic opinion as a sudden return to the pre-republican administrative pattern of government. For the President's motive was to dismiss a Chamber that refused confidence to a conservative ministry that he had named and desired to retain. When the new elections returned an even larger hostile majority, it became evident that genuine republicanism and the representative pattern of government had become rooted in public opinion. MacMahon bowed to the popular will, named a ministry responsible to the new republican majority, and the true political history of the Third Republic began. During the following years the growth of an industrial working class swelled the ranks of true republicans and as a result further increased the power of the parties committed to making the Republic truly democratic. Thus with the principle of ministerial responsibility to parliament established, the Prime Minister came to assume most of the executive power. But the reaction to MacMahon's "coup" had been so strong that vigor and initiative on the executive's part were henceforth discouraged.

From the constitutional point of view the history of the Third Republic may be divided by World War I. From 1877 to 1914 there was a marked trend toward revising the 1875 constitutional balance between the executive and the legislature in favor of the latter. From the first World War to the fall of the Republic in 1940, the governmental system, lacking an effective executive power, proved unable to meet new problems and there resulted a radical increase in ministerial instability. Again, informal means were found to institute a counter trend in which the executive was strengthened at the expense of the legislative.

The most permanent characteristics of French government, however, were developed during the earlier period. Prior to the first World War France was still far from being a fully industrialized nation, and her largely small-town and rural population had not only a poor opinion of the Paris government, which under dictators and revolutionary mobs had brought grief to the country, but also felt little objective need for government intervention in their everyday lives. After all, France was well endowed with natural resources, and was fairly independent of world trade. It was felt that government was necessary to keep order and protect the frontiers, but beyond that could only serve as a source of oppression and unnecessary expenditure by the nation. Indeed the victory of the middle class republicans after 1877 was accompanied by a victory of the economic principle of laissez faire that reached proportions unknown in other major powers, except for the United States. The scope of governmental policy was severely limited and this eliminated pressure for reforming the governmental system—of little importance in French life at the time.

These conditions produced traits that are still very much present in French government today. First there is the importance of ideological issues and verbal partisanship. This is partly due to the relative unimportance, in early Third Republic politics, of economic and social issues such as factory legislation and the income tax question. These questions were raised but were not resolved until after the last threat to the Republic was laid to rest in the Dreyfus Affair. Certainly, too, the verbal effervescence was in part born of a reaction against long years of censorship. For if France is today the nation of free speech par excellence, it is only because government control over political opinion and its expression had been so much a tradition during the long period in which the administrative pattern of politics prevailed.

Second, there is the amazing individualism of French politics—the importance of personalities, of local and regional issues, and hence the lack of discipline that pervades all levels of politics. Again reference to France's past provides the cause: personal discipline, intellectual consistency, the sacrifice of personal motives for collective ends, are all required in political systems where the politicians are actually responsible for most political decisions. But in France where no tradition of local government existed, where a powerful administration, with agents in every locality, determined the minutest matter, there was little objective need to be responsible. Things would get done the way "the state" wanted them whether political leaders acted responsibly or not. Most of them, outside of the few who held ministerial posts at any one time, conceived of themselves as members of either the opposition or a potential opposition, and thus no effort was made to moderate criticism or temper ambitions. Overturning a Government became as much a means of opening a general competition for ministerial posts as it was for registering disapproval of Government policies. French experience seems to suggest the rule that parliamentarism increases in irresponsibility and instability in inverse proportion to the role it has in actual determination of policy.

But if the continuing existence of a monarchical bureaucracy appeared to interfere with the full prerogative of the parliament, why did this supposedly sovereign body permit the conservative institution to flourish? Why didn't the victorious republicans decentralize French government, thus reducing the role of the ancient central bureaucracy in policy formulation? The Third Republic was produced in a compromise between conservative friends of the administrative tradition, who wanted as little democracy as possible, and progressives of the representative republican tradition, who wanted wide-sweeping social reforms and political changes. Neither having a clear majority in the early years, a compromise was necessary, the terms of which were neatly put by Thiers when he warned, in 1871: "the Republic will be conservative or it will not be at all."

This compromise provided for the retention of the centralized bureaucracy, which guaranteed order, in return for a representative assembly elected by universal suffrage and, later, limited local self-government. But by 1900 progressive republicans, finally in control of the government, became aware of the advantages of a centralized bureaucracy, with its police and local government organizations. In the aftermath of the Dreyfus Affair they learned that such institutions could be used as effectively against conservatives as the latter had used them against republicans in 1848 and 1871.

Moreover, the progressive republicans had slowly transformed the 1875 regime into something quite different from what it had originally been. After MacMahon's retirement only nonentities were chosen for President of the Republic. The true chief of the executive was the Prime Minister, who with his cabinet became totally responsible to the Chamber of Deputies. Nor did the President of the Republic attempt to reaffirm the independence of the constitutional executive by using the power of dissolution. Almost eighty years had to pass before a French parliament was dissolved before its term was formally reached. At the same time indirect methods were used to decrease the power of conservative forces in society. An attempt was made to insure the secular state school's monopoly on education. Then the powers of local government authorities were increased in an effort to withdraw at least some power from the conservatively recruited central administration. Finally, and most important, progressive republicans sought continually to decrease the power in France of what they considered the most potent conservative influence—Roman Catholicism, until 1905 recognized and supported as the official French church.

The climax of this struggle between those who had never accepted the Republic as permanent and the growing number of devoted republicans came in the famous Dreyfus Affair. Beginning in 1894, the affair became the last pitched battle between the social groups loyal to the administrative tradition of government and the politicians of the representative tradition. Captain Dreyfus was a victim of a judicial error in which the honor of the French army was at stake. The case was exaggerated out of all proportion because of the excellent opportunity it offered both friends and enemies of the democratic Republic to fight what they thought would be a decisive ideological battle. The army, along with the Church, remained one of the last strongholds of pre-republican and authoritarian sentiment. Everyone in France who opposed further democratization of society—and with the rise of socialism this had come to include many socially conservative republicans—opposed rectification of the error on the grounds of *raison d'état* (reason of state), the higher logic that must prevail over abstract justice and individual rights. Those who favored the trend toward separation of church and state and the general dominance of the representative tradition, urged revision of the error and a full pardon for Dreyfus even if it meant dishonor for the army—and often many urged this in order to discredit another bastion of conservatism, rather than in order to uphold the rights of an individual.

By the time the Dreyfus decision was reversed in 1906 important political changes had taken place that were partially responsible for the revision. The rise of the Socialist Party had brought a powerful ally to the
democratic forces, which helped assure the primacy of the Chamber over
the executive and thus seemingly neutralize a conservative civil service.
Church and state were separated in 1905, the influence of the army was
reduced, and the balance of political power shifted into the hands of the
lower middle classes, represented by the Radical Socialist Party. The great
battle of political reform had been won.

But at the same time France was slowly and almost unnoticeably losing
its world position. In the years before World War I her birth rate fell, her
industrial development lagged in relation to the major powers and her
colonial expansion was seriously challenged. The battle for a democratic
republic had so absorbed her political energies that the need for social and
economic reforms had been overlooked. Nor were the political reformers
who had won power in the years before the first World War prepared to
embark on these social and economic changes. Except for the socialists,
the progressive forces proved vehemently opposed to bestowing upon the
executive, necessarily the agent of social and economic change, the new
powers required for meeting the problems of an industrial society. Had
they not recently won the long fight to weaken its independent role in
France?

The war radically altered the conditions of French politics. Its enormous
physical and economic costs served further to weaken France's world
power. Yet wartime needs had demonstrated the virtues of strong executive leadership and Clemenceau's exercise of this power seemed to reveal
by contrast the impotence and irrelevance of the highly verbal parliamentarism of prewar politics. It was not surprising, therefore, that the
conservative partisans of the administrative pattern of politics should have
won a great victory in the first elections after the armistice. Hope was
rekindled for the possible reversal of the prewar victory of democracy after
the Dreyfus Affair. And the old ideological battles around the state
monopoly of education, around the influence of the Catholic Church,
around the power of the administration vis-à-vis parliament, were all
revived. But added to these were a new set of pressing political problems
resulting from the economic effects of the war and the Soviet revolution
in Russia.

[The rise of communism in France had two important influences on
French politics. It weakened the strength of the democratic Left by attracting socialist voters to an extremist party that kept aloof from the rest
of the nation.]And by frightening the more conservative members of the
democratic parties it inspired the formation of authoritarian political

groups on the Right that gained new strength for their old battle against the Republic. Now these groups could claim that the democratic parties were not strong enough to resist communism. These party developments made the formation of moderate Government coalitions more difficult than before the war and made their existence more precarious as well.

The real breakdown of French political institutions under the weight of problems for which they were not adapted did not come until the decade before World War II. Then a combination of domestic and international crises started the country on the road that brought the Third Republic to an end. The government had, after all, been conceived by nineteenth-century liberals, who had assumed that the scope of public policy and governmental power had been too broad under Napoleon III. While intentionally retaining his centralized bureaucracy as an organ of order and control, they allowed executive power to wither away, producing thereby a parliamentarism that had difficulty acting in times of stress. Under the vastly increased responsibilities of government created by economic depression and international troubles, the archaic structure of French government began to show serious signs of breakdown.

From 1932 on ministerial instability became chronic. The average life of a Government during the next eight years was four months, as compared to eight months in 1914-32 and ten months in 1870-1914. The growth of extremist groups on the Right that advocated direct and violent action against the government was a tangible sign of public disaffection from the regime. Indeed, as the Great Depression settled on the major industrial countries a feeling of revolutionary potential appeared throughout the world, which in France was encouraged by the rapidity and seeming frivolity with which Governments came and went. In February 1934, extreme Rightists rose in a mass demonstration on the Place de la Concorde in Paris to protest the government's incapacity to manage the country's affairs. They attempted to cross the Seine and invade the Chamber of Deputies, once again producing for posterity a "revolutionary day" in the spirit of 1789, 1830, 1848, and 1870. Though France was now thoroughly republican and democratic and no real threat to the constitution emerged, the Popular Front, a coalition of all the left-wing parties, was formed, ostensibly to protect the Republic against the resurgent Right, but in fact seizing the opportunity to enact long-needed social reforms.

The Popular Front, however, served largely to weaken French unity in a world threatened by war because it seemed to integrate the Communist Party into national political life. France in the 1930's was still very much an agricultural country, with 48 per cent of the population living off the land, and only a small minority of the remaining 52 per cent who could have been considered members of a modern economy. In a word, for all the hue and cry of its intellectual politics, very much in the revolutionary tradition, France was basically a conservative country in 1936. Yet since 1932 the Communist Party had gained over half a million votes in the election and over fifty new deputies. And in Germany and Italy another form of revolutionary movement, Fascism, was claiming that the wave of the future was behind it. In these circumstances Frenchmen of all opinions began to realize just how ill adapted to the twentieth century their country had become. The choice for many seemed to be between Fascism and Communism, but at any rate the viability of traditional liberal and republican government appeared to them doubtful. It was in this state of mind that the French were called upon to prepare for World War II. Amazingly, great efforts were made and when war came in 1939 France had an impressive war machine readied. But beneath the surface the divisions and unsettled problems of the preceding two decades created the potential of collapse. It remained only for the spectacular defeat of the French army and the *de facto* abdication of the country's leadership to make this potential a reality. In June 1940 the defeat of the army and the resignation of the Government of Paul Reynaud constituted indictments against which the Third Republic had no recourse. In July the authoritarian Vichy regime was created, led by Marshal Pétain, who re-established the administrative pattern of government in the best pre-republican tradition. The Chamber and Senate were replaced by an appointed advisory council and the civil service was put in complete charge of policy-making as well as policy execution. As in 1870, a regime that had increasingly lost the confidence of the people failed to survive a military catastrophe—only this time the regime was the Republic.

The Origins of the Fourth Republic: 1940-1946

During the critical last years of the Third Republic two groups of reformist critics of French political institutions appeared both in and out of party politics. One group, made up largely of conservatives and anti-Communists, urged that the old-fashioned parliamentary democracy be streamlined in accordance with the model presented by the new dynamic powers of Nazi Germany and Fascist Italy. Another group, drawn from among the younger members of the center and moderate left parties, as well as from civic reform groups outside of politics altogether, urged a rejuvenated and energetic Republic, reformed to meet the challenge of new problems, rather than scrapped in favor of a return to the authoritarian tradition of the monarchy and the Empire.

After the armistice of June 1940, France was divided by the Germans into a zone occupied and governed directly by them, and a zone, with its capital at Vichy, administered by a French government nominally free of German supervision. This non-occupied zone was ostensibly ruled by Marshal Philippe Pétain, the aged hero of World War I, who became the figurehead for a government in the hands of the conservative and authoritarian reformers of the Third Republic. At the same time, however, in both zones as well as in the French colonies overseas and among Frenchmen in London, there developed a spirit of resistance to both the Vichy policy of collaboration with Germany and its attempt to transform France into an authoritarian country. It was quite fitting, therefore, that the second group of democratic reformers should become leaders of this resistance. Within metropolitan France underground resistance movements were created and in London General Charles de Gaulle organized Free France, which was ultimately to become co-ordinator of all French efforts to re-enter the war at the side of the Allies.

De Gaulle's efforts, although at first primarily military, became inevitably political. He correctly reasoned that an appeal to continued resistance in the name of the discredited prewar Republic would inspire little enthusiasm. Moreover, he knew that the leaders of active resistance within France were almost exclusively young reformers or marginal politicians for whom defeat had come as a vindication of their long-standing demands for change. De Gaulle saw that to enlist their co-operation Free France would have to promise a Fourth Republic after victory. Thus from 1942 onward the general and the leaders of the internal resistance movements formally planned new economic and political institutions to be created after Liberation.

Since the Resistance was as much opposed to returning to the Third Republic as it was to the Vichy regime, constitutional and reform projects studiously sought to avoid the pitfalls of both a weak and anarchic parliamentary democracy and a tyrannical dictatorship. As in 1875, constitutional thinking during the war years sought to balance institutions of the administrative and representative patterns of politics. True mixed government was the goal: executive and legislative powers balanced and assured of a responsible yet independent coexistence by the separation of powers. When liberation came in 1944 hope was high, for the past four years had seemed to eliminate all the forces that favored one or the other of the extreme forms of government under which France had long suffered. On the one hand, the blind conservative partisans of government by an administrative and social elite had been thoroughly discredited by their roles in the collaborationist government of Pétain—truly the government of administration *par excellence*. On the other hand, the prewar parties and politicians, who had failed to produce the necessary leadership and had become identified with ineffective government and ministerial in-

stability, had also been discredited by the rapid collapse of the Third
Republic in 1940. What seemed to emerge in 1944 was a new political
elite, inexperienced, young, yet enthusiastic and in many ways more
realistic and adapted to modern times than had been the old cadres. This
was reflected in the first Constituent Assembly, elected in October 1945
in order to draft a new constitution: over 90 per cent of the members had
no previous national political experience.

And yet very potent seeds of the past were imbedded in the new French
politics. After having denounced de Gaulle and the Resistance as agents
of British imperialism, the French Communist Party hastily recanted in
1941 when Hitler attacked the Soviet Union. Subsequently the party became one of the most active and popular elements of the Resistance.
However, leadership of the Resistance remained firmly in the hands of the
moderate non-Communist reformers, who were committed to establishing
an efficient parliamentary government in which a strong executive balanced a vigorous legislative. De Gaulle, as leader of the French resistance
movements, naturally loomed as head of the first postwar French government. But for the Communists de Gaulle and the principle of a strong
executive represented the major obstacles to their assumption of power
after the war. Thus even prior to liberation the Communist Party urged a
truly "revolutionary" constitution that would assure a predominant representative assembly in which, of course, they expected presently to gain
a strong if not a near-majority position. As for de Gaulle, their only
formidable competitor for post-liberation popularity and organizational
drive, the Communists made an effort to discredit him with the moderate
reformers by encouraging a whispering campaign about his alleged plans
for dictatorship.

The Communist Party thus made itself heir to the pure revolutionary
tradition that during the nineteenth century constantly had urged an
"assembly regime" in which the legislature in effect performed executive as
well as legislative functions. Naturally their activity tended to inspire a
reaction of fear on the part of French conservatives. Many who had at
first hoped for a balanced constitution now reacted against Communist
extremism by reviving activity on behalf of a predominant executive and
bureaucracy. It was natural that General de Gaulle should become their
leader as he constituted the only other real focus of public sympathy in
the country. As a consequence, by the time debate over the exact terms of
the Fourth Republic's constitution began, French politics were once again
divided along the classic lines of the representative, democratic ideal of
authority versus the administrative, elitist ideal.

Of course neither de Gaulle nor the conservative parties supporting him sought to institute a dictatorial regime on the monarchist or Bonapartist models. Rather they sought simply to assure effective government by remedying the defect of a weak and unstable executive that the experience of the Third Republic had revealed. Yet the opposition of the Communists, who urged reducing the formal powers of the executive even further than they had been reduced by custom before the war, automatically thrust de Gaulle and his supporters into what appeared to be the anti-republican camp. Fearful that the Communists would be successful at the elections by posing as the only truly republican party, the moderate reformers abandoned both de Gaulle and their early intentions of creating a strong executive to balance the traditionally powerful legislature. Although the 1946 constitution does not incorporate the radical "assembly regime" of the Communists, it nonetheless goes far toward legally institutionalizing those customs of the Third Republic that had led to the weakening of the executive branch.

True, a token effort had been made to give the Prime Minister increased powers and to make the defeat of a Government more difficult. But in practice none of these new provisions prevented the reappearance of instability which soon approached the record of the Third Republic during the interwar years. The short period of social and economic reforms—including nationalization of the natural gas, electricity and coal industries, the major insurance companies, and the commercial banks—did not dispel the growing disillusionment over the fruits of the Liberation. Again as at the beginning of the Third Republic, the political system was the product not of consensus, but of a compromise between the two historical forces of French society. The new constitution, drafted by Resistance leaders who supported the representative tradition, established the legislature as the dominant branch of the government. But General de Gaulle and the more conservative political leaders around him managed to retain intact the highly centralized and essentially predemocratic bureaucracy, the institution essential to the administrative tradition. Nor did de Gaulle's departure from the Government change matters: the threat of a Communist coup made the Resistance leaders realize that a centralized bureaucracy, and especially a strong police organization, was absolutely necessary. Yet in the matter of positive government action to resolve France's many postwar problems, the partisans of the representative tradition continued to insist on the primacy of parliament's role. But parliament, divided among many parties and unable to produce stable Governmental majorities, showed itself incapable of acting swiftly and effectively. Soon after the Liberation period it became clear to many Frenchmen that there was arising a serious disproportion between the range of governmental responsibilities created by the constitution and postwar social reforms, and the authority, stability, and efficiency of the supposedly new governmental system.

In brief, defeat, occupation, resistance, and liberation had not liquidated the burden of the past in the French political system. They had simply created a number of new layers in French political culture that were further to complicate and hinder the already cumbersome operation of French government. To the ancient enmity between partisans of the administrative and representative traditions were added the vexatious issues of the German occupation and collaboration versus resistance; "Gaullist" and "Pétainist" were added to the collection of epithets that envenomed political debate. The new political personnel soon slipped into the classical categories of French politics, given new names but still fighting the ancient battle of the two opposing ideals of authority.

Those interests seeking economic and social changes looked to parliament and encouraged it to remain vigilant against attempts by the civil service to prevent "progress." Those interests opposed to such changes looked to the administration and hoped for a strong executive to protect them against "anarchy" and "revolution." Between parliament and the civil service, the cabinet, properly the source of policy-making, remained simply the changing agent of changing majorities in the legislature. The result of this struggle has been what the French call *immobilisme*—a lack of effective governmental action on pressing public problems because of a lack of agreement on the proper solutions. The prime beneficiaries of such a situation have been the various groups and the extremists of all colors who live on discontent. Thus, the continued absence of true mixed government, integrating administrative and representative institutions, is caused by the continuing divisions in French political culture, as well as being itself a cause of these divisions. This has consequences for our approach to the study of the French political system. In the study of the British system we may start with the Cabinet and the House of Commons, whose actual powers are based on a massive consensus on the constitution. This consensus and the general pattern of government it legitimizes have profoundly shaped the structure and methods of British political parties and interest groups, which, therefore, Dr. Eckstein has examined at a later stage of inquiry. In France, on the other hand, the constitution has had no such shaping influence. Hence, before the operations of cabinet and legislature can be discussed, we need first to understand the forces and interests that underlie the uneasy compromises of the French constitution.

CHAPTER 17

Political Forces

The Many Interests and Ideologies

[The variety of political opinions in France is as long-standing as her governmental instability.] But although this variety antedates the coming of parliamentarism, its responsibility for increasing instability was greatly heightened when the establishment of universal suffrage and the subsequent organization of mass parties brought public opinion directly into politics. In general, therefore, while French parties in their present form are of relatively recent origin, their ideas and their social bases developed during the nineteenth century. On the whole this is equally true of England, yet there only two major parties emerged, while multipartism developed in France. [It is true that the British tend to approach political problems in a more pragmatic and empirical manner than do the French.] This is not so much because the British shun all doctrine and ideology as because basic national purpose rests with them on such deep consensus that problems of policy can be approached pragmatically. France's lack of consensus, and hence her more sectarian and doctrinaire approach to politics, is, like Britain's consensus and pragmatism, the product of, first, a series of historical and political accidents, and second, certain social, cultural, and economic factors.

[Long before the nineteenth century, English kings had sought, or had been forced to seek, the opinion of others in the making of governmental decisions.] At first it had been only baronial councils, but by the late eighteenth century it had long been accepted that the king made his decisions "in parliament." While the British crown progressed continually toward greater self-limitation, the French monarchy in the early nineteenth century progressed just as steadily toward greater centralization of all political decisions in itself. [Because policy was made by the king and ✳ his administration, it was unnecessary for opinion to be organized effectively by parties in order to alter the administration's views—which in all

235

cases would prevail. Because of these situational factors political opinion became unrelated to policy-making, and, in its irresponsibility, tended to disperse along lines having more to do with general ideas, social interests, and personality cliques than with the pros and cons of concrete policy. Even with the limited introduction of parliamentary government and the limited extension of the suffrage during the nineteenth century, French kings were reluctant to share their sovereignty. The French Prime Minister remained a personal agent of the royal will, unlike his British counterpart, who gradually became a true party leader, mustering the support of a majority in parliament to which he ultimately became responsible. In France the king viewed parliament as an institution of the political opposition and he saw in its growing divisions into groups a guarantee of his own supremacy. Thus a vicious circle was created: the office of Prime Minister in France had little independent power and therefore attracted few men of talent and leadership; because few such men became Prime Minister the office was not expanded and an executive power responsible to parliament, yet effective and stable, failed to develop.

As for the variety and abstractness of French political ideas, especially those of the Left, it must not be forgotten that they originated in a long and bloody revolution which attempted to destroy not merely a Government, or even a political regime, but a whole society. When it succeeded, many revolutionaries sincerely believed that they had wiped the slate clean and could begin constructing French society anew. Consequently, they set about devising plans and ideologies that dealt not simply with the immediate problems of the day, but with grandiose plans for remaking the intellectual, economic, and political life of the country along radically libertarian lines. Naturally those who opposed the revolution opposed it totally and adopted the mode of thought of the revolutionaries to do so. Thus royalists and conservatives in general rejected the fact of the revolution and urged a return to a divine-right monarchy even more illiberal than that which preceded the Revolution. They too sought in politics a means of totally revising society rather than simply meeting problems of the day. To complicate matters further, the Napoleonic experience introduced a new theory that combined authority with consent and a limited social equality. This was meant to be as total a substitute for revolutionary theory as revolutionary theory had sought to be for the monarchical tradition—indeed all the more so since it claimed to be a synthesis of the two!

Finally it must be noted that the revolutions of the nineteenth century and the uncertain future of the Third Republic during its early years, all tended to nurture the hopes of partisans of the many political opinions that rejected the democratic republic. They were discouraged from compromise by the constant rise and fall of constitutions, and political crises such as the Dreyfus Affair. Thus France's chronic constitutional and political instability was a leading factor in the development of her many different political forces as well as being itself an effect of their multiplicity. [The structure of political power in France, being multiple and varied, encouraged a sectarian and ideological style of politics. This in turn prevented an easy integration of political forces even when circumstances were favorable for unity among partisans of rival ideals of authority.]

Social, Economic, and Cultural Origins

[It has been stated earlier that the most striking characteristic of French political institutions is that they are "unreformed," i.e., that they have not been adapted to changing conditions.] In large part this is the consequence, as we have seen, of French society itself being unreformed. Of all the great powers France presents the largest number of outcroppings of past economic and social ages. [By the end of the nineteenth century Britain and Germany were thoroughly industrialized while Russia was still very largely agricultural. But France, although largely agricultural, was already important industrially, and yet retained a large commercial and artisanal sector of its economy, representing a transitional stage of development.] Moreover, the bulk of her agriculture was not of the extensive, mechanized type arising in Britain and the United States, but rather was based on a large number of small holdings, exploited by individual peasant families who used methods developed during the seventeenth and eighteenth centuries. Yet some of French agriculture was modern, extensive, and oriented toward success in the competitive world markets. Clearly the interests of this commercial agriculture would not always be the same as those of peasant agriculture.

[Similarly France developed a few large, modern industries that operated alongside a majority of small family-owned plants that refused to modernize and amalgamate.] Thus, again there occurred a subdivision of interests within a sector of the French economy: alongside a small group of progressive businessmen whose productivity was high enough to allow them to make concessions to labor, was a large number of small businessmen whose high unit-cost of production prohibited a progressive wage policy if profit margins were to be maintained.

[Finally, the slow progress of industrialization and a low birth rate preserved a distribution of goods and services based on a huge network of small shopkeepers and artisans.] Without the pressure of a growing population there was no energy behind a reform of the distribution system. The shopkeepers and artisans shared no interests with either agriculture or industry; they felt that they were increasingly being deprived of their share in the national income by impersonal economic forces such as "big business" and "big labor."

[In terms of political opinions, such a kaleidoscopic economic and social pattern produced a number of irreconcilable forces which, unable and unwilling to compromise, continue to prevent movement toward fewer and larger political groupings.[First, there is a backward peasantry, tied to ancient production methods and having no more in common with any other group representing the producer's and property-owner's outlook in politics than a very general conservatism. Second,[there is a large group of marginal nineteenth-century family businesses whose owners will not and cannot form the core of a "reasonable" conservative party prepared to compromise with labor in order to increase productivity and profits. Nor are their interests rightly represented by the minority of dynamic modern businessmen whose high productivity allows them to be more supple in dealing with labor. Third,[there is a huge number of shopkeepers and artisans who, sensing that an evolving economy can bring them only disaster, readily support antiparliamentary movements that seem to give momentary promise of delaying if not upsetting the forces of progress. Fourth,[there is a large industrial laboring class, totally alienated from a society in which forces such as those mentioned above have retained power and still set the style of values and customs. Unlike the working class in Britain, the French proletariat is a revolutionary class with a long history of conflict with "capitalism." While in England the workers' interests were generally represented by the middle-class Liberal party until the twentieth century, in France the workers and the middle class broke irrevocably in 1848. From then on they became the most violent enemies; consequently all hope was lost for associating the French worker with a "reasonable" reformist movement led by the liberal bourgeoisie.

[Thus social and economic factors have produced at least three types of conservatism—that of the peasant, the successful businessman, and the marginal businessman;[and at least two kinds of progressives—the revolutionary worker and the middle-class reformer.]It should be noted that the demands of each of these groups are conditioned more by their role in France's political culture than by an objective economic or social grievance. French and British small shopkeepers may both suffer from the growth of large chain stores. But it is only in France, with her Jacobin tradition of sympathy for the little man against the big and powerful organization, that the shopkeeper can become such a powerful political force. Although Pierre Poujade organized France's shopkeepers into an essentially reactionary movement, much of his success was due to an appeal to this ancient, leftist, Jacobin hatred for *les gros* (the fat ones).

In addition to these basic socio-economic groups making for five distinct, class-based parties, two other cultural factors further increase the number of possible party groupings. For besides divisions along social and economic lines, a serious division along philosophical lines is caused by the continued existence of the Catholic Church question. To this day it remains difficult for two shopkeepers to belong to the same party if one is a practicing Catholic and the other a Freemason and an anti-clerical. The reason is that, although church and state were separated in 1905, the Catholic Church is still a partisan, political force for conservatism in the eyes of many Frenchmen. In 1789, of course, this was a fact, as it was during much of the following century when the Church openly supported anti-democratic and later anti-Republican parties and opinions. The Church is no longer solidly conservative, and indeed many individual Catholic leaders are among the most active reformers. Yet it cannot be denied that in the provinces, wherever the influence of the parish priest is strong, the resistance to progress is also strong. The fact that this is commonly due to the economic backwardness of the region and the inadequacy of secular state educational facilities is often not remembered, and the old image of an inherently conservative Church is preserved in the minds of many Frenchmen. Thus on all levels, from workers to business-men, class and occupational interest is further subdivided by attitudes toward Catholicism.

Clearly, then, many French political parties are associated with a limited historical experience and with often obsolete social groups. Even when they no longer fulfill a real representational need for these groups, however, they often live on because their leaders want to retain them as personal vehicles, exploiting a purely emotional attachment in order to keep the parties alive. The vanity and self-importance of French political leaders has itself been an important influence in perpetuating the multi-party system. With two parties, only two men can be supreme party leaders and potential prime ministers; in a multiparty system, producing frequent changes of coalition cabinets, the opportunities for top leadership are more numerous. This has been an important factor in preventing the success of most attempts to form permanent larger groupings of the relatively small French parties.

Present-day Parties and Pressure Groups

As in other democracies, political forces in France may be divided into political parties and pressure groups, the former contesting elections and represented in parliament and in the government, the latter organizing occupational interests to influence government policies. Since there are over ten national parties represented in parliament and countless pressure groups, some system of classification is important for purposes of analysis. To this end the eight major parties to be discussed, as well as the six pressure groups, will be grouped under four opinions that represent the basic political outlooks and hence the smallest number of categories into which French political forces may be divided. In only one case does a single political party fully represent such a basic political outlook—the French Communist Party can be said virtually to monopolize the representation of those in France who are discontented enough to consider themselves, at least on election day, "revolutionaries." However, many vote Communist without being revolutionary in fact.

French political opinion may be divided four ways: conservatism and authoritarian reaction, which support the administrative concept of authority; and reformist liberalism and revolution, which are associated with the representative concept of authority. Each tradition, it must be noted, is shared by a moderate and an extreme advocate of its institutional pattern, for as we have seen, there are still Frenchmen who feel justified in breaking the present constitutional compromise and resorting to violence as a means of establishing the "pure" regime founded on only one of the competing conceptions of authority. Today the extremes—of authoritarian reaction on the right, and revolution on the left—are represented by the Poujadists and Communists respectively. In strength and influence such extremist parties wax and wane with the health of the economy, the fortunes of French prestige on the international scene, and other factors. Moreover, the interests and ideologies of the parties representing these four divisions change greatly from one generation to another. Today's revolutionaries, the Communists, have vastly different social aims from the revolutionaries of 1848, who today would find themselves more comfortable in the company of the reformist liberals. Similarly, today's conservatives have an ideology reminiscent of the liberals of the late nineteenth century. What appears permanent is the basic fourfold division of opinion and the distribution between the two historic conceptions of authority.

Finally, it should be mentioned that while the French Communists are formally committed to an all-powerful representative assembly, it is most unlikely that they would actually allow such an institution to function once they attained power. Experience in the eastern European countries has demonstrated that the Communists simply use this revolutionary posture in order to muster popular support against an ineffective or oppressive government. Once in power, they establish a dictatorship of the Communist Party that, in fact if not in theory, follows the purest administrative tradition of politics.

Conservatism

In the general election of January 2, 1956, 31 per cent of the voters cast ballots for parties that may be considered more or less conservative. Conservatism represents the largest single bloc of opinion only because the Left is divided between Communists and reformers who together poll a clear majority of the vote. The fact that since 1947 Communists have been kept out of Governments has meant that conservatives in parliament have formed the majority of the remaining political forces available for making Government coalitions.

French conservatism is also more disorganized and dispersed than the forces of change and reform. Many more parties are needed to represent the variety of conservative viewpoints than to represent progressive opinion. French conservatism is like an attic: in it are accumulated various old and useless odds and ends of doctrine which are treasured along with a certain number of modern interests and ideas. Actually, most conservative parties are of relatively recent origin as organized groups. This is because, until the rise of the Socialist Party, no real threat was posed to the ruling-class status of the social and economic elites. The ideas and the aspirations of conservatism are, of course, of ancient lineage and today, although there is little royalist opinion left—though enough to make monarchy a subject of discussion—French conservatism still partakes of the pre-republican administrative tradition of politics. Much of the ideology of present-day conservatism dates from the nineteenth-century monarchical experiences and especially the middle-class July Monarchy. In particular French conservatism today embraces an essential desire to preserve the social status quo, an attachment to the values represented by Catholicism, and a faith in the elitist and administrative approach to resolving political problems.

The Independents and Peasants Party (Centre National des Indépendants et Paysans)

This is essentially a national electoral machine grouping the Paris leadership of a number of small conservative parties. But it can be considered a single party especially since in recent years its internal cohesion and even its party discipline have increased considerably. The *Centre* was the largest conservative party, after the last elections, polling over 14 per cent of the votes cast and having 80 deputies in the National Assembly—the third largest number of any party group in parliament. It was organized in 1948 in order to provide for conservative deputies the same sort of national organization that the left-wing parties had created at the liberation in 1944. The *Centre* grouped splinter parties that were themselves descendants of prewar organizations many of whose members and leaders had supported the Vichy regime and hence were in disgrace in the years following the war.

The Independents and Peasants Party is strong in those areas of France that have always voted for conservative candidates. Thus it is powerful in the eastern and western extremities of the country where the population, is rural, devoutly Catholic, or both. It is also strong on the central plain around Paris where agriculture is commercial and extensive and hence the businessman's outlook dominates. In urban areas the average French businessman votes for this party as do large shopkeepers and people living off corporate income.

The party leader is Antoine Pinay, who during his premiership in 1952 became associated in France, as in the world, with the popular image of the thrifty French middle class that makes its living in relatively backward family enterprises. A minority of the party looks for leadership to Paul Reynaud, the last premier of the Third Republic, who still represents more "enlightened" conservatism, in particular that of big business and finance, as well as the commercially oriented agriculture of northern France. The party's organization is very loose, based largely on local committees of notables—businessmen, professional men, landowners, and the like. It lacks, of course, the large corps of party militants or regulars associated with mass parties. And, needless to say, in such a party of notables party discipline is very low indeed. But until recently the party's lack of formal organization has been a matter of pride for the membership. In contrast to other parties in which policy is often determined by the wishes of a restricted group of active militants who control the organization, Independent and Peasant deputies are free to act upon their judgment of the national interest or in accordance with the wishes of their constituents. It must be noted, though, that these deputies, unhampered by the vigilance of a disciplined party organization, are also more available to serve as representatives of economic interest groups, which in fact many of them do. It is primarily in this party that business and agricultural pressure groups find their parliamentary spokesmen. When, for example, the president of the employers association of the road transport industry ran for office, he ran on the Independent ticket. The outstanding representative of the textile industry is also a deputy of this group, while the man who was in charge of lobbying activities for the French association of manufacturers was an Independent senator.

The Independents and Peasants are also proud of the fact that their party has no official "doctrine." Since they are in favor of the social status quo, and since a "doctrine" is usually an instrument of political attack against entrenched power, they have not considered this lack a handicap. Conservative politicians have depended on their "relations" in business and governmental circles to forward their interests and have not found it necessary to develop a doctrine with which to curry favor in public opinion. However, in recent years they have made an effort to develop some sort of doctrine, attempting at least to give a greater impression of consistency to their various policies and their general property owner's ideology. The party is energetically opposed to all forms of government intervention in economic affairs except for subsidies to marginal industries and high tariffs for agricultural and manufactured products. Otherwise they are for strictly free enterprise and opposed to the nationalization of any industry. The party has consistently fought attempts to reform the tax system in the direction of making it produce more revenue from personal income taxes, and it naturally opposes increases in government expenditure. On the other hand, it has urged state aid to Catholic parochial schools and has always supported a strong military establishment. In foreign policy it has generally been nationalist and opposed to the liberalization of France's ties with her overseas possessions.

In a word, the Independents are heirs to the opinion the French call "the classic Right." It is this heritage that makes them a distinctive political force and that makes their co-operation with parties to their left precarious. Most other French parties are unwilling to identify themselves for long with men and ideas so frankly committed to conservatism and the past.

The Christian Democratic Party or MRP (*Mouvement Républicain Populaire*)

Unlike the Independents and Peasants Party, the MRP is highly organized and has a well-defined doctrine. Indeed, ten years ago it would not have been considered a conservative party at all but rather a member of the liberal reformist group. Most of its leaders and its militants did not consider themselves conservatives then, nor do they now. However, MRP voters from the outset have been largely conservatives and in recent years they have obliged the party leadership to adopt conservative policies. The MRP polled somewhat more than ten per cent of the ballots cast on January 2, 1956, and its seventy deputies in the National Assembly made it the fourth largest party group.

The Movement is heir to the vigorous French political tradition of liberal Catholicism and in particular the movement known throughout Europe as Christian Democracy. Organized in its present form in 1944, the MRP's early leaders were associated with prewar Catholic youth organizations or were members of the small liberal Catholic party, the

PDP (*Parti Démocrate Populaire*). Liberal Catholicism had originally emerged as a political force during the July Monarchy when such Catholic writers as Lamennais and Ozanam protested against the open support given to the social status quo by the Church. Later on Christian Democrats urged French Catholics to pay greater attention to the social teachings of their religion, and early in the present century they besought their coreligionists to abandon their political hostility to the Republic and concentrate their efforts on social reforms. But Christian Democracy remained a small minority opinion until World War II, when the impressive resistance record of its leaders considerably increased its prestige. Leaders of the PDP and the Catholic youth movements were among the most active opponents of both the German occupation authorities and their Vichy collaborators. Yet the MRP's huge post-Liberation success—in October 1945 it polled over 20 per cent of the votes cast and sent 152 deputies to the first Constituent Assembly—was undoubtedly due to the support it received at the time from all segments of French conservatism. The normal representatives and parties of French conservatism had very largely been compromised by their support of Vichy and hence were not even allowed to run for office. For most traditional conservatives, voting for the MRP was the only alternative to voting Socialist or Communist. With the rise of more orthodox conservative parties, half of the MRP's voters abandoned the party for more congenial representatives who preached less about social duties and promised more in the way of concrete help to business and agriculture.

Today the MRP is like its prewar ancestor, the PDP—a largely regional party. Its main strength is focused in Alsace, Brittany, Anjou, and Touraine, where a powerful and doctrinaire attachment to Catholicism prevails among all classes. MRP voters in these areas, unlike their fellow Catholics who vote for the Independents and Peasants, are likely to be professional people and employees rather than farmers or businessmen. Elsewhere in France the MRP is strong among civic-minded professional people, white collar workers, and managerial occupations.

Because of their origin in an ideological movement, seeking to affect public opinion, Christian Democratic parties in Europe have been well organized. The MRP is no exception: in 1944 it sought to match the efficient and tight organization of the Left, with which it had to compete under an electoral system that awarded a premium to the large and well-organized national party. It has, therefore, a network of local sections, themselves organized into departmental federations. Policy is determined democratically by local and national congresses, which elect the president of the party and its executive committee. Alongside this organization is an allied series of occupational "teams" whose purpose it is to spread

Christian Democratic doctrine and perform good works within their respective occupations. The "teams," made up of representatives of various branches of a vocational group, are responsible for drafting much of the party's economic and social program and in keeping the movement close to its grass roots. But the influence of the organization, and in particular of its loyal and generally liberal militants, has decreased in recent years. In order to retain the support of its conservative voters, the party has played down the more reformist interests of the militants.

The principal leaders of the party are Georges Bidault and Robert Schuman, each of whom has served as Foreign Minister for a long period. Party doctrine is still liberal Catholicism, and theoretically reformist, but the decisions of the leadership on policy in parliament clearly indicate the party's recent conservative orientation. They have, for example, opposed extension of government welfare programs, fought attempts to raise taxes, and, of course, have supported government aid to Church schools. Most importantly, they joined conservatives in opposing a liberal colonial policy in Indochina, although at the same time espousing a policy of European integration and international co-operation. Although their formal doctrine prevents them from advocating free enterprise as categorically as do the Independents and Peasants, their actual policies have not seriously differed from those of the latter in recent years.

On the other hand, historical memories and the experience of both leaders and militants prevents the MRP from being thoroughly content in an alliance with the "classic Right." The party, as well as the leadership, was formed in a schism from the Right and during the occupation they were in open hostility to the Vichy regime, whose last defenders are among the present-day Independents. Moreover, Christian Democracy's interest in the social message of Catholicism is sincere and clashes with what they consider the coldly antisocial outlook of the "classic Right."

Conservative Pressure Groups

Two major pressure groups support the conservative viewpoint in France: the CNPF, or National Confederation of French Employers (*Confédération Nationale du Patronat Français*), similar to the American National Association of Manufacturers; and the CGPME, or General Confederation of Small and Medium Business (*Confédération Générale des Petites et Moyennes Entreprises*). The former has existed since 1936 and has roots going back to 1919, while the latter was organized for the first time after World War II in protest against the alleged neglect of small-business interests by the CNPF and the political parties.

Traditionally French business has sought to influence politics at the executive and administrative levels rather than at the level of public opinion or parliament.] Businessmen were reluctant to organize, relying on their social contacts with the high civil servants of the powerful administration to make known their views on public policy and to lobby for preferential application of the law. [The rise of Socialism and Communism and the increased activity of government in economic life, however, have caused them to organize formally, and the CNPF, representing primarily big business, now maintains extensive contacts with parliament as well as with the administration.] In 1946-49, when the Communist danger was at its height, the organization contributed heavily to anti-Communist parties and candidates. Since then it has subsidized the electoral campaigns of certain friendly deputies. The CNPF maintains an excellent legislative reference service which is available to any deputy and is highly attractive, given the inadequacy of such a service in the parliament and the understaffed offices of the party groups, the only official secretarial help available to deputies.

The CGPME represents smaller and more marginal business, which, because it is more numerous, is also more powerful in terms of actual votes controlled. [With fewer personal contacts among the high civil servants, the CGPME is obliged to focus its attention on the legislature. In parliament it has organized a series of informal "study groups" that include deputies coming from districts in which a given industry is important.] Representatives of these interests then come before the groups to present their views on pending legislation and try to impress upon the deputies the electoral consequences of failing to vote sympathetically.

Reformist Liberalism

[The forces arrayed against conservatism are equally disparate and unstable. They too were born in the intellectual turbulence following the Revolution and have rarely been unified.] Even in 1956, when the major parties representing reformist politics were together in an electoral coalition called the Republican Front, they hardly spoke with one voice. For this group includes the progressive wing of a former conservative coalition; parties that were once revolutionary but no longer consider themselves such; and groups that have little interest in doctrine and policy except as means to assure them of office. The Republican Front coalition, which after the 1956 elections included all reform parties, received 27 per cent of the votes cast in those elections. It consisted essentially of three parties that share in common a vague desire for movement and change in political and social institutions. Two of the three are anti-clerical, and all three accept government intervention, although admittedly in widely varying degrees. There is little agreement, therefore, on the kind and extent of the reforms necessary and needless to say the coalition is extremely unstable.

The Gaullist Party (*Centre National des Républicains Sociaux*)

[The Gaullists, who were on the right wing of the Republican Front, until recently would have been classed among the conservatives, if not among the anti-parliamentary forces.]Indeed, the majority of Gaullist deputies in the present Assembly voted with the conservatives more often than with their Socialist and Radical allies in the Republican Front government of Guy Mollet. This is due to the simple electoral fact that they were elected by conservative voters. [Yet since their national leaders and their party's program are reformist, and since the party was represented by members in the reformist Government of the Republican Front, the party may be discussed under the reform category.]

[The present Gaullist party is the pale and shrivelled successor to General Charles de Gaulle's political movement, the RPF (*Rassemblement du Peuple Français*)—hence the label "Gaullist."]The latter was founded in 1947 in order to promote radical constitutional change and to unify the country in the face of what de Gaulle felt certain was an approaching world war. In 1953 the general withdrew the RPF from politics and the Gaullist deputies were obliged to organize a new party. In the 1956 elections the party polled somewhat less than four per cent of the votes cast and elected 20 deputies to the Assembly.

In 1951, when the Gaullists ran under the direct patronage of General de Gaulle and the RPF, they polled almost 22 per cent of the vote and had 118 deputies, the largest single group in the lower chamber. Frenchmen who feared Communism above all voted for the Gaullists because they believed de Gaulle to be the only French leader capable of saving the country from a Communist strike for power. With the stabilization of the economic situation and the resultant recession of the Communist threat, the need for a "savior" declined and thus the *raison d'être* for the RPF seemed to disappear for most of the party's conservative supporters. They switched their allegiance to other parties, and what remained of the RPF was organized into a party that represents both new and prewar political currents. On the one hand, the party is a continuation of a type of small, centrist "party of personalities" that under the Third Republic served as the electoral machinery for a politician having powerful personal appeal in his constituency; on the other hand, it is also the representative of certain reform ideas from the time of the Resistance and, in particular, of the then widespread desire for serious constitutional reform to set up a strong and stable executive.] This has been and remains the prime goal of de Gaulle's own political activity—although he no longer concerns himself with party politics—and in the measure that today's Gaullist deputies are attached to the general's memory, they too support this principle.

[The Gaullists are an urban party and receive most of their support from towns in the eastern and western parts of the northern half of the country, or from a series of widely scattered departments in which their leaders have strong personal followings] Elsewhere the Gaullists are supported by urban professional people such as doctors, lawyers, and engineers; by former Resistance fighters and ex-servicemen; and apparently by the more enlightened and productivity-minded members of the business community.

The organization is still led by two of de Gaulle's closest wartime associates—Jacques Chaban-Delmas, who led the group into the Republican Front; and Jacques Soustelle, former Resident-General of Algeria. The party fell heir to the RPF's rather extensive national organization and hence it has a larger number of militants than such a small group ordinarily would. Moreover, [the RPF stoutly insisted that it had a doctrine and a program, based upon the Resistance, which it sought to impress upon public opinion.] Hence efforts were made, during the movement's heyday, to enroll large numbers of party workers who had been former resisters, and today many of these still work for its successor, the present Gaullist party. This doctrine, besides praising the virtues of a constitution that provides a strong executive, preaches a self-styled enlightened nationalism that aims at making France a great power once again. To this end it also urges more economic and social reform than do the more conservative nationalists in the Independents and Peasants party. But what primarily separates the Gaullists from much nationalist opinion, such as that represented by the Independents, is the fact that most of them were personally and bitterly opposed to the Vichy regime, whose remaining admirers are to be found among the Independents and Peasants. Although on colonial matters the Gaullists tended to be more conservative than the other parties of the Republican Front, the general spirit of firmness and movement which Pierre Mendès-France originally gave to the coalition assured their support during the elections. Besides, de Gaulle had named Mendès-France as the only premier he could admire since he himself left that post, and this "grace" was alone enough to assure the Gaullists' temporary loyalty to a coalition to which Mendès was at least nominally attached.

The Radical-Socialist Party (Parti Républicain Radical et Radical Socialiste)

[During the past ten years this party has evolved in an opposite sense to the MRP] In 1946 it was considered conservative. It vigorously opposed the nationalizations, and having been the governmental party par excellence of the prewar Third Republic, it generally damned all that had been done since the Liberation. But since 1951, and particularly while Pierre

Mendès-France was its leader, the majority of the party in parliament supported various economic and social reforms and led in the formation of the Republican Front coalition.

Almost ten per cent of the ballots cast in the last election went to candidates of the Radical-Socialist Party and to those of a few splinter parties that usually follow its lead, such as the UDSR (*Union Démocratique et Socialiste de la Résistance*), a small yet influential "party of personalities." Immediately after the election, and prior to the various splits in the party, the Radicals had 54 deputies in their Assembly group and the splinter parties allied with them had 22 deputies. The Radical Party is the lineal descendant of the "radical" wing of nineteenth-century liberalism, which championed political democracy, civil liberties, separation of church and state, and basic social reforms such as factory legislation—all before World War I. Between 1906 and 1940 the Radical Party was one of the most powerful in France and was the hinge party in most coalitions, the element without which a Government could not be formed. While the Republic was still being consolidated against attacks from the Right, the Radicals usually allied with the Socialists. But after 1919 they steadily became more conservative and except for their short co-operation with the Socialists in the Popular Front Government of 1936, almost always voted with the conservatives on social and economic matters.

After World War II the party had a number of bad years because it was associated in the public mind with the corruption and ineffectiveness of the declining years of the Third Republic. However, with the rise of the traditional conservative parties, it returned under Mendès-France to its earlier liberal position. One result of this has been that most of its conservative leaders have either been expelled or have voluntarily resigned to form splinter groups most usually allied with the Independents. Today, two groups of voters support the Radicals: the larger is made up of the provincial middle class—shopkeepers, farmers, teachers, minor professional people. Their strength is concentrated in southwestern and southeastern France, areas where there is relatively little modern economic activity. A smaller group is made up of urban intellectuals and professional people in Paris and in the larger towns of northern and eastern France. These latter are primarily voting for the "new" Radical party of Mendès-France and not for the dusty traditions of the party represented by its ancient strongholds in the south of France.

Like the Gaullists, the Radicals are also a party of personalities. But they are more loosely organized and are less committed to "doctrine." In recent years the leaders were Mendès-France, who, before he resigned in 1957, brought into the organization a large number of young, reformist intellectuals that consider him France's Franklin D. Roosevelt; and

Edouard Daladier, prewar Prime Minister and aged leader of provincial Radicalism. The local organization of the party is based on committees of "notables," which are often closely associated with Masonic lodges, far more active politically in France than elsewhere. These committees send delegates to an annual congress that largely rubber-stamps decisions taken by an executive committee. While traditionally the Radical Party had few formal members, the popularity of Mendès-France in 1954-56 caused membership to rise from 61,000 in 1953 to 150,000 in 1956. But again, recent divisions in the party and the decline of its former leader's popularity has undoubtedly caused a reverse trend.

The only constant in Radical doctrine and policy has been anti-clericalism, and even that gave signs of wavering in 1951 when many Radicals voted with the Right for government aid to Catholic schools. In economic matters the party, although it led the fight to introduce the income tax into France before 1914, has been fighing against its extension ever since. Under Mendès-France's reformist leadership it became mildly interventionist, urging government aid to foster economic reconversion of backward French businesses and to reduce the sprawling system of subsidies to other marginal sectors of the economy. It still considers itself the party of the "little man" and the most loyal protector of the ideals of the Great Revolution of 1789.

The emotional ties that bind the Radicals to the principles of political democracy for which it fought so long, and its rock-bound anti-clericalism, represent the chief obstacles to a comfortable coalition with the conservatives. Under Mendès-France the additional incompatibilities of a new-found liberalism in colonial policy and a professed economic reformism, were added. On the other hand, the Gaullists—on their right in the Republican Front coalition—were too nationalist and too committed to the person of a "great man" for most Radical militants, while on the Radicals' left in the coalition, the Socialists, because of their faith in deficit financing and massive government direction of the economy, make permanent co-operation precarious. This, of course, leaves the Radicals very much in the position they held before World War II: in the center of the French political spectrum and, incidentally, occupying a position that automatically gives them a role in almost any government coalition.

The Socialist Party or SFIO (Parti Socialiste—Section Française de l'Internationale Ouvrière)

The French Socialist Party is the largest and best organized of the reform parties. Formally its program still calls for the collectivization of all means of production according to Marxist principles. In fact, however, the party aims simply at reforming French capitalism so that a more equal distribution of the national income may be achieved. In January 1956 the party polled close to fifteen per cent of the votes cast and was represented by 94 deputies in the National Assembly.

Notwithstanding its formal attachment to Marxism, the SFIO—as it is usually referred to in France—can best be situated in the pre-Marxian tradition of the utopian socialists such as Proudhon and Louis Blanc. It is above all rigorously and emotionally egalitarian and democratic, more attached to the revolutionary mythology of 1789 and 1848 than to the "scientific" analyses of a German intellectual like Marx. By the end of the nineteenth century the various socialist groups in France were divided into two camps: one urged violent revolution as the means to power and the socialist society; the other advocated evolution and a victory at the ballot box instead. In 1905 the two camps formed the present organization by reaching a compromise in which the revolutionary doctrine was retained in theory, but the evolutionary methods were adopted in practice. The party became affiliated with the Second Socialist International—hence its official title as the "French Section of the Workers' International"—while the majority of its members remained patriotic and reformist rather than internationalist and revolutionary as parties in the International were supposed to be. Although the extremist revolutionary wing of the party broke off in 1920 to form the French Communist Party, the Socialist Party retained the loyalty of the great mass of the French workers until the early 1930's. At that time the growing economic crisis, splits in the party organization and leadership, and the relative failure of the Socialist-led Popular Front Government, all contributed to a sharp decline in the popularity of the party. The more dynamic Communist Party profited from these developments and after World War II completed the process by replacing the Socialist Party as the representative of the working class. By 1940 it was clear that the Socialists had fallen between two stools: they could neither be revolutionary enough to compete with the Communists nor were they willing to give up their revolutionary dogma in order to further co-operation with the middle-class parties on programs of piecemeal reforms.

The party today is strongest in the industrial north, where workers in the smaller factories still vote largely Socialist. They are also strong in all urban areas among white-collar employees, the personnel of the nationalized industries and other government workers. In the southwest and southeast many small farmers, traditionally attached to democratic socialism and the left-wing tradition, still vote Socialist as do teachers and other provincial notables of modest means. From 1946 to 1951 the Socialists declined in electoral strength and general influence. The party membership shrank and it became apparent that younger voters were turning from them. In large part this was due to a crisis of leadership. Ever since the death of its great prewar leader, Léon Blum, the party has had no outstanding personality at its head. Its nominal leader now is Guy Mollet, who became Prime Minister of the Republican Front Government after the 1956 elections.

The party organization is still powerful and highly bureaucratized. At its base is the local section. These sections are grouped into departmental federations which send delegates to an annual congress. At the top is a collegial executive which settles questions such as Socialist participation in Government coalitions. Since the war the party machine has controlled this body, thus reinforcing the power of the rather unimaginative party bureaucrats. After the postwar record of 335,000 regular members in 1945, the number dropped to about 113,000 in 1954. But in 1955 membership was said to have reached 120,000 and the relative popularity of the So-cialist-led Mollet Government in 1956 probably helped to preserve this trend of growth.

Unlike the conservatives, the Socialist Party prides itself on its doc-trine—democratic socialism. But otherwise, the party does little with its faith in the collectivization of all means of production. The attention of the party's program is focused rather upon social-welfare schemes and other means of redistributing wealth by government intervention in a basically capitalist economy. Thus while it led the Government coalition in 1956 the party extended social security benefits, increased paid vacation time by law, and talked of increasing personal income taxes and taxes on business in order to finance further aid to the lowest income levels. It is firmly anti-clerical and opposed to aid to Church schools, and at least its militants remain generally anti-colonialist. It differs from its neighbor party, the Radicals, primarily on economic and financial mat-ters, for the Radicals represent groups that are economy-minded and that oppose rises in taxation, with which welfare schemes are usually financed. But the Socialists' attachment to parliamentary government and their long experience of betrayal by the Communist Party makes co-opera-tion with the latter even more unthinkable than co-operation with the conservatives.

Reformist Pressure Groups

Two of the three major trade union organizations usually support reform policies, without being officially related to any of the reformist political parties. The larger of these is the French Confederation of Cath-olic Workers or CFTC (*Confédération Française des Travailleurs Chré-tiens*), which since 1919 has provided a haven for those workers whose strong religious sentiments prevented them from belonging to the militantly anti-clerical and Marxist French trade union movement. Of more recent origin is the smaller General Confederation of Labor—Workers' Force, or CGT-FO (*Confédération Générale du Travail—Force Ouvrière*), which was created in 1947 by dissidents from the third and largest labor union—the Communist General Confederation of Labor or plain CGT. In 1953 the strength of the CFTC was put at 600,000 members, that of CGT-FO at about 500,000—their combined strength being considerably below the estimated 1,500,000 members of the Communist CGT.

French unionism, however, is traditionally nonpolitical. The use of the CGT by the Communists for non-economic purposes such as politically motivated strikes has driven non-Communist workers to seek representation elsewhere. Thus Socialist workers and civil servants tend to join CGT-FO unions and during the days when the MRP still appealed to the working class its worker adherents joined the CFTC. In factories and on governmental advisory boards, representatives of these two union organizations tend to support the policies of the reformist party coalitions. The Catholic CFTC, for example, loosened its semi-official attachment to the MRP when Mendès-France formed his Government in 1954, even though he was a member of the anti-clerical Radical party. Its support was certainly one of the causes for the Republican Front's attracting a large number of liberal Catholic votes in the eastern and the urban sections of France in 1956.

The relative weakness of the French trade union movement in general —there are fewer than three million members out of a total force of wage earners of twelve million—and in particular the weakness of these two reformist organizations among union members, means that the trade unions are without the strength to be as potent a political force as are British trade unions. The low wage levels in France mean, furthermore, that union dues—when paid at all—must necessarily be very low, which makes for insignificant funds for political action and pressure-group activity. Finally, the small membership as well as the anti-political tradition renders union control of the political behavior of the working class very ineffective.

Revolution

The Communist Party (*Parti Communiste Français*)

The Communist Party represents the revolutionary Left. This, as we have seen above, is an ancient and respected French political tradition, dating from the Revolution of 1789 and from the brutally suppressed workers' uprisings of 1848 and 1871. The revolutionary Left like the "classic Right" existed long before the Soviet revolution of 1917 and the founding of the French Communist Party in 1920. Indeed, France's revolutionary experiences of 1789, 1848, and 1871 were themselves influences on Marxism and Russian communism. As a consequence, many of the 5,500,000 Frenchmen who adhere to the revolutionary Left by voting Communist are really expressing attachment to an old, home-grown political tradition which today happens to be, in their estimation, best represented by the Communist Party. After all, if more of them were in fact real, dyed-in-the-wool Communists, more would accept the party's discipline by becoming card-carrying members. As it is, however, even official party statements in 1956 did not claim more than 430,000 members, while unofficial estimates placed the number of members at about 200,000, of which at least a fifth were paid party functionaries.

Before 1920 the revolutionary Left was obliged to vote either for ineffective little splinter parties or for the Socialist Party. In the latter case they voted Socialist hoping that the revolutionary wing of the party would ultimately control it. After the Communist revolution in Russia the majority of the Socialist Party's militants—not simply voters, but rather party members and workers—voted at a congress to become Communist, and the minority of the militants re-created the prewar Socialist Party under Léon Blum's leadership. But since the overwhelming majority of Socialist voters in the 1920's remained loyal to the original democratic socialism, the Communist Party languished until the 1930's, when its participation in the Popular Front Government brought the party out of the self-imposed isolation of the previous decade. Formerly it had attracted only the poorest paid workers in the heavy industries of the urban north and the poorest farmers and peasants of southern France. After 1934, however, by posing as the most active anti-fascist force, it attracted professional people, intellectuals, and during the war its excellent Resistance record helped to attract further groups such as shopkeepers and white-collar workers, thus making its followers in general a cross section of the population from all parts of the country. No longer considered a "foreign nationalist party," as Léon Blum had called it, the Communist Party after the Liberation not only polled the largest vote but also was the party whose supporters were best distributed throughout the country. In large part the vote was a protest against both the prewar leadership of the country and the suffering of the occupation years. Radical solutions were desired by the poorer classes and the most extreme party was supported for this purpose. The amazing thing about the Communist vote until this day, however, is its stability, for although the party is no longer as national nor as popular as it once was, it still polls about the same number of votes as it did right after the war.

In January 1956 the party won 25 per cent of the votes cast—more than any other single party—and sent the largest group of deputies to the National Assembly—144 members. This represents practically the same percentage of the electorate as in 1951 and only 2½ per cent less than its percentage of the voters in 1946, the party's best year. In 1936, its best prewar year, the Communists polled only a bit more than 15 per cent of the popular vote. This huge success of the party is due first to its excellent organization and second to a combination of circumstances and adroit propaganda that has made practically all the discontented in France believe that the Communist Party is their only possible means of solving their problems.

Who, then, is the one out of every four French voters who believes this? The typical Communist voter is a factory worker, probably in a fairly large, heavy industry, and living in or around a town. Since most of French industry is in the northern half of the country, around Paris, Lyons and Lille, large concentrations of Communist voters are to be found there. Somewhat less frequently a Communist vote is cast by a poor farmer or peasant in the backward and mountainous center of France, an area that has always voted far left in protest against its low standard of living. Nor are these farmers necessarily landless; rather they hold tiny plots which provide them with such a meager living that they are often worse off than an agricultural wage earner on the large northern farms. Backward, ignorant, yet unwilling to merge their plots in co-operatives, they easily accept as scapegoats large landowners and big businessmen, who the Communist party assures them are the cause of their misery.

The organization that delivers this large and stable bloc of votes is brilliantly conceived and operated. It is a highly centralized machine that operates according to military discipline under central direction resembling an army's general staff. At the top are the leaders, members of the political bureau, the secretariat, and the central committee. Maurice Thorez, although ailing, is apparently still supreme boss, and Jacques Duclos, the party's parliamentary leader, is his chief lieutenant. Below this level are the departmental federations, themselves based on local sections. So far the organization is similar to that of the Socialist Party, although in the Communist Party there is no contact horizontally among sections or federations. Only vertical communication exists, thus assuring perfect discipline and preventing the formation of factions within the party as well as the kind of grass-roots debate that could lead to opposition to the leadership. The unique Communist institution, however, is the cell, existing below the section and bringing the party into factories, shops, offices, and city blocks. It rarely groups more than sixty members, of whom one is cell leader and alone has authority to communicate directly with the higher

echelon of the party, which in turn communicates only with him for purposes of passing down orders and decisions of the hierarchy.

[But finally the most basic reason for the party's success is that it is
ever-present in all the activities of society, giving a constant demonstration
of dynamism and seemingly practical accomplishment, not to mention
apparent interest in the little man's everyday concerns.]Thus when other
parties talk of lowering clothing prices the Communist Party actually goes
out and organizes a co-operative for selling clothes cheaply to workers. It
provides legal aid against landlords who seek to evict workers, organizes
sports and youth programs for underprivileged families. In short the party
does many of the things that the old-fashioned, big-city machines used
to do in American politics to "buy" the votes of the poor by tangible,
not verbal, activity. Indeed, the analogy is more apt than it would first
seem, for one could argue that had France ever had a real reform period
in her recent history, the essentially demagogic machine control of the
Communist Party over the lower classes in France would today be as
weak as the control of the big-city machines has become in the United
States.

[The Communist Party's doctrine is orthodox Marxism,] which is more
fully treated in the section dealing with the Soviet Union. It should be
noted here, however, that while the party still talks occasionally of the
violent overthrow of the government, in practice it is working for power
by either a clear victory at the polls or by an agreement for unity of
action with the Socialists, followed perhaps by a new edition of the 1936
Popular Front Government, which this time the powerful Communist
Party could clearly dominate. Naturally the party supports all policies that
increase the standard of living of the workers. However, in this respect
it is often faced by an embarrassing choice: either to support such reform
measures and then possibly lose the votes of those who are no longer discontented as a result of the reform; or to oppose the reform in question,
which also may result in defections, this time of those who had hoped
to gain from the change.

[Of course, the party is violently anti-colonialist and supports the "peace"
programs of the USSR.] But it cleverly masks its Soviet foreign policy in a
nationalistic disguise and consequently avoids appearing too obviously
as the Russian advocate in France. Until the Republican Front Government in 1956 the party was in an almost permanent and obstructive opposition in parliament. Recently it has become more co-operative on individual parliamentary votes in order to show the Socialists and other
reformers that joining the party in a Popular Front would not be too
dangerous. However, the extreme Stalinist position of the party on the
Hungarian revolution in the fall of 1956 effectively ruined its long-pre-

pared program to span the gap dividing it from the rest of the French Left, and today the party is more isolated than ever.

The largest French trade union organization, the CGT, represents the only important Communist pressure group. However, this means primarily that the leadership of the CGT is Communist, for a large part of its membership is either nonpolitical or votes for other parties, principally the Socialists. Often the worker, if he wishes to be protected effectively by a union, is obliged to join the CGT because it is either the only union existing in his plant, or the only active and effective one in bargaining with management. The Communist leadership of the CGT learned that many of their members were not Communists when it vainly tried to call them out on strikes for purely partisan political reasons, such as protesting the presence of American troops in France under the NATO agreement. Because therefore the Communist leadership does not fully represent the politics of its members, the value of the CGT as a political pressure group is limited. Even in purely trade union matters concerning wages and working conditions, the CGT occasionally loses the lead to the numerically smaller CFTC and CGT-FO because of the reluctance of its members to follow the leadership of men whom they consider to be primarily political agents and not legitimate union executives. Yet because the CGT fell heir to the traditional French union machinery, it still represents at least nominally the majority of organized workers.

The importance of the CGT is great, however, as a recruitment source for members of the Communist Party and as a propaganda machine in the working class. Moreover, for members of a party that claims to represent the workers, it is vital that the largest union organization should be at least nominally under its control. A Communist CGT, furthermore, is another institution in the Communist "state-in-potential" to which the party can point when it seeks to assure its supporters of its strength in the country.

Authoritarian Reaction

Authoritarian parties in France are also called anti-parliamentary parties, for they usually cite the existing political system, the major parties, and, in particular, parliament, as the causes of the nation's troubles. They center their attack on the constitutional system, unlike the Communists, who consider the economic system the root of all evil, and they indirectly suggest that what is needed is less talking in parliament and more authority and efficiency. There have been two kinds of anti-parliamentarism in France. The first appeared prior to World War I, when remnants of the royalist and Bonapartist opposition to the Republic organized in small leagues or around newspapers and exploited the occasional scandals and increasing political instability of the Republic to argue for their authoritarian alternatives. But only when a strong man like General Boulanger in 1889 appeared and struck the fancy of the great mass of opinion did these small groups become dangerous as the potential cadre for a powerful anti-parliamentary party based on the nation's malcontents.

After World War I French anti-parliamentarism became increasingly powerful. The rise of international Communism coupled with the economic crises that dislocated the economic security of the French middle class, inspired conservative politicians to adopt what they considered more effective and direct methods. Playing upon the fear that constitutional government and the moderate parties would not be able to withstand the Communists, they organized in the 1930's two large anti-parliamentary movements that grouped over one million members each: Colonel de la Rocque's *Croix de Feu* (literally "Crosses of fire," referring to the military decorations won under fire by the combat veterans who made up its nucleus), and the former Communist Jacques Doriot's French People's Party (*Parti Populaire Français*). Although these groups did not attain power, they did undermine confidence in the Republic for a large segment of the middle class at a time when international conditions required national unity. Add the fact that the Communists were engaged in a similar operation among the working class and it is not at all surprising that morale was low in the France of 1940.

After World War II an attempt was made to correct the deficiencies of French parliamentarism and thus eliminate the principal cause for the rise of anti-parliamentary movements. But by 1947 it seemed apparent to many Frenchmen that the new Fourth Republic would not be much more effective than the old Republic, and indeed perhaps even less, given the enormous increase in the tasks of government and the rise in Communist strength. General de Gaulle's RPF, although formed that year by him for reasons not directly related to Communism and the government's inefficiency, immediately became the vehicle for a new anti-parliamentary movement of opinion. Middle-class people who feared a Communist coup, who felt that the weak middle-of-the-road Governments could not keep order —either economic or political—rallied to de Gaulle. The return of normal economic and political conditions, however, saw these people abandon the RPF and return to their original conservative parties. But for large segments of the middle class engaged in commerce, marginal agriculture and various small and inefficient service occupations, prosperity never really came to stay. Poorly organized, living on a slim profit margin, the tax load—even when much of it was dodged—seemed to threaten their livelihood. The menace was now seen as coming from an unjust tax system, imposed by a parliament that was again considered to be the culprit. From this situation arose Poujadism in 1953 and at the 1956 elections 13 per cent of the voters supported Poujade and the other minor parties whose main goal is the radical overhaul of the representative government of the Republic in the direction of authoritarianism.

The Poujadist Party or UDCA (*Union de Défense du Commerce et de l'Artisanat*)

[This is a new party that has no roots in the past, save in the general tradition of anti-parliamentarism. Its leaders and militants are mostly former conservatives but there are also former Gaullists, Socialists, Radicals, and even former Communists among them.] It is really a pressure group turned political party, for it was founded by Pierre Poujade in 1953, on the suggestion of a Communist city councilor of his town, to protect shopkeepers and artisans from a new governmental tax drive. In January 1956 his party polled more than 11 per cent of the total vote and was represented by about 40 deputies in the National Assembly.

[The rise of *Poujadisme*, like the rise of Gaullism and anti-parliamentary movements of the past, is the story of one man—the leader of the movement.] For faith in the genius of one man is, above all else, the guiding principle of anti-parliamentary parties. In the case of the Poujadists the "one man" is Pierre Poujade, aged thirty-six, proprietor of a stationery store in a small provincial town in central France. As a youth he had contact with Doriot's French People's Party but during the war he escaped from occupied France to join de Gaulle's Free French forces instead of collaborating with the Germans as had Doriot. After the Liberation he dabbled in local politics as a Gaullist and ran successfully for the municipal council on a conservative ticket. He was a brash fellow, loud-mouthed, energetic, intelligent and sardonic. As a small shopkeeper himself, he had noticed the hardship caused by the increased pressure to pay taxes, the nonpayment of which alone saved many of his marginal colleagues from bankruptcy. During the postwar scarcity of consumer goods and the resultant inflation of prices, many of them had lived fairly well and had succeeded in avoiding taxation. With the economy stabilized after 1949, competition from new chain stores becoming fierce, and tax controls considerably tightened after 1952, for many shopkeepers the only hope for survival remained in continuing to avoid payment of taxes. To aid them in this endeavor Poujade formed his UDCA, which organized collective resistance to the tax collectors, and pressured deputies to revise existing tax laws. When the election was called in late 1955, [he quickly transformed his organization into a party that frankly appealed to the large commercial and artisanal sector of the backward French economy,] in which small shopkeepers alone number over two and a half million.

[The great bulk of the Poujadist vote comes from the economically backward regions of France—-the west, southwest and central regions where a low level of income makes the small shopkeeper's lot a hard one. In agricultural areas, former Communist and Socialist peasants switched their protest vote to Poujade in 1956, while in the cities former RPF voters, probably shopkeepers and white-collar workers, decided that Poujade was the strong man they would now vote for. Finally, a group that may be considered almost a fifth general political opinion—that of negativism toward politics, the non-voters—seemed to turn out in force in 1956 and vote heavily for Poujade. Non-voting in France is far from being as important a political attitude—given the large areas of social protest and the generally ideological and highly charged political life of France—as it is in the United States. Usually only about 20 per cent of the eligible voters in France fail to exercise their right to vote, and after the Liberation this percentage was reduced somewhat by the singular importance of the early election that decided the constitutional settlement. However, even then the percentage of non-voters never fell to the record low of 17 per cent attained in January 1956. Undoubtedly this was due to the dramatic circumstances of the election, the first since 1877 that followed a dissolution of the lower house of parliament. And studies have shown that many of these new voters, especially in departments where the percentage of non-voting fell to about 15 per cent, cast their ballots for Poujade in protest against conditions they had long borne in silence. By and large, however, the Poujadist vote is a protest by voters who have tried one or more parties in the past and have been continually disillusioned.

The leader of the movement, of course, eclipses all others about him. But he does have a competent staff and apparently has a well-financed organization. It is built around the old UDCA, the structure of which is loose and constantly in flux because of the instability of party cadres. The shopkeepers, artisans and occasional farmers who are members of this pressure-group-turned-party, act as its militants. Given their excellent channel of communication with the public in their shops, they are even more powerful than their numbers would indicate. No doctrine or coherent program has been presented, a fact consistent with the experience of anti-parliamentary movements of the past. However, Poujade has stated as his immediate goal—which he has suggested quite seriously—the convocation of the pre-Revolutionary Estates General in order to present grievances and propose a revision of the political system. The Estates General, of course, represents a vaguely corporatist concept in which occupations or classes are represented, rather than territorial entities, and in which there is no place for parties or traditional politicians. It is clear that a social group whose future is threatened, such as the small French shopkeeper, would prefer that type of representation, since it tends to "freeze" society on the basis of its present structure and provides a means of escaping the majority principle.

[Of course the Poujadists oppose plans for economic reconversion, all tax reforms and government intervention of any type, since such intervention could only be in favor of economic expansion. They are also violently opposed to liberal colonial policies, which has led some people to believe that the rich colonial interests are Poujade's prime source of funds. Nationalism is another resource of anti-parliamentarism, as is anti-Semitism. Although Poujade made some use of both these propaganda themes, he has since the election centered his fire on purely economic and occupational issues of interest to his shopkeeper and artisan clientele.

What makes co-operation impossible with other parties is above all Poujade's intransigent rejection of all their overtures—at least until the time of this writing. Conservatives would like to marshal Poujadist votes against their reformist opponents but Poujade has been too clever for them. He realizes that his support is in large part made up of disillusioned voters and militants from all parties and that only as long as he keeps aloof from them as well as from the parliamentary game of compromise and bargaining can he hope to retain their allegiance. Anti-parliamentarism represents primarily an emotional hatred for existing politics and political leadership and when its heroes cease "opposing" they lose their purely negative function for voters who among themselves are agreed on no positive program of government.

CHAPTER 18

Making and Unmaking
a Government

Under parliamentary government, in which the executive is responsible to a majority in the legislature, a disciplined two-party system makes the choice of a Prime Minister and his Cabinet a simple one. In this case a majority in public opinion is almost always reflected in the existence of a majority party and hence the choice of a Government is automatic: it is the leadership of the majority party. In a multiparty system having no single majority party, the Government must necessarily be responsible to a coalition majority. This majority is always potentially more unstable than a single-party majority, although when the majority coalition is long dominated by one large party, as in Germany and Italy, considerable stability can be achieved. In France, however, there is neither a clearly dominant party around which a stable majority coalition can be built, nor a potential majority in public opinion that can impose a coalition upon unruly parties. As a consequence elections do not produce obvious Government majorities. Instead the election of a Government by a clear mandate from the people, as in the two-party elections of Britain, is replaced by a process of finding a majority within the newly elected National Assembly and making a Government from the available leaders of this potential majority coalition. In spite of the similarity of constitutional forms, the patterns of power relations between Government, parliament and electorate in the two countries are radically different. The most serious consequence of this difference is that Government policy in France is more removed from direct accountability to public opinion than in England. The people sense this and as a result popular discontent in France is more often channeled into irresponsible political behavior.

But not only is it difficult to make a French Government; it is also notorious that French Governments do not last long. During the life of the legislatures elected on November 10, 1946, and June 17, 1951, there were over twenty Governments, or an average of ten per legislature, based on coalitions forged from among almost a dozen parties. During the same period Great Britain was ruled by the Labour Party, under Attlee, and by the Conservative Party under Churchill and Eden—the change in party being brought about by the election of 1951, which produced a Conservative majority. Generally it may be assumed that there will be but one Government per legislature in England, because a change in the political executive usually takes place only after a shift in the parliamentary majority following a general election. But in France the average of ten Governments per legislature means that only the first Government after the election—and perhaps not even that—has such a clear electoral mandate, while the other nine Governments are likely to have behind them parliamentary majorities quite unrelated to changes in public opinion.

[The central problem of the French political system is Government instability.] This problem, however, cannot be directly examined until the mechanism of French parliamentary practice is described and its influence on Government or ministerial instability determined. [For the main function of parliament in France is to make and unmake the Government, the body of ministers who with the Premier are delegated by parliament to direct the executive branch. Policy-making is a secondary function, which parliament dominates, to be sure, but shares with other institutions; the choice of the political executive, on the other hand, is wholly its function. Making and unmaking Governments, therefore, are the major events in the decision-making process.]

Elections

[To begin with, elections in France do not mean a choice between alternative Governments,] as they do in Britain. One obvious reason is that no single French party can amass anything approaching a majority of the vote and hence take complete charge of the executive. Nor has it been possible in normal times to create two national party coalitions before the elections, because of the vastly differing relations between the parties from one constituency to another. Historically, moreover, French parliamentary elections still retain the function assigned to them during the Revolution: to select an assembly that would check executive power or itself wield that power. With the return of the administrative tradition of politics under the monarchies and empires of the nineteenth century, this situation was not changed—that is, elections still were not meant to produce Governments. Under the kings and the two Bonapartes the elected deputies were, for practical purposes, excluded from any respon-

TABLE 3   French Governments 1945-58

PREMIER	DATE GOVERNMENT INVESTED	RESIGNED	PARTY COMPOSITION AT INVESTITURE (MINISTERS)
Elections Oct. 21, '45			
Charles de Gaulle	Nov. 21, '45	Jan. 22, '46	5 MRP, 5 CP, 5 SFIO, 3 UDSR, 1 RS, 1 Con.
Félix Gouin (SFIO)	Jan. 26, '46	June 11, '46	7 SFIO, 6 MRP, 6 CP
Elections June 2, '46			
Georges Bidault (MRP)	June 23, '46	Nov. 28, '46	8 MRP, 7 CP, 6 SFIO, 1 UDSR
Elections Nov. 10, '46			
Léon Blum (SFIO)	Dec. 16, '46	Jan. 16, '47	17 SFIO
Paul Ramadier (SFIO)	Jan. 22, '47	Nov. 19, '47	8 SFIO, 5 MRP, 5 CP, 3 RS, 2 UDSR, 2 Con.
Robert Schuman (MRP)	Nov. 24, '47	July 19, '48	6 MRP, 5 SFIO, 2 RS, 1 UDSR, 1 Con.
André Marie (RS)	July 26, '48	Aug. 28, '48	6 SFIO, 6 MRP, 5 RS, 2 Con.
Robert Schuman (MRP)	Sept. 5, '48	Sept. 7, '48	6 MRP, 4 SFIO, 4 RS, 1 Con.
Henri Queuille (RS)	Sept. 9, '48	Oct. 6, '49	5 MRP, 5 SFIO, 3 RS, 1 UDSR, 1 Con.
Georges Bidault (MRP)	Oct. 29, '49	June 24, '50	6 MRP, 5 SFIO, 5 RS, 2 Con.
René Pleven (UDSR)	July 12, '50	Feb. 28, '51	6 MRP, 5 SFIO, 5 RS, 3 UDSR, 3 Con.
Henri Queuille (RS)	Mar. 10, '51	July 10, '51	7 MRP, 5 SFIO, 4 RS, 3 UDSR, 3 Con.
Elections June 17, '51			
René Pleven (UDSR)	Aug. 10, '51	Jan. 7, '52	7 MRP, 7 RS, 7 Con., 2 UDSR
Edgar Faure (RS)	Jan. 20, '52	Feb. 29, '52	8 MRP, 8 Con., 7 RS, 3 UDSR
Antoine Pinay (Con.)	Mar. 8, '52	Dec. 23, '52	6 Con., 5 RS, 4 MRP, 2 UDSR
René Mayer (RS)	Jan. 8, '53	May 21, '53	8 Con., 7 RS, 6 MRP, 2 UDSR
Joseph Laniel (Con.)	June 27, '53	June 12, '54	8 Con., 5 MRP, 4 RS, 3 Gaul., 2 UDSR
Pierre Mendès-France (RS)	June 18, '54	Feb. 6, '55	5 RS, 4 Gaul., 3 Con., 2 UDSR, 1 MRP
Edgar Faure (RS)	Feb. 25, '55	Jan. 24, '56	5 RS, 5 Con., 4 Gaul., 4 MRP, 1 UDSR
Elections Jan. 2, '56			
Guy Mollet (SFIO)	Jan. 31, '56	May 21, '57	6 SFIO, 4 RS, 3 Gaul., 2 UDSR
Maurice Bourgès-Maunoury (RS)	June 12, '57	Sept. 30, '57	6 RS, 5 SFIO, 2 UDSR
Félix Gaillard (RS)	Nov. 5, '57	April 15, '58	4 SFIO, 3 RS, 2 UDSR, 3 MRP, 1 Gaul., 4 Con.

ABBREVIATIONS: CP—Communist Party · Con.—Conservative · Gaul.—Gaullist · MRP—*Mouvement Républicain Populaire* (Christian Democrat) · RS—Radical Socialist · SFIO—Socialist Party · UDSR—*Union Démocratique et Socialiste de la Résistance* (small center party of personalities) sibility in choosing the political executive. When the chief of state himself did not dominate the executive he chose a Prime Minister who did and who was usually independent of any majority in parliament. Coupled with a limited suffrage this exclusion of parliament from a share in choosing the political executive reduced the function of representation to insignificance.

Thus in neither the representative nor administrative ideal of authority was there room for the concept of an executive both responsible and independent. Hence the practice of elections that produced such executives did not develop. For partisans of the administrative pattern of politics, governing was the business of the king and his friends, and not a matter to be determined by a majority; for supporters of the representative pattern the executive was naturally an agent of tyranny, unnecessary once a sovereign assembly was elected to represent the public will. Elections came to be seen as simply the means of producing either a condensed substitute for popular sovereignty, or a delegation of notables, representing the various economic and social elite groups of the nation, whose docile presence in the capital served to attenuate the authoritarian appearance of royal or imperial rule.

The result of this electoral history was that when France suddenly received universal suffrage and representative government under the Third Republic, there existed no natural and tested system of elections that could link the popular will with the executive by means of a parliamentary majority. Instead there were a number of electoral systems that had been chosen by various rulers solely on the basis of their utility in producing a co-operative parliament, one having no real majority, thus no will of its own. One of these systems, perfected under Napoleon III's dictatorship, provided for single-member districts with the seat going to the candidate who won a majority of the votes on a first balloting, or, failing that, to the candidate having simply the largest number of votes on a second balloting held one week later. The traditional multiplicity of parties excluded the use of the plurality vote criterion on the first ballot, as was possible in two-party systems like those of England and the United States. Moreover, Napoleon III found that the two ballotings afforded the government an excellent opportunity for observing a free test of opinion in the first balloting, and then proceeding to the nomination of "official" candidates and an elimination of strong opposition candidates prior to the second balloting. It was this system essentially that the Third Republic employed for most of its elections from 1875 to 1940, although, to be sure, almost always without the intimidation and official candidatures between the ballotings.

The two-ballot majority system of the Third Republic did not facilitate the emergence of effective majorities. In most districts the first balloting simply served to set the odds on the various party combinations that could confront each other in the decisive second voting. [Party diversity was thus encouraged, since various economic and social groups used the first balloting as a preliminary test run to measure the weight of each group organized as a party,] Moreover, the system gave an advantage to the parties that were less encumbered with a formal doctrine and a national organization, since they were better able to take advantage of the bargaining that took place in the small local districts between the two ballotings. [In consequence the system produced parliaments made up of deputies who had been elected by local party coalitions having little or no relevance to national issues.] Nor were these deputies, once inside the Chamber, inclined to organize themselves in groups that reflected their electoral coalitions. From these arrangements it was the loose, largely programless center parties that profited most, for they alone could adopt any position dictated by local or parliamentary circumstances without risking accusations of doctrinal inconsistency.

During the Third Republic, therefore, the former manipulations of the emperor during the week between the ballotings were simply replaced by the manipulations of the local party bosses. The electoral system continued to encourage the party diversity and political irresponsibility that had existed under all patterns of French politics since the Revolution. And parliament, although elevated to the rank of the dominant branch of government, was unable to produce stable majorities. The founders of the Fourth Republic—Socialists, Christian Democrats and Communists— represented parties that had long opposed the traditional two-ballot electoral scheme. Not only did they consider it immoral, but they also knew that a system favoring center parties, organized locally and endowed with well-known personalities and professional cadres, would hardly help their new party machines, which were organized nationally and depended primarily on a national program and ideology rather than famous names. [As a consequence a system of proportional representation (PR) was adopted that favored large, nationally organized political parties such as the SFIO, the Communist Party and the MRP.] It was claimed, of course, that such a system was also the fairest and the most honest, for it assured some representation to all shades of opinion which a majority system definitely would not, and it furthermore eliminated the "deals" and obscure party bargaining which the two-ballot system had encouraged at the expense of purity of program. The new system, it was claimed, would thus never frustrate a true manifestation of the popular will.

The law governing the elections to the first legislature of the Fourth Republic in 1946 still largely applies today. It established the department as the basic constituency, although in the case of the more populous departments, two or even three constituencies were carved out. The number of seats for each constituency was apportioned according to the population, approximately one seat for each 55,000 registered voters. Parties in each constituency were obliged to present lists of as many candidates as there were seats in the department. [The voter cast his ballot for the list as a whole—thus actually voting for the party and the decision of its leaders in setting up the list, rather than for individuals.] For in effect the voter had no way of substituting names on the list or altering the order of the names as they appeared on the party lists. Seats were allocated to parties in proportion to the votes they received in each department. But instead of pure PR—mathematically impossible in the small constituency of the department—a complicated system based on the principle of the "highest average vote per seat" was employed. The effect of this system was to give the parties with the largest number of votes in each department a larger proportion of that department's seats than they would have deserved according to strict PR.

[By the end of the first legislature the Communists had passed into the opposition, and on the right there appeared the powerful Gaullist opposition.] Together these two dynamic movements threatened to attract such a large vote that no moderate majority would be possible. On the eve of the new elections in 1951, the then center parties—SFIO, MRP, Independents and Radicals—therefore decided to alter the election law so as to make sure that the huge Communist-Gaullist popular vote would not be translated into a "negative" majority in the National Assembly. [This was accomplished by permitting parties to make electoral alliances (*apparentements*) in departments and giving these alliances all the seats of any constituency in which they won an absolute majority of the votes cast.] Within such a winning alliance seats were allocated to individual party lists according to the 1946 version of PR, which, moreover, applied to departments in which no alliance won a majority or in which no alliances had been concluded. This new electoral system gave the center parties the opportunity to face the Gaullists and Communists as though the centrists were one unified party and to reduce the representation of these minority groups, as is done normally in plurality voting systems in the United States and Britain. The system worked as intended: the Communists won 71 fewer seats than they would have under the 1946 law, the Gaullists 26 fewer—enough in both cases to assure the center parties a slim but workable majority in the Assembly.

No changes were made in the 1951 law for the 1956 elections. The elections came suddenly after dissolution of the National Assembly by Premier Edgar Faure—the first time this power had been used under the Fourth Republic and indeed the first time it had been used by any French execu-

tive since 1877. There was, consequently, little time for making comprehensive alliances even if the center parties' "marriage of convenience" had
still existed. In fact, without the Gaullist threat, and as yet unaware of
the strength of Poujadism, the center parties failed to make broad enough
alliances to capture a majority of the vote in many departments. As a
result the 1946 method of distributing seats proportionally was applied
in most departments. Without the majority element of the alliances
working against them, the Communists in the 1956 elections radically
increased their representation in the Assembly, although their popular
vote remained the same as in June 1951.

[After the Liberation, the Resistance leaders had hoped that PR, party
lists, and the larger, departmental constituencies would help to stabilize
and purify French politics by obliging the voter to choose party and program
rather than personality and special promises.] By creating an electoral system that favored large, nationally organized parties, moreover, it was hoped
that the total number of French parties would be ultimately reduced.
The experience of a decade has shown these hopes to have been in vain.
The number of parties has not been reduced over the prewar figure and
Government stability has not increased. The alliances of 1951 moreover
reintroduced much of the bargaining and behind-the-scenes deals that PR
was supposed to abolish. Yet cleavages between the parties have, if anything, become more unbridgeable as a result of the extra power the list
system has given to the doctrinaire national party organizations and their
leaders. Finally, local issues still have a very potent influence notwithstanding the larger constituencies of the list system, for parties are
careful to construct a "balanced ticket" that includes representatives of all
the regions of the department.

Therefore choice of a party is today no more a choice of a Government
than was the choice of a personality under the single-member system that
prevailed before World War II. Indeed, since the 1951 election the choice
of a party has often represented nothing more than a vote cast for a popular
personality whose position at the head of the party list makes his election
probable. Electoral coalitions are rarely translated into stable majorities
in the National Assembly for the postwar system has eliminated the possibility of polarization between Left and Right which tended to occur
under the old system on the second ballot and which sometimes produced
a potential Government majority. Moreover, the old single-member constituency assured a personal contact between voter and deputy that made
the latter more sensitive to changes in public opinion than he now is, the
party organization being interposed between deputy and voter as a result
of the list system.

[In short, the present electoral system of proportional representation has neither reduced the number of parties nor led to more stable party coalitions. Instead experience has shown that coalition-making, the basic necessity and "fact" of French political life, is now more difficult and party cleavages more permanent than before the war. Added to this new rigidity has been the difficulty produced by a large Communist group in parliament which reduces the range of parties from which opposing coalitions are to be formed. With the existence of an anti-parliamentary group on the right like the Poujadists, the alternatives for moderate Governments are few and rarely cohesive, because in order to form any Government at all parties of very different economic and social outlooks are usually obliged to join together. For Governments based on unnatural and consequently shaky coalitions, the best policy is often no policy.

It is true that electoral systems may determine certain of the conditions under which party competition takes place and thus influence the development of a party system. But in France the powerful cultural and economic forces making for political diversity exclude the possibility of electoral reform producing a party system like the British. As was the case with the prewar single-member majority system, the modified proportional list system of the Fourth Republic has done little to mitigate the chronic divisions of political opinion and create majorities capable of governing effectively. It does allow Frenchmen, however, to continue voting for "delegates" of their economic, ideological, or temperamental viewpoints. These meet in the National Assembly to find a transient majority rarely reflecting a majority in public opinion, which, when it does exist, is unable to find expression thanks to an electoral law that has not been able to offset its underlying cleavages.

Parliament

The French parliament consists of the directly elected, powerful lower house, the National Assembly, and the indirectly elected relatively weaker upper house, the Council of the Republic. There exist two advisory semi-parliamentary bodies whose opinions are often requested by the two houses of parliament but that have no role in making and unmaking Government, and only a limited role in legislation. The Assembly of the French Union advises on colonial questions while the Economic Council prepares studies on economic and social problems, but neither is an important force in the pattern of power.

The National Assembly

As has been seen above, the present National Assembly is the product of an historical process that has made the legislative branch of government predominant in France. Underlying and reinforcing this development is an important concept of French political culture. Ever since the Great Revolution, directly elected representative bodies have been considered the sole agent of popular sovereignty. Since according to French political thought sovereignty cannot be divided, the idea of sharing ultimate decision-making with the executive branch has been rejected as alien to the revolutionary tradition. And since it has traditionally been conservatives who have sought to take power from the representative assembly, the republican tradition has jealously guarded the prerogatives of an all-powerful assembly. Modern arguments of government efficiency have not succeeded in weakening the faith of the French Left in the wisdom of this arrangement. Moreover, as has been seen, the revolutionary atmosphere of 1946 only served to reinforce opinion in favor of the all-powerful legislative branch in accord with the ideal of partisans of the representative tradition of politics.

The effect of this has been that unlike Parliament in Britain, the job of the National Assembly is primarily to decide Government policy and choose a Premier and cabinet to serve as its delegation and execute this policy. The great majority of its time is therefore spent in deliberation—debating general policy—rather than in simply casting policy received from the executive into the form of law. And its most vital single function aside from deliberation is producing the delegation from its midst that will serve as the Government and execute its will. But of course to produce a prime minister and cabinet it must first find a majority to which they will be responsible. This too is done by the National Assembly alone, unlike England where, thanks to a two-party system and disciplined parties, the majority is usually clearly indicated by the popular vote at elections.

This task is hardly an easy one for French deputies, elected by a public opinion that is severely divided and according to an electoral system that in no way helps the electorate produce a coherent parliamentary majority. But unenviable as it may seem to some, the job of deputy is much sought after in France. A deputy is elected to a five-year term and, given the weakness of the executive's power of dissolution, his chances of enjoying the full term are good. The job, moreover, is all the more desirable because the legislature is supreme and hence each individual deputy is guaranteed a fraction of sovereign power. As the king in the days of absolutism was surrounded by adulation and respect in "better circles" of opinion, so the fractionalized monarch of republican France receives, if not adulation, at least considerable respect and attention from the social and economic elites of the country. For to be deputy means that you are essentially a delegate of a regional economic or social interest group, posted to the capital with the mission of protecting your constituents against either an arrogant administration or a hostile parliamentary majority. You are, as in the United States, the recipient of constant petitions for help and counsel, and it is expected that you will spend a good part of your time intervening with the huge French bureaucracy in favor of your local constituents.

For some the attraction of the deputy's pay and emoluments is not without force: the deputy receives close to $6000 per year, far above the average French income, as well as a series of privileges such as the frank, a railroad pass, the right to wear a large tricolor sash at official functions, and, above all, the right to be addressed as, at the very least, *Monsieur le député* for the rest of his days. For it should not be forgotten that Republican France has preserved the love of privilege and honors born in the culture of Eternal France. To become a deputy a Frenchman or Frenchwoman must be at least twenty-five years of age and in possession of his or her civil rights. Until 1945 women in France were neither eligible to vote nor to run for office. Today there are over 25 lady members in the French parliament, fewer than in Germany, though more than in either Britain or the United States. Furthermore, the Resistance origins of much of France's political personnel has made the average age of French deputies in the Fourth Republic lower than that of their prewar predecessors. As for occupation, the legal profession is best represented, as in Britain and the United States. But unlike these two countries, the second largest professional group is agriculture, reflecting both the prestige and the continued importance of this sector of the economy. In third place come members of the teaching profession, always active in a country whose revolutionary tradition offers the teacher the status of a secular priest. Finally, and again unlike other Western democracies, business seems to produce few successful candidates for the National Assembly. This is undoubtedly because of the widely held assumption that private business interest excludes the ability to deal with the national interest. Recognizing this fact, politically ambitious businessmen assume for the elections another professional status, or contrive to disguise their social positions as did the scion of a prewar railroad magnate who described himself in his campaign literature as "the son of a railroad worker."

Finally it should be noted that French deputies often serve as local government officials in their constituencies at the same time they represent them in Paris. Indeed, deputies with the strongest personal positions are often those who have managed to parallel their jobs as deputies with positions as mayor of their town and member, or even chairman, of their department's General Council. The importance of local ties, notwithstanding the existence of national party lists in elections and the larger departmental constituency, is demonstrated by this custom, which has had the unfortunate side effect of giving the French parliament a very bad record of absenteeism. The maintenance of the proxy vote in the National Assembly—non-existent in other major parliaments—although recently limited, has been supported on the basis of this custom of local office for deputies.

Of the 596 members of the Assembly, elected in 1956, 544 were from the 90 departments of metropolitan France, the rest representing constituencies of overseas departments and other dependencies. These overseas deputies are elected by various systems and as a rule take little active part in either the legislative or the purely political activity of the metropolitan representatives. They do constitute, however, a block of votes that are eagerly sought after in close decisions and, on matters not immediately relevant to overseas questions, they often promise their vote to the major party group that commits itself to the relief of a particular local colonial grievance.

Deputies are organized formally and informally within the Assembly. The basic formal organization is the party group, recognized by the constitution and usually connected with a national party organization. More often than not, however, new national parties are actually extensions of groups of deputies that have broken with existing party groups. Thus in the fall of 1956 a group of conservative Radical deputies, rebelling against the reformist leadership of the party leader, Pierre Mendès-France, broke away from the Radical group and proceeded to bind those departmental organizations in which they retained power into a national organization, to which they gave a name confusingly similar to that which they had just abandoned. This is an index of the almost total lack of effective party discipline among all deputies except those belonging to the Communist and Socialist groups.

The other formal institutions are the Bureau, made up of the President, Vice Presidents, and Secretaries of the Assembly—all elected from among its membership; the specialized legislative committees whose members are distributed according to proportional representation of the party groups; and the "Conference of Presidents" (Conférence des Présidents), or steering committee of the Assembly, made up of the President, the Vice Presidents, the chairmen of the legislative committees, and the chairmen of the party groups—all called "presidents" in French. Legislative committees will be dealt with more fully in Chapter 19. The Conference of Presidents, however, must be considered immediately because it is especially typical of French parliamentarism. The purpose of the Conference or steering committee is to establish the provisional agenda of the National Assembly, for, unlike the British cabinet, the Government does not have control of the parliament's timetable or program of business.

The Assembly allows a representative of the Government to attend meetings of the Conference but his role is purely consultative. Final determination of the agenda, moreover, is with the Assembly itself, as befits a truly deliberative body.

The President of the Assembly has more prestige nationally than the presiding officer of the House of Representatives or of the House of Commons. This is due, first of all, to his important constitutional function as the immediate replacement of the chief of state, the President of the Republic, in case of a sudden vacancy in this office. In fact he is considered, according to official rules of precedence, the quasi-constitutional Vice President of the Republic and must be formally consulted at times of ministerial crisis as to likely candidates for the premiership. As presiding officer of the Assembly's deliberations, moreover, the President takes a more active role in debate than does the British Speaker, though on the whole he is less effective in controlling discussion. For the President is above all the guardian of the Assembly's rules of procedure and customs, both of which emphasize the individual deputy's inviolable right to speak. Moreover, debate is less restricted in the Assembly than in the British parliament because the French executive lacks the control over the parliament's agenda that is afforded by a disciplined party majority. Closure of debate in France is decided by a majority vote of the deputies, but both custom and the difficulty of quickly constructing a majority for closure, prevent its frequent use. However, limited forms of closure providing for restricted debate on urgent legislation are occasionally employed—though again a majority vote of the deputies is required.

Debate does not have to follow rigidly the subject on the agenda nor the decisions made by the Assembly's steering committee, the Presidents' Conference. As a member of a policy-making body, the deputy has the right and, as he sees it, the obligation to discuss any aspect of the subject under consideration, however far removed it may seem to others. Subjects for debate, furthermore, are not necessarily presented in the form of motions, resolutions or bills, but are often simply broad problems, such as "the Algerian question," which have been agreed upon for a general debate, at the end of which agreement is reached on the actual form the Assembly's disposition of the matter will take— be it a resolution, a motion to pass on to the next matter on the agenda, or a decision to continue debate at a later time.

Certain sessions of the Assembly are set aside for a special debate known as "interpellation," which constitutes the chief parliamentary device for criticizing the executive. An interpellation is a formal question, put to the Government orally by a deputy, and followed by a general debate in the course of which the Government answers the question and other deputies add their views, whether hostile or not, of the Government's position. Because of the provision for general debate, absent in the British question procedure, interpellation represents an ideal and constantly available opportunity to enemies of the Government to harass it and even to force it from office. For by the end of a long interpellation on a detail of Government policy, the debate may have developed into such a general critique of the Government program that the Premier may be prompted to consider the vote following the debate as one of confidence in order to test the seriousness of the hostility generated. In recent years interpellations have rarely led to a Government's resignation, although they do remain a potential threat.

Voting in the Assembly is supervised by the President and in most instances is accomplished by placing in a box, passed among the benches by an usher, cards bearing the deputy's name—white for yes, blue for no. Only in the most serious votes, such as votes of confidence or investiture, is a roll-call vote stipulated, requiring actual presence in the chamber, the proxy vote being permitted in other cases. The proxy voting system has meant that most votes on legislation are attended by only a handful of "service deputies" (*députés de service*), many of whom are the group "box men" (*boîtiers*). The latter are usually secretaries or presidents of the party groups, who simply place a package of cards in the box, including the cards of all their group, voting them as had been decided at a previous meeting of the group. Although this would seem to introduce a measure of party discipline, in fact it simply allows mass absenteeism among deputies, for any member may "rectify" his vote during the voting, thus nullifying the action of the group's "box man."

But while having little influence on party discipline, the proxy vote nonetheless does reinforce the power of the party leader in parliament, the man who represents the most important informal institution of the National Assembly: the *ministrable*. Literally the word means "capable of becoming a Minister." It refers to roughly ten per cent of the deputies, who make up the pool of likely Ministers and Premiers. England has its shadow cabinet representing the one alternative Government, that of the opposition. In France the *ministrables*, representing the parties from which possible coalitions could be formed, are all members of the multitude of shadow cabinets a system of many undisciplined party groups could produce. The *ministrable* is, therefore, one of the informal leaders of the Assembly's main activity—making and unmaking Governments. His interest in this activity is, of course, direct, as he is himself a member of the pool from which the next government coalition is necessarily chosen. And of course the fact that a given party is represented in an outgoing Government does not exclude *ministrables* in that party from trying their best to become members of the succeeding Government, even if they held a ministry in the defeated cabinet.

To become *ministrable* three personal qualities are necessary: a sharp political judgment, usually provided by long experience in parliament, that readily indicates to you when and under what conditions a change in the executive will take place; an undoctrinaire approach to policy problems, which facilitates your being included in cabinets of differing political complexions; a personal prestige and magnetism that insures you a following among deputies in your own group as well as in other groups, and thus makes your inclusion in cabinets a matter of decided value at the time of the investiture vote. The holding of certain formal positions, such as the presidency of a major party group or of an important legislative committee, automatically make of you a *ministrable* because of the power inherent in them. The chances are, however, that you would not have been named to the post unless you had been already a *ministrable* in your own right.

Many veteran *ministrables* do not need formal office to increase their desirability in cabinets. The master *ministrable* of the early Fourth Republic, for example, had already established the record for ministerial posts held during the Third Republic—nineteen times minister from 1920 to 1940. The holder of this record, Henri Queuille, moreover was Premier of one of the two longest governments of the Fourth Republic—almost thirteen months in 1948-49. Queuille entered the old Chamber of Deputies in 1914 and was continuously re-elected from his rural constituency Naturally, a "safe seat" is a prerequisite for long continuity as a deputy, which itself is vital if one is to build up the wisdom and friendships necessary to be a *ministrable*. Queuille also served as a Senator for a few years, thus gaining useful experience and contacts in the upper house, which, under the Third Republic, had an indirect influence on making and unmaking Governments. Then naturally Queuille belonged to a moderate center party, the Radicals, and among them he had the reputation of being a peacemaker and completely devoid of doctrinal prejudices—this in a party not known for its strong ideological bent! Above all, Henri Queuille is a man who inspires confidence: of peasant background, simple and beloved by his constituents, he nonetheless is a professional man—a doctor by training; while a member of a party formally considered as liberal, he is personally known to be among its more conservative members; quiet, gentle, hardly a great orator, he is a skillful buttonholer and a respected judge of political behavior. In early 1951, for example, he predicted the effects of the complex new election law, of which he was the principal author, within a margin of a few seats.

As in Britain, the symbolism and unwritten social code of the National Assembly are vital influences on its activity. Deputies are acutely aware of the dominance of the Assembly in the making of public policy and of the jealousy this causes on the part of the main competing sources of power, the cabinet and the civil service. These and the pressure of public opinion represent the main threats to the authority of the deputies. Their reaction historically has been to draw closer together among themselves in order both to defeat attempts at strengthening the power and stability of the administration and to prevent reforms that could tie parliament more closely to changes in a volatile and uncertain public opinion. The life of the deputy in the Palais Bourbon, the great building in Paris that houses the Assembly, encourages this impression of proud and embattled isolation. Unwritten law specifies that every deputy must address his colleagues in the familiar form. Soon the average deputy, no matter what his origins, feels at home and in time an important transformation of his outlook takes place.

There is room for all the deputies in the Palais Bourbon's chamber— far more spacious than Parliament in London. The premises are divided into public and private areas. The sittings chamber or *hemicycle*, as the French call it, after its form, has a tribune facing the members, who are distributed according to political complexion from left to right. Such a setting naturally encourages oratory, flamboyance and theatrical exchanges, largely for public consumption, and indeed sittings of the Assembly, attended by large groups of the press and public, are often more amusing and exciting spectacles than are the more conversational and soft-spoken sittings of the House of Commons. But all around this great public chamber are deployed corridors, lounges, vestibules, a bar, a small library, writing and reading rooms, where members who come from berating each other publicly in open debate can be seen walking arm in arm, or sitting huddled together, discussing perhaps the probable effect of their exchange and the chances of the Government for survival. The new deputy soon learns that this curious ambivalence of attitude is of central importance to the workings of a sovereign assembly whose members, save for the Communists, all realize that their collective power must never be sacrificed to an argument among themselves. As a representative body the Assembly must be the scene of political debate which reminds the voter that the Government is being watched and criticized and that his political faith is being defended. But unlike the House of Commons, the Assembly is also a deliberative body that must come to a number of concrete decisions. It would therefore be foolish to perpetuate intransigent partisan behavior beyond the public chamber, for in a political system in which decision-making is dominated by the legislature, intransigence might mean that problems would receive no solution whatsoever. Thus both public opinion, with its vagaries and violent partisanship, and the influence of the civil service, with its equally extreme nonpartisanship, must be kept out of the "closed arena" if it is to function as deputies wish it to. It is for this reason that to an astute observer in 1913 it appeared that "there is less difference between two deputies, one of whom is a revolutionary and the other is not, than between two revolutionaries, one of whom is a deputy and the other is not." [1] And it is for this reason that present-day revolutionaries, such as Communists and Poujadists, bend all their efforts toward bringing violently partisan matters into the debate and in general toward disregarding the rules of the game, for it is precisely the paralysis of the Assembly's policy-making function that they seek.

The Council of the Republic

[In the French political tradition the upper chamber has a definitely undemocratic reputation.] The great revolutionary assemblies were unicameral and it was not until Thermidor and the Empire that an upper house was created, precisely in order to limit the action of the popularly elected lower house. Indeed, Napoleon I frankly called his upper house the "Conservative Senate," and the authoritarian regimes of the nineteenth century all used a Senate as a counterweight to a more broadly based lower house. The constitution of the Third Republic did not alter this tradition but in fact continued the imperial practice of providing for lifetime Senators. Although this provision was soon abandoned and the Senate developed into a thoroughly republican body, it did retain its more conservative character thanks to the mode of election of its members. [Senators were then elected for nine-year terms—over twice as long as that of a deputy—and not by direct popular election, but by an electoral college made up of the deputies, members of departmental councils and delegates chosen by municipal and township councils.] The last dominated the group and as a consequence the Senate became very much the "grand council of the townships of France," as Gambetta put it. But this was its purpose, for part of the price republicans had to pay for the 1875 constitution was to assure the royalist and conservative majority in the founding assembly that the popularly elected Chamber of Deputies would be checked by an upper house in which more conservative provincial France would have a permanent majority. Indirect election by a college in which the more numerous rural townships had a natural majority seemed to guarantee this. The result was a Senate that throughout the life of the Third Republic was more traditionalist in economic and social matters than the Chamber of Deputies.

In the revolutionary atmosphere of 1944-46 the first reflex of the drafters

[1] Robert de Jouvenel, *La République des Camarades* (Paris, 1913) p. 17.

of the new constitution of the Fourth Republic was to omit an upper
house all together and return to the unicameralism of the true "assembly
regime." But the prospective power of the Communist Party in a single,
all-powerful legislative body led Socialists and Christian Democrats to
agree that a counterforce of some sort would be necessary, if only to delay
passage of legislation. [A drastically weakened version of the prewar Senate
was therefore created and named the Council of the Republic in a further
attempt to indicate its special status.] [Until 1954 the Council was a purely
advisory body without the right to initiate legislation and in theory unable to delay the Assembly's version of a text for more than two months.]
The constitution specified clearly that the Government was responsible
only to the Assembly, which alone invested a cabinet, and it allowed the
lower house to reject any of the Council's amendments by simply adopting
its own version of a law by the same majority the Council had used. At
the same time the mode of election, being substantially the same as that of
the Senate, had made the Council the preserve of elder statesmen and the
representatives of provincial and agricultural and small-town interests.
Given the undeniable importance of these sectors of French society and
the growing strength of parties sympathetic to them, the advice of the
Council became increasingly respected, and in 1954 the constitution was
amended to return to the upper house much of the power of the old
Senate.

[The 320 members of the Council, whose seats are distributed among
the departments according to population, serve a six-year term, half being
renewed every three years. Like members of the prewar Senate, they are
not elected directly by the people but rather by electoral colleges in each
department, made up of the department's deputies, its locally elected departmental councilors, and delegates chosen by the department's township
councils. [To be eligible for election to the Council of the Republic one
must be thirty-five years of age, ten years older than for the Assembly.
Election is by party lists and proportional representation in the eleven
most populous departments, and by the majority system and the double
ballot in the other departments. Because the electorate is relatively small,
the influence of personality and personal connections is even greater than
in Assembly elections. The successful Council candidate is, therefore, usually a local "notable," well known to the politicians of the department
and supported by one or more of the important interest groups of the
region. [Party affiliation is less important than it is for candidacy to the
Assembly,] for very often it is the party that must offer terms to a popular
notable if it is to be represented in a department at the Council elections.
Of course, party discipline is less important in the upper house, since the
Government has no political responsibility toward it.

Yet with the accretion of the Council's power, Governments have tended increasingly to draw one or two of their members from the upper house. This has been partly to show courtesy but also in order to forestall delay of its legislative program in the Council by having a few ministers who can "talk the Council's language." Like the prewar Senate it has also become, in the matter of drafting legislation, the "chamber of reflection," correcting and often improving the draft of laws presented by the Assembly. However, it almost invariably changes laws in a more conservative direction, and this underlies the reason for a continued demand for reforming the mode of election of Council members. Finally, as a constitutional part of parliament, the Council joins the Assembly every seven years to elect the President of the Republic, the French chief of state. As a source of elder statesmen and seasoned politicians, the Council can provide candidates as well as strategists for this election. This was also the case with the old Senate, but its weaker successor has, in fact, played a minor role in the two presidential elections since the war.

The President of the Republic

The holder of this office is chief of state, not chief executive or head of the Government. He is elected by parliament in a special joint meeting of both houses at the royal chateau of Versailles, where deputies and senators ballot in great pomp until a majority is finally arrayed behind a candidate. The President's term of office is seven years and he may be re-elected once. This relatively long tenure of office is important to his constitutional role, which is to serve as an element of continuity—in a parliamentary system noted for its unstable executive—and to serve as guardian of the constitution. This last duty is accomplished primarily by mobilizing public opinion against any party or group that threatens the constitutional order.

The President of the Republic performs the many ceremonial duties of any chief of state and this constitutes the bulk of his day-to-day activities. Although he also officially promulgates laws, bestows pardons, and presides over the French judicial system, his acts in these connections must all be countersigned by a member of the Government. Most of these decisions he takes as chairman of the body that presides over the judicial system—the Superior Council of the Judiciary (*Conseil Supérieur de la Magistrature*), or as chairman of the Council of Ministers (*Conseil des Ministres*), the name given to the more formal meetings of the Premier and his ministers at which the chief of state is in attendance. It is in this latter capacity that the President is entitled to be informed of all foreign relations and matters of national security. This is very important, for his major independent and personal activity arises in time of national emergency when, as the highest officer of the French Republic, he must appeal for national unity and self-sacrifice.

Almost as independent is his role in time of Government crises when he presides over the election of a new Premier to head the executive. Following a Government's resignation, defeat on a vote of confidence, or censure by the National Assembly, there occurs what the French call a "ministerial crisis" (crise ministérielle—after ministère, or ministry, i.e., Government). The outgoing Government simply takes care of current business while a new Premier, cabinet, and majority coalition are sought. This process of finding a Premier who can put together a cabinet and a program that will have the support of a majority in the Assembly is conducted by the President of the Republic. He receives advice on likely candidates and likely party coalitions from the President of the Assembly and others, but he alone—and herein lies his power—decides on the order in which the various candidates for the Premiership are called before the Assembly. It is possible therefore for a President to ruin a candidate's chances by sending him before the Assembly too early, or by ignoring the potential candidacy of a leader toward whom he is hostile.

Because of this power it is no exaggeration to say that the making of a Government in France is inaugurated by the President of the Republic. This, as well as his function as guardian of the constitution and of the national interest, depends for its full exercise on the personality of the incumbent. Although constitutionally the President under the Third Republic was far more potent than at present, the abuse of the office—and in particular of the right of dissolution—by the second President, Marshal MacMahon, led to a parliamentary custom that assured the election to the Presidency of only the most pale and noncontroversial political personalities. While this emasculated Presidency was formalized by the constitution of 1946, the two incumbents since that time have, paradoxically enough, been relatively strong personalities who have increased the influence of the office by establishing certain precedents. Vincent Auriol, the first President of the Fourth Republic, had been an active and forceful Socialist politician who gave no sign after his election of considering himself a figurehead retired from everyday politics. Auriol created a secretariat for the Council of Ministers which became the "memory" of the French government's deliberations in foreign affairs and, by keeping individual ministers aware of their stated opinions at times when political expediency indicated the need for forgetfulness, served as a force for consistency. He even participated in party politics by openly encouraging the organization of a strong and moderate conservative party to reduce the attraction of the Gaullist movement, which he considered a threat to the constitution.

The present incumbent, René Coty, was a respected and little-known conservative member of the Council of the Republic until, to the surprise of seasoned politicians, he was elected President in December 1953. Although, like Auriol, a partisan, he had a reputation for fairness and for constructive and responsible behavior in the upper house. Like so many Presidents of the Republic before him, René Coty was elected partly because his outlook and personality symbolized the political mood of France at the time, as interpreted by its parliament. In choosing a President, deputies and senators are not only interested in choosing a seasoned politician who will be able to preside over the delicate process of making a Government; they also seek a man who at the time of election has the attributes of a national unifier and whose possible acts in defense of constitution or national interest would most likely be considered legitimate by the great majority of the people. Thus in the left-wing enthusiasm of the post-Liberation period only a moderate Socialist like Vincent Auriol could have hoped to achieve this position of respect, while in the more contented and prosperous atmosphere of 1953 a reasonable bourgeois like Coty seemed indicated. In both cases the choices, although deplored by the shrill voices of ideologues, have been ratified by the genuine affection that developed for both men and their families during their terms. With this popular affection and a personal sensitivity for parliamentary life reinforcing his authority, the President of the Republic is endowed with considerable influence upon the conduct of the French government and the content of its policies.

The Government: Premier and Cabinet

The real chief executive is the Premier—who is also called President of the Council of Ministers (*Président du Conseil des Ministres*). Although the present constitution clearly makes him effective head of the executive branch, his lack of influence over the Assembly and the relative independence of the civil service continues to make of the office of Premier the single most unreformed element in the French political system. More than any other institution the political executive's status illustrates the continuing cleavage between the administrative and representative traditions. It demonstrates most strikingly the absence of a true "mixed government" in France—that is the absence of an effective separation of powers that guarantees the strong and independent executive necessary to the modern state, alongside a vigorous and unfettered legislature, constantly ready to criticize policy.

The office of Premier is really founded upon a contradiction that lies at the heart of French parliamentarism: as in Britain the Prime Minister and his Government are responsible before a majority in the legislature and serve only as long as this majority exists; in contrast with British practice, this majority is never controlled by a firm coalition of disciplined parties, let alone the single disciplined party that usually assures a stable majority in Britain. Nor does the French Premier possess that supplementary control over the loyalty and coherence of a majority—the British Prime Minister's unquestioned and constantly available right to dissolve parliament. The necessary coalition nature of Government majorities, the lack of party discipline, and the Premier's lack of effective dissolution powers, all mean that Assembly majorities for legislation are usually short-lived, casual majorities. To pass a legislative program the Premier must bargain with the *ministrables* for a series of casual majorities, often composed of different parties. To remain in office he must see to it that no hostile majority develops in the Assembly and that the existing unwillingness to upset him lasts as long as possible.

This situation of unstable majorities, based on a coalition of undisciplined parties, arose historically from the fact that the French party system evolved without playing a responsible role in organizing Government majorities in parliament. Up to the Third Republic the Premier and his ministers were usually responsible only to the king or emperor. The Premier was thus hardly ever the responsible leader of even a coalition majority in parliament. Thus the practice of an executive responsible to, yet independent of, the legislature, had no echo in France during the years when it was becoming established in England. Indeed, so unimportant was the Premier considered in France that the Third Republic's constitutional laws, admittedly drafted by a monarchist assembly, contained no mention of this office. The President of the Republic, considered to be the temporary replacement for a king, was declared explicitly to be head of the executive as well as chief of state, and indeed Adolphe Thiers, the first incumbent, combined these two functions in his person. Until 1877 the President and the Chamber of Deputies competed for control of the executive power as embodied in the Ministers and their Premier. The victory of the Chamber after the May 16 crisis led to the emasculation of the Presidency of the Republic by the customary, yet effective, bar to the President's power of dissolution.

Unfortunately, partisans of the administrative tradition of politics have never given up hope of re-creating a pre-republican executive, one independent of parliament and the representative power. And since France still has executive instability and ineffective government, their argument in favor of a strong and independent executive has never lost at least a superficial relevance. Today, however, an increasingly wider circle of political leaders are calling for a stronger Premier, one who has the means

of controlling coherent parliamentary majorities and who, as a consequence, has both authority and longevity in office. Indeed, the heart of
the debate over constitutional reform in France deals with the role of the
executive: shall the Premier be given a discretionary right to dissolve the
Assembly? Shall the Premier be elected directly by the people in order to
give him an authority approaching that of an American President? But
while the debate continues the Premier and his cabinet still occupy a
buffer zone between the civil service and the legislature. For unlike the
British model—and indeed quite opposed to it in effect—the French cabinet is today still a delegation from a temporary Assembly majority, and
not the leader or executive committee of a stable majority.

Because the Government is based on a majority created casually in
parliament, and not on a majority laboriously constructed by agreement
among national parties and sectors of public opinion in the country, it is
quite removed from a potential source of strength—the support and mandate of public opinion. Between the office of Premier and the people lie
the barriers of the National Assembly, the President of the Republic, even
the Council of the Republic, and finally the national party organizations.
These forces together prevent the choice of a man who could by force of
personality make contact with opinion and thus become somewhat independent of the changing humors of parliament. Prospective Premiers
realize, therefore, that longevity in office depends on raising few divisive
problems, avoiding pressure on parliament, and refusing all temptations
to appeal over the heads of the deputies to public opinion. In short, the
French Prime Minister remains in office as long as he remembers that
he is the delegate of a majority in parliament and, unlike the British Prime
Minister, has no rights against its will. In the rare cases when a Premier
and a Government coalition have been given a mandate in a general election—as in 1936 and 1945—or when crisis requires obvious governmental
energy, as in the case of Pierre Mendès-France and the Indo-China problem—then, for a brief moment, French parliamentarism may become similar to the British. For then special conditions have counterfeited for
France the *sine qua non* of effective parliamentary government: a coherent and disciplined majority.

Making a Government after Elections

The constitution envisages only three occasions for choosing a new
Premier and cabinet: after the election of a National Assembly; after a
Government has been defeated in a vote of confidence; or after a Government has been formally censured by the National Assembly. There have
been since 1946 only three elections; only five Governments, as of early
1957, have fallen on a vote showing lack of confidence; no Government

has ever been formally censured. Yet the National Assembly has had to make more than twenty new Governments under the Fourth Republic. We shall examine below the extra-constitutional conditions under which most French Governments fall. First, however, let us begin by examining the way in which a Government is made in the simplest case, that following a general election.

As in Britain the results of an election point to a winner, although in France it is not a single party. Rather it is a potential Government coalition made up of parties that either were formally allied in the election campaign or share a common political tendency that gained more seats relatively than did any rival tendency. For instance, in the elections of January 1956 the reformist parties allied in the "Republican Front"—the Socialists and Radicals—gained more seats than any other combination of parties, excluding the isolated Communists, and hence they were judged the winners. Soon after the first meeting of the new Assembly, the President of the Republic begins his conversations, calling upon the Presidents of the Assembly and of the Council of the Republic, as well as the heads of the party groups in the Assembly. This is a formality after an election for the first *ministrable* called to try to form a cabinet is bound to be the parliamentary leader of the strongest party in the winning coalition. Thus in January 1956 President Coty called first upon Guy Mollet, leader of the Socialist Party, the largest party in the Republican Front coalition, and this even though Pierre Mendès-France was clearly the strongest and most popular personality in the formal coalition.

When no large party is clearly dominant among the parties that made relative gains, one of the leaders of a small "hinge" party, which itself may have made no gains but is situated between parties that did gain strength, is chosen. This shows why membership in a small splinter group, located between large groups, is so popular. Typical of such a splinter party in the Republican Front coalition would have been either the small UDSR group, situated between the Socialists and the Radicals, or the small Gaullist group, on the right of the Radicals. However, whoever the President chooses, he is certain to be a member of the Assembly, for although constitutionally he can choose anyone—including a private citizen or senator —it is an almost unbroken custom to choose only deputies as candidates for Premier.

If the first *ministrable* called accepts, he becomes "Premier designate" (*Président du Conseil désigné*) and immediately sets about finding the other *ministrables* to serve in his cabinet and to reflect the majority he hopes and plans to represent. The choice of individual deputies and the distribution of the various ministerial posts among them is most critical. The choice of *ministrables* must necessarily be made among the parties that are going to form the majority coalition indicated by the election. But the so-called winning parties do not always possess among them an absolute majority of the seats in the Assembly. Therefore, what they must usually do is to form a center of attraction to which marginal deputies from small hinge groups add the needed extra votes. Guy Mollet, for example, benefited from the support of a sizable number of conservative deputies and representatives of overseas constituencies. Naturally, this is a source of instability, but given the fairly even distribution of seats among the groups, there is no alternative; often a ministerial post has to be offered to a deputy who is formally a member of a party that not only did not belong to the winning coalition but actually fought the coalition at the polls.

The *ministrables* chosen must not only agree with the Premier designate's program, but also be able to "deliver" as many votes of their party group as possible. If the "wrong" party leader is chosen these votes may not be available at the time of investiture. Or if the "wrong" post is offered to the "right" party leader, he may refuse to enter the cabinet and the votes may thus become unavailable. Not only is this whole process of matching deputies and ministerial posts a highly delicate one, based as it is on a number of personal judgments, but it also requires considerable time. Moreover, with the increasing power of the Council of the Republic it has become necessary to seek out one to three ministers from among the influential members of the upper house. A frequent source of delay may also arise from the need for protracted bargaining with party leaders, who sometimes may not be *ministrables* or even deputies, over aspects of the Government's proposed program or over the distribution of posts. During these negotiations, seldom lasting less than ten days, there is a caretaker Government in office that naturally cannot take a lead in policy. Consequently no policy is made other than that made silently by the day-to-day decisions of the civil service.

With the cabinet finally assembled and his program drafted, the Premier designate goes before the Assembly to make his program speech and solicit its "investiture"—as the vote of approval is called. It should be remembered that immediately following an election is one of the few times when a fairly clear popular mandate exists, and hence the Premier who presumably represents the winning political tendency is justified in presenting a coherent and fairly comprehensive program. This is not usually the case after a number of Governments have been made and have fallen, for then the Premier is elected on a single issue and not because he has an apparent mandate from the electorate.

After the Premier designate has made his program speech a general debate is opened during which representatives of all parties comment on the speech, question the Premier designate, and explain why their group will or will not vote for him.]The debate is used by the groups who oppose the Premier designate in order to dislocate his expected majority, although no one can be quite certain what his majority will be until after the vote. Moreover, before, during, and after the speech and debate there is great behind-the-scenes activity in the corridors and halls surrounding the public chamber. Opposition deputies buttonhole marginal members of the potential majority and try to influence them to change their votes; the members of the Premier designate's cabinet and their friends try to enlarge the expected majority by promising minor and as yet unawarded ministerial posts, or desired legislation, to important deputies whose groups are still "on the fence." The whole process is a powerful demonstration of the absence of party discipline and the already burgeoning divorce between decisions made in the "closed arena" of the Palais Bourbon and the popular mandate as expressed in the elections. For often, as a result of these conversations, parties that had been chastised by the voters are quietly invited to support a Government based on the winning majority in return for support of parts of their program, presumably a program that had also been rejected by popular opinion.

[After the general debate is closed a roll-call vote is taken in which only a simple majority of votes cast is required for investiture.] Prior to the 1954 constitutional revision an absolute majority of the total membership was required but this was often difficult to attain from among the deputies remaining after the permanent opposition of Gaullists and Communists was discounted. [If the Premier designate fails to receive a majority, the President of the Republic inaugurates a new round in the process of making a Government. In his choice of a new candidate, however, he takes into account the reasons for the failure of the first Premier designate.] The process now resembles the making of a Government after one or more have already lost the confidence of the Assembly. It therefore must be treated after an examination of how a Government is brought down by the Assembly.

Unmaking a Government

[The French constitution provides that, after investiture, a Premier and his cabinet will remain in office throughout the five-year life of a legislature save in the two exceptional cases when they are formally obliged to resign.] As in Britain, a Government must resign after it has been censured, which in France means by an absolute majority of the membership; or after it has lost a vote of confidence, which in France implies a more formal procedure, requiring announcement by the Government that it places a question of confidence on a given piece of legislation or on a specific procedural motion. [Following this announcement a twenty-four-hour cooling-off period must elapse, after which a general debate takes place and the vote of confidence is taken. Under recently revised rules of procedure in the Assembly, this vote must be a roll-call vote in which only votes cast personally by the deputies present are counted. This was to increase the solemnity of the occasion and, like the twenty-four-hour cooling-off period, prevent a snap decision or even a completely haphazard majority, which voting by proxy formerly allowed. Given the continuing high rate of absenteeism in the Assembly, the roll-call vote provision has served to make it more difficult for a Government to lose a vote of confidence because unless an absolute majority of the membership votes against the Government, according to the constitution the Assembly has not legally withdrawn its confidence.

From the beginning of the Fourth Republic in 1946 to early 1958 no Government suffered a vote of censure and only five Governments failed votes of confidence and thus came under the obligation to resign. Yet in that time over twenty Premiers and their cabinets resigned, the vast majority having "fallen" under circumstances not explicitly foreseen by the constitution. The average life of a Government from 1947 to 1956 was as a consequence six and a half months. During the hectic last twelve years of the Third Republic, from 1928 to 1940, Governments lasted an average of six months, and for the one hundred governments of the Third Republic, from 1870 to 1940, the average life was seven months, twenty-five days. Governments fell during the Third Republic, and indeed during the monarchies and empires of the last century, under circumstances similar to those of today and of course executive instability is in no way peculiar to the Fourth Republic. Nor must the significance of a French Government's resignation be closely compared to the resignation of a British Government. After all, it does not mean, as in Britain, the end of the majority party's rule, brought about by a breach in party discipline, which itself usually reflects a serious disaffection of public opinion from the Government.

Before trying to assess the significance of the French cabinet crisis, however, it is necessary to observe the three ways in which the great majority of these "non-constitutional" Government crises occur. Most resignations, and hence Government crises, take place following simple rejection of an important Government bill or motion by a majority in the Assembly. This of course includes those Government bills and motions that were deemed important enough to become questions of confidence and were rejected by less than the absolute majority of the membership required to create a formal obligation to resign. For example in March 1952, Edgar Faure's first Government resigned after defeat on a vote of confidence by only a relative majority. But Faure noticed that his defeat was due to the sudden defection of certain conservative and Radical deputies on whom he had formerly counted for a majority and hence judged the future of his legislative program to be very doubtful.

Some resignations occur after defeat on an entirely secondary bill or motion, or indeed even after simple rumors and conversations in the corridors indicating that as a result of possible defections the Government would be defeated on a forthcoming vote, whether put as a confidence vote or not. Thus in December 1952, the Government of Antoine Pinay resigned on the eve of an important vote because the Premier learned that the MRP, one of his two major Government parties, although for some time an unwilling partner in his generally conservative coalition, had decided to abstain. Realizing that this abstention was simply a prelude to the MRP's leaving the coalition altogether by voting against him, and knowing that their abstention in this instance would ruin his chances of success in the forthcoming vote, Pinay decided to hand in his resignation.

Finally, when there is serious disagreement over a matter of policy within the cabinet, whether simply a matter of personality or a reflection of doctrinal differences between the parties in the coalition, the Government often decides to resign. And when a member of the cabinet resigns his post for personal reasons, it is often seized upon as an opportunity to strengthen the cabinet and forestall a decline in its majority by reshuffling its members and perhaps even taking in representatives of new parties. In cases where the party coalition remains the same, however, the cabinet may resign in order that new and "unused" *ministrables* from the same parties may become ministers and try to continue the coalition's general program. A change in political circumstances often requires more conservative or more progressive representatives of the parties in the cabinet so that different marginal deputies may be attracted to vote with the Government on new legislation. It should be noted that this reshuffling can take place without a collective resignation of the cabinet. This is in fact the process followed in Britain where bringing in fresh personnel rarely leads to a cabinet crisis, given the strict party discipline and the Prime Minister's position as the recognized majority-party leader. In France, however, a more serious reshuffling does become a cabinet crisis because it drastically revises the Premier's original choice of ministers and implies a change in emphasis, if not in policy itself.

If in all the above cases there is no constitutional obligation to resign, why then have the great majority of resignations occurred in these circumstances? The answer of course is that the official, constitutional relations of the Premier with the National Assembly have little bearing on his real relations with that body. Constitutionally his position is similar to that of his British counterpart: he is obliged to retire only if censured or defeated on a confidence vote, and he is armed with the right to pose the question of confidence on any matter, thus introducing at least a threat of dissolution.] In fact, however, most French Premiers use the question of confidence only to get the appropriations bill or budget passed quickly, and they shy away from using it as a means of "disciplining" their majority by increasing the possibility of dissolution. The reason for this of course is that the French Premier is not the true leader of a parliamentary majority as the constitution describes him, but rather is the delegate of a prevailing majority. By tradition, moreover, he does not have the right to discipline his majority, because, unlike his English counterpart, he is the majority's emanation and not its respected leader. To remain in office after his majority has changed or has indicated its disapproval means not only that chances are small for getting further policies approved, but also that the Premier's future as a *ministrable* may be jeopardized, having thus seemingly proven himself to be intractable, and unmindful of the informal but all-important rules of the game. Only on the rare occasions when the Premier has great personal popularity in the country does his position approach that of the British Prime Minister. For under those conditions he can count on the pressure of public opinion to discipline his majority, momentarily giving him the weapon that party discipline continuously makes available to the British leader.

If then an indication of the Assembly's decreasing confidence, or threat of decreasing confidence, underlies most Government crises, what are the reasons for this instability of confidence and of majorities? Clearly the fact that the majority is a coalition of three or more different parties makes it inherently more unstable than a one-party or even two-party majority. The Premier often does not even control his own party's policy, let alone that of the others in his coalition. Even a strong party leader, such as the Radical Mendès-France, was unable to marshal the total Radical group in the Assembly on the vote of confidence of February 1955, the loss of which caused his resignation as Premier. But more important than this coalition problem is the fact that, for a deliberative body like the Assembly, shifting majorities are natural and inevitable. An attitude towards each public issue is formed by a parliamentary majority—not always the same majority, to be sure—and if the Premier sees that he is no longer in agreement with the majority or if the debate on the issue has produced a new majority, the Premier bows to parliament's deliberative will by resigning.

The shifting or casual majority and the deliberative function of parliament are common to both the American and French legislatures. However, in the United States the rigid separation of powers isolates the executive from being affected by the instability of congressional majorities. In Britain the two-party system, and a stable parliamentary majority based on party discipline, assure stability to the executive. In France none of these safeguards of stability exists. The Assembly is by tradition an undisciplined body of political groups, jealously guarding their supreme decision-making power. Elections are rarely able to bestow a mandate on one party or even on a coalition of parties. Coherent Government programs are not likely in coalitions and as a result party groups change their attitudes and hence their allies according to the issues before the Assembly. If the Government in office is unwilling to obey an emerging majority, it soon learns that it no longer has the Assembly's confidence. No formal vote is needed for this and, as seen above, the Assembly is usually displeased by a Premier's insistence on a formal vote of confidence, for this indicates an intention to threaten or discipline the Assembly. The Assembly prefers Governments that accept its will and the Governments that have lasted longest are like Monsieur Queuille's, which saw to it that few new issues came before parliament on which serious shifts in majority could occur, or, when they did arise, accepted the verdict of the new majority without protest.

With the election receding into the background the Assembly tends to become more and more isolated from public opinion and changes in group membership take place that further jeopardize the life of a Government. It is not unknown for a party group to lose half its deputies during the term of a legislature as a result of a revolt against party leadership. If a Government regularly depended on the votes of the whole group such a "dissidence," if it passed to the opposition, could oblige the cabinet to resign. Again the multiparty tradition and the lack of party discipline create an element of instability that British parliamentarism does not know, thanks, among other things, to the Prime Minister's power of dissolution, which is particularly useful against just such threats of dissidence. The French deputy's personal ambition for ministerial rank and the ease with which it can be satisfied in France's multiparty system clearly constitute other reasons why Government crises are more frequent in France and why the task of making a Government during the course of a given legislature is more usual than making Governments after elections.

Making a Government between Elections

Between elections the process is similar to that following a general election save for two points: first, the lack of popular mandate requires a number of additional stages during which a majority is "found"; second, the process, no longer dominated by the immediate results of the election, is now controlled by the struggle among groups within the Assembly over a solution to the problem or issue that brought down the previous Government. After the usual round of official consultations, the President of the Republic calls upon the leader of the group he believes, or has been advised, was principally responsible for bringing down the previous government. This is often a ritual act, because it usually means calling upon a party that has regularly opposed the Government and as a consequence is too isolated to form a cabinet with the party groups that have been in the defeated cabinet and most probably will be in the new cabinet as well.

After this step begins the serious effort to make a Government. With no obvious Premier designate available, the President asks a party leader to undertake a "mission of information" (*mission d'information*) which involves taking a "turn around the track" (*tour de piste*) of French parliamentary life, as well as making calls upon important government officials. The purpose of this is not primarily to see whether the leader undertaking the mission can marshal a majority and hence become Premier designate—although this is not to be excluded as a possibility. Rather it is simply to draw up a list of potential candidates who would be acceptable to the largest number of party and parliamentary leaders, given the political circumstances. With this slate in hand he returns to the President, who then calls one of them to his office in order to sound him out as a possible Premier designate. This man is immediately dubbed, quite literally, the "Premier sounded-out" (*Président du Conseil pressenti*), and he proceeds to take a "turn around the track" similar to the one accomplished during the mission of information, except that the Premier sounded-out is able to talk a bit more concretely about the prospective Government's program and can even bargain, in a general way, for the support of different groups in return for particular program concessions. Since various groups must be solicited, the concessions tend to be of all kinds and indeed are often contradictory in content, something that is less common in setting up a Government program after elections. But the incoherence of policy is the normal price of finding a majority and setting up a Government.

If the results of these talks indicate that notwithstanding promises of program concessions and ministerial posts, no majority would be possible for the first of the Premiers sounded-out, the President of the Republic sounds out other men on his list, taking into account the reasons—or what he thinks are the reasons—for the previous failure. Occasionally the President will choose first to sound out a party leader who he feels certain has no chance of getting a majority behind him. He does this, as in the case of President Auriol's choice of Antoine Pinay in March 1952, because he wishes to "raise the mortgage" (*lever l'hypothèque*) weighing upon the

Assembly as a result of corridor gossip about a certain kind of majority that he considers impossible—in this instance a conservative majority, which Auriol hoped to show was an absurdity by giving Pinay, its potential leader, the chance to fail ignominiously. Pinay, however, was successful, Auriol was obliged to name him Premier designate, and he went on to receive the Assembly's investiture as a result of an important dissidence in the Gaullist group, the possibility of which—unknown to the President at least—had suddenly made a true conservative majority feasible for the first time since the Liberation.

[A crisis is usually extended by the failure of a number of Premiers sounded-out to become Premiers designate.] The longer the crisis lasts the better the chances of the man who is named Premier designate late in the crisis and, of course, the President can hold out his personal candidate until the critical moment when he feels that the Assembly's growing anxiety over the length of the period without a Government will come to the aid of the next candidate. Here, as in the case of premature nomination of someone he dislikes, the hidden power of the President appears. The length of the crisis is naturally extended if the Assembly rejects a Premier designate after all indications during the "turn around the track" of the sounding-out stage had pointed towards ready approval. The reasons for this happening are legion, including, unfortunately, simple capriciousness on the part of many deputies and the bruised feelings of *ministrables* who had not been consulted. A more justifiable reason, however, is that the Premier designate's solution to the problem on which the previous Government fell, as described in his program speech, no longer accords with what the groups had thought he meant when he sketched it in brief outline at the sounding-out stage. This in turn may be due to simple bad faith on the part of the Premier designate or it may reflect changes deemed necessary at the last minute to placate a particularly intransigent yet valuable *ministrable* who brought up his own objections somewhere else along the line of conversations. In the case of the failure of a Premier designate, the President may return to any of the previous stages, including the earliest one—sending out a "mission of information." For it should be noted that this whole seemingly Byzantine and faintly malodorous process is based on easily adaptable custom and exists solely to "find" a majority in a group of men sharply divided. This can only be done by laborious, constantly crisscrossing conversations, and it is the job of the President to see that the "right" majority is found. If he so chooses, however, he may dispense with all preliminaries and name another Premier designate right off, but he will do this only if the crisis has gone on long enough to reveal that the temper of the Assembly is such as to make the chances of a second rejection slight.

The Government Crisis as an Institution

[With its factious bickering, its personal intrigues, its cynical bargaining, its general confusion and haphazardness, the French ministerial crisis is nonetheless central to the politics of the Fourth Republic.] But it should be remembered that the crisis is not the cause of this confusion and intrigue, but rather the result of them. It reflects the underlying and unreformed defects of French political life—the permanent flaws and continuing weaknesses of a political system still torn by a conflict between two rival patterns of institutions. It is a reflection of the lack of a constitutional settlement, a true separation of powers, and the endemic diversity of French political forces that employ the rival institutions of parliament and the administration to perpetuate their discrete existences. In the abstract one could say that French political institutions are too contradictory in purpose, and French political forces too incompatible in ends, to allow for any sort of government whatsoever. But in fact decisions are made by the system, for thanks to the safety valve of ministerial crisis short-term compromises can be made between parties over the content of policy, and between rival institutional patterns over the means of policy. For in effect the ministerial crisis is a miniature, bloodless, and highly routinized palace revolution in which executive power is passed from one group of political leaders to another group, with the tacit understanding that the turn of still others will soon arrive, thus obviating recourse to more violent strikes for power. With respect to a constitutional settlement and a real political consensus France is perhaps closer to a South American republic than it is to Britain and the United States. But the existence of the routinized ministerial crisis allows France to escape the serious economic and political dislocation that accompanies shifts of power in Latin America.

[A French Government's resignation is in no way comparable to one in England because in France the same *ministrables* usually come back in different posts, no important policy changes need occur, and, in any event, a highly efficient permanent civil service manages affairs quite competently during the crises.] In Britain the crisis occurs at a time when an election, following a dissolution of the Commons, would be fairly certain to produce a strong executive, either by returning the Government party or by bringing the opposition party to power with a clear mandate for new policy. In France the crisis is almost always independent of an expression of public opinion and thus neither increases nor decreases the stability of the new Government. Instability is accepted as the price for persisting in the luxury of unreformed politics and the crisis is simply the manifestation of this instability. Moreover the fact that many of the same *ministrables* return after a crisis to the new cabinet does not at all mean that policy remains consistent: as delegates of a new or modified majority they are agents of a new or modified policy. The personality price a *ministrable* pays to remain always near the exercise of governmental power is the constant subordination of his own doctrinal or policy views to the demands of the parliamentary majority then prevailing or on the point of emerging. A number of years of this continual compromise with one's values may permanently affect one's character, as we shall see in the following chapter.

[The cabinet crisis is the only means of making French parliamentarism viable,] lacking as it does the coherent majorities of the British model upon which it was patterned. The crisis is a "time out" during which a new team, usually fairly divided and lacking a real captain, comes into the game without any basic strategy for the rest of the half, but simply a tactical agreement for the play at hand—the issue on which the Government is formed. The resulting pattern consists of a multiplicity of partially effective executives instead of one stable and effective executive; a multiplicity of casual majorities instead of one majority based on a single party or on a firm coalition with a coherent program. French constitutional development has provided no place for a stable executive that is both responsible to parliament and yet independent enough to frame and pursue policy. The Premier has been either the docile agent of the true executive, the chief of state—as under the kings and emperors, in which case he was not responsible to parliament—or he has been the wholly dependent delegate of a casual majority of the parliament, as under the Third and Fourth Republics. This lack of a strong institutional leader of a parliamentary majority has in part been responsible for the continued existence of small, irrelevantly divided party groupings. For it is conceivable that the creation of a strong Premier's office, endowed with the full power of dissolution and based on a direct popular mandate, might ultimately lead to the creation of two relatively disciplined party coalitions. Casual majorities are, in turn, the only kind of majorities a much-divided party system can produce. In the United States a similar state of affairs does not affect executive stability, thanks to the presidential system of separate election. In France, however, it is at the heart of ministerial instability, for a new cabinet is required for each change in the majority. Clearly, however, the two factors are intertwined: the multiplicity of parties makes the creation of a stable executive, able to discipline his majority, unpopular with the leaders of the party factions, whose authority depends on the lack of discipline within a majority; the absence of a true executive makes it unnecessary for the parties to form more coherent groupings with which to support such an executive. Yet when a solution for a problem can no longer be put off, limited agreement on policy among the parties, as well as immediate executive action, must be provided for. [It is the cabinet crisis, the institutionalization of making and unmaking a Government, that promotes limited agreement and discovers a Premier to whom limited authority can be given] Short of radical constitutional reform this is the best a political community divided on basic means as well as on ends can hope for.

Meanwhile, [the institutionalized ministerial crisis serves as a safety valve against explosive pressures generated by France's fragmented body politic.] For this, however, the French pay a high price. In a country without consensus the very existence of the regime depends on its essential neutrality or lack of impact on the life of the nation. [Ministerial instability, by preventing Governments from doing much, paradoxically produces great social and economic stability.] Yet it is this rigidity of the French social fabric in the face of new internal and external problems that creates the potential of instability in the regime itself. For, unable to govern effectively, the French political system is always threatened with being overwhelmed by either hostile forces within or more powerful enemies from without. This was the case in 1870, again in 1940, and there is no indication that the future of the present constitutional arrangement is assured.

CHAPTER 19

Policy-Making

Scope and Process

The process by which French public policy is made is so conditioned by the politics of making, unmaking and preserving the cabinet that it is completely subordinate to the latter in importance and its product is often inferior to that of the other major powers. This product—legislation and administrative regulation—suffers primarily from three defects. First, the instability of Government coalitions based on undisciplined parliamentary groups has encouraged Governments to postpone action on problems that threaten to divide the coalition. Second, policy, when made, tends to be a rather pale compromise of the views of the innumerable interests that are active in parliament, thus losing the coherence it may have had when proposed by the cabinet. This is because of the executive's lack of control over the legislative process and the serious influence of pressure groups upon deputies. Third, the final form of important policies is often more the reflection of the will of the executing civil service than of either the responsible executive or the responsible legislature, or even the pressure groups that may have participated in the policy-making process. This is a result of the frequent inability of parliament to muster a positive majority in favor of a solution for a particular policy problem and of the cabinet instability which leaves the civil service without political direction for long periods, or under the supervision of short-term and inexperienced ministers. The net result of this diffuse and incoherent policy-making is that in French government the important democratic principle of accountability is often neglected. It is difficult for French public opinion to know who is responsible for a given government act or failure to act, and, therefore, to know which party, person, or institution can be held accountable for its effect on society. Indeed, the very complexity of the policy process in France discourages the precise and probing critique that could mobilize parliamentary opinion to reform policy-making institutions and break the vicious circle.

These defects in policy-making have long been characteristic of the pattern of power in the French political system. However, in the last decade the extent to which these defects have become responsible for preventing effective policy from being made has increased to a dangerous point in the face of the growing scope and complexity of the problems confronting government. Thus it is not only because the process of making policy has produced incoherent policy or no policy at all that Frenchmen are still so discontented with their Governments. For in large part the process of policy-making has been crippled by the kind of policies and the content of Government programs adopted since the Liberation. Obviously the attempt to reconstruct French war damage primarily by government initiative made normal policy-making processes all the more overloaded. Along with large-scale nationalization of industry and the creation of new social welfare services, reconstruction under government sponsorship brought government policy-making under the early Fourth Republic into far closer contact with the complex interests of French society than was the case with the laissez-faire processes of the Third Republic. The demands of interest groups have therefore found a much larger role in policy-making than ever before. Then too the complexity of economic and social legislation has obliged parliament to relinquish much of its power over the details of policy. In the case of tax laws in particular, parliament, if it wanted any tax reforms at all, was forced to extend the regulatory powers of the administration to the point where they verged on policy-making. Finally, the failure of a number of important government policies, such as the attempt to keep the French colonial empire intact or the vain efforts at playing the part of a great world power, has resulted in increased talk of revising the constitution in order principally to strengthen and stabilize the executive. In this case the nature of policy—its failure—has inspired, if not actually a change, at least a discussion of changes in the process of policy-making itself.

The postwar demand for policy was channeled in three directions: a demand for reforms of the structure of the French economy, in order to repair war damage quickly as well as to create a sector of socialized industry; the creation by the government of a vast program of social services and economic controls in order to maintain internal economic equilibrium during the difficult postwar years as well as to move toward a more equitable distribution of the national income; ambitious foreign and colonial policies in order to maintain France's great-power position and her "presence" throughout her traditional overseas possessions. The effects of these policy demands on the policy-making process were striking. Debate over the social welfare services, the controls on the economy and the structural reforms such as the nationalized industries served further to intensify party battles for the many conservative Frenchmen who still did not accept the Resistance leaders' goals of partial socialization. The nationalized industries, as well as the new social services, have added heavy responsibilities to the government, straining further its already limited ability to act. Finally the attempt to maintain France in her overseas territories, against the wishes of rebellious and nationalistic indigenous populations in Indo-China and Algeria, has placed a serious strain on the French economy and upon the national psychology. For with a declining overseas empire, many Frenchmen feel France's future as a great power is bleak and hence all efforts at reform and expansion are futile.

[In French foreign policy as in economic and social policy, the problem has not been one of mistakes as much as it has been one of not making decisions at all—one way or another.] Thus Tunisia and Morocco, now independent states, would still be part of the French Union had a French Government decided once and for all either to subdue the nationalists by force, as France is attempting to do in Algeria, or to embark upon a policy of negotiation and compromise that would have extended autonomy to the two countries within the French community. But instead of these policies, no decisions were made at all since there existed no stable majority for one or another of the two alternatives. This *immobilisme*, or lack of positive policy, is even more strikingly illustrated in the economic sphere, where it has often taken the form of policies that cancel themselves out.

Frenchmen still recall with irony the effects of one such political compromise in economic policy in January 1948. Conservatives in the first Schuman Government urged the immediate re-establishment of a free gold and foreign exchange market in France, ostensibly to make the return of expatriated capital more attractive to investors, and thus contribute toward promoting the much sought-for "confidence" in business circles. Socialist opposition to such a "class policy" immediately threatened the life of the coalition cabinet. In order to restore confidence yet keep the Socialists within the majority, Finance Minister René Mayer decided to accompany the reopening of the gold market by the recall of all 5000-franc notes—which had been the principal instrument of hoarders, speculators, and black-marketeers, all sworn enemies of the Socialists. The measure, moreover, was to serve as an anti-inflationary move as well, supposedly offsetting any possible inflationary effects of freeing gold and capital trading. But the net economic result was that confidence was not restored, thanks partly to the government's delayed program of reimbursement for the withdrawn 5000-franc notes, and inflation and speculation were encouraged by the effects of freeing the gold and capital markets. True, both Socialists and conservatives did remain within the cabinet.

[More than anything else French economic, social, and financial policies since the war illustrate how much the nation's ills are traceable to the defects of her political system.] Dependence on shaky and fundamentally incoherent majorities—such as one binding Socialists and conservatives together—makes very slim the margin of policy decisions that are acceptable to all members in such a coalition. As a consequence energetic decisions to undertake effective or simply technically correct policies are avoided in order to remain in power. But there comes a point in living with an unsolved economic or financial problem when a decision must be taken, and it is at that point that French Governments invariably fall. Some sort of decision is then proposed by the new Premier designate, very often the very policy proposal that the parliament refused to approve for the previous Government. In any case one can be sure that the proposal will almost never be so sweeping as to jeopardize his chances for investiture. Meanwhile, changes in French society are slow and the ancient economic and social interests that underlie the basic party divisions and that nurture the unreformed political system remain intact. Thus the circle is closed, within which France allows herself the luxury, as one acute observer has put it, of keeping time by her own steeple clock.

Role of the Government: Policy Initiation

One of the major differences between English and French parliamentarism is that while in France the Government also initiates most policy-making, it loses control of final determination to the legislature.] Thus the executive's role in the process is decidedly limited, a situation produced by the conscious effort of the drafters of the 1946 constitution as well as the slow accretion of custom that has been encouraged since the early Third Republic by partisans of the pure representative tradition of politics. Nor can the Government's role be enlarged at the final stage of policy execution, for although the bureaucracy is nominally under the cabinet's direction, it has traditionally shown an independence and a will of its own in interpreting and applying the law. The consequence of this is that French policy-making somewhat resembles the American in its diffuseness, and in the difficulties involved in knowing exactly whom to hold accountable for policy decisions. For, given the limited role of the French cabinet in policy determination, the natural inclination to hold the Government responsible is not always justified in fact even if it is in theory.] One of the causes of ministerial instability is the habit of parliamentary majorities insisting on the responsibility of cabinets for policy, thus using the Government as the scapegoat for policy failures and thereby shifting responsibility from their shoulders to those of expendable coalition cabinets.

The Ministers and Their Departments

[Most proposals for taking governmental action originate with the executive and in particular with the specialized government departments.] Thus during the first legislature, 1947-51, of the 1289 laws enacted, 937 originated in ministries while only 352 originated as private members' bills in parliament. Each ministerial department is headed by a member of the cabinet assigned by the Premier—that is, a *ministrable*, whose political attributes have been described above. [In recent years cabinets have been made up of ten to fifteen full Ministers and another ten to twenty Secretaries of State (*Secrétaires d'Etat*) and Under Secretaries of State (*Sous-secrétaires d'Etat*).] The Ministers head the most important departments such as Foreign Affairs, Justice, and Finance, and are drawn from among the more powerful *ministrables* in the Government coalition. The Secretaries and Under Secretaries head lesser departments such as Public Works, Post, Telegraph and Telephones, and Information, or they serve as second in command in a ministerial department.

[Both the number and rank of the departments vary according to the political requirements of the Government in power.] If an important *ministrable* insists on heading the Merchant Marine department, the Premier may elevate it to the rank of a full ministerial department in order to satisfy the *ministrable* in question. If a Premier wishes to cut down the number of cabinet members, he may amalgamate a number of lesser departments and attach them to one of the larger ministerial departments. Finally, if he wishes to demonstrate his Government's particular interest in a special problem, say delinquent youth, he is perfectly free to create a new department of delinquent youth affairs. Similarly, if political necessity requires a large number of *ministrables* in the Government, he may split up a number of departments or create new departments just to make room for the precious *ministrables*.

When a *ministrable* becomes a member of a cabinet, he is liable to undergo a serious change in outlook. As a deputy his efforts were bent toward becoming a Minister and hence even in cases of Governments whose general policies he approved, he did not overly regret their fall. For a cabinet crisis at least offered the opportunity of becoming a Minister and hence much of his time as deputy was spent in devising means for bringing about this opportunity. [But once that exalted station has been attained his object is to remain there as long as possible, since the job can be very attractive indeed. In many ministerial posts the incumbent receives, aside from a most adequate salary, a handsome apartment in the ministry's building, usually situated in the center of Paris and endowed with a generous entertainment allowance. There is of course a certain amount of "spoils" available to the Minister for distribution to his friends in the form of minor posts in the Parisian and provincial services of the department, appointments to the Legion of Honor, and an unlimited supply of promises to change regulations in order to help certain groups and individuals. Further, there is the respect that surrounds a Minister and in title-conscious France the constant pleasure derived from being henceforth referred to, whether in office or not, and until the end of his days, as: *Monsieur le Ministre.*

Increasingly the post of Minister requires a real professional, an administrator having considerable *expertise.* Yet the necessity of choosing *ministrables* for their political rather than their administrative talent works against this. And once in office the cabinet's unstable majority does not allow its members to be overly inventive or energetic in their posts if the cabinet and their own jobs are to last. So although the requirements of substantive policy have created the need for a new kind of Minister, the requirements of traditional parliamentarism more often than not lead to the appointment of the political artist and not the expert administrator.

Under the Fourth Republic the situation of the *ministrables* has produced a number of striking individual personality transformations. Most of the current *ministrables* come from among the crusading Resistance leadership. Originally they saw in ministerial posts the means of participating in the construction of the new France dreamt of during the occupation. Many of them developed considerable technical skill in their first posts, and in the early days they fought hard to get Assembly approval for what they considered the "necessary" policy, no matter what the parliamentary situation was. But with the re-establishment of traditional French politics they learned that the life of a coalition Government often depends more on the problems it avoids than on the policies it succeeds in guiding through parliament. Compromises such as Finance Minister René Mayer's bargaining the deflationary policy of withdrawing the 5000-franc notes against the inflationary policy of freeing the gold market, became the price of cabinet, and therefore ministerial, longevity. And since they were human and enjoyed power, many of the former idealists found themselves rationalizing their continual compromises with principle by openly insisting there was no alternative to their policies. It is to this process that Frenchmen critical of the present political system refer when they add to a long list of defects the final and unforgivable sin of "gobbling up men."

Like the Minotaur of the ancient legend who devoured his offspring, the Fourth Republic has taken a heavy toll among the youthful—or those who were youthful and hopeful at its foundation.

A few *ministrables* have escaped this fate, thanks to long tenure in a single ministerial post through various Governments, which permitted them to follow a positive program through to completion. One former Resistance leader, Eugène Claudius-Petit, did a good job in his five years (under eight Governments) as Minister of Reconstruction and Housing. The Socialist Resistance leader Robert Lacoste achieved much during his four years as Minister of Industry, as did his MRP successor Jean-Marie Louvel, in his three years in the post. But these were essentially technical jobs, dealing with such administrative matters as rebuilding war damage and allocating scarce raw materials, and controversial political problems were rarely dealt with. Similarly the continuity of one party in a given ministry—such as the long tenure of the MRP in the Foreign Ministry, or of Radicals and Socialists in Interior and Education—reflect more the power of the parties in insisting on their retention of ministerial plums than a continuity of policy in line with the doctrines of the parties concerned. There is in fact considerable stability in the personnel of French Governments, for, after all, outstanding *ministrables* constitute a group whose composition changes slowly. In the fourteen cabinets between 1946 and 1951 there was an average of only six new faces among the twenty or so Ministers in each succeeding cabinet. However, and here is the significant point, it was in the vital posts of Finance, Defense and Colonial affairs that the new faces cropped up and in which the greatest turnover of *ministrables* occurred. It was in certain politically sensitive jobs that the least continuity of personnel existed, reflecting, in fact, the slight continuity of policy in those fields.

The Minister has contact with the bureaucrats of his department not through a permanent under secretary as in Great Britain, but through a large personal office staff he brings with him from his political party or his circle of friends. This is known as the "ministerial cabinet" (*cabinet ministériel*) and is made up of assorted high civil servants on leave, bright young men from the universities and business, journalists, members of the minister's family, and faithful party workers. The bureaucrats in his personal staff are employed to "speak the language" of the civil servants in his department. They are the ones who aid the Minister in choosing from the Government bills and programs suggested by the civil servants those he will urge the cabinet to adopt as Government policy. They also aid the Minister in approving or rejecting the many ministerial regulations, decrees, and orders that are constantly brought to him for his signature by the permanent staff.

The bright young men and journalists are the Minister's eyes and ears in parliament, in the ministry, and among important circles of opinion and influence. They inform him as to which measures have a chance of parliamentary approval, what parliament thinks of his record as Minister, how influential interests are reacting to a Government policy of which he was the author, and which *ministrables* in parliament are "out to get him." With the help of the permanent bureaucracy, these members of his personal staff also prepare his speeches and draft answers to the innumerable questions on his department's activities posed in writing or orally by the deputies, usually on behalf of their constituents.

The Premier's Office and Policy Co-ordination

The policy proposals selected by a Minister are brought to the cabinet meetings for discussion and decision. But the complexity of modern governmental problems customarily requires that other departments be brought into the final drafting of the proposal for action, especially if it involves a large expenditure of government funds, for this might mean cutting the appropriation for another department. Under the Third Republic the Premier alone was responsible for this co-ordination, a task that became increasingly difficult for him to accomplish in the last crisis-ridden years of the regime. Moreover, although he was chief of the executive, the Premier had then no permanent staff, but was dependent primarily on his personal cabinet or on the civil servants of the regular ministerial department he chose to head along with the Premiership. Today, the French Premier has his own regular government department of bureaucrats, a division of which is called the General Secretariat of the Government. This performs the important task of co-ordinating the policy proposals of Ministers, and after cabinet approval transforms them into Government bills. The Secretariat also submits Government bills to the Council of State (*Conseil d'Etat*), a body of high civil servants who act as the government's permanent legal advisers, empowered to redraft bills if they seem improper or unconstitutional.

To assist the Premier in co-ordinating the initiation of Government policy and supervising the executive branch, a number of other important government services are also grouped under the Premier's office (*Présidence du Conseil*). Besides the Secretariat there is the successor to the Monnet Plan organization, which offers the Government long-range economic advice; the government publications office; the personnel office of the French civil service; an office for co-ordinating defense and security policies (*Secrétariat Permanent de la Défense Nationale*); the Atomic Energy commission; the general accounting office; and finally the little known and mysterious SDECE (*Service de Documentation Extérieure et de Contre-*

Espionnage), which is roughly France's equivalent of the American Central Intelligence Agency.

[Collective responsibility for Government policy is taken in meetings of all the members of the Government in what is known formally as the Cabinet Council] (*Conseil de Cabinet*). The Premier presides and it is in this group that the day-to-day program is hammered out. The civil servant head of the Premier's Office is present to take the minutes and present the agenda. Unlike the British cabinet, the French is not truly a deliberative body in the sense of making policy decisions that have a good chance of being enacted into law. Rather it is a general strategy board that advises the Premier as to the political ways and means of marshaling a parliamentary majority for a given Government policy, and the political liabilities or assets of presenting a certain Government bill. Here again the all-pervading problem of preserving the Government's unstable majority obliges the cabinet to discuss policy proposals more often in terms of their effect on parliament and the Government majority than in terms of their intrinsic value to France. Cabinet meetings, though they may start with a discussion of the substance of a Minister's proposed bill, almost necessarily have to end with a discussion of the chances for its passage and the effect of the parliamentary reaction on the cabinet's future. After all, even if the Government decides to present the bill to parliament, the basic determination of policy rests with the parliament, its committees, and the majority that develops for or against the measure. [The cabinet is reduced to the task of devising strategy for retaining as much as possible of its original proposal without endangering its majority in the National Assembly] a prospect the British cabinet rarely has to worry about.

[Occasionally the Premier and those members of his Government who are full Ministers meet under the chairmanship of the President of the Republic as a body called the Council of Ministers (*Conseil des Ministres*). The purpose of these meetings is to deal with the most vital matters of national security, defense, and foreign policy, matters so important that it is felt that the highest officer of the state must be consulted.] As the prime element of continuity in French government, the President of the Republic is entitled to know of commitments made by a Government that might affect France in the future. His wisdom and experience, moreover, are sought at these meetings and indeed Presidents Coty and Auriol have both used them to expand their role in policy-making by acting as spokesmen for the nation's long-term interests.

Relations with Parliament

[Although parliament makes the basic policy decisions, the Government has much influence upon the legislature's ability to make these decisions, if only little influence upon the content of such decisions in comparison with the British cabinet. This limited influence is derived, first, from the right to demand that certain procedures be followed during debate upon legislative proposals and in the conduct of parliamentary sessions; and, second, from the fact that parliament often gives the Government the power to make rules having the force of law in connection with problems that it cannot itself resolve.

In debate on any bill before the Assembly the Government can demand that an amendment increasing expenditure or reducing revenue, proposed by a deputy, be separated from the bill in question and transformed into a separate measure. This allows the Government to protect the integrity of its version of a bill until it has been passed or rejected by parliament. Probably the most useful power of the Government is the simple right to participate in open debate in both houses. For if the Premier has a brilliant mind and is an accomplished orator the chances are that his pleas in favor of or against a bill will influence a few of the marginal deputies. Logical and well-styled argument and the force of personality carry more weight in the French parliament than in that of any other major legislative body. The career of a great Third Republic parliamentarian like Aristide Briand was made by his "violoncello voice" coupled with the arguments produced by a shrewd, ironic and well-trained lawyer's mind.

Another procedural power is the Government's right to transform a vote on any bill into a vote of confidence, either positive or negative. If a previous Government has fallen in the constitutionally prescribed pattern within the preceding eighteen months, this right can provide the Premier with the power to threaten dissolution. But even when no such situation exists, which is the normal state of affairs, the possibility of calling for one vote of confidence after another on various parts of a Government bill, or on a few Government bills, in the context of the twenty-four-hour cooling-off period required before the balloting on a vote of confidence, can cumulatively create an atmosphere of urgency that often comes to a Government's aid in getting support for its program. A third tool of the Government against the legislature is its recently re-established right to close the annual parliamentary session by decree after the minimum of seven months has been attained, or to adjourn parliament for varying periods of time during the session. This aids the Government directly in only a negative way by eliminating for a few weeks or months the possibility of defeat following a sudden adverse vote in the Assembly. Indirectly, however, it can be of vast use to a Government by allowing it a period of time, free of the constant need to answer questions and criticism in parliament, free of the demands of a parliamentary agenda over which it has no control, during which the Government can exercise its broad regulatory powers. These are the powers all executives possess to write detailed regulations applying the broad principles set forth in laws passed by the legislature. In France these powers are often extended by the Assembly, just prior to adjournment, with the express understanding that the Government will use them to take a number of quasi-legislative decisions on matters that parliament was unwilling or unable to decide.

Governments also are occasionally given powers of delegated legislation —the right to make rules having temporarily the force of law. In France this practice dates from the 1920's, when economic crises presented problems that parliament was unable to resolve even after long debate. Thus the Poincaré Government of 1924 asked for and received the power to make important financial reforms by means of decrees, called decree-laws (décrets-lois). The abuse of this institution in the 1930's led the constitution drafters of 1946 to declare formally that parliament could not delegate its lawmaking power. But the institutional malady for which decree-laws were a cure remained: less than two years after the constitution was adopted the Assembly found itself unable to agree on a reform of tax legislation. In order to get the needed policy changes on the law books, the Government persuaded the Assembly to pass a "framework law" (loi cadre) empowering it to draft the tax reform and deposit it with the Bureau of the Assembly. If at the end of a certain period of time the latter had not rejected the Government's "contents" for the "framework," the draft would automatically become transformed into law—the Assembly thus having passed it by default!

It was for a similar purpose that later Governments persuaded the Assembly to transform part of this rule-making power into what was, in effect, true legislative power. This was done by a law that arbitrarily declared certain policy matters to be in the realm of executive regulation rather than legislation. Unlike the prewar decree-laws, which were of a temporary nature, this extension of regulatory powers, exercised formally by the Premier's office, has no time limit and succeeding Governments can, within the scope of the policy matter to which regulatory power has been extended, alter or abrogate the rules made by past Governments. Usually the Government will seek advice from such advisory bodies as the Economic Council and the Assembly of the French Union, as well as from the Assembly's Finance Committees, as to the content of these regulations.

In 1954, however, a complete return to the procedures of the decree-laws took place. At the present writing the constitutionality of these methods has not been challenged, probably because they were surrounded by far greater safeguards against abuse than were their prewar predecessors. The temporary power to alter laws by decree is now given only to a specific Government and the areas of policy that can be affected by decree are carefully enumerated. Moreover, the advice of the Council of State is often required and of course the usual requirement that decrees ultimately be presented for parliamentary ratification is again stipulated. Thus through the new decree-laws, the framework law, and through extensions of executive regulatory powers, Governments are able to make progress toward achieving their programs independently of parliament. Yet it should be remembered that a Government employs these powers only with the express permission of the legislature. Parliament knows too well that the greatest threat to its prestige is its own frequent fits of policy-making paralysis. Letting the Government have its way on specific matters through these procedures is a small price to pay for its unchallenged authority on most decisions of public policy. Moreover, framework laws and the rest are all useful ways in which a parliament can shift responsibility to the Government for controversial policy-making such as tax laws. These easily produce bad electoral results yet are necessary for the conduct of government. Nor does the executive protest these shifts of responsibility, for its coalition nature allows each party in turn to shift the blame for the necessary yet unpleasant policy to one of its partners.

Finally mention must be made of the many opportunities Ministers have for meeting deputies and senators, legislative committee chairmen, and party group leaders, in the course of parliamentary proceedings. These will be discussed in detail directly below; however, it should be noted here that in certain political situations, especially if the Premier is leader of a large party group, he can exert considerable influence over his coalition majority by promising small groups or individual deputies that he will incorporate their policy proposals in the Government program. As we have seen earlier this constant bargaining over policies for the preservation of a majority is the principal reason for the incoherence and inconsistency of French policies and for the phenomenon of *immobilisme*.

Role of Parliament: Legislation

While most policy is initiated by the executive and over seventy per cent of the laws are proposed by that branch, it is the parliament that is most influential in determining the ultimate content of Government policies. It has been seen in the previous chapter that the drafters of the constitution meant the Assembly to have this predominance, and it has been argued above that the incoherence of French policies is a reflection of the instability and incoherence of the majorities in the Assembly. To this legal superiority in influence has been added a large body of custom and procedure surrounding legislation, much of which dates from the

Third Republic, and all of which supports the predominance of the Assembly.

An obvious index of this superiority is that the French parliament insists upon being more involved in the bulk of policy-making than does the British parliament. Thus French laws are not only more detailed in application than British laws, but, above all, they are more numerous and refer to a greater variety of subjects. Between 1946 and 1951 the National Assembly passed an average of 286 laws per year, while the House of Commons passed only an average of 56 per year. This is explainable by the fact that in England a much greater use is made of delegated legislation, which allows cabinet ministers to make fairly important policy by "statutory instruments" or, in French terms, by decree. Thus whereas in England important changes in the social welfare services have been made by decree, in France the Government has been obliged to ask parliament for laws to make roughly equivalent reforms.

The natural superiority of the Assembly in policy-making comes from the fact that the cabinet's life is implicity placed in jeopardy on almost every important piece of legislation it considers. Whether a bill is of private or Government origin, the Assembly's disposition of it invariably reveals the condition of the Government's majority. Moreover, the making and unmaking of a Government usually is closely related to the legislative process: a Government falls because the Assembly refuses to pass a law it considers vital or insists on passing a law it opposes; a new Government is made because its promised version of the law or policy is acceptable to an Assembly majority. Often this attitude toward vital Government proposals is developed in the Assembly's committee system, which has the power to revise Government bills completely, or in the Assembly's open debate on legislation, during which, as we shall see, Premier and Ministers are in a relatively weak position, although not without some powers.

The Government's position in the lawmaking process is that of an accused man under cross-examination by judge and jury, as well as by the prosecutor. Indeed, its position is even more limited, for the Government does not have the accused's right to present his side of the case in full: unlike the British parliament and the American Congress, the French Assembly provides the Government with no regular opportunity for presenting a complete and interrelated annual Government program such as can be presented in the Address from the Throne or the annual State of the Union message. Nor would there be much sense in such a declaration, given the short life and unstable majorities of French coalition Governments. But it is indicative of the jealously guarded predominance of the legislature that such an opportunity for the Government to state its case is not allowed.

For the Government, legislation is essentially a piecemeal, catch-as-catch-can affair. At every stage fragmentation of its program and alteration of its proposals face it. In the committees interest groups find an arena for urging changes that are of benefit to them. In the general debate individual deputies, representing interests or their own eccentric views, have a further opportunity to alter the Government's text. Since there is even less party discipline in the Assembly than in Congress, the Government can rarely fall back on its coalition for support against such depredations. It usually must bargain one amendment against another in order to retain the heart of a bill, the result being the pallid compromises on policy spoken about earlier.

At all stages of legislation the parliament can oblige the Government to modify, or even withdraw, policy proposals by simply threatening their defeat. Only by posing the question of confidence can the Government discover whether the Assembly is really willing to upset the cabinet in order to oppose the specific policy. But it has been seen that few Premiers are willing to use the vote of confidence on legislation other than the budget because by custom it connotes an attempt to coerce the sovereign Assembly. Usually if a Government encounters serious opposition in the committees, and if in debate there is indication that its majority will not support it on the bill, it may use defeat on the measure—even though confidence has not been officially put in question—or even the threat of defeat, as the occasion to resign.

The Committee System and Pressure Groups

As in the United States Congress the life of a piece of legislation begins in one of the specialized legislative committees, called by the French "permanent general committees" (*commissions générales permanentes*) in order to distinguish them from *ad hoc* committees that are sometimes appointed for investigative purposes. There are nineteen of these permanent committees in the Assembly, each corresponding to a subject of legislation usually parallel to a ministerial department. A committee has forty-four members elected according to proportional representation of party groups. The members elect their chairman from their midst. Both Government and private members' bills are assigned to the proper committee by the professional staff of the Assembly.

Although membership and chairmanship in committees is by election, an informal system of seniority operates somewhat, for certain important *ministrables* are repeatedly elected to the more powerful committees. They build up, as a consequence, considerable technical competence in the subject matter of the committee. This as well as their general prestige as *ministrables*, prepares them for specific ministerial posts and makes them formidable critics of Government bills, their *expertise* indeed often serving their ambitions as *ministrables*. In practice, however, neither committee chairmen nor committee actions on Government bills are serious threats to a cabinet's life, although potentially the committee stage can serve as the beginning of a decided campaign to defeat the Government by blocking legislation it considers vital.

[Assembly committees meet on Wednesdays when the Assembly usually does not convene in plenary session.]After a committee receives a bill it has two weeks in which to name one of its members as the *rapporteur* (reporter) for the bill. The *rapporteur* then has a maximum of three months during which to prepare a report on the pros and cons of the proposed legislation; this report, when he submits it to the committee, serves as the basis for its deliberations. The Government has the technical right to oblige a committee to report out a bill once the three-month limit has been reached, but this is never necessary, for on important legislation the committee acts with considerable speed.

[In the preparation of his report the *rapporteur* has the facilities of a small committee secretarial staff plus one permanent civil servant from the appropriate ministerial department.] Only in the case of the Finance Committee is there a research staff comparable to the large staffs attached to American congressional committees. Thus if he should require documentation to write his report, the *rapporteur* must turn either to the relevant ministry—a source he is likely to suspect of favoritism toward the cabinet version of the bill—or to sources outside the Government. The report is largely a personal task in which the deputy serving as *rapporteur* has considerable opportunity for showing his abilities. If he is ambitious he may choose to use an important Government bill to show off his critical gifts, naturally more appreciated by a body that is institutionally hostile to the executive than would be an analysis emphasizing the positive qualities of the legislation.

[The deliberation of the whole committee on a piece of legislation begins, then, with this original report. It ends with the drafting of a general committee report passed by majority vote.]It is during these deliberations that a committee fills its historic role as an institution of the "assembly regime." Committees in France originated as the practical means of permitting an all-powerful revolutionary assembly to discharge its policy-making functions effectively. When in the nineteenth century the legislative branch was turned into a rubber stamp by kings and emperors, the committee meetings, closed to the Government by tradition, remained the last preserve of parliamentary criticism and independent judgment. When under the Third Republic the partisans of the representative tradition gained dominance, they reinforced the power of the legislative committees in order to insure the legislature's general superiority over the executive and its bureaucratic agents. Indeed, they made the committees permanent and specialized so that they would be all the more effective as watchdogs of government operations. For the committees were specialized microcosms of the Assembly as a whole, which was itself the agent of the sovereign will of the people. Situated at the heart of the legislative process committees became the target for the pressure of interest groups working for or against the adoption of certain laws. After all, committees seemed to have been originally intended to "democratize" policy-making by allowing the representative branch to develop its own expert view of a measure proposed by the administrative branch. What could be more "democratic" than incorporating the views of the people as represented by economic and social interest organizations? This process of "hearing" the views of economic and social interest groups, however, remained informal, without the organized and public hearings that legislative committees in the United States conduct.

This democratic origin and traditionally anti-Government function of the French committee system has made of it the prime channel for pressure-group penetration of the policy-making process. Under the Fourth Republic pressure-group activity has, if anything, been increased because of the proliferation of legislative subcommittees that deal with laws affecting individual industries. Thus the most direct access to legislation for an interest group is to elect an employee of their professional association to the Assembly, who then may succeed in becoming chairman of the legislative committee or subcommittee dealing with laws affecting their interests. There is, indeed, the case of the president of the petroleum industry's trade association who became chairman of the subcommittee dealing with legislation concerning that industry. Similarly an official representative of the trucking industry and one for the clothing industry became deputies and immediately found themselves active in the committees concerned with their former occupations. Nor is this universally condemned, because it is seen as a sensible way of providing the committee with *expertise* and the views of the "consumers" of the legislation, both useful in criticizing the proposals of the Assembly's real adversary—the Government.

Less direct is the influence pressure groups exert by exploiting the most serious material and technical deficiency of the French lawmaking process: the lack of adequate research and secretarial assistance for the individual deputy. Neither the *rapporteur* in writing his original report, nor the committee in deliberating on the report and on the bill, nor the individual deputy in making up his mind on how to vote in committee and later in the Assembly debate, has access to the kind of documentation and expert advice available to American congressmen. The Assembly's small library is more for browsing than for research and the Assembly's staff is not adequate for the research needs of committees. Moreover the secretarial help available to a deputy is wholly inadequate and the overworked civil servant attached to the committee has only his highly suspect home ministry as a source of documentation.

Into this vacuum pour masses of carefully and attractively prepared information originating in the offices of trade unions, professional and trade associations, chambers of commerce and the many small private research organizations that work for industries or individual businesses. Less frequent, yet almost more attractive to deputies, are the outright offers of secretarial help from a private organization—the offer of the services of a secretary three times a week, or of a bright young man who will help the rushed and relatively inexpert deputy with his work. Some of the information and research is distributed in the informal "study groups" (*groupes d'études*) for particular industries or sectors of the economy that are made up of deputies of all parties coming from districts in which these interests are powerful. Roughly analogous to the American "cotton bloc" or "farm bloc," these study groups are more specialized and organized, being founded usually by a deputy who has a close tie to the industry. Although they are formally prohibited by the Assembly's rules they meet regularly in rooms of the Assembly or Council of the Republic, at which time representatives of the industry may address them, documentation may be distributed and a discussion held on the current legislation affecting the industry or interest concerned. Then the members return to the Assembly or the committees, presumably enlightened and technically prepared to criticize the bill up for consideration—although the enlightenment can hardly be said to come from an unbiased source.

By all odds the most important, although the most indirect, means by which a pressure group influences legislation is the normal practice of deputies seeking places on committees that deal with the economic and social interests of their constituents. This results in the exaggerated overrepresentation of certain regions on committees dealing with matters relevant to their interests. Thus on the new beverages committee of the Assembly the four winegrowing departments, while theoretically entitled to one seat on the basis of population, managed nonetheless to get nine seats. Furthermore, it is traditional that the labor committee be dominated by former trade union officials and the education committee by former schoolteachers. The result of this is that deputies committed to the particular points of view of economic and social interests, dominate the deliberations of legislative committees. Thus the nature of the committee membership, as well as the nature of the documentation and research available, tends to influence committee deliberations in the direction of the particular interest.

[But what makes the committee stage especially destructive of a coherent government policy is the complete absence of any formal Government representative in committee deliberations.] Indeed the Government is even more at a disadvantage with its legislative proposal than is the private member, for the latter may attend at will all committee meetings and take part in all proceedings save the final vote. To be sure, a Minister can state the Government's case in committee meetings and the committee can call upon a Minister or a civil servant from a department to explain a Government bill. But in both cases the Minister is in the role of an expert and not the defender of Government policy in the committee's discussions. This custom was adopted originally to protect the weak parliamentary committees from the pressure of an all-powerful executive. With the evolution of French parliamentarism it has simply encouraged parliamentary fragmentation of Government policy and protected particular interests from any effective counter arguments by a Minister representing, at least nominally, the general interest. The continued absence of Government spokesmen during committee deliberations is another illustration of how unreformed institutions of French government tend to serve functions quite different from those for which they were originally intended. Excluding the Government from committee deliberations affects the efficiency of the policy-making process by preventing the Government from explaining the need for a proposed piece of legislation before it is revised by the committee.

[These additions and substractions made by a committee take the form of amendments,] motions asking the Government to revise portions of the bill, and even "counter-bills" (*contre-projets*), which are often complete revisions of the original Government proposal. These modifications are requested by either the *rapporteur* or by members of the committee; they are then voted upon by the committee and if they are accepted the bill is modified accordingly. [After all changes have been made the bill is voted on as a whole, the committee deciding for or against recommending its adoption by the Assembly.] When this decision has been taken—usually after many Wednesdays of deliberation—the bill, in the form of the general committee report, is sent to the Bureau of the Assembly. The Conference of Presidents then proceeds to find a place on the Assembly's agenda during the following two weeks for the bill's first reading.

Assembly Debate on Legislation

[No matter how much a legislative committee changes a piece of legislation, it is the Assembly as a whole that determines its final form and disposition.] Debate, motions, amendments from the floor, and "counterbills" drafted during debate can all change the committee's draft or disregard it entirely by adopting the legislation as originally proposed, or reject both committee and original versions to adopt a third. In the case of Government bills, the implicit jeopardy in which the cabinet's life is placed by the legislative process appears during the debate and the voting of the Assembly. Here, unlike the committee stage, the Government is well represented by Ministers and loyal deputies, and, as mentioned above, it has a number of procedural weapons available to protect the original version of its proposal. But ultimately, if it insists on a piece of legislation, it must risk its life in order to mobilize its maximum strength from a recalcitrant Assembly.

[The program of the Assembly—its agenda—is determined by the Conference of Presidents, in which the cabinet is represented.] As committees report bills out, the Conference assigns them a place on the agenda on Tuesdays, Thursdays and Fridays, when the Assembly usually holds its plenary sessions. In the case of pressing legislation the Government can demand, under the rules of urgent procedure, the immediate presentation of a committee report. If this is refused the Government can ask the Assembly for immediate discussion of the bill without assignment by the Conference or even without the final committee report. Since this procedure, however, is complicated and implies Government pressure on parliament, it is little used. Normally, therefore, the Government will simply try informally to urge the chairmen of the committees and the Conference of Presidents to report out an important bill quickly and place it upon the agenda immediately.

[Debate on a bill always begins with the reading of the committee report by the *rapporteur*.] This is followed by a general debate in which any deputy may make a speech, for or against the draft presented in the report, or for that matter on another version that he has drawn up himself. It should be noted that unlike procedure in the British parliament, debate on a Government bill is not opened by a statement of purpose by the interested Minister, nor is debate centered upon the original Government draft. In the Assembly the Minister's role is at first restricted to what the French call "making the synthesis" (*faire la synthèse*) at the end of the general debate. This is a speech in which the Minister summarizes the various positions taken on the report, reiterates the Government's position, and attempts to answer criticisms of the Government draft. It is hardly the direct and open advocacy of the original Government bill that takes place in Britain, but rather an effort at demonstrating, largely by rhetoric alone, that the Government's position is not too different from the views expressed in debate. It is therefore an appeal to compromise, an effort at persuading the majority to accept some of the Government's original views in exchange for the Government's acceptance of parts of the Assembly's revisions. Again the inferior power of the Government in policy-making is demonstrated: not only must the Minister wait until after the general debate to expound the Government case, but also when his turn to speak comes he must not urge the Government's original position too energetically for this would indicate an effort by the Government to discipline the all-powerful Assembly and it might inspire the latter to show the Government who is "boss."

After the general discussion the bill is debated article by article, a vote being taken on each. As at the committee stage, amendments and even counter-bills may be moved by individual deputies. The Government, however, is not allowed to move amendments or to ask for reconsideration of its original bill. Although entitled to speak in debate the Government can only act to modify the committee's version of its bill through the agency of an individual deputy loyal to the cabinet. Besides the right to participate in the general debate, all a Minister can do to win reconsideration of the Government's initial legislative text is to propose it as a "counter-bill" to the committee version contained in the report before the Assembly. But this usually means that the initial text must go back to committee again and probably suffer the same changes it did on its first passage through that stage, not to mention the additional delay involved in resubmission.

When all amendments and counter-bills have been discussed and voted upon, the bill as a whole is debated and put to a vote. Discussion at all these stages is theoretically limited in time by general agreement, and is announced by the President of the Assembly. But rare is the deputy who does not exceed the time limit for speaking, or who does not freely wander from the specific article or even bill being discussed. French canons of parliamentary courtesy prevent the President or the Assembly from cutting short a lengthy speech. True, the Assembly's rules of procedure do provide for closure of debate by a majority vote, as well as a form of limited debate similar to the British closure by compartments or "guillotine." But the request for closure, available to both Government and individual deputy, is never made under normal circumstances. And limited debate, which in Britain serves to expedite Government-initiated legislation, in France only serves to deprive the Government of an adequate opportunity to persuade marginal deputies to adopt the motion or amendment it endorses.

The Advice of the Council of the Republic

While the Assembly is alone responsible for making laws, no law can be finally promulgated by the President of the Republic until the upper house has given its advice. The Council, moreover, has acquired, since the constitutional revision of 1954, the right to have legislation first introduced there, save for bills ratifying treaties, the appropriations law, and any bill providing for a decrease in revenue or an increase in government expenses. Otherwise an individual senator or the Government, through a senator, may introduce a bill in the Council, and if it is passed it may be transmitted to the Assembly for passage into law.

Most bills, however, are first introduced in the Assembly and after being voted on first reading are sent to the upper house. There the bill follows a procedure analogous to that of the Assembly: the bill is considered by a Council committee, reported to the Council by a *rapporteur*, debated by the senators in detail and in general. Amendments are proposed, voted upon, and the bill as a whole is finally accepted or rejected by the Council. This action must take place within two months after the Council has received a bill from the Assembly or else the Council loses the right to present its version. But if the Council has sent its version back to the Assembly for a second reading within the prescribed time limit, there begins a "shuttle" (*navette*) between the two houses, the purpose of which is to develop complete agreement between the two drafts of the bill. This "shuttle," however, is limited: if an accord is not reached on the final version within 100 days after the Council has begun its second reading, the Assembly again has the last word. It can then cut short any further readings by the Council, but only in order to vote the final passage of its own original version of the bill.

Clearly the Council does not have a veto over legislation that the Assembly insists upon passing, other than the delay involved in the shuttles, which, it is true, may serve as bargaining power to force the Assembly to accept parts of the Council's draft. The procedure does, however, allow the Council to fulfill its prime function as a "second chamber"—that of polishing and improving laws and providing the highly political Assembly with a cooler and often more mature version of a policy proposal. After all, the Council is made up of older, often more experienced, men. It is a smaller body whose agenda is less encumbered than the Assembly's, thus allowing more careful debate and amendment. Since the Government is not responsible to a majority in the Council, a more objective and less politically charged atmosphere prevails. Although the Government's position in Council deliberations is no stronger than in the Assembly, the very absence of a threat to its life in the Council's proceedings allows it to be more active and more forceful in arguing its case in open debate. Indirectly elected, less responsible to party machines and public opinion, relatively divorced from the intrigues of making and unmaking a Government, the senators can listen to the Government with greater attention to the strict merits of a policy proposal and less attention to its purely political implications. Consequently when a Government bill has been badly deformed by Assembly action, the cabinet may look to its Minister-senators or loyal supporters to help it modify or even reverse much of the Assembly's action on the bill.

Naturally if the Assembly's version of a bill reflects real hostility to the Government, the Council cannot hope to change this attitude. But in the case of hasty drafting, or of the adoption of inconsistent amendments, or simply of momentary hostility to the Government, the delays offered by the shuttle and the many useful amendments of the senators, can serve both the Government's legislative program and the purposes of improved lawmaking. The only thing now needed to make the Council a completely positive and constructive influence on legislation is a change in the system of electing its members. At present rural and generally conservative districts of France are overrepresented in the Council, thus making its action consistently suspected of being biased. When its political complexion is more in accord with the national pattern, the Council will undoubtedly increase its powers even further.

Relations with the Government

The foregoing discussion of the legislative process has centered upon the relations of parliament with the Government and the various means available to parliament for obliging the Government to accept its version of a policy proposal. Similarly, in the discussion of the role of the Government in policy-making the means were described by which the executive could influence parliament to acquiesce in its independent policy-making. Finally, the process of making and unmaking a Government, described in Chapter 18, also concerns the power relations between the executive and the legislative branches of French government. As was pointed out, in all these relations the life of the Government is implicitly, or in the case of confidence votes and censure votes, explicitly, placed in jeopardy. Most relations between the two branches, therefore, are essentially a test of political wills: the will of the Government to risk its life in order to insist on the importance of certain legislation; the will of the Assembly to open a cabinet crisis at a particular juncture in internal or external politics. Although most of these relations take place in open Assembly debate there are of course also informal conversations in the corridors of the Palais Bourbon and the offices of the government departments. Here

Ministers, high civil servants, and deputies loyal to the cabinet attempt to influence officers and members of committees and marginal members of their majority. Here too individual deputies attempt to influence the government to adopt one policy or drop another.

But aside from this general area of relationships that involve lawmaking, there exist certain critical functions of parliament that bring it into contact with the executive, without implicitly or explicitly jeopardizing the life of the cabinet. These functions are primarily carried out by the parliamentary question procedure, which obliges the Government to answer deputies' and senators' questions on any subject pertaining to the execution and interpretation of laws. Unlike interpellation, question procedure can never go beyond criticism to become a wholesale condemnation of Government policy by the parliamentary majority, since it is accompanied by neither a general debate nor a vote that may be considered by the Government one of confidence. For this reason, interpellation is allowed only in the Assembly, to which the Government is alone responsible, while questions may be posed in both houses. Because of the overshadowing importance of the interpellation, and the general pre-eminence of the legislative branch in policy-making, regular question procedure in the two French houses is hardly comparable to its British counterpart. The French procedure deals primarily with technical and administrative questions, usually asked by the deputy at the request of a constituent or interest group affected by the Government act or regulation. Questions may be put to a Minister orally at the regular hour on Fridays, in which case the Minister may answer directly or ask for a delay in which to develop his reply. No debate is allowed and questions are dispatched quickly—when indeed they are treated at all, for very often the Assembly decides to forgo question hour on Fridays. The great bulk of questions, therefore, are submitted by deputies and senators in writing, published in the Official Journal of parliament and answered in the Journal by the Minister.

While of little immediate political significance, questions without debate, both written and oral, provide parliament with a useful control over arbitrary administrative acts. For, paradoxically, while parliament has vast powers over the cabinet—the political executive—it has relatively few direct controls over the actual wielders of the executive power, the bureaucracy. Indeed it has often been argued that parliament insists on a "delicately poised" cabinet, closely responsible to a parliamentary majority, because this is the only way in which to neutralize the vast administrative corps. If there were an independent and stable cabinet, it is argued, the French bureaucracy would be capable of promoting far greater changes in society than could the relatively smaller and less all-pervading British or American central bureaucracies. Unable or unwilling to go to the heart of the matter—curbing France's traditionally powerful central-ized bureaucracy—her politicians satisfy their desire to control the execu-tive by toppling the cabinet—that is, the controlling body of the bu-reaucracy. Having seen that so much of parliament's relations with the Government is conditioned by this fear of the power of its bureaucratic arm, it is now important to turn to the final and executory stage in the French decision-making process.

Role of the Bureaucracy: The Last Word

The French Administrative Tradition

In the discussion of the scope of the problems facing French Govern-ments it was argued that the policy-making process was inadequate to deal with them successfully. Of course, reference was being made to the purely political part of the process—that of the predominant yet often paralyzed parliament and the unstable political executive. For paradoxically, the actual executing agent of policies, the central bureaucratic administration, would be able to deal with almost any problem efficiently if it received coherent and clear directives from the executive and legislative branches. The national administration is potentially one of the strongest bureauc-racies in the world and, even as it is, has responsibility for a wide variety of activities such as local government, some manufacturing, administering the whole court system, most education, all police powers, all public works anywhere in France, and many other matters that in Great Britain, Ger-many or the United States are handled by independent local authorities if not by private enterprise.

This widespread responsibility of the central bureaucracy is not simply a reflection of the increase in social services and government regulation of the French economy since the war. Instead it is a testimony once again to the survival of an unreformed administrative pattern of policy-making for large sectors of French life. It is, moreover, the reason why the representative tradition of parliamentarism has not developed an efficient distribution of power between the political executive and the legislative. For supporters of this tradition have feared that an independent execu-tive, armed with such a powerful bureaucratic machine, would easily be tempted by the possibility of making policy by itself. Why then have the Third and Fourth Republics, founded by partisans of the representative tradition, allowed such a powerful arm to remain available to their ene-mies? The answer lies in factors of political culture as well as historical circumstance.

A centralized, permanent and powerful bureaucracy is the oldest and most characteristic institution of French public life—far antedating democratic institutions. Born in the absolutist days of the seventeenth century, the bureaucracy was from the start associated with that originally French contribution to political thought: the idea of sovereignty. This held that in every political community there had to be one ultimate source of decision-making in public affairs. Prior to the Revolution this source was, of course, the king, the creator of all laws, who exercised these powers, through his personal bureaucracy or administration. The Revolution was fought to substitute the people for the king as the ultimate source of law. Logically, then, it should have followed that the unitary state and the centralized bureaucracy, which aided the king in making and executing decisions, would also be swept away by the Revolution. Indeed, the more moderate and perhaps far-sighted of the revolutionary leaders saw that the wise corollary of popular sovereignty was local self-government and rigorous administrative decentralization. But the Jacobins, who soon came to power, felt that it was important to retain a central bureaucracy for practical as well as doctrinal reasons.

On the practical level a strong central bureaucracy was needed to prosecute the war revolutionary France was obliged to wage against most of the dynastic powers of Europe. The Jacobins also needed a centralized governmental mechanism in order to impose the victory of the Revolution, largely a Paris affair, on a conservative and generally hostile provincial France. To permit regionalism and administrative decentralization would also have meant allowing many of the last vestiges of the old hierarchical and even feudal society to survive. Most of the hatred of the revolutionaries and indeed much popular discontent even in the provinces had been directed against social inequalities under the old regime. Only a powerful Paris-directed administration, with its regulations and enforcement procedures, could insure equality before the law in a country used to inequality and privilege.

On the doctrinal side the revolutionaries and their republican successors were never able to rid themselves of a general French cultural compulsion to have a single source of authority in public affairs. According to their interpretation of the ideas of Jean Jacques Rousseau, apostle of the Revolution, the king's single sovereign will was to be replaced by the people's single sovereign will, and the king himself replaced by a representative assembly. Since this assembly could neither be in continuous contact with the people's will nor alone both make and execute the law, there developed the theory that it would act in favor of an abstract collective good and its laws reflecting that good would be executed by a permanent administration.

Such a theory presumed a pure "assembly regime," in which policy would be made by the all-powerful sovereign assembly and executed by a neutral bureaucracy. But as we saw in Chapter 16, events of the nineteenth century did not allow such a regime to develop. Napoleon made the bureaucracy more than ever the center of the policy-making process, although he did retain the revolutionary idea of the collective good in the place of the clearly obsolete ideas of divine right and feudal order. Furthermore, by organizing a regular bureaucratic career, rendering the administration omnipotent, and encouraging an *esprit de corps* for servants of the state, he strongly reinforced the principles of centralization and permanence, and produced a new and much respected occupational category in France.

[Down to the Third Republic, then, the administration remained an adjunct of the all-powerful executive, both in making and executing policy.] Naturally, it also became the sworn enemy of the more extreme supporters of the revolutionary idea of a dominant assembly. But when the republicans finally came to power after 1877, they again failed to destroy the essentially undemocratic centralized administration. The early leaders of the Third Republic were not the revolutionary hotheads of 1794, but were representatives of the rising industrial middle class that had chafed under the economic and foreign policies of Napoleon III and had suffered under the new system of privileges created by the emperor. They feared a "strong man" and the return to power of the old aristocratic elites, but they feared equally the radicals in their own party who talked threateningly of a "social and democratic republic." In the realm of economic and social policies, they disliked a strong, interventionist or positive state, based on a centralized and permanent bureaucracy. But for purposes of defense against a return of the aristocratic elites or a revolutionary threat to private property, they allowed the bureaucracy to remain as the heart of a "policeman's state" which could protect the status quo. However, to guard against the possibility that the bureaucracy, under the leadership of the cabinet, would develop an independent will, they created a dominant role for parliament in policy-making and even introduced limited local self-government.

Unfortunately, they neglected to change the personnel, duties and methods of the old imperial bureaucracy, whose values consequently remained, during the Third Republic, much what they had been under the kings and emperors. The stability of French bureaucratic personnel in the nineteenth century is indeed amazing: between 1847 and 1852, from the July Monarchy to the Second Republic to the Second Empire, there were hardly any more changes in personnel than in a normal five-year period under one regime. This was again the case for the years 1869 to 1875, when a dictatorial empire became a liberal empire, turning into a royalist provisional republic and becoming finally a true and permanent republic. Most

high civil servants, therefore, remained loyal to the traditional administrative concept of a single collective good which they as servants of the
state could alone determine and promote—an idea developed under Napoleon I. France under the Third Republic was, in this sense, as "statist"
as she had ever been under the empire.

But the growing power of the deputies and the calls for reforms from
labor and other interest groups which were soon transformed into electoral pressures and victories—all left the high bureaucrats more convinced
than ever that they alone were right. Since they were almost exclusively
recruited from the upper middle class and the aristocracy, they tended to
resist reforms that were demanded by the rising lower middle and working classes, represented by the Radical Socialist and Socialist parties. Aware
of this, these parties attempted to weaken the bureaucracy by fighting for
parliament's complete control over the executive. But, as has been noted,
the effect of destroying an independent political executive was only to
produce ministerial instability, which, if anything, increased the power of
the permanent bureaucracy committed to the social and economic status
quo. By striking at the political executive the leftist parties actually were
missing their mark, for they weakened the institutions—the Premier and
his cabinet—that could control the conservatively oriented bureaucracy.
The latter was, moreover, protected from overhaul and reform by the
parties and interest groups that agreed with the bureaucracy's conservative outlook and that saw in its power a means of offsetting the threats
to private property inherent in universal suffrage during the rise of an
industrial working class. These business and agricultural interests were
thus the new supporters of the administrative tradition of politics. Taking
the place of the aristocratic elites of the monarchies and empires, they
formed new social elites that profited from the existence of a centralized
bureaucracy, imbued with the traditional bureaucratic pride of office and
a self-confidence in its superior policy-making wisdom.

The partisans of the representative tradition who founded the Fourth
Republic in 1944-46, were once again faced with the problem of the
bureaucracy, the stability and continuity of which through the nineteenth
century, the Third Republic and even the Vichy regime had, as one com-
mentator has put it, "led to the survival within administrative life of
principles belonging to vanished political systems." [1] Strong pressures from
the Left, led by the Communist Party, urged the complete purge of the
bureaucratic personnel and its replacement by the revolutionary cadres
of the Resistance. A small reformist minority urged some renewal of personnel, but primarily argued for the institution of more democratic and

[1] William A. Robson, ed., *The Civil Service in Britain and France* (New York, 1956)
p. 161.

representative methods of recruitment plus a rigorous decentralization of administrative functions, so that the central bureaucracy would no longer have such sweeping powers over all sectors of public life. This, they felt, would eliminate the congenital fear of a strong political executive, which, with a less centralized and omnipotent bureaucracy, would be allowed more stability and thus be able to do a better job of policy-making within the proposed narrower scope of national government action.

Although methods of recruitment were democratized in 1945, neither the wide scope of bureaucratic action nor the upper-class monopoly on the high civil service posts was, in the end, seriously modified. For again the threat of a revolutionary Left, this time the Communists, militated against disorganizing the "policeman's state" at a time when everyone was talking of a possible Communist coup. Even more justifiably, it was argued that the new structural reforms voted, plus the broad and necessary governmental powers for directing the economy during the period of reconstruction, both required the retention of a centralized and experienced bureaucracy. Necessity, therefore, also militated against decentralizing administrative functions, and even against a serious purge of prewar bureaucrats, for fear of a shortage of much-needed *expertise*. Notwithstanding the desire of the Resistance leaders to eliminate the threat to representative government and democratic policy-making constituted by a bureaucracy that still believed in its independent right to determine government policies, such a bureaucracy still exists in France today. As a result the bureaucracy remains the focus for the hopes of partisans of the pure administrative tradition of politics and it prevents progress toward true mixed government in which the parliament and an independent political executive co-operate in making policy which is faithfully executed by a neutral administration.

The High Civil Servants and Their Outlook

The most influential members of the bureaucracy are naturally the permanent directors of those government services most directly related to policy-making. These services are in major ministerial departments like Foreign Affairs and Finance, or they are in the new administrations such as the social services or the nationalized banks, which, while independent of the cabinet, are in close contact with economic and social policy-making. The high civil servants in departments such as Interior, Education, Justice and Commerce are important, to be sure, but since their duties are largely either technical or purely executive, they are not considered influential in the policy-making process. Unlike these bureaucrats, those involved in economic, social, and foreign policy-making are principally drawn from four groups of civil servants generally referred to as the "Grand Corps of the State" (*Grands Corps de l'Etat*). These are the Inspectors of Finance, the diplomatic corps, the Court of Accounts, and the Council of State. In theory Inspectors of Finance are the top career officials of the Ministry of Finance, as members of the diplomatic corps are in the Ministry of Foreign Affairs. Similarly members of the Court of Accounts are usually occupied with verification of government expenses, while the Council of State serves as the Government's principal source of legal advice in drafting legislation, as well as an administrative court and supervisor of the civil service. However, many members of these corps of high civil servants are officially "detached" from their ministry or service in order to serve as directors of important offices located in other departments or in the newer administrations. In addition, members of these corps are chosen by Ministers for their personal cabinets and brain trusts, while others serve as staff directors for the major legislative committees. Thus wherever Government policy is drafted, turned into law, and finally cast into administrative regulations, there members of the Grand Corps are to be found.

For this reason it is important to inquire into the background, training and values of these "mandarins" who direct France's potent and active state apparatus. They are recruited, in the main, by a very rigorous written and oral competitive examination, which requires, above all, intellectual ability, plus a liberal education, presence of mind, very articulate written and oral expression, and an undefinable polish or self-confidence born of intelligent, yet persistent cultivation of the ego. These were the requisite qualities of the Grand Corps before the war, when recruitment was almost exclusively from the upper classes, for then as now these qualities were usually products of an education and cultural breeding available only to the well-to-do. Attempts were made in 1946 to democratize the high civil service by allowing subaltern functionaries from modest backgrounds to take examinations, and by creating a National School of Administration to provide a uniform training for all new candidates. However, the oral examination boards were from the start necessarily in the hands of veterans of the prewar Grand Corps who, unconsciously and also for reasons of *esprit de corps*, set standards that closely approximated those that had obtained in the past. As a consequence 65 per cent of the young Frenchmen who passed the supposedly "new" examination in 1945-51 were from business, professional, managerial and high civil servant families. Only 3 per cent were recruited from agricultural and industrial working class families, while the bulk of the remainder came from fairly well-off artisanal and independent farmer families. There is evidence, moreover, that considerable inbreeding exists since 40 per cent of the candidates are children of fairly well-placed civil servants.

In a country where the standard of living for wage earners is still relatively low, few families of the lower classes can afford to do without the earning power of a son. Hence only 5 per cent of secondary school students and 4 per cent of university students are from the industrial and agricultural working class. Since higher education is absolutely vital to success in the competitive examination, educational experience and its financial implications provide a sort of prior selection for the high civil service.

Ever since the beginning of the century the incomes of even the highest civil servants have failed to keep up with the rise in the cost of living. As a consequence the government service throughout the 1920's and 1930's continued to lose prestige and saw many of its most talented members leave for lucrative jobs in private industry. This was understandable, for, after all, high civil servants were drawn largely from the same class as management and the training and *expertise* derived from government jobs served them well in managerial positions. After World War II this trend continued and in 1951, 60 per cent of the candidates for the competitive examination admitted that government service for them was but a stepping stone to business and financial careers. Many of the most important private banks and manufacturing companies are directed by former high civil servants. Indeed the heads of the fifteen top private and public banks are former Inspectors of Finance. This brings up the question of whether the community of background between "Big Business" and "Big Bureaucracy" does not represent a threat to democratic processes of policy making.

There is unquestionably a similarity in outlook and values between the top bureaucrat in an important economic service of the administration and the top officer of a large business. Both are managers and highly competent technicians; both are interested in an efficient and productive French economy; both are slightly contemptuous of unstable and ineffective parliamentarism; finally both have a great faith in technical, empirical, "realistic" solutions to problems. Unlike his nineteenth-century predecessor, today's high civil servant has come to appreciate the need for considerable economic and social policy-making by the central government. Naturally, he has especially come to appreciate the increase in power this trend has given experts in government. More than ever, therefore, the top echelons of the bureaucracy are sensitive to their duties as servants of the "positive state," the administrative tradition that for centuries has served the national interest, as it saw this interest. Today the influential bureaucrats see this interest as modernization of French society and a rise in French economic production. Hence it is alleged that they are relatively accessible to pressure from representatives of the modern and efficient sectors of the economy, such as the big manufacturing companies. Certainly by background and experience a community of viewpoint does exist between these groups. Furthermore, thanks to the many advisory committees of businessmen attached to government departments and to the close personal relations between bureaucrats and their former colleagues in private business, there also exists ample opportunity for Big Business pressure upon the source of the rules and regulations that give law concrete meaning.

How Bureaucrats Influence Policy

Discretion and secrecy are essential characteristics of all bureaucracies. Hence very little is written about the actual day-to-day workings of a government department and even less about what a high civil servant does to affect government policy in his daily routine. The matter must therefore be discussed in general terms, with reference being made to those sectors of the policy process where it appears the civil service could have great influence.

Relations with the Cabinet

[Most day-to-day policy originates with the permanent civil service and is simply shepherded through parliament by the Ministers.] Formally the Council of State examines all Government bills and advises as to their drafting, the compatibility of their content with previous legislation, and their probable effect in accomplishing their goals. The Council also serves as a court to which individuals can appeal if they believe administrators or agents of the government have executed a law in a way contrary to its purpose and have, as a consequence, done them damage. Thus the Council of State has a function of judicial review of regulatory acts by the government that may have important aftereffects on Government policies. In 1953, for example, the Council quashed regulations barring Communist students from the National School of Administration, on the ground that it was a misuse of administrative powers, tending to infringe upon the legislative prerogative.

[Even policy of a reforming and controversial nature, which may appear to have originated with the politically responsible Minister, more often than not will be found to have come from a member of his personal staff who has been "detached" from a Grand Corps job.] In this capacity many civil servants have the chance of serving as the powers behind the throne in many cabinets. Below the Ministers there are the directors of the department's permanent divisions and offices, whose job it is to adapt laws for execution throughout the country. We have seen that this job of interpretation, of exercising the important rule-making powers of the executive, is very much part of the policy-making process. Indeed, in their efforts to get laws modified to suit their interests, certain pressure groups consider it the most vital part of policy-making. Besides this day-to-day rule-making, however, there has been an increase in quasi-legislation by bureaucrats thanks to parliament's continued use of "framework laws," slightly disguised delegations of legislative power, and the repeated extensions of normal rule-making power. As seen above, all this has been in an effort to escape the need to deal with very controversial economic and financial problems that threaten to shatter the tenuous political majority and thus defy any legislative solution at all. Similarly in times of cabinet crisis when the defeated Ministers remain in office only to carry on current matters until a new cabinet is invested, it is again the bureaucracy that decides policy on these matters. The defeated cabinet has lost the confidence of the Assembly, while a new cabinet has yet to take office: during the crisis, which can last from one to four weeks, only the bureaucracy is available to decide, for example, pressing diplomatic questions; and the bureaucracy remains to inform and advise the new Government on immediate problems after the crisis.

[Now, the inclination of the average bureaucrat in the decision-making situation is invariably toward maintaining the status quo.] Not only does his background and training tend to make him dubious of romantic, highly "political" suggestions for change, but also his technical knowledge of the complexity and unpredictability of social affairs tends to make him skeptical of all reforms that promise quick solutions to problems he knows are permanent. Thus a Minister of Reconstruction and Housing may urge sweeping legislation to modernize the construction industry while a Minister of Finance may propose a new tax law to control tax evasion. It will be the bureaucrat's job to take these proposals and "cut them down to size," pointing out to the Minister the uselessness of such legislation, given the many technical problems involved. This innate conservatism, this resistance to an overly reformist use of government power, is not always a reflection of political conservatism on the part of the civil servant. Often it may reflect his realistic and slightly cynical conviction that real social change can never come from the manipulations of the bureaucracy or the passage of the usual "façade legislation" of a coalition majority, amended beyond recognition and "corrected" by competing pressure groups. Most bureaucrats realize that change must come from a strong political executive, supported by a coherent parliamentary majority that can pass effective legislation and make it stick. [Bureaucrats cannot be expected to be reformers or initiators of policy because they can only execute policy made by the responsible political authority.] When a coherent Government policy does not exist they must necessarily mark time and "manage" the status quo, which to impatient reformers often seems a conservative policy of defending entrenched interests. Naturally, bureaucrats are pessimistic about the ability of most cabinets to get vigorous reforms passed by parliament, and hence their automatic resistance to ambitious calls for change from Ministers. But their generally conservative influence on Government policy might well disappear if the executive was stable enough to conceive coherent and vigorous policy and remain in office until it was enacted into law by a disciplined majority. Were this kind of government to develop in France her bureaucracy would perhaps become as neutral and as loyal as is that of Great Britain.

Relations with Parliament

[The expert advice of bureaucrats is constantly being sought by the two houses of parliament in their consideration of legislation] On the staffs of committees and of the advisory semi-parliamentary bodies, bureaucrats may have a direct role in the legislature's rewriting of Government bills. More directly, however, bureaucrats can influence parliament by becoming elected as deputies and senators, using their *expertise* and talent in committees and in debate. For, unlike British civil servants, [the French bureaucrat may run for public office.] Thus in the National Assembly alone twenty-seven high civil servants, temporarily "detached" from service, held seats in 1951.

[Less formally, but no less directly, the bureaucracy influences deputies by its own pressure-group activity, akin to that of any economic or occupational interest.] Generally contemptuous of the parliamentary game, bureaucrats nonetheless offer their expert aid to deputies who support policies they consider "technically" sound, or who oppose policies they consider unwise and dangerous—either to their own occupational interests, in the case of civil service personnel questions, or to their interpretation of the national interest. Like most pressure groups working on parliament they too exploit the average deputy's lack of a regular source of unbiased information and advice. A bureaucratic coterie, having failed to persuade the cabinet to modify the draft of a Government bill, may go directly to the legislative committee that is considering the bill and through friendly deputies or their civil servant colleagues on the committee staff, may manage to make their views prevail at another level of the policy-making process.

All these cases of bureaucratic influence exist in the United States and Britain in varying degrees. But the lack of authority of the French Premier and his Ministers, who are the regular source of direction for the bureaucrats, encourages the latter to pursue their ends on the more potent level of policy-making, the parliament, more vigorously than is usual in other countries. This leads to an unfortunate confusion of legislative and administrative power which makes French Ministers very suspicious of their civil servants, the civil servants contemptuous of their regular chiefs, and the French parliament unsure whether the bureaucrat is speaking for himself or as a disguised representative of cabinet pressure. This again highlights an unfortunate by-product of a governmental system in which executive instability, a lack of discipline, and an independent administration can be most dangerous for democratic policy-making.

Relations with the Public

It is the administrative action of lower-level bureaucrats that is the aspect of national government closest to the individual Frenchman. Unlike in Britain, the United States, and Germany, every act of a public authority in France has long been the act of an agent of the highly centralized administration. Local government is in the hands of a bureaucrat who works for the Ministry of the Interior in Paris. The social services depend on a Paris office. The schools and the courts in the most remote parts of France are standardized and directed respectively by the Ministries of Education and Justice. Finally, the police in every part of the country obey orders from the Ministry of the Interior. All matters of public policy from French membership in an international alliance to whether an extra day of vacation may be given to the grammar school students of La Roche-sur-Foron, are decided in Paris by law or by ministerial regulation. And since the closest the average Frenchman gets to participating in policy determination is the election of a deputy every five years, it is not surprising that he should feel that most policy is decided by a monolithic, inhuman and faraway administrative machine.

The immediate effect of having such a centralized bureaucracy in direct contact with the people is that policy decisions are promptly and efficiently carried out. Whatever is decided in Paris today, by law or regulation, is executed tomorrow or the day after in every part of the country. There is no local authority that stands in the way of the swift and uniform execution of government policy. The principal agent of the central government at the "grass roots" of the policy process is the Prefect, a high civil servant who, as an employee of the Ministry of the Interior, is responsible for local government. For while elected departmental and municipal councils do exist, the serious decisions of local government policy are all made by the Prefect in consultation with his Paris Ministry. If the local elected councils resist these decisions the Prefect can report this to the Minister of the Interior, who can, if he so chooses, dissolve the recalcitrant elected bodies. Moreover, an individual with grievances or a request for special treatment can go to his elected local government official or even to his deputy, but the chances are he will first go to see the Prefect. The first objective will be to get a special dispensation from him, such as the suspension of a law or rule in his own particular case. If this fails he will appeal to his deputy to intercede with the central administration in question or with the relevant Minister himself.

Thus the Prefect applies laws and regulations to the local population. To assist him in this task he has the services of a small staff of bureaucrats, who, like the Prefect, depend on Paris although they live and work in the provinces. This bureaucracy is made up of tax collectors, inspectors of various kinds, and a corps of police, whose job it is, beside the usual law enforcement duties, to keep the Prefect informed of the activities of political parties, economic and social developments such as strikes, and of the general "mood" of the citizens. French police organizations are grouped under the central control of the Ministry of the Interior, the Ministry of Defense, and the Paris police department. Under Interior there are the French equivalents of the American F.B.I. as well as a national riot police. Under Defense there is a military police (*Gendarmerie Nationale*) responsible for order in the countryside where there is no municipal police, and for executing the orders of the military courts, which in France have jurisdiction over civilians as well as military personnel. Under the Paris police department is France's equivalent of the American Secret Service as well as a corps of "economic police," whose job it is to enforce economic and currency controls. This plethora of police organizations grew, not as a result of rational planning, but in consequence of need.

For, given France's highly centralized government and her administrative tradition of universal governmental regulation, each time a new area of public policy is taken over a police organization to assure execution of policy is required. This, for example, explains why the rise in government economic regulation required an economic police, and why the rise of Communist agitation called forth the creation of a new riot police. Since local authority is an extension of Paris authority the police must necessarily be centrally organized.

In the case of infractions of the laws or regulations the Prefect or his police inform the local agent of the Minister of Justice, the public prosecutor. This bureaucrat then proceeds to draw up a case which is tried in a court system that is administered by the Ministry of Justice, although nominations to the bench are made by the Superior Council of the Judiciary, hence assuring the independence of judges. There is no jury, save in the most serious criminal cases and the defendant is tried before one or more judges, who are hardly his "peers" but rather are civil servants whose job it is to see whether in fact there was or was not a breach of the rule or the law. In its handling of most civil and criminal cases, the French court system typifies the heavy administrative tradition in which the individual for practical purposes is considered guilty until he proves himself innocent. Since a cautious bureaucratic mentality pervades the court system, judges are generally mediocre and the process of justice is often slow and painful for the accused. The public, as a consequence, has little more confidence in the judiciary than in any other agent of the central power.

Given the many functions of the Paris bureaucracy, it is no wonder, then, that the average Frenchman should feel "cramped" by the constant presence of the administration. While, as we have seen, this may lead to efficiency, it also has helped produce the widespread public disaffection from governmental authority that is referred to usually as France's "lack of civic-mindedness." But one is usually civic-minded from a sense of participation in policy-making and a feeling that government is truly responsive to the needs and demands of the people. A centralized bureaucracy that regulates all aspects of public life, and a parliamentary system that produces ineffective legislation, do not contribute to this sense of participation or this belief in the responsiveness of government to the public good.

CHAPTER **20**

Prospects

[The fact that the Frenchman is so surrounded by an all-pervading bureaucracy has tended to underline his discontent with his country's political institutions.\For if government is so incoherent in its policy-making, so patently unable to solve problems, why should it have such an onerous administrative extension that impinges on everyone's freedom? For some —predominantly the parties of the Left—the fault lies with the administration and the executive, which, by serving hidden economic and social interests, disorganize and confound policy-making by the sovereign parliament. Their solution is, of course, continued strengthening of parliamentary dominance over the executive and its administrative arm. For others— usually conservatives—the fault lies with a hopelessly divided parliament whose congenital incoherence prevents the administration from doing its job properly and therefore only makes it seem onerous. Their solution is a strengthening of the executive and an extension of the area of policy- making decided upon by the administration.

Actually the attitude of all Frenchmen toward this question is ambivalent and hence the continued division between representative and administrative traditions even within the individual[The Frenchman loves order, and a systematic approach to public problems that, according to experience, only a single, all-pervading administration can provide] The moral side of this love of order, stressed by the Revolution, is of course, the equality of treatment by public authorities, which again French experience has shown can be provided only by a central administration. Yet, the Frenchman also loves freedom, individualism, and the possibility of having his own particular way with things as much as possible—all of which self-government and representative institutions have protected since the coming of the Republic. But this basic ambivalence has itself contributed to the coexistence of the two political patterns: concretely, when

332

the Frenchman is contented he is glad to allow the Prefect to keep order and protect private property; but when he has hard times or when he is bothered by the administration, he is glad to have a parliament to which he can appeal for redress. And at all times Frenchmen who are attached to the status quo look to the administration for protection against Frenchmen who are unhappy with the status quo, and these in turn look to parliament for reforms and improvement of their lot.

The ambivalence of the French toward the role of the bureaucracy in policy-making is perhaps the most suggestive key to an understanding of the general problem of French government. They like the administration because in a governmental system of weak and unstable cabinets, and vacillating and ultimately ineffective national policies, it seems to be the only stable, dependable, and effective force for public order. Yet they fear the administration because it is too "present," representing thereby a constant threat of arbitrary rule and the limitation of individual freedom. Since the Third Republic, the expression of this ambivalence has been in the preservation of a monolithic "policeman's state," staffed by a centralized bureaucracy, controlled by a weak and easily removed executive, itself responsible to a powerful legislature. Such a compromise between the two traditions of politics seemed to provide the desired order in society along with a guarantee of individual freedom, for the instability of the controlling executive left the administration free to preserve a stable society, but nothing more.

In recent years, however, the need has been for a dynamic order in society, one that could be adapted to new problems and new demands from the evolving social groups such as an urban working class. France is becoming increasingly industrialized, her production and population are both expanding vigorously. In this context, the old French desire for order in freedom, born in an earlier social setting of small businesses, a predominantly agricultural economy, and a stable population, must find expression in new political institutions or face frustration.

France can acquire these new political institutions by allowing crisis and circumstance to impose the necessity of reform upon her. It is argued by some students of French government that only a serious transformation of French society through continued industrialization will ever create the conditions of effective government. For, it is claimed, only by eliminating the remnants of past social structures, such as marginal shopkeepers, can political forces be reduced in number or be obliged to form stable governing majorities. And, it is further argued, only by continued prosperity can the working class be wooed from the Communist Party and thus brought to participate in the French political community. These observers argue, in short, that only through changes in the social order outside the political system can the pattern of interests be so altered as to make possible the desired pattern of power.

But granted that France has prospered and is becoming more "modern" every year, there is still the problem of widespread public discontent. Over eight million out of twenty-two million French voters in 1956 cast ballots for parties hostile to representative, democratic government—the Communists and the Poujadists. To wait until natural growth makes France modern enough for effective government is to risk a sudden rise in discontent in the case of a temporary setback in this growth. For this reason other students of French government argue that conscious and immediate reform of French political institutions is required if French government is to be made effective and this danger avoided.

There are signs in France today that the latter course might be chosen. The dilemma that led reformers to remain hostile to a strong and independent executive because they feared a socially conservative administration seems to have run its course. It is slowly being accepted that reforms in society can only be brought about by a strong political executive, responsible to a coherent majority in parliament. And such a majority is at least in part produced by the existence of a premiership and cabinet worthy of their names and, therefore, worthy of making a firm party coalition in order to capture them. France has long had parliamentary government without its most important prerequisite. Like Britain, France has an executive responsible to parliament, but, unlike Britain, there is neither a disciplined two-party system nor even a disciplined set of party coalitions to provide the executive with stable governing majorities. The instability and incompatibility of French party coalitions necessarily makes for instability of cabinets based upon them. Only by isolating the executive from the effects of constantly shifting parliamentary majorities can French government regain much-needed stability and power. This might be accomplished by making the chief of the executive, the Premier, responsible to the people and not to parliament; or it might be accomplished by giving the Premier the unfettered right to dissolve the Assembly and call for new elections when a stable governing majority has disappeared.

While partisans of the representative tradition are discovering the virtues of "strong government," French conservatives, partisans of the administrative tradition, are finding the bureaucracy less amenable to their backward economic views and hence are making greater use of representative institutions to pursue their goals. This is shown by the stronger and more national organization of the major conservative party and the growing pressures upon parliament. The administration is itself beginning to become slowly more representative of the population as a whole and thus will become ultimately less menacing to partisans of the pure representative tradition in politics.

As a consequence, the means of producing mixed government in France, government that is stable and independent yet responsible to the popular will, may finally be in prospect. To satisfy the French love of freedom and individual self-expression, the administrative tradition is being democratized and should ultimately be decentralized. More local self-government should be introduced and a certain amount of economic and political regionalism encouraged. This would help to rid Frenchmen of the feeling of being "cramped" by the all-encompassing bureaucracy. Divorcing the idea of the central government from the ancient image of a "policeman's state" would allow the politically responsible part of the executive, the cabinet, to become more effective, although within a narrower sphere of activity, limited to national affairs alone. In this way the French desire for order and effective policy-making could be met, but no longer by an obsolete and top-heavy administration which encourages a purely negative vigilance by a dominant yet divided parliament. By reducing, instead, the area of central government activities, by encouraging administrative decentralization and regionalism, the way would be cleared for making the most vital activities of central government cut deeper, thus dealing more successfully with the problems of adapting French society to modern economic, social, and international problems. This would be accomplished by strengthening the political executive, giving the Premier the discretionary power of dissolution and making him directly responsible to the electorate instead of to an easily shifting parliamentary majority, impossible to discipline, given the nature of France's multiparty system. At the same time by decentralization of government activities this newly strengthened executive would no longer be feared, for its strength would clearly be exercised in a limited area of national policy. French parties, faced with the possibility of conquering a real bastion of responsible and effective executive power, capable of getting things done, would perhaps organize themselves in more stable electoral and Government coalitions. From these changes would emerge a political system no longer divided between a representative and administrative pattern of politics. For with both parliament and the administration weakened, the forgotten man of French political institutions—the Premier—could be strengthened, thus combining and linking the necessary elements of both traditions in his person: authority yet responsibility. Thus may yet be resolved the ancient hostility of the two Frances which has produced victory for neither, but only humiliation for the single France, long beset by the discontent of her citizens over their political life.

PART FOUR

THE GERMAN
POLITICAL SYSTEM

by Herbert J. Spiro

Excerpt from a debate on the film industry and censorship in the Bundestag, April 2, 1954.

DEPUTY PAUL   (Social Democratic Party):

It is another matter that movie people are interesting for the press—just as interesting as for instance politicians, including the Federal Ministers. In this connection it must, however, be remarked that the former are usually more rewarding for the press than the latter, because they are as a rule—I underline as a rule—more beautiful in figure and face. [*Hilarity in the center.* DEPUTY PELSTER: Can't always say that!] In the film industry, too, business is sometimes made with dirty things. [*Calls of "Aha" from the center.*]

But, my most esteemed ladies and gentlemen, we Social Democrats have not invented this order of society [Very good! *from the SPD. Laughter and calls from the center*] in which one coins gold out of dirt. [*Sustained hilarity.*] After all, it is your view that everything in the world and in the economy should be subjected to Liberalism. [*Laughter in the center and right.* DEPUTY PELSTER: Socialism is after all the legitimate child of Liberalism.] But Federal Minister Dr. Wuermeling is not just concerned with the movies, he is only looking for arguments for his ambitions, and these ambitions are of a shady, very shady sort. [*Laughter and calls from the center:* Oh! Oh!] Herr Federal Minister Wuermeling, in seeking to castrate the movies [*The President's bell*], is leading an attack on liberty of the spirit and of artistic creation. [*Applause from the SPD. Contradictions from the center.*]

When problems of marriage and family life may no longer be treated, then a part of their intellectual substance is being withdrawn from the movies. Artists of all times and nations have represented not only the average fate. They were stimulated to create the unusual, the tragic, and the problematic. Thus it was from Sophocles to Shakespeare and Goethe [*Hilarity and calls from the center—the President's bell.*], thus it was from Schiller's *Luise Millerin* through Ibsen, Strindberg, on into our time.

. . . .

DEPUTY MENDE   (Free Democratic Party):

When the movie *Trip to Marakesh* was shown in Neumarkt-St. Veit, Father Stehlböck had the penitential bells rung and prayed for the poor

339

sinner Frau Mayerhofer, owner of the movie theater and wife of Bundestag Deputy Mayerhofer of the Party of the Bavarians. [*Great hilarity*.] In his Sunday sermon, there occurred the words: "Let us pray against the delusion of this woman," and "By their fruits ye shall know them." [*Renewed great hilarity*.]

In Bardenberg, on the occasion of the performance of the film *Grosse Freiheit No. 7*, a picket line was formed around the movie theater in order to prevent the public from entering the theater. This was done under the leadership of the local clergyman, who had equipped himself for this purpose with a poster, by members of the Catholic Film Commission.

Benjamin Constant has proclaimed that democracy, when carried to its extreme, can degenerate into the most terrible steppingstone to despotism. Let us therefore if possible avoid this association of people's sentiments, people's censorship, and people's democracy. A politician and a responsible person in public life must do more than merely listen to the *vox populi*. He has the responsibility, before his conscience and God, to let his actions be determined in the sense of the categorical imperative of Immanuel Kant. [*Vigorous applause from the FDP and the SPD*.]

It seems to me that it would be best to stay with Blaise Pascal, whose *Pensées* the Herr Federal Minister knows as well as I do, too. To the question, whether man is good or evil, whether Jean Jacques Rousseau is right with his *"retournons à la nature,"* Blaise Pascal replies: Man is neither good nor evil; only misfortune wills that he often becomes a devil when one wants to force him to become an angel. [Very good! FROM THE SPD.]

21

Continuity and Discontinuity in German Politics

The Constitution of the Federal Republic of Germany was proclaimed only in May 1949. The government based on this Constitution controls only about two thirds of the territory and three fourths of the population of Germany. The rest of the country is a satellite which has been subjected to a forced process of sovietization. It calls itself the "German Democratic Republic."

Until 1955, the government of the West German Federal Republic did not even exercise sovereignty over its own territory, but was under strict control by the Allied High Commission. This body consisted of representatives of the United States, Great Britain, and France. Even after sovereignty was granted to the Germans, troops of these three powers remained on the soil of the Federal Republic. Its Constitution was actually written to meet specifications and a deadline, set for 1949 by the Military Governors. The deadline had been preceded by four years of military occupation and military government following the most colossal military defeat and the greatest human migration in history—it brought ten million refugees and expellees into Germany. Before these catastrophes, their "cause": twelve years of totalitarian dictatorship, National Socialism under Adolf Hitler. In 1933, he had destroyed the Weimar Republic, Germany's first experiment with constitutional democracy. The Weimar Republic, in turn, had been born out of the country's first great modern defeat, at the end of World War I, in 1918, and lived—often on the brink of death or suicide—for only fourteen years. Before that, there were the forty-seven years of the Second Empire, an absolute monarchy with some vestiges of constitutionalism. And before 1871, Germany had been little more than what Metternich called it, "a mere geographical expression."

Can there be any basis for comparing German with British or French government? Off-hand, we might well deny it. The differences in historical raw material are simply too vast. Compared with Britain, France appears unstable. But at least France had already had forty-seven years of her *Third* Republic, when the German national state was only forty-seven years old and the Germans were trying to build their *first* Republic at Weimar. At that time, one could have said: Constitutional politics in Britain has tradition; constitutional politics in France is supported at least by the revolutionary tradition; but constitutional politics in Germany does not even have that. Thus, the Weimar Republic had to start virtually from scratch. Since World War II, in France, one speaks of an easy return from the Fourth Republic to the Third. In Germany, a return from the Bonn Republic to that of Weimar, short-lived as it was, would be much less likely. French society is deeply divided, but at least there seems to be general acceptance of the procedures that produce *immobilisme*. German society, upon recovering self-government, faced so many problems that it should have been rent by even more cleavages. Moreover, it lacked experience with political procedures by means of which these gaps could be bridged and differences compromised. The Germans had not only to reconstruct government, but also to create the procedures by which disagreements about the goals of reconstruction could be either resolved or deferred. And this at the same time at which they had to deal with the much more immediate and serious problems of reconstructing the physical basis of their very existence.

The amazing thing is that they seem to have mastered all these tasks. Today their economy expands faster than those of France and Britain. The government of the Federal Republic is much stabler than that of the Fourth French Republic. After the general elections of September 1953, one of the parties, the Christian Democratic Union, controlled an absolute majority of the seats in the second Bundestag and a two-party system may be in the offing. Both neo-Nazis and Communists have made poor showings at the polls. The competing regime in the Soviet Zone of Germany would collapse immediately upon the withdrawal of the military and police forces on which alone it rests. If the outside observer did not know that West German political institutions and processes were created virtually out of nothing, he might think that the present order and stability must have been preceded by a long, slow, gradual, and peaceful evolution. But he knows that this was not the case, and this leads him to ask: Is the present appearance of stability a mere illusion? Or is there after all something in German politics that has provided a thread of continuity through all the changing tides of disunity, absolutism, wars, totalitarianism, and economic and political catastrophe? How effective is government in West

Germany, both in terms of its capacity to put its policies into effect, and in terms of the likely longevity of the constitutional regime?

The Jagged Curve of Modern German History

[Politics has been stable so far during the young life of the Federal Republic of Germany.] But eight years is hardly enough to permit a sound judgment about the endurance of this political stability. For such a judgment, a longer period would have to be considered. The longest period available starts in 1871. Since the German states were not unified until that year, one cannot properly speak of "German" politics before then, but only of the politics of Prussia, Bavaria, Baden, Hamburg, etc., and of the external relations of these states. [German politics since 1871, if viewed in terms of its scope and goals, its structure and policies, has been anything but a paragon of stability.] Thus, if we were to picture in a graph the evolution of each of the four political systems considered in this book, the British curve would undoubtedly be the smoothest. The German curve would probably be the most jagged—more jagged, that is, than even the Russian, because Germany achieved national unity so much later than Russia. Since 1871, at least seven major changes have affected Germany. Each of these was bound to be, and was in fact, reflected in German politics, so that there was little opportunity for a stable pattern to evolve.

Of these seven changes, the first and the last were perhaps the most radical, because the first created a unified German political system, and the last destroyed it by division. Bismarck's founding of the Second Empire, at the end of the Franco-Prussian War in 1871, brought together into one state the many diverse political units of the member states, to the exclusion of Austria.] The division of the country, formalized by proclamation of the constitutions of the Federal Republic and the German Democratic Republic in 1949, in effect created two German states, of which the Eastern has far less continuity than the Western with their common predecessors. In terms of effects on German politics, the first change was probably more important than each of the subsequent ones before the last. The other changes were brought about by rapid industrialization, abolition of monarchy, inflation and depression, establishment of Nazi totalitarianism, and the consequences of defeat in World War II.

National Unification

[Before the unification of Germany under Prussian leadership, nothing that could be called a German political system had been in existence.] There was, to be sure, an area of German culture where the German language was spoken and where German literature and thought were predomi-

nant. But this area had little political significance, because it was criss-
crossed by many barriers of different kinds, some of them insuperable for
the forces of political unification. Thus the area of German culture included the German-speaking territories of the Austro-Hungarian Empire,
which were to become a part of the German state only for the brief period
of the last seven years of Hitler's Third Reich. It included also more than
half of Switzerland, among whose German-speaking population there was
never much sentiment in favor of political unity with any state outside
the Swiss Confederation. Nevertheless, ever since the French Revolution
and the elimination of many smaller German principalities under Napoleonic occupation, the goal of national unification of as many of their
compatriots as possible under one crown had inspired many Germans,
especially the liberal-minded among them. During the revolutionary year
of 1848, a National Assembly met in Frankfurt and was dominated by
such liberals, among them many academic professionals. It offered the
German crown to the King of Prussia, Frederick William IV, who rather
contemptuously turned it down. During the next two decades, Prussia built
up the North German Customs Federation, but it was not until Prussia's
victory over Austria in the War of 1866 that the political unification of
the German states "from above"—on the initiative of their rulers and
under Prussian leadership—became a real possibility. Their common military effort against Louis Napoleon's Second Empire finally gave Bismarck,
the Prussian Chancellor and Foreign Minister, the opportunity to bring
into being the German Empire as a federation of princes presided over by
the King of Prussia, William I, as German Emperor.

Before this happened, one could only speak of several diverse political
systems existing in the member states. Their diversity can hardly be exaggerated. Little, for example, was shared in common by people from the
eastern provinces of Prussia, dominated by the Junker aristocracy with
their large landed estates and their ethics and outlook molded by Luther-
anism and traditions of military service, and people from the southern
parts of the Kingdom of Bavaria, ruled by the Roman Catholic dynasty
of the Wittelsbachs, which was much more ancient and "cultured" than
the Prussian Hohenzollerns. The lower classes did not even share an
easily understandable language. Again, there were great differences between
the Catholic peasantry and coal miners of Westphalia, a Prussian province,
and the trading population of the Hanseatic city-states of Hamburg, Lü-
beck, and Bremen, with their centuries-old traditions of patrician republicanism and world-wide commercial contacts. Yet all this diversity was
merged in one national state and given central representation in the first
effective national German parliament in history.

Before 1871, there had been no occasion for setting up political parties or procedures national in scope. Unification thus resulted not only in the establishment of a new structure of government that was wider in its scope than any previously set up in the German area. It also created the need for political practices and parties of similarly unprecedented scope. It also created a single economy. And all of this set in train developments that led toward *one* German society, with less diversity than before and with fairly general agreement on this new German nation as the proper unit of political authority.

Industrialization

In 1871, the Third French Republic was also born, though under less auspicious circumstances than the Reich, and without any agreement on its republican character. In France by this time, however, national unification was an achievement of the dim past, and a useful stock of procedures of self-government had been built up since the Revolution. Even though this was not the case in Germany, political developments there might have taken much the same course as in France. That they did not is due in large part to the compression into a relatively short period of time of the radical social changes that followed unification. Of these, industrialization came first, and it came belatedly and rapidly, and as in other countries accompanied by urbanization. Without the founding of the Reich, industrialization would not have come about in the way in which it did. In Britain and France, industrialization took place earlier than in Germany; in Britain, after both national unification and the constitution had ceased to be controversial, in France long after national unification had been achieved, though at the same time as the establishment of her modern constitution. In Germany, on the other hand, the spacing in time of these three problems was much closer: national unification, establishment of a constitution, and industrialization. Moreover, the solutions to all three problems, which were made in the second half of the nineteenth century, were pushed forward under the leadership of the Prussian government. Even industrialization received much more support from the government in Germany than in either of the other two countries. One reason for this was precisely the Germans' conviction that they had to catch up with their neighbors' head-start in this field, and that they could do so only by means of a deliberate national effort. One result of this was the close alliance from the outset between the rising class of industrialists and the old Junker aristocracy, often strengthened through intermarriage. Partly because of this, and partly because of the increasing size and importance of the military establishment during the period that culminated in World War I, it continued to be the Prussian Junkers who largely "set the tone" for the newly industrialized German society. Among other things, this made the orientation of industrialist employers toward their workers much more paternalistic than that of their French or British counterparts. This was to have a lasting influence on the organization and aims of the industrial working class, whose growth was itself an important consequence of industrialization. The longer life, in Germany, of pre-industrial and prenational ways of doing things, of forms of organization, and of habits of thought, combined with the need to modernize these radically and rapidly, was later to cast German politics in its own mold, and to introduce some of its more peculiar characteristics. Among these are the desire to revamp in a thoroughgoing way institutions regarded as inade-quate and, therefore, to blueprint the reforms beforehand with the help, and in the manner, of academic scholars; the persistence or frequent revival of corporate habits of thought and action, and the desire on the part of corporate groups to be aided and legally regulated by the state; and the lack of a conception of political authority either fully developed or gen-erally agreed upon.

Abolition of Monarchy

While the second great change had primarily economic causes, the third was once more due to political action. Abolition of monarchy—Imperial German, royal Prussian, Bavarian, etc.—and of the duchies and principal-ities was one of the first acts of the new revolutionary regimes that took over power in Berlin and other German capitals when defeat ended World War I in November 1918. This abolition of monarchy was formalized the fol-lowing year in the republican Constitution adopted by the National As-sembly at Weimar. It was designed to do away with the many remnants of feudalism still contained in the previous system, and especially with the continued social and political predominance of the old Prussian aristocracy. Though the former ruling families were not deprived of their often vast land holdings, they lost their political power and prerogatives. But some groups had to replace them in their functions of leadership. The make-up of one of these groups is suggested by the Article of the Weimar Consti-tution that, in its first paragraph, abolishes all titles and, in its final para-graph, specifically exempts academic titles from this prohibition. In any case, though the social revolution that was involved in this abolition of monarchy was nowhere near as radical as had been the revolution of 1789 in France, it did change German society and had strong repercussions on German politics.

Economic Crises

This third major change had hardly been consummated and the new Weimar Republic was just beginning to get on its feet, when another change, once more of economic origin, began to weaken the very social groups that had taken over from the aristocracy. First, the great inflation wiped out most of the savings of the middle class. Then, beginning in 1929, the great depression made millions of workers unemployed and dependent upon relief for their livelihood. The effects on the social structure of these two economic catastrophes were reflected, almost as in a fever chart, in politics in general, and in voting behavior in particular, as will be seen later.

Totalitarianism

In the society that had been ravaged in this way, Hitler established his totalitarian dictatorship, starting in January 1933, when President von Hindenburg appointed him Chancellor. Hitler and his henchmen deliberately engineered the fifth change. It consisted of the attempt to break down all the varied articulation of society, so that nothing would stand between themselves and the vast mass of individuals they sought to control absolutely. The Nazis' attempt was largely successful, though only for the time being, i.e., until their disappearance from the scene in the *Götterdämmerung* of 1945. Virtually all private and public associations and organizations not dependent upon the National Socialist Party were destroyed; so also were other political parties, trade unions, professional, sports, trade, and cultural associations, masonic orders, private clubs, and so forth. Only the Protestant and Roman Catholic churches withstood this onslaught, and they often at the cost of confining their activities completely to the realm of the spirit. Before millions of Germans were killed on the battle or home fronts of the War, Germany's 600,000 Jewish citizens—about one per cent of the population—were either forced to emigrate or were exterminated

Defeat

We will never be able to gauge the independent effects of twelve years of totalitarianism on the social structure, because these effects were intermingled with the consequences of total, unconditional defeat in World War II. The society the Nazis had tried to level completely was now subjected to three years of hunger and privation. It had to absorb ten million German expellees and refugees, having harbored, just previously during the War, almost that many foreign slave laborers and prisoners of war. Moreover, all this happened under the stern watchfulness of the victorious Occupation Powers, who were themselves intent upon remaking German society by means of the so-called "four D's"—denazification, demilitarization, decartelization, and democratization. The economic consequences of defeat also made necessary another wiping out of small savings, effected through a currency reform in 1948.

Division

The seventh major change—the division of the country—has brought into being two German economies, two social structures, and two German states. It means that each of the contemporary German governments controls a territory, a population, and an economy, that are completely new units and never before had an independent existence. For Western Germany, in particular, this has created a social structure different from any in previous German history. Moreover, it is not only different, but it differs in ways that could not have been foreseen by projecting earlier developmental trends. For example, while the population of Germany before World War II was made up of Protestants and Roman Catholics roughly in the ratio of 2:1, the two denominations are of fairly equal strength in the Federal Republic of today. Its territory contains a relatively higher proportion of the total German population than before division, but it also has to get along without the food traditionally supplied by Germany's eastern breadbasket, which is now located in the eastern Democratic Republic and under Polish and Soviet Russian administration.

Thus runs the jagged curve of modern German history. The character of society in the Federal Republic is very different from that of society under the Weimar Republic, and that again from the 1870's. Therefore, we may expect a similar lack of likeness between the main problems faced in each of these three periods, the cleavages running through society, and also the party systems by means of which the controversies arising out of these problems have been fought out. In the 1870's, the main problems consisted of consolidating the new nation, industrializing the economy, expanding the military establishment and generally strengthening Germany's international position. In the 1920's, they consisted of consolidating the new democratic constitutionalism, keeping the economy on an even keel despite reparation payments under the Treaty of Versailles and despite the effects of an erratic world economy, and making the best of military defeat and the consequent loss of territory and restriction of military strength to 100,000 men. And in the 1950's, the main problems concern constitutional reconstruction in the aftermath of totalitarianism and occupation, rebuilding the destroyed and divided economy, and seeking reunification of a Germany that was split in two by the division of the whole world into two hostile camps.

Two Germanys

This brings us back to the questions about stability, continuity and effectiveness. An approach to some answers may lie by way of comparing the politics of West Germany and East Germany. These two systems are radically opposed to each other in virtually every respect: genesis, goals, popular support, political organization and procedures. If they nevertheless have some outstanding characteristics in common, this may cast light on the stable elements in German politics, the more so because both regimes were established in the wake of the great catastrophe of 1945. At first glance, this common point of departure and the strong revulsion against anything that smacks of the abhorred Nazi regime seem to be all that the Federal Republic of Germany (*Bundesrepublik Deutschland*) and the German Democratic Republic (*Deutsche Demokratische Republik*) share. Otherwise, they are true opposites and indeed prototypical of all the differences between politics inside and outside the Soviet orbit, because they came into being at one of the main focal points of the Cold War.

The Democratic Republic was established under the aegis of Soviet occupation authorities and the leadership of German Communists who had been specially trained for this task in the Soviet Union. Its evolution has followed a pattern very similar to that of the other Soviet satellites in Central and Eastern Europe. Its leaders have been wholly dependent on the support of the Red Army for their survival in power. In the Federal Republic, on the other hand, a Constitution had to be written before the Western Occupation powers would permit the establishment of a German government for the territory of their three Zones. This "Basic Law" was designed to measure up to the highest standards of democratic constitutionalism as practiced in France, Britain, the United States, and elsewhere in the Western world. Its first nineteen articles contain a bill of rights that was meant to be really effective. Several free statewide and federal elections have been held under this Constitution. These elections produced stable and efficient coalitions of parliamentary majorities. Peace, prosperity, and good government prevail in West Germany. The population supports its political leaders, who enjoy respect throughout the world, even in Moscow.

A greater contrast than that between the governments of East and West Germany could hardly be imagined. It is so great that all those situational barriers seem to have been overcome that are usually believed to stand in the way of reaching collective goals by means of deliberately "engineered" political institutions. After all, the raw materials with which politicians started in the Eastern and Western Zones, in 1945, were fairly similar. And yet, 'the two governments are radically different not only from those that preceded them in Germany, but even more from one another. In this sense, contemporary Germany could serve as a superb example of the feasibility of "constitutional engineering."

There is, however, at least one belief on which both systems are based— a faith in precisely this feasibility of constitutional engineering, or in the capacity of men to shape their common fate in a rational way through the deliberate construction of political institutions. Some such faith can be found in all modern societies. The American Founding Fathers certainly held it. So did the authors of the first and all subsequent French constitutions, and the creators of such international organizations as the League of Nations and the United Nations. This faith is one aspect of the rationalism that has pervaded Western culture, especially since the eighteenth century. And it seems quite natural that it should be stronger in a country like Germany, where the need to create a whole new set of political institutions and procedures arose after both World Wars—just as it seems natural that it should be weaker in Great Britain, where no urgent need to make sudden and vast changes in ancient procedures and institutions has arisen in the course of many centuries. Nevertheless, there are two unusal aspects to the strength of this belief in contemporary Germany: first, its adherents might well have been disillusioned by the failure of the Weimar Constitution, which did not survive although it was written by some of the best legal, political, and social scientists of the time. And second, the intense legalism that accompanies this conviction as to the feasibility of constitutional engineering is not a necessary concomitant, i.e., the conviction could be held just as well with a less legalistic view of politics. In West Germany hardly anyone in any sphere of public life is willing to experiment with new institutions or processes by a method of trial and error unless explicit, detailed, comprehensive, and constitutionally sanctioned legal authority can be established beforehand.

Some sound explanations for this legal formalism can be found in recent German history. One is the absence of anything resembling the rule of law in the Soviet Zone. This has made the West Germans want to put on a blameless performance on this score. Another is the flagrant flouting of the Weimar Constitution and laws by the Nazis, which was obvious to everyone despite the Nazis' efforts to maintain a façade of constitutionality and legalism. The present legalism is in part a reaction against that lawlessness. A third reason is the historical sequence, Weimar Republic–National Socialism, which led many to view the one as the "cause" of the other. This turned some Germans against constitutional democracy in general, but they were barred from participation in politics by Occupation fiat during the first few postwar years. Those who were licensed for politics during this period concentrated on the construction of a system of government that would be foolproof against another Hitler, by correcting the alleged shortcomings of the Weimar system. All the novel constitutional provisions of the Basic Law are such corrections. The constitutional fathers of Bonn were able to go about this work of constitutional reconstruction in a fairly objective way because the Occupation Powers had at that time not yet returned much political responsibility to the Germans. As a result, political disagreements did not distort their constitutional deliberations to any great extent. They were not forced simultaneously to forge both new policies *and* the new methods by which such policies were to be compromised out of the divergent views of the parties. The constitutional authors at Bonn had to produce only the procedures of compromise, not policies. They were able to rebuild the constitutional system, starting at the state level, some time before they were put on their own politically by the Occupation Powers.

As the Occupation Powers slowly took the lid off West German politics, numerous previously dormant disagreements made themselves felt. Many of these were the common garden variety of political issues that exist in most modern industrial societies and that have existed in Germany ever since industrialization: economic organization, distribution of income, social security, the role of organized labor, relations between the state and the churches, educational opportunities, and the like. Other issues were of a potentially more explosive and divisive nature because they arose out of the National Socialist experience, out of the War and its aftermath, Occupation and division of the country. The positions that people took on these issues were determined largely by their attitudes toward the Weimar Republic and the Hitler regime. As a result, additional cleavages were created in German society. Just as politics is complicated in France by the fact that the social, religious, and constitutional cleavages have usually not coincided, so in Germany today, because there, too, the social, religious, and the several constitutional cleavages present a crisscross pattern.

There is another resemblance between the politics of France and Germany: the tendency to justify one's stand on any issue in ideological terms, that is, by reference to a comprehensive, closed, consistent system of knowledge. The two tendencies—toward ideologism and toward legal formalism—mutually reinforce each other. The ideologists believe that *the* truth exists, that it can be known, that they themselves know it and therefore have the answers to all questions and solutions to all problems. Legal formalism persuades them that the inconsistencies, irregularities, and vicissitudes of politics can be replaced by a consistency, regularity, and certainty provided by law and administration. Both orientations, the legalistic and the ideological, lead to a high esteem for the powers of knowledge and for its possessors, the academically trained intellectuals.

In these attitudes toward politics, held almost subconsciously, and mutually related to and reinforcing each other, lies a thread of stability that does run through the discontinuity and institutional and constitutional instability of German politics. Legal formalism, faith in the feasibility of constitutional engineering, ideologism, and faith in the powers of knowledge—all these are marked in the political culture of all of contemporary Germany. They have been manifest in German politics since even before the time when such a thing as German politics can properly be said to have existed—for example, during the Liberal "Revolution" of 1848 and the National Assembly of Frankfurt. Under the Empire, the values and beliefs on which these attitudes were based were further elaborated. At the birth and during the short life of the Weimar Republic they bloomed forth fully. And under the Bonn Republic, one of them, legal formalism, has become more marked than ever before, in reaction to both the previous Nazi, and the present East German Communist totalitarianism.

Political and Constitutional Stability

The stability of politics in the Federal Republic since its establishment in 1949 is outranked as a "miracle" only by the West German "economic miracle." But it is of such recent vintage that it may well be deceptive, especially since it has followed a historical development in which the constitutional pendulum oscillated from one extreme to the other, while the political pendulum—when it was permitted to oscillate freely at all, i.e., under the Weimar Republic—had a most irregular beat. How can we tell how long political stability will last? Will it survive Chancellor Adenauer? More important, can we speak of any constitutional stability in the 1950's? Does the one stable thread we have found, at the semi-conscious procedural level, augur well for continued constitutional stability?

The fourteen years of the Weimar Republic were a period of political instability. The average life of cabinets was but little longer than under the Third French Republic. Out of the many parties represented in the Reichstag, majority coalitions capable of agreeing on positive policies were hard to forge. The "Weimar Coalition," consisting of the Marxist Social Democrats, the Roman Catholic Center, and the liberal Democratic Party, agreed only on the need for the defense of the Republic, but not on social, economic, or cultural policies. This situation was made even more tenuous by the anti-republican attitudes and the anti-constitutional activities of the conservatives, monarchists, nationalists, and Nazis on the right, and the Communists on the left. For opposed reasons, these two extremes of the German political spectrum wanted to destroy the Republic—and in the end they did. Before that, they sought to sabotage political stability in order to put an end to the temporary constitutional stability the country was enjoying. In the process, they often resorted to open violence, the very antithesis of legal formalism. Violence and terror finally won out and, behind the thin veil of feigned legality, they reigned supreme during the period of Hitler's Third Reich.

The very strong contemporary legalism of German political culture arises out of the desire to insure permanent stability, both constitutional and political. But by an ironical twist of logic, the results are often the very opposite of the intentions. To the legalistically oriented, there seems to be no better way to insure constitutional stability than to include a great many provisions in the constitution, and then to make this constitution hard to amend. And there seems to be no better way to straighten out the complexity, and to contain the potential violence, of politics, than to divert as much as possible of the raw material of politics into the administrative and judicial machinery. This is being attempted in West Germany today.

Meanwhile, however, economic, social, cultural, and foreign-relations problems continue to change in a world that is anything but static. These changes then call for political and constitutional adjustments. Most political processes and institutions have been crystallized by explicit and detailed legislation, or even by inclusion in the Basic Law. The need for change, which could be satisfied by informal adjustment in a less legalistically oriented society, in Germany often requires legislation or even constitutional amendment. It follows that both those who favor and those who oppose some change frequently call on the constitutional courts for legal interpretations of issues that are really political. The courts, however, have neither a tradition of constitutional interpretation nor great popular respect to fall back on in exercising this function. The Basic Law is hard to amend. Therefore, those who are involved in constitutional controversies —of which there are more than would be the case without legal formalism —feel cramped politically, and the intensity of their conflicts is thereby increased. The courts are overloaded with constitutional cases. Politicians who are dissatisfied with a verdict vent their spleen on the judges and seek to insure having their way in the future through revamping the court system and judicial powers. Any minor issue is easily raised to the level of a constitutional conflict, and thus some of the most fundamental institutions of the Federal Republic are potentially less stable than they might be if their life were not anchored in the Constitution itself.

Other institutions, which were kept out of the Basic Law precisely in order to keep them more flexible even though they are by nature basic, fundamental, or organic, are subject to frequent revision. This has been true especially of electoral laws, through which the parties believe they can engineer more advantageous representation for themselves in parliament. It applies also to the territorial organization of the states, which can be changed without constitutional amendment. The drive for constitutional change, enhanced by the scope of the Basic Law, is thus deflected to institutions not included in this Constitution, which are just as basic but are as a result brought into a condition of constant flux.

This situation is further aggravated by the explicitly tentative status of the Basic Law. Its authors at Bonn were afraid that the title "constitution" implied permanency to such an extent that it might be viewed as an acceptance of the division of Germany. The document consequently provides that it is to be superseded by an all-German constitution once the country is reunited. Thus the Federal Republic denied itself the kind of permanent constitutional stability for which most of its citizens yearn. Of course, it is considered less reprehensible to criticize or attack a constitution of which one may legitimately hope that it will be short-lived. Moreover, anticipation of the eventual reunification of the Soviet and Western Zones stimulates theoretical speculation about the all-German constitution that will then have to be drafted. Widespread public discussion of these "iffy" constitutional problems of the future further enhances constitutional consciousness and constitutional litigiousness, without at the same time furthering the cementing of a "constitutional myth."

The outcome of all this is a high degree of potential constitutional instability. All that seems stable and well-established is the pervasive legal formalism, which determines the manner in which issues are perceived, stated, and fought over. This means also that the political leadership is made up of people who by education and background fit into this way of doing things. In this respect there is often more resemblance between the leaders of politically hostile organizations than between leaders and followers on each side of the fence.

West German society is still rent by many divisions, based on present interest, traditional ideological convictions, and recriminations about the past. The one need concerning which there is the most general agreement is the need for the rule of law and order, and this agreement arises out of the revulsion against the experience of lawlessness. Political order has been insured so far through constitutional engineering. For this reason and because of the importance of legal formalism, we will examine the structure of the Constitution and the procedures for which it provides before we look at the parties and interest groups that operate within it, the policies they espouse, the scope of the policies the government actually puts into effect, and the effectiveness of government itself.

CHAPTER 22

The Formal Structure
of Government

By and large, the structure and process of government in West Germany are what the Basic Law says they are. This is the case neither in Great Britain nor even in the United States, with its written constitution. An American professor of government can tell his students not to bother reading the Constitution, because it does not describe the actual operation of American politics today and might therefore confuse them. His German colleague often has his students read nothing but the Basic Law and learned commentaries on it, and from such a study they can actually get a fair idea of the operation of their political system. Britain, of course, has neither a written constitution nor even its functional equivalent, partly because the need to construct a whole system of government, or even parts of one, never arose. This need did arise in the United States, but only once, and that before the nineteenth century. In Germany, by contrast, the repeated need for complete reconstruction, combined with the recent frequency with which this has occurred, means that the Basic Law does give a description of government in the Federal Republic that is both accurate and adequate. Another reason for this is the high value placed on strict observance of constitutional and legal provisions, and the high expectations Germans generally hold that political stability will be the necessary consequence.

As a result, it would be difficult to get an understanding of parties and pressure groups and their functioning without prior acquaintance with the constitutional framework within which they operate. This is true even of such organizations as the Social Democratic Party and the German Trade Union Federation, which are older than the German national state and can pride themselves on their traditions and ideologies. Since they, too, have shared the prevalent faith in the feasibility of constitutional engineer-

355

ing, they have adjusted their modes of operating to the demands of the
new constitutional order, to the shaping of which they contributed at least
as much as their less democratically inclined political opponents.

The Lapse of Politics

This new constitutional order was built from the bottom up. In this
respect it is in contrast with the work of constitutional reconstruction
undertaken by the French during and after World War II. That is one of
the reasons why there are more differences between the Bonn Basic Law
and the Weimar Constitution than between the Constitutions of the
Third and Fourth French republics. There is, however, a more important
reason: while republican *government* lapsed in France during the years of
the Vichy regime, republican *politics* in one form or another continued
throughout the period between the death of the Third Republic and the
birth of the Fourth. Thus, while the new constitution was being drafted
the very men who were doing the drafting were interested not only in
creating a sound set of institutions, but also in their own more or less immediate political aims. In other words, even if there had been agreement in
France on long-run constitutional goals—and there was not—disagreement
on short-run political goals would have affected the drafting labors. In
West Germany, on the other hand, was there not only as yet no weighty
and acute disagreement about long-range constitutional objectives, simply because the Occupation Powers did not let anti-constitutional elements
participate in public life at this time, but there was also little short-range
political disagreement that could to any very important extent influence
the work of constitutional reconstruction, simply because there was relatively little German politics going on at the time.

German politics, as carried on during the four years from the end of
the war to the founding of the Federal Republic, was severely restricted
by the Occupiers in almost every respect. The enumeration of the several
functions of government given in the Preamble to the Constitution of
the United States may serve as a convenient check list for finding out
just what the Germans were allowed to do on their own.

First of all, the Germans were not able to do anything at all toward
"forming a more perfect union." On the contrary, the country was not only
divided into four Zones of Occupation, but two of these were governed
by Powers that, for different reasons, were intent upon further decentralization inside their territories: the French because of fears of a German
revival and hopes of encouraging separatist leanings on the part of some
Germans; the United States because of convictions about the virtues of
grass-roots democracy and a necessary connection between democracy and

federalism. Since the British held neither of these prejudices, their Military Government was the first among the three Western ones to permit the organization of political parties and trade unions with zonal scope. The Americans, by contrast, kept German politics confined to the local and state levels for much longer.

"To establish justice" was a task assumed by Military Government. For a while, German courts were not permitted to function at all and were replaced by Military Government courts. Even after German jurisdiction had been largely restored, the Occupation Powers continued to control such important areas of judicial activity as denazification. The courts also applied much new law that was made by Military Government.

"To insure domestic tranquillity" was the job of the Armies of Occupation, and when the German police did begin to reappear on the scene, it was reorganized, retrained, supervised, and controlled by Military Government.

"The common defense," down to 1957 at least, was provided by the armies of the Western victors of the war, though the Germans have been able to contribute to maintaining this defense establishment by bearing some of the costs of the Occupation and making, after 1955, an equivalent contribution to the North Atlantic Treaty Organization.

"The general welfare" was the one thing the Germans were allowed to help promote, through clearing away the debris and rebuilding their towns and industries. But even on this score they received a great deal of Allied help, especially from the United States; and all the important policy decisions—economic, fiscal, with regard to public health, and otherwise—were made or at least supervised by Military Government.

Finally, the Occupation Powers, since they had just defeated the Nazi regime, saw *themselves* as bringing "the blessings of liberty" to the Germans and, presumably, their posterity. That was why one of them, the United States, soon "ordained" that the several states, newly organized as units of government in the American Zone, should "establish" constitutions for themselves.

The basic functions of government were thus not being taken care of by the Germans themselves. They could address their collective efforts to the pressing problems of their immediate material needs, and this they had to do at the level of the grass roots, whether they wanted to or not. The needs were such that not much disagreement arose as to the best ways of meeting them. Those men and women who, as former Nazis, were now considered accountable for contributing to bringing about these disastrous conditions in the first place, were either in Allied concentration camps or else kept out of public affairs. As a consequence of all this, on a zonal or national scale politics was lacking.

Constitutional Reconstruction

When the task of constitutional reconstruction was taken up in earnest, the builders were able to ask themselves what sort of institutions would best serve the public interest, without too much concern for narrow partisan considerations, because concrete partisan interests were not yet as clearly evident as later and partisan conflict had not yet generated among them strong mutual antagonisms or mistrust. On the contrary, in some cases bitter enemies of earlier and later periods were firm collaborators during the first three or four postwar years. Many of them had learned to know and respect one another as common opponents of the National Socialist regime, despite different class, party, or religious backgrounds; others, in the course of the reconstruction labors; still others had co-operated in resisting some of the more unpopular Occupation measures, such as the dismantling of industrial plants for demilitarization or reparations purposes. All of them, except for the minute minority of Communists, were tied by the further bond of opposition to the Sovietization of the eastern part of their country.

Their task began at the level of the states, in the United States Zone, on American prodding to write constitutions. The men who drafted these first state constitutions had sufficient perspective to realize that their work would influence, and perhaps set the pattern for, the constitution that, they hoped, would sooner or later be written for the whole of Germany. They were deeply and fully conscious of the historical importance of their task. They went about it by asking themselves what constitutional flaws had brought about the failure of the Weimar Republic. To correct these flaws, they produced many ingenious devices. There were, of course, many different and often mutually exclusive interpretations of the life and death of Germany's first experiment with constitutional democracy. But despite this fact they turned out constitutions that were generally sound when judged in terms of internal consistency.

The Occupation Powers had their theories, too. Of these, the American were particularly important for their influence on German federalism. After the Americans, the British and French permitted the establishment of state governments in their Zones as well, even though some states in the British Zone did not get constitutions until after their delegates had helped to write the Federal Basic Law and their parliaments had ratified it. As a result of this American-initiated reconstruction at the level of the states, the first postwar German representative organ was also established. This was the Economic Council (*Wirtschaftsrat*), which was composed of 52 representatives elected by the state legislatures. The Occupation Powers gave it some jurisdiction over the combined Zones of the United States and Great Britain—the so-called "Bi-Zonia"—and later also the French Zone. Later, the Parliamentary Council (*Parlamentarischer Rat*) was created to draft a federal constitution. It consisted of 63 members who were elected by the state parliaments and then appointed by the Ministers-President (*Ministerpräsidenten*), who were and are the chief executive officers of the states. It was these same Ministers-President to whom the Military Governors addressed their instructions about the constitution.

Federalism

As a result, the Basic Law had a truly federal genesis. The several member states (*Land*, pl. *Länder*) were in being before the Federal Republic. Its Constitution was drafted by delegates from the states and ratified by all the state legislatures, except that of Bavaria. The degree of federalism to be written into the constitution was one of the major bones of contention in the debates of the Parliamentary Council. And since the Basic Law has come into effect, one of the most persistent issues of West German politics has been the balance of powers between the states and the federal government. Besides the circumstances surrounding the birth of the Basic Law, there are good reasons for the persistence of this issue in German history. The Bismarckian Constitution was federal. In 1871 it unified, under Prussian leadership, eighteen grand-duchies, duchies, and principalities, three Hanseatic republican city-states, and four kingdoms. The Weimar Republic, too, was a federal state. But federalism had been one of the obstacles in the path of the centralizing ambitions of Hitler's totalitarianism, so that the governmental wreck that was left on the hands of the Germans at the end of the war was that of a unitary non-federal state. The Soviets would have preferred to leave it that way, judging by the scrapping, in 1952, of the federal structure provided by the Constitution of the Democratic Republic in their Zone. British preference also tended toward a non-federal setup. But American and French leanings and advice in the other direction fell upon sympathetic ears with those Germans who believed that a more federalistic Weimar Republic could have better withstood its enemies, and/or that the Nazis' centralism was both against German constitutional tradition and a principal tool of totalitarian control.

They therefore designed each of the federal provisions of the Basic Law as an improvement on the Weimar Constitution. This is true of the territorial structure of the new federalism, the provisions for reform of the federal structure, the Bundesrat as the federal house of parliament, the distribution of legislative powers, federal emergency powers against the states, the Federal Constitutional Court, and the symbolism of the new Republic.

Territorial Structure

Many interpreters of German history have seen its major blemishes in Prussia, the dominant state both before and after unification in 1871. Under the Imperial Constitution, the Prussian government had 17 of 58 votes in the upper, federal chamber of parliament, and could command a majority by exerting pressure on her smaller neighbor states. The Prussian government in turn was responsible to its king—who was also German emperor (*Kaiser*)—and nominally also to the Prussian state Diet (*Landtag*). In this Prussian parliament, representatives of the poorest class of the population had only one third of the seats, so that it was always controlled by the representatives of the other two thirds, a conservative or reactionary minority of the people. Under the Weimar Republic, this Prussian class-franchise was abolished, and Prussia's predominance in the Reichsrat, the new federal chamber of parliament, was reduced. Prussia now had 25 of 66 votes. But some half of these 25 were not cast by the Prussian state government, but by the governments of the provinces into which Prussia was divided. Nevertheless, after the Nazi experience there were still people who blamed the failure of the Weimar Republic on Prussia's relative predominance. They did this despite the fact that the Prussian state government had, throughout the years between 1919 and 1933, been controlled by the pro-republican parties of the Weimar Coalition. The Allied Powers, too, were so convinced by this argument that the breakup of the Prussian state was one of their war aims, which was restated in the Potsdam Declaration of the Big Four in 1945. Prussia was officially dissolved by an Allied Control Council Law of February 25, 1947.

The constitutional fathers at Bonn were generally agreed on the need for a reasonable balance of territorial size and population among the member states of their new Republic. Since much of the old Prussia was under Soviet or Polish administration, or located in the Soviet Zone of Germany, and because the breakup of the rest had been made mandatory upon them, they were able to achieve such a balance without much trouble. The boundaries of the states did, however, present a problem. As these existed at the time of writing the Constitution, they were partly the result of Zonal boundaries between the Occupation Powers, drawn by the latter without much regard for German tradition, or administrative and economic efficiency. There was some doubt as to the viability, in the long run, of a federalism whose member states had as weak a basis in traditional attachment and utilitarian rationale as, for instance, North-Rhine-Westphalia, the largest of them. Considerable sentiment existed in favor of immediate boundary revisions. On the other hand, the states had already been operating long enough for the formation of groups that had a vested interest in their continued existence and in maintenance of the federal *status quo.*

A compromise was born out of these conflicting considerations. For the time being, the territorial *status quo* was to be kept, but Article 29 of the Basic Law made provision for a general federal reorganization. This was to be concluded within three years after promulgation of the Basic Law. But since the Allied High Commission withheld permission for initiating this procedure, the deadline had to be postponed. Only in the fall of 1955 did the Federal Government receive the report of a commission, headed by one of the surviving Chancellors of the Weimar Republic, which made recommendations concerning this problem. No action had been taken on this report by 1958. Article 29 also contains a provision for the use of initiatives and plebiscites, but for the purpose of federal reorganization only. The contrast with the Weimar Constitution on this score is marked, because it characteristically permitted use of these two ultra-democratic devices for all but budgetary purposes. Anti-republicans several times abused the provision in order to launch publicity campaigns against such measures as the Dawes Plan and the building of naval vessels. The men at Bonn did not want to give enemies of their Constitution a similar opportunity.

In the southwest corner of the Federal Republic, the effect of Occupation zoning on state boundaries was particularly noticeable, and clearly went against both tradition and efficiency. Therefore, Article 118 provided that the territorial reorganization in that area should be accomplished by means of a special procedure involving negotiations among the three state governments concerned, federal legislation, and a subsequent plebiscite. This procedure was actually followed and, after a great deal of controversy —including litigation in the Federal Constitutional Court—the three states combined into one, Baden-Württemberg. It adopted a new constitution in 1953.

Thus some of the states that established the new German "federation" had not existed for long and had little reason for existence. It was partly in order to emphasize this temporary character that the "Basic Law" (*Grundgesetz*) was called that instead of "Constitution" (*Verfassung*). It provided for federal reorganization, including the possibility of absorption of one state by another, and this actually happened within the first three years of the life of the Federal Republic. Considering this along with the foreign forces that encouraged the Germans to build a federal structure, one may well ask whether their federalism is not a pretty artificial affair—especially when compared with the federalism of, say, the United States or Canada. If this is true of the federalism of the Federal Republic, is it not likely to be true of contemporary German constitutionalism as a whole? And does not this Constitution itself, by provisions such as those for federal reform, encourage institutional instability?

The answers are: "Yes, but . . ." The "yes" is suggested by the tremendous self-consciousness with which the Germans attacked the whole problem of constitutional reconstruction. Having been unused to political responsibility for such a long time and having not yet assumed its full burdens, they were able to approach their task almost as an academic exercise. If political institutions that were conceived and built up in this spirit failed to live up to expectations, this could easily lead to disillusionment.

"Yes, but . . ." The "but" is required as a qualification because new institutions need people to run them, and these people may develop both sentimental attachment to, and material interest in, them. As a result, they will fight more or less fiercely against any attempts at change or abolition. If enough time is given for the development of such attachments and interests, advocates of reform may become aware of the potential explosiveness of their schemes, and therefore desist from proposing them in the first place. Under favorable conditions, German federalism may lose its present potential fluidity, the more so because there are real economic and cultural differences among the populations of the various parts of the country, though the present arrangements do not do complete injustice to these differences by any means.

The states served an important purpose as the proving ground not only for the rebuilding of German constitutionalism, but also for the revival of German politics. Nevertheless, partly because of their somewhat artificial character, some prophets of the doom of German federalism predicted that state politics would lose all vitality once the federal government really got going. Able and energetic politicians would leave for its greener pastures, the attention of the parties would be completely concentrated on capturing control of the federal government, and the states would become mere administrative branches of the central bureaucracy. But these predictions have turned out to be wrong. The main reason for this is the make-up, the position, and the role given to the Bundesrat by the Basic Law.

Bundesrat

The government of each state is represented by three, four, or five members in the *Bundesrat*, the upper chamber of the Federal Parliament, depending on the size of its population (See Table 4). Its votes there must be cast as a unit; that is, even though the state is governed by a coalition of parties that take opposed stands on an issue in the Bundestag, the lower house, all the state's votes must be cast together in the Bundesrat. This has forced the representatives of state governments in the Bundesrat to behave much more like the state delegates they are than like representatives of the political parties to which they happen to belong. Largely as a result of this constitutional provision, the deliberations of the Bundesrat have been structured around true issues of federalism, such as the perennial question of the distribution of revenue between federal and state governments and among the several states. Of course, this might have happened even without the requirement for block voting, since the states have "natural" common interests. But without the requirement party discipline would probably have overcome these considerations. As things actually stand, the state governments have developed so much interest in their common problems, as distinguished from those of the Federal Parliament, that their Ministers-President hold regular conferences very similar to the Governors' Conferences held annually in the United States.

Because of the continued vitality of government at the state level, neither the Bundestag nor the Federal Government can afford to treat the Bundesrat as either a silent or a minor partner. If the Weimar tradition had been followed, the upper house would have performed a useful function as a body of expert civil servants for the revision of technical details of bills and regulations. Under the Basic Law, the states participate in federal legislation through the Bundesrat. All Bills that deal with matters on which the states have the right of concurrent legislation, as well as regulations that implement laws, must be passed by the upper house before they become law. If the Bundesrat rejects a Bill by a simple majority, the Bundestag can override this veto by a simple majority of its votes. A two-thirds veto of the upper house requires a two-thirds vote of the lower house to be overridden. Disagreements between the two houses may be resolved by a standing committee consisting of ten members of each. Since the range of items listed under the concurrent category is wide, and because of the relative independence of the state governments, this committee has often been busy. Members of state governments have made a point of attending meetings of the Bundesrat personally and regularly. Its presidency rotates annually among the Ministers-President. As a result of all this, the Bundesrat has become more important than the Reichsrat, its predecessor of Weimar days.

TABLE 4   Representation in the German Parliament (1954)

STATE	POPULATION	VOTES IN BUNDESRAT	SEATS IN BUNDESTAG
Schleswig-Holstein	2,305,500	4	24
Hamburg	1,752,100	3	17
Lower Saxony	6,569,300	5	66
Bremen	623,000	3	6
North-Rhine-Westphalia	14,561,300	5	138
Hesse	4,520,800	4	44
Rhineland-Palatinate	3,266,900	4	31
Baden-Württemberg	7,008,100	5	67
Bavaria	9,158,300	5	91
TOTAL	49,765,300	38	484

Federal Emergency Powers

The strength of the new German federalism is also due in part to the allocation of legislative powers. This allocation was revised for two reasons: to correct the shortcomings of the Weimar Constitution, as interpreted by the members of the Parliamentary Council at Bonn, and to compensate for the evils of centralization under the Nazis. The Basic Law does not reserve any legislative powers exclusively to the states. But it does contain a long list of twenty-three fields subject to concurrent state and federal legislation.[1] On these matters, the federal government has juris-

[1] Following is the list of legislative powers of the Federation and the States. It is of interest also because it gives an idea of the considerable scope of governmental functions, a matter to which we will return in Chapter 24.

Basic Law, Article 70:

(1) The States have the power to legislate insofar as this Basic Law does not vest legislative powers in the Federation (*Bund*).

Article 71:

In the field of exclusive legislation of the Federation, the States have the power to legislate only if, and insofar as, they are expressly so empowered by federal law.

Article 73:

The Federation has exclusive legislation on:
1. foreign affairs;
2. citizenship in the Federation;
3. freedom of movement, passports, immigration and emigration and extradition;
4. currency, money and coinage, weights and measures and regulation of time and calendar;
5. the unity of the territory as regards customs and commercial purposes, com-

diction when individual states cannot effectively regulate them, when regulation by one state might be prejudicial to the interests of others, or

mercial and navigation agreements, the freedom of traffic in goods, and the exchanges of goods and payments with foreign countries, including customs and border control;

6. federal railways and air traffic;

7. postal services and telecommunications;

8. the legal status of persons in the service of the Federation and of public law corporations directly controlled by the Federal Government;

9. industrial property rights (including patents and trade marks), author's copyrights and publisher's copyrights;

10. co-operation of the Federation and the States in the field of criminal police and in matters concerning the protection of the Constitution, the establishment of a Federal Office of Criminal Police, as well as international prevention and repression of crime;

11. statistics for federal purposes.

Article 74:

Concurrent legislation extends over the following fields:

1. Civil law, criminal law and execution of sentence, the constitution of courts and their procedure, the Bar, notaries and legal advice;

2. census and registry matters;

3. law pertaining to associations and assemblies;

4. the right to sojourn and of settlement of aliens;

5. the protection of German works of art and of cultural (historic) significance against removal abroad;

6. matters relating to refugees and expellees;

7. public welfare;

8. citizenship in the States;

9. war damage and compensation;

10. assistance to war-disabled persons and to surviving dependents, the care of former prisoners of war and the care of war graves;

11. law relating to the economy (mining, industry, power supply, crafts, trades, commerce, banking and stock exchange, insurance to which civil and not public law applies);

12. labor law, including the constitution of enterprises, the protection of workers and provision of employment, as well as social insurance, including unemployment insurance;

13. the furtherance of scientific research;

14. law regarding expropriation insofar as it is concerned with the matters enumerated in Articles 73 and 74;

15. transfer of land and real estate, natural resources and means of production to public ownership or to other forms of publicly controlled economy;

16. prevention of the abuse of economic power;

17. furtherance of agricultural and forestry production, safeguarding of food supply, import and export of agricultural and forestry products, deep-sea and coastal fishing and the guarding and preservation of the coasts;

18. transactions in real estate, law concerning land and matters concerning agricultural leases, housing, settlements and homesteads;

19. measures against epidemics and infectious diseases affecting human beings and animals, the admission of medical and other healing professions and healing practices and the traffic in drugs, medicines, narcotics and poisons;

20. protection concerning traffic in food and stimulants as well as in necessities of life, in fodder, in agricultural and forestry seeds and seedlings, and protection of trees and plants against diseases and pests;

21. ocean and coastal shipping and aids to navigation, inland shipping, meteorological services, sea waterways, and inland waterways used for general traffic;

22. road traffic, motorized transport and the construction and maintenance of highways used for long-distance traffic;

23. railroads other than federal railroads, except mountain railroads.

when the requirements of legal or economic unity call for it. The Federal government has exclusive powers of legislation in eleven fields.

The Federal Government can force a state to fulfill its obligations to the Federation, but only with Bundesrat approval. This provision for federal interference in state affairs is similar to the one contained in Article 48 of the Weimar Constitution, which some have considered one of the main contributors to the end of the Weimar Republic. Under Article 48, the Reich President could use federal troops against a state and/or suspend civil rights. Such measures had to be reported at once to the Reichstag and could be rescinded at its request. In the 1920's, Article 48 was used several times with success against states in which extremists were using violence. But during the last three years of the Republic, and especially under the chancellorships of Brüning, von Papen, and von Schleicher, these powers were abused, both by circumvention of the need for parliamentary approval and by their exercise while the Reichstag was either in recess or dissolved. It was also under Article 48 that the Reich Government could issue decrees having the force of law, as it did continually during the years of parliamentary deadlock starting in 1930. The Basic Law, through its Article 67, discussed below, was designed to safeguard against a repetition of the abuse of similar powers, but even more against the possibility of parliamentary deadlock. If such a stalemated situation should nevertheless arise, the approval of the Bundesrat is once more required (under Article 81) for decrees issued by the Federal Government. So long as the representatives of the state governments in the Bundesrat retain the independence of viewpoint that the constitutional position of that body has virtually forced upon them, and that they have displayed so far, these safeguards should be adequate.

However, in 1948 and 1949, while the Basic Law was being drafted, the maintenance of public order was still mainly a task of the Occupation Powers, and it was then anticipated that that state of affairs would prevail for fairly long, the more so since the demilitarization of Germany had been one of the victors' primary war and occupation aims. These hopes were shattered when, after the outbreak of the Korean War in 1950, the Western powers called for German rearmament. After the treaties on Western European Union came into force and the Federal Republic was admitted to the North Atlantic Treaty Organization, the parliament had to consider the constitutional position of the armed forces that were to be brought into being. On this issue, some extreme federalists, especially from Bavaria, advocated the establishment of separate militias, if not armies, in the several states, but they lost out in the face of the exigencies of modern defense requirements. The Basic Law was amended in March 1956 to permit the creation of Federal Defense Forces. In peacetime, these are to be under the supreme command of the Federal Defense Minister. This command is transferred to the Federal Chancellor once a "state of defense" (*Verteidigungsfall*) has been proclaimed, normally as the result of action to that effect by the Bundestag. Legislation concerning the organization and administration of the defense forces requires Bundesrat concurrence.

Umpire of Federalism

Sooner or later, however, this and other questions of constitutional revision will come up again. When this occurs, parliamentarians are likely to ask the Federal Constitutional Court (*Bundesverfassungsgericht*) to give opinions on the most controversial questions. Some of the functions of this Court, especially judicial review of the constitutionality of parliamentary legislation, are among the new constitution's most daring innovations in German practice. But this is not true of its function as umpire of the federal system. This function was also exercised by the State Court (*Staatsgerichtshof*), the supreme federal tribunal of the Weimar Republic. To cite the most important example: after Chancellor von Papen abused Article 48 in order to oust the pro-constitutional state government of Prussia in 1932, the ousted state government brought suit against the Reich Government in the State Court. The Court found von Papen's action partly unconstitutional, but by the time it did so, it was already too late. The authors of the Basic Law consequently tried to strengthen the position and increase the prestige of the highest court in several ways.

First, they raised it one level in the governmental hierarchy in order to make it the equal of the highest legislative and executive organs. They accomplished this goal by reinstituting the equivalent of the old State Court, in the form of the Supreme Federal Court, but then creating the new Federal Constitutional Court and placing it at the apex of the judicial hierarchy. Second, they provided for the election of its judges by the Federal Parliament, half of them to be elected by each House from among the federal judges and other qualified persons, such as professors of jurisprudence. By contrast, the old State Court had been manned by career judges appointed by the Ministry of Justice. And third, they made it in effect the guardian of the Constitution by giving it the power of judicial review. Thereby they both enhanced its prestige and made its role more controversial, as will be shown later. Although the Court has had to decide several cases of a mainly federal character, these have not so far made up the most important part of its work. This has consisted rather of interpreting basic rights and reviewing legislation for constitutionality.

Symbolism

Finally, under the general heading of federalism, there is the matter of federalistic symbolism. The title of the country is, of course, *Federal* Republic of Germany (*Bundesrepublik Deutschland*). Its principal officers are officially—and are almost always referred to as—*Federal* President, *Federal* Chancellor, and *Federal* Ministers, in the *Federal* Government. Parliament consists of the *Federal* Diet and the *Federal* Council and meets in the *Federal* House. The new defense establishment is called the *Federal* Armed Forces. In each case, the word *Bund* has been substituted for the word *Reich*, used in the Weimar constitutional vocabulary. This terminology has helped create a general awareness of living in a federal system. At the same time, it has also led some politicians to suggest that the *Bund* is merely a temporary organization, to be replaced once more, after reunification, by the *Reich*. Revival of the state of Prussia is being advocated by some in the same connection.

The Federal President

Preoccupation with titles and formal positions has strongly influenced the constitutional role assigned to the head of state of the Federal Republic, the Federal President (*Bundespräsident*). In the Weimar Constitution, an attempt had been made to combine in the presidency both power and restraints—power, in order to provide an adequate substitute for the monarch; and restraints, in order to prevent irresponsible conduct of the kind in which the last Kaiser, Wilhelm II, used to indulge. The Reich President was popularly and directly elected, and served for a term of seven years. His functions were those commonly assigned to Continental heads of state: he was commander in chief of the armed forces, signed laws and decrees, convened and dissolved Parliament, but always with the counter-signature of the Reich Chancellor or a Reich Minister, and these last were to be subject to parliamentary control.

The first President of the Weimar Republic, Friedrich Ebert, a Social Democrat, performed his duties in a solid if colorless manner. His successor, Field Marshal von Hindenburg, Germany's great commander of World War I, turned out to be more colorful throughout, but during the last years of the Republic either unwilling, or—because of senility—unable to live up to the spirit of the Constitution. He dissolved the Reichstag on the request of Chancellor von Papen, who was supported by a minute parliamentary minority and should for that reason never have been appointed in the first place. Then, von Hindenburg permitted use of the emergency powers of Article 48 without parliamentary approval. Ultimately, he was to preside over the establishment of Hitler's dictatorship, remaining President until his death in 1934.

The authors of the Bonn Constitution clearly believed that the President's constitutional position facilitated or even accelerated the downfall of the Weimar Republic. As a result, the powers of the Federal President are but a pale shadow of those of his Reich predecessor. To begin with, his plebiscitary base was removed. He is now elected by the Federal Convention (*Bundesversammlung*), a body that is convened solely for this purpose. It consists of the members of the Bundestag, joined by an equal number of electors, who are elected by and are representative of the political make-up of the state parliaments. His term now runs for only five years, i.e., only one year longer than that of a full-term Bundestag. Most of the discretionary powers that had previously led to abuse, have either been abolished completely or severely curtailed. In effect, the main constitutional functions remaining to the President are the symbolic and ceremonial ones and the giving of counsel and advice to the Federal Chancellor and other parliamentary politicians. The soldiers of the new German military establishment no longer take an oath to obey the President. He has the power to find that a "state of defense" exists, but only when the Bundestag is prevented from doing so, and even then only with the Federal Chancellor's counter-signature and after consulting with the presiding officers of both Houses of Parliament. He is no longer supreme commander of the defense forces.

The Federal Chancellor

The fathers of the Bonn Constitution thus weakened the presidency because of their retrospective orientation. But they clearly had to place somewhere the powers they took away from the President. Portions of them ended up with the Bundesrat, as has already been noted. Most of them, however, were lodged in the chancellorship, which was clearly intended to become the keystone of the whole constitutional edifice. However, to make it that, the concentration of powers in the hands of the Federal Chancellor (*Bundeskanzler*) would not suffice unless at the same time something was done to stabilize his tenure in office. The Weimar chancellorship did not compare unfavorably in strength with the premiership in the Third Republic. The trouble was not its lack of strength, but its instability. And this in turn was due to the political fragmentation of the Reichstag and the difficulties connected with producing positive parliamentary majorities, ready and able to support coalition cabinets. Under the Weimar Republic, as under the Third and Fourth French Republics, it seemed easier to obtain a parliamentary majority that would vote lack of confidence in a ministry than to find one that could agree on its successor.

To remedy this situation, the constitutional engineers of Bonn invented an ingenious device—or rather they applied it, because it had previously been patented in the state constitution of Württemberg-Baden. Article 67 of the Basic Law provides that the Chancellor, who is to be elected by a majority of the members of the Bundestag, cannot be forced out of office simply because a majority of the deputies vote against him on a question of confidence. On the contrary, the

> Bundestag may express its lack of confidence in the Federal Chancellor only by electing, by the majority of its members, a successor, and by submitting a request to the Federal President for the dismissal of the Federal Chancellor. The Federal President must comply with the request and appoint the person elected.

One may well ask what effect a similar provision would have had on French politics, had one been included in the present French Constitution. But the question would be purely academic, because the French politicians who drafted their Constitution could never have agreed on its inclusion. It was precisely the main advantage of the drafters at Bonn over those at Paris that they were not yet involved in the full-blown battles of everyday politics and were, therefore, able to function more as engineering consultants to their public, which had ordered a blueprint for a stable structure, than as self-service builders of their own edifice, who like the French drafters, were at odds as to the purpose of the building.

Another question concerning this "constructive vote of lack of confidence" makes better sense: Can such a constitutional device, by itself, result in the harnessing of divisive social and political forces? If there are deep cleavages in the society, these are likely also to find their reflection in Parliament. There they may perhaps not result in the overthrow of a ministry, because of Article 67, but nevertheless cause refusal to pass the ministry's legislative program. Then the old problem of negative majorities would be revived, further aggravated by the frustrations caused by the artificially continued life of an unwanted ministry.

But the founding fathers at Bonn thought of this eventuality, too. First, they provided for Presidential dissolution of the Bundestag if it fails to give the Chancellor a requested vote of confidence, and if the Chancellor makes a request to that effect within three weeks. But suppose that the subsequent election returns a Bundestag similarly incapable of producing a positive majority? This situation was also anticipated. For if the Bundestag refuses to pass a bill the Government has declared to be urgent, "the Federal President may, at the request of the Federal Government and with Bundesrat approval, declare a state of legislative emergency with respect to a bill." Then, according to Article 81,

> If the Bundestag, after a state of legislative emergency has been declared, again rejects the Bill or passes it in a version declared to be unacceptable to the Federal Government, the law shall be deemed passed provided that the Bundesrat approves it.

The same procedure may then be applied to any other Bill within one period of six months—and one such period only—during one Chancellor's tenure of office. But, in contrast with Article 48 of the Weimar Constitution, the Bonn Basic Law explicitly forbids use of these provisions for the purpose of amending, repealing, or suspending the Basic Law or any part of it.

This scheme seems to be foolproof, and the first seven years of the life of the Federal Republic suggest that it actually is. In 1949, Adenauer was elected Chancellor for the first time by a bare majority—202 of 402 votes. Some bills were passed with the votes of the Social Democratic opposition against those of some members of the Government coalition. But this did not break up the coalition, as is usually the case in similar circumstances in France. In 1953, after the election of the second Bundestag, these provisions appeared to be less important, because Adenauer's own party, the Christian Democratic Union, controlled a majority of the seats by itself and was allied with other parties in a coalition that for some time held two thirds of the seats.

This situation, in turn, suggests that the explanation for recent West German political stability must be sought in electoral conditions as well as in constitutional provisions. If the voters had been very much divided, chances are that their parliamentary deputies would have been just as much divided. And in that case, the six months' grace provided by the constitutional article dealing with legislative emergency might have been of little and only temporary help. Still, the problem is not quite as simple as all that. The first Adenauer coalition and, to an even greater extent, the second were representative of a "natural" stable popular majority of what may be described as the lowest common denominator of non-socialist middle-of-the-road opinion. The point is that the second coalition, which emerged out of the election of 1953, would not have been as large as it turned out to be, and the CDU itself would not have received 45 per cent of the popular vote, if the politics of the first Bundestag had not clearly been conducted between *the* Government facing *the* Opposition. And this continual confrontation of two alternative programs was largely forced upon the parliamentarians—especially those of the minor parties—by

Article 67. If something resembling a two-party system is indeed evolving in West Germany, the inventors of this clever constitutional gadget are entitled to a good deal of the credit for having brought it about.

The Federal Government

According to Article 62, "The Federal Government (*Bundesregierung*) consists of the Federal Chancellor and the Federal Ministers." According to Article 64, "The Federal Ministers are appointed and dismissed by the Federal President upon the proposal of the Federal Chancellor." And according to Article 65, "The Federal Chancellor determines, and assumes responsibility for, general policy. . . ." The cumulative effect of these provisions, combined with those of Article 67, has been to make the Chancellor much more than *primus inter pares*.

Adenauer has in fact run his Cabinet in a much less collegial fashion than British Prime Ministers usually do. It was partly out of resentment over the one-man show the Chancellor was running that his first Minister of Interior resigned, even though disagreement over rearmament policy probably played a more important role. But while the Chancellor does not always consult his Cabinet colleagues before making policy pronouncements, he has usually backed them against attacks in the Bundestag. This happened, for instance, when the Bundestag voted to continue a bread subsidy in opposition to the policy of the Finance and Economics Ministers, and passed a vote of censure against the former. In this case, the Government was able to make use of the provisions of Articles 112 and 113 of the Basic Law, which make increases in budgetary expenditures dependent on Cabinet approval in a manner reminiscent of the rule of the House of Commons, which restricts initiative in increases in expenditure to Ministers.

The relative lack of collegiality in the Cabinet has been due not only to the constitutional and personal dominance of Chancellor Adenauer, but also to the fact that each of his three Cabinets has been a coalition. The first of these, during the period of the first Bundestag (1949-53), consisted of thirteen Ministers, the "classic" ten (Foreign Affairs; Interior; Justice; Finance; Economy; Food, Agriculture, and Forestry; Labor; Transport; Postal and Telecommunications; Home Construction plus three additional, dealing with Questions Concerning the Whole of Germany, Economic Co-operation, and Bundesrat Affairs. It was made up of eight members of the CDU/CSU, three of the FDP, and two of the German Party. After Adenauer's victory of 1953, he created two new Ministries, one for Expellees and another for Questions Concerning the Family. He also added four Ministers without Portfolio to his Cabinet, in order to assure himself of a smoothly functioning two-thirds' majority, sufficient to pass the constitutional amendments required for the European Defense Community. This Cabinet was composed of ten members of the CDU/CSU, four of the FDP, two of the Refugee League, and two of the German Party. The Minister for Postal and Telecommunications was a member of neither the Bundestag nor a party. After the breakup of both the Refugee League and the FDP, and because of dissatisfaction with the Minister of Defense, Adenauer again reorganized his Cabinet late in 1956. It was especially during the two years preceding the last shakeup that disagreements among the members of the Cabinet occasionally received public airing. When the Government was considering the stand it should take on the Saar Agreements, for example, even the results of a vote taken in the Cabinet were publicized.

The Bureaucracy

Both the provisions of the Basic Law and the composition of the first and second Bundestag have enabled the Cabinet to dominate the Bundestag. Seating arrangements symbolize its position of leadership. It has at its disposal a tier of benches to the right of the presiding officer and facing the deputies. Here, Federal Ministers are usually joined by the chief civil servants (*Beamte*), the so-called *Ministerialbürokratie*. These men are even permitted to address the Bundestag and, as representatives of their Ministers, to participate in meetings of the Bundesrat and of committees of the Bundestag. Members of the Bundestag sometimes resent this. On one occasion, a Social Democratic deputy complained about the fact that some civil servants were making faces at the Bundestag, in order to demonstrate their reactions to members' speeches. He claimed that the Minister of Labor had promised that he would bring the bad parliamentary manners of the *Ministerialbürokraten* to the Cabinet's attention, but in the end Adenauer denounced the Social Democrat for trying to be a "censor of manners."

This kind of outburst against bureaucrats does not arise from any deep hostility between the "administrative" and "representative" traditions, as in France. No such opposition exists. Many—roughly about a quarter—of the ministers and deputies have themselves had administrative careers and the status of the *Beamte*. Many are on the inactive list as civil servants for the duration of their parliamentary service and expect to return to active duty at a later date. Because of the almost identical educational prerequisites for legal, judicial, and administrative careers, parliamentarians and bureaucrats generally "speak the same language." People in West Germany are, as a result, not so aware of the problems of parliamentary con trol of the bureaucracy as in France or Britain. And this, in turn, makes it hard to estimate the actual power of the bureaucracy in German politics. Moreover, because the CDU dominated the Federal Government during the first eight years of the life of the Bonn Republic, one cannot tell whether the civil service would loyally serve a Government headed by the present Opposition. However, ministry changes at the level of the states indicate that the bureaucracy is loyal and neutral in this respect. And these state turnovers should be adequate test cases, since the state bureaucracies, in most instances, come under the ultimate jurisdiction of the relevant Federal Ministry.

With some exceptions under the Nazis, the German civil services have had a long tradition of political neutrality and of loyalty to the incumbent regime. This tradition goes back to the seventeenth century, when the Great Elector brought into being the Prussian bureaucracy, which was to serve as the model for most other bureaucracies for more than three centuries. Next to military service, civil service for the king was looked upon as the highest calling. This administrative tradition is so much older in Germany than either constitutionalism or parliamentary democracy that it still carries great prestige. In many respects it serves as the model profession. For example, the ranks and grades of the bureaucarcy are often used to classify the exact status of ordinary citizens. In part, this is due to the great scope of public services, which include, among other branches, the Federal railroads and all public school teachers and university professors. However, not all of these civil servants are *Beamte*. A majority have the lower status of public employees, which is broken down further into salaried and wage-earning groups (*öffentliche Angestellte* and *öffentliche Arbeiter*). Questions about the class basis and bias of civil servants have not played nearly so important a role in Germany as in Britain. Because of the assumed neutrality of both the State and its officials, these officials themselves form an estate, according to their own opinion and that of the public. The assumption is that once an individual takes the civil servant's oath to the State, he leaves behind his previous class or corporate interest.

These traditions, taken together with the presence of many *Beamte* in Parliament, must in part account for the general preference for administration or adjudication over politics. Orderliness is of the very essence of administration. To anyone brought up to become an administrator, parliamentary politics would naturally appear disorderly if not chaotic. Hence the defensive attitude, even on the part of its strongest backers, toward the Weimar Republic. The stability, on the other hand, that has so far prevailed in the Bonn Republic has made this defensive attitude unnecessary. That is why the authors of Article 67 are entitled to so much credit.

Three rival claimants for the plaudits due the authors of political stability might also speak up: those whose efforts were concentrated upon electoral laws; those who made constitutional amendments more difficult to pass than had been the case under the Weimar Constitution; and those who gave a firm constitutional anchor to basic rights by establishing the Federal Constitutional Court as the protector of these rights. Election law is not properly a part of the Constitution, except in a negative sense. The Weimar Constitution provided for proportional representation, whereas the Basic Law contains no such requirement, thus leaving to the legislature greater discretion as to the kind of electoral system they wish to devise. For this reason elections will be discussed later, together with another non-constitutional subject, parliamentary procedure.

Basic Rights

Not only are citizens' rights included in the Constitution, but its entire first Chapter, consisting of nineteen Articles, is devoted to them. Article One sets the tone for the rest:

> The dignity of man is inviolable. To respect and protect it is the duty of all state authority.
>
> The German people therefore acknowledges inviolable and inalienable human rights as the basis of every human community, of peace and of justice in the world.
>
> The following basic rights are binding on the legislature, on the administration and on the judiciary as directly valid law.

The catalog of rights is long and detailed. Particularly interesting here are the authors' efforts to prevent the abuse of these civil and political rights to subvert or overthrow the constitutional order. This desire was again due to their retrospective orientation. They asked themselves, in effect, "Why did the Weimar Constitution fail?" One answer they found in the abuse of the rights of free speech, free press, and free assembly by partisans of both the Nazi and Communist extremes of the political spectrum—abuses that finally led to the outbreak of open violence and then to the end of the Weimar Republic. Consequently, a right such as that of forming associations and societies carries with it a qualification:

> Associations, the objects or activities of which conflict with the criminal laws or which are directed against the constitutional order or the concept of international understanding, are prohibited. (Article 9)

Article 18 is even more explicit on this score:

> Whoever abuses freedom of expression of opinion, in particular freedom of the press, freedom of teaching, freedom of assembly, freedom of association, the secrecy of the mail, of the postal services and of telecommuni-

cations, the right of property, or the rights of asylum, in order to attack the free democratic basic order, forfeits these basic rights. The forfeiture and its extent shall be pronounced by the Federal Constitutional Court.

And Article 21 makes a similar provision with respect to political parties. Moreover, Article 20 proclaims the Federal Republic to be a "democratic and social federal state," in which "Legislation is subject to the Constitution; the executive power and the administration of justice are subject to the Law." Finally, in order to make these "basic principles laid down in Articles 1 and 20" as fixed, fundamental, permanent, and unalterable as humanly possible, an amendment to the Basic Law affecting them is "inadmissible," according to Article 79.

Constitutional Amendments

The amending procedure is set down in Article 79. Here the constitutional fathers were again intent upon correcting their forerunners. The Weimar Constitution could be amended by a two-thirds' majority of a two-thirds' quorum of the members of the Reichstag, i.e., actually by four-ninths, or less than one-half, of the deputies. This made the passage of constitutional amendments relatively easy, at least before the Reichstag was completely fragmented. The procedure was used fairly often. The resultant constitutional instability was, moreover, further aggravated. A bill that was passed by an amending majority did not have to specify whether or not it was in fact intended as a constitutional amendment. And if it was so intended, it did not have to specify just which provisions of the Constitution were to be affected by it. It therefore soon got to be quite difficult if not impossible to tell just what the Constitution consisted of.

In contrast, the Basic Law, according to its Article 79,

> may be amended only by a law expressly amending or amplifying the text of the Basic Law.
> Such a law requires the approval of two-thirds of the Bundestag members and two-thirds of the Bundesrat votes.

In the Federal Republic, there can thus be no doubt as to the content of the Constitution. An amendment to it can be passed only on matters about which there is substantial consensus. One result has been that only relatively few amendments have been passed so far. One of these dealt with a technical matter assigning jurisdiction over administration of a law designed to equalize the burdens of the war; this was not a matter of controversy. Another made provision for the conduct of foreign affairs and defense and was otherwise meant to give effect to the contractual agreements connected with the abortive European Defense Community.

The Allied High Commission used its suspensive veto against this amendment. As things turned out, since these agreements never entered into force, because of French failure to ratify them, the amendment was not then needed. After the Western European Union came into being as a substitute for E.D.C., however, a whole series of amendments was required to fit the new defense establishment into the framework of the Constitution.

These defense amendments were promulgated in March 1956. They established permanent committees of the Bundestag to deal with foreign affairs and defense. They gave the Bundestag the power to find that a "state of defense" exists. They also created the position of Defense Commissioner (*Verteidigungsbeauftragter*) of the Bundestag, copied from a similar Swedish model. The Defense Commissioner resembles the Inspector General of the United States Army, with the important difference that he is not a member of the military establishment itself but is instead responsible to Parliament. The strong desire of the Bundestag to insure civilian control over the military is reflected throughout this series of amendments. This is largely due to the fact that they could be passed only with the support of the Social Democratic Opposition, which drove a hard bargain. The SPD, like other constitutional engineers involved in these efforts, was once more haunted by its interpretation of the fall of the Weimar Republic and the role of the military in that catastrophe. That is why it insisted on an addition to the Basic Law according to which the individual's "freedom of conscientious decision" may not be limited if he has conscientious objections to war service. In that case, opportunities for substitute service must be provided for him. This addition was also made necessary by the original version of Article 4, according to which "No one may be forced against his conscience to perform war service." And in order to make quite certain that these basic rights would be considered binding upon the now strengthened executive, Article 1, which originally declared them to be binding as directly valid law "on the administration," was amended to read "on the executive power."

The Federal Constitutional Court

The difficulty of the amending procedure has thus contributed substantially toward the stability of the institutions anchored in the Basic Law and of the fundamental rights the Basic Law protects. This is one of several reasons why the Federal Constitutional Court has been assuming an increasingly important role. For, if there is disagreement in parliament on the proper meaning of a constitutional provision, clarity can no longer be produced by simply elaborating the controversial paragraph by means of a bill passed by a majority of four-ninths, as was the practice in the Weimar period. In most cases, the constitutional passage has to be left unchanged and an interpretation of its meaning obtained from the Constitutional Court. Going to the Court for this purpose is further encouraged by Article 93. This Article obligates the Court to render anticipatory advisory opinions on questions of constitutionality if it is requested to do so by the Federal or a state government, or by one-third of the Bundestag members. (This of course contrasts sharply with the Supreme Court of the United States, which early in its existence refused to render verdicts on anything but actual controversies at law.) In the Federal Republic, where the latent tendency towards litigiousness is already strong, this has meant that the Court's docket has been constantly overcrowded. Its wide and varied jurisdiction has further complicated its task. The Court is not only the final interpreter of the Constitution and the guardian of citizens' rights, as already mentioned. It also has the final say on Bundestag election controversies. Impeachment trials of the Federal President would take place before it. It has also had the burdensome task of deciding the constitutionality, not merely of contemporary legislation, but also of laws still on the statute books from the days of the Nazis, the Weimar Republic, and earlier periods. Besides that, it is the umpire of the federal system and the interpreter of Article 31, according to which "Federal law overrides state (*Land*) law."

Although the Basic Law provided for the Court, the law establishing it was not passed by the Bundestag until February 1951, a year and a half after the first Bundestag convened. This law provided for a Court consisting of two chambers (*Senate*) of twelve judges each, which are elected half by the Bundestag and half by the Bundesrat. The procedure for nominating the judges is quite complicated. The political parties have had a hard time arriving at compromises as to the composition of the Court, so that the appointment of the first slate of judges, and the filling of vacancies that have arisen since, was delayed, often many months at a time. Originally, the two chambers were assigned jurisdiction over different types of cases. One of them was believed to favor the political outlook of the Government, the other that of the Opposition. They were popularly referred to as the "black chamber" and the "red chamber." Since the Court does not publish dissenting opinions, there was no way of gauging the accuracy of this widespread belief. As a result, when parliamentary delegations of political parties had occasion to request an opinion from the Court, they tried to frame their case so as to have it decided by the "friendly" chamber. Needless to say, these practices did not tend to promote the prestige of the Court.

The Court's effectiveness as guardian of the Constitution and of citizens' basic rights is very hard to gauge. For one thing, it has been in operation for only five years. For another, many of its non-federal functions were such innovations for German government that they were bound not to find general acceptance right away. For the first two years of its life the Federal Republic functioned without a supreme constitutional court. But this gap in the constitutional structure was not a serious handicap. The Occupation authorities, under the Occupation Statute, had retained the power to disapprove legislation that "in their opinion . . . is inconsistent with the Basic Law, a state constitution, legislation, or other directives of the Occupation Authorities themselves or the provisions" of the Occupation Statute. In this sense, the Allied High Commission served as the ultimate guardian of the Constitution, and the Occupation Statute as a sort of super-constitution, until the abolition of both and the attainment of sovereignty by the Federal Republic in 1955.

During the first four years of its existence, the Court rendered about 120 decisions, but invalidated only two Federal and five state laws. Among its major cases was one finding the neo-Nazi Socialist Reich Party anti-constitutional and resulting in that Party's dissolution; another—a very prolonged one, decided in 1956—that had the same effect for the Communist Party of Germany; a case that found unconstitutional all those parts of the German Civil Law Code dealing with family law, because they violated the constitutional provision guaranteeing equal rights to the sexes; and others settling the claims of military personnel and civil servants of the former Reich. The two last mentioned types of opinions have generated the greatest amount of controversy, because they forced the judges to use wide discretion and to come very close to "judicial legislation." In the decision on family law, for example, the Constitutional Court instructed lower courts to judge in terms of the equal-rights provision of the Basic Law until such time as the Federal Parliament should pass legislation replacing those parts of the Civil Code that it found no longer valid. This opinion produced sharp criticism from German jurists and others who believe that the judicial function should properly be confined to the impartial, mechanical, automatically rigid application of existing law. The cases dealing with former civil and military servants of the Nazi regime were controversial, not only because of the highly charged concrete political interests at stake—the treatment to be accorded to men some of whom had been Nazis—but also because it pronounced on the question of legal continuity between the Nazi Reich and the Federal Republic. Its critics again considered this an excursion beyond the Court's proper sphere of jurisdiction.

Thus the Federal Constitutional Court has had to contend with hostility toward its substantive actions, as well as with criticism of its procedure, organization, and the method by which its members are selected. Some of this criticism has come from the Court itself, which in 1955 worked out proposals for its own reorganization, and submitted these to Parliament. The Bundestag did pass a bill reforming the Court's setup in 1956, and took into account some of the Court's own proposals. The division into two chambers, with their unequal work loads, was abolished, and at the same time the number of judges reduced. The three-fourths' majority of the Bundestag committee that had previously been required for the election of the Court's judges was reduced to two-thirds. However, these reforms received a mixed reception from the political public, and some have urged further reforms—or even the Court's abolition. It seems only natural that an institution involving so many novelties should need some reform after a period of experimentation. But if it were not for the tendency toward legalism, many of these reforms might have been accomplished in an informal way. As things actually stand in Germany, however, these requirements could be met only by deliberate legislative reform. In the course of the debates on the reform Bill, politicians naturally raised political issues. As a result, the reformed Court—which will continue to get much of its business because of the general preference for adjudication over politics—may enjoy less prestige than required for the adequate performance of its task.

The Periphery of the Constitution

The organization of the Court, as distinguished from its powers, is one of those matters that fall into the border area between the Constitution and mere legislation, the no man's land between what Oliver Cromwell distinguished as "fundamentals" and "circumstantials," between those matters that it generally requires some kind of extraordinary majority to change and those that can be passed by an ordinary majority. Besides the organization of the Court, two other important questions are to be found in this same ill-defined periphery of the Constitution: parliamentary procedure and the electoral system. In Great Britain, as Dr. Eckstein has shown, the scope of things considered constitutional and fundamental is very wide indeed. The fact that so many institutions are ancient, and accepted as virtually unalterable precisely because of this antiquity, has lent great constitutional stability to British government. On the other hand, the absence of a written constitution actually places no institution beyond Parliament's power to change or even abolish it by a majority of only one vote. Nevertheless, it is to the credit of British parliamentary procedure that such changes are made but rarely, and that when they are made, they usually do not serve only the immediate political advantage of the majority of the day. The British electoral system is as stable as parliamentary procedure with respect to its most important features—election by plurality vote and in single-member constituencies. The extent of the franchise, however, has been subject to occasional parliamentary changes, which Governments felt free to push through since they could claim a "mandate." This relative constitutional stability in both these fields has gone along with a widespread unquestioning consensus among politicians and public alike on the propriety and fairness of these very important "rules of the game."

Parliamentary Procedure

Nothing approaching this degree of consensus exists in either France or Germany, though parliamentary procedure has been more stable than electoral systems. Thus the Bundestag at Bonn initially adopted the Rules of Procedure of the Reichstag of Weimar days, at the same time adapting them to the constitutional changes that had occurred. It was able to get along on this basis for two years after its first meeting, until it passed a new set of rules in December 1951—and these did not differ very much from the older ones. The rules are long—132 paragraphs and close to 10,000 words—detailed, and comprehensive. They take account of the strong constitutional positions of both Cabinet and Bundesrat by providing that members of either, or their deputies, must be listened to by the Bundestag on their request. The Cabinet, on the other hand, does not have to accede to demands for a major interpellation (*grosse Anfrage*), though its refusal may be debated in the House if at least 30 members so request.

The Bundestag, voting by secret ballot, elects its own President by a majority of votes cast. But if the first two ballots do not produce a majority, a plurality choice is made between the two top contenders on the second ballot. The three men who have so far served in this capacity have all been members of the CDU, and have for the most part tried to preside over the business of the Bundestag in an impartial manner. The third holder of the presidency was elected by only a plurality of its votes. The President, his deputies, and representatives of the officially recognized party delegations (*Fraktionen*), together form the Council of Elders (*Ältestenrat*), which fixes the agenda of the Bundestag. For this reason, and also because party representation on committees is proportioned to the strength of these groups, the rules governing their recognition are important. The Rules of Procedure themselves, however, do not specify the minimum number of members required for purposes of recognition as a *Fraktion*. Rather they state that this minimum is to be fixed by a resolution of the House. This provision was designed to provide maximum flexibility on this point, in order to facilitate discrimination against minor parties—especially the anti-constitutional ones. In the Reichstag, the minimum used to be 15 members, but the Bundestag at first fixed it at 10. Then, in January 1952, it raised it to 15, so as to exclude the Communist deputies from the Council of Elders and the committees. This was made possible by the fact that the Communist *Fraktion*, though originally 15 strong, usually had a smaller number of deputies in the Bundestag, since some of them were frequently barred from the House because of disorderly conduct.

Unparliamentary behavior was quite a problem during the life of the first Bundestag, from 1949 to 1953. At one point, the President even excluded the late leader of the Social Democratic opposition, Dr. Schumacher, from the chamber. The Communists occasionally started near-riots. But since none of them was returned in the general election of 1953, things have got relatively quiet and restrained. During the first year of the second Bundestag's tenure, not a single reprimand was issued to members by their presiding officer. In fact, many of the debates have been so orderly as to bore some people—and this despite the fact that deputies must attend sessions and are not allowed to vote by proxy. When the Social Democrats have really wanted to show their disapproval of parliamentary proceedings, they have walked out of the chamber as a group, instead of resorting to the more rowdy tactics that are often used on such occasions in Paris.

One reason for this orderly parliamentary atmosphere is the fact that the function of the Bundestag is more propagandistic than deliberative. Speakers for the various parties usually do not try to convince one another of the merits of their several antagonistic programs—quite a hopeless task for anyone who would attempt it. Nor do they really try to hammer out policies based on reasonable contributions from all those capable of making them. They rather use the forum of Parliament to get publicity for their party's position. The speeches they deliver sound more like the policy declarations delegates of sovereign states make before certain international assemblies, such as the General Assembly of the United Nations, than like attempts to persuade. And although parliamentary reporting in the West German press has not yet reached the same high level as in Great Britain, the publicity value of debates is high. Some of the more important debates are reported verbatim in the better newspapers, some debates are broadcast, and a few are even televised.

The Rules of Procedure themselves conduce to this non-deliberative, propagandistic character of the debates. They do this by providing that speeches are to be delivered from the rostrum, which is located below the

President's high pedestal. A speech should last not less than five minutes nor more than one hour, and should not be read but delivered extemporaneously, with occasional reference to written notes permitted. However, this latter rule is often broken. Parliamentary leaders have been quite conscious of the resultant lack of liveliness of Bundestag proceedings. Because of their general wish to "bring Parliament closer to the people," they have instituted some formal changes designed to further this aim. One of these has affected the question period, during which floor microphones may now be used by deputies for asking supplementary questions. But this does not seem to have reduced the formal atmosphere of the debates in any marked degree. Another change was intended to increase respect for the Bundestag and the dignity of its business, by enhancing the prestige of its presiding officer. He is now attired in white tie and tails, and members rise as he enters the chamber. To some observers of contemporary German parliamentarism, this has seemed merely to add to its artificiality. After all, white tie and tails are but a pale image of Mr. Speaker's wig and knee breeches. It is true that some presidents of the French National Assembly have also affected this attire. But the National Assembly at least meets, and has been meeting since the Third Republic, in the Palais Bourbon, which was built in the eighteenth century. By contrast, the modernistic Bundeshaus does make a somewhat artificial, untraditional, and even temporary, provisional, rootless, and unstable impression.

If the plenary sessions of the Bundestag do not in the main have a deliberative function, where in the West German Parliament does deliberation take place? Partly in caucuses of the parties, discussed in the next chapter; and partly in specialized parliamentary committees (*Ausschüsse*). The Rules of Procedure provide that each bill must have three readings before it can be sent on to the Bundesrat and/or the Federal President for his assent. Debate for the first and third readings is about the general principles of the bill only, except that on the third reading detailed consideration is permitted of those parts of a bill that have been amended in the course of the second-reading debate. After the first reading, the bill is normally sent to one or more committees, whose report is then considered in the course of the detailed discussion on its second reading.

The first Bundestag had as many as 39 committees, whose membership varied, some having 27, others 21, 15, or 7 members. The most important committees (e.g., the one on questions of European security) were kept down to the minimum number of seven, so that only the three largest parties were represented on them. In this way, the minor *Fraktionen*—especially the Communists, while they were still recognized officially as a delegation—could be kept away from these frequently secret deliberations. Manipulation of the rules of the parliamentary game, in this case of the size of committees, thus served as means of discriminating against particular parties. Since none of the extremist parties returned any deputies to the second Bundestag, this particular concern has ceased to play a role. The second Bundestag established 36 committees (as of November 1953). Their memberships were 17, 19, 23, 29, or 31. Those with 17 members were made up of party members in the following proportion: CDU 9, SPD 5, Free Democratic Party (FDP), Refugee League (GB/BHE), and German Party (DP) one each; those with 29 members: CDU 15, SPD 9, FDP 3, and GB/BHE and DP one each. Every committee elects its own chairman. In many cases he is not a member of the government coalition but of the opposition party.

Committee members are often noted experts in the committee's special field, so that they can accomplish a good deal of quiet and businesslike legislative work. The work is quiet, because committee meetings are not normally open to the public or the press, and committee reports do not contain full transcripts of the proceedings, but only the committee's legislative recommendations to the Bundestag. However, while the meetings are closed to the public, members of the Cabinet or the Bundesrat, or their representatives, have access to all committee meetings, according to Article 43 of the Basic Law, which is reinforced further by the Rules of Procedure. As a result, committees are neither able secretly to hatch bills in order to compete with the Cabinet's legislative initiative, nor likely to become strong centers of parliamentary power, as in the case of their counterparts in the French National Assembly or the United States Congress. The best opportunity for this to occur in the Federal Republic would seem to exist in the case of the newly created Defense Committee, and its constitutional position has, for this very reason, been criticized a good deal.

The Committee for Petitions is an interesting innovation, based on citizens' right to petition or complain in writing to Parliament, anchored in Article 17 of the Basic Law. Of course, the Bill of Rights of the United States Constitution contains a similar provision, though the Congress has not thought it necessary to establish a special committee on petitions. That the Bundestag should nevertheless have done so, and made formal provision for its operation in the Rules of Procedure, is another expression of the tendency toward legal formalism: the constitutional right exists; therefore, there must be a legally sanctioned institution designed to make the right effective. German citizens are not likely to exert informal pressure on the deputy from their district or to use other informal contacts. During the four-year life of the first Bundestag, the Committee on Petitions actually had submitted to it, and dealt with, some 25,000 petitions.

On the whole, the Rules of Procedure and character of proceedings of the Bundestag do not differ very much from those of the Reichstag during the less troubled years of the Weimar Republic in the mid-1920's. The extreme kind of disorderliness that marked Reichstag debates after 1930, while it may at times have been approached in the first Bundestag, has been inconceivable in the second, between 1953 and 1957. But this is due to the absence of anti-constitutional elements in the Bonn Parliament and has little to do with changes in its rules. The largely non-deliberative, declaratory character of the debates has changed very little, and could be noted before in the Bismarckian Reichstag, the Prussian and other German parliaments of the nineteenth century, and such conventions as the National Assembly of 1848. The intellectual level of the debates was usually very high, the historical self-consciousness and seriousness of the speakers intense, and their general learnedness admirable. All this is still true. But the Bundestag, in contrast with its predecessors before 1918, and even in comparison with the Reichstag of the Weimar Republic, is constitutionally endowed with considerable legislative powers, and politically with many real opportunities for making contributions to shaping the material fortunes of the German people. But debates are still carried on, to a large degree, in the same old rather abstract and theoretical manner. Mention of material interest is still avoided in favor of learned historical and ideological justifications. And as before, the Bundestag often tampers with important provisions of the not-quite-fundamental periphery of the Constitution, in order to achieve immediate political objectives. All that really seems to stay stable at the bottom of this often deliberately created condition of general flux is the way of doing things—the retrospective orientation, the legalistic manner of discourse, the desire to formalize. These habits are not written down in any document. Those who have them are not even conscious of being dominated by them. And yet they seem to be just about the only factors of relatively continuous stability in German politics.

The Electoral System

The electoral system, by contrast, is one of the most unstable institutions, in Germany as in France. In the Weimar Republic, the Constitution itself provided for proportional representation. The scheme had already been prepared by an election law passed during the last year of World War I, which brought to fruition one of the Social Democrats' principal constitutional demands of the Imperial era. It was designed to make the Reichstag an exact mirror of political opinion in Germany. It divided the whole country into thirty-odd large constituencies. In each of these, the several parties submitted lists of candidates, whose names then appeared on the ballot in the order determined by the party bosses. Votes were cast for a party's list, not for individual candidates. Once the votes were counted in each constituency, each party was given one seat in the Reichstag for every 60,000 votes cast for its ticket. The seats were assigned to candidates in the order in which they appeared on the party's list. After all the votes cast for the several parties in each of these large districts had been divided by 60,000, the remainders, if greater than 30,000, were pooled in electoral district-unions, which consisted of two or three separate constituencies. Here the same process of dividing by 60,000 was repeated, and then remainders were dealt with once more in another pool at the Reich level. As a result, the membership of the Reichstag varied in size from one general election to the next, depending on the number of votes cast.

But this was by no means the most important consequence of the system. It placed the possibility of parliamentary representation within reach of minor groups whose support was geographically scattered rather than concentrated. Consequently, organizations that resembled interest groups more than parties were encouraged to put up candidates and able to get them elected. The system also tended to prevent much real contact between individual deputies and their constituents, since candidates were dependent upon their party bosses for the all-important position assigned to them on the party's list, rather than on the personal good will of the voters of their district. If placed at the top of the constituency list, or, even better, of the Reich list, a candidate was virtually assured of election. The system was also believed by some to have contributed to the splintering of the party system. This seems to be a questionable allegation, since the Weimar Reichstag contained almost the same number of significantly represented parties as the Imperial Reichstag before it, and that body had been elected from single-member constituencies.

In any case, whatever may have been the effects of the system of almost perfect electoral justice under the Weimar Republic, most of the men who had the task of reconstructing constitutional democracy in West Germany had very definite theories as to what these effects were—and their theories were not all in agreement. Some went so far as to assert that proportional representation was the principal cause of the failure of the Weimar Constitution. They tried to prove that without proportional representation the Nazis would always have remained a minute minority in the Reichstag, if indeed they could ever have succeeded in getting any candidates elected to that body at all, and that perhaps they would never have entered politics at all, because they could have entertained little hope of electing candidates in single-member districts. Moreover, if more personalized candidatures had been encouraged instead of the list system, it was said, people in the Weimar Republic might have felt greater loyalty to the constitutional regime as such, and been less easily swayed by demagogic denunciations of the futility of parliamentarism.

Most of these views are, at best, debatable. And debated they were in the Parliamentary Council at Bonn, which, having drafted the Basic Law, next drafted the first federal election law. It did not have to concern itself with provisions for the election of the Federal President, since the plebiscitary selection of the head of state had been eliminated by the Basic Law. Under the Weimar Constitution, the Reich President was elected by a majority of those voting on the first ballot and, this failing, by a plurality on the second. The additional general elections made necessary by this provision had further contributed to the intensity of political excitement during the last years of the Weimar Republic. In 1932, von Hindenburg, as the candidate for re-election, failed to get a majority on the first ballot, so that a run-off had to be held. In addition to these two elections there were three for the Reichstag between September 1930 and November 1932, which followed three dissolutions. Under the Bonn Constitution, this kind of piling national elections one on top of the other was not going to be repeated.

But what kind of electoral system would be used? The CDU favored single-member districts and election by a simple plurality. This position was based not only on relatively "objective" retrospective interpretations of the Weimar setup, but also on a fairly accurate estimate of the party's electoral strength in the country. The Social Democrats, on the other hand, were ideologically committed to proportional representation, since they believed it to be the only scheme embodying true democratic justice. And they, too, had reasons of interest, because of the heavy concentration of their supporters in urban industrial centers.

The outcome of this struggle between divergent views was a compromise. The basis for this compromise came, like so many other parts of the Federal constitutional machinery, from experimentation carried on in the laboratories provided by the member states. The first election held in the British Zone of Occupation was conducted on the basis of single-member plurality constituencies, as used in Britain and the United States. The results strongly favored the CDU over the SPD. Consequently, the "sixty-forty" system—to be explained below—was later introduced. The Parliamentary Council had first agreed on using a "fifty-fifty" system, having half the seats allocated to single-member districts and half to state lists.

The Military Governors, however, insisted on having this proportion changed to one of sixty-forty, as used in the British Zone.

The trouble was that the Occupation Powers, too, had theories about the failure of the Weimar Constitution and about the necessary institutional prerequisites for the survival of constitutional and democratic government. These theories were expressed in different ways, for example, the influence on the election law, just cited. Then there was the Military Governors' refusal to permit that part of the draft election law to stand that allowed civil servants who were elected to the Bundestag to go on the inactive list instead of permanently retiring from the service. The Military Governors insisted on permanent retirement, partly because of the suspicious view they took of the bureaucracy that served the Weimar Republic—not in fact much different from that which had served the Empire before—and partly because of American notions about the separation of powers. In practice, this provision tended to discriminate against the Social Democrats. Many of their potential candidates for parliamentary office have traditionally come from the bureaucracy, have no independent income, and would consequently hesitate to run for office unless they had the insurance of being able to return to the security of their career if defeated. In any case, as soon as the Occupation Powers put the Germans on their own in this respect, they proceeded to legislate as they would have in the first place.

Under the first Federal election law, 60 per cent of Bundestag seats were assigned to single-member constituencies in the several states, to be won by the individual candidates who got the largest number of votes. The remaining 40 per cent were assigned to state-wide party lists on the basis of proportional representation (using the d'Hondt maximum figure procedure).[2] In order to benefit from the proportional representation pro-

[2] Example of the d'Hondt procedure: Assume thrat 460,000 voters have cast ballots and there are 10 seats at stake, the votes being distributed among four parties as follows:

PARTY	VOTES
A	210,000
B	140,000
C	80,000
D	30,000

These figures are successively divided by 1, 2, 3, etc., i.e., by the number of seats already assigned to the party plus one.

÷1	÷2	÷3	÷4	÷5
A 210,000(I)	105,000(III)	70,000(V)	52,500(VII)	42,000(IX)
B 140,000(II)	70,000(VI)	46,666(VIII)	35,000	28,000
C 80,000 (IV)	40,000(X)	26,666	20,000	16,000
D 30,000	15,000	10,000	7,500	6,000

visions, a party had to win either at least one single-member district in the particular state, or 5 per cent of the total vote cast in the state. This provision was clearly designed to discourage minor parties. The election returns August 14, 1949, showed both the CDU and the SPD to have been right in advancing their respective schemes. The CDU won 114 constituency seats and only 24 from state lists. The SPD won 96 from state lists and only 35 constituency seats. But the Free Democrats, which joined the CDU in Adenauer's first coalition, won 40 of its 52 seats from state lists. In other words, the CDU was able to form a majority coalition in the first Bundestag as a result of the proportional representation provisions which it had opposed. (Of course, if proportional representation had not been provided for at all, the seats that actually went to the FDP might instead have gone to the CDU in the first place.)

The law under which this first Bundestag was elected was not meant to be permanent. An independent citizens organization, the Voters' Union, early expressed the hope that Parliament would soon replace it with a permanent measure. However, the Bundestag did not get around to this task until just before the end of its term. Then another makeshift compromise was passed after rather heated debate, this time by a voting coalition consisting of both the Social Democrats and the Government parties, against the votes of the Bavarian branch of the CDU, called the Christian Social Union (CSU), and the German Party. This law provided for the election of 484 deputies, in contrast with the first law's 400. Half of these were to be elected in single-member districts as before. To elect the other half, who were put on state lists nominated by the parties, each voter was given a second ballot, on which he voted for one of the party lists. With his first vote, he voted for an individual candidate running in his district. The second votes were counted on a state-wide basis, again using the d'Hondt procedure. From the number of seats thus allocated to each party in a state, there was deducted the number of seats already won on the basis of the first ballots in the individual constituencies. But this

---

First, the figures in column (÷1) are divided by 1. A has the highest quotient and gets seat I. A's votes are therefore divided by 2 the next time around, giving it 105,000, less than B's 140,000 in the first round; hence B gets seat II. In the end, the seats are distributed as follows:

PARTY	SEATS
A	5
B	3
C	2
D	0

From Hans Trossmann, *Der zweite deutsche Bundestag* (Bonn 1954), p. 90 f.

time, in order to benefit from the proportional representation provisions, a party had to win either one single-member seat, or 5 per cent of the total votes cast in the whole Federal Republic (instead of just the state involved, as previously).

The result was that the minor parties either elected no deputies at all to the second Bundestag, or suffered substantial losses. The German Reich Party, the Communist Party, the Party of the Bavarians, and some other small groups, which had placed 5, 15, 17, and 12 deputies, respectively, in the first Bundestag, received fewer popular votes and won no representation at all in the second Bundestag. On the other hand, the Refugee Union (GB/BHE), which had run no candidates in the federal election of 1949, won 27 seats, all from state lists and by means of proportional representation. The CDU/CSU won 243 seats, of which 71 were from state lists. The SPD got 150, of which 105 were by proportional representation. Of the FDP's 48 deputies, only 14 were elected in single-member districts, in contrast with 10 of the German Party's total of 15. Since Adenauer's coalition, as of 1953, consisted of the CDU/CSU, FDP, GB/BHE, and DP, supplemented by the Center Party, its majority in the Bundestag consisted of 198 deputies elected in single-member constituencies and 140 elected by proportional representation from state lists. The surprising thing was that, despite the complicated voting procedure employed, only 3.3 per cent of the ballots cast had to be rejected as spoiled.

During the debate that produced the second electoral law, several speakers said that they hoped for passage of a more permanent electoral law early in the term of the next Bundestag—before political considerations motivated by an imminent election would outweigh "objective" considerations. These hopes turned out to be in vain once more. In the spring of 1956, the CDU threatened to push a still less proportional election law through the Bundestag. This move was largely responsible for causing the FDP's branch in the state of North-Rhine–Westphalia to leave the state coalition in which they had been with the CDU. Using the constructive vote of lack of confidence, for which that state constitution provides, they formed a new coalition government together with their erstwhile opposition, the Social Democrats. Other branches of the FDP threatened to execute similar maneuvers in other state parliaments. Partly because of these threats, the Adenauer Government reneged on its plan to reform the electoral system. The federal elections that were held on September 15, 1957, were governed by a law that differed from its forerunner in only one important point: this time, a party that did not receive at least 5 per cent of the total popular vote cast in the whole Federal Republic had to elect three single-member seats instead of one, as previously, in order to benefit from proportional representation. As a result, the Refugee League, which received 4.6 per cent of the popular vote but elected no candidate in a district, was not represented in the third Bundestag. In contrast, the German Party, which received only 3.4 per cent of the popular vote but elected six constituency candidates, placed 17 deputies in the Bundestag. The Free Democrats and allied splinter groups got 7.7 per cent of the total vote, elected one district candidate, and were represented by 41 deputies. The Social Democrats (31.8 per cent and 169 seats) and the Christian Democrats (50.2 per cent and 270 seats) now had more than four-fifths of the electorate supporting them and controlled almost nine-tenths of the seats in parliament.

Election systems in the member states have, in most cases, not been stabilized either, so far. Usually a state legislature passes an election law just before the next election, sometimes by a small majority. Occasionally, the constitutionality of provisions of these laws is challenged in state courts or in the Federal Constitutional Court, and the general institutional instability is thereby intensified. Basically, however, this instability is the result of two factors: first, the difficulties involved in, and the fear of, including detailed electoral provisions in the Constitution, which is so much harder to amend that its Weimar predecessor; and, second, the prevalent belief in the feasibility of constitutional engineering, whether its ultimate purpose be immediate partisan advantage or the presumed long-run public interest of the whole country. Because of the first, election laws can be changed by mere parliamentary, rather than amending, majorities. Because of the second, the parties encourage such changes, hoping to gain thereby. As a matter of fact, however, the causal relation between a specific election law and the results of the election governed by it can never be demonstrated with accuracy. This is so because the electorate might have behaved differently with a different law. But if the Germans become aware of this truth, the instability of electoral systems may only be increased.

Politics *versus* Government

In any case, the relatively unpolitical period of German constitutional reconstruction has now definitely gone, with the same wind which blew out Allied eagerness for German "demilitarization." No longer can the West Germans enjoy the luxury of academically discussing the merits and demerits of various constitutional provisions, in assemblies that are necessarily in general agreement on the authority of constitutionalism as such, and unconcerned with the purposes for which political power is exercised, simply because they have little influence on its exercise. Since 1955 at the latest, constitutional and policy issues—issues of authority and issues of purpose—have been inextricably interwined. Each issue of predominantly one kind is likely to generate its counterpart, predominantly of the other kind. The belief in the feasibility of constitutional engineering, far from waning, will wax—and that in both parts of the divided country, so long as it remains divided. For both systems seem to have accomplished the goals they set themselves largely as a result of the governmental machineries that they deliberately and rationally engineered into existence. The intentional seems to have shaped the situational, rather than the other way around. This is true especially in the Federal Republic. One of the main objectives of its constitutional fathers was political stability— the opposite of the situation that prevailed under the Weimar Republic. They got political stability, marked by its contrast with the rapid succession of cabinets in neighboring France. There is, of course, no proof positive that this is the result of constitutional provisions, such as the one for the constructive vote of lack of confidence. But since nothing succeeds like success, people easily jump to the conclusion that they are the architects of their own current state of relative political bliss.

Moreover, constitutional re-engineering is likely to continue. Changes in the political situation of the Federal Republic—such as attainment of internal sovereignty and accession to N.A.T.O.—would call for making readjustments even without the existing predilection in favor of making them. At the same time, the increasing urgency with which demands for the reunification of the country are being voiced tends to strengthen the public's awareness of the provisional character of their constitution. The value of the prizes at stake for the different political groupings constantly increases, together with their awareness of the possibility of having one's way by means of changing fundamental institutions of government. Consequently, the potential explosiveness of both constitutional and policy issues increases as well, and so, therefore, does the desire to avoid friction by the old method of substituting adjudication or administration for politics. We have suggested that this desire is more likely to produce the reverse, namely the politicization of everything constitutional instead of the constitutionalization of everything political. In any case, politics—the resolution of conflicts of interest—has become increasingly more important than government—the framework within which conflict takes place— in the Federal Republic. And it is in the way in which politics is conducted that we can best search for that stability which we have so far failed to find to our satisfaction in those very institutions that were designed to insure stability.

CHAPTER 23

Parties,
Issues, and
Political Style

"The parties participate in the forming of the political will of the people." This sentence is not a quotation from a textbook on comparative
government, but from Article 21 of the Basic Law of the Federal Republic of Germany. It illustrates once more the extent to which the formal
constitution in West Germany includes matters that in other countries
would come under the heading of "informal political processes." Even in
Germany, we must admit, much of what the parties do is not explicitly
regulated by law. However, this legal gap is regretted by many Germans
and was not intended by the authors of the constitution, which in this
same Article provides for passage of a "party law." By the beginning of
1958, no such law had yet been passed. One reason for this is said to be
the reluctance of party politicians to make public party finances, as would
be required by such legislation.

The sentence is interesting for another reason: its emphasis on "political will" and the parties' relation to this. British political vocabulary does
not assign an important role to the notion of political will. That the reverse is true on the Continent may be connected with the crucial character
of the concept of sovereignty in Continental political theory, and the fact
that will has generally been viewed as the main function of the sovereign,
e.g., by Rousseau. Of course, any government has to produce a will in the
sense that it must make decisions. This is just as true of British as of French
and German government, but the English-speaking peoples have never

been as self-conscious about the problem. This in turn may be because of the historical fact that they have never had as much trouble finding and expressing their political will as most of the Continentals.

While this criticism cannot be leveled at contemporary West German government, the explicit linking of parties with forming the political will has created some difficulties. Only parties—not interest groups—have been assigned this role among non-state organizations. In other words, the parties have a constitutional monopoly in this participation. Politics, however, is a continuous and comprehensive process and does not admit of this kind of compartmentalization. Interest groups in many cases have to become involved in politics. Indeed, politics would often not work without such involvement. But formalism leads many Germans to condemn "political" activity by organizations other than parties. The Basic Law itself enables them to make a constitutional issue out of such cases. On the other hand, the parties' constitutional monopoly of this role often leads them to differentiate their function excessively, or unrealistically, from the function of other organizations that are also a part of the structure of effective power. This self-differentiation has a further consequence in that it enables party politicians to claim that they are really not concerned with material interests, since such a concern belongs in the proper sphere of the interest groups. Since they thus exclude material interests from their domain, that leaves ideal interests. And ideals in turn—for reasons already been mentioned—often tend to be ideologized in Germany.

In this chapter, we are interested in the structure of effective power, and for that purpose the constitutional statement about the forming of the political will of the people provides a useful focus. After all, the Basic Law and the other laws described in the last chapter cannot really subsume all that we would want to know. Nor would we expect that the ideologies of the various parties really tell us enough about the aims and methods of their members and supporters. There must be other factors that go into making the German political will. This is likely especially because of the radical novelty of the contemporary West German political situation. Many of the problems and issues the West Germans have been facing since the end of World War II differ fundamentally from those which Germans have ever faced before and from those which Britons, Frenchmen, or Russians are facing today. Political parties are among the instruments by which issues are formulated, solutions for them advanced, and controversies about them fought out. Changes in problems and issues, therefore, should result in changes in parties and in the party system. Has this been true of the Federal Republic?

The Changing Party System

In Chapter 21, we saw how often and how profoundly German society has been subjected to changes since national unification in 1871. Of the last three of these changes—totalitarianism, defeat, and division— we would expect that the cumulative effects must have been so revolutionary that there could be little, if any, continuity between the present party system and its predecessors. National Socialist totalitarianism might have had this effect by itself. The Nazis started out as just another member of the multi-party system of the Weimar Republic. Officially, theirs was the National Socialist German Workers' Party (N.S.D.A.P.). By 1933, they had become the strongest single party, though they were still short of having a majority in the Reichstag. Nevertheless, President von Hindenburg was finally persuaded that Hitler might be able to bring order out of the political and economic chaos that reigned in Germany during the last years of the Weimar Republic. On January 30, 1933, he appointed him Reich Chancellor, and Hitler proceeded to form a cabinet of National Socialists and Nationalists. He outlawed the Communist Party on the pretext that alleged Communist arson had caused the fire in the Reichstag building. In the election of March 5, 1933, the Nazis had won 288 seats, the Nationalists 53, and the Communists 81, out of a total of 647. Since the Communist deputies were excluded from participating, this meant that the Nazi coalition held 341 of 566 seats, a majority, though somewhat short of an amending majority. Nevertheless, and partly as the result of violent intimidation, the other parties in the Reichstag, except for the Social Democrats, joined the Nazis in passing the so-called Enabling Act, which transferred full legislative powers to the Reich Government. Thus Hitler could claim with some justification to have attained full power by constitutional means. He proceeded to use this power to outlaw all parties but his own, and eventually, upon von Hindenburg's death, to combine the office of President with those of Chancellor and *Führer* (leader) of the Party.

The history of Nazi totalitarianism lies beyond the scope of this book. For our immediate interests here, it suffices to state that most anti-Nazi politicians were silenced, often by being killed, imprisoned, or exiled. The Nazis attempted to revolutionize German society completely; the war and its aftermath brought about further changes. Hence, though some men who had been active in politics before 1933 returned to it after the war—the SPD, for example, had maintained a headquarters in exile—there was little cause for them to return to the methods and goals which they had pursued during the Weimar period. There were many reasons for this. The bankruptcy of the old methods and goals had been clearly demonstrated by Hitler's success. He evidently offered things to the German electorate that the other parties did not offer, or that the voters did not believe them capable of achieving. The Germans had by now passed through the crucible of Nazi totalitarianism, which had deeply affected their values, their beliefs, and their expressive symbols, either because Nazi ideological indoctrination had succeeded, or—in the majority of cases— because of their negative reaction to this indoctrination. Half of one generation had died during the twelve years of the Nazi regime, and half another generation had reached voting age. And these reasons for the expediency of devising new political methods and goals could be further multiplied.

The ravages wrought by the war, and the subsequent division of Germany, point at least as strongly to the likelihood of discontinuity in the German party system. As a result of the war, millions died in addition to those who met their end by natural causes between 1933 and 1945. Allied bombings of German cities resulted in tremendous material destruction. The expulsion of ethnic Germans from Eastern Europe and from formerly German territories which were taken over by such countries as Poland and the Soviet Union, resulted in the influx into the now smaller Germany of somewhere between eight and ten million people, many of whom had not been German citizens under the Weimar Republic—e.g., the Sudeten Germans from Czechoslovakia. Establishment of the totalitarian Soviet regime in the eastern part of the country further added to this migration. The occupation of the country by Allied military forces acquainted the Germans with new political and administrative methods, especially in consequence of the Western effort to "educate" the Germans for democracy. Incidentally the Occupation also provided an outside enemy, in opposition to which the Germans could wish to unite, or with regard to which the issue of opposition or support could further divide the German population.

Thus, as the outcome of these largely intentional efforts on the part of the Nazis, and the largely circumstantial effects of defeat and division, the social structure of West Germany today is certainly not the social structure of the Weimar Republic; neither are the party system and the pattern of interests in general. And this can hardly come as a surprise to anyone who recognizes any connection between social structure and political structure—and in order to do that one need not be a Marxist but simply a realist. The connection may not be very evident in a country such as the United States, where class-consciousness has been weak. But in most

European countries, where class-consciousness has been quite strong, this relation between social structure and political structure is correspondingly marked. There, even Roman Catholic parties, which have the avowed aim of surmounting the class-struggle or of denying its reality, are affected in their strength, aims, and methods by changes in the social structure. Nevertheless—and this should come as a surprise—there does seem to be a high degree of continuity about the West German party system. At least this is true so far as the subjective feelings of the leaders and members of most of the contemporary parties are concerned. Most of them think of themselves as carrying on with an old political tradition that goes back at least to 1871, and often beyond that. Of all the parties operating at the federal level, there is only one of which this is not true—the Refugee League (GB/BHE), and understandably so. The masses of refugees and expellees living in the Federal Republic are a novel phenomenon, the direct consequence of the colossal defeat of 1945, and the division of the country. Nor is it true of the Christian Democratic Union to the extent that it is of the remaining federal parties, and again for evident reasons: the changes in the denominational make-up of the Federal Republic, along with other factors, made possible the organization of a Christian rather than a merely Roman Catholic party. Nevertheless, the predominantly Roman Catholic element of the CDU, and even more its Bavarian branch, the Christian Social Union, usually make them sound as though they were the legitimate heirs and continuators of the Roman Catholic Center of Weimar and Imperial days, and of the Bavarian People's Party of the Weimar period, respectively.

Traditional Parties

The remaining federal parties are, if one is to take their self-estimates at face value, virtually identical in long-range aims with their predecessors. The contemporary Center, reduced though it was to 10 deputies in the first Bundestag, and 4 in the second, claims to be the true residuary legatee of the old Center, though it is farther to the left on social and economic issues. Similarly, the German Party, first represented by 17 and later by 15 members, considers itself the true heir both of the Hanoverians of the two previous German political systems and of other Conservatives outside of the area of the former kingdom of Hanover, which Prussia annexed in 1866. The Free Democratic Party looks back on what is probably the oldest tradition, that of German national liberalism. This liberalism dominated the abortive Frankfurt Assembly of 1848, split into National Liberals and Left Liberals under the Empire, and continued this bifurcated existence as the German People's Party and the Democrats in the Weimar Republic.[1] The Social Democratic Party has not even changed its name since 1871, when it placed one deputy in the Reichstag. By 1912, it had become the strongest single party in Parliament, which it continued to be until 1932, with one brief exception in 1924. The Social Democrats still consider themselves the Party of Marx and Engels, Lassalle, Bebel, and the other socialist saints.[2] And the Communist Party, even though it appeared in strength in the Reichstag under that name for the first time in 1924, and is not represented in the second Bundestag, claims to have even purer ideological blood in its veins.

⌈The Social Democrats and the Communists, as also the other self-styled traditional contemporary West German political parties, use many of the slogans and symbols of their predecessors of Weimar and Imperial times⌋ Much of their appeal to the electorate is couched in terms of the vocabulary of these older ideologies. Leaders, members, and supporters are often thoroughly conscious of their own and others' political and in-

[1] The Chairman of the FDP, Dr. Thomas Dehler, who was Federal Minister of Justice in Adenauer's first Cabinet, demonstrated this traditionalist orientation at a congress of the Party in March 1955. Shortly after the Social Democrats and other opponents of German rearmament had held a symbolic rally in St. Paul's Church in Frankfurt, he denounced this use by Socialists of the birthplace of German liberalism as "blasphemy." "We are the heirs of the Paul's Church," he said. He called the Free Democrats "guardians of the heritage of the Frankfurt Parliament, which had sought unity and freedom." A socialist economy could never be combined with liberty. All the attempts of socialism had not led to liberty, and this was true of any form of socialism, including the Ahlen Program of the CDU (which was directed against the excesses of capitalism). Then he denounced denominational parties and said, "German democracy can become healthy only when the last Socialist recognizes that only the free economy can be social, and when the last Christian refrains from carrying on the political battle in the name of Christ. . . . We consciously created parliamentary democracy, but we know how threatened this democracy is today, because there are only a few free men and women in Parliament." This was meant as an attack on parliamentary party discipline, which was followed by an attack on the two-party system as unsuitable for countries with socialist and denominational parties. (*Frankfurter Allgemeine Zeitung*, March 26, 1955)

[2] In November 1953, Erich Ollenhauer, Chairman of the SPD, wrote that it was the task of the Social Democrats to analyze the present social structure in the spirit and with the method of Karl Marx, and to draw from the results of these investigations consequences for political work. A Social Democratic party without the Red Flag would be a party without heart. "A party without the *Lieder* and fighting songs, which have grown close to our hearts in the course of ninety years and which . . . may be supplemented by newer timely ones; without the comradely '*Du*' or the binding and obligating form of address, '*fellow*' (*ohne die verbindende und verpflichtende Anrede* '*Genosse*')—that would be a party without blood." At the same time, he denied that the SPD was an ideological party (*Weltanschauungspartei*), because it did not compete with the great religious currents. But the socialist labor movement had released great ethical power among millions of human beings, who had previously been a stolid mass because of the unscrupulousness of capitalist society and the failure of Christianity in the face of the practical tasks of neighborly love. Ollenhauer admitted that Marx had erred in his prognosis of future social development, but added that Marx had never proclaimed his theory to be a dogma of faith. Only the Communists and reactionary opponents of Social Democracy had done that. (*Frankfurter Allgemeine Zeitung*, November 13, 1953)

tellectual pedigrees. In some cases, specific solutions to concrete problems are justified by them by reference to statements made by the party's ideological forebears.

Now, if we are at all right about the tremendous difference between the problems facing the Federal Republic today and those that faced its predecessor regimes, then contemporary German politicians must be deceiving themselves and their public with their claims of traditionalistic affiliation. Mendès-France may claim to be the legitimate heir of Gambetta—though he would hardly stress the point—and Churchill of Disraeli. But does Adenauer have anything concretely in common with Windthorst, Ollenhauer with Lassalle, or President Heuss with the men of Frankfurt in 1848? (Perhaps this subjective feeling of continuity serves merely as subconscious window-dressing, which hides the real discontinuity of German politics and parties) Or perhaps it is the result of the reappearance in Bonn, in 1948 and 1949, of some of the men who had served in the Weimar Reichstag for many years. In any case, it does seem to cover up the relative newness and rootlessness of politics in the Federal Republic, while at the same time exploiting the considerable residue of sentimental and traditional attachments to the political symbolism of older days, which may be remembered by some voters as the good old days.

The Decrease in the Number of Parties

Some answers to these questions about the artificiality of such claims to continuity may be found by taking a look at the evolution of the German party system and by examining the aims of individual parties since national unification. Table 5 shows the relative stability of the Center throughout the Imperial and Weimar periods, but a great increase in the percentage of votes garnered by the CDU/CSU, whose Catholic members claim descent from the Center. The Social Democratic vote and representation in the Reichstag, once it had reached the level of 1912, is also very stable. But it seems more continuous than the CDU/CSU in the Bonn Republic, even though some of its former strongholds are now in the Soviet Zone, whereas the old Center owed very little of its support to those areas that are not now part of the Federal Republic. This would suggest that, in order to maintain its Weimar level of strength, the SPD must have obtained additional electoral support, some of it possibly from former Communist voters.

(The Conservatives (later the German National People's Party) also present a fairly stable curve from 1871 to 1933, with occasional oscillations). But it would be hard to tell which of the contemporary parties is receiving the support of its surviving former supporters or similar social groups

TABLE 5 Party Strength in the German Parliament*

| | EMPIRE | | | | | | | | | | | | |
	MAR. 1871	JAN. 1874	JAN. 1877	JULY 1878	OCT. 1881	OCT. 1884	FEB. 1887	FEB. 1890	JUNE 1893	JUNE 1898	JUNE 1903	JAN. 1907	JAN. 1912
National Socialist													
Conservative	54	21	40	59	50	78	80	73	72	56	52	60	45
Free Conservative	38	33	38	56	27	28	41	21	28	23	20	25	13
Hanoverians	7	4	4	10	10	11	4	11	7	9	5	2	5
National Liberals	119	152	127	98	45	51	99	42	53	47	52	56	44
Other Liberals	30				47								
Left Liberals (Democrats)	47	50	39	29	67	74	32	77	48	50	36	50	42
Middle Estate													
Peasants										6	1	7	3
Bavarian Peasants									3	5	6	1	3
Bavarian People's Party													
Center	58	91	93	93	98	99	98	106	96	102	100	104	90
SPD	1	9	12	9	12	24	11	35	44	56	82	43	110
KPD (Independent Socialists)													
Others	28	37	44	44	41	32	32	32	46	43	43	49	42
Total	382	397	← - →										397

* The important points to note are: the relative stability of the Center's strength throughout the Empire and Weimar periods; the waning of Liberal strength under the Weimar Republic; the relative stability of the Conservatives; the fixed number of deputies under the Empire, and its fluctuations under the Republic; the decrease of the number of parties from 1949 to 1953.

Under the Empire and the Weimar Republic, there were actually more parties than the table indicates. The category "Others" includes Alsatians, Poles, Danes, and Independents, who, in

JAN. 1919	JUNE 1920	MAY 1924	DEC. 1924	MAY 1928	SEPT. 1930	JULY 1932	NOV. 1932	MAR. 1933	AUG. 1949	SEPT. 1953	SEPT. 1957	
					WEIMAR					BONN		
		32	14	12	107	230	196	288				
42	66	106	111	78	44	39	54	53				
									—	27	—	Refugee League
3	4	5	4	4	1	—	1		17	15	17	German Party
22	62	44	51	45	30	7	11	2				
									52	48	41	FDP
74	45	28	32	25	14	4	2	5				
			7	11	23	23	2	2				
				9	19	1						
5	4	3	6	8	6	2	3	2	17	—	—	Bavarian Party
	20	16	19	17	19	22	19	19				
									139	243	270	CDU/CSU
89	69	65	69	61	68	75	70	73	10	4	—	Center
165	113	100	131	153	143	133	121	120	131	150	169	SPD
22	83	62	45	54	77	89	100	81	15	—	—	KPD
1	4		3	24	4	5	4		21	—	—	Others
423	466	472	493	491	577	608	584	647	402	487	497	

1878, a fairly representative year, placed 14, 14, 1, and 14 deputies, respectively. It also includes "Anti-Semites," also known as the German Reform Party, who in the last seven elections under the Empire elected between one and 17 deputies.

The election of January 1919 was that of the National Assembly at Weimar, which adopted the Weimar Constitution.

today. This difficulty arises mainly from the absence from present-day German politics of a party of conservatives or primarily nationalist voters. Some of these people may be voting for the German Party today, since it now has more deputies than the Hanoverians ever had under either Empire or Weimar Republic. But most of them probably vote for the CDU or the FDP. The FDP also gets some of the votes of both the former Liberals and Left Liberals, whose fortunes suffered a steady decline in the years before 1933.

[It is, of course, hard to tell just how the German electorate has redistributed its party allegiance, for several reasons. First among these is the decrease in the number of federally active parties.] Under the Empire, there were as many as thirteen represented in the Reichstag—and that was before the introduction of proportional representation. The number was about the same under the Weimar Republic. In the first Bundestag at Bonn, there were nine parties, and in the second, only six (seven after the split in the FDP). Above all, the two extremes of the political spectrum have been eliminated from the federal Parliament, and when one considers the combined strength of Communists and National Socialists in the four Reichstags elected after 1929, the difficulties inherent in any attempt to estimate the electorate's reallocation of votes among the remaining parties will be evident. Nor can one do more than guess on this question for all those areas of the Federal Republic in which many newcomers have settled from other parts of the country, or from Central and Eastern Europe. And since the present election districts do not coincide with those of the Weimar Republic, the task is made still more difficult.

Nevertheless, (an over-all impression does emerge right away: whether for constitutional or other reasons, the party system has changed drastically, simply in terms of the smaller number of parties with parliamentary representation, and the fact that the CDU and SPD together hold more than three-fourths of all the seats in the second Bundestag.] This means that the relative strength of the remaining parties has also changed radically. From this it follows, finally, that each of the parties must have a clientele that differs a good deal from that of the particular Weimar party from which it claims to be descended. If we add to this the further fact that a whole new generation of voters grew up and reached voting age during the sixteen to twenty years that separate the first and second Bundestag elections from the last Reichstag election, then we must recognize how different from their predecessors the present parties are bound to be.

The Parties' Goals

Refugee League

To begin with the youngest of the West German parties, the "Refugee League" (literally "All-German Bloc/League of the Homeless and Those Who Have Lost Their Rights,"—*Gesamtdeutscher Block/Bund der Heimatlosen und Entrechteten*—abbreviated as GB/BHE) cannot claim legitimate descent from any predecessor organization. Since there is no precedent for the expulsion into Germany of millions of ethnic Germans (*Volksdeutsche*) or for the division of the country, there is also no precedent for the existence of this kind of political clientele. No previous group of people has faced the same problems as these displaced persons—unless it be the vertically displaced victims of the economic crises of the twenties and thirties, whose lot bore some resemblance to that of the vertically *and* horizontally displaced Germans of the forties and fifties. Consequently, the political aims of the League are also novel. It was first formed in the state of Schleswig-Holstein, which had been flooded by the heaviest concentration of expellees. The Occupation Authorities—the British, for this state—would not license it as a political party. This refusal was prompted by their desire to prevent the direct participation in politics of organizations that seemed to them to be nothing more than economic interest groups. This, therefore, is another instance of the importance of political theory and of interpretations of the fall of the Weimar Republic for postwar German politics. Not only the Germans in their Basic Law, but also the Occupation Authorities in their licensing policies, made a distinction between political parties and interest groups. In the case of the British and the Americans, this distinction was derived from the experience of the two-party system. Superficial views of this kind of party system generally assume that interest groups apply pressure on the parties or representatives, while parties are concerned mainly with capturing control of personnel and policies of the government. People with a background of a multi-party system, such as the French or the Swedes, would be less inclined to exclude interest groups from political activity for this reason. The Germans would not have refused to license the Refugee League on these grounds, either, though they were anxious to prevent the kind of parliamentary fragmentation into splinter groups that had occurred under the Weimar regime.

In any case, the Refugee League was not able to participate in the first federal election of 1949. After being licensed in Schleswig-Holstein and subsequently in other states as well, it had at the outset some remarkable electoral successes. Its professed goals were directed mainly toward the improvement of the lot of the potentially large segment of society toward which its appeal was aimed. It wanted to make it possible for refugees to move out of the squalid camps, in which hundreds of thousands of them were living, and into new housing units, to be constructed with government subsidies, or onto farms to be provided by government aid. The League also favored revisions in the Law to Equalize the Burdens of the War, in order to favor expellees and refugees. At the same time, it also sought to appeal to groups of socially displaced people by urging legislation favorable to former soldiers and civil servants. It established close contacts with the geographically based organizations of expellees, many of which favored revisions in Germany's present eastern boundaries. In this connection, the party's policies sometimes appeared to be informed by strongly nationalistic strands with an ideological tinge.

After the first electoral victory of the League, several of its leaders became ministers of a coalition government in Schleswig-Holstein. In these positions, they made themselves unusually accessible—by German standards—to their constituents, by having regular open-house office hours. As a result of such tactics, the League won 27 seats in the Bundestag elected in 1953—all of them via state lists and proportional representation. They joined the Adenauer coalition Government, and two of the leaders became Federal Ministers, one of them in charge of the Ministry for Displaced Persons (Vertriebene). Gradually, however, the special public to which the Refugee League had appealed began to lose its identity and to be absorbed into the West German society and economy as these recovered their stability and prosperity. With that, the League began to lose votes in state elections and to show internal rifts. By 1955, these tendencies brought about a split in the party and in its parliamentary delegation. More than half the delegation, led by the two Federal Ministers, joined the Christian Democrats. The rest have usually voted with the Opposition. By the end of 1956, the Ministers had left the Cabinet. In the 1957 election, the Refugee League failed to elect any deputies.

Thus the Refugee League was brought into being by the existence in society of new groups with new problems, which led it to advocate new policies and even to employ novel political methods. But with the gradual disappearance of these groups and their problems, the party is likely to disappear, too. All of this speaks for the greater absorptive capacities of the major parties, and especially the two largest of them, CDU and SPD. In the Weimar Republic, there were no political procedures that forced people to think in terms of the dichotomy, Government-versus-Opposition. This encouraged each of the parties to retain the purity and consistency of its ideological and material appeal. In the Bonn Republic, this is no longer true. Consequently, its party politics is not only a horse of a different color, but a new kind of animal in German experience. And this, in turn, means that it has had to evolve new codes of conduct and is still doing so all the time. While this has so far made for political stability, it has also made for political unpredictability.

Center

The Center (*Zentrum*), smallest of the parties represented in the second Bundestag, appeals to a potential electorate that has not changed appreciably since the 1870's, when Roman Catholicism first organized politically in order to fight the *Kulturkampf* in defense against Bismarck's attacks on the Church. Among the voters who traditionally supported the Center in Imperial and Weimar days, there were always many Roman Catholic workers of the industrial Rhineland and the Ruhr area. But because the dominant wing of postwar political Roman Catholicism was willing to join with other Christian groups in the "Democratic Union," and therefore had to dilute its denominationalism and to accept middle-of-the-road social and economic policies, those former Centrists who were unwilling to accept dilution stayed out of the Union. This was true especially of those who were unhappy about dilution of social and economic policies. On cultural questions, the Center has taken an orthodox Roman Catholic line, but on social and economic issues it is usually quite close to the Social Democrats. As a result, the Center has lost so much support that the second Bundestag elections would have left them completely out in the cold if the CDU had not agreed not to oppose the Center's strongest constituency candidate. He was thereupon elected, so that the party's land-list in the state of North-Rhine–Westphalia could benefit from the second votes it received in that state. It gained these benefits despite the fact that its total for the Federal Republic was far below the minimum of 5 per cent—actually only 0.8 per cent—which is required for that purpose of parties that do not elect a district representative. Even in North-Rhine–Westphalia, the Center received only 2.7 per cent of the votes cast in 1953. But as a result of this satellite type of alliance, the Center lost both independence and support, mainly because it alone among these parties tried to resist the prevailing trend, which is towards dilution of appeal to a lower common denominator, by further distilling its doctrine to a purer elixir than even that of its predecessor, the Center of the Weimar Republic and earlier days. It, too, disappeared from the Bundestag as a result of the election of 1957.

German Party

The German Party (*Deutsche Partei*) has suffered a somewhat similar fate. But its support has been numerically stronger and geographically more concentrated than that of the Center. Consequently, its Bundestag representation was reduced by only two from 17 to 15 as a result of the 1953 election. Ten of these were elected in single-member constituencies in the states of Lower Saxony (8) and Hamburg (2). This suggests some similarity between the electorates appealed to by the German Party and the pre-Nazi Hanoverians, Conservatives, and National Liberals in Northern Germany. This amalgam has given the party a program that makes identification with any one of these alleged predecessors somewhat spurious. The Hanoverian Party, for example, arose out of opposition to Prussia on the part of supporters of the Guelph dynasty, which had ruled the kingdom of Hanover until its annexation by Prussia. Yet the German Party, much of whose present strength draws upon these traditional Hanoverian loyalties, nowadays favors the colors black-white-red over the Republic's official black-red-gold—and black-white-red are precisely the national colors that symbolized the unification of the German states under Prussian leadership. Since the German Party's strength is thus highly localized, its aims are, too. They focus mainly on the needs of the agricultural population of Lower Saxony, and the commercial interests of the port city-states of Hamburg and Bremen. One of the Party's leaders fittingly headed the Federal Ministry for Traffic. Another was Federal Minister for Bundesrat Affairs until he left the Cabinet in order to head a coalition government in the state of Lower Saxony.

Free Democratic Party

The aims of the FDP (*Freie Demokratische Partei*), third strongest party at the federal level, are pitched so as to suit the interests of industrialists, businessmen, shopkeepers, professionals and white-collar people, and more especially those among them who have qualms about casting their votes for the CDU because of its Roman Catholic majority component. Its platform and campaign appeals have emphasized the virtues of free enterprise in its post-1948 West German version, the "social market economy." With regard to the "cultural" issue, the FDP has opposed denominational schools. In the field of foreign policy, it has tried to work out an independent West German policy, sufficiently differentiated from that of the CDU to make it distinguishable, but not so much as to make it coincide with that of the SPD, or to leave the CDU without the support of its coalition partner when foreign affairs came up for votes in the Bundestag. This latter aim was held to at least until part of the FDP left the coalition. On the whole, the FDP has tried to combine programs somewhat reminiscent of those of two earlier liberal parties: the right-wing nationalists and the left-wing democrats. It also gets much of its support, especially financial, from the type of big industrialists that occasionally provided leadership and funds for the conservative German National People's Party of the Weimar Republic. The two wings of German liberalism never held more than 107 out of 466 seats, the high of the Reichstag elected in 1920, and sank to a low of seven out of 647, in the last election of 1933. In the first and second Bundestag elections, the Free Democrats received 11.9 and 9.5 per cent of the total vote, respectively. The loss appears to have redounded to the benefit of the senior coalition partner, the CDU. The FDP thus also suffered from those institutional pressures that make for the dilution of party programs, and its own platform bears no direct resemblance to any one of those of its claimed predecessors.

In the early part of 1956, the FDP split in two. The first step in this process took place when its branch in North-Rhine–Westphalia brought down its own CDU-dominated coalition government by joining the Social Democrats in a constructive lack-of-confidence vote. As already mentioned, this was done partly in protest against the threatened new electoral law. Soon thereafter, the Bundestag delegation of the FDP split into two wings, the majority withdrawing support from the Adenauer coalition, while the minority, led by the four FDP Ministers in Adenauer's cabinet, stayed loyal to it. The minority subsequently founded its own party under the title Free People's Party (*Freie Volkspartei*). By the end of 1956, its Ministers had withdrawn from the federal cabinet, which the Chancellor revised so as to give his own CDU greater strength. Meanwhile, the fight of the two remnant organizations of the FDP for a continued independent existence began to look more and more desperate. Its orators still use many phrases borrowed from the liberals of Germany's past, but the problems the Free Democrats presently face are too different for them to find much aid or comfort in that quarter. Along with the other minor parties, the FDP is threatened with annihilation by the two giants, CDU and SPD.

Social Democratic Party

Of the SPD (*Sozialdemokratische Partei Deutschlands*), we might legitimately expect that it would have changed its goals less than the other parties. It started out as a class party with a definite ideology. It maintained a headquarters organization in exile during the Nazi and war years. And there is, after all, still an industrial and working class in West Germany today. For these reasons, the SPD more than the others can afford to behave very much as it used to behave in earlier times. And on the whole, this seems to be true. Nevertheless, considerable changes have occurred. One of the most noticeable has been the Socialists' stronger tendency toward nationalism, which was particularly marked before Schumacher's death in 1952. This emphasis on nationalism can be explained partly again in terms of a retrospective interpretation of the

SPD's history in the Weimar Republic. If it had been more nationalist then, its leaders were thinking after the war, Hitler might have been less successful in his efforts to exploit nationalist aspirations among the masses. Also, the SPD figures that it stands to gain more than the CDU from reunification, at least in terms of electoral support in the predominantly Protestant eastern part of the country. Again, the SPD has feared the domination of a United Europe of six states (the Federal Republic, Italy, France, and the three Benelux countries) by Christian parties, and has therefore sometimes opposed Adenauer's European integration policy with rather nationalist-sounding arguments. In part this has undoubtedly been simply because of the SPD's oppositional role, which encouraged it to take a different if not wholly opposite stand from that of the less national-ist, more Catholic, and "little-European" CDU. The SPD has become less doctrinaire about its Marxism, partly in order to try to win back electoral strength lost as a result of partition, and partly in response to the more obnoxious manifestations of East German Communist Marxism. The Party has more than flirted with Protestant theology, and its theorists have written a good deal about the compatibility of Marxism with Chris-tianity, especially Protestant. This has led to a lowering of emphasis on socialization and nationalization as major Social Democratic goals, which they had always been in the Weimar years, and even more so before 1919. Officially, the SPD today insists on socialization of basic industries only —especially coal, steel, chemicals, and banking. Some of its leaders and most of the rank and file are not even keen on that. Many of them are relatively satisfied with such "social" but hardly socialist measures as co-determination, which tend to improve the atmosphere in which workers live and their relations with their superiors, without, however, changing the structure of the economy by affecting property rights.

Explanations for this toning down of ideology and abandoning of earlier goals on the part of the SPD are not hard to come by. Loss of its strongest concentration of electoral support in the present Soviet Zone seems to be the most important factor. The SPD of the Soviet Zone was forcibly merged with the Communist Party there to form the Socialist Unity Party. In West Germany, some of this loss was made up for by the weakening of the Communist Party, which was a direct result of the reign of terror conducted by the East Zone Communists, as well as their obvious de-pendence upon the Russians. When the Federal Constitutional Court outlawed the West German Communist Party as anti-constitutional in 1956, it was expected that some of its votes would switch to the SPD, but in the federal election of 1953, this had been a mere 2.2 per cent of the total. The changes in the SPD's program have, however, been far greater than this change in its situation would by itself have called for. The main reason for this seems to lie in the fully oppositional role the SPD is playing today. In the Weimar Republic, the SPD could never hope to obtain a majority of Reichstag seats. It could participate in a Government only as one member in a coalition with at least two other parties. It therefore never had occasion to formulate a comprehensive program both consistent and realistic, because it knew that it would never have sole responsibility for putting such a program into effect. Under the Basic Law, however, the institutional pressures—especially because of Article 67—are such, that there is not only the tendency to conduct political debate in terms of the dichotomy, Government-*versus*-Opposition, but also the possibility of an SPD Government or at least one dominated by the Social Democrats.

In the first two postwar federal elections, the SPD was within 0.2 per cent of getting 29 per cent of the vote cast. Despite the truncation of the country, the party thus got a higher proportion of the vote than at any time since the Reichstag election of 1928-30, in which it held just over 31 per cent of the seats. On the programmatic side, the SPD has achieved this success by pitching its appeal to wider circles than merely the working class, i.e., really to all those who are for almost any reason (excluding subversive reasons) opposed to the policies of the governing coalition at Bonn. As in the case of the other successful party, this has meant a dilution of its goals, a reduction of the ideological content of its program, and a general attempt to find the lowest common denominator of the predominantly material aspirations of its potential supporters. Again, as for these other parties, this has had the effect of changing the character of the SPD, despite its relatively high degree of continuity with the past, so that its future strength, goals, and possible political allies can hardly be projected.

Christian Democratic Union

Of no party is this as true as it is of the Christian Democratic Union (*Christlich Demokratische Union*). In the first federal election (1949), it received 31 per cent of the vote. In the second Bundestag, it held a majority of the seats after receiving 45.2 per cent of the popular vote. In the third, it was further strengthened. Some of its leaders make no claim to direct descent from any party of Weimar or Imperial days, although many of its outstanding founders came from the old Center. But their desire to surmount the Center's narrowly Catholic orientation was precisely the leading motive for founding the CDU. "The Union"—as, characteristically, it is usually referred to, rather than as a party—was born out of the desire of men who had been opponents of Nazi totalitarianism to reconstruct German society on the basis of general Christian ideals, both Catholic and Protestant. Their success was immediate in the state elections which they entered. The bi-denominational nature of the CDU's electoral appeal is demonstrated by the fact that its support is just as strong (within 0.7 per cent) in predominantly Catholic Bavaria as in predominantly Protestant Schleswig-Holstein. The composition of its parliamentary delegation shows that it contains both industrialists and trade union officials, both small farmers or peasants and aristocratic estate owners (such as Prince Bismarck), both descendants of ancient Rhenish families and displaced persons from the Sudetenland. Naturally, in order to attract all of these diverse elements, with their different interests, the CDU has had to formulate a very general sort of program. And whenever the program has been couched in more specific terms on controversial points, actual policy has tended to deviate to that level at which a compromise among all of these often antagonistic interests could be found. This has been true, e.g., of its social and economic policy, which originally opposed capitalism in favor of a "social" economy, but ended up by establishing the "social market economy," which blends free enterprise with social security and well-placed subsidies. Similarly, on the issue of centralism-*versus*-federalism, where the Union leadership in the federal government has leaned toward centralism, some of its state organizations, such as the autonomous Christian Social Union (*Christlich Soziale Union* or CSU) in Bavaria, have espoused the cause of states' rights. The same is true of foreign policy, with regard to which the Western, Catholic, wing tends to be more preoccupied with the priority of European integration, while the Eastern wing, including refugee leaders and former heads of the CDU of the Soviet Zone, is more concerned with reunification.

However, the goals of the CDU are such that it gets support from all these sectors of West German society. Consequently, its clientele is a completely new entity in German politics, and its future behavior one big question mark. Thus some students of German politics believe that this conglomerate coalition of a party has no cement of its own, being held together by nothing but the firm and grandfatherly personality of its leader, the Federal Chancellor, Dr. Adenauer. When he passes from the political scene, they say, his creation will crumble to bits—an event for which they claim to be witnessing previews whenever Adenauer leaves the country for a while, occasions which are often used by his lieutenants for quarreling among themselves. But others have opposite fears, ill-founded though these seem. They claim that their compatriots have retained so strong an aversion to parliamentary politics because of the failure of the Weimar Republic and because of the Nazis' anti-parliamentary propaganda, that they hunger for strong leadership and wish to submerge themselves in one great party and, eventually, another one-party system. In any case, the make-up and the goals of the CDU make it a novelty for German politics. In part this is the result of radical changes in social structure and consequent changes in political values that have taken place in Germany. To a greater extent, however, this novelty seems to be the effect of constitutional provisions, which set off a chain reaction that is evolving in the direction of something resembling a two-party system. The CDU has been the political anchor of the amazing political stability that has prevailed in the Federal Republic during the seven years since its founding. All the novel aspects of this party once more underline the tentative character of this stability: If the anchor should crack, the crew of politicians would almost certainly grow panicky, and the whole ship of state might either be put in dry dock for a radical overhauling or re-designing, or just be abandoned to sink, as earlier German models have been.

Political Methods

Germany's changed social and economic problems have thus generated new and different political issues. These new issues have brought into be-ing potential cleavages within the electorate that neither existed before, nor had any counterpart in earlier cleavages. Nevertheless, the effects of the constitution have been to contain these potential divisions and not to permit them to fragmentize the electorate or parliament. Consequently, the contemporary party system bears little resemblance to its forerunners. There is, nevertheless, the tendency to preserve continuity with the past in at least one respect, the manner of political discourse. Here we have noted especially the traditionalist and ideological verbiage with which the voters' favor is sought. This suggests that there may be a higher degree of stability in the methods by which politics has been conducted in Ger-many. Speechmaking, platform-writing, and pamphleteering are, after all, an important part of politics. This relative stability in political methods must be traced partly to the continuity of political personnel, both inside and outside of parliament. The continuity may be of two kinds: return to politics of the same persons who were active in it before 1933; and serv-ice by men with educational and professional backgrounds similar to those of German politicians of the past.

Political parties were organized, or reorganized, in West Germany be-fore there was a great deal of politics in which they could engage, as already mentioned. This was so because most of the really important deci-sions were still being made by the occupation authorities, at least until

1949. The occupation powers also controlled most of the material means by which policies could be put into effect. This situation partly explains the attempt of the parties to put on traditionalist clothes. There were few concrete contemporary issues on the basis of which they could effectively differentiate themselves from one another. All of them had to be *for* constitutional democracy and *against* Nazi totalitariansim. If they were not, they would not be licensed by the occupation powers. They could exert but very little influence on current domestic events, had hardly any patronage to give away, and could not at all affect Germany's relations with foreign states other than the four that occupied their country. And even those they could not influence to any great extent. To achieve any noticeable degree of differentiation at all, therefore, they had to project their programs into either the past or the future, and they proceeded to do both. The parties' attempted self-identification with their predecessors of the Weimar period thus made good sense, at least until the revival of German politics in 1949. Both leaders and followers during this period actually wanted to take attitudes that were fairly identical with those of their traditional forerunners. Only when the parties began to be effective instruments of self-government did this cease to be so. Then these old and in the main ideological outlooks became obsolete, simply because they were largely irrelevant to the novel problems with which the Federal Republic had to come to grips. By this time, however, the new or revived political organizations had already been identified, and their leaders had identified themselves, with the earlier approach. As a result, this approach was retained, by and large, at least on the surface. The uninformed observer might, therefore, get the impression—even in 1958—that West German politics revolves in the main around ideological, legalistic, and "scientific" issues, when it is in fact quite as much concerned with concrete conflicts of material interests as politics in the United States or the United Kingdom. And even the informed German participant may labor under the same illusion, because he mistakes the style of his own political discourse for the substance of his political goals.

The relatively lengthy and non-political incubation period through which the parties had to pass has had an important long-run effect on the way in which issues are formulated, and this in turn naturally affects the methods by which politics in general is carried on in the Federal Republic. Of course, political issues are not formulated by parties alone. Interest groups also play a role, and sometimes a large one, in this first stage of the political process. Since interest groups are supposed to be in the game for the sake of their more or less immediate material interests—regardless of whether these be of an economic or cultural character—we might reasonably expect interest groups at least to see to it that issues are formulated in more concrete and pragmatic, less abstract and ideological-legalistic terms. This expectation would be disappointed in most cases. Relatively little difference is to be found between the way in which parties on the one hand, and interest groups on the other, formulate political issues. Indeed, it almost seems as though everyone in German politics were afraid that he would get no hearing for his cause, unless he garbed his goals in ideological, legalistic, and scientific verbiage.

If this were mere façade, and if everyone were aware of this fact, it would not be very important. After all, in other systems politicians also profess the idealism of their motives, point to the superior legal or constitutional validity of their own claims, and occasionally support these with the learned opinions of lawyers, economists, historians, and other men of science. In Germany, however, these practices are not mere façade, but rather part and parcel of the political style. This means that when essentially the same problem arises in Great Britain and Germany—for instance, trade union demands for a higher real income for their members—it is treated very differently in the two countries. In some cases it means that issues of a purely ideological or legalistic nature take on great independent importance in German politics, even though they seem to the outsider to be purely artificial and to have no relevance to any real or concrete problems the society actually confronts.

Ideologism, Legalism, Scientism

The demand of trade unions for higher wages shows the effects of the ideological, legalistic, and scientistic orientation. In Germany, as elsewhere, many different means are at the unions' disposal for pressing such a demand: direct negotiations with employers or their organizations; direct or indirect pressure on parliament for passage of such measures as food subsidies, rent control, a more favorable tax law, or wage legislation; support of or affiliation with a party; and ultimately the strike. Before the Nazis outlawed free trade unions and supplanted them with their own National Socialist German Labor Front, there had been three trade union organizations in Germany: a Liberal, a Christian, and a Marxist, affiliated respectively with the Democratic, Center, and Social Democratic party. The Marxist union had been by far the strongest. After the war, former leaders of these organizations came together and decided to found one German Trade Union Federation (*Deutscher Gewerkschaftsbund*, or DGB). It was to be neutral in partisan politics, even though Social Democrats outweighed "Christians" among both leaders and members by a ratio of about four to one. They thus ruled out the Labour Party path. This increased the DGB's bargaining power, since it could in any case count on the support of the SPD, and would on some issues also get the support of the CDU, whenever that party could be swayed by its labor-friendly left wing.

Until 1954, no major strikes for better wages, hours, or working conditions took place. The DGB concentrated rather on getting the Bundestag to pass pro-labor legislation. It made a special effort on behalf of a set of laws granting labor the right of codetermination. This involved participation by labor representatives jointly with stockholders' representatives in the supervision and management of privately owned industrial and business corporations. The practice of codetermination had first evolved for very concrete and practical reasons in steel corporations that were being reorganized under supervision of British occupation authorities. Nevertheless, a systematic ideology was soon built around this institution, lengthy legal arguments were elaborated both for and against it, and learned legal, economic, sociological, and other scientific treatises were produced in its defense and denigration. Practically everybody involved in these controversies was convinced that these pragmatically evolved practices needed nothing more than a solid legislative foundation—and this would not be an unusual thing to provide after a period of trial and error. But these people believed firmly that it would have been better if such legislation had preceded experimentation in the first place, and that no further experimentation in other industries could be carried out without prior legislation in detail. Given a similar situation in Great Britain, chances are that many years would have passed before passage of a law designed to recognize the existence of something that had grown up by the method of trial and error. And once labor had adopted some such goal, it would hardly have justified it in such elaborate ideological terms.

In Germany, this controversy involved the threat of a strike by the Metal Workers and Miners Unions. As a result of this threat, Chancellor Adenauer pushed the demanded legislation through the Bundestag. It was passed by an unusual coalition of his own CDU/CSU and the SPD. More interesting here is the immediate and violent denunciation of the unions by all those who were opposed to the substance of the legislation, and by many others. On the occasion of this and almost every strike or threat to strike since then, the opponents of labor have attacked what they termed political action by economic interest organizations.

Such arguments are based on the generally accepted assumption that public life consists of a number of watertight compartments, and that different public organizations should confine their activities to their respective spheres. German parlance refers to *Staatspolitik, Wirtschaftspolitik, Kulturpolitik,* and so forth, and most Germans would assign parties to the first compartment, trade unions and employers' associations to the second, the churches to the third, and so forth. Any overflow from one compartment to another is frowned upon. That all such questions can ultimately become issues of partisan politics in any modern representative democracy—that it is indeed entirely normal and healthy for the political system for them to do so—is something many Germans would deny. And when such an overflowing occurs, this fact itself rather than the substantive disagreement at hand often becomes the primary issue of the controversy. Thus, in the case of strikes, those opposed to them raise the question whether the stoppage of work is not meant in some way to apply pressure to parliament and, if so, whether this is not anti-constitutional. If it is not, they ask, "Why not? It should be made anti-constitutional," —whereupon a constitutional issue has been more or less artificially created out of a disagreement over material interests. Similarly, when opponents of rearmament held a protest convention in the same St. Paul's Church in which the first German National Convention of 1848 had held its fruitless meetings, proponents of rearmament argued that this kind of extra-parliamentary consideration of a question that was then before the Bundestag was designed to undermine the constitution, if it was not outright unconstitutional.

Political Recourse to the Courts

Frequently, issues that in France, Great Britain, or the United States would be initiated and fought out in the legislative forum are, in Germany, initiated, fought out, and settled in the courts. This is true of matters of a wide variety of importance, from the sublime to the ridiculous. Two mutually hostile politicians often try to get even with each other by means of libel and slander suits on the basis of campaign statements that, in most other countries, would probably do little more than draw laughs from the other fellow and the public. Seemingly harmless jokes about a "monopoly of divine support" allegedly enjoyed by the Christian delegation in the Bundestag led an outsider to initiate proceedings by the state prosecutor to ascertain whether blasphemy had not been committed. When Federal Ministers think that they have been insulted by a newspaper or magazine, they often sue and have the offensive issue confiscated on court orders. When the Social Democrats were obviously going to be outvoted on the question of ratifying the abortive agreements on the European Defense Community, they tried to stop their promulgation on constitutional grounds through the instrumentality of the Federal Constitutional Court. When the state government of Bavaria threat-

ened to unbalance the budgetary equilibrium of the Federal Minister of
Finance, himself a Bavarian, by paying civil servants under its jurisdiction
a Christmas bonus that was higher than he deemed defensible, the Federal
Government tried to get an injunction against Bavaria from the Federal
Constitutional Court—in vain, as it turned out.

Political Issues

The problems that give rise to issues in West Germany are, on the
whole, very similar to those that give rise to issues in other European constitutional democracies, especially those on the Continent. This is only
natural, since all of them share more or less similar backgrounds, so far
as their economies are concerned, their social structures, their cultures,
and their foreign relations. German political issues differ to any significant extent only where the German problems are unique. This has been
true of all the issues arising out of the National Socialist experience, the
Occupation, and the division of Germany. Beyond that, the principal dis-
tinctiveness of German politics lies in the methods by which these largely
similar issues are dealt with, i.e., the style of politics, and in the predominance of different kinds of issues at different levels of politics, attributable
to the constitutional structure of the Federal Republic.

Economic and Social Issues

We may classify issues under the main headings, social and economic,
cultural, historical, foreign relations, and constitutional. Of these, all but
historical and constitutional issues are mainly of a substantive nature, i.e.,
they deal with the substance of interests that are in conflict. The other
two types of issues are more concerned with the means by which substantive conflicts are being or have been dealt with. Until the occupation
powers surrendered their last political controls to the Germans in 1955,
historical and foreign policy issues played a minor role in German politics.
The main concern of the parties was to push through their demands concerning such questions as the distribution of income, social security, relief
for economic victims of the war, reconstruction of productive capacity and
of housing, the educational system, relations between schools and churches,
and the like. And these are roughly the same issues as those that matter
in the politics of other Continental countries, such as France or the Neth-
erlands, or even in insular Great Britain.

During the initial period of postwar reconstruction, economic and social
issues were generally dealt with at the lowest level, mainly because the
occupation powers did not permit any higher levels of government to come
into existence for some time. After the founding of the Federal Republic,

this ceased to be true. There was virtual unanimity on the desirability of a fairly even economic development for the whole country, despite federalism and the selfishness of the better-off states. Consequently, many of the early political battles of the Federal Republic dealt with the abolition of those inequalities that had been created by differences in the aims of the three Western occupation powers. Economic and social legislation that had been passed in the several states before 1949, e.g., concerning pensions or labor relations, was superseded by federal laws. Since 1949, federal politics has been the main arena for economic and social issues in German politics.

Cultural Issues

German politics differs from that of neighboring countries as a result of the federal character of the German constitution. Because of this federalism, some issues are important mainly at the state level, others mainly at the federal level. Cultural questions, for example, have to be settled at the state level, in the absence of federal authority in this field. There is no Federal Minister for Education or Culture. The issue of whether to have secular schools, "Christian community" schools, or denominational Protestant and Roman Catholic schools, all of them state financed, has been an explosive one in the Federal Republic. But given the provisions of the Basic Law, themselves prompted by revulsions against Nazi practices in this field, this issue has had to be settled in each of the member states. As a result, the denominational issue, and such related questions as anti clericalism, which have always made for the existence of multi-party systems in Continental countries, have been relatively unimportant at the federal level. But for the deflection of this potentially divisive set of issues to the state level, the cohesiveness of the bi-denominational CDU probably would not have lasted as long as it in fact has. And friction between the strongly Catholic CDU and its strongly Protestant coalition partners in the first and second federal coalition Governments would probably have been greater.

This situation also explains the different composition of governing coalitions at the federal and state levels. During the life of the first and second Bundestag, while in Bonn the CDU was allied with the FDP, the DP, and the Center, against the oppositional SPD, practically all the possible combinations existed in the various state cabinets: the "Great Coalition" of CDU and SPD; an even greater coalition including all the parties from SPD on the left to the DP on the right; another of SPD and Refugee League; another of SPD-FDP-DP; and several other types. This also casts light on the existence of parties whose electoral support is confined to one state only. Of this, the Party of the Bavarians is a good example. It was represented in the first Bundestag, but failed to win a place in the second because of the federal five per cent provision. In Bavaria, it joined the SPD, FDP, and minor groups in a government whose opposition consists of the CSU.

Historical Issues

Historical and foreign policy issues were not permitted to figure overtly in West German politics until the occupation powers restored sovereignty to the Federal Republic in 1955. By historical issues we mean those that arise out of a nation's past, in Germany's case, especially the recent Nazi past. Since denazification was controlled by the occupation—administered at first by its officials, later by Germans on their instructions—and because of the licensing requirements for political parties, recriminatory controversies of this type could not bubble up seriously until former Nazis regained their civil and political liberties. As soon as this did happen, they were able to try to revive their discredited ideology and to denounce their opponents as unpatriotic, un-German, or traitorous. This some of them did, for instance, with regard to the executed and surviving participants in the plot on Hitler's life of July 20, 1944. Ex-Nazis also tried to identify constitutionalist enemies of totalitarianism with the occupation powers and hold them responsible for such events as the division of Germany.

Recriminatory historical issues of this kind also play a role in French politics, e.g., in connection with the Resistance movement, as Dr. Wahl shows. Some of these issues have been petrified into ideologies, which often no longer bear any direct relevance to concrete problems of real current significance. This is true of issues of such old vintage as those arising out of antagonism between supporters of the French Revolution and defenders of the *ancien régime*, or critics of clericalism and supporters of the Church. In Germany, issues of this type played a role in earlier periods, too. Their political manifestation, however, differed from that of similar issues in France, because they often had an ideological character *before* the parties were able to do anything about them. And it was precisely because of their lack of power to influence the position the German state would take toward them, that their attitudes on these issues became parts of rigid ideologies in the first place. This reversed sequence, in turn, tends to make historical recriminatory issues more divisive in contemporary German politics than in France. This situation is, moreover, further complicated by two facts: The latest experience giving rise to one such issue, Nazi totalitarianism, happened so recently and with such vehemence as to be very much a part of German political memories—more so than the Vichy experience in France. And the policies of the occupation powers on this issue during the early postwar years of German political impotence postponed its settlement, and for that very reason stimulated ideologism on this score.

Foreign Policy Issues

These conditions similarly affected the treatment of foreign policy issues. Politicians who were expressly opposed to the occupation regime were at first simply not admitted to renascent German politics. The Military Governors and, later, their successors the High Commissioners, were in full charge of Germany's relations with other countries, even to the extent of representing Germany on international bodies, such as the Office of European Economic Co-operation. When control over her foreign policy was given to the Federal Republic, this was done as the Western Allies' part of the bargain, by which the West Germans were to contribute to the defense of Western Europe and the "Free World" against Soviet Communism. Under this bargain, the Federal Republic, having just been subjected to five years of Allied propaganda and re-education on the evils of German (or Prussian) militarism, was required to rearm and to become a member of the North Atlantic Treaty Organization. But meanwhile Germany had been divided into the Western Federal Republic and the Eastern Democratic Republic. Every question of foreign policy consequently became entangled with the problem of division and the means for bringing about reunification. To some of the related questions the parties had already given much thought and study during the period of their relative impotence. The Social Democrats, for example, had always viewed themselves as the most anti-militarist party. They were therefore quite in sympathy with the earlier Allied demilitarization policy. At the same time, they also evolved theories about collaboration with other European countries, especially those in which their sister socialist parties, members of the Second International, were strong, such as the United Kingdom and the Scandinavian countries. During the first Bundestag, and particularly before the death of the SPD's postwar leader, Dr. Schumacher, they saw tactical advantage in identifying the Adenauer government with the Occupation Powers. Schumacher at one point even referred to Adenauer as "the Chancellor of the Allies"—for which the President of the Bundestag excluded him from the chamber for using unparliamentary language. The Socialists also believed that they had better reasons than the CDU for actively pushing a policy of reunification, because of the strong electoral support their Party had traditionally received in the areas now in the Soviet Zone. In addition to this, the new, constitutionally encouraged, tendency to conduct politics along the pattern government-

versus-opposition, led the SPD to oppose both of the main facets of the CDU's foreign policy, rearmament and European integration in the predominantly Catholic "little Europe," by contrast with the predominantly Protestant "great Europe."

Constitutional Issues

Constitutional issues may arise in a political system, when it has no constitution; for example, when it is a newly founded system, such as the United States during the Independence period; when there is lack of consensus on the "rules of the game"; or when there is lack of consensus on substantive issues of material interests, in the fighting over which parties find that they can use constitutional issues to their advantage—as has often been the case with filibusters in the United States Senate. The dividing line between the last two cases is hard to draw, although one can usually tell whether the emphasis of consensus, or its lack, tends more toward the substantive or the procedural side. In the Federal Republic, constitutional issues arose for each of these reasons, which is one explanation for the extraordinarily important role they have played.

To begin with, West Germany had no constitution, so that constitutional issues were the only ones that were taken up at one level of politics, that of the constitution-drafting Parliamentary Council. After the Basic Law was adopted, its novelty made for a relatively weak consensus on these new rules of the game, so that new constitutional issues were likely to be raised frequently. Moreover, for both of the preceding reasons, virtually any substantive issue was likely to be converted into a constitutional issue, whenever an opportunity for such a conversion appeared. This has been particularly true of foreign policy issues. The process began with the hesitancy to constitutionalize the division of the country, a hesitancy that produced the title of Basic Law instead of Constitution. It was easy to make this conversion in the case of the treaties on the European Defense Community. On this issue, the Social Democrats insisted that they contained constitutional amendments and should therefore be passed by a two-thirds' majority of Parliament. They also insisted on this with regard to the contractual agreements that brought the Federal Republic into the substitute Western European Union, but by this time, after the election of 1953, Adenauer had the support of two-thirds of the Bundestag. However, he also needed the support of two-thirds of the Bundesrat, whose votes are cast, it will be remembered, by representatives of the state governments.

Issues in State Politics

The requirements for passing constitutional amendments and the federal make-up of the upper house then had the curious effect of making foreign policy the principal issue in campaigns preceding the elections of state parliaments. Normally, problems within the jurisdiction of these state legislatures such as cultural, educational and administrative ones, would present the main issues for these campaigns. As things actually turned out, however, both Government and Opposition sent their chief leaders from Bonn into the state campaigns in order to get some kind of mandate on foreign policy. During the last federal election of 1953, the restoration of German self-government had not yet gone far enough on this score to make foreign policy the one overshadowing issue. In that campaign, it was just one issue among several. During the next few years, however, foreign policy did become the main issue, both because of its intimate connection with the question of reunification and because of the relative satisfaction that prevailed regarding most other potential issues. Since the Adenauer coalition could not claim to have a mandate on the conduct of foreign policy, and because W.E.U. and rearmament required constitutional amendments, it sought to get temporary mandates in the state campaigns. Moreover, something similar happened even between such campaigns, as the case of the use of the constructive vote of lack of confidence in North-Rhine–Westphalia, in early 1956, illustrates. The FDP had been restive in its federal coalition with the CDU, felt itself threatened by the draft of a new electoral law, and also disagreed with Adenauer's foreign policy, preferring more active negotiations with the Russians and even with some East Germans. On all these grounds, it left its coalition with the CDU at the state level in North-Rhine–Westphalia, joining instead in a coalition government dominated by the SPD. All of this happened, not because there was dissatisfaction with the administration of the incumbent Minister President, Karl Arnold, or even because SPD or FDP parliamentarians in Düsseldorf, the state capital, "lacked confidence" in this CDU politician. On the contrary, the SPD had been his coalition partner during early postwar years. Arnold himself, who has a "Christian" trade union background, would have preferred to continue this kind of "Great Coalition," since he distrusted the state's FDP organization, with its industrialist, capitalist leanings. He entered into the coalition with the FDP only under pressure from Adenauer as federal chairman of the Christian Democratic Union. On the other hand, having lost his minister-presidency, he was able to "get even" with Adenauer: At the next federal party convention of the CDU, Arnold was elected one of four deputy chairmen of the party, even though Adenauer told the convention that he wanted to continue with only two deputies, in which case Arnold would not have been one of them.

In any case, the over-all outcome of this situation has been to make the Bundesrat more immediately responsive to public opinion than the Bundestag, since elections of the nine state parliaments take place at irregular intervals during the life of one and the same Bundestag. Some German constitutional experts consider this an anomaly. Partly in order to give state-wide issues their rightful place in state politics, and partly in order to simplify politics in general, they have urged synchronization of federal and state elections. In other respects, too, some of them have advocated similar measures of defederalization, e.g., by doing away with differences among school curricula and admissions requirements in the various states and establishing uniformity throughout the whole Federal Republic.

Vocabulary of Politics

Campaign speeches and pamphlets, and parliamentary debates, are, of course, not couched solely in terms of constitutional or legal arguments. Nor are they by any means always learned historical, legal, economic, sociological, or ideological treatises. Often they are designed to appeal to the material interests of the voters quite as much as, say, in the United States. In the Bundestag campaign of 1953, for example, CDU speakers emphasized many concrete achievements of their government: the "economic miracle" of recovery under the free "social market economy" since the currency conversion of 1948, the building of homes, the absorption of refugees and expellees, and the return to a position of respect and influence in international politics, so shortly after defeat. Similarly, the SPD, on the other side of the fence, pointed to economic inequalities created in the course of recovery, promised greater government subsidies for home construction and better social security schemes, and blamed the continued division of Germany on Adenauer's foreign policy. Some of the studies made of voting behavior in various parts of the Federal Republic suggest that such material considerations influence German voters almost as much as American voters.

But even when the core of German political campaigning is concerned with such material interests, this is more often than not camouflaged by the trappings of learnedness, historical traditionalism, ideologism, and legalism. This is noticeable in the setting of campaign rallies. The halls are usually decked out with national flags. There is of course nothing distinctively German about that, but each of the parties has its own flag, which is also much in evidence. Rightist and leftist parties often begin and end their rallies with trumpet fanfares, blown by a band belonging to the party's youth organization. CDU rallies are sometimes preceded by a brief concert of classical music; SPD meetings, by marches played by a band of "Falcons," the party's youth organization. Usually, half a dozen or so members of the party's local executive committee are seated at a table on the speaker's platform or stage, facing the audience. But even though the local candidates are among them, it is not the normal practice to have them speak before the main speaker. In most cases, they are not even introduced, an indication of the high degree of centralization and discipline of the parties. Since discipline and control are usually exercised by the party's state rather than its federal organization, this relative lack of direct contact between local candidates and their constituents is the more remarkable. The speaker, especially when he is the party's state or federal leader, rarely speaks for less than an hour and often for more than two. He rarely indulges in "local color" oratory, designed to warm up his audience to him. As in the Bundestag, his speech may be punctuated by hostile interruptions from listeners. These he may ignore or respond to. Sometimes there are counterattacks upon the interruptor—occasionally physical and to the point of violence—from loyal members of the audience. At the conclusion of the meeting, the singing of the *Deutschlandlied* is standard operating procedure for all parties but the Social Democrats, who sing the socialist anthem. At CDU rallies, the official third stanza of the *Deutschlandlied* is the standard, while parties further to the right prefer the more nationalist first stanza. But even Christian Democrats can often be heard singing the first stanza, probably less for reasons of nationalism than because of their ignorance of any part of their national anthem other than it.

Just as in the parliaments, so in campaigns, the intellectual level of speeches is usually quite elevated (if not elevating), at least when compared with equivalent American political addresses. In fact, to an American observer, some of them would seem very much like university lectures, if it were not for the fact that many of them exceeded the standard fifty-minute duration. Similarly, some political pamphlets resemble scientific monographs in both thoroughness and dullness. When they deal with material interests, both speeches and pamphlets often recite lengthy statistics—a practice, incidentally, of which Hitler, too, used to be fond in his harangues, which sometimes lasted for four hours. When concerned with economic questions, SPD speeches especially seem to assume a level of economic knowledge for the acquisition of which the equivalent of at least a college freshman course in economics would be needed. Since the Social Democrats have always stressed training in Marxist theory, and offer courses on this sort of thing in their party schools, their speakers are probably wise to pitch their appeal at this level. Campaign speeches often—almost regularly—delve back into the history of the problem with which they are concerned, to demonstrate the consistency of the party's "right," and its opposition's "wrong" attitude toward it. The practice of citing supporting opinions by professors of jurisprudence, economics, sociology, history, etc., is often observed by campaign orators. The dead saints of the parties, both of the recent and the dim past, are often with them in spirit. In the campaign of 1953, both the SPD and the CDU used dicta of the late Socialist leader, Dr. Schumacher, in their campaign slogans. While SPD speakers do not directly quote Marx or Engels—in line with their general policy of toning down overt evidence of Marxism—their whole approach to current problems is heavily informed by Marxist theory. Such phrases as "class struggle," "imperialist domination," "capitalist exploitation," "proletarian solidarity," and the like, figure prominently in their speeches, and are understood in terms of a sort of vulgar Marxism by the audiences.

Door to door canvassing is not a common campaign practice in West Germany. But often meetings are held by local organizations of interest groups, at which candidates most sympathetic to the group make speeches. Voters are registered automatically and receive the card they have to present at the polling place through the mails. Since German law has traditionally required individuals to register their residence with the police, this method of automatic voters' registration does not present any organizational problems and is handled with great efficiency. It also offers one explanation for the relatively high participation in elections, despite the early fears of some who expected apathy or revulsion because of the enforced voting under the Nazi terror. And even though most Germans, both academic types and others, usually display an inferiority complex with regard to the average German voter's interest in and information about political questions, most American observers would give them a higher grade in both subjects than their counterparts in the United States.

Education for Politics

Where do the voters get their political education, and what is its nature? Answers to these questions may also help to explain the formalistic peculiarities of German politics which have already been noted. In the United States, people get what is probably the most important part of their political training at a very early age, during their school years. While they are getting it, neither the children nor, very often, the teachers are aware of the experience in the processes of American democracy that is being provided. Americans become familiar with these methods in a very informal way, for example, by electing class officers, collecting and spending class dues, or deciding with a minimum of adult interference or guidance where and when to hold the class picnic or which orchestra to hire for the school dance. In the course of all this, they virtually have to acquire familiarity with the kind of procedures contained in Robert's *Rules of Order*, even without being exposed to a course in "civics." The unconsciousness of this process of political education is one of its most important aspects and largely responsible for its effectiveness. On this score, the contrast presented by German education for politics is most marked. Even at this early stage, the whole thing is a very self-conscious, deliberate, planned, and, for these very reasons, formalistic affair. Given the German historical background, and especially the recent Nazi experience, no other approach may have been feasible on a large scale. No one in Germany who reached political maturity after Hitler's access to power in 1933 had any experience with even the most elementary democratic practices. This meant, among other things, that hardly anyone knew how to work on a committee, or how to arrive at common decisions on the basis of more or less rational contributions made by individuals who were initially in disagreement. The "leader principle" (*Führerprinzip*), one of the ideological hallmarks of National Socialism, made committee work rare and difficult to conduct under the Nazi regime. Compromise was not recognized as a virtue and therefore not openly practiced. The same was generally true of most of the other means by which disagreements are resolved and common policies arrived at in democratic societies.

To this, we must add the occupation powers' express desire to "educate the Germans for democracy" and the prevailing traditionally formalistic atmosphere, in order to understand the formalistic approach to political education in West Germany. Since the war, German high schools have also given civics courses to their students, but—to exaggerate the contrast between them and their American counterparts—there students are made to memorize the Basic Law and state constitutions, while here they are taught how government actually works by means that include mock "youth legislatures." In most German classrooms, a strong teachers' paternalism prevails regarding concrete decisions which, in the United States, would be made by the students. The consequence of this is that Germans are usually more familiar with the law than with the practice of the political process. This has its effects on adult politics. For example, in German committee meetings—in politics, business, and elsewhere—several copies of pocket-book editions of the relevant laws and by-laws are prominently displayed on the board table and frequently referred to, so that much time is often spent in parliamentary squabbles. And these quarrels arise, not because different committee members are necessarily in disagreement about policy, but because they feel a yearning to use the right legal procedures in formulating their agreement, while they are at the same time unsure of themselves in the use of these procedures. Even at this low level, as a result, substantive issues or "non-issues" are often transformed without need into procedural, constitutional issues.

Academic Political Personnel

All of this means that the equivalent of the "parliamentarian" plays a very important role. Given the civil and code law tradition, it further reinforces the crucial role of the jurist as one who is learned in these political procedures, which are in most cases reduced to "made" and systematized law. The jurists in turn—and not necessarily out of selfish motives —often encourage this tendency to enhance their prestige by demonstrating their own indispensability to the political process. Moreover, this situation has implications that reach even farther and operate more subtly: It also encourages ideological thought and action. Perhaps because of the methods of legal education used at the universities, and the influence of these methods on pedagogy in general, there is a general tendency toward systematic, comprehensive, codified teaching and learning in other disciplines, some of them far removed from the law itself. With this goes a very high degree of respect for, and deference to, those men and women who are officially certified, by their academic degrees, as having acquired all—literally "all"—this knowledge in a field.

Significant also is the comparatively high proportion of academically trained persons in the Federal Cabinet, the Bundestag, executive committees of the several parties, and politics in general. Adenauer's second Cabinet, for instance, consisted of nineteen Ministers, of whom eleven were listed as holding a doctorate, two as professors, but only eight without an academic degree. The Federal President is officially listed as "Professor Doktor Heuss," and generally referred to as "Professor Heuss." In the first Bundestag, 114 of 402 deputies were listed as holding doctorates, three of them as holding two doctor's degrees each. These last, incidentally, are often addressed as "Herr Abgeordneter (deputy) Doktor Doktor Schmidt." In the second Bundestag, the proportion of academics was even higher. Of course, people with some kind of university education predominate in other modern parliaments as well. For example, the predominance of lawyers in the United States Congress has often been noted. The difference here is, however, twofold: In the first place, these men are trained in the common law, which discourages a codified view of the world. And secondly, they are not in politics primarily because they advertise themselves as academic men. On the contrary, an American candidate for elective office would probably find an exclusively academic background a great campaign handicap. In Germany, it is the other way around: The case of Chancellor Adenauer illustrates this. Though always referred to and addressed as *"Doktor* Adenauer," his doctorate is actually honorary, and postwar at that. Similarly, the late leader of the Trade Union Federation, Hans Böckler, after having been awarded a doctorate *honoris causa*, was generally referred to as "Dr. h.c. Hans Böckler." Just think of the many honorary degrees conferred on President Truman (and most other Presidents of the United States and British Prime Ministers), or the case of Woodrow Wilson, and how ridiculous it would have sounded to Americans had they made use of these titles. But in Germany since politics at all levels is conducted to such an important extent by men who are supremely conscious of their academic training, to which they often owe their political status in the first place, politics is cast in an academic mold.

Stability of Political Style

This has been true of parliamentary politics in Germany at least since the National Assembly of Frankfurt in 1848, as we have already seen. And this seems to be the one constant and stable factor throughout all the different regimes that have succeeded one another since then. The academic cast of mind and tone was sloughed off neither when the parties got political responsibilities after 1918, nor when self-government was restored to the Germans after 1945. Continuity in the political style after World War II was due in some measure to continuity in political personnel. Most of the leading figures received their training in the Weimar Republic. But even those who reached political consciousness under the Nazis were then exposed at least to the trappings of a similar atmosphere. Some of the Nazi leaders, despite the generally anti-intellectual orientation of the regime, also boasted of their academic background. The most striking case in point is the Minister of Propaganda and Popular Enlightenment, who was always referred to as *"Doktor* Goebbels." The National Socialists always claimed that their ideology—which they considered as important as the Communists theirs—was based on scientific reasoning and the facts of race, blood, soil, and so forth. The façade of legalism that they tried frantically to preserve through the twelve years of their rule of lawlessness has already been mentioned.

Are these three aspects of the style of German politics, scientism, ideologism, legalism, still equally noticeable in the Federal Republic today? That scientism and legalism are as strong if not stronger should have become evident by now. With regard to ideologism, however, some weakening may be detected. In part this is again the result of the general revulsion against all things connected in German memories with the National Socialist period, and especially those of them that are once more also characteristic of the hated Soviet German dictatorship. Both under the Nazis and the Soviets, courses in political *Weltanschauung* were and are a regular part of the school curriculum. This by itself would provide sufficient reason for many Germans for turning away from an ideological approach to politics. Beyond that, there is the dis-ideologizing effect of politics that is conducted along the pattern, government-*versus*-opposition, although the weakening of party ideologies may have strengthened the ideologies of interest groups, with which we deal in the next chapter. Increased contacts with the predominantly unideological Anglo-Saxon occupation powers may also have had their effects in this direction. And, finally, the realization has dawned upon many Germans that their comprehensive systems of knowledge are not of very much help in solving the concrete problems with which they have had to come to grips. In some cases this has not yet reached the level of full consciousness, and the ideological vocabulary of politics has been retained, even though it often merely hides material interest politics. With other people, however, one finds such a high degree of awareness of the vicious consequences of ideological politics on Germany's past, that they have executed a complete about-face, to the point at which they openly advocate pure interest politics. When this position stops short of actual advocacy, it is reflected in a kind of detached cynicism about politics, which sees in it or behind it nothing but naked struggles for power and influence among interest groups, no matter how idealistic or ideological parties and politicians may sound in their protestations.

This suggests that the German attitude toward politics is dominated by a curious ambivalence between extremes, as is German political history. People either believe that politics should be thoroughly subjected to the restraining regulation of laws and the constitution; or they believe that might makes right. Similarly the Empire is followed by the Weimar Republic, the Republic by Hitler's Third Reich, and that once more by the Bonn Republic. It may be that the experience with violence and the consequent fear of violence has made people want to abolish anything that resembles violence even only slightly, as politics undoubtedly does. So they try to substitute administration and adjudication for politics. But when they subsequently discover that politics is with them inescapably, they throw up their hands in despair or disgust, and say, "We might as well be honest instead of hypocritical about this. It's all just a matter of power." And while the individual or the whole nation is passing through one stage, there is the fear of reversion to the other, so that the characteristics of the present stage are exaggerated even more in order to prevent this regression.

We have seen that the parties do "participate in the forming of the political will of the people," as the Basic Law provides. They help to formulate the issues, to marshal support for alternative solutions, and to make the resultant policies. But in order to see whether they are doing this in ways that are more or less ideological than formerly, and whether or not somewhere underneath naked power is the final determinant of policy, we shall have to take a look at the content and the scope of policy in the Federal Republic. To this we turn next.

CHAPTER 24

The Pattern of Policy

The main difficulty facing the student of contemporary German government is the lack of firmly established traditions, institutions, and procedures. Since the Germans themselves are painfully aware of this shortcoming, they display a sort of conscious yearning for tradition. This yearning would be both weaker and less conscious if more real traditions actually did exist. In other constitutional democracies, where institutional and political continuity is quite real, politicians do not need to make such contrived efforts to appear as authentic representatives of ancient traditions as in Germany. We have seen in our study of the German parties how unrealistic these claims to represent tradition necessarily are, in view of the fact that most of the problems the country faces today are radically different from those it confronted when modern parties and their ideologies first grew up. Besides, the constitutional framework within which these problems are dealt with differs just as much. Their lack of tradition thus produces this very yearning for traditionalism, which they seek to satisfy by adopting the old ideologies and the old ideological style of conducting politics. They lack a generally accepted conception of authority, or, to put it differently, they lack constitutional consensus, except on two levels: There is agreement on Germany, the geographic and national entity, as the unit of authority, and there is agreement on the style of politics. But there is no equal degree of agreement on the all-important rules of the political game, because the rules have been switched on the players too many times, and usually to the advantage of the most powerful group, whether it existed inside or outside German society. Consequently, anyone who wants either to justify the present constitution or to impose another set of rules upon his compatriots, must try to do this by appealing to the nation, and legalism, ideologism, and scientism. But this raises all sorts of stumbling blocks for the student, for it means that much of what the Germans say about their own politics cannot be taken at face value.

This is what makes it so hard to find a sound answer to questions about power in Germany: How effective is government? What stability is there in this effectiveness? How much can it do? For how long are its policies likely to be accepted? Since their accepted concept of authority is not fully "filled in," it is even more difficult to find out the extent to which there is an accepted conception of purpose, that is, substantive consensus. This is so because two antagonists may claim to be disagreeing about the purpose of government, when actually the same substantive policies would be acceptable to both; they are actually only trying to fight out their conflicts about conceptions of authority. To put it differently, the trouble is that the present "constitution" is only of the vintage of 1949. Many Germans prefer to see it as the direct continuation of the serial, whose first installment ran from 1919 to 1933, under the title of "Weimar Republic." This interpretation sees the twelve years of Nazi rule as a foreign and extraneous interlude. Thereby it unduly minimizes both the causes and the effects of those twelve years on present politics. If those who hold this view were right, there would be much more material on which to base answers to these questions about effectiveness. There is more in the case of the three other governments dealt with in this book. For Germany, we have so far only been able to show how government is organized, why "constitutional engineering" organized it this way, and how the parties operate within the framework of government. In the course of all this, we have been looking for those factors that really do seem to be stable, that are not merely superficial, but, because they are firmly rooted in German history, have the backing of a sufficient consensus so that they may be expected to survive any future changes, such as the reunification of West Germany and East Germany.

It would seem that the best way to find out how effective government can be in Germany would be to ask how effective it has been since the founding of the Federal Republic. Why not just ask: How much does government do? How does it do these things? Does the population readily accept government policies? We are going to deal with these questions presently, but we should not expect them to answer the basic questions about effectiveness, because these questions also contain the dimension of time, and this brings us back to our earlier difficulty. Government may have been extremely effective during the years between 1949 and 1958, and the scope of its policies very wide. However, because of the lack of stability and continuity in the past, and because of its tentative present make-up, our answers, too, must be very tentative.

The Scope of Concrete Policy

How much does government do in the Federal Republic? What sort of things does it do? Governments can try to control virtually all spheres of life, as we have seen in the case of the Soviet Union. Even in Great Britain, the scope of policy is and has been wide, especially since the years of World War II and the Labour Government which followed it. In the Federal Republic, it is certainly not as wide as in the Soviet Union. One reason for this is again most Germans' revulsion against the Nazi and East Zone totalitarianisms. They have wanted not only to restore the rule of law, which those regimes destroyed, but also to make government less total and all-engulfing. Furthermore, the Federal Republic only recently emerged from the control of the occupation powers, under which—as we have seen—many of the normal functions of government were performed by these non-German authorities. But how does the scope of government policy in the Federal Republic compare with that in Great Britain and France? This comparison cannot be as clear-cut as that with the Soviet Union. The scope of policy is at the same time both wider and narrower. There are some matters handled by the national government in those two countries that in Germany are not taken care of by the federal government or any government at all. But in other areas the reverse is true.

Here, as with regard to constitutional provisions, present arrangements are to a large extent the product of deliberate efforts to improve previous arrangements, whether of the Nazi or the Weimar period. This applies, for instance, to the West German economy. The official label describes it as a "social market economy" (*soziale Marktwirtschaft*). That is, it is an economy of the market or of free enterprise, which at the same time also aims toward the goal of social justice. This kind of economic policy is attractive both to the Christian elements in the CDU, because of its social justice component, and to the "liberal" elements in the CDU and its coalition partners, by virtue of its economic liberalism. At the same time, it is not as offensive to many Social Democrats as would be a policy of purely capitalist private free enterprise. Moreover, we have already seen how the SPD itself has considerably toned down its socialism. It wants only the basic industries to be socialized, and even those to be controlled by public corporations, on whose boards the government would have only one third of the seats, the other two thirds going to consumers and labor. The SPD has come out in favor of competition wherever "feasible." But even this toned-down socialism has not so far been attractive to any more of the electorate than that portion that supported it in the Weimar Republic.

Statism

Does this relative lack of socialist enthusiasm in the Federal Republic —when compared, e.g., with Britain even after the Conservatives re- turned to power—mean that government stays out of the economy al- together? It does not, but rather that government legally regulates even its own non-interference. In this respect, the Federal Republic is, of course, not unique by any means. Even before the advent of what has been called the "mixed economy" in the United States, there were a good many regu- latory agencies in the federal government. It seems safe to say, however, that the proliferation of codified governmental regulation of most spheres of life has not gone as far in either the United States or Great Britain as it has in Germany. Of neither of those countries could one say, "The people abhor a legal vacuum." And yet this statement seems to charac- terize the West German situation. Moreover, the fact that the German electorate has given no mandate to socialize the steel or coal industry— as did the British—does not imply that it is in any way "anti-statist." On the contrary, the tradition of economic statism is fairly old in Germany, as was noted in the discussion of the country's rapid industrialization. Thus railroads, which were nationalized in Britain only after World War II, were in Prussia built by the state in the beginning. And Bismarck introduced a social insurance scheme that was the most advanced of its time, partly because it was designed to take the wind out of the Socialists' sails. Also, the close and friendly relations prevailing between the old *Junker* and the new industrialist aristocracies eliminated from the outset the kind of hostility between the state and captains of industry that has played such an important role at various stages of the political evolution of Britain, the United States, and France. Finally, private enterprise without state help and direction would not have been capable of undertaking the enormous task of physical reconstruction that lay ahead at the end of World War II.

The Social Market Economy

The Germans thus have no tradition of principled opposition to state interference in the economy, or to state ownership of industry. Nor do they share the Americans' belief in the virtues of free economic competi- tion. And yet the Federal Republic is today described officially as having an economy of the market. Just what does this mean with respect to the role of government and the scope of its policies? It can be understood only if projected against the background of the first three postwar years, when the parties, because of their lack of real power or influence, were still mainly ideologizing. Because of the destruction, dislocation, disorganization, shortages, and hunger of those years, practically all of the physical wartime controls were retained. Food, fuel, housing, just about everything was subjected to strict rationing and equally strict price controls. All of this further increased the shortages, by encouraging a flourishing black market. Then in 1948, largely on the initiative of American Military Government, and against Russian objections which were connected with the subsequent beginning of the Berlin Blockade, the great currency reform was engineered. Overnight, the show windows of stores were filled to overflowing with goods, and a great burst of economic activity was unleashed. The CDU and the FDP rode to electoral victories on this wave, while the SPD, because of many economic injustices allegedly involved in the currency conversion, recriminated and favored a return to physical controls. The Government parties tried to meet these criticisms by labeling their market economy as "social." By this they meant that the underprivileged would be helped and cared for. Thus one of the major legislative products of the first Bundestag was the unique Law on the Equalization of the Burdens (*Lastenausgleich*) arising out of the war and its aftermath. Out of the proceeds of a capital tax levied over several decades, victims of the war or expulsions are being compensated for their losses. Others receive pensions, and the whole social insurance and social security system, whose beginnings go back at least to Bismarck, has been retained and in many respects expanded. For example, a Children's Allowance Law, which benefits especially families with many children, and is reminiscent of Nazi policies in this respect, was passed by the second Bundestag—incidentally by the votes of the CDU alone, unsupported by any of the other parties. There is also a comprehensive system of subsidies to various sectors of the economy, such as agriculture. The price of coal as a home fuel has been kept artificially low by means of such a subsidy. The initial phases of the housing reconstruction program were financed mainly out of public funds and achieved remarkable results. A system of tariffs complements these arrangements.

There were other measures designed to insure that the market economy should provide not only prosperity but also social justice. Outstanding among them is the scheme known as codetermination, which has already been mentioned. Under it, representatives of labor have an equal share with stockholders' representatives in the management of privately owned corporations in the iron-, steel-, and coal-producing industries. Its main avowed purpose was to improve labor relations in these industries and to give labor a check on irresponsible industrialists who might finance extremist political groups, as some of them did finance Hitler before 1933. Codetermination first came into being about 1947, in the steel industry in the Ruhr, which the occupation powers wanted to get back into production and to decartellize at the same time. In 1950, both CDU and SPD voted for the bill that provided the legal basis for retention of this scheme in the steel industry, and its extension to coal. The CDU supported codetermination because it could easily be considered an application of the modern social doctrines of the Catholic Church. Two years later, a milder version of codetermination was voted for the rest of the economy, this time against the votes of the SPD. Under its provisions, employees furnish one third of the members of the supervisory boards of directors of private corporations. The Adenauer coalition parties support such measures as part of their effort to temper the free enterprise economy with what they consider to be social justice. And this comes with particular ease to the CDU, which, according to its official program, is opposed to unrestrained capitalism because it fails to do full justice to the human qualities and human needs of human beings.

Government Regulation

The government's interference in the economy does not end with these measures which are designed to insure social justice. On the contrary, there is a vast volume of regulatory legislation covering all aspects of economic activity, regulating competition to such an extent that one can hardly consider it competition any more, setting standards for vocational and professional qualifications, and much more. Nor is all this regulation in any sense imposed by government upon an economy that resists it or is restive under it. In the majority of cases, it is rather given to the various trades, industries, and professions at their own request to be regulated. The attempt on the part of United States Military Government to introduce professional and vocational freedom (*Gewerbefreiheit*) in the American Zone of Occupation may serve as an example. Under the American policy, licensing requirements for such trades as baker, butcher, barber, grocer, etc., were reduced to a minimum. The first thing the Germans did, when given sufficient "sovereignty" to do so, was to restore the whole network of old regulations, which in many ways resembles the medieval guild system. In fact, many of the regulatory practices are hangovers from the age of feudalism and, for this reason, by no means confined to Germany alone, but to be encountered all over Europe, where their most notable effect is a much lower degree of social and economic mobility than prevails in the United States. But there are differences in this respect from one European country to the next. Thus, the French Revolution tried radically to abolish all organizations of the guild type by means of the *Loi le Chapelier* so that the vocational, trade, and labor organizations that do exist in France today have a less traditional and more rational and interest-oriented character than their German counterparts. In Britain, there remain a few such associations—such as the City of London Companies—which are of very ancient vintage indeed, but these perform "dignified" rather than "efficient" functions. In Germany, many associations have kept both sorts of functions, but they are not really efficient in any contemporary sense. They have not been fully assimilated to industrial capitalism, as it were, and still have about them much of the aura of the *Ständestaat,* the hierarchical state organized in functional estates, each of which is in turn hierarchically organized within itself.

In this way, even saleswomen in department stores and business secretaries are affected by patterns of corporatist thought. There is much less switching from one job to another than there would be in the absence of so much comprehensive and detailed regulation. The tendency to view life in general and politics in particular in a compartmentalized fashion is also due in part to these institutions. Individuals prefer to do only those things, and to be active in only those fields, to which their "role," their "station and its duties," entitle them. And because, both in their schooling and their economic activity, they are accustomed to having a clear course prescribed for them, they expect to have the same kind of order in politics, too. So far as making a living is concerned, this setup provides a great deal of security and—at least as important—a *feeling* of security which is highly prized, especially after the several catastrophes through which the Germans have passed in the twentieth century. The fact that they value security more and freedom of opportunity less than Americans is both a cause and an effect of this organization of the economy.

For the younger generations, especially of workers, who do not remember the political battles for more social security, or the period of vast unemployment before Hitler came to power, there is a general tendency to turn as a matter of course to the state for security and help. This attitude also received stimulus from the Nazi regime. The older generation, on the other hand, frequently complain that the youngsters "go to sleep in the ready-made bed" of material comfort which their fathers, fighting for their ideals, prepared for them. The oldsters recall the ideological—or, as they would have it, idealistic—struggles of the past and criticize the alleged "materialism" of their sons and grandsons. Because these did not have to fight for either their freedom or their security, older men often raise doubts as to whether they would be willing to fight to defend them, if the need should ever arise.

This is another form taken by the criticism of contemporary German politics on the ground of its materialistic orientation. To the extent that it points to the fact that the younger generation of Germans did not have to make a great effort in order to bring about the present political and economic stability, it points to an important truth, one of the great differences between contemporary Germany and France. The French fought for their freedom, against both the Nazi German occupation and the Nazi-supported Vichy regime. Dr. Wahl describes the great impetus given to the French reform movement by this experience of the Resistance. The Germans, with minor exceptions, have not fought for freedom for a very long time. They never had an equivalent of the French Revolution. The "revolution" that established the Weimar Republic, at the time of defeat in World War I, was so much a part of that defeat and otherwise so limited in its consequences, that many have denied that it was a revolution at all. There was no effective violent resistance against the Nazi system, which was after all a German, not a foreign, regime. The attempt on Hitler's life of July 20, 1944, failed and had the result of eliminating thousands of the most convinced fighters for freedom from later participation in German politics, since the Nazis executed them. There was no overt, violent resistance worth mentioning against the occupation powers after the war. In many ways, the heroic and tragic uprising of the East German workers against the Soviet regime of the Democratic Republic in Berlin and elsewhere, on June 17, 1953, was unique in German experience for over a century. In France, in contrast, there was not only the revolutionary tradition, but also the memory of successful violence used on behalf of freedom, recently enough to be remembered by all. France has made "progress on the barricades." Progress in Germany has come through orderly action, usually from above, or from the outside. National unification was achieved largely by Bismarck and sealed as a compact among the German princes. Social insurance, too, was introduced from above, by Bismarck. The first constitutional republican regime was introduced in the wake of defeat and under foreign influence. The same was true of the present second Republic. In Germany, legality, not violence, has paid off.

Interest Groups

But is German politics today really material-interest politics? We have seen that government does a great deal that affects and even controls citizens' material interests. We have yet to see how the policies are made that determine whose interests are to be served, and to what extent. The last chapter showed the role of the parties in the process of policy-making. Different parties appeal to different parts of the electorate in their professed and/or actual goals. Given the present electoral systems in the Federal Republic and its member states, no party that wants to survive, and certainly none that wants to grow in power, can afford to appeal to only one interest, whether it be economic, social, denominational, sectional, or other. Under the election law of the Reichstag of the Weimar Republic, this was not so. There was at least one party that managed to seat twenty-three deputies on the basis of a rather narrow interest-group appeal, in the elections of 1928 and 1930. It called itself the Reich Party of the Middle Estate (not middle class, characteristically). And there was a Peasants Party, and even a Bavarian Peasants Party. In other words, under the Weimar system, interest groups could and did go directly into parliament, in order to participate directly in policy-making there. Present institutions make this virtually impossible. The interests, however, still exist, and they are still organized. How do they try to get for their members what these want?

Bonn became the capital of the Federal Republic in 1949. By 1952, at least 270 interest groups of various kinds had established offices there. The variety represented among them is exceedingly great and ranges from industrial and scientific research groups, labor unions and employers' organizations, to refugee groups and taxpayers' leagues. They have their offices in Bonn in order to influence both the making and the implementation of policy. The latter can best be done through contacts of "lobbyists" with members of the "ministerial bureaucracy," i.e., civil servants in the Federal ministries concerned. Such contacts are facilitated by the fact that many organizers and representatives of interest groups are themselves former civil servants on leave of absence, who may intend to return to their government jobs at a later date. Most members of the civil service at these upper levels have a background of university juristic training. So do many representatives of interest organizations. After studying law at a German university, and passing a series of state-administered examinations, a student has a legal right to government employment. He may opt for a career in the judiciary or public administration, or for a private career, either as a practicing lawyer or in business or organizational work. If he chooses an administrative career, he can usually leave it for private business or politics but still retain grade and seniority for a later return to the civil service. This opportunity is often availed of. It not only facilitates communication between the interest groups and the Federal ministries, it also makes it possible for the interest groups to have as their representatives in the Bundestag men with a background of public administrative experience. Furthermore, it provides some politicians with a safe civil service berth to which they can always return in case they are defeated at the polls or fired from their private or organizational jobs.

United States occupation authorities objected to those provisions of the Basic Law and the first election law that kept civil servants from having to resign from the service upon accepting elective office. But in the long run the Germans had their way, on this as on other matters. For the first Bundestag, this meant that about one quarter of its members had a civil service background. In many instances, these deputies are also officers of professional civil service organizations. The political parties, in order to obtain the support of these associations or interest groups, nominate such men as their candidates. The same thing happens with representatives of other types of interest organizations, sometimes with their presiding officers. These have many opportunities for influencing policy, both in their party caucus and in committee meetings. The committee meetings are especially useful for this purpose. In contrast with Congressional committees, they hardly ever take testimony from representatives of groups that are particularly interested in legislation under the committees' consideration; nor do they hold public hearings. But because these groups often have leading officers on the committee as members, they are represented perhaps even more effectively in the Federal Republic than in the United States, although—and because—there is less accompanying publicity. For example, as of March 1953, 13 of the 27 members of the Committee on Nutrition, Agriculture, and Forestry were officers of interest organizations active in these fields. At least 10 of the 21 members of the Labor Committee were connected with labor organizations, and 6 of these 10 held leading positions in the DGB. Sixteen of the 21 members of the Committee on Civil Service Law (*Ausschuss für Beamtenrecht*) were civil servants. Some of the lobbies have recently begun to operate in a very modern, "American" way. They have run great publicity campaigns, promoting their cause by means of advertisements in the press and short films in movie theaters. This was done, for example, in relation to legislation on transportation, the automotive, oil, and rubber industries wishing to keep transportation taxes low and to expand the road network. (The close connection between these German industries and their counterparts in the United States may account for this largely unprecedented use of American methods of public and legislative relations.)

Modern methods do not characterize the majority of interest organizations, however, but in the main only those that really are modern simply because they do not have a long life to look back on. Many of the organizations that have offices in Bonn do have long traditions and are rather proud of them. This is true, for instance, of the German Trade Union Federation. Even though this is the first time that there has been one unified and politically neutral labor movement in Germany, the members of the DGB like to trace their origins back at least to the beginnings of both socialist and Christian trade unions in the middle of the last century. Similarly, the various trade, craft, and professional organizations have traditions that they consider to be both ancient and honorable. Membership in some of them is compulsory for the practice of a trade or profession. This is true, for example, of the chambers of commerce and industry (*Industrie-und Handelskammern*), which carry out some of the state's regulatory activities, such as supervision of apprentices and their training, administering apprentices' examinations, setting fair trade practices, and the like. Commercial and industrial businesses have to belong to these local chambers, which in turn belong to a hierarchy of state chambers, topped by the German Diet of Industry and Commerce. The interests the chambers represent often bring them into conflict with the trade unions, membership in which is not compulsory for workers, and which themselves are not admitted to membership in the chambers of commerce and industry. Now, we might expect that the unions would therefore advocate that the chambers be stripped of their semi-governmental character and their governmental functions. However, the reverse has been true. The unions have advocated that they themselves be made compulsory members of the chambers, by federal legislation. In addition, some of the trade unionists would like to have membership in the unions made compulsory for employees and to have governmental functions assigned to the unions as well.

The Desire to Be Regulated

This points to one characteristic that most of the German interest groups seem to share in common: the desire not for less government regulation but for more, both of their own affairs and interests, and of their relations with others. Another reflection of this desire may be found in the several systems of specialized courts that exist alongside the regular courts and the administrative courts (*Verwaltungsgerichte*). There are labor courts (*Arbeitsgerichte*), which deal with relations between employees and employers; and "social" courts (*Sozialgerichte*), which handle cases arising out of the administration of the social security system. These specialized courts have the virtues that go with speedy proceedings and judges who are technically informed. At the same time, these very virtues also encourage litigation.

Thus, even though the scope of material policy in the Federal Republic today may not be as great as in Great Britain—e.g., the coal industry is not government owned or operated—the scope of regulatory policy is very great indeed. In Britain, there is less demand on the part of interest groups to be formally regulated by government than in Germany. There is not so widespread and powerful a conviction as in West Germany that the creation of "social peace" is an urgent task for government, which could best be fulfilled by having government organize and regulate most social relations.

One explanation of this desire for comprehensive formal regulation may once more lie in the lack of any long German democratic and parliamentary tradition. In Britain people generally know how to conduct negotiations, say, in collective bargaining or at a meeting of a parent-teacher association. This is less often the case in Germany, and hence the yearning to have procedural rules for such and any occasion laid down once and for all in explicit legislation. Because agreement on authority is incomplete, the attempt is made to engineer it into existence. Because there is no procedural consensus, one has to be created artificially. But this yearning goes even further. People are reluctant to have relations with others that are not part and parcel of the status their vocational or political standing gives them. Therefore, many of them would prefer to have their contacts with other social, economic, and cultural groups formalized as well.

The most overt manifestation of this line of thought is advocacy of a revival of the Reich Economic Council (*Reichswirtschaftsrat*). This was the third, functional, economic house of the parliament of the Weimar Republic. It was not particularly effective. Nevertheless, today many trade unionists, both Social Democrats and Christian Democrats, are convinced that a series of economic councils, topped by one at the federal level, would serve the cause of social justice by extending labor's rights of co-determination above the level of the individual business corporation. It would also ease "social tensions" by defining clearly mutual rights and obligations between the "social partners," i.e., employers and employees. Constant contact and exchange of views between representatives of divergent economic interests is going on all the time, of course, in the Bundestag among other places. But because of their tendency to compartmentalize public life, the advocates of a re-established economic council tend to overlook this fact. Parliament, so they argue, deals exclusively with *Staatspolitik*. *Wirtschaftspolitik* therefore requires a separate, functionally specialized, deliberative body. Existing informal contacts between different economic groups do not suffice to promote "social peace," mainly because they are informal. Therefore, they should be formalized.

Are parties more ideological than interest groups? In West Germany, the reverse may well be true. The parties can no longer afford to remain as ideological as they used to be, because of the institutional pressures toward something resembling a two-party system, especially the pattern of government-*versus*-opposition. Unless they conform to this pattern, they are likely to be snowed under by the two great parties which are conforming to it. Now, this seems to have the consequence of deflecting ideologi-

cal patterns of conduct "down" to the level of interest organizations. This
need surprise us only if we think of interest organizations in British or
American terms, i.e., as being concerned mainly with obtaining material
gains for their clients. If that were their chief concern, then they would
have to operate in a rational manner, applying pressure wherever it is
likely to bring results, compromising, log-rolling, making alliances with
other groups regardless of the convictions of these groups, and so forth.
In other words, such interest organizations could not afford to be ideological, nor would there be any incentive for them to be ideological. But this
does not apply to German interest organizations, except for the very modern ones. The older organizations, since they have good reason to think
of themselves as bearers of ancient corporatist traditions, already have the
ready-made ideology of their estate or guild to fall back upon. In this connection, it is significant that even the SPD, for which class has always
been the most important social phenomenon, has referred in many an
official party program throughout its history, not only to the working class,
but also to the workers' estate (*Arbeiterstand*). And the Nazis, when they
spoke of the social leveling that would be carried out in order to establish
the true national community, attacked "*Klassen und Stände.*" If we combine the ready-made ideologies of the old estates with the deflection of
ideologies from the party level, we can understand why the interest groups
may be becoming more ideologized. Moreover, since ideological habits of
thought and action are direct and obvious obstacles to bargaining and
compromise, we can also understand why the interest groups may have
more of a stake in explicit government regulation than the less ideological
parties. They are afraid of the lack of consensus, the possible outbreak of
violence, and therefore want to engineer consensus into existence by constitutional means.

Policy and the Constitution

In Germany as elsewhere most trade unionists are interested above all in
improving their standard of living. But in order to get an increase in economic influence or power, they demand a change in the constitution
through creation of the Federal Economic Council. In making this demand, they are also inviting an increasing amount of government regulation of their own affairs. The situation is further complicated by their
additional desire to get the prestige that would go with membership in a
federal economic council or the chambers of commerce and industry. In
this sense, they want to return to something resembling the corporative
Ständestaat, the state in which the different functional estates were represented, in which the guilds largely regulated themselves with power

delegated to them for that purpose by the state, and in which no one had to worry very much about competition. The preference today is for regulation over competition. On this point, American occupation policy also clashed with German traditions and desires, and the Germans by and large restored the restraints on competition which Military Government had earlier abolished.

A further explanation for this preference may be found in the important role in politics played by civil servants, officials, bureaucrats (*Beamte*). We know that many members of the Bundestag are of this professional background, which generally involves legal training. These people tend to bring into politics in general and parliament in particular the legalistic, bureaucratic habits of their profession. The same is also true of many of the officials of large organizations, such as trade unions and large business corporations, who enter politics. Moreover, since the civil servants are assured of being able to return to the service in case of need, they are likely to retain a high degree of self-identification with "the state" (*der Staat*), which is certainly one of the most formidable terms in the German vocabulary. This is quite as true of the "progressive," lately revolutionary, Social Democratic Party as of the more conservative FDP. The image many German Socialists have of a socialist society is that of the State of Civil Servants (*Beamtenstaat*), in which everything will be orderly, regulated, and legalized. A functional, hierarchic organization would be indicated for such a state, and in it conflict, bargaining, competition, compromise, would have no legitimate place. Ideally, there would be no politics. In any case, whether they are hopeful for the socialist state of the future, or nostalgic about the corporatist state of the past, the Germans generally state their aspirations in legal or constitutional form.

Because government regulation is actually desired to such a great extent, the actions of government are respected, that is, effective. If a policy has been arrived at by the prescribed legal and administrative procedures, very few Germans would resist it in any way. There have been many illustrations of this. When the victorious Allies first began to occupy Germany at the end of the war, they expected resistance of the type the French had offered the Germans before the Liberation. There turned out to be virtually no German resistance—not even to the denazification policies, at least overtly. Part of the explanation undoubtedly lies in the sheer exhaustion of the German population, but part of it also in the fact that the Germans realized that the Allies were wielding "sovereignty" over German territory, that they were the source of law, and that they therefore had to be obeyed. The law always has to be obeyed—even in a revolution. The best illustration of this is Professor Sigmund Neumann's delightful story about SPD "revolutionaries" in Leipzig, in November 1918. Following sound revolutionary tactics, they wanted to take over the railroad station. But they did not take it by storm, as the French might have in a similar situation. They knew—as what German does not?—that the law requires that one buy an admission card to the platform, for ten pfennig, and get this card punched at the turnstile before going out on the platform. And that is exactly what they did in order to "seize" the railroad station!

In the recent history of the Federal Republic, even the most controversial policies of the Federal Government were accepted readily after they had been passed by parliament and/or found constitutional by the Constitutional Court. This was true, for example, for the several acts on codetermination. It was true of the European Defense Community and Western European Union treaties, and of the rearmament and conscription policies. So far, at least, government policies have been respected regardless of their substantive purpose, so long as they are backed by the authority derived from legal origins. The authoritative origins of policies are considered more important than their concrete consequences. This means that the best way to attack a proposed policy is through criticism of its legal source, and, ultimately, by questioning its constitutional basis. This route of argument makes for potential constitutional instability.

We may now return to our original question about the comparative scope of policy in Germany and Great Britain. In some substantive respects, government does more in Britain. But if a Social Democratic majority should ever come into power in Germany and pass socialization legislation, there would be little fear that anyone would resist any more than the Tories resisted after 1945. As a matter of fact, socialism might be accepted more readily in Germany than in Britain. The tradition of state regulation of the economy might have this result, as also the high prestige of the civil service. After all, if major industries were socialized, then practically everybody would be a *Beamter*. About one-ninth of the total labor force, incidentally, is already in the public services. On the other hand, the effective scope of regulatory government policy is much greater in Germany than in Britain. In Germany, almost any substantive issue is likely to be raised to the constitutional level. Many issues arise on the constitutional level in the first place. Many constitutional changes are also likely to be accepted by the population as authoritative, so long as they are arrived at in a legal way. Many others may be of such potential explosiveness that the discussion of them would have very divisive effects on German politics. This would seem to be likely in the case of issues dealing with that part of the concept of authority that has not yet been fully filled in, i.e., the basic rules of the political game. Certainly future years are going to present many opportunities for conducting such debates.

CHAPTER 25

Prospects

What are the prospects for German government? This question presents a double difficulty, because it involves not only the record of past instability, but also the uncertainties of relations between the Soviet World and the Free World. Germany lies athwart one of the main focal points of the Cold War. Its division into two states, the Federal Republic and the Democratic Republic, is a direct consequence of that struggle. Every change of temperature in the cold war is soon reflected in German politics. Whether, when, and on what terms the country will be reunified—all this depends on the international policies of the Soviet and Western governments. Of course, similar contingencies have to be taken into account in talking about the prospects of any governmental system. Nevertheless, by now it should have become clear that it is easier to foresee with some degree of accuracy the shape of future politics in the United States, Great Britain, France, and perhaps even the Soviet Union, than in Germany, where no stable pattern of institutions has emerged.

Can anything be said about specific questions such as these: What will become of the CDU after Adenauer leaves the political scene? Will this conglomerate coalition party of Roman Catholics and Protestants, Bavarians and North Germans, industrialists and workers and peasants, stick together, or will it break up? If it breaks up, into what kind of new groupings? Has the habit of conducting politics along the pattern government versus-opposition, become sufficiently well established to survive any radical changes within either of the two major parties? Are the constitutional provisions against extremist parties enough to prevent the overthrow of constitutional government, even if a grave international or economic crisis should arise? What will happen in the event of reunification? Would an All-German constitution contain a provision for a constructive vote of lack of confidence? Have constitutional practices, and loyalty to them, become so firmly ingrained in West Germany that they could be commu-

445

nicated by contagion, as it were, to the population of East Germany, which has been indoctrinated in Soviet Communism since 1945?

The student of government is throwing academic caution to the winds, even when his forecast is as limited as ours here will be. We have looked for elements of relative stability and continuity in modern German politics. We have not found them in the institutions of government, and could have found them there only by ignoring twelve years each of Nazi and East German Soviet totalitarianism. We have not found much stability or continuity in the party system, either, and could hardly have expected to. The changes to which German society and economy, and even the very entity, "Germany," have been subjected since national unification in 1871, have been too radical and revolutionary. These changes have completely transformed the problems faced by the Germans. Since their present constitutional system is also different from any preceding one, the issues that play central roles in German politics are also novel. Of course, problems in France and Great Britain have also changed, but they are still being dealt with by means of the same institutions that served that purpose in the 1870's.

Not so in Germany. Therefore, in looking for something stable and continuous we have had to go beyond the institutions of government, beyond parties and their programs, to attitudes toward politics. These are expressed in the ways in which people see their problems and formulate the issues arising out of them. In this respect, we have found elements that seem not to have changed very much over the decades. People are still unhappy rather than cheerful about the necessity of politics. Order is considered a virtue. Politics is disorderly. By substituting adjudication and administration for politics, order may be established. Knowledge alone can provide those principles, by means of which order can be established. Complete knowledge is available to those who devote themselves to study. Social order can be established through application of their knowledge by students of society and the law. "The Law" is one of the several, often competing, comprehensive systems of knowledge, on the basis of which politics can be transcended—to the extent that this is at all possible.

These attitudes of legalism, scientism, and ideologism, and the desire to get away from politics altogether, are reflected in the pervasive wish to foreorder all possible future disputes by means of detailed institutional engineering, and in optimism about the likelihood of reaching desired objectives through this instrument. This in turn tends to aggravate further the leanings toward constitutional instability. And it is strengthened even more by the understandable anti-totalitarian desire to establish the true *Rechtsstaat*. As a result, consciousness of the provisions of both constitutional and ordinary law is widespread. Preoccupation with constitutional problems is frequent. Many ordinary disagreements about substantive interests, which elsewhere would be handled within the constitutional framework, tend to become in the Federal Republic issues about the constitutional framework itself.

The tendency to make constitutional issues out of questions of interest might not be too important, so long as the questions of interest themselves are not of a very divisive nature. This was the case in West Germany until full self-government was returned to its citizens by the Western occupation powers. The Allied High Commission continued to function as the supreme guardian of the constitution against anti-constitutionalist forces, and some of the most important policies were imposed upon the Germans from the outside. By now, however, the Germans can no longer blame things on the occupation—nothing, that is, except the aftereffects of older policies. Rearmament and reunification policy, each directly dependent upon the other, have become the principal current issues in West German politics, as of 1958. Political battles about these two main issues will often be carried on at fever heat. Politicians will make use of many tactics in order to have their way or to obstruct the opposed majority from having its way. One of the best established and most promising tactics is constitutional controversy. Much of this may be expected. Much of this controversy and politics in general will be carried on by men of academic status in positions of leadership. Political discourse will abound with the vocabulary of old, and perhaps some new, ideologies. Even if the worst should happen and violence break out between East and West Germany, legalistic arguments and considerations will play an important role. These attitudes are likely to continue to be expressed—that much seems sure. But what the policies will look like that German government will produce, or what course Germany's future constitutional development will follow —that is uncertain.

PART FIVE

THE RUSSIAN
POLITICAL SYSTEM

by Adam B. Ulam

"Accounting and control—that is the *main* thing required for the 'setting up' and correct functioning of the *first phase* of Communist society. *All* citizens are transformed into the salaried employees of the state, which consists of the armed workers. *All* citizens become employees and workers of a *single* national state 'syndicate.' All that is required is that they should work equally—do their proper share of work—and get paid equally. . . . The whole of society will have become a single office and a single factory, with equality of labour and equality of pay." Lenin, *The State and Revolution, August 1917*.[1]

"In every branch of industry, in every factory, in every department of a factory, there is a leading group of more or less skilled workers who must be first and foremost attached to production if we want to make sure of having a permanent staff of workers. . . . And how can we manage to attach them to the factory? It can be done by advancing them, by raising their wages, by introducing such a system of payment as will give the skilled worker his due. . . . *And so our task is to put an end to the instability of labour power, to abolish equalitarianism, to organize wages properly, and to improve the living conditions of the workers.*" J. V. Stalin, speech delivered in June 1931.[2]

[1] V. I. Lenin, *Selected Works*, Moscow, 1947, vol. II, p. 210.

[2] J. V. Stalin, *Leninism*, vol. II, pp. 430-31, New York, 1933.

CHAPTER 26

The Origins of Soviet
Political Culture

When we speak of Soviet Russia (for it takes too long to say or write The Union of Soviet Socialist Republics), we underline the twofold character of the history and government of the communist state. There is Russia the builder and dominant part of the empire: "An unbreakable union of free republics was forged forever by the great Rus" proclaim the first words of the Soviet national anthem adopted during the second World War.[1] The earlier ideological scruples were then fully displaced by proud glorification of Russia's past and the *Internationale* was no longer deemed suitable for the national anthem. And there is "Soviet," the term that brings to mind the complex of ideas and institutions having to do with Marx, Engels, and Lenin, with the Revolution of 1917, and with a movement that claims to be universal and supranational and has an ideology that claims to present a picture of the future of all of mankind.

Thus the political culture of the U.S.S.R. contains elements of the history of the state and nation that trace their beginnings to the tenth century A.D., yet at the same time it has the imprint of an ideology that has developed within the last century. The history of the Russian people and of Marxism-Leninism are the two major foundations of the Soviet political system.

How to assess their relative importance has been the major point of dispute among the commentators on Russian affairs and Russian historians themselves. Is Marxism merely a thin veneer for the latest manifestation of forces apparent throughout the course of Russian history, or is the communist regime a definite break with the historical tradition of Russia? The proponents of the first view have stressed the parallel between Soviet totali-

---

[1] The word *Rus* has been used traditionally to describe the medieval Russian state in contrast to its modern form: *Rossiya*.

tarianism epitomized in Stalin and the high points of despotism and reform in Russian history found under Ivan the Terrible (1533-84) and Peter the Great (1682-1725). Even such characteristic institutions of Soviet Russia as the *kolkhoz* (the collective farm) are for them but a continuation of the old system of peasant tenancy—the *mir* of old Russia. The proponents of basic continuity of Russian history have not infrequently characterized the dictatorship of the Communist Party as the up-to-date expression of the traditional organization of Russian society where the sense of community and social union, often with religious undertones, has assertedly been prized above the "Western" values of personal freedom and individualism.

It has been pointed out with equal force that there is but a faint resemblance between modern totalitarianism and old despotism; that the *kolkhoz*, which is an attempt to apply the factory system to agriculture, has nothing to do with the *mir;* and that it is a gross oversimplification to take the relative absence of liberal and representative institutions in Russian history as an indication of something inherently undemocratic or collectivistic in the Russian national character. And indeed, though no revolution can destroy the accumulated weight of ten centuries of history, both Marxism and totalitarianism are modern phenomena. Russian history explains why they came to Russia, and the modifications they have undergone there. But neither Marxism nor totalitarianism are "typically" Russian. To understand them we must look at the social and economic forces that gave birth to the doctrine and have guided its growth and that of the most influential socialist movement.

Marxism

There has always been a feeling in some circles, both Marxist and non-Marxist, that the victory of a Marxist party in Russia was something of a historical "mistake." Marxism was born in the West. It is the product of political and economic conditions of Western society in the nineteenth century. By its own premises the doctrine of Karl Marx (1818-83) and Friedrich Engels (1820-95) was supposed to triumph in a fully industrialized society. How can one explain, then, the popularity of Marxism in pre-1917 Russia, and finally the victory of a Marxist party in a largely peasant economy undergoing but the intermediate stages of industrialization? Does it make any sense to talk about historical forces and the role of ideologies, or should we consider the prevalence of Marxism in pre-1917 Russia an intellectual fad, and the victory of the Bolsheviks in 1917 a historical accident?

What characterized Marxism in its beginning both as a theory and a political movement were three main elements: (1) an economic theory; (2) a philosophy of history; (3) a philosophy of revolution. [The economic doctrine is based on the famous labor theory of value. Capitalism, resting as it does upon private ownership of the means of production, is not only, or mainly, unjust, but primarily self-destructive.] The capitalist's profit is considered an unjust extortion from the worker, who has the right to the total product, since labor is the only source of value. But far more important than the ethical aspect of the problem are its economic consequences: [the inevitable exploitation of capitalism creates periodic and successively more severe crises of overproduction.] [Mature capitalism cannot but lead to increasing unemployment, increasing poverty of the masses, since in order to retain their profits the capitalists must keep depressing the level of wages.] At the other end of the social scale this leads to increasing monopoly and concentration of the means of production in fewer and fewer hands. It was the economic aspect of their doctrine that led Marx and Engels to differentiate sharply between their own and other brands of socialism. The others, they held, pleaded for socialism on ethical or political grounds, while only Marxism saw that, quite apart from moral postulates and political conditions, socialism—the ownership of the means of production by the community—is the *inevitable* sequel of fully developed capitalism.]

Marx and Engels produced their work at a period when it was widely believed, and not only among socialists, that the social sciences could have the validity and predictability of the natural sciences, and that the laws governing the development of society could be laid down with the rigor of physical laws. That conviction was likewise the basis of their philosophy of history and politics. ["Scientific socialism" was built on the broad framework of economic determinism, which provided the main clue to the workings of history.] Material factors, and more specifically the character and ownership of the principal means of production, constitute for the Marxist the master key of the social development of mankind. [Hegelian dialectic and nineteenth-century materialism are joined in Marxism to provide the gigantic framework of history where, as their economic underpinnings change, civilizations develop, mature, and then collapse.] The economic forces determining the content of history are then, themselves, triggered off by changes in science and technology. The industrial use of steam spells the final end of feudal society, where land was the principal means of production. Further inventions and the adoption of industrial techniques bring about the triumph of a new civilization and economic organization—capitalism. Yet *when fully developed*, capitalism is doomed by the same technological and economic forces that had predestined its success, and it must yield to a new way of life—socialism. Whatever its philosophical and political postulates, Marxism is unusually sensitive to and conscious of the development of science and technology. Its frame of mind is both historical and scientific.

The forces of history find their tangible embodiment in the social classes. Hence "the history of all hitherto existing society is the history of class struggles." [2] For the dominant class does not capitulate once its economic basis becomes less important and its political role obsolete. In Marx's lifetime the middle class in Western Europe, and especially in England and France, was winning political concessions from the landowning aristocracy and became the dominant political class in the state. The struggles for parliamentary and social reforms, for the ending of aristocratic privileges, and for civil rights were viewed by Marxism as mere reflections of the basic and immemorial class struggle—itself echoing the evolution of the forces of production. To Marx, the triumph of the middle class (which he witnessed and in a way applauded as rendered inevitable by the forces of history) was but a prelude to the ultimate class struggle between the bourgeoisie and the new class produced by the Industrial Revolution: the working proletariat.

The intricate combination of philosophical, historical, and economic arguments culminated in Marxism in a plea for political action. Even before its theoretical structure was fully complete, Marxism appeared in the *Communist Manifesto* (1848) as a philosophy of revolution. Though Marx considered as inevitable the eventual destruction of the capitalist system by the forces of history, he worked for and at times expected the imminent overthrow of capitalism by the workers. The language of the economist and philosopher is often subdued by the language of the politician and revolutionary who wants to give history a push. If the theoretical part of Marx's writings is flavored by one word: *inevitability*—the inevitability of the Marxian scheme of history, of forces dwarfing human efforts and making the downfall of capitalism certain—then the political side of his argument is colored by the word *exploitation*: the capitalists and industrialists are not mere agents of historical forces, but also malevolent oppressors and exploiters of the workers. The latter, once they gain the consciousness of their real situation, will smash decaying capitalism and its props, the state and organized religion.

Throughout his life the need for a revolution in which the working classes would seize the reins of the state remained for Marx an article of faith. As to the character and methods of this revolution he did not remain of one mind. When the revolutionary excitement in Western Europe began to subside after the forties and fifties of the nineteenth century, Marx's revolutionary optimism subsided with it. At one point he was ready

[2] *The Communist Manifesto.*

to grant that in some highly industrialized countries with parliamentary institutions revolution might come through non-violent and parliamentary means; i.e., the working classes securing a majority in the parliaments of their countries. After his death, his *alter ego*, Engels, was to go even farther in the expectation of a peaceful transition to socialism. But the most persistent element in original Marxism is its appeal for revolution and its diffidence toward the institutions of the modern state, whether parliamentary or judicial, as being based not on impartiality but on the vested interests of the economically dominant class. Only when the workers capture the state will democracy and equality become a reality. Until then they are for Marx but hypocritical phrases used by the bourgeoisie to strengthen its political and economic oppression.

Any large-scale social doctrine is open to many interpretations. Translated into political action, it becomes, of necessity, detached from the mere opinions of its author and his immediate disciples. Marxist parties, and not only in Russia, have justified actions most inconsistent with one another in the name of the same theory and the same body of writings. Already in Marx's life economic and political facts were impinging upon some of his principal theories and prophecies. It was a cardinal point of Marx's theory that the growth of capitalism brings with it the inevitable lowering of the standard of living and increasing unemployment for the workers. Yet the second half of the nineteenth century, which saw the flourishing of capitalism and industrialism in Western Europe, witnessed also an undeniable increase in the material well-being of the masses. Along with it came the widening of the parliamentary franchise, rudimentary measures of social security, and the legalization of labor unions—measures that Marx had held unlikely to be allowed by the bourgeois state. Socialist parties, even when they adopted the "orthodox" Marxist program (as in Germany) and refused to dilute it with liberalism, tacitly discarded Marx's more revolutionary and undemocratic prescriptions. Marxism in Western Europe appeared toward the end of the nineteenth century as merely a radical expression of the cosmopolitan, democratic, and egalitarian tendencies of the era, capable of being absorbed into the mechanics of a constitutional state. It was as such, clothed in democratic and constitutional phraseology, that it traveled into the economically and politically backward regions of Eastern Europe.

Even a summary account of Marxism provides some clues as to what made it so important to Russia, then a predominantly agrarian country, and what caused Marxism *as a political movement* to be born in the context, not of a fully industrialized society and of democratic institutions, but of the initial stages of industrialization and of semi-feudal political institutions. Its revolutionary appeal echoed the discontent of the former peasant or artisan whom mysterious economic forces had deprived of his previous livelihood and had compelled to seek employment in industry. Here he found himself, even if better paid, without the security of his previous occupation, usually unprotected against sickness and accident, unprovided for in old age, and prohibited by the state and his employer from joining a labor union. Politically, the industrial worker was then without the right to vote, and it is logical that parliamentary institutions must have appeared to him merely as an arena of struggle between the middle and the upper classes. By the end of the nineteenth century the status and material conditions of the working class *in the West* presented a considerably different picture, and precluded a ready response to the revolutionary appeal of Marxism. But the Russia of 1900 was similar in some respects to the West of the 1840's and 1850's, so that Marxism, in its original revolutionary and conspiratorial form, could well take root in Russian soil.

A critical analysis of Marxism and of the validity of its postulates is not needed to perceive its twofold significance as a political movement. In a society undergoing the transition from the agricultural to the industrial order, Marxism offers the lower classes an effective and appealing exposition of their grievances and frustrations. It shares this characteristic with many other socialist and anarchist movements. But unlike the latter, Marxism does not not urge blind opposition to the necessary phenomena of modern life: the state and industry. On the contrary, while it advocates the destruction of capitalism and the bourgeoisie by revolution, it also speaks of the inevitability and benevolent effects of both industrialism and the state after capitalism has been destroyed.[3] Marx's qualifications about the withering away of the state and about complete economic equality, both of them inconsistent with modern industrial society, were to provide a useful rationalization to Stalin when he was building his totalitarian state and grossly inegalitarian society. But without burdening Marxism with the full responsibility for totalitarianism, it is clear that Marxism has considerable tactical advantages over other forms of socialism and radicalism. In a society where the mass of inhabitants are denied the right of participation in politics, and where the birth pangs of indus-

[3] Though Marx believes, as do the Anarchists, that the state should wither away, the practical consequences of this notion are nullified by his admission that victorious socialism will need the state, for a while, and a powerful centralized state at that, owner of all the means of production. A similar admission takes most of the strength out of Marxism's message of egalitarianism: complete equality cannot be achieved immediately after the victory of socialism and destruction of capitalism. Only communism, the final stage of socialism—the time schedule is again not specified—will realize the slogan "from each according to his ability, to each according to his needs."

trialism are in evidence, Marxism appeals both to the past, in denouncing the evils of factory discipline and the wage system, and to the future, in promising that in a socialist society industrialism will bring with it democracy and abundance.

Russian Traditions

That Russian history is in some sense "different," that it does not fit into the categories employed for other countries, has been the assumption of many writers, Russian and non-Russian, conservative and socialist. To the nineteenth-century historian with a liberal bias, history meant steady progress from despotism and superstition to democracy and enlightenment. Since Russia did not appear to conform to the pattern, Russian history had to be qualitatively different from that of the West. Today we no longer share the optimism that made such overgeneralizations possible. Nor do we believe in the notion that every country has its own "genius" and historical mission imprinted in the unique character of its political institutions. That Russian history *is* different from that of the West is due not to the "Russian soul" or to the presence of factors absent elsewhere, but to the same social and economic forces found in the West, but appearing in Russia at different times and with different intensity.

We should not minimize the importance of the most obvious differences: a religion accepted from Constantinople rather than Rome, and a Church and society that had undergone neither the Renaissance nor the Reformation; a social system in which the mass of the peasants was not emancipated from serfdom until 1861, long after Western Europe; and the relative absence or fragility of representative institutions and of an independent judiciary. But we need not resort to mysticism or the exaggerated theory of the uniqueness of the Russian national character to explain the heritage of Russian history that the Soviets took over in 1917. The analytical apparatus of the social sciences is quite adequate for that purpose.

The most striking characteristics of Russian society on the eve of the revolutions of the twentieth century were: centralization and the autocratic character of political authority; a social structure in which the mass of the freshly emancipated peasantry was still under severe economic and political restrictions and the middle class far weaker than and different in character from its Western European counterpart; and the rudimentary character of institutions of political and economic representation. The sources of these "peculiarities" that leave an undeniable imprint on today's Soviet institutions can be found in Russian history. Let us therefore spotlight some problems in the development of Russia and examine how the social and political forces that agitated the rest of Europe made their appearance in Russia.

Centralization of Political Authority and the Autocratic Tradition

In the West the principal beginnings of the modern state date from the Renaissance. Every student of history knows how the Tudor monarchy in England and figures such as Louis XI and Richelieu in France strove to overcome the heritage of feudalism and dispersion. The necessary elements of a modern state—a sense of national unity and centralization of political authority with the attendant institutions of the bureaucracy and the standing army—began to emerge only slowly and painfully toward the end of the Middle Ages. Roughly at the same time the task of state- and nation-building also confronted Russia but under vastly different conditions.

Ever since its recorded beginnings in the tenth century, the Russian state struggled for survival and expansion against its neighboring Finnish- and Turkish-speaking tribes and states. After the Mongol invasions, the most notable setback in this struggle resulted in the subjugation of most of the country to the Tartars. For two centuries (from the middle of the thirteenth to the middle of the fifteenth century) most of Russia was isolated from the rest of Europe, with her previous and quite extensive commercial and cultural intercourse almost entirely interrupted, and her princes reduced to Tartar vassals and tribute collectors. Only in the fifteenth and sixteenth centuries did modern Russia begin to take shape, around the nucleus of the Grand Duchy of Moscow. This building of a state took place under conditions that, much more than in the West, facilitated, if not demanded, the erection of a strong and despotic monarchical authority. There was continuous warfare with the Tartars and sporadic wars with Russia's northern and western neighbors: Sweden and the kingdom of Poland-Lithuania, which contained extensive Russian-speaking lands. It is no wonder that even in sixteenth–century Europe, where absolute monarchy was the rule, the government of the Russian tsars epitomized in the reign of Ivan the Terrible became the byword for despotism.

In the West the Middle Ages had bequeathed to the Renaissance states social and political institutions that, centuries later, became the bases on which constitutionalism and representative institutions could, and did, grow. Such institutions were not unknown in medieval Russia. The monarchy was counterpoised by the Church with the Metropolitan of Moscow, later on the Patriarch, as its head. The Estates and Diets of the rest of Europe were paralleled by the Russian Assembly of the Land, and the Council of the Magnates. Even the rising middle class, in Western Europe the fermenting element of the social and political change, found its counterpart in the merchant republics of Novgorod and Pskov, which acknowledged but nominal sovereignty of the prince. But in Russia these institutions were considerably weaker and lacked a wide enough social basis. They were eliminated (as in the loss of autonomy by Novgorod and Pskov), or subjugated through terror and economic sanctions by Ivan III (1462-1505) and Ivan the Terrible (1533-84). The latter's reign is not atypical of certain other great periods of Russian history: though he was a great social and political reformer and the military leader who finally destroyed the Tartar power, his reign abounds in instances of violent and systematic terror. It is a pattern to be found again in Peter the Great and Stalin, and one that is not entirely absent from the reigns of the great state builders in the West—Louis XI in France and Henry VIII in England.

Ivan's reign, with its centralization and despotism, was followed, again not atypically, by a period of reassertion by the nobles, internal anarchy, and foreign invasions. Early in the seventeenth century it appeared as if Russia were to be joined to her western neighbor, the Polish-Lithuanian state. It was at that point that something approaching modern nationalism was born in Russia. A wave of popular feeling, largely religious in its foundations, since the rival Polish monarchy was Catholic, established the Romanov dynasty in Russia and preserved the independence of the country. The inheritance of a prolonged national or religious struggle is likely to be an exaggerated and parochial sense of nationalism. The struggle against the Poles erected the autocracy and Orthodoxy into national symbols, and strengthened the isolation from the political and cultural currents from the West.

It fell to Peter the Great (1682-1725) to modernize the Russian monarchy, but also to clamp tighter the shackles of absolutism. One aspect of his reforms was to impose the externals of Western civilization upon his subjects, symbolic of which was the enforced shaving of beards by the nobility. Modern industry and technology were imported into Russia, not through the action of private citizens, but by the state. In one reign, Russia, a backward and ignored country, became a major power and a member of the European community of states—a historical development unparalleled until the rise of Japan in the late nineteenth century. Peter's reforms, however, also resulted in the destruction of the still existing social and political particularisms, and, consequently, in the strengthening of the principle of autocracy. The Church was deprived of the Patriarch and subjected to a lay official appointed by the emperor. Noblemen's privileges were made dependent on their direct service to the state, and the nobility, as a class, was amalgamated with a bureaucratic caste. Violent repression followed the slightest sign of semi-feudal or religious (one is tempted to say "counterrevolutionary") reaction against the reforms. Serfdom remained the main prop of the economy, and the gap between the upper classes, forcibly westernized and educated, and the mass of the people, became wider.

In a sense the pattern established under Peter has characterized Russian history during the past two centuries and its traces are evident under the Soviet regime: the state became the main planner and executor of social and economic policy. In the West a similar situation prevailed during the heyday of mercantilism in the seventeenth and eighteenth centuries, but it was drastically changed in the nineteenth century when the social classes developed stronger viewpoints and pressures of their own. As compared with western European countries, a sharp contrast marks Russia's development down to our own times. Russia was now in the forefront of the European community of nations. From Peter's time onward her upper classes participated in the most advanced European intellectual and political currents. Yet the mass of the people were left far behind. Revolutionary outbreaks, in which seventeenth- and eighteenth-century Russia abounds, are like medieval risings and *jacqueries*, sporadic outbreaks of disgruntled nobles or oppressed peasants or Cossacks, rather than modern revolutionary movements with their specific political and economic postulates.

The principle of autocracy, now embellished with the latest bureaucratic techniques, remained unimpaired throughout the reign of Catherine the Great (1762-96). Contacts with Europe increased and indeed the partitions of Poland brought Russia much farther West. But if Catherine and her advisers thought of modernizing the state, they thought so in terms of the enlightened absolutism of the century, which sought to increase education and efficiency but neither decentralization nor the subjects' rights. The French-speaking and Westernized nobility was tied more firmly to the throne by economic and social concessions, but any half-hearted attempts at basic social reforms were defeated by the fears arising from the outbreak of the French Revolution.

Only at the beginning of the nineteenth century was the possibility of modern representative assemblies first discussed by the Russian government. This brief era of liberalism under Alexander I and his minister, Speransky, was succeeded by a period of reaction and the fundamental parts of the latter's constitutional proposals were shelved. At the end of the Napoleonic wars the empire was increased by the addition of Finland

and a part of Poland. In these areas the tsar was a constitutional monarch and representative institutions functioned while he remained the Autocrat of a Russia that did not possess anything remotely resembling a parliament!

[The reign of Nicholas I (1825-55) began with the first modern revolutionary attempt.] The Decembrists of 1825, who failed in an armed *putsch*, were composed mostly of young aristocrats and army officers. They had some constitutional and reformist notions gathered from the West and they stand at the beginning of the great Russian revolutionary tradition. Their abortive attempt provided the justification for a new technique and routine of repression. The Russia of Nicholas I became an autocracy in which the passivity of the citizen was no longer taken for granted. The police state, with its administrative judgments, its secret police, and its all-embracing censorship, became the means through which the tsarist bureaucracy strove to preserve the *status quo* and to repress the social and intellectual ferment. [The tsarist state under Nicholas considered itself, and was so considered by Europe, as the bulwark of absolutism.] The Polish uprising of 1830-31 was put down by arms and Poland's constitutional privileges abrogated. A Russian army helped the Austrian emperor to put down the Hungarian rebellion of 1848-49. In contrast with a Europe bustling with democratic movements and liberal reforms, Russia stood as the fortress of militarism and of national and social oppression, a seeming exception to all the rules of historical development as propounded by liberalism.

A cursory look at Russian history reinforces one's first impression of the passivity of the population and the consequent ability of the government to exercise absolute and at times tyrannical power. [The revolutionary movement of the second half of the nineteenth century, though now almost continuous and punctuated by violent incidents, such as the assassination of Alexander II in 1881, was the work of small groups drawn for the most part from the thin layer of the educated and upper classes.] At the end of the nineteenth century, just as at its beginning, Russia was an autocracy. The reforms of Alexander II supplied the rudiments of local government and judicial independence, but they did not affect the reality of the police state and the absence of civil rights. Into this society, politically static but in an economic and social revolution, came Marxism.

The Social Structure and Representative Institutions

Russia's political development becomes intelligible only in terms of her social history, the main characteristics of which are familiar in the history of the West, though the parallel development stops at a certain point. [Social classes and their status became frozen in Russia and it was only the coming of the Industrial Revolution in the second half of the nine-teenth century that propelled society forward at a feverish speed, ultimately creating a political crisis. An oversimplied explanation, not without ele-ments of truth, would run in a circle: society was weak in Russia because the government was strong; the government could be so strong and op-pressive because society was so weak. The actual story is more complicated.

Economic conditions peculiar to eastern Europe made Russia lag in her commercial and industrial development. By the same token, the struc-ture of Russian agrarian society relied on serfdom. A great majority of the cultivators of the soil—hence a majority of the population—were unfree: they belonged to the state or to the landlords. These serfs, besides work-ing their own land, had to work for their masters. The latter had a variety of powers over their peasants amounting almost to that of life and death. In direct opposition to what happened in the West, the legal status of the Russian peasant had deteriorated since the Middle Ages. The build-ing of modern Russia that took place in the eighteenth century did not lead, as one might have expected, to the destruction or alleviation of serf-dom. On the contrary, the submission of the nobility to the new autocratic system was won not only through force but also through concessions, at the expense of the peasants. The alliance of the government and the nobility made serfdom far more rigid and the powers of the landlords more extensive. A Russian landowner of the eighteenth century, and in-deed until 1861, could whip his serfs, send them into the army (where until 1874 the term of service was twenty-five years) or, in extreme cases, into exile to Siberia. He was not allowed, at least in theory, to ruin them economically or to evict them from their land, as could be done to the tenant farmers in England or Ireland. In short, the lack of rights was miti-gated by an extremely low but still real form of economic security, a sit-uation that was to recur in Russian history.

Serfdom and its consequences were the central facts of tsarist Russia's politics and economics, just as the collectivized agriculture of the U.S.S.R. constitutes the main dilemma of the Communist regime. Largely because of serfdom, the nobility remained an obedient tool of the government and could not assume an independent posture toward the throne. It made social mobility almost impossible and hampered commercial and indus-trial progress. Last but not least, in an age of nationalism as well as lib-eralism, serfdom was felt to be, and was, a derogation of human dignity, an institution that set a majority of Russians apart from the national community. Yet the government could not bring itself to abolish the in-stitution on which the whole social order was grounded, and the destruc-tion of which might threaten the survival of autocracy.

It was as much the pressure of economic forces as a deliberate decision of the government that led to the Emancipation Edict of 1861. The action of the government of Alexander II was greeted at first with enthusiasm, and was considered, even by some of the political exiles, as a rebirth of Russia. Yet the manner of emancipation was to have grave results for Russian society.

[Economically, the result of emancipation was far from being satisfactory to the peasant.] The government took all too great care to protect the landlords. [The peasants were given land, but in many places not even all the land that they had held as serfs.] The government paid off the landlords, while the peasants were to be weighed down for years with redemption dues to the state. But the main point of grievance was to remain the scarcity of land and the peasants' feeling that somehow they had been cheated because so much land remained in the hands of the landlords. The impact of the industrial age was already felt in Russia through a prodigious growth in population. Even with the growth of industry, and with mass migrations to the new lands in Asiatic Russia, the need and hunger for land was deeply felt among the peasant masses.

[Politically and socially, the Act of 1861 preserved some of the features of the old village system: a decision endowed with far-reaching consequences.] We may be justified in using a twentieth-century term and speak of "nationalization" of the peasants rather than of "emancipation." For the reform of 1861 did not give them full civic and social rights but made them more directly wards of the government. Equally important, [the old form of village organization, the *mir*, was preserved and even strengthened. The *mir* was a form of communal self-government that exercised a variety of economic as well as judicial decisions] although in tsarist Russia its more important decisions were naturally guided, first by the landlord and then by the government agent. The *mir* collected taxes, sent recruits to the army, judged minor disputes, etc. But in addition it periodically redistributed the land of the peasants, decided on the character and methods of cultivation, and in general acted as the joint possessor of both the land and labor of its members. To a conservative the *mir* appeared as the bulwark of old Russia, which preserved the peasant in his "native" customs and allegiances and saved him from the contamination of modern ideas. But even some of the revolutionaries thought of the institution as a Russian form of socialism and democracy that should be preserved. Karl Marx said in a weak moment that the *mir* could enable Russia to pass into socialism without undergoing the full rigors of capitalism.

The truth is that the *mir* had nothing to do with democracy or socialism, certainly Marxian socialism, as the terms are properly understood. It was an institution at once egalitarian and conservative, but in both senses running against the tendencies of modern times. It was certainly different from the *kolkhoz*, the collective farm, imposed by Stalin, which is based on the application of industrial factory methods to agriculture. The *mir* prevented the application of better agricultural methods and inhibited the development of enterprise among its members. It hampered social mobility and the growth of an enlightened farmer class. It was, in brief, a powerful anti-industrial influence and hence not only anti-capitalist but also anti-socialist in spirit. Its preservation in 1861 for reasons of expediency and conservative ideology did not help the regime but was bound to prevent the rise of a strong middle class such as both enlightened conservatism and liberalism require. It was only a few years before the first World War that the tsarist regime made a resolute attempt to remedy the mistakes of 1861. On the initiative of Peter Stolypin, the ablest social statesman of prewar Russia, the peasants were enabled and encouraged to break up the *mir* and to develop into individual farmers. But the war interrupted what would have been the building of a peasant middle class.

The imperfect emancipation of 1861 was but one of the measures by which the government belatedly recognized that an economic and social revolution was going on in Europe and that Russia could not escape its effects. The lament of a provincial governor is characteristic: the building of railways is dangerous to established institutions, because railways enable people to travel and travel in turn exposes them to subversive ideas! Railways, however, had to be built, and with them came manufacturing and banking and other disturbing paraphernalia of progress. The growth of the middle class never caught up with the advances in industry and commerce. Russia entered the Industrial Revolution during its more advanced stage. The average size of a manufacturing or commercial unit was much greater than during a corresponding period of the industrial development of the West. Hence there was very little in the country in the way of the self-made small and medium manufacturers of France and England. Rather, the Russian middle class of the late nineteenth century had an educational and intellectual status and was composed mainly of members of the liberal professions and of the middle and lower bureaucracy. The intelligentsia was unusually susceptible to the intellectual currents and political ideas of the West. Their frustrated thirst for political activity often found its expression in literature and journalism, which flourished both at home and in exile.

To the growing social aspirations of its educated classes the tsarist government, even in the reforming period of Alexander II, offered but half measures of reform. The jury system and a very limited scheme of local self-government, in the country (*zemstvos*) and cities, heavily weighted in favor of the propertied classes, were substantial advances over the past but insignificant when compared even with recent reforms in the former fellow autocracies of Austria-Hungary and Prussia. Instead of becoming a safety valve, Alexander's reforms stimulated the pressure for more basic reforms. The latter half of his reign (from the late sixties to 1881) was full of revolutionary activity and violent repression. The revolutionary movement was as yet the work of small groups, but it reflected the discontent of several sections of society. Western anarchist and socialist ideas, which in the West had become tamed or insignificant, were being adopted in Russia in their original revolutionary and violent character. When Alexander II fell to the last of several attempts on his life by the revolutionary group called the People's Will, his assassins included a man of peasant antecedents, the daughter of a high tsarist official, a scientist, a Pole, and a Jew. The composition of the group symbolized the diversity of revolutionary premises within the Russian Empire.

It is useful to insert a note of caution: Because the Revolution came in 1917 we tend to think of many preceding years as being years solely of oppression on one side and of revolutionary strivings on the other. A more balanced view would take into account the strength of the nationalist and conservative tradition in nineteenth-century Russia, and popular attachment to the tsar and the Orthodox Church as the symbols of Russian nationhood. The century was also the period of the great flowering of Russian culture, which, in literature, music, and even the sciences, made imperishable contributions to European civilization.

Once Russia entered the industrial race the growth of her economy was rapid indeed. The *rate of growth* of Russia's industry between 1890 and 1914 does not compare unfavorably with that of the U.S.A. for the same period. Perhaps the total picture points up one of the "contradictions" of which the Marxists love to speak: a vigorous and growing society and economy shackled by obsolete political forms. But even in politics the picture is not of one color. After 1905 Russia had a degree of constitutionalism. Her parliament (*Duma*) was neither democratically elected nor very effective, but it provided the promise of political progress. Censorship was relaxed. The lot of political prisoners, while still grim, was considerably better after 1905 than it was to be in Stalin's Russia. In the Constitutional Democrats (*Kadets*) liberalism was the most potent influence among Russia's educated classes.

In brief, the coming and popularity of Marxism in Russia are explicable in terms of historical and social forces, but the Revolution of 1917 and the triumph of the Bolsheviks are as much if not more the result of a fortuitous arrangement of events and personalities.

CHAPTER 27

The Party That Became the State

The history of the Soviet state begins, paradoxically, nineteen years before the Revolution. For it was in 1898 at a meeting in Minsk that a handful of delegates organized the Russian Social-Democratic Party, out of which grew the Bolsheviks—the Communist Party of our day. The years of clandestine activity, of conspiracy against tsarism, and of internal strife, that characterized the growth of Bolshevism left their indelible imprint on the state the Party created. Hence the "prenatal" period of the U.S.S.R. and with it the habits of thought and action the Bolsheviks acquired before their coming to power, are of much more than academic interest. The Marxism that has stamped its imprint upon the minds of millions of Soviet citizens is not the Marxism of Marx. Much as Soviet ideology today owes to Marx, it owes perhaps even more to the powerful genius of Lenin, who boldly interpreted, altered, and distorted the original doctrine. In so doing he not only dictated the tactics of the revolutionary movement in Russia, but also formulated the political values and beliefs upon which the Soviet dictatorship was founded and in large measure still rests. To follow the fortunes of the tiny handful of conspirators that he led is to witness the emergence in embryo of most of the essential ideals, structures and practices of the massive Soviet state of today.

Marxism in Russia

The genealogy of Russian Marxism runs back at least to the small groups of revolutionaries who fought and conspired against tsarism during the last decade of Alexander II's reign. In 1879 the most notable of these groups, the People's Will, split into two factions. One of them conducted a campaign of terror that culminated in the assassination of the tsar in

1881. The other, the so-called Black Partition, under the leadership of George Plekhanov, abandoned terrorism and became the nucleus of the Marxist movement in Russia. The original People's Will, like its predecessor the Land and Freedom group, had but a vague populistic ideology that did not go much beyond a plea to summon a constitutional assembly for Russia. Though socialistic in character, the ideology of the group centered upon the peasant and paid but scant attention to the rising industrial proletariat. The People's Will perished in the wave of repression that followed the assassination of the tsar, though some of its ideas and terrorist tendencies were reborn shortly after the turn of the century in the Social Revolutionary Party. Black Partition, on the other hand, became the progenitor of Liberation of Labor, the first Russian Marxist group, formed in 1883 by Plekhanov, Paul Axelrod, and Leo Deutsch. In a series of books Plekhanov laid the foundations of theoretical Marxism in Russia. Thus from the beginning the attitude of the Marxists toward populism, indeed toward the peasant, was an ambivalent one. Marxism in Russia sprang up from a *narodnik* (populist) movement, and inherited some of the latter's conspiratorial flavor as well as a preoccupation with the peasant. On the other hand, the separation from Black Partition meant that Plekhanov and some others felt that conspiring was not enough and that the vague, partly sentimental and partly utopian, philosophy of populism had to be replaced with the systematic philosophy of history and economics of Marxism. While recognizing the revolutionary potentialities of the peasant problem, the Marxists came to feel that the *active element* in a revolution would be provided by the rising working class, and not by the discontented but dispersed and basically conservative peasantry. As we have seen, Russia in the eighties and nineties of the last century was a rapidly industrializing country. Since Russia had entered the industrial race late, her industry was of the new large-unit type, which created large conglomerations of workers in the main cities of the empire. Thus Moscow, St. Petersburg (today's Leningrad), Warsaw, and Lodz in Russian Poland, Baku in the Caucasus, and others became highly industrialized, and these large concentrations of workers of many nationalities provided fruitful ground for revolutionary propaganda.

Little circles of mostly young intellectuals, some of them university and high-school students, were the first to absorb, and then spread, Marxian propaganda. The oppressive intellectual atmosphere of Russia in the nineties, with its censorship and suppression of all political activity on the part of students merely increased resentment among young people and led them to search for a revolutionary solution. Marx's doctrine, with its intellectual intricacies, its comprehensive scope and theological flavor, was the very thing to appeal to young intellectuals living in revolt against their society. They in turn carried a simplified version of Marxism to the workers, who, scantily protected by the state and forbidden to form unions, were equally responsive to the revolutionary call. In contrast to populism Russian Marxism did not rely on terrorism nor did it expect a sudden and dramatic reversal in the government and society. Its propaganda was of a long-range nature. It worked through discussion and persuasion; it stressed the need of organization, teaching that the struggle, though it would be long and arduous, was bound to end in victory, because the forces of history were on its side. Economic distress and political persecution combined to create a wave of strikes in 1895-98 and they in turn increased the influence of the socialists among the workers.

The foundation of the Social-Democratic Party in 1898 was an attempt to unite the different strains of Marxism within the Russian Empire. The new party was to house not only the various shades of socialism but the Marxist groups based on nationality associations such as the Jewish Bund and various socialist groups in Russian Poland, the Caucasus, etc. The very diversity of the elements the Party was attempting to hold together augured from the outset that its internal life was to be one of ideological and tactical quarrels, of schisms, divisions, and expulsions. There arose a situation quite paradoxical at first glance, and yet common among ideological and revolutionary parties: a group of conspirators pitted against a powerful state was so rent by discords and quarrels that the various factions at times tended to make their struggle against the autocracy secondary to their internecine quarrels. What became known as Bolshevism emerged from two such struggles within the Party: one over the issue of the meaning of Marxism in Russian society; the other over the character and organization of the Marxist party.

Orthodox Marxist doctrine held that as capitalism progresses the working class will organize itself *spontaneously* and the workers will acquire the class viewpoint, that is, will realize the necessity and inevitability of putting an end to capitalism. Drawing upon this interpretation of Marxism, a group of Russian socialists who were to become known as "Economists," held that the primary task of the socialist party in Russia should be to operate not on the political but on the economic plane. Trade unions, not conspiracies, should be the weapons with which to fight for the immediate *material* interests of the workers: better pay, shorter working hours, the legal right to organize, and social security. Inherent in the position of the Economists were two assumptions: First, that Russia was as yet unprepared for socialism, as she was just entering the capitalist stage of development. They interpreted Marxism as meaning that a fairly long capitalist development, with the state dominated by the middle class and parliamentarianism, must precede any successful attempt to set up socialism.

The second assumption of the Economists was equally repugnant to revolutionary socialists. In line with the ideas then prevailing among Western socialists,[1] they appeared to hold that the very logic of economic and social development would bring about democracy and then socialism, and that revolutionary activity was consequently unnecessary, if not harmful. Industrialization and social pressures would first temper, and ultimately abolish, the barbarities of Russian tsarism. The road to socialism lay through peaceful organization and education and not through coups d'état.

Had the ideas of the Economists prevailed and become basic to Russian socialism, it would have followed the democratic and evolutionary path of many socialist parties in western Europe and elsewhere. But as a matter of fact, the Economists, though influential among the intelligentsia, were soon to find themselves outside the pale of the Social-Democratic Party, and their subsequent story belongs to the history of Russian liberalism rather than to that of socialism. The reasons for their defeat were fairly obvious. In the first place Russian autocracy was not willing, at least not until after the Revolution of 1905, to allow any political activity even of the most moderate kind. The tsarist bureaucracy was also blind enough to prohibit independent labor unions, and to hesitate long before extending the most rudimentary type of protection to the worker. The soil of parliamentarianism, social legislation, and progress in which democratic socialism could grow, simply did not exist in Russia at the time, and even after 1905 there was to be but little opportunity for free political and professional life.

The answer of the revolutionary wing of the Party to the Economists was uncompromisingly hostile. The great authority of the founder of Russian Marxism, Plekhanov, was thrown against them. The future Bolsheviks and Mensheviks combined in denouncing the Economists as traitors to Marxism. And it was in this polemic that Vladimir Ilich Lenin laid the theoretical foundations of the Soviet version of Marxism.

In 1902 Lenin was but thirty-two, already a veteran revolutionary, his membership in the socialist circles dating from the early 1890's, and his career having included a period of exile in Siberia. Since he came from an intellectual middle-class family one of whose members (his elder brother) was executed for participation in a plot against Tsar Alexander III, his choice of the life of a revolutionary was neither atypical nor difficult to understand. It was the reading of Plekhanov that had drawn him toward Marxism. He had already established himself as a theoretician, and in 1900, with Plekhanov and others, he began to edit in exile the Social-

---

[1] Best illustrated in the writings of the Fabians in England, and of Eduard Bernstein and other Revisionists in Germany.

Democratic paper *Iskra* (Spark). In 1902 Lenin came out with *What Is To Be Done?*, probably his most important work, fundamental to the understanding of the history of the Bolshevik Party and the Communist state.

What Is To Be Done? was a pamphlet addressed to the current problems of the Social-Democratic Party, which was at that time, we must repeat, a small group of revolutionaries, partly in Russia, partly in exile. Neither their most pessimistic enemies nor they themselves would have dreamed that this group would grow in the course of one generation into a party of millions and into the absolute master of a vast state. Yet the argument and the flavor of *What Is To Be Done?* have remained imbedded in the values and beliefs of the Soviet system. They are evident in the pronouncements of Khrushchev as they were in those of Stalin and Lenin.

First, the flavor and tone of the book. We are struck by its *dogmatism*. The theory of Marxism is not to be trifled with. The use of Marx's writings as if they were infallible scriptures, the heavy pedantic tone, and the vituperation of those who would dilute or modify Marx (i.e., those who disagreed with Lenin's interpretation of the master) are already in evidence. We can already see in the book the *undemocratic* temperament that Lenin was to implant in the movement. When he wrote it Lenin was officially and by conviction a Social-Democrat, i.e., his socialism was coupled with the belief in and postulates of democratic institutions. But temperamentally he was opposed to the premises of democracy: in particular its rationalism, which teaches that the mass of people are capable of seeing and resolving the main issues of politics; and its humanitarianism, which holds that human values and feelings should not be sacrificed too readily even at the altar of social and economic progress.

The argument of the book revolves about the concept and the role of the Party. In a remarkable passage in which he attacks the main theses of the Economists, [Lenin lays the foundations of Bolshevism. The masses, if left to themselves, he argues, cannot acquire the proper class consciousness or work out a revolution. They must be led by a body of professional revolutionaries.] In fact, Lenin is quite ready to reinterpret Marx, while claiming, of course, that he is merely following the letter of the doctrine. Marx had assumed that class consciousness comes to the workers in the course of their economic struggle with the capitalists. But, says Lenin, *spontaneously* the workers will develop only *trade union consciousness*, i.e., the desire to improve their economic conditions, to legalize their organizations, and to secure other material and status concessions. To rely on the spontaneous growth of class feeling among workers, as the Economists would have done, is to abandon the hope for revolution, the hope for socialism, and to resign oneself—though Lenin does not say it in so many words—to a slow *evolutionary* development toward something which, though an improvement on autocracy, will be neither socialism nor Marxism. The first task of revolutionary socialism, therefore, must be the creation of a disciplined party of professional revolutionaries who will instill revolutionary consciousness into the masses. This party cannot be a debating society or a party on the Western model, but must possess a conspiratorial as well as legal organization. Lenin's concept of the Party— that of a quasi-religious order of conspirators devoted to revolution— harks back to the traditions of revolutionary groups of Russian populists. Thus the tradition of a conspiratorial group ready to undertake a coup d'état was linked with the doctrine of Marx—the mixture that constitutes Bolshevism.

What Lenin had to say about the composition of his ideal revolutionary party has likewise been imprinted on the history of the Communist movement, not only in Russia but elsewhere. The workers constitute the best material for the membership, not only because of the reasons Marxism traditionally gives, but also because their very mode of life—the routine of the factory—accustoms them to discipline and organization. Thus they make good soldiers of revolution. Yet the class origin, Lenin implies, is of secondary importance as a qualification for the revolutionary. A socialist party devoted to the cause of revolution must send its detachments into every segment and class of society. Intellectuals as a rule may be too individualistic and opportunistic to submerge themselves in a group, but, by the same token, they have the necessary intellectual tools for conducting revolutionary propaganda. In a sense a revolutionary party must disregard the class origin of its members and must look to the qualities of mind and will, and the capacity for obedience.

In short, the recipe is for a centralized hierarchical and conspiratorial organization whose highest organs will lay down not only organizational directives, but the doctrine as well. To repeat: this is not a political party in the Western sense of the word, not even in the sense in which the contemporary German and French Socialists were parties, but a quasi-religious, almost military, order of revolutionaries. The notion of *elitism*, of subordination of the mass of members to a small directorate, is clearly here. Marxism, born in the era of rationalism, receives in Lenin's hands a definitely irrationalist twist. If the majority of the people cannot see clearly their real interest, i.e., the necessity of revolution, but have to be propagandized and shown the path, does it not follow that the mass of mankind will always have to listen to the dictates of a few? Such a conclusion is not spelled out by Lenin but it is inherent in the argument of *What Is To Be Done?*

In its totalitarian intolerance of differences of opinion, in its anti-democratic contempt for the capacities of the masses and its stress on disciplined obedience to an elite, Lenin's pamphlet formulated the conception of authority that was to triumph in the Soviet dictatorship. This conception defined the role of the Communist Party in relation to the rest of society, endowing it with the unquestioned right to govern. At the same time it also set the movement on its way to a centralization of authority in the top leadership of the Party itself, unchecked by any effective participation from below. This is not to say that Lenin had already conceived the dictatorship of Stalin. There were still traces of democracy and freedom within the Party, if not in the Party's relation to the masses. In time these remnants of liberalism were eliminated from the structure of Soviet absolutism. Still, for the house that Stalin built, Lenin laid the foundation well.

The Bolsheviks before November

The Second Congress of the Russian Social-Democratic Party, which met in 1903 in Brussels and then in London (after the Belgian police drove the delegates out), was the decisive turning point in the history of Russian Marxism. The Economists had for the most part been defeated or had left the Party. The splits that appeared at the Brussels Congress were, thus, between various branches of *revolutionary socialists*. The most notable among them was the controversy and the division between the Mensheviks and the Bolsheviks. These names, meaning respectively "Minoritarians" and "Majoritarians," do not convey accurately what happened at the Congress, for on some issues the Bolsheviks, led by Lenin, were in a minority. So, for example, the definition of a Party member followed the Menshevik draft rather than that of the Bolsheviks. [Lenin wanted the Party membership restricted to those who were *actively* participating in the political and conspiratorial work. His Menshevik opponent, Martov, sponsored a slightly different phrase that would have allowed sympathizers as well as activists to enroll in the organization, and he carried the day.] On some other issues, notably on the personnel of the Central Committee and the Party organ (*Iskra*), the Bolsheviks, supported by Plekhanov, prevailed, but only after some of their opponents had walked out and refused to participate in the balloting.

It should be kept in mind that in view of conditions then prevalent in Russia, it had not been possible for the delegates to the Party Congress to be elected in any regular and orderly fashion. The Congress that produced the Party program and crystallized the two main tendencies of Russian Marxism was composed of the revolutionaries who happened to be abroad at the time or who had been able to smuggle themselves out

of the country. The basic split in the Party between the Bolsheviks and
the Mensheviks was to persist until 1912 when the former declared themselves a separate Party.[2] It is difficult to give a simple reason for the split:
the causes are not exhausted either by the ideological differences or by
the personalities involved. Thus it would be erroneous to assume that the
Mensheviks were, as a body and on every issue, less radical than the
Bolsheviks, or less prone to a revolutionary action. It is by and large correct to say that the Bolshevik faction was Lenin's group and that he dominated it to an extent not even approximated by any single leader within
the Menshevik group. Thus Lenin's dictatorial ways led to an early split
with Plekhanov, who soon joined the Mensheviks, thereby isolating Lenin
on the editorial board of the *Iskra*. Many other prominent socialists, some
of whom were to rejoin the Bolsheviks in 1917, became estranged from
them in the pre-Revolution days simply because they felt that the Party
was unduly dominated by one man.[3] In fact, it was being said among the
European socialists that Lenin was ruining the cause of Russian Marxism,
and that his personal ambition and vindictiveness would destroy Social
Democracy in the empire. Yet it should be kept in mind that *prior* to the
victory of Bolshevism in November 1917 Lenin did not have at his disposal
any instruments of coercive power, and if a sizable body of Marxists followed him both inside Russia and in exile, it must have been because his
arguments appealed to them. It would not be far wrong to discern two
opposing temperaments in the camp of pre-Revolution Russian Marxism:
on the one hand, the Bolsheviks, more akin to the old populist groups
in their revolutionary impatience, less democratically minded and more
prone to divest Marxism of its elements of humanism and rationalism;
on the other hand the Mensheviks, who were closer in spirit to their Western colleagues—revolution in their minds did not take an absolute priority
over democracy.

We have to keep in mind that such judgments are really based on hind-
sight. It was in 1917 and afterwards that the full extent of anti-democratic
tendencies lurking in Bolshevism was exposed. Prior to the Revolution
neither of the two Marxist groups appeared as dangerous and radical, either
to the government or to the upper classes, as did the Social Revolutionary
party, the inheritor of the populist tradition. One branch of the Social
Revolutionary Party conducted a systematic terroristic campaign against
the government and several high officials fell prey to assassination.[4] The

---

[2] Though on many issues, especially within Russia, the two factions continued to
collaborate until the Revolution.

[3] The outstanding example is Leon Trotsky.

[4] The attitude of the Bolsheviks toward terror was not without ambiguities. Thus
Lenin evidently countenanced terroristic activity in some areas, e.g., in the Caucasus,
which was designed to secure funds for the Party. Sporadic acts of terror against

Social Revolutionaries, though led by intellectuals, were mainly a peasant-oriented party and their influence on the peasants, still a decided majority of the population, was a matter of profound concern to both Marxist groups.

The revolution of 1905 was a sign that revolutionary feeling was endemic in Russian society. That revolution was a preview of the conditions that were to destroy tsarism in 1917. First, a wave of peasant unrest, reaching its crest in lootings, land seizures, etc. As usual the peasant rising was unco-ordinated, elemental and ineffective in its character. Nationalist stirrings of revolutionary character came into the open in Russian Poland. Other non-Russian parts of the empire also experienced trouble. The defeat of Russia in the war with Japan became the catalyst of tension. Peasant unrest proved to be merely the broader canvas against which the decisive revolutionary action took place in the cities, especially in the two capitals, St. Petersburg and Moscow. It was among the workers that the revolutionary movement that had permeated all classes of society took the most drastic expression. The striking workers of St. Petersburg formed a *soviet*. The word is merely Russian for *council*, but its more specific meaning illustrated in 1905 and 1917 could be loosely translated as "a workers' council of action"—a revolutionary body elected *ad hoc* in a time of crisis from among the delegates of factory workers.[5] The soviet in a revolutionary situation was elected with but little attention to democratic safeguards. It tended to be a fluid group in its composition, not unlikely to be dominated by a party that possessed the advantages of strict discipline and superior techniques of agitation. The latter characteristics were to be fully evident only in 1917. In 1905 the almost spontaneous growth of soviets astonished the Russian Marxists and especially the Bolsheviks. The latter could not be expected to be too friendly to the new phenomenon. Didn't Lenin distrust "spontaneity"? Yet they joined in the movement. In the St. Petersburg soviet the leadership was assumed by the Mensheviks but soon a brilliant newcomer, Leon Trotsky, then only twenty-six and temporarily estranged from both factions, became its moving spirit. For a time St. Petersburg was ruled by the soviet, the authorities being fearful of moving against it. The general strike, followed by an insurrection, broke out in Moscow.

The revolution failed for several reasons. In the first place the government disarmed the more moderate of its opponents by promising constitutional concessions. Secondly, the armed forces had not been demoralized

---

government officials were held by Lenin, along with other Marxists, to be harmful to the revolutionary cause. Even before the Revolution some of the Bolsheviks indicated that they were not opposed to *preventive terror*, i.e., the use of extralegal and drastic punishments against political opponents once the socialists were in power.

[5] In 1917 delegates of soldiers were to join the workers in the soviets.

as they were to be in 1917 by three years of a sanguinary war, and remained, with a few notable exceptions, disciplined and obedient to the government.[6] In the third place, the process of social dissolution had not reached the level of 1917. With its opponents divided, the government proceeded to arrest the soviet of St. Petersburg and to suppress in blood the Moscow uprising. The revolution of 1905 had proved to be a great rehearsal.

Viewed as such, it is difficult to overestimate its influence on the Bolsheviks. For Lenin and his followers it was an eye-opening revelation that in a revolutionary situation one has to transcend Marxist formulas and employ flexible and daring tactics. One must swim with the revolutionary current and seize its direction. The discontent of the peasant masses (and peasants furnished the majority of soldiers) could not be channeled into Marxist slogans. Hence, when an opportunity arises the Bolsheviks must forget Marx for a while and appeal to the peasant with a slogan that will assure them of, at least, his benevolent neutrality. The middle classes showed themselves ready to abandon the revolution when promised parliamentarianism. But bourgeois parliamentarianism is less suitable as an arena for revolutionary action than the flexible and volatile system of representation embodied in the soviets. The idea of an alliance with the progressive part of the middle class became for the Bolsheviks entirely secondary to the need of winning the support of *workers and poorer peasants*. Unlike the Mensheviks they decided that liberalism was *not* a natural ally of socialism.

The period of 1906 to 1917 is the only period in the history of modern Russia when something resembling constitutionalism and free political life was in existence. The tsarist government did not have the slightest intention of introducing democracy, nor even a constitutional and parliamentary system in our own sense of the word. The *Duma*, or parliament, convoked in 1906 had very limited powers. Since there was no ministerial responsibility, executive powers continued to reside in the tsar and his advisers. Even in legislative and budgetary fields, the government could still by-pass the parliament. Most important of all, the complicated electoral law was rigged in favor of the more conservative classes, and when the first two parliaments proved unduly radical and obstreperous, the law was still further changed so that the Third and Fourth Dumas were dominated by moderate conservatives. But if Russia in the period immediately preceding the War and Revolution did not become a democracy or shed the vestiges of despotism, it must be kept in mind that for the first and only time in the twentieth century (excluding the short period between March

---

[6] That revolutionary stirrings were particularly potent in the Russian navy was already demonstrated in 1905. Thus there was a mutiny in the naval fortress of Kronstadt, and the famous revolt of the battleship *Potemkin*.

and November 1917) political parties could operate in the open and literature critical of the government could be distributed legally. In the Duma there was at least the germ of genuine national representation and a platform for voicing social and political demands. Those who hold that the Bolshevik regime, while repressive, freed Russia from unrestrained monarchical absolutism forget that between 1906 and 1917 the civic freedoms, while not sufficient or considerable, were infinitely more extensive than they were ever to become in the Soviet period.

The fortunes of the Bolsheviks during the period illustrate the axiom that the party was already so constructed both ideologically and organizationally that it was bound to prosper in periods of acute revolutionary excitement and decline in periods of political and economic progress. Like the Mensheviks and the Social Revolutionaries the Bolsheviks finally agreed to participate in the work of the Duma, though, with their radical colleagues, they considered the emasculated parliament as a platform for propaganda rather than a genuine parliamentary forum. It is significant—bearing in mind that the franchise was far from being democratic and the elections could not portray accurately the division of political sentiment in the country—that in the elections to the Second Duma the Bolsheviks obtained half as many deputies as the Mensheviks, and that in the subsequent elections they never topped the number of deputies elected by their socialist rivals. Both Marxist parties were outdistanced by the Social Revolutionaries and their allies, who had what amounted to a monopoly of political influence among the radically-minded peasants. The middle class followed the "Kadets" (the Constitutional Democrats), the leading party in the first two Dumas, who professed liberal ideas and who would have been content to transform Russia into a constitutional monarchy on the English pattern. Even in the freest and most democratic elections, the Bolsheviks would never have got more than a small minority of votes, and they and their sympathizers were a minority even among those who saw a drastic revolutionary change as the only solution.

This fact in itself never bothered the Bolsheviks, who considered the parliamentary struggle as entirely secondary to clandestine revolutionary activity. Lenin reproved some Bolsheviks who would have boycotted the Duma elections, but he was much more severe with those who would have liquidated illegal activities and concentrate on open political life. What was profoundly more disturbing to the Bolsheviks than their numerical weakness or the government's tampering with the electoral law, was the possibility that revolutionary feeling would abate and that reform, whether put into effect by the government or forced by the moderates, would relegate them to a small uninfluential group.

Such prospects were quite real in Russia in 1906-17. For once, the tsarist government adopted the policy of intelligent reform in addition to repression to deal with the revolutionary situation. [The new premier, Peter Stolypin (1906-11), while a man of the most conservative and reactionary ideas, saw clearly that the police, the Cossacks and the *agents-provocateurs* would not by themselves preserve the monarchy and the social order] He realized that the source, if not the active carrier, of the lingering revolutionary feeling was the peasant imprisoned in the *mir*, denied more land, and kept under all sorts of social and political disqualifications. The solution was to free the more enterprising peasants from the *mir*, to give them some semblance of civic rights, and, most important of all, to transform them into farmers, with land of their own and opportunities of acquiring more. The peasant would then have a stake in the political and social order, and Russia would have a rural middle class antagonistic to revolutionary changes. A series of laws enabled and encouraged the peasants to break up the *mirs* and to set themselves up as individual proprietors. The peasants' remaining financial obligations to the state (dating from the time of the emancipation) were canceled, and the government now extended credit facilities to the peasants so that they could buy up the nobles' lands. [The peasants' land hunger was being at least partly satisfied, and a new peasant class, more conservative in its outlook, was rising in the villages]

Had Stolypin's social engineering been accompanied by a willingness on the part of the regime to introduce genuine constitutionalism and to invite the moderates into the government, there is little doubt that Russia would have been launched on a period of peaceful liberal reform. There was an undoubted decline of revolutionary feeling beginning with 1907. Membership in the revolutionary organizations, especially among the Bolsheviks, declined. Some Party leaders turned to other pursuits. Even though there was a renewal of radical feeling in 1912 and Lenin reorganized his faction into a separate party in the same year, it appeared as if no major chance, on the order of 1905, for a dramatic overthrow of the regime would ever recur. Lenin himself, while not abandoning Bolshevism, more than once indicated that he did not expect an overthrow of tsarism in his lifetime.

[All such calculations were completely upset by the outbreak of the war in 1914. The war brought for Bolshevism the sense of final and complete separation from the main current of Western socialism. It had been fondly imagined prior to the summer of 1914 that the working masses in every country would make a world war impossible, and that, under the leadership of the socialists, they would refuse to fight in the quarrels of their capitalist masters. The war demonstrated, on the contrary, that the Marxist notion of the workers' solidarity transcending national boundaries was largely a dream and that the appeal of nationalism was infinitely greater than that of any other social or political idea. The majority of socialists in

France, England and Germany followed their country's policy, some of them entering the war governments. Especially painful and disillusioning to Lenin was the "defection" of the German Social Democracy, until 1917 the leading Marxist party in Europe, whose spokesmen now vied with the bourgeois and conservative parties in the intensity of their chauvinism. Nor was Russian socialism free of the same influence: many radicals, including Plekhanov, urged that the political struggles be postponed until the war was brought to a victorious conclusion.

To Lenin and his followers the war marked the end of a stage in the development of socialism. Marxian socialism had to be reborn in a more radical and revolutionary form. The body uniting all the socialist parties, the Second International, had to be replaced by a new international uniting the "true Marxists." In neutral Switzerland, where he spent the first three years of the war, Lenin held conferences with other socialists who opposed the war. His position, a radical one even within the context of a radical assembly, was that pacifism and prevention of war was not enough, and that the world war should be utilized for the purposes of a socialist revolution. More and more he considered the world-wide struggle as the final and suicidal convulsion of world capitalism—an opportunity for revolution and socialism.[7] During the early stages of the war there was little to justify his hopes. It was socialism and not the old order that seemed to be disintegrating. But the collapse of tsarism in Russia provided a new and unexpected opportunity for Bolshevism and, as it seemed then, for a world-wide socialist revolution.

The Revolution

The first Russian revolution of March 1917 was in no sense the work of the Bolsheviks nor of any organized political movement. Exhausted by its military defeats, its corruption and inefficiency, the tsarist regime simply collapsed in the face of some riots and strikes in Petrograd that at another time could have been easily suppressed. The blood baths of the war, in which after the initial successes Russian armies were being continuously beaten, had deprived the regime of the army's support. The soldier's disgust with his leaders and the scandalously inefficient and corrupt system

[7] During the war years Lenin wrote his *Imperialism*. The main thesis of the book—that imperial expansion and hence wars are a direct result of the search for investment markets and sources of raw materials by the capitalists of advanced industrial countries—was taken verbatim from the book of the same title by an English radical, J. A. Hobson (with Lenin barely acknowledging his debt). But in Lenin's formulation, Hobson's argument was to serve the Marxist cause: imperialism is the last critical stage of capitalism: the quarrels and wars of rival imperialist powers present a wonderful opportunity to revolutionary socialism, which in backward colonial territories should exploit local nationalism and anti-colonialism.

communicated itself to the villages. The moderates and even conservatives now saw tsarism as an obstacle to a military victory and a barrier to a reform that would save them from a revolution. Hence it fell easily after a slight push.

What was to take its place? [The Duma formed a Provisional Government composed of liberals (the *Kadets*) and moderate conservatives. The war, it was thought, would continue and in due time Russia would have a constitution and a democratic state.] Yet revolutionary pressures soon gave the lie to such hopes and pushed toward a more radical solution. A war period is not the time for successful constitutional experimentation. The Provisional Government was from the beginning but a shadow authority, political power having become fragmented and distributed among the *soviets*, which sprang up all over the country. This time the soviets extended to the army, being called the Soviets of the Workers' and Soldiers' Delegates, and even into the front lines. In the villages the *mirs* received a new lease on life, the peasants who under the Stolypin reforms had become "separators" being in many cases forced by their less progressive and less prosperous brethren to come back to the traditional organization. [In retrospect it is easy to see that Russia between March and November of 1917 was in a state of anarchy, and that only a very determined action on the part of the democratically minded politicians could have prevented a dictatorship of the right or the left.] Yet the democratically minded politicians both in the Provisional Government and in the Soviets were of divided counsel and separated by ideological differences. Popular sentiment was in favor of an end to the war, but the liberals and some socialists felt that they were bound to their allies, and were now fighting in the cause of liberalism against Germany. The peasants as usual wanted land, but the Provisional Government was unwilling to carry out an agricultural reform during the war. [The leading person of the "Government" was a moderate Social Revolutionary, Alexander Kerensky, who in July became Prime Minister and who secured for a while the collaboration of the leading Mensheviks and Social Revolutionaries.] But the temper of the times was revolutionary and the most extreme suggestions were likely to become most popular. The Bolshevik Party, which in the beginning of the Revolution was a tiny element in the political picture, was to become within a few months, through revolutionary audacity and unabated demagoguery, the state.

Before March the Bolsheviks' numbers are estimated as between 20,000 and 25,000. Its leaders were in exile (like Lenin and Zinoviev), or in Siberia (like Kamenev and Stalin), or in jail. [In the first elections to the Soviets they ran a rather poor third behind the Mensheviks and the Social Revolutionaries.] In the villages the latter still overwhelmed both the

Marxist groups. Until Lenin's arrival in April, the Bolsheviks were in a quandary as to what their policy should be. According to the Marxist scheme, here was the bourgeois-democratic revolution. Presumably the socialist revolution was to come, but not in the immediate future. Should not the Bolsheviks in the meantime collaborate with the Mensheviks and other radical groups? The first Bolshevik leaders to reach the capital were Kamenev and Stalin, who as members of the Central Committee assumed temporary command and pursued a rather hesitant and ambiguous policy both on the issue of collaboration and on the continuance of the war.[8]

In the middle of April Lenin arrived in Petrograd and in his very first words at the railway station indicated the new tactics. No compromise with the Provisional Government, "all power to the Soviets"; and immediate peace, confiscation of privately owned land, and abolition of the coercive organs of the state. It was clear that to Lenin the Bolsheviks should, Marx or no Marx, try to seize power at the first propitious moment, and for that purpose should not hesitate to outbid everybody else with the most demagogic and anarchist slogans. Lenin's postulates were, at first, greeted with amusement by his enemies and with incomprehension and protests by the Bolsheviks. The "old man" seemed to have lost touch with reality and once again his fanaticism was going to doom Russian Marxism. By the force of his personality Lenin gained the majority among the Bolsheviks, though tactical and ideological scruples lingered on among his closest associates until and after November.

The ridiculous dream of a fanatic who thought that he and his small group could conquer and rule Russia soon became a real threat. The Provisional Government was losing what little power and prestige it had; the armed forces, demoralized by the bloodletting of an unsuccessful offensive and undermined by the revolutionary agitators, were in a mutinous mood. The Bolsheviks' peace agitation was especially effective in gaining converts among the garrison of Petrograd and among the sailors. The moderate leaders of the Social Revolutionaries who in May joined the Provisional Government were being undermined in their own party because of their failure to carry out a land reform. The Bolsheviks in the summer of 1917 received an accession of strength from a group of socialists who had previously oscillated between the Bolsheviks and the Mensheviks and who now brought into their ranks a group of brilliant leaders, the outstanding among

[8] Joseph Vissarionovich Stalin was at the time neither an obscure Party hack, as he has been pictured by some, nor the leading collaborator of Lenin, as he has been presented in servile official biographies. Since 1912 he had been a member of the Bolshevik Central Committee and one of the leading Bolsheviks. In the over-all hierarchy of Bolshevik leaders he occupied an intermediate position. Certainly people like Kamenev, Zinoviev, and Trotsky were much more prominent during and immediately after the Revolution, and the first two had been much closer to Lenin.

whom, Trotsky, was to be, along with Lenin, the moving spirit of the Bolshevik Revolution and of the first few years of the new regime. The Bolsheviks gained vastly in membership. On the eve of the second revolution, they were still a decided minority in the country. But they were now a sizable and strategically located minority that enjoyed the advantages of almost military discipline while their enemies were divided and confused.

The Government, composed of people with democratic doubts and hesitations, was unwilling, even if it had been able, to proceed resolutely against the Bolsheviks, who made no secret of their intentions. Only in July after an unsuccessful Bolshevik rising were some Bolsheviks imprisoned and was Lenin forced to go into hiding. The structure of the Party was left undamaged. An attempted rightist rising by General Kornilov in September forced Kerensky to relax his half-hearted attempts against the Bolsheviks. The unsuccessful insurrection showed the weakness of the army as a political instrument, but also the hopeless position of Kerensky's Provisional Government and the moderates. Russia was in the throes of anarchy. By late September the Bolsheviks obtained the majority in the Petrograd and Moscow Soviets. On October 23, 1917, the Bolshevik Central Committee decided upon an uprising. The plans for the uprising became a public secret since they were revealed by Zinoviev and Kamenev, who had opposed them within the Central Committee. Still, the Government was powerless to prevent it. On November 7, 1917, the "Government," which by this time meant the city of Petrograd and the control of some arsenals and offices, fell to the Bolsheviks, who had presumed to act in the name of the Petrograd Soviet. The struggle was brief and almost bloodless. Kerensky's Government fled the city, and the Bolsheviks could appear before the All-Russian Congress of Soviets as victors. The Congress, in which the Bolsheviks and their temporary allies, the left wing of the Social Revolutionaries, had a majority, proclaimed the transfer of power to Soviets throughout Russia, in fact to the Bolsheviks. The new Government, the Council of Commissars, was purely Bolshevik in its composition, with Lenin as chairman. The opposition—the Mensheviks, the moderate Social Revolutionaries—left the Congress. The Bolsheviks had "power." At the end of 1917 power meant a strategic position in the civil war that was to engulf Russia for the next three years and that began while the German armies were advancing deeper into Russian territory. The new regime had no army to speak of and no administrative machinery. In the country as a whole the Bolsheviks, at the end of 1917, when they were more popular than ever before or after, were still a decided minority. The proof came in the elections to the Constituent Assembly held before the Bolsheviks established their monopoly of power. The elections produced a majority for the Social Revolutionaries, with the Bolsheviks getting about

25 per cent of the vote. Thus the only free and democratic election held in the twentieth century in Russia produced a decided anti-Bolshevik majority. In January 1918 the Assembly met for its only session and was promptly dissolved and driven out by the Bolshevik Government. January 1918 marks the demise of the last lingering democratic impulses in Bolshevism. No more *free* and *multi-party* elections were to be allowed, and the Party self-professedly assumed an absolute dictatorship.

The rise of the Bolsheviks to power and final stage of victory offer certain lessons that are of importance in understanding the Soviet Union and the Communist movement of today. Lenin had succeeded in creating a party that, unlike so many socialist and radical parties, managed to preserve discipline and to follow its leaders in all their tactical and ideological shifts and maneuvers. The price paid for the achievement was to give up what was left of the democratic element in Marxism. But the Party *itself*, though run dictatorially, had not as yet achieved the totalitarian spirit characteristic of the Stalin period. Zinoviev and Kamenev, although they had disagreed with Lenin on the eve of the revolution, were immediately after the November coup again his closest collaborators. A few weeks after the November Revolution some Bolshevik leaders still felt that the Government should include representatives of the other socialist parties and they felt so strongly about it that they resigned, temporarily, from the Council of Commissars. It would take several more years before the Party, now the instrument of dictatorship, would in itself become so monolithically totalitarian that honest disagreement with the dictator would be branded as treason. But the foundations of totalitarianism were already there.

Another point to be stressed is that the Party did not win power and relative popularity under the banner of Marxism but with anarchist slogans that appealed to the war-weary and demoralized nation. Lenin had preached defeatism and desertion; the taking over of the land and factories by the peasants and the workers; abolition of the bureaucracy and the standing army; and complete economic egalitarianism. Once in power the stark realities confronted the Bolsheviks. Like any Government, they had to defend the country against the enemy, keep the national economy going, and reconstruct the machinery of the state—all tasks that would have been made impossible by literal fulfillment of their own slogans. Powerful brakes had to be applied, and the manner of their application is the history of the decades that followed the November coup, until from the most thoroughgoing, most anarchical, of all revolutions, was born the most dominating and exacting state of modern times.

CHAPTER **28**

The Development of
Soviet Policy

The Struggle with the Peasant

The Bolsheviks seized power in November 1917 with the idea of instituting a new type of society in Russia and eventually in the world. The basis of that society was to be Marxian socialism and its eventual aim communism. We have already seen[1] why Marxian socialism should have won in a society that Marx and Engels thought unlikely to be among the first seized by socialism. But whatever doubts, conflicting schemes and theories the Bolsheviks might have had before November 1917 as to whether Russia was ripe for a socialist revolution or not, whether the bourgeois revolution should not be prolonged, whether they should share power with liberal and other socialist parties, and whether the Russian Revolution could survive in the absence of a world-wide revolution, etc., they were faced in November with the fact of having power and of being called on to build a socialist society from the ruins of what they regarded as having been, not a fully developed capitalist society, but a mixture of feudal and capitalist elements.

Now there was precious little in their own ideology to facilitate the task or to guide them through the first step. Marx and Engels had been socialists but they had written mostly about capitalism. There is very little in Marx to indicate *concrete* steps that a socialist party should undertake upon seizing power in a predominantly agricultural country. There is no discussion in the scriptures of Marxism as to how a *socialist country* should *industrialize,* how the mass of small peasant holdings can be brought into large-scale units run by the state, or what kind of price system a socialist administration would evolve. And beyond the vague and contradictory

[1] In Chapter 26.

484

hints in those same scriptures there is but little to indicate, economics aside, what kind of society the dictatorship of the proletariat would bring about. What about the family under socialism? What kind of arts and amusements would the new society have? Of bourgeois ideas and institutions under those headings Marx had written voluminously and scathingly. But he offered no blueprints for the future except to assert that socialism would free man from all his bonds and release his highest creative powers.

All this, understandably, did not help the Communists, who inherited a government and society in complete ruin, had civil and foreign wars on their hands, with industry and agriculture producing at a fraction of their pre-World War I level. As to all revolutionary leaders, so it fell to Lenin and his colleagues to restrain the revolutionary impatience of his followers; to point out that first things come first, that reconstruction and victory in the war must precede social experimentation and the building of a new life. Yet, at first, the broad sweep of the revolution poured past all the cautions and restraints. The peasants seized the landlords' lands, and in effect reinstituted the communal organization of the villages. The workers drove out their employers and directors and attempted to run factories on an ideological rather than technical *expertise*. The more militant among the Communists pushed the official policy of repression of the church to the point of severe persecution of religious cults and their faithful. Wars, famines, and the collapse of established social values led to the decline of the family, to drastic experimentation in the arts, education, etc. In the midst of all the troubles the most stringent measures had to be resorted to, and sometimes they gave the impression that the regime, prompted by the crisis, as well as by its ideological scruples, was drawn despite its better judgment to install socialism and communism right away, skipping several historical periods. Thus in agriculture all land was legally nationalized and the heavy grain requisitions imposed upon the peasant gave the impression that he was to be communized by compulsion. Agricultural communes with land, implements and dwellings held in common were encouraged. In industry a high degree of egalitarianism was in fashion, with any disparity in pay, or difference in status, even if justified by function, considered unproletarian if not outright counterrevolutionary. This was the period (1917-21) of "War Communism," when the inexperience of the new rulers, their ideological premises, and most of all the social and economic chaos, gave rise to the impression that the Communists were impractical fanatics determined to establish the final stage of communism without having industrialized their country, without having gone through the stage of socialism.

A halt was called in 1921 with the institution of the New Economic Policy, the period of 1921-28 taking consequently the name of the *Nep.*

Aside from the need for an economic reconstruction, Lenin and his associates were motivated in establishing the Nep by the anarchistic tendencies they saw in the Party (the Workers' Opposition) and the Kronstadt Revolt. Hence their decision to eschew the most radical policies for the moment. The peasants were to be appeased by being required to pay to the state only a specified portion of their crops, rather than an arbitrary quota to be met regardless of the size of their crop. Trade, and even small-scale industry, run by private operators was legalized. In brief, the state reserved for its ownership banking, transportation, and heavy industry, and allowed free enterprise elsewhere. The march toward socialism was not given up but merely suspended until the country could catch its breath and fully recover from the ravages of the preceding years.

The Nep represented a strategic retreat, during which the forces of socialism in Russia would retrench, recuperate, and then resume their march. Yet both within Russia and abroad the adoption of moderate economic policies was often condemned or praised as indicating that the Bolsheviks had realized the "impracticability" of socialism and were content to establish a mixed economy or state capitalism. Such judgments were based on a gross misunderstanding of the basic ideological premises of the Soviet leaders, or—in the case of those who argued the point in Russia—on purely political motivations. Being by temperament as well as by conviction Marxists, the Soviet leaders, whether led by Stalin, Trotsky, or Zinoviev, were bound in the long run to insist on a full-scale industrialization and socialization of the country. The reasons for their determination were found not only in their ideology and their economic views but also in their most deeply held *social* and *political* opinions. It is almost axiomatic for a Marxist to hold that socialism can come only in an *industrialized* country. It was equally axiomatic for Russian Marxists to have held that the power of any socialist party must be based on a mass of industrial proletarians, and that in a country where the mass of the population was composed of petty landholders, no matter how strong the dictatorship of the Party, no matter how exclusive its monopoly of political power, the forces of history would act against socialism and would eventually bring about the downfall of the Soviet regime. This obsession of the Communists against the individual peasant holder was held with the tenacity of a religious dogma, the strength of which no one who does not share it can fully appreciate. The Communists of all factions held this belief: in the long run Russia must be industrialized, and private ownership in agriculture must be abolished. If not, Soviet power would collapse, either before an external enemy, for a non-industrialized state is weak; or before the internal one, for peasants, no matter how poor, if they have land, are against socialism and have all the instincts and aspirations of the petty bourgeois.

Thus the Nep, during its short duration, 1921-28, was obviously an expedient. Yet even as such it was bitterly assailed by various factions of the Communist Party, especially when to their ideological scruples was joined the resentment of the ruling clique. First Trotsky and then Kamenev and Zinoviev attacked the ruling group and its policy as favoring the peasant and especially the rich peasant, the *kulak*, while neglecting the industrial worker. Stalin and his then ally, Bukharin, were accused in 1924-25 of encouraging the growth of rich peasants by their policy which legalized the leasing of land and the hiring of help by peasants who could afford it. This was decried as the legalization of exploitation of man by man, a fine state of affairs for the first socialist country in the world!

The reasons that brought the Nep to an end and that determined the regime to proceed full speed with collectivization and industrialization are manifold and complex. The ensuing period, 1928-33, has been called with a great deal of justice the "Third Russian Revolution" (the first one being in March, the second in November, 1917). In the space of five years individual ownership of land was practically eliminated, collective farms and state farms taking its place; and Russia was launched on a gigantic industrialization drive that was to make her over from a mainly agricultural country into one of the two leading industrial countries of the world. The scope of this program and the speed with which it was to be accomplished involved tremendous dangers. The regime declared an open war on the majority of the population—the peasants. Industrialization was financed by lowering the standard of living of the masses and thus imperiling the Soviet regime. Why should a power-conscious regime embark on such a perilous course? And if so, why the feverish and reckless pace?

There are three *groups* of reasons behind the decisions reached in 1927 and 1928. *Economically*, by 1927 Russia had recovered from the ravages of war and her production, both agricultural and industrial, had reached the prewar level. Further advance could, the Soviet government became convinced, proceed only on the basis of thorough industrialization. Furthermore the type of economy that became stabilized during the Nep did not allow the Soviet government that *full control over the economic life of the country that every Communist government craves.* The tempo of economic development was dependent not only on the government but on the peasant. If the peasant felt that he was getting enough money for his crops, and if with that money he could purchase some goods, then he would sell his grain. If not, he could consume it on the farm or feed it to his animals rather than sell it at the government-fixed price. In 1927 and

1928 on the basis of such reasons the peasants were reluctant to sell. The socialist government in bondage to the peasant! The Communists forced to appease the peasant economically, and if he is appeased economically, won't he tomorrow demand political concessions as the price for his grain? It is no wonder that Stalin's regime fell upon the peasant with the same fury that it displayed in fighting its opponents within the Party.

[Politically, then, the decision to industrialize and *collectivize* was based on the natural aversion of Communism against any independent source of economic or political power in the state.] Instead of millions of individual farmers with all their anti-socialist instincts there would be fewer but more efficient collective and state farms. Labor would be released to industry, the government would, so it was hoped, be able to control the production and distribution of food; and, most important of all, the Soviet regime would not be dependent upon the good will of millions of peasants.

[*General power and international considerations* were also not lacking behind the resolution.] Stalin's dictatorship was firmly established. But it was a dictatorship over a relatively weak and backward country. Until Russia was industrialized, until she had reached the industrial level of the West, she would be, so ran the thinking of the Communists, at the mercy of the capitalist world. Hence Stalin's slogan that the U.S.S.R. had "to catch up and to leave behind" the leading capitalist countries in the industrial race. Hence his appeal to national pride in evoking the memory of Russia's past defeats because of her weakness, and the pledge that a powerful industrialized and socialized U.S.S.R. would never have to endure a similar fate.

Thus economic, military and politico-social reasons, as well as the natural impulse of a totalitarian system to grow stronger and vaster, all played their part. In view of the weak position of agriculture and the lack of capital the decision to industrialize rapidly and to telescope into ten years what in the West took generations undoubtedly represented a vast gamble. But the gamble was undertaken by the regime confident of its ideological premises and conscious of its great resources, among which not the least important was coercive power almost, but not quite, unlimited, as the resistance of the peasants was to show.

The decision to industrialize a country involves a choice not unlike that before an individual who decides to buy a house or a car. He will finance it out of a loan, his savings if he has any, or simply by curtailing his expenditures by reducing his standard of living. To the Soviet government beginning its industrialization in 1928 the last choice was the only feasible one. The sinews of industrialization—mainly heavy industry—had to come out of the internal resources of the U.S.S.R., a country that in 1928 already enjoyed, if that is the phrase, one of the lowest standards of living in Europe. From then on the Soviet workers had to work harder and longer. For a time, and it turned out to be quite a long time, fewer among them would be producing commodities to feed, clothe, and shelter people, and more of them would be producing heavy machinery, and the commodities that could be sold abroad, and for which the Soviets would acquire foreign machines and foreign experts. To repeat, none but a totalitarian system enjoying vast powers of compulsion would have attempted to squeeze the wherewithal of industrialization out of the already pitiful standard of living of its people.

The First Five Year Plan was authorized by the Fifteenth Party Congress in 1927 and was to cover the years 1928-33. Many of the delegates to the Congress believed that they were sanctioning a cautious progress toward collectivization and industrialization. The mechanics of planning were theoretically to be worked out by the planning organs, and especially the Gosplan, or the State Planning Commission, an organ staffed mainly by economists, cautious beings aware of resources, rates of growth and other economic realities. But the actual planning and supervision of the plan was soon snatched out of the economists' hands. Decisions as to the goals of economic planning, the pace of industrialization and collectivization, the means to be employed, came to be arrived at—and still are—in the Politburo of the Communist Party, with the planning experts just filling in the details. Thus sometime in 1929 the dictator and his entourage reached the conclusion that the original pace of collectivization prescribed in the First Five Year Plan was too slow. It was decided to accomplish the major part of collectivization before 1933. The ostensible slogan was to exterminate the *kulaks* as a class. But the fury of the Party and the state fell not only upon the rich (by Russian standards) peasant, but upon the broad masses of peasantry. In his incredible tenacity for his land, the peasant refused to be propagandized or "educated" into the collective, where his land and his livestock would be pooled. The government increased its compulsion and the peasant resisted by the only means he knew: by refusing his grain to the state, by slaughtering his animals. In 1929 and 1930 the conflict became violent. Wholesale deportations transferred to Siberia and elsewhere hundreds of thousands, if not millions, of *kulaks*, now a catchall term for any peasants who resisted collectivization. Famine gripped the Ukraine. The losses of livestock endured during those terrible years have not, in some categories, been made up even today.

The war against the peasant was not merely an incident in Russia's industrialization, and the problem requires a few words. Deeply ingrained in the Marxists has been the habit of thought that socialism cannot be achieved, nor can the power of the Communist Party be secure, if there is in society a considerable element that owns one of the means of production. Thus the millions of peasant households, each tilling its small plot, were not only a bar to rapid industrialization but the breeder of anti-socialist attitudes. The collective farms, on the contrary, Communism believes, are not only more efficient, as they can produce more with less labor, and can be profitably worked with mechanical appliances because of their larger size, but they give the peasant the psychology of the worker rather than that of the small property owner—deadly enemy of socialism. But complete elimination of the private element from agriculture proved beyond the means of even the Soviet regime. True, by 1936 more than 90 per cent of the land in Russia was in the collective and state farms, and as of today there are practically speaking, no individual farmers in the U.S.S.R. But the government and the Party had to make two important concessions to the peasant.

In the first place, the bulk of arable land is in collective farms rather than in state farms. The latter, the Communists believed early in the first Five Year Plan, would play a more important role than they have actually assumed. A state farm, where the peasants are just hired hands, is the closest thing in agriculture to an industrial factory, hence preferable to the Marxist, and disliked by the peasant. The dominant role of the collectives over the state farms, or *sovkhozes*, is thus a concession.

In the second place the structure of the collective farm has been modified so as somewhat to appease the peasant. True, the collective farm is not a co-operative farm in our sense of the word. Though theoretically it is run by an assembly of its members, it is subject to the most centralized direction. Its manager in many cases comes from outside the *kolkhoz*. Insofar as the nature of its crop, the norm of work and its organization are concerned, the *kolkhoz* is most stringently subject to regulations that emanate, in the last instance, from Moscow. As the medieval baron's castle stood overawing his serfs in the vicinity, so does the local Machine Tractor Station stand guard over several *kolkhozes*. The M.T.S. not only provides machinery for the *kolkhoz* but supervises its plans and performance.[2] Attached to it are special Party workers who carry on propaganda and ideological indoctrination among the villagers. "Collectivization," then, is a euphemism for land nationalization and direction from above. But in the collective the devil—to the Communists the element of private ownership—has not been entirely chased away. In the prevailing type of the *kolkhoz*, the so-called *artel*, though most of the land is pooled together the peasants

[2] In the spring of 1958, the government and the Party decided to allow the *kolkhozes* to purchase their Machine Tractor Stations. If the reform is carried through and the M.T.S. become the property of the collective farms, rather than—as they are now—agencies controlling them, the collective farms would receive, at least on paper, a considerably greater amount of autonomy. The reform, sponsored personally by Khrushchev, is yet another expedient to gain popularity among the peasants, and hence a better economic performance from them.

still retain their dwellings and little garden plots where they grow fruit and vegetables, which they can sell in the open market, and—faced with the implacable resistance of that powerful personage, the peasant woman —even Stalin had to yield and grant that peasant households might own fowl and even a cow. Yet, in the main, the *kolkhoz*, in its structure and principle, reminds one of the factory. Peasants work in teams and brigades according to an assignment by the chairman. Their remuneration is adjusted according to the type of the job and their individual performance. The net income of the *kolkhoz* is divided among the members both in cash and in kind. Special bonuses are allotted to the workers and teams that surpass their output quota, and corresponding deductions penalize those who fail to meet the plan. Jobs that require some technical skill, e.g., that of the tractor driver, may have a base pay several times that of an unskilled laborer. In brief, insofar as his collective work is concerned, the peasant is simply in the position of a hired hand rather than a member of a co-operative.

Ridiculous as it may seem to us, the peasant's garden plot and the few pitiful remaining elements of private property in agriculture have been a source of major worry to the Soviet leaders and a matter of major concern to the Soviet economy. For one thing, peasants have spent disproportionately large amounts of time in working their own plots as against working on communal land. For another, the remaining plot, smaller than one acre, and its few appurtenances, stand as a link with the past and with the peasant's nostalgia for individual ownership. Soviet agriculture has not shared in the prodigious growth of the rest of Soviet economy. While Russian industry (and especially heavy industry) has increased its production many fold over its pre-1928 level many sectors of agriculture have not advanced substantially beyond that year. Collectivization has centralized Soviet agriculture at the disposal of the Government, it has released labor for industry, but it has not solved the problem of agricultural production in a country with a growing population, and it has not eradicated the peasant's longing for his own land.

Confronted with this problem, the Soviet regime has pursued the familiar zigzag course between compulsion and concession to the popular feeling. Thus at times the government would limit more sharply the size of the garden plot, tax its produce more heavily, and tighten the discipline of the collective farm. At other times the peasants would be granted tax benefits and encouraged to grow more on their plots. A major debate on the future of Soviet agriculture must have divided the inner circle in 1949-50. One Soviet leader, Andreyev, came out publicly for a loosening of the *kolkhoz* structure in a direction that might transform it into a genuine co-operative farm rather than a government grain factory. But Andreyev was publicly denounced and the opposite tendency prevailed for a time. A great movement to merge collective farms into larger units combining perhaps several villages was initiated and carried through. The main objective was clear: in a gigantic *kolkhoz* the peasants working in brigades some miles away from their homestead would find it impossible to devote much time to their individual plots. Nikita Khrushchev in 1950 formulated an even more drastic remedy. He advocated *agrogorods*, or agro-cities, in which the collectives would be combined into still larger units, peasants would live in apartment houses and be taken out to cultivate the outlying fields. The garden plot and its appurtenances would now completely disappear, and the Communists' dream would be realized: the peasant would be assimilated in his habits, way of living, and psychology to the city dweller. But Khrushchev's plan was in turn repudiated.

The post-Stalin era inherited the dilemma of agriculture. Again a variety of remedies has been tried: tax concessions, promises of more consumers' goods under Malenkov's primacy, reduced requisitions from the *kolkhozes* to the government so that the rest of their produce could be sold in the open market, etc. To increase total agricultural yield, the regime, and especially Khrushchev, who identified himself with the project, has sponsored the settlement and cultivation of "virgin land"—lands in Kazakhstan and elsewhere that were previously thought unsuitable because of their climate and soil for agricultural production.

In a country where the ordinary political processes are denied or are meaningless, people will often express their satisfaction or dissatisfaction with the regime by their economic performance. In that sense the Soviet peasant has "voted" up to now against the government. It remains to be seen whether any structural changes in Soviet agriculture, or a greater flow of consumers' goods, or a greater liberality of the regime, would change their vote. In Russian history up to now the peasant has been the central, though passive, figure. Most of the social and political problems, though often fought out by others, had their source in the status and feelings of the preponderant majority of the nation who dwelt in the villages. Today, with industrialization, the peasants no longer constitute that majority. Yet with their status not entirely satisfactory to the regime and unsatisfactory to them, they constitute a vast social segment that has not quite fitted into socialism and hence a question mark in the uncertain future of the Soviet regime.

How were the Soviet leaders able to win their long and bitter struggle with the vast majority of the population? What was the source of their power? Their principal instrument was the Communist Party, whose weapons and techniques of control we shall examine in detail in Chapter 30. But how did the leadership hold together this huge organization and win from it the emotional commitment and the disciplined devotion necessary to carry out their grandiose plans? We can understand this only if we look at the drive for industrialization, which, under Stalin, became for millions in and outside the Party a compelling national purpose, inspiring fanatic loyalty and legitimizing privation, terror, and rigid conformism.

Industrialization

The appeal of Soviet Communism to people in other countries has often reflected not so much the attraction of the ideas of Communism, but the admiration for a country that in the space of one generation has raised itself from a backward agricultural community to a great industrial power. Though the achievement of the Soviets has undoubtedly been great, it should be kept in mind that it was not created from nothing. Pre-Revolutionary Russia, backward as she was in *absolute* terms in comparison with the West, was in *relative* terms a rapidly growing industrial country. Entering the industrial race very late in the nineteenth century, Russia progressed very fast; her industrial production in some years prior to World War I grew at a faster pace than that of the most advanced Western countries, including the United States. It is reasonable to assume that with some industrial base and with her scientific talent post-World War I Russia under any social and economic system would have become a major industrial power. Still the achievement of the Bolsheviks in absolute terms, and in view of the two devastating wars that have intervened, is very great—as great as their ability to squeeze the sinews of industrialization out of the already pitiful standard of living of the Russian masses. The price in human terms has been enormous but in one respect the fondest expectations of the authors of the November Revolution have been fulfilled: Russia is an industrial power, one of the two greatest in the world.

The original impulse to industrialize was for the Bolsheviks grounded in their Marxist ideology but also in something else. By and large the Communist leaders hated—and their hatred was shared by many non-Communist intellectuals—pre-Revolutionary Russia with its backwardness, its social torpor, and the majority of its population sunk in passivity and superstition. Those exotic social traits that charm many a Western reader of nineteenth-century Russian novels were exactly the ones that the Bolsheviks detested. From the intelligentsia, which, as the saying went, "knew about everything, but could do nothing," to the peasant masses clinging to their immemorial habits, the Russian Marxists saw nothing but backwardness and apathy. Their view, as we have seen, may have been exaggerated, but they were impatient to "give history a push," to establish a modern scientifically organized society. Though they detested the capitalist West, they looked with admiration upon its industry, and its scientific spirit. Years after the Revolution, when the pendulum had swung back and when Russian history was again being glorified, Stalin could still speak with approval of the American spirit of enterprise and wish for its presence in the Russians—together, to be sure, with socialist consciousness.

It is no wonder then that the first years of rapid industrialization after 1928, the years of great suffering, of the persecution of the peasantry, were also years of great ideological fervor and élan, especially among the Communist young. If it had not aroused strong enthusiasm among at least part of its supporters, the regime, cruel and in many ways inefficient, would undoubtedly have collapsed. But the Communists, for all their transgressions and inefficiencies, managed at the time to convey the impression that they were doing something—lifting Russia by its bootstraps. And from the despot himself came the slogans that underlined the grandiose task: "To catch up and to overcome" the West; the U.S.S.R. must within a decade perform the work of industrialization that elsewhere took generations. And since every struggle needs a visible, tangible enemy to justify the privations and sacrifices, Stalin proclaimed the thesis that as socialism progresses the class struggle becomes sharper, the "enemy" becomes more desperate and unscrupulous—the "enemy" being whoever it was convenient to brand as such at the moment: the rich peasant in Russia, the capitalist powers, etc. Hence the great question was, in Stalin's words: "Who will get whom?" Shall "we," the Communists, succeed in building a modern industrial state, or shall "they" defeat our attempts to collectivize, to industrialize, and to destroy the hostile classes and forces? "They" were then not only the *kulak*, or a foreign paid saboteur, but those Communists of little faith who pitied the peasant, who felt that industrialization was proceeding too fast or too inhumanly, "they" were all the traditional forces of apathy and backwardness in Russian society.

The drive toward industrialization proceeded then at a high pitch and, initially, with a kind of religious fervor. But beyond the initial fervor the campaign to industrialize rapidly and at a high cost in human freedom and comfort obviously requires other things. If you want a whole nation to strain everything to produce more and more, to measure success in life and national well-being by production figures, then you must adjust the whole mentality of the nation to the task. Thus industrialization cannot be performed rapidly in a society that is permeated by ascetic values. Nor can it come easily where people believe that equality is the highest social good, and that it is ignoble for a man to strive to have more in goods and services than his neighbor; or that comfort and leisure are more important than production. The Soviet leaders accordingly set about creating a system of sanctions and incentives that had as its main objective the maximization of production. [At the altar of industrialization there had to be sacrificed those parts of the Marxist dogma that proclaimed equality, and the protection of the worker against the employer, for industrialization demands incentives based on performance, and a very rapid industrialization demands at times the sacrifice of the worker's health and comfort to the demands of production.]

[The first to go overboard was the remaining autonomy of the trade unions vis-à-vis the state. In 1930 the Stalinists acquired complete control of the Soviet trade unions. From then on they became but an auxiliary branch of the government with their main function not the protection of the worker against the employer, i.e., the state, but the maximization of production and the indoctrination of the workers in attitudes appropriate to rapid industrialization. The right to strike, though legally not abolished, in fact disappeared, and we hear of no strikes until the post-Stalin era. In 1931 Stalin spelled out a few more of the consequences of the drive for industrialization: workers must be subject to some discipline; they cannot be allowed to flounder from one job to another, and their pay must correspond to their performance at work. Thus arose the institution of labor passports, which limit the worker's freedom of choice of work, and the institution of work norms, which the worker has to meet to earn his full pay, and the excess over which is rewarded by a bonus. Both these devices have always been resisted by the trade unions in every country on the ground that, unless in a real emergency such as wartime, they make the worker into a beast of burden and are likely to limit his freedom and injure his health. But in the socialist state they became the basis of labor relations, and evolution away from them began only two years after Stalin's death. Indeed, they were soon supplemented by a rigorous labor code that subjected the worker to fines for absenteeism or lateness to work, and, for repetition of these offenses, to imprisonment. It goes without saying that the length of the working day was extended. Since the thirties filled the Soviet forced labor camps with a mass of inmates, the government could utilize millions of slave laborers for particularly hazardous tasks such as mining and construction in unfavorable climatic conditions, and could rely upon prison labor for a large part of its scheduled production.[3]

In 1934 Stalin summarized the whole trend in theoretical terms.

[3] The number of people in forced labor camps has always been a matter of dispute among foreign experts. Some have given fantastic estimates like 20 million, but the most modest guesses for any year between 1932 and 1941 have never gone below 3 million. Authentic Soviet documents, like the secret economic plan for 1941, which was captured by the Germans and then found its way to the West, authorize the assumption that the inmates of the forced labor camps constitute a sizeable proportion of the Soviet labor force. Partial dissolution of the camps began with the amnesties following Stalin's death.

Marxism, he proclaimed at the Seventeenth Party Congress, has nothing to do with egalitarianism in wages. This is a petty-bourgeois prejudice. Nor had Marxism anything to do, according to the same authority, with the workers' interfering with management. There had already been proclaimed the dissolution of the "trio" (*troika*) that had used to run the factory, i.e., the manager, trade union secretary, and the local Party secretary: the manager assumed full authority with the latter two becoming his helpers in the task of expanding production. The Soviets have used extensively that bane of the working class in the West—the speed-up system. The middle thirties were full of well-publicized workers who would suddenly break the working norm. The heroes would be properly rewarded and the *average norm would then be raised* for all the workers in the given occupation. The shock workers became known after one of the first as the Stakhanovites—and they became the aristocracy of Soviet labor, rewarded by higher pay, bonuses, orders, etc. "Socialist competition," or factories and industrial regions as well as individuals "spontaneously" challenging each to a race in production, became a regular feature of the Soviet labor scene, both in industry and in agriculture. Thus those two proverbial methods of driving the labor force in a capitalist state, the carrot and the stick, found their fullest application in the socialist state. Gone in the process was even the pretense of building a classless society in the real sense of the word. For now a huge difference in the economic status and in the opportunity to obtain the amenities of life separated the common worker from a Stakhanovite, not to mention an industrial director, a successful engineer, or a popular author. The disparities in income grew and they were fully authorized by the changes in the Soviet tax structure. The change was symbolized by the quiet disregard of the old principle, operative until the late twenties, that a Party member should not be paid more than the equivalent of the wages of an *average industrial worker*. The visible symptoms included the restoration of ranks, orders and more colorful uniform in the army and navy; and soon, during the second World War, certain branches of the civil service were put in uniform.

In 1936 Stalin proclaimed that socialism had been achieved in the U.S.S.R., and that now, instead of the exploiters and the exploited, there were left only two friendly classes: working peasants and workers, and the Soviet intelligentsia, not a class, but sprung from the other two. The statement was true insofar as it referred to the abolition of private ownership of the means of production. But it was emphatically untrue insofar as it implied that the Soviet Union had achieved a society in which the difference in income and status had narrowed down or even that it was moving in that direction. It was true that hereditary distinctions had been largely obliterated, and that careers were now open to talent on a scale unimaginable in pre-Revolutionary Russia. But it was and is emphatically untrue that the exploitation of man by man—and its source, the exploitation of man by the state—has been abolished in the U.S.S.R.

The sociologists have noticed that very often a given stage in the economic development of society is accompanied by very specific social customs. Marx and Engels in writing of their contemporary bourgeois societies decried the "philistinism" of their social and moral values. The emphasis on the family tie and on religion; the horror of illicit love and unconventional behavior, even the optimistic and moralistic tone of the literature of Victorian England—they all appeared to the makers of Marxism as hypocritical devices through which the exploiting classes kept the workers content with their miserable lot. Yet all those symptoms appeared, and with official encouragement, during the period of socialist industrialization in the thirties. There was one exception: a Marxist regime could never encourage religion. Yet even so the struggle against the Orthodox Church was relaxed, and militant propagation of atheism was discouraged.

Prior to the thirties divorce was extremely easy to obtain, and abortion was legalized. No sanctions were invoked against unconventional sexual relations. Again the change is drastic in the decade of Great Industrialization. Divorce was still legal but the courts discouraged it and it became expensive. Abortion for reasons other than health was declared illegal. Heavy penalties were prescribed for homosexual acts. The sanctity of the family tie was invoked both in official pronouncements and in Soviet literature. It would be too simple to assume that at a certain point the regime had suddenly decided that the grandiose task at hand required social stability and moral orthodoxy. But certainly in comparison with the immediate post-Revolutionary era, the "line" officially sponsored in the thirties and up to now has been extremely conventional and moralistic. It is as if the individual were told that this is no time to indulge personal whim and life: the state and society expect everyone to have a stable and decorous life and to devote his energies to the important social tasks.

The early Bolsheviks included among themselves, or attracted, experimenters in art, literature and the theater. Every social revolution breeds and brings the desire for the new in the arts. But as in the case of morals, the arts, and literature and even science became increasingly subject to the authority of the Party. And in the thirties and forties the official line turned heavily toward traditionalism and conventionality. Soviet writers were told, then ordered, to depict the problems and successes of socialist construction. The depiction of the unusual or the morbid, stress on individual problems unconnected with the building of socialism or the defense of the socialist fatherland, became in effect prohibited. The arts and literature became subjugated to the Party, to the extent that distinguished authors were forced to rewrite their works if they did not meet with the Party's approval. The prevailing line became *socialist realism*. Its principal motif in contemporary novels and even poetry was the striving by the new Soviet man toward—and eventually his attainment of—collectivization and industrialization and the subordination of individual life to society. In Plato's *Republic* the author anticipates totalitarianism by prescribing what music a well-ordered state should allow. The rulers of Russia followed by prescribing or banning various styles of musical composition and by requiring the artists to celebrate patriotic or social motifs in their music, e.g., Shostakovich's composition celebrating Stalin's afforestation plan. The Party's control over the artistic and scientific life of the country duplicated its control over every other aspect of life of the population. Scientific and artistic disputes would be settled not by the judgment of the public but by the dictum of a Party authority, with the dictator himself making pronouncements on the most unexpected subjects.[4]

The main import of the change during the thirties, quite apart from the strictness of totalitarian controls, was the emphasis on stability, conventionality, and optimism, in the arts and literature. The question must be posed whether this tendency can be ascribed solely to the dictates of the Party, or whether the artistic fashions of the period—which is not yet ended in the U.S.S.R.—are not also due to the natural reactions of a society undergoing industrialization, and acquiring thereby, for all the Marxian phraseology, middle-class values reminiscent of Victorian England. The paradox is hard to stomach if we look at Russia as a socialist state and a totalitarian society. And yet the effect of great changes that were imposed upon Soviet society beginning with the first Five Year Plan was to inculcate in a considerable part of society the good bourgeois values of the nineteenth-century West: the importance of hard work, of saving, of measuring one's station in life, among other things, by one's income and the quantity of one's material goods, etc. True, all these things have been drilled into the Soviet people in the name of socialism, and, true, no one in the Soviet Union may own a bank or a factory. But otherwise the logic of modernization and industrialization has played a strange joke on Marxism: Decades of socialism and of the "dictatorship of the proletariat" have instilled the attitudes and aspirations of a middle-class society. "Become prosperous," said Stalin to the peasants in 1934. Soviet literature and newspapers are full of moralistic stories—really the Soviet version of the Horatio Alger stories—of poor working or peasant boys who,

---

[4] Thus in 1950 Stalin all of a sudden delivered himself of a judgment condemning the then leading linguistic theory in the U.S.S.R. and coming out for another one. The baffled sycophants, not quite knowing why, what, and to whom Stalin was addressing his pronouncement, declared his commonplace views to be one of the most important philosophical and scientific documents of the era!

through hard work and study, advance in life, becoming engineers, doctors, or "shock workers," i.e., reaching the status where they have a car of their own, a television set, and enjoy, as the phrase goes, "all the amenities of a rich and cultural life." Such is the ideal set before the youth of Russia by the Communist Party of the U.S.S.R.!

The return to the traditional values,[5] has been accompanied by a *qualified* rehabilitation of Russian history. Soviet historians in the immediate post-Revolutionary era and up to the middle thirties depicted pre-November Russia as a barbarous country, sunk in despotism, poverty and obscurantism. Except for the revolutionary tradition reaching to the beginning of the nineteenth century nothing was presented in a positive light. Tsarist Russia was an oppressor of nations, her population groaned under poverty and superstition, whatever was good and progressive, whether in ideas or technology, came from the West. In this respect a fundamental change was ordered in the mid-thirties. The history of the Russian people was to be extolled. Even some of the imperial rulers were classified as having been "progressive" for their period. Thus, Peter the Great, for all his depotism, was now a man who reformed Russia and made her a world power (and a Soviet reader could not be unmindful of a contemporary parallel). Even Ivan the Terrible, it was discovered, was terrible and terroristic always toward the nobles, but solicitous of Russia and her people. The dangerous international situation and the imminence of war was the major but not the only reason for this rewriting of the past. In a period of great reconstruction and of great purges, the regime was also instinctively reaching for all the elements of stability it could find, and one of the most important ones was Russian patriotism. It seemed to be saying to the dominant nation of the Soviet Union: "The regime may be tyrannical, and it may be subjecting you to all kinds of sufferings and privations, but it is your government, and it is doing it for the greatness of your country."

This note was, of course, sounded even more loudly during the war. During its first, and for the Russians most catastrophic, phase, all the invocations and appeals to stand against the invader were made in the name of *Russian* patriotism, rather than of socialism, Marxism, or even of the more inclusive *Soviet* patriotism. And at the end, at a victory banquet at the Kremlin, Stalin pronounced a famous eulogy of the *Russian* people, again assigning them major credit for the victory, and acknowledging their tolerance toward their government, which, the despot stated—an unusual modesty in Stalin—has made mistakes. Russian patriotism was then rediscovered by the Soviet regime to be their major asset, and the natural instinct of the people to fight for their government, no matter how

[5] Or rather to the traditional values of the West, since, as we have seen, these values were not shared very widely in pre-Revolutionary and pre-industrial Russia.

oppressive, against a foreign foe, to be a surer basis of their power than even Marxism-Leninism.

Following the war the Russian nationalist motif was not muted but on the contrary intensified. The damages of the war had to be made good in a feverish haste. Instead of easier living and greater liberties, the Soviet people were subjected after 1945 to continuing deprivations, and the continuation of the totalitarian rigor was no longer masked or rationalized by the war effort. As if to offset and justify the disappointed illusions and continued hardships a violent propaganda of Russian nationalism was launched. The non-Russian nationalities of the Bolshevik empire were reminded that the Russian nation even in tsarist times not only did not oppress them, as the earlier Communist "line" had proclaimed, but even then had brought them civilization and progress. Some of their national heroes previously extolled by the Communists as "progressive" fighters against Russian and tsarist oppression now were declared to have been reactionaries and traitors. The past traditions of the Russian people in the arts, science, literature—in a word, in everything but pre-Revolutionary politics—were extolled and declared to have been in advance of those of other nations. A violent campaign was conducted against "cosmopolitanism," by which for a time was meant any feeling that there was anything in the outside world worthy of admiration or emulation. And, an invariable element of extreme chauvinism and xenophobia in any society, an anti-Semitic note crept into even official pronouncements. It is clear from the admissions made by Soviet officials since the Twentieth Party Congress that discrimination was practiced against people of Jewish origin.

The tightening of totalitarian curbs and the officially sponsored chauvinism appear in retrospect to have been prompted by two major reasons. The first one was the recollection of the war, in which Russian nationalism proved to be intense, even on behalf of a tyrannical regime, while in the non-Russian areas of the U.S.S.R., especially the Ukraine during the first stage of the war, capitulation and even collaboration with the invader occurred on a fairly large scale.[6] But above and beyond the experience of the war, its end signified the end of the hopes for more liberal policies and for a more abundant life. Barely pausing for a period of reconstruction, the march toward more complete industrialization was resumed, and with it the continuation of a low living standard for the masses. The victory of the state, which made it one of the two superpowers in the world, which expanded its territory, gave it satellites in Eastern Europe, and won a Communist ally and protégé in Asia, brought no benefits to the people,

---

[6] Though German brutality and exactions soon dissuaded the Ukrainians from the notion that the Nazis were a lesser evil.

save the freedom from the invader. It is not inconceivable that to allay and redirect the popular grievances, the Communist authorities sponsored the nationalist campaign with its distinctly anti-Semitic undertones.[7] The movement that has always boasted of its international orientation and that had vowed unyielding struggle against all national and social prejudices has thus lent itself to a campaign of chauvinism.

The story of Soviet society between 1945 and 1953 is that of a society that has largely matured economically and socially, leaving behind the backwardness of old Russia, and showing both in its resistance to the invader and in the economic recovery and progress its great adaptability and strength. But against this social and economic picture the political system still remained geared to the task of running a primitive society that needs the whiplash of totalitarianism to make it into a modern industrial state. Totalitarianism, fastened on Russian society in the name of social and economic reconstruction, has remained and become intensified even though the major task of reconstruction has been accomplished.[8]

Policy after Stalin

The period since 1945 and especially since Stalin's death in March 1953 has been thus not so much a period of great social changes in the U.S.S.R., as one in which the regime, though still totalitarian, has not been able to suppress at will and control *all* the social aspirations and popular demands for reasons that are spelled out elsewhere,[9] the regime has adopted a the new society has expressed. Thus in the wake of Stalin's death and series of "liberal" measures. In the main they consist in lopping off the *extremes* of terror and controls over the citizens' lives. Successive amnesties have largely emptied the forced labor camps. The well-advertised stress on *socialist legality* has narrowed (though not entirely abolished, for in a totalitarian state terror can never be abolished entirely) the range of cases in which penalties are dispensed administratively without juridical procedure. Thus the special panels of the secret police that dealt out summary justice were officially abolished, and the powers and role of the secret police curtailed. Greater latitude of views and fashions has been allowed in the

[7] Another reason is found in the fact that the propaganda authorities had to overcome the effects of their own *wartime* efforts, when, of course, friendliness toward and appreciation of the U.S.S.R.'s Western allies was the officially sponsored line.

[8] The other and the major justification for the stringency of police controls and the continued sacrifices in the standard of living, as given by the regime, has always been the alleged "capitalist encirclement" and the hostility of the outside world to the U.S.S.R. That argument has lost much of its propaganda value after World War II and especially since the Russians' acquisition of nuclear and hydrogen weapons in 1949 and 1953 and the subsequent realization that a *major* war would involve universal and unprecedented destruction.

[9] In the section on the power structure of the Communist Party.

arts, sciences, and literature. Citizens of the U.S.S.R. are no longer trained hysterically to avoid foreigners or foreign contacts for fear of being branded as spies. At times, as after the Geneva conference in the summer of 1955, positive friendliness toward, and even contacts with, the West were encouraged. In brief, the regime, while still totalitarian in its controls and attitudes, has sought to behave sanely in all such matters, in contrast with the extreme of Stalin's despotism, which undoubtedly imparted something of the psychopathic to the whole society.

But all these are mere externals. The important developments are those that have taken place in respect to the most important aspects of the Soviet citizen's life: his mode and his standard of living. Here the regime of Stalin's successors has recognized certain social pressures and in a way responded to them. Under the leadership of Malenkov (roughly from Stalin's death until the end of 1954) it has promised and in some ways began to furnish more in the way of consumers' goods. The grandiose plans of capital construction initiated or planned under Stalin, expensive in man power and capital, have been largely modified or abandoned. Malenkov's demotion was accompanied by strong admonitions that heavy industry still has the priority in the Soviet system and that the consumer's demands must wait. Yet in the long run the new interests centering on the demand for a rise in the standard of living cannot be ignored and must be appeased by the Communist Party, for such is the logic of the social and economic situation of the U.S.S.R. Following the Twentieth Party Congress a general increase was scheduled in the retirement and old-age benefits. In December 1956 the current Five Year Plan was ordered revised to curtail some of the capital investment projects. The most stringent pieces of Stalin's labor legislation have been abolished, including the system of labor passports, thus according the worker, at least formally, the right to move from his job without incurring penalties. The same trend is reflected in the reduction of working time in industry and the increase of the wages of the lower paid workers. And an important concession to the yearning for a higher standard of living is the recent extension of legal abortion to cases other than those for reasons of health. An important and far-reaching concession, still difficult to assess, is the proposed sale of the Machine Tractor Stations to the collective farms—a reform which, if carried through, could give a greater degree of freedom to the members of the collective farms in planning and executing their work.

The sum total of these concessions is not very great. It certainly does not mean that the Party and the government are not capable of continuing or imposing new restraints or sacrifices upon the Soviet peasant and worker, should they deem it to be necessary. But the changes are not due simply to the fact that "Stalin died." They demonstrate that Soviet society has reached the stage where its future growth and economic and social order can hardly be secure or uninterrupted unless some of the benefits of the economic progress are passed on to their producers, i.e., the Soviet workers and peasants. The logic of industrialization that has made the U.S.S.R. the second greatest industrial country in the world, has required an alteration in the traditional pattern of incentives offered by the rulers of Russia to their people. [This country, whose *rate of growth of industrial production* still runs at two or three times the corresponding figure for the U.S., and which has produced miracles of technology such as the first release of the earth satellites, still has a pitifully low standard of living.]That the people expect an improvement, though they are not yet in a position to demand it, can be gathered from incidents such as Khrushchev's promise in July 1957 that the aim is now to catch up with and surpass the U.S. in a few years in the production of basic foodstuffs. But if consumer goods are to be encouraged, will industrial production remain capable of expansion at the present rate?

There are two pertinent questions about the recent trends. One is whether Stalinism could not be reimposed, and the other touches on the political consequences of these socio-economic changes. After all, in his social and economic policy Stalin did move in a zigzag course: once the limit of compulsion was reached, a relaxation was ordered for a time. Thus compulsory and brutal collectivization was arrested in 1930 to be resumed after a breathing spell and the Second Five Year Plan was kinder to the consumer than the First. Could not the present rulers of Russia also use a similar technique? In the first place it is unlikely that the combination of personality and circumstances that created Stalinism could be reproduced in today's U.S.S.R. One is reminded of the fable of the sorcerer and his apprentice. The sorcerer could evoke a giant of enormous strength but could also render him harmless at will. Lenin and the Bolsheviks activated the masses of the Russian people and carried through a revolution. The task accomplished, they fastened on the people a bureaucratic and oligarchic regime. Stalin poured the enthusiasm and energies of the Communist Party into the task of industrializing and of collectivizing the countryside. The foundations of a new industrial society having been laid, he decimated the Party. The sorcerer's assistant, it will be remembered, could evoke the monster but forgot how to control him and the giant threatened his maker with destruction. The fable should not be taken too literally, but it suggests the difficulty of reimposing the full weight of past despotism upon a society that has changed so much in the past generation.

Politically there is nothing to indicate that there can arise in the U.S.S.R. a nucleus of political power to compete with the Communist Party. The weakness of Communism in the satellites, the events in Yugoslavia, Poland and Hungary—all these phenomena have appeared in countries where Communism is of recent domination and where the powerful force of nationalism opposed it, and especially its Soviet connection. In the U.S.S.R. *Russian* nationalism has been exploited by the Communist regime, while the nationalisms of other peoples inhabiting the U.S.S.R. have yet to begin to play their full role. Communism and the Communist Party have been fastened on the country for forty years, and it is reasonable to assume that no Soviet citizen has a clear-cut idea of an alternative political and social system. It is possible that the regime may be subjected to increasing social strains, and that the immediate future will not see a violent revolution or upheaval (save probably changes within the ruling hierarchy), but that the pressure of economic and social forces will relatively weaken the Party and its unlimited powers of compulsion toward the people. In time perhaps something like semi-autonomous status might be won by institutions like the *state* bureaucracy, the trade unions, and the armed forces. The prospect, always keeping in mind the possibility of a *temporary* attempt to return to Stalinism, is of an evolution of the regime toward a greater responsiveness to the people's needs and aspirations. But there is no prospect in the foreseeable future of the U.S.S.R.'s evolving into a democracy, or achieving the rule of law rather than that of men and a doctrine.

Considerations of foreign policy may appear to be out of place in a discussion of social and economic factors that shape the Soviet system. Yet no political system has been influenced so much *internally* by its appraisal of and attitude toward the world outside it. The November Revolution took place amidst the vivid expectations of the Bolsheviks that it would be but a prelude to a world-wide *socialist* upheaval in which industrialized societies of the West would follow the Russian example. For years afterwards the Soviet regime lived in the fond expectation of capitalism crumbling and soviet regimes springing up all over the world, thus fulfilling the promise of its ideology, which holds that socialism is the eventual destiny of all mankind. A visible expression of this hope has been the *Communist (Third) International,* or *Comintern,* with its seat in Moscow and comprising Communist parties in most civilized countries and dedicated to the overthrow of non-Communist regimes. The Soviet government, though for diplomatic reasons it often insisted that the Third International was an independent organization that just happened to be situated in Moscow, never really made a secret of its own intimate connection with and then domination of the international Communist movement. From the middle twenties on, the International, like political life in the U.S.S.R., came under the very stringent domination of the Stalinist faction. And in turn the devotion to Moscow of the various national Communist parties and their total subjugation reached the point where their internal disputes, problems and leadership were settled not in their countries but by a decision in Moscow. The Soviet Union has thus been in a very peculiar position insofar as her foreign policy and its instrumentalities have been concerned: In addition to the usual influence exerted abroad by a great power, her policy has been helped and supported by groups of devoted followers in every country in the world. Soviet foreign policy has thus had two strings to its bow: the Foreign Commissariat or Ministry and the international Communist movement, which even after the dissolution of the Comintern in 1943 [10] remained firmly under Moscow's thumb. The Comintern was supposed to be a genuinely international body with equality of the participating parties. Yet quite apart from and beyond the fact that Soviet Russia was the only state in which Communism was in power during the duration of the Comintern, the Soviet regime dominated foreign parties such as the French Communists over whom it had no physical hold, with almost the same facility with which it could tell the Communists in the Ukraine or the Caucasus what to do.

Two quite different questions are posed by this tie-in between the Soviet state and the international Communist movement. The first touches on the strange phenomenon of the subjugation of the movement to the dictates of the rulers of the U.S.S.R. How could the foreign Communist parties, which often included courageous and intelligent people in their ranks, submit so tamely to summary orders? How have they been able to ignore the excesses and brutalities of the Soviet regime, its frequent violations of its Marxian premises, and its equally frequent sacrifices of international Communism to its own power interests? [11] To answer fully would require an elaborate psychological and political treatise. A very simple explanation would see in the hard-core Communists outside the U.S.S.R., not so much partisans of a political movement, as devotees of a religious cult with Russia its spiritual as well as power center.

A more germane question from our point of view is how far the connection has influenced Russia's policies both externally and internally. Do the Soviet leaders subordinate their policy to the aim of establishing Communism everywhere in the world? Do they look at the world through Marxian spectacles, or simply as rulers of a great and expanding state?

The answer must acknowledge that political motivations, just like per-

[10] The gesture was one of courtesy toward Russia's allies and otherwise meaningless, since the habit and mechanism of obedience to Moscow were too much ingrained among the foreign Communists to be disrupted by it.

[11] The Russo-German Pact of 1939, which opened the way for the German invasion of Poland and hence World War II, is, of course, the most notorious example of the latter.

sonal ones, are a complex business and cannot be explained in single-factor terms. Certainly there has been a vast change from the very earliest days of the Soviet regime, when the Bolsheviks expected a world revolution and when their every policy was discussed with that aim in mind. In the succeeding years the support given to the foreign Communist parties was given increasingly only in return for their absolute obedience, and with the idea that they were a *valuable asset to the Soviet state*. Thus from the middle of the twenties to the present the U.S.S.R., instead of being the servant of international Communism, appeared increasingly as its master, and conversely the international Communist movement became its servant. The trend was fully demonstrated following World War II when Communist regimes in Eastern European countries (Poland, Hungary, Bulgaria, Czechoslovakia, Rumania, Yugoslavia, and Albania) were established either largely or completely with the help of the Red Army. Quite apart from their ideological character and policies they were treated as appendages of the Russian state, and those Communists who were, or even appeared to be, more nationalistically minded were purged as mercilessly as any opponents of the Communist regime. The defection of Yugoslavia in 1948, which was due to the determination and ability of the ruling Yugoslav Communists not to submit unconditionally to Moscow, opened a new era in international Communism. For it demonstrated that while Communists *out of power* are likely to be fanatical followers of the line laid down by Moscow, once *in power* they like to augment and consolidate their position, think in their own *national terms*, rather than continue being humble and ever-ready-to-be-dismissed servants of another state and its leaders. Titoism is then an organic disease of successful Communism rather than a phenomenon making a sporadic appearance in Yugoslavia.

As to the broader question whether the Soviet leaders always see foreign countries and policies through the prism of Marxism, the answer, with qualifications, must be in the affirmative. No matter how cynical or power-oriented a group of people may be, it is likely that they will view an unfamiliar situation in terms that reflect their upbringing, their deeply ingrained habits of thought and speech. Thus it may be impossible for even unusually well-informed Soviet Communists to view Western politics as being run in the main by something other than what Marxism-Leninism teaches them it is being run by: the class interests of the big-business circles. While *their experience* may teach them to be skeptical about their regime's propaganda about the conditions in the U.S.S.R., they are much more likely to believe in it when it "explains" the outside world.

This problem should not be confused with another one: whether the ruling circles in Russia believe in the inevitable armed clash between the

U.S.S.R. and the capitalist world, or whether they believe that social (read: Communist) revolutions abroad are likely to have a violent rather than evolutionary character. The Soviet leaders' pronouncements on those two subjects ever since the earliest and most ideological phase of the Communist regime was over in the early twenties, exhibit a familiar zigzag pattern: whenever a useful propaganda point could be scored at home or abroad by depicting an armed clash as inevitable, that was done. Thus the haste and sacrifices of rapid industrialization were rationalized by Stalin in the late twenties and early thirties on the grounds of an approaching war. During World War II, on the contrary, the virtues of coexistence of the U.S.S.R. and the Western world were extolled, and foreign Communists were told to collaborate even with "progressive" capitalists! Just as the people are being periodically scared by the prospect of the return of the internal enemy, i.e., their erstwhile capitalists and landowners (though it is never explained from where!), so the vision of a foreign aggressor and imperialist is a necessary device in the propaganda armory of the totalitarian regime, one that is periodically exhibited and retired. Insofar as *their actions* are concerned, the foreign policy of the U.S.S.R. has for a long time been characterized by a *determined but cautious* policy of territorial aggrandizement, of expanding its sphere of influence, and yet avoiding the risk of an all-out war with the main power of the West that would undoubtedly be catastrophic to both sides in the present age.

The post-Stalin foreign policies of the Soviet Union fall into a pattern parallel to her internal development. Just as inside the U.S.S.R. the absolute rule of terror has been relaxed for reasons spelled out elsewhere, and an attempt has been made to revivify the Communist Party, so with foreign Communist states and parties the stress has been laid more on the ideological bonds and less on sheer physical domination by Moscow through the Red Army, etc. The effort, abroad as at home, has been made in the conviction that the new social and economic forces no longer permit the existence of the old Stalinist-type controls; and that among the Communist states there is now at least one, China, that, because of her sheer size and potential strength, cannot simply be run from Moscow.[12] Hence the attempted reconciliation with the Yugoslav Communists, the relaxation in the other satellites, and the attempt to normalize the relations with the United States at a low rather than high level of tension, symbolized in the "Geneva spirit" and Khrushchev's and Bulganin's visit to Great Britain in the spring of 1956, etc.

Within the Communist bloc the relaxation has already produced two

[12] Though for the time being, because of the backwardness of their economy and because of the international situation, the Chinese Communists are content to remain junior partners to the U.S.S.R.

setbacks from the Russian point of view. The seizure of the leadership of
the Polish Communist Party in the fall of 1956 by its nationalistic wing
and the ejection from its top councils of the most pro-Russian Communists gave a spur to similar attempts in Hungary, which led, however, to
a general anti-Communist revolt. This it required Russian troops to suppress, the local Communist regime thus exhibiting, after more than ten
years in power, both its extreme unpopularity and its inability to run the
country without Russia's military might behind it. The events in Poland
and Hungary are symptomatic. Even the reversion to the more stringent
policy of Soviet domination of its European satellites is unlikely to change
the *long-run prospect* of those regimes' attempting to emancipate themselves from the Soviet Union, and thus in the meantime of being sources
of worry to, and possibly an economic drag on, the imperialist power, instead of being additional elements of strength to the U.S.S.R.

Neither the internal relaxation nor the external defeats of the U.S.S.R.
should infuse one with the idea that the Soviet system is crumbling or
that Soviet territorial or ideological expansion is at an end. Both at home
and abroad the Soviet regime is being challenged and weakened, to some
extent, by its successes. At home the success of industrialization has created
new classes with new aspirations and needs, which impinge on the role and
monopoly of power of the Communist Party. And in the satellites the very
forces released by the work of the Communists themselves have combined
with local nationalism to challenge Soviet domination. Since the U.S.S.R.
is a great and still rapidly expanding industrial power, none of these developments threatens the Soviet regime with collapse. But the new social
forces at home, the nationalisms of the non-Russian nationalities within
the U.S.S.R., and the ferment in the satellites, dictate inexorably the modification of the role of the Communist Party at home, and that of the
U.S.S.R. in the international Communist movement. For a time an attempt may be made to revert to the pre-1953 methods of control at home
and abroad. In the longer run social forces will assert themselves.

TABLE 6 The Formal Structure of the Soviet Government

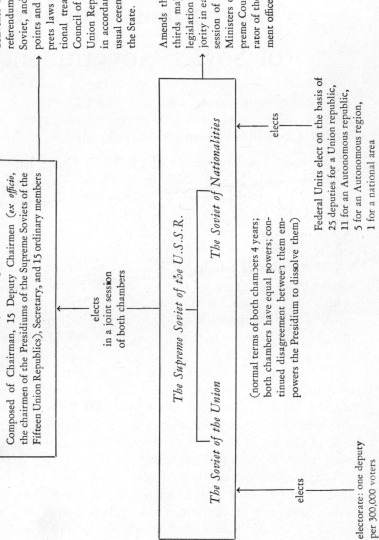

THE ORGANS

COMPETENCE

The Presidium of the Supreme Soviet

Composed of Chairman, 15 Deputy Chairmen (*ex officio*, the chairmen of the Presidiums of the Supreme Soviets of the Fifteen Union Republics), Secretary, and 15 ordinary members

Convenes the Supreme Soviet. Can order a referendum. Between sessions of the Supreme Soviet, and subject to its confirmation, appoints and dismisses Union Ministers. Interprets laws of the U.S.S.R. Ratifies international treaties. Can rescind orders of the Council of Ministers of the U.S.S.R. or of a Union Republic "in the event they are not in accordance with the law." Performs the usual ceremonial, etc., duties of the Head of the State.

elects
in a joint session
of both chambers

The Supreme Soviet of the U.S.S.R.

The Soviet of Nationalities

The Soviet of the Union

(normal terms of both chambers 4 years; both chambers have equal powers; continued disagreement between them empowers the Presidium to dissolve them)

Amends the constitution by at least two-thirds majority in each chamber. Passes legislation and the budget by a simple majority in each chamber. Appoints (at a joint session of both chambers) the Council of Ministers of the U.S.S.R. Appoints the Supreme Court of the U.S.S.R. and the Procurator of the U.S.S.R. (the chief law-enforcement officer of the U.S.S.R.).

elects

Federal Units elect on the basis of 25 deputies for a Union republic, 11 for an Autonomous republic, 5 for an Autonomous region, 1 for a national area

elects

electorate: one deputy
per 300,000 voters

CHAPTER 29

The Formal Structure
of Soviet Government

Soviet Constitutionalism

[The constitutional structure of the Soviet Union has always been an elaborate façade behind which one-party rule and totalitarianism have occupied the political scene. No meeting of the Supreme Soviet has ever even faintly approached in importance a Party congress. Neither the Council of Commissars nor the Council of Ministers has ever rivaled the role of the Central Committee or the Presidium-Politburo of the Party as the supreme maker of policies. It is almost superfluous to add that Stalin, during much of the period of his dictatorial power (1925-41), never held a high state position. Lenin's function as the leader of the Soviet state was predicated on his personal and Party stature rather than only on the fact that he was Chairman of the Council of People's Commissars. Malenkov's brief primacy after Stalin's death was again based on a number of factors, only one of which was that he headed the government as the Chairman of the Council of Ministers. If the formal aspect of Soviet politics is to be studied, then the Statute of the Communist Party is a more important document than the Constitution of the U.S.S.R. From the top to the bottom of the Soviet structure the Party has played a more important role than the corresponding state organs.

The question that occurs right away is: why have an elaborate constitutional structure in a totalitarian regime? Is the Soviet constitution, the whole apparatus of elections, representative bodies, etc., merely "propaganda" of no significance whatsoever in the total picture of Soviet politics? And if so, why study the Soviet constitution and its appurtenances?

There can be no simple answer. The evolution of Soviet constitutional institutions has reflected an important evolution in the thinking of the

Bolsheviks about the state and its organization. Although, in practical terms, the state institutions have usually been subordinate to those of the Party and the representative bodies have usually had functions of a declamatory rather than political or deliberative character, the over-all significance of the representative institutions has transcended the "propaganda" aspect that is usually stressed by the outside commentators on the Soviet system. Soviet representative institutions as well as Soviet constitutionalism as a whole have several aspects of usefulness for the Communist regime, and by the same token several points of interest for those who want to understand the spirit and mechanics of Russian totalitarianism.

Constitutionalism and the Soviet Philosophy of the State

The Soviet regime has inherited the ambivalent attitude of Marxism toward the state and bourgeois constitutionalism. As for some Christian philosophers the state was a necessary evil and a consequence of our sins, so for Marx and Engels nineteenth-century Western constitutionalism, if not the state itself, was the product of the specific conditions of the class struggle. Economic exploitation by the possessing classes was protected by the state, while constitutionalism with its fictions of civic equality and legality was designed to appease the non-propertied masses. Yet Marxism, unlike anarchism, never maintained that victorious socialism would be able to dispense with the machinery of the bourgeois state right away. Presumably constitutions, elections, and the administrative machinery of the state would continue until socialism turned into communism, i.e., until production, liberated from the fetters of capitalism, became able to provide abundance for everybody, and thus dissolve classes and make the state, even the democratic state, superfluous. The (presumably) long transition from socialism to communism would be characterized by real— as opposed to bourgeois-fake—democracy; in contrast to the conditions of bourgeois democracy, elections, civil liberties, etc., would flower under the conditions of "proletarian dictatorship," which Marx somewhat paradoxically specifies as the dictatorship of a vast majority of the people.

Marxism, then, offered very little by way of concrete prescription for constitutional experimenting under the conditions of Russia of 1918 or, for that matter, of 1958. It offered several paradoxes: the distrust of Western parliamentarianism, and yet the conviction that under socialism "real" parliamentary institutions and "real" democracy should flourish; the final aim of the withering away of the state, and yet the transitional period during which the socialist state would be extremely powerful, since it would run the economy of the country as well as exercise the usual functions of the state. Within the thinking of Bolshevik leaders, these para-

doxes were reflected both before and after the Revolution, in a variety of
ideas running the whole gamut from the "abolition" of the state to the
most centralized and authoritarian structure. Some problems resolved
themselves. Like most secular religions, Bolshevism was for freedom but
the "right" kind of freedom, for democratic elections but elections that
would end in the "right" side's, i.e., their own, winning. Thus one-party
rule became both the reality and the theory of the Bolshevik government
a few months after the November Revolution, though at first a few Bolsheviks grumbled and objected that other bona fide revolutionary parties
should be allowed to share in the government. The issue was determined
when the Bolsheviks drove out the Constituent Assembly in January
1918. Within a few months the temporary alliance of the Bolsheviks and
the Left Social Revolutionaries was ended. Up to about 1920 there were
still a few stray Mensheviks and Social Revolutionaries in the representative organs (soviets). In effect, however, the two years after the Revolution witnessed the repression and liquidation of *all* other parties including
even those elements in the Social Revolutionary and Menshevik parties
that offered qualified submission to Soviet power.

While building the one-party state Lenin and his associates, even in the
midst of a civil war, still considered it supremely important to settle the
constitutional framework. No idea of a revolutionary directorate or complete absence of constitutional forms entered their minds. They set about
devising a structure of government in which the Party dictatorship would
operate within the context of democratic institutions. Their own form of
democracy, it was felt, should represent something new and different from
Western parliamentary institutions. Yet for all the nomenclature and all
the pyramidal arrangement involved, the network of representative institutions evolved in the Constitutions of 1918 and 1924 bore more than a
superficial resemblance to the Western pattern. Though the electoral
appurtenances favored the workers over the peasants, and members of the
former possessing classes and clergy were banned from voting, the base for
elections was the mass of people. The Bolshevik leaders thus felt themselves to be heirs of the Western republican tradition. They early rejected
the notion that professional representative institutions, i.e., trade-union
councils, should replace wider popular assemblies. The new nomenclature,
soviets, for representative institutions, "commissars" for ministers, had the
revolutionary flavor about it, but the structure of assemblies, provisions
for amending the constitution, and parliamentary practices, indicated the
link that, on paper and in theory, existed with the main current of Western
constitutionalism.

The first two Soviet constitutions, prepared in the early days of the
regime and considered as transitional documents until the final triumph

of Communism in Russia, illustrate, then, one of the uses of studying the formal side of the government of the U.S.S.R.: Soviet constitutions reflect the basic philosophy of the state of the actual rulers of the Soviet Union— the leaders of the Party and the state—and their estimate of the people's aspirations. Soviet politics is like a vast painted canvas: Action and movement take place on the first plane but they are balanced by a serene background. Thus the actuality of Party politics, of the real pattern of power, is balanced by the background of constitutionalism.

The trend toward "normalcy" in constitutional institutions was emphasized even more in the Soviet Constitution of 1936. The Stalin Constitution, as it was then called, abandoned the unwieldy network of elections of its predecessors. Instead of a huge Congress of Soviets that seldom met, its also overlarge Executive Committee of two chambers, and the Presidium—the only steadily functioning representative organ—the new Constitution returned to the bourgeois simplicity of two normal-sized parliamentary chambers: the Council (Soviet) of the Union and the Council of Nationalities, which designate the Presidium, the collective president of the U.S.S.R. Under this Constitution suffrage is direct, and equal, and the former disqualification from voting of certain classes is abandoned. The Constitution of 1936, adopted incidentally in the period of Popular Front, and the drawing together of the Western democracies and the U.S.S.R. in the face of the threat from the Axis, reflected the conviction of the regime that the Soviet Union should receive a "normal" constitution with the echoes of the early revolutionary struggles and revolutionary romanticism muted. As Stalin proclaimed, socialism had been achieved in Russia. There were no longer any exploiting but only two friendly classes: workers and peasants. Hence there was no longer any need to discriminate against the former landowners, the clergy, etc., nor to weigh the worker's vote more than that of the peasant. The Constitution, which acknowledged the leading role of the Communist Party, proclaimed an impressive list of civil rights guaranteed to the citizens, in which the "bourgeois" freedoms of press, speech, inviolability of the person, were joined by the socialist rights, the state guaranteeing every citizen the right to work and leisure. Again, the value of the Constitution as a beautiful background to the stark political reality is enhanced if we keep in mind that the Stalin Constitution came into effect during the most intense period of terror in the history of the U.S.S.R., when the holocaust, not only within the Party and the state apparatus, but also among the population at large, made a mockery of the civil rights and liberties so emphatically guaranteed in the Constitution.

The background is not without its uses. The regime, unlike the Fascist and Nazi philosophies, does not in theory repudiate the democratic and humanitarian tradition of European political thought. It does not explicitly base its claims on an irrationalist philosophy, or elitism. It claims that political democracy *does* exist in the U.S.S.R. When it becomes necessary or convenient to repudiate a particularly sordid period of Soviet history, it can put the blame on wanton behavior of individuals and their lack of respect for Soviet legality and constitutionalism. None other than the head of the police forces and presumably one of the main supervisors of terror, Lavrenti Beria, blossomed out after Stalin's death (though not for long) as the advocate of legality. In the campaign against the cult of personality and in the general repudiation of the excesses of the Stalinist era, the Soviet leaders led by Khrushchev again based their emphasis on the illegality and unconstitutionality of Stalin's actions and the system of terror from 1934 on. Thus the Constitution and the legal underpinnings of the system enable the regime to have their cake and to eat it too, and to present all the hard political facts that are, in reality, of the essence of the Soviet political system, as temporary and transient aberrations arising out of the willful and illegal acts of individuals, rather than as being imposed by the logic of totalitarianism.

Does not Soviet constitutionalism work against the regime in the sense that the rights proclaimed in the Constitution are belied every day by the facts of Soviet politics? Does not the average citizens resent the gap, say, between the provisions of the Constitution as to free elections and the reality, in which the Communist Party nominates a single list of candidates who are then elected without opposition? Up to now the Soviet regime has not betrayed any apprehension that the gap between the theory and the reality of Soviet politics will undermine the foundations of the dictatorship. Throughout the worst periods of the totalitarian terror under Stalin, the Constitution of 1936 was proudly extolled as the most democratic in the world. Western constitutionalism has been proclaimed as a sham and Soviet liberties have been exalted. Elections to the national representative bodies have always been celebrated as holidays and the foregone results, with over 90 per cent of the electorate voting for the official and unopposed lists, have been hailed as demonstrating the strength and popularity of the regime. Seen from one point of view, Soviet representative institutions and constitutionalism as a whole are a tribute that totalitarianism pays to universal human aspirations for freedom and democratic institutions. Though in practice they are limited by the requirements of the dictatorship, and even in theory they are expounded as consistent with the superior requirements of the ideology and the one-party state, Soviet constitutional institutions are not negligible in the spectrum of Soviet politics, and, under certain circumstances, as will be discussed below, they may acquire a real as distinguished from symbolical importance.

Soviet Constitutionalism as a Unifying and Educational Factor

In their origins Western representative and constitutional institutions had but little to do with any abstract theories of democracy or with the practical necessities of giving the people an opportunity of expressing their preferences as to the system of government. They existed to provide a framework of national or state unity. The monarchs of the Middle Ages summoned parliaments in order to consult their subjects on the most expeditious ways of obtaining money, and to give a select body of their subjects an opportunity of acquainting themselves with the complexity of the problems facing the state. This rudimentary function of constitutional institutions is of great importance in assessing the working of the constitutional framework of the U.S.S.R. In the Supreme Soviet of the U.S.S.R. the delegates from Uzbekistan and the Soviet Far East sit alongside Russians and Ukrainians; factory workers and collective farm peasants who have distinguished themselves in their work are fellow delegates with the highest Party leaders, marshals of the Soviet Union and academicians. Thus unity and cohesiveness of the Soviet state finds its tangible expression in the constitution and its organs.

The Supreme Soviet serves as a platform for the announcement and demonstration of national policies. Once a motif is thrown out by a leader, the other delegates, in a fashion common to all totalitarian parliaments, join in a chorus expounding and intensifying the official pronouncement, be it a warning to the "warmongers of the West," or, contrariwise, a profession of Soviet friendship and wish for collaboration with the U.S.A.; the need for further development of the Soviet consumer industries, or the reassertion of the superior needs and requirements of heavy industry. In an "activist" totalitarian regime, in which the citizen is expected to be not merely a passive subject and observer but a convinced and enthusiastic participant in the official policies and sentiments, the tribune of the national legislature is one more instrument for enmeshing the common man with the machine of the state, of expounding and amplifying the policies that come from above. The same holds for the Soviet courtroom: the dictator, whether an individual or a group, reserves for himself alone the right to proceed extralegally, while the mass of the citizens in their dealings with one another are bound by general rules and regulations. Thus in a highly developed totalitarian regime constitutionalism and legality become themselves handmaidens of the dictatorship.

In the same vein in a country of the vastness of Russia, of the complexity and ubiquity of the Soviet state machinery, the network of representative and legal institutions serves as one of the most useful devices through which the rulers check both on the behavior of their subordinates and on the sentiments of their subjects. A deputy from Odessa will not criticize Stalin, or, at different times, Malenkov, or Khrushchev, or any of the main figures of the regime, but he will not be restrained but on the contrary encouraged to speak of the administrative deficiencies or shortcomings in his city, or the failure of some ministry to provide an adequate volume or quality of goods. Legal remedies will not avail against officially sponsored terror, but a worker persecuted by his manager or trade-union secretary will have his day in court. Beyond the rigid frame of the dictatorship itself, and beyond the wide scope of official policies, the grievances and aspirations of the people can be aired and redress can be sought.

Soviet Constitutionalism as a Political Factor

We come to the third major consideration of Soviet constitutionalism: its use as a *major* political factor. Admittedly, as implied here throughout, *in a stable totalitarian situation*, the legal and constitutional framework is secondary to the real complex of political, police and social forces upon which the regime rests. Yet examples are not lacking in which in a situation of crisis an institution that has existed on paper without interfering with the essence of political power has suddenly become endowed with importance. Throughout many years of the Fascist regime in Italy, it would have been inconceivable for the Grand Fascist Council to have repudiated Mussolini or for the figurehead king to have dismissed the dictator. Yet following Italy's defeats in Sicily in 1943, the constitutional and legal fictions became endowed with temporary reality and the Fascist regime crumbled at the bidding of those institutions it had so long and so readily commanded.

It is rather far-fetched to draw any possible parallels with the Soviet Union. Throughout the long years of the consolidated Bolshevik reign the representative institutions never registered any but a unanimous vote, the courts never rendered a political verdict but in accordance with the desires of those in power. When the great struggle for power rocked the Communist Party and the country in the middle twenties, no reflection of it penetrated the All-Union Congress of Soviets or its Executive Committee, so unimportant were they in the over-all political picture. Legal institutions were used during the purges of the thirties as convenient places in which to publicize and denounce the alleged crimes of the former and potential opponents to Stalin. Nor has the use of such extralegal devices died with Stalin. Beria and his henchmen were tried and sent to death without observing any of the constitutional provisions about guarantees against arbitrary arrest and trial in open court. It is not too much to assume that many a humbler citizen has met with an arbitrary arrest since

March 1953, though the frequency of such incidents must have diminished considerably since Stalin's death.

Yet when all is said, the importance of Soviet constitutional devices has increased since the despot died. Essentially the dictatorship has been in transition and constitutional offices are endowed with *potential* political significance. On the morrow of Stalin's death a group of senior Communist Party officials, after (it is reasonable to assume) some bargaining, rearranged the highest offices in the Party and the state. The new arrangements were in obvious violation of both the Party statute and the Soviet Constitution, though *post facto* they were ratified by the competent body. One office that changed hands was that of the chairman of the Presidium of the Supreme Soviet, i.e., the titular head of the Soviet state. Now, that post was never of any political significance, having been held during Stalin's last years by a faithful but undistinguished Stalinist, Nicolai Shvernik. It is significant that with the opening of a new era it was thought important by the highest Party leaders to change the incumbent, and to entrust the presidency to the senior member of the Party Presidium; a man who, because of his age and past role would not be directly involved in the coming struggle for power, Marshal of the Soviet Union Kliment Voroshilov. In an unstable situation the post of the titular head of the state became of consequence.

Totalitarian systems are unable to endow their constitutional systems with vitality, not only because of the unwillingness of the rulers, but also because of their real inability to conceive how free representative and legal institutions can operate. Political struggle thus *has* to assume the aspect of intrigue, of matching physical and organizational forces at the disposal of the factions, rather than of a free interplay of ideas and a test of strength within the constitutional framework. It is not too much to say of the rulers of the Soviet Union that they do not wish to grant the real prerequisites of democracy to their people; that they could not afford to grant them if they wished; and, most important of all, that they would not know how to go about instituting *real* constitutionalism and a *really* independent judiciary even if they could afford to. By the same token, the habits of mind and action, and the social and political setting that enable constitutional and democratic institutions to operate, have at present no root among the peoples of the U.S.S.R., having been extirpated by four decades of dictatorship and having had but a rudimentary development before. Yet history teaches that as the most intensive form of absolutism recedes, social and economic aspirations become translated into political demands. Representative institutions, as asserted by one of their most famous theorists, are a tender growth and it may take a very complicated pattern of events and conditions to bring them to maturity. But the seeds of democratic ideas and institutions possess a vitality that makes them begin their growth even within the freshly opened cracks of totalitarianism.

Federalism

The Constitution of 1936 guarantees each of the fifteen[1] Union republics that constitute the Soviet state the right "freely to secede from the U.S.S.R." More realistic on the subject is the Soviet national anthem when it speaks of "an *unbreakable* union of free republics." The most poignant illustration of both the freedom and the right to secession is seen in the fact that no more serious charge could be preferred against a real or alleged enemy of the regime, whether under or after Stalin, than that of plotting to separate one of the national republics from the U.S.S.R. As for tsarist Russia, so for the U.S.S.R., the problem of the non-Russian nationalities remains a master factor of its politics. The mosaic of nationalities is reflected by the gradations of legal status from the Union Republic, to the Autonomous Republic, to the Autonomous Region and the National District. The intricacies of formal federalism are counterbalanced by the fact of political centralization assured by the totalitarian system. As is the case with other political institutions the nationality problem is an example of the peculiar dialectic of Soviet politics: the theory grounded in the democratic side of Marxism and embodied in the constitution confronts the antithesis of totalitarian reality. The interplay of the two will provide one of the keys to the future of the Union of Soviet Socialist Republics.

This dialectic confronted the Bolsheviks at the time of the Revolution, when the Russian empire was in a state of dissolution and when the Soviet leaders by their own declaration had been committed to the principle of self-determination. Though the discussion about the nationality problems had in the past divided the Russian Social-Democratic Party, Lenin and his partisans had firmly embraced the principle of a free option by each nation as to its remaining within a multi-national state or separating from it. Definitely repudiated was the view of Rosa Luxemburg that national independence is a problem of secondary importance to the working class, and that the triumph of socialism will render superfluous the national question. The official view enunciated, under Lenin's supervision, by young Joseph Stalin had clung to the territorial principle and independence of nations. Yet power brought with it the immediate posing of concrete questions: Should the Bolsheviks sit idly by and see large parts of the Russian empire slip from their grasp? Should self-determination extend to

[1] The number was reduced in 1956 to fifteen through the absorption of the Karelo-Finnish S.S.R. in the Russian S.S.R.

cases in which "reactionary" (i.e., non-Bolshevik) elements would form states out of the former territories of the Russian empire? At first, in view of its weakness, the Bolshevik regime could not but find it good politics to adhere to its announced principles, and to agree to the independence of various nationalities of the old empire. The defeat of Germany freed the Soviets from the oppressive conditions of the Treaty of Brest-Litovsk, which, among other things, would have detached the Ukraine, and have made her in effect a German satellite. Soviet successes in the Civil War infused the regime with more self-confidence and made it solicitous of restoring to the government most of the old empire's territory. There were still in 1919-20 expectations of a Europe-wide revolution, and hence the independence of Poland, of Finland and of other Baltic states would presumably be but an interlude to their reintegration as Soviet republics. The 1920-21 period saw the end of such hopes. The task was now to reconstruct the Soviet state on a new federal basis, and to implement in practice the Soviet nationality principle.

This principle was to be enunciated later on by Stalin, the first Commissar of Nationalities and one of the architects of Soviet federalism, as requiring a state "proletarian in content and national in form." The expression "proletarian in content" signified in effect that the various "union" and "autonomous" republics could not expect bona fide political self-determination once they found themselves within the spectrum of Soviet power. The Ukrainians, Georgians, Armenians, the Turkic nations of Central Asia, etc., would no longer—this is speaking from the perspective of the early twenties—be submitted to forcible russification and denial of cultural rights, but they would be subject, together with the Great Russians, to the political and economic monolith of the Soviet system.

In the early days of the regime, when the foundations of Soviet federalism and their theoretical underpinnings were being laid, ideological considerations still possessed a vitality that only much later gave way to power considerations. Lenin, the supreme revolutionary pragmatist, was anxious that the practical task of consolidation of the Soviet state and its centralistic organization should not be combined with an underestimation of the potent force of nationalism. Before, as a leader of a handful of revolutionaries, he had adhered to a nationality policy that would avoid a disintegration of the revolutionary movement into its national segments while at the same time it endorsed the spirit of nationalism. Now, as the leader of a multi-national state, he sanctioned forcible incorporation of the Ukraine and Georgia by the Bolsheviks, while at the same time he warned against the excesses of Great-Russian chauvinism. At the Eighth Party Congress in 1919, angered by the arguments of Bukharin and Pyatakov who disparaged self-determination as being strictly secondary to the dictatorship of the proletariat, he exclaimed: "Scratch some Communists and you will find Great-Russian chauvinists." Practically on his deathbed in 1923 Lenin denounced Stalin's and Dzherzinski's repressive policies in Georgia with the observation that people of non-Russian ethnic origin sometimes became the most intense Russian chauvinists, a remark particularly suitable in view of Stalin's subsequent career.

The theoretical disagreement thus paralleled the differences among personalities of Soviet leaders. Dzherzinski, the Pole, and Stalin, the Georgian, could be the warmest advocates of political centralization and, in effect, of Russian predominance in the Soviet Union. Others, like the veteran Ukrainian Communist, Skrypnik, and the Georgian, Budu Mdivani, professed their native nationalism no less intensely than their Communism. Out of the ideological crosscurrents, out of the specifically Russian conditions following the end of World War I and the Civil War, was born both the theory and the practice of Soviet federalism.

The theory was militantly nationalistic insofar as the cultural rights of each, even the tiniest, nationality, were concerned. Not only were the great and ancient non-Russian nations to be given the fullest autonomy in the use of their language, free development of their culture, etc., but similar rights were to be extended to the Chuvash and the Ostyaks, primitive Asian tribes. Siberian tribes barely emerged from the Stone Age were to be encouraged to have their own written language and literature, and to have some form of national organization. The early most ideologically tinged days of the Soviet state were the days of enthusiastic nation-building, when federalism was to join in a harmonious union nationalities at most disparate stages of development and to guide them in a joint socialist experiment. The Bolsheviks went out of their way to provoke and establish the feeling of national separateness, even in such cases as that of the Byelorussians, where this feeling was not very strongly developed. If socialism was eventually (and "eventually" in the early twenties was thought to mean rather soon) to unite all nations of the world in one great union, why be afraid of Ukrainian, Armenian, or Kazakh nationalism? Remove economic exploitation, proclaimed Marxism, and the state becomes an instrument of progress and of social justice, the progress that will gradually make the state itself superfluous. By the same token, remove national oppression, which is but one form of economic exploitation, and various nationalities will abide peacefully together, and through their free development will hasten the day when the triumph of socialism will secure one supranational socialist culture and language. Russia, the jailer of nations under the tsarist regime, would become a Soviet federation, a prototype of the future universal union of socialist states.[2]

[2] It is a highly academic question, but one that has occasioned some debate, whether

The practice of Soviet federalism saw at the end of the Civil War several state units nominally independent of each other, but in fact already united, or about to be united through the agency of the Communist Party and the Red Army. By the end of 1922 the process of consolidation, either peaceful or forceful, by the Bolsheviks transformed their empire into four units. The giant among them was the Russian Socialist Federated Soviet Republic, which received its constitution in July 1918. The R.S.F.S.R. contained several autonomous republics and districts, many of them created out of the Turkic-inhabited territories of Central Asia. United in fact, but nominally entirely independent, were the Ukrainian, the Byelorussian, and the Transcaucasian Soviet Socialist Republics. The last one was composed of three previously separate and really independent states, which the Bolsheviks conquered once the Civil and Polish wars were over. The edifice was crowned by a formal union, and as of January 31, 1924, the Soviet state became the Union of Soviet Socialist Republics.

The formal pattern of Soviet federalism has changed but little between 1924 and 1958. The number of Union republics had grown from four to eleven on the eve of World War II, and is now fifteen. The sources of accession have been: "promotion" of autonomous republics to the status of Union republics, as in the case of the Central Asiatic republics; subdivision of existing republics, as in the case of the Transcaucasian republic, resolved into its historic components Azerbaijan, Georgia, and Armenia; and conquest, as in the case of the Moldavian republic (part of which had been in the Ukrainian S.S.R. before 1939) and the three Baltic states annexed to the U.S.S.R. in 1940. Some changes of status have taken place among the lesser gradations within the federal structure. The most noteworthy has been the dissolution during and after the war of some autonomous republics and national regions, the inhabitants of which allegedly collaborated with the Germans. This fate has befallen, among others, the Volga German and the Crimean Tatar autonomous republics, and has been accompanied by a wholesale deportation and dispersal of the surviving population throughout Russia.

Within the framework of the constitution the federal principle is represented in one of the two representative chambers, the Council (Soviet) of Nationalities. Within this Council each of the Union republics is represented by twenty-five members, autonomous republics by eleven members,

Marxism postulates that the final stage of socialism-communism will see not only the withering away of the state but also of national differences. Certainly Stalin in one of his speeches once forecast the development of a universal language superseding the national one. Late in life, as in his famous article on linguistics, he repudiated the view that the progress of socialism would erase cultural separateness of nations or construct one nation. Like all the more extreme and utopian prognoses of Marxism, the notion of "the withering away" of the state and of national differences has been allowed in the Soviet Union to fall into desuetude.

autonomous regions by five, and each national district sends one member. The 1936 Constitution thus enthrones the federal principle in a more clear-cut form than its predecessor of 1923-24, in which the Council of National-ities was one of the two branches of the Executive Committee of the un-wieldy Congress of Soviets. The council of Nationalities has coequal powers with the Council of the Union, which is elected on the basis of population. The attractiveness of Soviet federalism was enhanced during the discussion of the 1936 Constitution by Stalin's pointed references to the right of secession of the Union republics, and the need, therefore, of their being fairly large and homogeneous units.

The division of competence between the All-Union and the republic authorities was sketched again in an atmosphere of unreality that has pervaded the whole history of Soviet constitution-making. The adminis-trative organs are divided into three large classes: the All-Union ministries (e.g., heavy industry[3]) reserved to the competence of the central organs; the Union-republic ministries (e.g., agriculture), in which the adminis-trative organs in the republics report to the corresponding ministries in Moscow; and finally republican ministries (e.g., education), where au-thority is theoretically vested exclusively in the hands of the republics. The Union-republic governments parallel the central organs with their single-chamber Supreme Council, and the Council of Ministers. More or less the same arrangement prevails in the case of the autonomous republics.

Political literature has been rich in discussion occasioned by problems of federalism. Thus the American, Swiss, Canadian, and German systems have since their beginnings been characterized by conflicts and debate as to the extent of federal vs. state or province powers. Within the Soviet Union the secondary character of the constitutional arrangements has pre-vented any possibility of such conflicts and has rendered almost superfluous a serious discussion of the division of authority between the center and the Union republics. It is still appropriate to make some remarks con-cerning the problem. Even within the letter of the Constitution the au-tonomy of the constituent units appears shaky. The Union republics have the right to secede from the Union (Article 17), but the Presidium of the Supreme Soviet of the U.S.S.R. has the power to rescind decisions of the Councils of Ministers of the Union Republics (Article 49-e), and similar powers belong to the Council of Ministers of the U.S.S.R. (Article 69). The Procurator of the U.S.S.R., the chief law-enforcing official of the state, *appoints* the procurators of the Union and autonomous republics (Article 115). The amount of centralization envisaged in the Constitution is so

---

[3] Some heavy-industry ministries have recently become Union-Republic ones, and thus the trend toward greater decentralization of economic organization still continues in the U.S.S.R.

considerable that an argument could be advanced that, even if one takes into account the strict letter of law and disregards everything else, the Soviet Union is more of a unitary than a bona fide federal state.

The federal aspect of the Constitution is largely a backdrop against which is played the real and vital problem of nationalities. Whenever foreign or domestic exigencies require it, Soviet federalism is dramatically exhibited to the world as proof that the nationality problem has been solved in the Soviet Union. It is difficult to interpret otherwise the amendment of the Constitution in 1944 whereby the Union republics were granted the right to conduct foreign relations and to possess military forces, and the ministries of defense and foreign affairs were transformed into Union-republic agencies. No federation in the world grants its federal units the right to conduct independent foreign and defense policies. Behind the amendment were obvious political reasons: Soviet Russia was soon to claim seats in the United Nations for each of her sixteen constituent republics, and was actually to obtain two additional seats, one for the Ukraine and one for Byelorussia.[4] Stalin's ingenious reasoning at the Yalta conference, that he might have political trouble in the Ukraine if that war-devastated republic did not become one of the charter members of the world organization, illustrates one of the uses to which the regime has put its federal pretensions. Nobody in his right mind, either in the U.S.S.R. or abroad, is today willing to believe that Kiev or Minsk have policies, or even agencies, capable of conducting policies independent of Moscow.

Even more mysterious has been the fate of the Union-republic defense ministries. The inextricable combination of fiction, propaganda and potential importance that is Russian federalism was given yet another illustration in 1954. On that date, in celebration of the three-hundredth anniversary of the first union of the Ukraine and Muscovy, the Crimea, which is geographically part of the Ukraine, but which until then had been a district of the Russian Socialist Federated Soviet Republic, was ceremoniously transferred to the Ukrainian S.S.R. The practical political consequence was somewhat parallel to the gesture of a man transferring some change from one pocket to another, but it served as a reminder that the nationality-federal problem remains of great significance for the Soviet state.

The problem of non-Russian nationalities has three main foci in the Soviet Union. The most important non-Russian ethnic group is the Ukrainian. Numbering more than forty million and closely related to the

---

[4] The U.S.S.R. is thus represented in the United Nations by three member states: the federation and the two republics. The paradox, which escaped comment at the time, is that the largest federal unit, the R.S.F.S.R., was not pushed for admission, while two smaller ones were.

Russians in speech and culture, the Ukrainians are still a separate nationality with national consciousness and national aspirations that originated at least a century ago.

The two main nations of Transcaucasia, the Armenians and the Georgians, though much less numerous, have memories of a national existence and culture dating back to the first centuries of the Christian era. And both in the Caucasus and in Central Asia there are several Turkic-speaking nationalities: the Uzbeks, Azerbaijanis, Kazakhs, Turkmens, and others, all closely related and with a common background of Moslem culture.

In all three cases local nationalisms have been watched eagerly by the Soviet regime to detect and inhibit any signs of a desire for separate statehood or even a real, as distinguished from a paper, autonomy. This supervision has reached deeply even into the cultural life of the non-Russian nationalities, with anything suggesting past as well as present incompatibility of interests between the given nation and the Russians being declared treason. The process of russification of national cultures and of the indoctrination of the youth in the primacy of and the indissoluble union with the Russian nation have been especially pronounced since World War II. Yet while these means can be effective in the case of small, until recently primitive tribes, or smaller nations like the three small Baltic countries annexed during the war, they cannot be entirely efficacious when dealing with multi-million national groups like the Ukrainians and the Turkic peoples.

In some cases the Soviet regime has resorted to or allowed demographic changes to strengthen the preponderance of the Russian element. Thus in the enormous Kazakh republic, the Texas of the U.S.S.R., the Kazakhs are now in a minority with more than half of the population being relatively recent settlers from the Ukraine and Russia, and this process is likely to go on with the progress of industrialization and the settlement of the "virgin lands." The Russian element seems to predominate also in the larger industrial cities of the Ukraine. Yet in the age of nationalism even the most powerful totalitarian regime cannot resettle, extirpate, or completely eradicate the national feelings of a group of twenty or forty million people.

Here it is necessary to pause once again to observe the use of Soviet "constitutional formalism." The letter of the law stands in stark contrast with the reality of politics. Whether in Uzbekistan, the Ukraine, or Georgia, political authority proceeds from Moscow. But at times the grant, on paper, of national sovereignty has served to relieve the fissiparous tendencies of non-Russian nationalisms, and even to gain enthusiastic adherents for Communism from among the more backward nationality groups, for whom even a paper sovereignty represented an advance and promise over their pre-Revolution status. By the same token, the institutions and liberties that exist on paper sometimes have the knack of becoming transformed into live and menacing demands. No other aspect of the Soviet system is a likelier candidate for this role of Frankenstein monster than its national and federal problem.

Administration

The Soviet state has been, because of the size and complexity of its administrative structure, *the* administrative state of recent times. Modern technology and the consequently enormously involved economic and political systems under which we live have everywhere increased the importance of administration: the art and procedures of doing things political and economic. Some have argued that the very focus of politics has shifted from the public forums and halls of legislatures, where politicians discuss principles and enact laws, to the offices and institutions, where administrators devise the ways and means of keeping going the complex economic and political machinery of the modern state. This development in the pattern of policy has been noticeable even in the democracies. It has reached its highest point in the Soviet Union. The totalitarian state is also the administrative state: a hierarchy of administrators—whether they be Party bureaucrats, officials charged with the planning and development of the economy, army and police officers, etc.—rules Russia. They are accountable, in the last resort, to the highest group of administrators. In the Presidium of the Communist Party the old revolutionary leaders (who themselves had served as Stalin's deputies over a large administrative domain) now play a secondary role to the new generation, whose whole career had been within the administrative apparatus of the state and the Party until their ability or the whim of the dictator, or both, endowed them with a political significance as well.

It was not as a charismatic leader or a victorious general that Stalin ascended the pinnacle of power. Though most accounts of his rise neglect his considerable political ability, it is generally true that his main avenue was his skill as an *"apparatchik,"* a man of the "apparatus" (of the Party) who through his ability at running the routine business of the Party gained an upper hand over his competitors, who shone more brilliantly as theoreticians or orators. Several years of anonymous work in Stalin's secretariat preceded Malenkov's emergence as a major Party figure. Khrushchev had been an obscure Party worker before he was selected by the dictator, at the height of the purges in the thirties, to be the head of the Ukrainian Party organization. Bulganin's career may serve as a prototype of the *curriculum vitae* of a successful politician in the Soviet Union: a

stint with the Secret Service, work at the managerial level, director of the
State Bank, chairman of the Moscow City Soviet, and finally national
prominence as a political general and minister of war, accompanied, of
course, by membership in the highest Party councils. The new generation
of the highest Soviet leaders, the Pervukhins, Saburovs, Kirichenkos, and
Suslovs, are for the most part people who have arrived at prominence
through long years of administrative work and whose political prominence
was a prize for their technical (in the broad sense of the word) usefulness.
To be sure, (the ability to advance or even to survive within the Soviet administrative system cannot have been unconnected, especially during the
period of the Great Purge of the thirties, with political ability, at least in
the sense of choosing the right protectors, special usefulness and docility
to the dictator, etc.) But the fact remains that the ascent to high posts has
been apolitical in the Western sense of the word "political" (no struggle
for votes, no interplay of political ideas, has enabled a man in the Soviet
Union to achieve prominence during the last generation) Politics in our
sense of the word has atrophied during the Stalin era. Administration has
become pre-eminent.

That this should be so, is one of the poignant ironies of the history of
the Soviet state. For, along with the conviction that, under Socialism, the
repressive and military tasks of government should wither away, the early
Bolsheviks have inherited the notion that there is nothing specialized or
special in the task of governing. Lenin's dictum that a kitchen servant can
easily be transformed into a political expert is well known. That amateurs
could perform the most involved functions of government was clearly
expressed in Lenin's *State and Revolution*. Administration would wither
away before the state. (Popularly elected councils would run the whole
complex of governmental functions, executive and legislative, and even
judges would be elected) Thus members of the local city soviet (i.e., city
councilmen) would give part of their time freely to the task of administering various branches of the city administration. The principle of separation
of powers, *at any level*, was felt by the Bolshevik to be obsolete and smacking of fraudulent, bourgeois parliamentarianism. The highest administrative organ could not be dispensed with even in the early beginnings. But
no bourgeois-sounding title of "minister" for the land of the soviets. The
official appelation was at first the "Provisional Workers' and Peasants' Government." Branches of the central government were called Commissariats,
presided over by the People's Commissars, each assisted by a council-
collegium. The Soviet of People's Commissars soon became in effect a
council of ministers, and the fact was officially recognized when in March
1946 the name itself was changed to conform to the accepted world-wide
usage. About the same time uniforms were introduced for members of

various branches of administration including those the most "bourgeois" countries are content to leave ununiformed. The symbolism of titles and uniforms has reflected the great change both in actuality and in official thinking on the subject of administrations.[5]

(Russia is, then, a much-administered country.] It is proposed here to examine the structure of state administration, leaving for the subsequent chapter the structure of the Party. [The interrelationship of the Party and state machinery is one of those topics in politics that cannot be described by laying down a set of rules. The Party leads and controls the government. All the state officials, even of the middling rank, are its members. The highest officers of the state are important Party officials (though the converse is not always so). Yet the exact way in which the two machines intermesh and react upon each other varies with each important change in the political atmosphere, the personality of the incumbents of the given positions, etc.]A few examples will illustrate the problem. Though they are chosen from the highest ranks of the Party and state administration, they find their parallels at all levels of the hierarchy.

The Chairman of the Council of Commissars, i.e., the prime minister, following Lenin's death, was Alexei Rykov. As early as 1928 Rykov disagreed with Stalin, then already in complete ascendance, over questions of agricultural policy, and fell into disgrace. Yet Rykov retained his chairmanship until December 1930. The head of the executive branch of the government was powerless when confronted with the hostility of the Secretary-General of the Party. While still in office, the former had no alternative but to carry out policies and instructions of which he disapproved. Rykov was succeeded by Molotov, a faithful pupil and follower of Stalin. It was not until May 1941 that the dictator himself assumed the chairmanship. It is possible that the general European situation—Russia was to be plunged into war within a few weeks—may have persuaded Stalin that he should assume immediate and overt leadership of the government. But in terms of real power, the chairmanship was in fact insignificant. No one would argue that Stalin was more powerful on May 6, 1941, when he assumed the office, than he had been on May 5.

In February 1950 an article in *Pravda* attacked A. A. Andreyev for his views on the organization of the collective farms. Andreyev was then a member of the Politbureau but, what is more important from our point of view, he was also Chairman of the Council on Kolkhoz Affairs, then the highest governmental organ dealing with collectivized agriculture. A simple notice in the Party organ was a sufficient indication that Andreyev's

---

[5] That the first generation of Bolsheviks should have believed the problems of governing to be relatively simple at the same time that they espoused the notion of a *professional* and *centralized* revolutionary party, is one of those paradoxes that illuminate the twofold character of their Marxist heritage.

views no longer had the support of the very highest Party circles. Andreyev promptly recanted his views and was replaced as the chief spokesman for the regime on agricultural affairs by N. S. Khrushchev. The latter in turn was criticized within a year by a Party official much inferior to him in status, but who was obviously acting on instructions from higher quarters. The incident, which is discussed in another chapter, illuminates not only Soviet politics in the last years of the Stalin era, but also the atmosphere in which policies are formulated and executed under the Soviet system. Neither the ministry of agriculture nor the Council on Kolkhoz Affairs is an independent policy-formulating organization. They go along formulating and supervising policies, until at a crucial point the highest Party organ, or, in Stalin's days, the dictator himself, steps in. Here a matter of great economic and, incidentally, ideological, importance was settled by a decision of one, or at most a few, persons. The Party then lays down the policies and provides the "tone" in which they are administered. What is true at the top is also true lower down. The secretary of a local Party committee is likely to be a more important person than the chairman of the given city's council. The former attends, not only to Party matters in the strict sense of the word, but economic, educational, and other problems of the city or district are also within his responsibilities.

The enormous growth of administration in the Soviet Union is a logical consequence of the concept of the state, which controls and administers every aspect of the national economy. If the state strives at the same time to direct all forms of its citizens' activities from their beliefs to chess playing, then it cannot dispense with a vast army of officials. The logic of totalitarianism as well as that of socialism makes the U.S.S.R. a bureaucratic state.

The administrative history of the Soviet state has exhibited one of those "inherent contradictions" of which Marxists love to talk when they discuss non-socialist countries. Socialism, in the Soviet concept of it, means "doing things": increasing production, expanding the industrial plant, training scientists, athletes, soldiers. Action rather than deliberation, construction rather than the reconciliation of conflicting interests, has been the desired characteristic of the Soviet administrator. The emphasis on quantitative achievement has characterized not only economic administration. It would be comical, if it did not involve so huge a number of human tragedies, to relate how at the height of the Great Purge, 1936-38, Party and security officials set themselves regular quotas of "enemies of the people" and "wreckers" they "had" to discover and liquidate to gain the approval of their superiors. The emphasis on production, in the widest sense of the word, that has characterized Soviet society in the last generation has necessitated the institution of one-man direction in most administrative institutions and the discarding of many devices designed to prevent administrative abuse of powers and corruption. Gone or diminished in importance are the collegial arrangements in ministries whereby the minister was merely a chairman of a collegium of senior officials. The same has happened to the famous *troika*, the arrangement under which major industrial enterprises were run by a committee composed of the director, the secretary of the Party cell, and the trade-union representative. One-man management was prescribed in a famous speech of Stalin's in 1931 as an imperative in the struggle for rapid industrialization, and it has been a rule ever since. But vesting of complete authority for a certain area of administration in one man is an excellent incentive for efficiency *only up to a certain point.* After that point has been reached the lack of institutionalized restraints is liable to breed complacency, corruption, and, a cardinal sin in a totalitarian regime, a feeling of independence vis-à-vis the central organs. The story of Soviet official utterances on public administration and administrators has consisted in the interplay of two ostensibly contrasting *motifs.* One has been the harping on the need of one-man management, and the inadmissibility of diluting authority, whether in a ministry or in a plant. The other insistent note has been the complaint of officials' "losing touch with the masses," of nepotism and high living among Party and state officials, of their arbitrary behavior, contempt for the rank and file of their subordinates, etc. In place of normal administrative restraints, a system of controls peculiar to a totalitarian state had to be constructed. Officially, the task of control lies in an institution, like the Ministry of State Control, which checks administrative performances of various agencies and has the right of auditing their books; and the Procuracy of the U.S.S.R., which checks on the legality of administrative actions and ordinances. But in fact the most, if not the only, effective way of controlling high officials has been the fear of political disgrace and liquidation that could befall them upon discovery of an administrative failure. Failure, under Soviet totalitarianism, has often been equated with political heresy and treason. A high official—say a Party Secretary of a sizable region or a minister controlling an important segment of the economy—was, especially in Stalin's era, like the proverbial Oriental vizier. While in favor he enjoyed unlimited power over his subordinates, and, if he so desired, the appurtenances of luxurious living. An incautious utterance, an administrative mistake or bad luck that could be seized upon by the envious or by his rivals, could bring his instant downfall, followed by imprisonment or worse.

The system under Stalin, as his successors who had sweated it out were perceptive enough to realize, did not really *control* the administrators, it *terrorized* them. It was not the control agencies and regulations that exercised restraints over the body of bureaucrats, but the secret police and the fear of denunciation. Thus in the last resort the system often defeated itself. [For an administrator endowed with the power to make a prompt decision in an economic or other matter would yet be so terrified of making a miscalculation, which might cost him not only his job but also his head, that he would refer the matter to his superior, he to his, etc., until relatively trivial decisions would have to be decided by the Politburo or the dictator himself.] The secret police spread its network of informers over all administrative institutions. From a less dramatic viewpoint the obsession with fulfilling and overfulfilling production quotas—the main avenue of success for an ambitious manager and director—often resulted in falsifying statistics, shoddy quality of the product and corrupt practices in the struggle to obtain scarce raw materials. Soviet administration worked in an atmosphere of nervous tension, conducive to success over shorter periods and emergencies, like the War, but insufferable and self-defeating as the long-run practice.

It is this fact, among others, that persuaded Stalin's successors to carry out their campaign against the "cult of personality," i.e., to spell out and to publicize the crimes and abuses of their great predecessor. Their objective has *not* been to change the totalitarian character of the regime, but to reintroduce a degree of "normalcy" and legality into the Soviet system. Some German political theorists of many years ago formulated the concept of *Rechtsstaat*, i.e., of a state that, while not democratic in character, would yet be ruled by laws, and whose bureaucracy would have its powers and competence strictly defined. The objective of the new masters of the Soviet Union has been to have a form of Communist *Rechtsstaat*. The campaign against Stalin's ghost had the concrete result of exposing thousands of little Stalins who in their spheres acted arbitrarily and corruptly. The relaxation of terror and the imposition of stricter controls on the power of the organs of state security has served to relieve the tension and to assure the rank and file of Soviet administrators that they could now work with at least a modicum of physical security. The new regime has grasped the dangers and inefficiencies of overcentralization. While not for a moment relaxing the totality of political centralization, the bosses of the country—members of the Presidium of the Communist Party of the U.S.S.R.—have allowed and encouraged a degree of economic and administrative decentralization. More emphasis on the quality of work and production, and the restoration of the morale of the administration—these have been the aims of the new leaders, and, as we shall see, behind the new policy there has been not only the desire for administrative efficiency but political considerations as well.

In brief, the objective of the rulers has been what might be called sane Stalinism: policies oriented to preserve the totalitarian character of the state and to assure its economic growth but stripped of the aberrations and excesses that emanated from the despot's personality. It is legitimate to pose the question whether it is in the nature of things political to have a halfway house between unbridled totalitarianism and government of laws; and a related question: what effect have the new policies had up to now? No simple answer will suffice. It is reasonable to assume that in the administrative sphere as elsewhere, Soviet totalitarianism is in a fluid condition and capable of retrogressing into some of the excesses of the Stalin era as well as progressing to a pattern more closely approximating bureaucracies of the West. The lessened fear of the secret police, greater freedom of criticism, and the encouragement of more initiative and decision-making at the lower and local levels of administration: all these reforms cannot but improve the morale and efficiency of Soviet administration. But the Soviet official, especially in a crucial economic sphere, is still expected to perform at a feverish pace. The analogy of an Oriental potentate may no longer be suitable, but insofar as his security and peace of mind are concerned, he may not unfairly be compared to an American baseball manager or football coach. Failure to produce may not always be excused by references to the poor material available or to the hard schedule. He may find himself accused of an improper attitude or the inability to work with people, and no civil service regulations will protect him from a curt dismissal. And the element of terror has not of course been entirely eliminated. The main subordinates of Beria were hunted down and eliminated with the same thoroughness that in Stalin's times characterized the persecution of real and alleged Trotskyites and Bukharinites. Malenkov's replacement as the top man of the regime by Khrushchev was followed by a shakeup in several important Party and state positions. Should Khrushchev be replaced or removed, the change would reverberate throughout the Soviet administrative machinery.

Ministers and Ministries

The structure of the Soviet administration bears witness to the complexity of functions assumed by the state and to the undercurrents of totalitarian politics. Thus, since the state controls *directly all* the spheres of economic life, the Soviet administrative apparatus includes all the agencies of production and consumption. Every store and every factory in the U.S.S.R. is owned and administered by the state. Every acre of land is under control of the state, while most cultivated soil and forest is owned and run either by state agencies or by collective enterprises like the collective farms, which for all purposes are units in the state economic administration.

[To supervise this vast network of enterprises the Soviets until recently resorted to centralized economic administration as well as planning.] The number of ministries both of the U.S.S.R. and the Union republics was consequently large, for they included in addition to departments common to all states, such as finance, war, interior and commerce, ministries covering every region of economic activity, such as ministries of chemical and heavy industry, of the automobile industry, etc. The total roster of central ministries (i.e., both All-Union and Union-republic) has oscillated between twenty-five and fifty and the number would be considerably larger if we included a number of special commissions and committees whose heads have ministerial status (e.g., the Gosplan—the committee to plan national economy; the committee for state security, etc.). Some of the ministries used to be, and a few still are, not administrative agencies in the Western sense of the word, but headquarters of gigantic economic enterprises that cover all of the Soviet Union.[6] Others are great preserves of political power, and their heads are, by virtue of their position, among the leading men of the regime. Thus, at the height of his power in the late forties and again for a few months after Stalin's death, Lavrenti Beria was clearly more than just a deputy prime minister and minister in charge of security matters. He was a man who controlled a vital segment of power in a totalitarian state. The police and the special armed forces of his ministry were at his disposal. Some of his closest subordinates were his personal protégés and friends. It is only gradually and cautiously that Stalin himself moved to diminish the enormous concentration of power in Beria's hands, and the security chief's ultimate downfall evidently required a concerted action of all other major leaders of the regime. In a somewhat similar sense the Ministry of Defense, for so long jealously preserved by Stalin against any potential Bonaparte, enjoys, under currently fluid conditions of Soviet totalitarianism, a special status. Its head had been for a long time Stalin's crony, Voroshilov, followed by ministers who were either technicians or political generals. That the ministry of armed forces has now become a preserve of political power and its incumbent a figure of great influence has been demonstrated in both the political rise and downfall of Zhukov. Elected an alternate member of the Presidium at the Twentieth Congress, he was promoted to a full member in the July 1957 crisis and removed as well as dismissed as Minister a few months later. While the reasons for his dismissal are not clear, the Party bosses obviously did not enjoy the presence in the highest organ of a man who

---

[6] Something like the Atomic Energy Commission in the U.S.A., which is charged with the production of atomic products as well as the extraction of fission-producing materials, comes close to the *type* of economic agency in the U.S.S.R.

was primarily a general and only secondarily a Party man, and who, worst of all, enjoyed a wide popularity in the country.

The problem of co-ordination and of relative competence of various ministries is again posed in a sharper focus in a totalitarian society than it is in the framework of democratic administration. In England a war minister who feels that he is being imposed upon by the Treasury will carry his case to the Prime Minister and the Cabinet or, as a last resort, he can resign and explain his case to Parliament. In the U.S.S.R. the major decisions are reached outside the context of the ministerial council, and the given ministers participate in them only insofar as they are important members of the Presidium of the Communist Party. Thus in the middle thirties when Russian transportation was in a deplorable state and was proving to be a major obstacle in rapid industrialization of the country, Lazar Kaganovich was appointed Commissar of Transportation. Kaganovich has the reputation of a capable administrator, but what is more important, he was then a person of enormous political importance: a member of the Politburo and right hand of Stalin in economic affairs. He had thus the ability to make decisions and commandeer resources far beyond the reach of an "ordinary" minister of transport.

The Council of Ministers even from a mechanical point of view is not the proper body to debate and determine policies. Even in the post-Stalin days it remains a large body to perform the functions, say, of the British Cabinet, which, though only between one-third and one-half of its size, has been accused of being too large for efficient policy formulation. It may be assumed that insofar as *administrative* policies are concerned they are determined by a smaller group, composed of the Chairman, first deputy chairmen, and deputy chairmen.[7] This in October 1956 gave a group of fourteen, of whom seven were until June 1957 members of the Presidium of the Communist Party, and all of whom were members of the Party Central Committee. The Chairman of the Council is traditionally, though as we have seen not always, one of the highest men in the regime. The Premier until March 1958, Bulganin, was for the most part of his tenure considered second man in the Soviet hierarchy. Khrushchev's assumption of the office is significant, not for its own sake but simply because it shows a considerable deviation from the current theory of collective leadership, in so far as the highest positions both in the Party and in the administration are for the moment combined as they were during the latter part of the Stalin era.[8]

[7] The Chairman and first deputy chairmen constitute the Presidium of the Council.

[8] The relative ranking of the Soviet oligarchs was for a long time easy to assess by simply following the official order of names at a function as given in the Soviet press.

The administrative reforms and the party crisis of 1957 have affected the structure of the Council of Ministers. Most of the deputy chairmen happened to be in a group opposed to Khrushchev and lost their ministerial positions as well as their party posts. Thus, the two senior first deputy chairmen, Molotov and Kaganovich, were dismissed, as well as deputy chairmen Malenkov, Saburov, and Pervukhin. Previous reforms had added to the All-Union Council of Ministers (not inconceivably to increase Khrushchev's influence) chairmen of Councils of Ministers of the Union Republics. At present there is a small number of deputy chairmen, and the title first deputy chairman is no longer used. Bearing in mind the constant pattern of constriction-expansion of Soviet administration, it is most likely that the current set-up will not remain stable. For one thing, it is difficult to see how, if the Council of Ministers is a frequently meeting body, the chairmen of the Councils of Ministers of the Union Republics can be in regular attendance, and their original addition may have represented a tactical move rather than a definite change in the pattern of administration. Also, considering the vastness of the Soviet administrative machinery, it is quite likely that the number of deputy chairmen of the Councils of Ministers will again be expanded. Each of the deputies is likely to wear several hats: some are still heads of ministries or committees; all of them are high Party officials. Multiplication of offices in one person is not as pronounced as in Stalin's time. Jealous though he was of his subordinates' becoming too prominent, the dictator, himself a man of enormous energy and industry, required his lieutenants to imitate his working habits. L. Kaganovich, for instance, was at one time in the thirties Secretary of the Moscow Party organization, member of the Central Party Secretariat, in addition to being in over-all supervision of heavy industry. But Soviet administrators still are, as a rule, overworked.

There have been but a few glimpses of the decision-forming process at the highest levels of Soviet administration. We know, for instance, that important decisions used to be reached under Stalin (and there is no reason to believe that the procedure is now greatly different) at a meeting of either the plenum or a committee of the Politburo. The specialists, i.e., the ministers in charge, would report or recommend, and the Politburo would decide. In his "secret" speech denigrating Stalin at the Twentieth

---

Thus in the thirties the names of Molotov, Voroshilov and L. Kaganovich invariably followed that of the dictator. Stalin's death brought about the ranking (1) Malenkov, (2) Beria, (3) Molotov. Sometime after Beria's imprisonment in the summer of 1953, the pattern was set whereby members of the Presidium of the Party are listed first and alphabetically, then members of the Party Secretariat, then deputy chairmen of the Council of Ministers who are not members of the preceding bodies, etc. Official etiquette thus conforms to "collective leadership."

Congress, Khrushchev criticized his erstwhile boss for, among other things, his completely chaotic way of assigning responsibility for various matters or of simply by-passing even the Politburo and settling vital decisions on his own. Yet there is little to indicate that, administratively, things have changed very much. There is no more Stalin to act completely arbitrarily but there has not been and there cannot be in a totalitarian system a nice division of functions between the government and the Party. Khrushchev has not found it inconsistent to address himself to matters of administration as well as policy. Thus, he spelled out the way in which new areas are to be brought under cultivation and prescribed the main crops for them, etc. He has upbraided the Soviet construction industry for not using enough structural steel and cement. And so it will be as long as the Soviet system continues; the Party will not leave any branch of administration to its own devices, whether its head is Khrushchev or anyone else.

The same confused line of authority runs through the ministries and through the councils of ministers of Union and autonomous republics. One might imagine that the improvement of dairy cultivation in the Ukraine is the primary responsibility of the Minister of Agriculture of the Ukrainian S.S.R. But it will be the First Secretary of the Ukrainian Party who will make the authoritative statement on the subject. Somewhat in the manner of a dog chasing its tail the regime is forever trying to establish clearer lines of authority and to free its administrative machinery from the insufferable amount of red tape the system entails. Ministries are merged into larger units to assure greater flexibility and more scope of action, then it is found that the unit is too large and unwieldy, or that, for political reasons, it is unwise to concentrate so much authority under one minister. It is useless to recount how many times light industry has been split and then reunited into one ministry, or how, for different reasons, the Ministry of the Interior has fissioned into Internal Affairs and State Security, only to regroup again.[9] Right now decentralization is the slogan of the day in Soviet administration and industry. In the summer of 1956 several Union-republic ministries were transformed into republican

[9] The Ministry of Internal Affairs was re-created on the morrow of Stalin's death out of the ministries of Internal Affairs (N.K.V.D.) and of State Security (M.G.B.). The former had specialized in the more routine functions of the Ministry of the Interior; the latter's functions were devoted to the more political tasks: the tracking down of espionage and subversion, the supervision of the forced-labor camps, and so on. Their reunification in the hands of Beria indicated his reassertion of power, just as their previous separation reflected the realization that complete and immediate control over *all* the security apparatus made its incumbent dangerously powerful. Following Beria's downfall the political importance of the security apparatus was decisively reduced and the still important segment of police and security powers again split up. Thus there is now the Ministry of Internal Affairs, with its usual tasks and supervision of ordinary police, and the Committee of State Security (K.G.B.), which has inherited the function of the old M.G.B.

ministries, i.e., put within the full competence of the Union republics. The list included ministries of justice and automobile transport. At the same time greater decentralization was prescribed within some of the remaining Union-republic ministries. Thus the Ukrainian press reported in August 1956 that several thousand coal, oil, metallurgical, etc., enterprises were turned over from the central organs to the control of the Ukrainian ministries.

A very drastic measure of decentralization was promulgated in June 1957 after several months of discussion and preparation. Sponsored personally by Khrushchev, the new pattern of economic organization envisaged the abolition of most of the central economic ministries both Union and Union-republic. Such central agencies as the ministries of the chemical industry, food products, textile industry and so on were abolished. Most of the functions of the former industrial and construction ministries were split up among a number of economic councils corresponding to the major industrial and production regions of the country. Each territorial council was to administer multiple economic enterprises within the region. In May 1957 it was planned to set up 92 territorial economic councils: 68 of them within the Russian S.S.R., 11 within the Ukrainian S.S.R., and one for each of the remaining federal republics. Thus huge industrial districts like Moscow and Leningrad, as well as Kazakstan and Byelorussia, would each constitute a separate economic unit but would all be subordinate to the State Planning Commission as well as to the U.S.S.R. Council of Ministers, which was expanded to include *ex-officio* chairmen of the councils of ministers of the fifteen Union republics.

The reform is likely to have important effects politically as well as economically. Under the latter heading the regional economic councils may well increase the efficiency of the industrial machine of the U.S.S.R. The reorganization brings administration closer to the units of production. Under it a chemical plant, say, in Minsk, would no longer be directly administered from Moscow, but would be run by the chemical department of the Byelorussian Economic Council with its seat right in Minsk. Savings on personnel, the avoidance of wasteful duplication of production facilities, and greater powers of initiative and direction for the people on the spot are also likely to be among the gains of the new system. On the other hand, since a totalitarian system lives by centralization, while there may be *administrative* decentralization there is no room in the Soviet system for a bona fide decentralization of economic *policy planning*. Over-all economic plans will continue to be worked out by the highest councils of the Communist Party and the Gosplan, and the Ukrainian or Kazakh economic council will not be allowed to develop the economy of its region according to its own economic ideas. In time even administrative decentralization may prove too much for the framework of totalitarian politics. It does not take much prophetic sense to envisage Communist officials in the near future grumbling about the fact that there is too much decentralization in Soviet administration, and that industrial enterprises in the Ukraine or Georgia fail to respond promptly to the directives from Moscow, the culprit being the unsound and un-Leninist practice of diluting the powers of the central organs. In a sense this is the common dilemma of all modern industrial states: how far can the intricate and intertwined industrial machinery be consolidated under the same management. We hear complaints about the nationalized industries in Great Britain and about the huge corporations in the United States. But in the absence of democratic institutions and of private enterprise, the problem is much more fundamental in the U.S.S.R.

Politically and administratively the new organization of Soviet industry confers enhanced powers and responsibilities upon the organs of local government and especially upon the Union republics. As we have seen, the decentralization is more apparent than real: there is in the background the centralizing and unifying apparatus of the Communist Party. But even a decentralization of management may in due time lead to claims for partial economic autonomy on the part of various national regions of the U.S.S.R. Administrative decentralization thus increases the importance of the national and regional problem in the U.S.S.R. For the time being the reform is proclaimed in the name of efficiency, with its authors not unmindful of its favorable reception among the local Party and state leaders. But the future evolution of Soviet industrial administration will affect, even more than up to now, the crucial problem of totalitarian controls by the Party of all aspects of Soviet life. The new pattern of Soviet industrial organization is based on regionalism and decentralization, with only a few branches of industry retained under the old economic ministry setup (e.g., the aviation, radio and defense industries preserve All-Union ministries). Above the network of territorial economic councils is the Gosplan and behind it the Council of Ministers of the U.S.S.R. and ultimately the Presidium of the Central Committee of the Communist Party of the U.S.S.R.[10]

[10] To show that decentralization will not mean the lack of strict central control here is a quotation from Khrushchev's speech on the reorganization to the Supreme Soviet: ". . . The U.S.S.R. State Planning Commission (Gosplan) will have in addition to its general departments for over-all planning, specialized agencies, divisions and specialists for various branches of industry, thus co-ordinating and directing the development of specialization and co-operation in separate branches of the national economy in co-ordination with the plans for economic development on a national scale. These specialized agencies and divisions will have to work out plans for the development of different industries and *supervise their implementation*" (my italics). To some extent the abolished economic ministries thus reappear as subdivisions of the Gosplan.

Behind the problem of Soviet administration stands the larger issue of the Soviet administrator. In the early days of the regime they were of two varieties—the specialist taken over from the tsarist or pre-November days, indispensable because of his technical qualifications but watched and suspected by the regime; or a professional revolutionary, well-versed in Marx and Plekhanov but not necessarily competent to run a ministry or factory. Both types are now extinct, either through natural attrition or through the Great Purge of the thirties. In their place has arisen the new Soviet bureaucrat, a product of the Stalin era. He is a man almost equally distant from pre-Revolutionary society and from the struggles and ideological excitement of the Revolution and the first years after it. His training, often even in the non-economic and non-technical branches of the administration, is likely to have been scientific, or in the social sciences. Questions of ideology, the great doctrinal disputes of the past, are for him matters of, at most, historical interest. He is, in brief, not terribly dissimilar from a bureaucrat, business executive, and army officer in the West *insofar as his training* and his *objectives* in life are concerned. If he belongs to the Party, it is more often than not a consequence of his job and the desire to advance, rather than of a deeply thought-out ideological preference. Communism in Russia has managed to produce in its officialdom a new middle class not startlingly different in its aspirations and viewpoint from the middle classes elsewhere, though it is superficial to speak of a managerial revolution and unwise to consider this new class as a monolithic whole in its attitudes and interests.

Soviet administration is thus an important factor in the changing social scene of the U.S.S.R. Here, as in other aspects of the Soviet political scene, the relentless terror of the Stalin era has obscured but has not stopped the growth of new social forces and aspirations. Russia's industrialization and growth as a great world power would have been inconceivable without the creation of the enormous and intricate administrative machinery. For all its shortcomings, for all the tenseness and insecurity in which the Soviet administrator has worked, this machinery has performed the day-to-day tasks of administration and planning. It has served the state well, and the Soviet administrator may soon feel and demand that his rewards should go beyond the enhanced social status and relative physical security accorded to him by the post-Stalin regime. His technical ability and his vital function in the system give him a base of power from which to press such a demand.

CHAPTER 30

The Communist Party
of the U.S.S.R.

The Character and Function of the Party

In the years that have passed since Lenin wrote his *What Is To Be Done?* the Bolsheviks have grown from a handful of conspirators partly in exile abroad and partly in the underground in Russia into a huge party of several million members. No longer fugitives and in the background, the Communists rule Russia, control or guide other Communist parties that have sprung up in all countries of the world and some of which have since World War II achieved power in their own countries. It is certainly no longer the party of the hunted, of the Marxian intellectual and the revolutionary worker. Its resources are in effect the resources of the largest country of the world and for its funds it no longer has to beg from rich sympathizers or to stage "expropriation" raids on banks like the ones in which young Dzugashvili–Stalin first achieved revolutionary renown. Over the years the Party has grown and changed until it is today the party of business managers, ministers, generals; of the elite of skilled workers and collective farm officials; of professors and engineers. Membership in the Party has become almost synonymous with achieving success and status in Soviet society. The symbolism that the Party retains, of being the representative of the oppressed, of the "prisoners of starvation," as the *Internationale,* the Party hymn, still proclaims, is clearly obsolete and paradoxical.[1]

[1] The evolution of the name of the Party is an interesting story. Until 1918 the Bolsheviks remained the "Social-Democratic Workers Party–Bolshevik faction." To demonstrate the Bolsheviks' drastic break with the "reformist" Socialists of the West as well as with the Mensheviks, Lenin prevailed at the Seventh Party Congress (not without protests from some Bolsheviks) in having the name changed to the "Communist Party (of Bolsheviks)." The change was designed to emphasize that while the Bolsheviks remained Socialists and Marxists, they repudiated the name allegedly stolen

And yet if the Party's composition and its function have changed, the spirit of its organization and its professed aims still remain based on the principles postulated by Lenin in 1902, fought for and evolved by him in 1903 and in the succeeding years. Democratic centralism: i.e., strict discipline and unquestioned and absolute authority of the central organs of the Party, remain the official dogma for the six to seven million Party members, just as they were for a few thousands before the Revolution. The Party is still officially the vanguard of the working class, and as such it cannot be content just to express and execute what the masses want: its official aim is to propel them to what they "*really*" want (i.e., what they *ought to* want), and as such it is the teacher and censor of the people. Officially, again, socialism in Russia has been achieved, but the final goal of the Party remains as it was in 1903—further expansion, and strengthening of socialism, and, eventually, its transformation into communism where "from each according to his ability, to each according to his needs" will become the basis of social relations. Thus the split personality of the Communist Party—the party of conspiracy—in power; the champion of the oppressed, now an organization thoroughly bureaucratized, its high officials enjoying the privileges and perquisites of good living; the party aiming to bring about the most absolute and perfect democracy, which is yet organized with the strictest discipline and lack of inner democracy surpassing that of the most rigorous military organizations and religious orders.

The Communist Party of the U.S.S.R. is, then, many things. It is certainly not a political party in the American, English, or French sense of the word. It does not seek and solicit members the way a democratic party does. To gain membership in the Party is an achievement and privilege. There is a period of probation, and any member who fails to live up to the standard of behavior set for the Party member, whether in his public or private life, faces expulsion. In theory, even the rank-and-file member is an "activist"—a man who takes a leading part in public activities of his city, town, or village, who on any job is an example to his fellow workers in industry and diligence, who has at least a rudimentary knowledge of Marxism-Leninism and hence is capable of explaining political situations in his country and the world at large. The Bolshevik is, then, expected to be a *superior citizen*, if not a superior type of human being. There are many descriptions of this idealized version of Party member in Soviet literature. In Sholokhov's *Upturned Virgin Soil* [2] the author describes the

by "opportunistic" and non-Marxist socialist parties, and by their new name emphasized *revolutionary* and non-reformist Marxism and socialism. At the Nineteenth Party Congress the parenthesis "(of Bolsheviks)," so full of history, disappeared from the Party's name, which is now officially the "Communist Party of the U.S.S.R."

[2] Published in the U.S. under the title *Seeds of Tomorrow.*

struggle for collectivization in a small Cossack village. The period is that of the great collectivization drive of the late twenties and beginning thirties. The Party representatives encounter all sorts of opposition in their attempt to persuade the peasants to join in a collective: sabotage by the rich peasants, "wrecking" activities of the emissaries of counterrevolution, and simply ignorance and attachment to their own land on the part of the mass of peasants. One *non*-Party man stands out in helping the Party officials to overcome these obstacles and to make the peasants see the justice and wisdom of pooling their land and cattle in a communal organization. At the end of the book this patriotic Soviet citizen is invited, as a reward, to join the Party. He begs off for the moment, saying that he is still not worthy of membership in the Party of Lenin and Stalin, because whenever he sees his cow, now a part of the communal herd, he still has a twinge of regret that his property has been "communalized." The old Adam of bourgeois mentality is not entirely dead and until he is laid to rest, the new Communist man cannot take his place!

The process of indoctrination begins not too long after the cradle, with the organization of the Little Octobrists following which Soviet children may at nine (!) join the Young Pioneers. But the burden of indoctrination of the young falls upon the *Komsomol*, the League of Communist Youth, with its membership ranging from the age of fourteen to twenty-six. An organization patterned in its structure upon the Party itself, and strictly controlled by it, the Komsomol is even more numerous, having over fifteen million members. The organization has its congresses and central committee. Though, as their relative size indicates, by no means all of the Komsomol graduates join the Party, the former is the main recruiting ground for the ruling group.

Totalitarianism is especially watchful in indoctrinating the young. And the young are perhaps less convinced by paper theories than by the romanticism of action, of working and playing together. Hence to the Komsomol have been addressed the special calls for action, as during the First Five Year Plan, during the War, when the membership in it grew by leaps and bounds in the Armed Forces, and most recently when the call went out to settle and cultivate "virgin land" in Kazakstan and elsewhere. Physical culture and paramilitary training emphasize the "activist" character of the Komsomol. It is definitely *not* merely a discussion group, or an assembly of political sympathizers of a "grown-up" party like the Young Conservatives or the Young Republicans.

In brief, the mystique of Communism is propagated from the earliest days. It is a mystique of an active and devoted life—devoted to the service of the Party and the Soviet Fatherland. The young Komsomol member is supposed to be a junior replica of the image of the Communist: enthusiastic, eternally watchful (against the enemies of the Party and the state), and joyfully creative and enterprising at whatever post he finds himself in.

This mystique of Communism, again strange in an ideology claiming its descent from the most rationalistic and materialistic creed of the nineteenth century, is very deeply ingrained in the official myth. The Communists, as the popular saying has it about the Seabees in this country, are supposed to be able to do the impossible in only a little longer while than it takes them to do the difficult. The Communist is a dedicated builder of a new society and a new life. He is a man whose mind is free of superstitions about private property and religion, a perfect repository of the scientific truths inherent in Marxism-Leninism. So much for the official picture, the picture the Party presents especially to its ancillary youth organizations, the Pioneers and the Komsomol, which are designed to train young devotees for its membership. The actual picture is more complicated.

The concept of the Communist Party emphasizes that it is the party of workers. In the early days before the Revolution, while most of the leaders came from the intelligentsia, the bulk of membership was in fact found among the factory workers. After the Revolution, when the Party was in power, it still put a premium upon recruitment among workers. The Party was now governing a predominantly rural country yet it shrank from admitting too many peasants into its ranks. They were a "hostile class element." The Bolsheviks in order to govern had to employ tens of thousands of former tsarist officials, engineers, officers, etc. Yet these also as a group were debarred from membership. In the rules about admission to Party membership until the middle thirties one finds inherent the theory of what might be called hereditary and occupational taint: except in unusual circumstances, no one who had been born into a middle-class environment, or who had at one time possessed real property, even if only a few acres, could be expected to become as trustworthy a Communist as a *real worker*, himself a son of a worker or of a landless peasant.[3] The more the prospective candidate was removed from the worker, the more difficult were the conditions for admission and the longer was the probationary period before full membership. Already in the early days there were voices on both sides of the question: The Workers' Opposition[4] cried as early as 1921 and 1922 that the Party and the country were run not by workers but by bureaucrats. Zinoviev and Kamenev in 1924 and 1925 exclaimed

[3] The injunction did not apply of course to the old Bolsheviks themselves, among whom could be found: Lenin sprung from a family of tsarist bureaucrats; Trotsky, son of a *kulak*, i.e., a prosperous farmer; Leonid Krassin, who had before World War I been an engineer and industrial manager; and even somebody like V. V. Ossinsky, whose real name was Obolensky, and who came from the famous princely family.

[4] See below, in this chapter.

that the rich peasants were penetrating the Party. On the other side Leonid Krassin, an early Commissar of Trade, an old Bolshevik but an engineer by profession, protested that a country like Russia could not be run without the help of a technical intelligentsia, and that the Party should not scorn the administrators, industrialists, and engineers. Yet the Party's attitude on qualifications for membership continued substantially unchanged into the thirties. The beginning of the great drive for industrialization and collectivization and the first Five Year Plan were bound to have an effect on the problem. In 1936 Stalin proclaimed that exploitation of man by man was extinguished in Russia. Socialism had been achieved and instead of *antagonistic* classes, two friendly classes now existed—the peasants and workers—and the intelligentsia was not like the old intelligentsia, the product of a class society, but came out of the working classes and hence was entirely trustworthy. The change in the attitude of diffidence toward the non-worker was coming about slowly even amidst the tremendous revolution that was transforming Soviet society and the vast purge that was decimating the old revolutionaries among the Bolsheviks.[5] The watershed was represented by the Eighteenth Party Congress, held in 1939. The discriminatory regulations about accepting new Party members from among the non-workers were abolished, and the attitude of diffidence toward the intellectuals, engineers, etc., was proclaimed to be non-Soviet.

The Party has thus abandoned both in practice and in theory social discrimination when it comes to accepting new members. With industrial growth and the passage of years, the Communists no longer feel as they most certainly did in the 1920's, that they are a garrison in a country peopled either by the class enemy or the ignorant and that consequently it is courting disaster to let the enemy or wavering elements into the ruling group. What does remain is the conviction that the broad basis of the Party must still remain the worker. Even amidst the most total terror and most absolute one-man dictatorship, the Bolsheviks paid more than lip service to this principle. Stalin expressed it when in a speech he compared the Communists to Antaeus of Greek mythology: Antaeus was invincible when he was in contact with Mother Earth; only by lifting him up and depriving him of this strength-giving connection could Hercules defeat

[5] The late twenties and the early thirties thus witnessed quite a series of trials of engineers accused of "wrecking" the growing industry of the Soviet Union. Quite apart from the substance of the accusations, the trials represented a propaganda effort to picture the failures and privations of the First Five Year Plan as being largely caused by the "class enemy" rather than by its inherent defects. In the purges of the thirties, including the trials of the old Bolsheviks, a subsidiary charge leveled against the accused was the concealment of their class origin upon joining the Party. X joined the Party pretending to be the son of a poor peasant while in reality his father was an exploiting *kulak*. Not surprisingly, X, several years later while a high official, turned out to be a "wrecker" bent upon sabotaging the Soviet people's victorious march toward socialism!

him. And so this thoroughly totalitarian and oligarchically run organization
is forever seeking to have its contacts with the masses of the population.
Clearly an elite body, it still sees it supremely important to have the
workers and the collective farmers as the bulk of its membership. In his
report to the Twentieth Party Congress Khrushchev again pointed out that
unless the Party penetrates every sphere of national life, and unless it has
its members everywhere, both Soviet power and Russia's economic progress
will be endangered. The standard complaint reappears in Khrushchev's
remarks: The Party is becoming too bureaucratized, too distant from
the common worker: "It is an abnormal state of affairs that in a number
of branches of national economy a considerable number of Communists
working in these branches are doing work which is not directly connected
with the decisive sectors of production. For instance, at coal industry
enterprises there are nearly 90,000 Communists, *but only 38,000 are employed underground*. Over three million Party members and candidate
members live in rural areas, *but less than half of them are working directly
on collective farms, M.T.S.,[6] and state farms*." [7] And in an attempt to
revivify the Party that recalls the terrible sufferings and oppression of the
Stalin era, the Party boss once again emphasized the cardinal point of the
Communist creed: nothing can go well in Russia unless the Party is directly connected with it and unless every Party member has a sense of
mission and responsibility: "The C.P.S.U. is a governing party, and what
is done in our Soviet land is of vital interest for the Party as a whole and
for every Communist. *A Communist has no right to be an onlooker*." [8]
The attempt to spread its membership widely in the occupational sense
is emphasized in the renewed attempt to strengthen the Party organization in the villages. Traditionally, and still distrustful of the peasant and
peasant mentality, the Party believes that the performance of the agricultural sector of Russian economy, which still lags behind the industrial,
would improve if there were more Communists and more Party activity
in the countryside. The Twentieth Party Congress approved that every
machine tractor station—the focal point of a rural region's economy—
should have a Party organization. Again, the problem and proposed solution are nothing new. The beginning of the great collectivization drive of
1928-29 was signalized by thousands of Party activists' and agitators' being
sent out from the cities to the villages to explain to, to cajole, and, as it
turned out in most cases, to coerce, the peasants into pooling their land
and cattle in collective farms.

The injection of the Party into the most crucial sectors of the nation's

[6] Machine Tractor Stations.

[7] The italics are mine.

[8] My italics.

economy has been paralleled by saturation with Party members of the most important segments of the power structure. [It goes without saying now that a vast majority of high-ranking officers in the Army are now card-carrying Communists.] The situation is thus drastically different from the days of the Civil War and the twenties, when a majority of officers were still outside the Party circle, many of them still veterans of the tsarist army, and when the institution of the political commissar was created largely to watch over the apolitical officer. The security organs have always been the part of the state apparatus most heavily saturated with Party members, and in the early days of the regime they were, at the higher level, a special preserve for the old Bolsheviks.

The story of the changing national composition of the Bolsheviks is another interesting sidelight of the changing function of the Communist Party. Along with other revolutionary movements in pre-World War I Russia, the Bolsheviks drew heavily, especially within their leading circles, on the national minorities within the tsarist empire. It is not surprising that disproportionate numbers of Jews, Poles, Letts, Georgians and Armenians flowed into the ranks of the revolutionary movement.[9] [The national character of the Party immediately after the Revolution and throughout the twenties continued to reflect the numerically disproportionate contribution that the erstwhile persecuted minorities and nations had brought into the Bolshevik Party. The trend began to be reversed with the growing ascendance of Stalin.] A Georgian by birth who to his death spoke Russian with an accent, Stalin became in effect an exponent of Great-Russian chauvinism within the Party. In the struggle for leadership, first against Trotsky and then against the so-called Left Opposition,[10] the Stalinist faction was not above using anti-Semitic arguments capitalizing on the fact that the "left" leaders, Trotsky, Kamenev, Zinoviev, and many of their supporters were Jews. The purges of the thirties fell with particular vehemence upon non-Russian Communists. The Party had now clearly embraced Great-Russian nationalism, and what was implicit in Communism before now became explicit: the continuation and intensification both within the country and externally of Russian imperialism.

In the early days of Soviet power a fugitive Hungarian or Polish Communist would be welcomed in the Soviet Union and quite often pass into a high Party or even state position. In the mid and late thirties the majority of these honored guests were liquidated, often after an absurd charge that they were spies for the very governments from which they had fled.

---

[9] If any generalization is possible then it could be stated that the Bolsheviks were more "Russian" in their leadership and composition than their rivals the Mensheviks, and, insofar as the leadership was concerned, than the Social Revolutionaries, the representatives *par excellence* of the peasants.

[10] See below, pp. 563 ff.

While the purge hit the Party hard as a whole, it was particularly ferocious in the Ukraine and the Central Asian republics. By the end of the thirties the Party was overwhelmingly and disproportionately Great-Russian in its composition. One expert concludes that numerically the Party was especially strong in Russia proper and in Transcaucasia, weaker in the Ukraine, and especially in Byelorussia and in the Central Asian republics, and presumably even in these last Great Russians accounted for a considerable proportion of its membership.[11] The trend continued unabated until Stalin's death. While victory over the Germans was officially the triumph of all nationalities of the Soviet Union, it was to the Russian nation in particular that Stalin raised his toast at the famous victory celebration at the Kremlin in 1945. The last years of the tyrant's life witnessed a renewed campaign against the alleged nationalist aberrations among the non-Russian nationalities, and a clearly officially sponsored anti-Semitic campaign.

A fuller story of these events belongs to a discussion of social changes in Russia. What should be stressed is that the Communist Party has become predominantly Russian. It is an ironic fact that the Party that claims to represent the proletariat of the whole world, and in its ideology the humanistic tradition of all mankind, conducted in the late 1940's a deliberate campaign against cosmopolitanism and for, in effect, Russian chauvinism. The years that have passed since Stalin's death have brought some changes in the nationality policy of the Party. Russian chauvinism has become muted. In the local Party organizations, especially in the Ukraine, more prominence is given to the natives. It is impossible to say how far this policy has been reflected in the national distribution of Party members. It is clear, however, that the Russian predominance within the Communist Party as a whole is here to stay. One factor that worked against Beria in his struggle for Party leadership was undoubtedly his non-Russian origin. And Russian nationalism, as well as its broader version, Soviet patriotism, remains one of the leitmotifs of the Party.

The evolution of the character of the Communist Party and the distribution of its membership among various social and national groups already throw a considerable light on the role of the Party in Soviet society. But in what sense are its some seven million members the "governing party," as phrased by Khrushchev? To be sure, *all* office holders in Russia in every branch at every level of government are either Party members or in fact nominees of the Party. To be sure, *all* political and economic decisions in Russia are made either by the Party directly, or indirectly through the state organs staffed and led by Party members. But, as distinguished

[11] Merle Fainsod, *How Russia Is Ruled*, Cambridge, 1953, p. 229.

from the small group at the top, be it the Politburo, the Presidium, or the Central Committee, how do the millions of individual members "govern"? And what is the basis of their power as a party?

We have seen the idealized concept of the Party member, and we shall see in the next section how an individual Party member fits into the machine of Party organization. Here we want to define the personality and the role of the Party member in Soviet society. For all the machinery of terror and police, for all the armed might of the state, political power rests in Russia, in some sense, upon these some seven million members. If their sense of identification with the Party weakens or disappears, if the Party member who is a trade unionist thinks of himself mostly as a unionist, the one who is an officer mostly as an army man, and so on, then the structure of monolithic totalitarianism will be weakened beyond recovery. History is full of examples of revolutionary parties that carried through victorious revolutions and ruled for a while until their revolutionary élan weakened or degenerated and they themselves atrophied, eventually yielding to new social or political forces. The regime has always boasted and boasts today, forty years after the November coup d'état, that in the Communist Party there is still enshrined the *Revolution*; that the revolutionary regime has not given way to a military dictatorship or a bureaucratic clique, that the Communist Party—the spirit of Revolution—not only reigns but rules.[12] An impartial observer will not accept the regime's self-estimation. He will point out that Russia is in fact ruled by a clique, or, today, by several cliques, of Party bureaucrats and that the high idealism of the Revolution has often given way to disenchantment, cynicism, and, in the high places, cynical enjoyment of the fruits of victory and power. But he will also be forced to admit that there has been some truth in the regime's boast: the Party's composition has changed, its rule has become vested in dictators and oligarchies, but the Communist Party, even during the worst periods of oppression and terror, has remained the catalyst of the vital forces in Russian society. It has led the Soviet Union through enormous economic growth and to the position of a great world power. The Party has often succumbed to corruption and terror, but never to lassitude. And if the Party is to continue to be the vital force in Russia, then the rank-and-file members must continue to see in their Party card something meaning-

[12] It is interesting to note how the Communists have clung to the democratic and progressivistic symbolism. Their periodical organs have traditionally borne names like: *Forward, Truth, Worker's Cause*, etc. Their propaganda, even at times of the greatest terror in the Soviet Union, has always been couched in terms of democratic and humanitarian trends bringing to mind the dynamic, forward-moving character of the movement. And those who are, or who are alleged to be, opposed to the Soviet regime are branded not as revolutionaries, but as *counterrevolutionaries*, implying that they are not only traitors but people who stupidly and vainly oppose the inevitable march of history.

ful beyond an acknowledgment of status and an open door to personal success.

["A Communist has no right to be an onlooker." The individual member must have a sense of mission.] Is this as true today as it was in the days of the Revolution, and in the days following it? The average member of the Party throughout the twenties was still very much of a revolutionary. Any party in power will attract careerists, and even pure opportunists, but in its general tone the Communist Party of the earlier years was still very much like a religious order with a special mission. An average member, even if a laborer with no formal education, was still assumed to be something of an intellectual, with a knowledge of the principles of Marxism and an acquaintance with the politics and economy not only of Russia but of the capitalist world as well. In theory no Communist, no matter what his official position or formal salary, was supposed to live on a scale surpassing the income of the average skilled worker. Marxism in its most theoretical aspect was still very much a live force in Party life. The great struggle for power that took place following Lenin's death was accompanied by the protagonists' tossing citations from Marx, Engels, and Lenin at each other. Not only Party congresses but small Communist cells debated the theoretical as well as practical aspects of such problems as whether socialism could be fully realized in Russia before a proletarian revolution took place in the West; whether a social revolution could succeed a national one in China and what the role of the Communists should be in it, etc. [Of freedom of discussion, in the wide sense of the word, there was always very little in the Communist Party, but there was certainly a lot of *ideological* excitement, which must have seeped down to the humblest member.] The Party, then, in the earliest days of the regime was bound by the cohesive force of ideology and the sense of mission both in Russia and in the world at large. This embryonic political culture enabled the Communists to preserve their power, while still weak numerically, first against their Civil War foes, and then in a country beginning to recover from the ravages of the wars, and still weak and rather primitive in its economy.

The ascendancy of Stalin, which must be marked as definitive from the Fourteenth Party Congress in 1925 and as absolute from the Sixteenth Congress in 1930, brought a different emphasis. The age of discussion, of ideological fervor, was over. What replaced it was the fascination of concrete tasks, the gigantic enterprise of collectivizing Russian agriculture and industrializing Russia. The average Party member in 1930 already felt the tightening of Party discipline and the beginning of relentless terror, which was directed against anybody who opposed the dictator. In the country at large terroristic measures were in full swing against the recalcitrant peasants. But for all the sufferings and famines and privations the Party had a new and concrete task to uphold its élan: the vision of a Russia full of factories, of manufactured goods, with all the major means of production really socialized—a gigantic step in the realization of socialism. It is doubtful that any society in modern times has undergone such a shock of privation, of a lowered standard of living, and of oppression as did Russia during the years 1928 to 1933 without overthrowing the regime that was causing the sufferings. The tightness of police controls does not provide the entire explanation. Part of it must be found in the fact that throughout the terrible years the ruling order—the Communist Party—could still operate with zeal and cohesion inspired by the awesome task.

The ability of Stalin to push the country and the Party close to the brink of disaster and yet to avoid a catastrophe was vividly demonstrated again in the middle and late thirties when, while the economic situation was considerably improved (over the conditions of the early thirties) and industrialization was gathering momentum, terror of unprecedented proportions gripped the party and society.[13] But aside from terror, the Communist Party was kept as a functioning organism by the magnitude of the task still at hand and by the knowledge that to slacken in the effort toward economic power would be to risk defeat in a war that was clearly approaching. To the incentive of socialist construction the regime added the note of Soviet—and even plain Russian—patriotism. Russia's past was rehabilitated. No longer was Russia's history to be presented, as it had been in the twenties by official Marxist historians, as a story of backwardness and oppression. The Bolsheviks were now cast in the role of the continuators of the great figures of Russia's past, like Peter the Great. The Russian nation was allowed to have had a great history, with some of the most tyrannical tsars being presented as having played a "progressive" role for their time. In other words, through the most trying times the Communist Party could still play a leading role, and through its existence assure the regime and the state of a degree of cohesion. The second World War and its immediate aftermath recharged the Party with patriotic élan. The struggle against the invader and then the reconstruction of the ravaged country were again the kind of aims to spur the Communists, to give them some feeling that they were still a "governing party" and not onlookers.

[13] Incidents illustrating the extent of terror were given by Stalin's right-hand man Zhdanov at the Eighteenth Party Congress in 1939 when the most acute phase of terror had been concluded, and the regime had piously denounced its excesses. In some Party organizations regular quotas were set for the percentage of "wreckers" and "spies" that had to be discovered in the Party membership. In one district hysterical Communists would provide themselves with medical certificates testifying that Comrade X, because of the poor state of his physical and mental health, could not conceivably become a tool of the class enemy! Stalin himself acknowledged that some errors had been made.

In some sense the Communist Party through its long years in power has been like an athletic team that preserves its morale throughout all the privation of training, and despite all the bullying by the coach or manager, as long as the aim is concrete and visible, and the performance of the team satisfactory. But if there is no game in sight, or the discipline and privations are obviously excessive for the desired purpose, the spirit of rebellion or sullen apathy replaces that of purpose. That in some way has been the story of the Communist Party in the last years of Stalin's rule. The Party had long before ceased to be a revolutionary corps, a handpicked elite of activists. It was, and it is now, composed mostly of people who have grown up under the Soviet regime and for whom the old ideological struggles and issues have no meaning. The asceticism of old days and the feeling of a special mission are also gone. Russia has been modernized and industrialized, and an average Russian does not have to be a fervent Communist or a reader of Marx to feel that it is a good thing for his country to produce more steel or to have more institutions of higher learning. During the last generation Russia has leaped into the front rank of modern industrial states. But this success of Communism has by the same token created its greatest problem: What is the rationale for the iron discipline within the Party, or for privations in terms of the standard of living, if the main struggle has been won?

The fondest dream of the Communist leaders of a generation ago was to create an administrative and technical elite that should not yield anything in terms of competence and skill to its Western counterpart. That elite has now been created and its members comprise a large part of the Communist Party membership. But by the same token, why should an engineer or an administrator or a factory manager who is also a Communist have aspirations different from those of his Western confrere? In what sense is he different *because he is a Communist?* To be sure, though socialism has been realized in Russia the officially proclaimed goal still remains ahead: communism. But how realistic or how desirable is it to an average member of the Party to conceive a society where the state will "wither away" and where "from each according to his ability, to each according to his needs" will be the fundamental law? What does Communism have to offer now to justify further privations, the continuance of the police state, the stringent duties inherent in being a member of the Party? The desirable achievements of Communism from the point of view of a convinced Communist—public ownership of the means of production, the widespread system of social security, modernization and industrialization of Russia—do not have to be fought for any more. They are, and they will go on of their own momentum even if the Communist Party disappears tomorrow.

The problem that faces the Communist Party is, then, the problem of preserving cohesion and the sense of purpose without which the Party, though it would continue to exist, would degenerate in importance and would ultimately yield as the ruling organ to some other force—the bureaucracy, the army, or something else—with incalculable consequences for the whole Soviet system. The problem is not new. What marked its existence in Stalin's last years was the reign of terror exerted by the dictator. By the same token the degree of suppression exerted by the despot, while it masked the crisis deepened its nature, and it was inevitable that with Stalin gone and a more fluid situation confronting the leadership in the country and in the Communist Party, the crisis would appear with full force.

Another part describes in some detail how the late dictator appraised the nature of the crisis in the Party and the means that he proposed to undertake in order to deal with it. To his successors it appeared imperative to lift, as the first step, the excessive amount of terror exerted within and without the Party by Stalin and to demonstrate to the rank and file of the members that while the Party would continue to be run according to "democratic centralism" i.e., from the top, a certain degree of latitude and freedom would be allowed in intra-Party relationships. When the Presidium of the Party took their seats on the opening day of the Twentieth Party Congress in February 1956 they were greeted as during the Stalin days by the servile applause of the delegates, but Nikita Khrushchev admonished the members to act with more dignity and restraint since they were masters and not servants of the Presidium! Nothing could be more symbolical of the changed times. Under Stalin a frenetic applause for the Leader was the prescribed form at a Party Congress, and his closest subordinates would receive ovations, the intensity of which was proportionate to the official's closeness to the dictator.[14] Apart from the official etiquette the charted course of the new leaders of the Party became obvious from two speeches by Khrushchev, first his official report as the First Secretary of the Party and then his speech to the closed session of the Congress in which he berated the late Joseph Stalin and attacked the "cult of personality," a euphemism for the craven worship of the despot in which Khrushchev along with all other Communists had to engage for more than a generation. The same leitmotif appeared in other speeches at the Congress.

[14] Thus at the Sixteenth Party Congress in 1930 Stalin was greeted according to the official transcript by "loud, long lasting applause turning into a long ovation; shouts 'Hurrah'; the whole Congress greeting him standing up." Molotov and Kaganovich and a few others received "long applause," while a mere member of the Central Committee in good standing (with Stalin) had to be content with "applause." In the subsequent Congresses the art and nuances of "spontaneous ovations" become considerably more developed.

By hacking at the Stalin legend the leaders were in effect undermining their own position, for had they not been the most servile helpers of the despot, and did they not reveal the abject terror in which the Party, along with the whole society, had lived for more than twenty years? Why? Part of the reason must be sought in the developments in the Party leadership just before and after Stalin's death. But beyond those reasons it is clear that the partial denigration of Stalin had a wider and more profound reason. Because of the developments we shall discuss later, it is no longer possible to exert, either in Russia or among the foreign Communists, the degree of terror with which the late dictator had ruled. If the Communist Party, the Soviet state, indeed the whole Communist world, is to be held together, then a new spirit, a new sense of mission, a new conception of purpose has to be poured into the Communists. What Khrushchev and other leaders attempted to say could be translated as follows: ["Look, Communism is not terror, forced labor camps, and the whole nation prostrate before one man. Those things were just an accident traceable to the personality of one man. Communism is a live, creative doctrine; it requires discipline and privations to be sure, but not servility and complete negation of legal and rational processes. We as Communists still have great tasks to perform, and we can perform them best if we return to the Leninist purity of our Party and its doctrine."] In other words, in place of terror, though its *moderate* use can never be abandoned by a totalitarian regime, the Soviet leaders are trying to revive ideological fervor and a sense of mission. Khrushchev quoted approvingly the criticism of Party officials by the great Soviet poet, Mayakovsky. Though written many years ago, it has become particularly applicable to the Stalin and post-Stalin era: "They have rooted themselves in their own spot and see nothing beyond their own nose. Having passed his exams on Communism according to the book, having learned 'the isms' by heart, he has finished forever with thoughts about Communism. What is the use of looking further? Sit and wait for the circular. You and I do not have to think if the leaders think." It might be added that under Stalin it was not always safe "to look further." The current line is to encourage initiative of Party members and to appeal especially to the youth. Great tasks like the settlement and agricultural development of new virgin lands are designed, quite apart from their economic desirability, to rekindle the sense of mission among young Communists.

It might be objected that the post-Stalin leaders want to have their cake and to eat it too. They do not dream of abandoning the substance of the police state or of replacing oligarchical rule by real Party democracy. At the same time they want all the advantages that in a democratic system accrue from free discussion and individual initiative. In a sense this has been a perennial dilemma of the Soviet system, hence the alternative periods, even under Stalin, of relative liberalization, and of extreme terror. What makes the present system different is that there have been economic and social changes in Russia that impinge upon the Party and that make a return to full-fledged Stalinism impractical.

The role of the Party as the guiding force of the Soviet state and society is, then, in a state of flux. There is in the foreseeable future no alternative but the rule of the Communist Party. But to repeat, if the Party does not recover its vitality and *esprit de corps*, it will lose ground to other social forces, and other institutions, like the army, and eventually the point will be reached when it would be "a governing party" only in name and its members would feel a prior loyalty to other social and political groups with which they were associated. It is often said that the monopoly of education and propaganda enjoyed by the regime can ward off such dangers, and can continue to bring up generations of Communist fanatics. But the most powerful and penetrating propaganda machinery in the world will still be ineffective if social and economic conditions make its postulates unrealistic and distant from the circumstances of life of the persons being propagandized. The regime is quite explicit in its concept of the Communist Party. It wants an active and ideologically motivated elite, or, as Mikhail Suslov, member of the Presidium, stated at the Twentieth Party Congress: "The Party does not admit all who declare their wish to join its ranks. It selects for itself the most advanced and active people; it regulates admission in conformity with the tasks facing it at one or another stage of its work. During the industrialization and collectivization of agriculture, the Party admitted mainly workers and peasants; during the years of war preferential admittance to the Party was given to whose who were at the front line. It is hardly necessary to prove that at present, when the problem of a steep improvement of material benefits is being solved, it is wise to lay stress primarily on the admittance of the direct producers of these benefits —workers and peasants." But will the new members, under changed social and economic conditions, respond as readily as of old to indoctrination and the old appeals of Communism? Suslov himself—and it is well worth noting that for many years he had been in charge of propaganda and agitation for the Party—gives examples of how boring the old stock in trade of Communist propaganda is to the average member. Thus he quotes approvingly the criticism of a rank-and-file member: "I am now in my thirteenth year of study of the history of the Party, and for the thirteenth time propagandists are talking about the Bund. Have we no more important problems than the criticism of the Bund? We are interested in the problems of our MTS, *rayon,* and *oblast. We want to live in the present and future.*[15] Yet our propagandists are so stuck in the bog of the affairs of the Narodniki and Bund that they cannot get out of it." But if Party members are bored by the stories of what was after all the heroic period of the Party, are they likely to be more interested in the intricate theories of Marx and Engels? If they begrudge the time spent at countless educational and prop-aganda meetings are they likely to remain attached to the Party that forces them to go through what are now largely meaningless motions? They want to live in the present and the future as engineers, students, workers, men with concrete needs and aspirations, and they will remain attached to the Party only if the Party shows that it responds to those needs and aspira-tions.

The future of the Communist Party is thus bound up with the changes the whole Soviet society is undergoing. And in turn this future is bound up with the wider question whether Communism has still something to offer to Soviet society or whether it, instead of the state, will "wither away." By relaxing one of the traditional levers of power in a totalitarian society, terror, the regime hopes to use more effectively the supplementary mecha-nism of propaganda and indoctrination. It explains to the millions of Party members that Communism is not blind obedience or bureaucratic self-satisfaction or learning by rote, but healthy self-criticism and accomplish-ment of great tasks of socialist construction. The success or failure of the new campaign will go a long way in determining the future of politics in the U.S.S.R.

The Power Structure

In its structure and the spirit of its organization the Communist Party bears an indelible stamp of having been born as the party of conspiracy, pitted against the resources of a powerful state, and forced to operate in secrecy and illegality. Today it is the ruling party, a body of several million members that monopolizes all political power in the Soviet Union, and yet its organization preserves the tone inherited from the years of illegality, of the struggle against overwhelming odds, of the years when the Party, in power but still a small group, was transforming the social and economic character of the vast country. The character of the struggle many years ago imposed upon the Party the need of deliberating in secret. Today, though the Party is no longer a group of hunted conspirators but the ruler, still, insofar as the deliberations of its highest bodies are concerned, the Presidium or the Central Committee, it reaches its decisions in secret, the mass of the membership and the world outside learning only the final

[15] My italics.

conclusions—and not always even that. The conditions of the revolutionary struggle were presented by Lenin in 1902 and 1903 as necessitating iron discipline and firm control of the central organs. But the victory of the Bolsheviks and then, by their own account, of socialism in Russia, has not weakened the discipline nor relaxed, up to now, the iron grip of the central organs over the whole organization. The early Bolsheviks could not have bothered, even if they had wanted to, about the niceties of the democratic process. Terror, though not considered by them as a major means of reaching their objectives, was still held to be legitimate and useful under certain circumstances. And terror both within and without the Party was never used as extensively as during the period when the Communist rule was unchallenged in the 1930's, and, though relaxed, it was not abandoned either in theory or in practice by Stalin's successors.[16]

Thus the early pattern has perpetuated itself, and though in recent years it has begun to give way under the pressure of new social forces being generated in Russia, the "ruling party" is still the party of conspiracy.

The statements above cover the general behavior of the Communist Party in the forty years that it has been in power. Yet within the general pattern there have been considerable variations in detail: periods when there was savage struggle for power within the ruling oligarchy; times when the hand of one man lay heavily upon the whole organization; times when there was, at least, a semblance of inner party democracy; other times when terror and intimidation restrained a member of the Politburo as well as a rank-and-file worker.

Like the Soviet state institutions, so also the Party institutions and laws exhibit a twofold character. The language of the statute, the concept of organization, is, more often than not, democratic. The reality behind very often limits or negates the democratic phraseology. Thus the cardinal

---

[16] In his speech to the Twentieth Congress denouncing Stalin, Khrushchev contrasted the circumstances justifying terror as practiced by Lenin with Stalin's illegitimate use of the technique: ". . . Lenin without hesitation used the most extreme methods against the enemies. Lenin used such methods, however, only against actual class enemies and not against those who blunder, who err, and whom it was possible to lead through ideological influences and even retain in the leadership. Lenin used severe methods only in the most necessary cases, when the exploiting classes were still in existence and were vigorously opposing the Revolution, when the struggle for survival was decidedly assuming the sharpest forms, even including a civil war. Stalin, on the other hand, used extreme methods and mass repressions at a time when the Revolution was already victorious, when the Soviet state was strengthened, when the exploiting classes were already liquidated and socialist relations were rooted solidly in all phases of national economy, when our party was ideologically consolidated and had strengthened itself both numerically and ideologically. It is clear that here Stalin showed in a whole series of cases his intolerance, his brutality, and his abuse of power." Yet the speaker himself and his colleagues, despite the fact that "the Revolution was already victorious" applied methods not much different from Stalin's against Lavrenti Beria and his associates. Beria and his real or alleged associates were denounced as guilty the day after their arrest, tried in secret, and executed.

organizational principle of the Party is "democratic centralism." As defined
in the Party statutes its meaning is: "a) Election of all Party governing
bodies from bottom to top. b) Periodic accountability of Party bodies to
their Party organizations. c) Strict Party discipline and subordination of
the minority to the majority. d) The decisions of higher bodies are unconditionally binding upon lower ones." [17] There is nothing in the bald
statement of the principle with which a democratically minded person
would quarrel. But the crucial word is "election." Here our usage of the
term and its meaning within the Communist Party differ sharply. Just as
in the election to the Supreme Soviet, or for that matter to any legislative
body in the Soviet Union, there is only one list; thus the pattern of election to any Party office is monotonously simple: one candidate, or one
list, and a unanimous election. It is likely that a small Party cell of a few
members would be free to elect any one of them to be the secretary of the
cell, but—and in this "but" there is the whole story of the Party structure
—his election would not be binding until and unless it received the sanction of a higher Party organ. When we reach the upper levels of the Party
organization the picture becomes even clearer. Nobody in the Soviet Union, at least for a generation, could have imagined the election of a secretary of a sizable Party unit, be it territorial or a great factory, as the result
of a free play of sentiments and interests of the members of the given
organization. The secretary of the Party, say in the city of Krasnodar, will
be selected by a higher Party organization, most likely by the central secretariat of the Communist Party of the U.S.S.R. At the time of his selection, he will not necessarily be a resident of the area. Quite likely he will
be doing Party work thousands of miles away from Krasnodar, which he
may have never visited in his life. An emissary of the central organs will
appear before the Party committee of Krasnodar with the "suggestion"
that Comrade X be elected, and elected he will be unanimously! The same
procedure applies with variations to the bureaus, committees and other
organs of the Party at the local and national levels. To be pedantic, those
officials are *elected* by members of the given organization, but *selected* by
somebody else, the somebody else being in the last resort the dictator, or
the ruling oligarchy.

If the word "election" is a euphemism for something else, then the next
principle of democratic centralism, "periodic accountability of Party bodies
to their Party organizations," also requires an appraisal. Again, there is no
doubt that members of a small Party cell would ordinarily feel no com-
punction about criticizing or removing their secretary or their bureau (i.e.,
the executive committee) for inefficiency or corruption. When, however, it
comes to a "higher up"—an official who is a considerable Party functionary

[17] Quoted in *Current Soviet Policies*, ed. Leo Gruliow, New York, 1953, p. 29.

—criticism or removal will have to come from above. An institution of which the Soviets are very proud and which they cite very often as a proof of their superiority over the Western forms of democracy throws a glaring light on democratic centralism. This is the famous "samokritika," or self-criticism. As applied to Party organization, a typical example would be a letter by a worker to a local or national newspaper pointing out that the Party secretary in the factory is falling down on his job, or is a person of low moral standards, and inquiring why *the regional or central Party committee does not undertake a corrective action.* The letter will be published or spoken criticism allowed, but not before the responsible Party officials determine that there is enough substance in the accusation. What is most characteristic is the fact that the call is always for *superior* Party organization to take action. Our worker will seldom or never start agitating against the official within the Party organization and call for a free vote of members to remove or chastise the culprit. Again, it is an emissary of the higher Party organs who is to investigate and chastise. It hardly needs to be added that this form of self-criticism is not infrequently a put-up job to remove for political reasons somebody who has become suspect or inconvenient to the higher-ups. And if the person concerned is really in the upper levels of the Party hierarchy, say a regional or republic secretary, the chances are overwhelming that his liquidation, through self-criticism, is at the orders of the ruling hierarchy.

Democratic centralism has, thus, meant in practice centralism and domination of the Party by a small group at the top, which, *as long as it is united,* can and has been able to exercise an absolute sway over the whole vast body of the membership and hence over the U.S.S.R. The qualification is important, for as we shall see, the pattern might be altered only during periods when a serious breach occurred within the very top group—this group usually being smaller than the membership of the Central Committee and usually identical with the Politburo (renamed "Presidium" at the Nineteenth Congress in 1952). Then politics, or rather politicking, could take place within the Party, and various factions reflecting the views of the leaders would try to gain adherents at the Central Committee and local levels, offering in effect competing ideological and political platforms, with the consequence that, as in earlier times, heated debates and conferences would take place at the Party Conferences and Congresses. Some writers in referring to such periods, especially the years following the November Revolution and up to the beginning of Stalin's dictatorship (usually dated from the Fourteenth Party Congress in 1925), have seen in them an intra-Party democracy, which was then restrained and finally destroyed only by the iron hand of the dictator. Yet it is stretching the term a great deal to see in disagreements and struggles within a narrow elite an essential part of the democratic process. It is true that under Lenin those Party members who disagreed with the leader and the majority group in the Central Committee were not physically liquidated or instantly imprisoned, or forced to degrade themselves by humiliating recantations. Yet in most cases they were demoted from their Party posts and sent to diplomatic posts abroad, or to do Party work in remote parts of the U.S.S.R. What Stalin often accomplished through terror and arrest, his great predecessor often did through lesser chicanery and through persuasion. The return to Lenin's ways as advertised by Stalin's successors is a return to more humane, more rational ways of ruling the Party, but still ruling it undemocratically.

The problem of power in the structure of the Communist Party is then a subject of considerable fascination. How was it that a group of revolutionaries—people who, we are always told by social psychologists, are unstable, liable to be quarrelsome, and, as history always has shown, liable to fall out among themselves once the victory is secure—managed to preserve an organizational unity and over so vast a country? To pose the question thus is partly to answer it. For the magnitude of the task as well as of the danger held the Bolsheviks together. And before the instruments of terror and bureaucratic controls could be perfected by his successor, the Party had been held together by the extraordinary personality of Lenin. He had held his flock together not only during the wanderings in the wilderness of exile, the Revolution, and the Civil War, but also, what was even more difficult, during the first years in the promised land of absolute power and the beginnings of the recasting of Russia's economy and society. By his very success in being a moderate dictator, he laid the foundations for a thorough despotism.

The development of the power structure in the Party and the shifting role of the Party organs can best be studied in the light of the major crises that have shaken the Communist Party ever since its victory and the latest of which, a crisis of ideology, as well as a struggle for power, is still continuing as this is being written.

The first crisis, for all its undramatic resolution, and in spite of the fact that among the Bolsheviks it claimed no human sacrifices, was in a sense the most important one in the forty years that the Communist Party has been in power. For in breaking, though through fairly humane methods, the various factions and opposition groups in the Party, and reaffirming the organizational principles postulated in 1902 and 1903, Lenin cut off all the possibility that a different, democratic, spirit might begin to grow in the Party. The methods employed had none of the perfidy that Stalin exhibited in outmaneuvering the "Left Opposition" in 1924-25 and the Right Opposition in the late twenties. Certainly they had none of the bloodthirstiness and sadism of Stalin when he sent the old Bolsheviks, then already discredited and impotent, to their death by the thousands during the Great Purge. Yet the latter phenomena would not have been possible except for the developments in 1920-22 which determined that there could be no "loyal opposition" within the Communist Party; that any disagreement on political or ideological grounds would be branded by the prevailing group in the leadership as heresy, and then treason, and that the defeated faction would be forced to recant or face expulsion or worse. The crisis had as a far-reaching side effect Lenin's sanctioning the erection of an elaborate apparatus of Party bureaucracy that would help prevent the recurrence of dissidence and of his entrusting the leadership of it to Joseph Stalin, who in 1922 became the Secretary-General of the Communist Party.

The arena of the struggle was twofold: the Party Congress and the Central Committee. The Party Congress was then, as it is now officially, the sovereign organ of the Communist Party. During the first post-Revolutionary era the Congress was no longer the motley assembly it had been before, of a few exiles and revolutionaries who managed to get out of Russia to hold a conclave on foreign soil, nor was it yet the assembly of delegates summoned to worship and applaud the great man and his lieutenants that it was to become under Stalin. It was still a live and reasonably democratically elected body. Under Lenin it met every year, and, for all the dissonances and bitterness of debate, the magic personality and enormous prestige of Lenin was still sufficient to secure a majority for the leader's postulates and policies. But increasingly the focus of power was shifting to a much smaller group, the Central Committee elected by the Congress but liable to be more subservient to Lenin than the parent body. Those organs of the Party that were to be manipulated so skillfully by Stalin to secure his predominance—the Secretariat, the Organizational Bureau and the Party Control Commission—were during the period 1919-23 thought of as mainly of administrative importance, inferior to the Central Committee in fact as well as in theory. The Congress as the sovereign policy-determining body, and the Central Committee as the executive and policy-formulating organ, enjoyed real importance during Lenin's postwar leadership. Beginning with Lenin's incapacitating illness in 1922, their real political importance declined, until they eventually were to serve as additional tools of personal dictatorship of Stalin or of the oligarchy that succeeded him.

The issue of the struggle was nothing else than the character of the Soviet state being born, and consequently of the Communist Party that was guiding it. The Communist Party, as we observed before, inherited from Marxism its twofold character. It was the Party of revolution, of opposition to the state, the party that embraced the anarchistic slogans of complete equality, of abolition of all social distinction and rank and of the standing army. At the same time, and paradoxically, it was the party that believed in the creation of a modern industrialized state as a prerequisite to socialism. Such a state, especially under the conditions of Russia of 1920, required many things directly opposed to the anarchistic side of the postulates of Bolshevism, the postulates under which it won the Revolution and the Civil War. Instead of weakening the state and hence the central organs of the Party, the vision of an industrialized and socialist Russia required a strong state, hence the unchallengeable authority of the central Party organs. Instead of economic equality and socialism right away, it required economic stability and reconstruction and incentives for hard work. Instead of the dissolution of bureaucracy and the standing army, it required the erection of an administrative and planning machinery. Lenin very early perceived the necessity of abandoning the "campaign oratory" in which the Bolsheviks indulged during the Revolution and of facing the facts. When the Kronstadt sailors, who in the crucial days of the fall of 1917 had been the staunchest supporters of the Bolsheviks, revolted in 1921 and tossed in the face of the Bolsheviks the very same anarchistic slogans they themselves had employed, their uprising was mercilessly suppressed. In 1921 Lenin had sanctioned the New Economic Policy, which was premised on the belief that before Russia could advance toward socialism her economy must be reconstructed and hence private trade and private ownership in agriculture must be tolerated for an indefinite period of time. The same line of reasoning persuaded Lenin and, especially, Trotsky that the Red Army could not become a revolutionary mob but had to have officers and discipline, and that the factories had to have skilled workers and engineers and they in turn had to have salaries above the wages of a common laborer.

These common-sense conclusions were opposed by a number of Bolshevik leaders, not only because of the persistence in the Bolshevik ranks of anarchistic and egalitarian sentiments, but also because of their more reasonable belief that the ruling group among the Communists was already settling down in the enjoyment of power and its appurtenances, and was inclined to defer the realization of socialism to an indefinite future. As in all dissensions within the Communist Party, we find in those early struggles an inextricable mixture of the power drive and ideological and temperamental dissonances. It would take too long to give a reasonably full story of the early Party schisms. The most characteristic and important were those of the Workers' Opposition, which provides the best opportunity for study of the early structure of the Party and the ways then employed in managing it.

At the Eighth and Ninth Party Congresses in 1919 and 1920 there were

already voices decrying bureaucratization of the Party, admission of former
tsarist officers into the Red Army, etc. With the end of the Civil War the
discontent within the Party found an expression in a new movement sponsored by some Party leaders. The two most prominent names were those
of Alexandra Kollontai, an upper-class intellectual who had joined the
Bolsheviks,[18] and Alexander Shlyapnikov, a true proletarian in origin and
a member of the Central Committee. The Workers' Opposition had as its
first and most important postulate the plea that the trade unions should
be fairly independent of the state and the Party, that they should run the
economy of the country. As secondary postulates they advocated scaling
down the wage differential,[19] and democratization of the Party. Repeated
in the Workers' Opposition's propaganda was the charge that the Party
was run by an oligarchy and that the country freshly freed from the rule
of landlords and tsarist officials was in the process of getting a new official
caste of Communist functionaries.

Their position was condemned by Lenin, not unjustifiably, as being
anarchist-syndicalist rather than Marxian. At the Tenth Party Congress,
which met in 1921 in the shadow of the Kronstadt revolt, Lenin's position
that the trade unions should be autonomous but not independent of the
Party received overwhelming approval. Lenin's motion prevailed not only
against the Workers' Opposition, but also against the views of Trotsky,
who would have made explicit what was implicit in Lenin's motion and
what became an accepted maxim in Stalin's period, namely that the trade
unions are strictly subordinate to the Party and are to help carry out the
government's economic policies rather than to have any policies of their
own. Sentiments akin to those reflected by the opposition were strong
among the rank and file of the Party. Yet characteristically the Workers'
Opposition could muster only a handful of votes at the Congress when
the great prestige of Lenin was thrown against them, and they had almost
no support within the Central Committee. The Tenth Congress condemned the Workers' Opposition as a "syndicalist and anarchist" deviation
and forbade further propaganda of their ideas.

The dispute had its most concrete application in the adoption by the
Congress of a provision still in the Party statute in a revised form, stating
that a joint plenum of the Central Committee of the Party and its Control Commission could by a majority of two-thirds expel a member of the
Central Committee from his post or even from the Party. Thus was formalized a provision that enabled the Party oligarchy, without recourse to

[18] Mme. Kollontai gained notoriety also by her strenuous advocacy of free love, and
literary efforts dedicated to the same theme.

[19] Though from our point of view, or from that of the U.S.S.R. since the thirties,
Russia in the period under discussion was economically as close to an egalitarian society
as you can get.

the Congress, to deal summarily even with Party notables should they set themselves in opposition to the dominant fashion. This weapon was to be used frequently by Stalin. The Tenth and Eleventh Congresses sanctioned an extended purge of the Party and of its "anarchist and syndicalist" deviationists. Thus, what began as a common-sense position of Lenin's against extreme radicalism ended as the negation of any democratic opportunities in the Party, the consolidation of the position of the Central Committee, and the forging of the weapon of the Party purge, by which the leaders could always rid the Party of elements they did not desire. It is not accidental that at the same time Lenin entrusted the direction of the Party apparatus to a man he did not particularly like, but who among the top Party leaders showed the least propensity for ideological quarrels and the most for quiet organizational work. In 1922 Joseph Stalin, already a member of the Political and Organizational Bureaus, became the Secretary-General. The expectation was that he would bring order out of the chaos into which routine administrative affairs of the Party had fallen, and also that he would help curtail the factional strife the Tenth and Eleventh Congresses had demonstrated.

[Stalin's emergence as the top administrator of the Party was the culmination of an organizational career] Before 1922 he already belonged to the Party's Organization Bureau and had held various important political posts, chief among them the Commissariats of Nationalities and of the Workers' and Peasants' Inspection, the latter devised as a control organ to check the performance of Soviet administration. His rise to power coincided with and was partly based on the growing importance of the administrative and control organs within the Party and the state. An indefatigable worker, master of detail and routine, Stalin struck a vivid contrast with the rest of the first-rank Communist leaders, who were much more impressive as speakers or writers but lacked the patience or temperament to attend to dull administrative work. Within a short time the Secretariat of the Communist Party ceased to be a simple organization where a few people received provincial delegations and attended to the grievances and problems of various local Party organizations, and became the veritable nerve center of the Party. The Secretariat assumed the responsibility for instructional and propaganda work, it sent out emissaries to check on the performance of Party organizations. The Secretary-General was in a position to determine who was to head Party work in various organizations (except, during the first few years, for the capitals of Moscow and Leningrad), and his work gave him an enhanced opportunity to make wide contacts and recruit partisans among the important Communist activists. If, in addition to Stalin's supremacy in the Secretariat and the Organizational Bureau, is added his considerable influence in the Party Control Commission, the body charged with standing watch over the activities and performance of the Party members, then it becomes understandable how an ambitious and able man was capable of building a tremendous power base and the foundations for an absolute dictatorship.

But the explanation cannot be given entirely in terms of Stalin's mastery of the apparatus. At any time between 1922 and 1925 the Central Committee or the Party Congress could have dismissed Stalin from his powerful position as Secretary-General. None of those bodies was dominated as yet by Stalin. Shortly before his death, Lenin, irked by Stalin's rudeness to his wife, Nadezhda Krupskaya, and alarmed by the reports that Stalin was building a personal machine, did in fact propose the replacement of the Secretary-General in a letter that was certainly known to the Central Committee.[20] But none of the aspirants for Lenin's mantle could be enticed to take on the strenuous job of day-to-day administration of the Party. Among the Party leaders of secondary importance, Stalin did at the time enjoy a certain popularity. In the light of what was to happen later this reputation of Stalin in the years 1922-25 may appear incredible. But his views and activities were, as a matter of fact, of the kind to appeal to a Communist administrator. He appeared then as a man of moderate views, desirous of rebuilding the Russian economy before taking drastic steps, such as the expropriation of the peasants. In brief, he was the advocate of moderate social policies. While the others were planning grandiose foreign revolutions, Stalin, while all for the support of foreign Communists, directed attention primarily to the tasks of socialist construction in Russia.[21] In terms of personality, Stalin, for all his scheming propensities, had, so it seemed at the time, none of Trotsky's intellectual arrogance, or Zinoviev's and Kamenev's vacillation. He stood—and it is not surprising that so many Communists were taken in—as an advocate of Communist "normalcy," of moderate policies, neither too much to the left nor too much to the right, in brief, for the continuation of Lenin's policies and tactics. It is no accident that after Lenin's death it was mainly Stalin who inaugurated a veritable cult of the dead leader, who for all his faults had detested sycophancy and religious veneration of personalities.

For all its democratic phraseology the Communist Party was then, as it

[20] The new generation of Communists heard of it for the first time in Khrushchev's indictment of Stalin at the Twentieth Party Congress.

[21] Stalin's position on this issue, his famous "socialism in one country" plea, is almost invariably misrepresented. It is made to appear as if Stalin, in the period under discussion, was for the abandoning of the revolutionary work abroad, while his antagonist Trotsky believed that a socialist reconstruction of Russia must be postponed until after a world revolution. The position of neither man was that categorical and one-sided, and as a matter of fact there was but little difference between their real views on the subject. Once in opposition Trotsky was maneuvered into arguing that Stalin was betraying the revolution, an argument that further weakened Trotsky's position, for it gave Stalin an opportunity to present Trotsky's followers as adventurists who, instead of attending to concrete tasks at home, wanted to engage in dangerous adventures abroad.

is now, an organization calling for a united leadership.⟩ Stalin's management of the problem of succession combined all the elements necessary to
the guidance of a totalitarian movement: the seizure of the administrative
structure, a degree of acceptance and popularity among the Party activists,
and the erection of a quasi-religious cult of the departed leader that would
facilitate the acceptance of a new one. Within the highest circles of the
Party he skillfully exploited the distrust of the majority of the top Communist leaders toward Leon Trotsky. The latter, the leader of the Red
Army and Lenin's right hand during the Revolution and the Civil War,
aroused the admiration of certain circles of the Red Army, the Soviet youth
and foreign Communists. A brilliant and many-sided man, Trotsky proved
to be poorly equipped for the kind of infighting into which Communist
Party politics resolves itself at times of transition. To the Party hierarchy
he appeared as a potential Bonaparte of the Russian Revolution, a man
who was not "really" a Bolshevik, as he had rejoined Lenin only on the eve
of the Revolution, and all his enormous services to the cause did not diminish their envy and fear of his brilliant abilities. In contrast with Trotsky,
Stalin stood out as a solid but rather drab personality, capable through
hard work and attention to administrative detail of warding off the brilliant rhetoric and charismatic personality of the Commissar of War. It was
thus that the two senior Communist leaders Kamenev (a brother-in-law
of Trotsky) and Zinoviev joined with Stalin to provide the collective
leadership of the Party during Lenin's incapacity and after his death. The
triumvirate (in Russian *troika*) was the product of the fear of Trotsky and
of the assumption that through a division of leadership personal dictatorship could be avoided.

The story has often been told how Stalin maneuvered his allies into
committing themselves too far against Trotsky, and how he disposed of
them in turn with the help of the right wing of the Party, and how then,
in sole possession of power, he crushed his erstwhile right-wing allies in
1929-30.[22] But personalities and personal struggles provide only part of

[22] The discussion of Communist leaders and policies in terms of right and left wings
and deviations is likely to appear puzzling. Thus Bukharin, when he opposed Lenin
on the signing of the Treaty of Brest-Litovsk in 1918, was described as the leader of
the Left Communists. In 1929 and 1930 we find Bukharin denounced by Stalin's
faction as a "right opportunist" for his opposition to rapid collectivization. In line with
the usual semantic jugglery at which the Communists are so adept, the Party's course,
i.e., the course of the prevailing faction of the Party, is *always* correct and *always* in
the middle. Those Communists who are fearful that the policies are too drastic or
rapid are denounced as the "right opportunists"; those who at other times believe them
to be too cautious are branded as "left-wing adventurists." Most of the proposals
advanced by Trotsky, Kamenev, and Zinoviev in 1924-25 and decried by Stalin as
senselessly "left," were put into effect by him in *much more drastic form* in 1929-30
but as emanating from himself alone. These policies were no longer either "left" or
"right"—they were "correct," and any criticism of them (often in the very words of
the Stalin of 1925) was piously described as "right-wing" opportunism.

the story. What is necessary for the understanding of the mechanics of Party politics is the realization that personal factors, ideological issues, and administrative controls all play their part and it is impossible neatly to separate one factor from the others. Thus Stalin's ambition and diabolical cunning are usually isolated as the key factor in his rise to power. Stalin's defeated enemies have traced his perfidy and deception throughout his whole career. Charges have been made, some of which are absurd and others unverifiable, about Stalin's early career, such as the stories of his poisoning Lenin or having been a tsarist police agent. But at the crucial point—to repeat—Stalin stood as morally no better and no worse than the other would-be successors of Lenin. Far from the future author of purges that decimated the Old Bolsheviks, it was he who restrained his allies, Zinoviev and Kamenev, from taking too drastic steps against Trotsky, whom they wanted to expel from the Party. When in 1925 Zinoviev and Kamenev turned against Stalin and his new allies, the future right opposition, Stalin the moderate again presented his erstwhile allies as extremists. In a dramatic moment at the Fourteenth Congress he exclaimed that Zinoviev and Kamenev wanted the "blood of Bukharin," his then ally on the Politburo, and having aroused the horror of the Congress at the idea of a revered Bolshevik leader's being assailed as if he were a counterrevolutionary, he announced that "we will not give you the blood of Bukharin." [23]

But Stalin's personal skill and the equally sordid but less skillful intrigues of his opponents provide just one part of the picture. In 1923-25 the policies embraced by Stalin, his political "platform," were of the kind to appeal to the great mass of Communists: cautious progress toward socialism, but certainly no drastic break with the New Economic Policy designed to set Russia on her feet before a wholesale socialist transformation. When Zinoviev and the Left finally turned on the Secretary-General, they pictured the country as reverting to a capitalist economy, with rich peasants becoming stronger and stronger and dictating the pace of Russia's economy. Stalin imperturbably met the charge by justifying his policies, as he justified everything he did, in the name of Leninism. Thus in 1925 private property in agriculture, and the allowing of richer peasants to hire help and lease more land (strange doings under a socialist regime!) was Leninism, just as in 1929-30 it was Leninism to expropriate the peasants and to force them into collectives. On the previous occasion Stalin informed the assembled Communists that Zinoviev and Kamenev obviously intended to force and rob the peasant, to attempt to coerce him into socialism instead of educating him through example and persuasion as Vladimir Ilich Lenin had taught should be done! And in the spirit of revolutionary

[23] In 1938 Bukharin and a whole group of Old Bolshevik leaders were tried and shot, thus following the fate of Zinoviev and Kamenev.

pragmatism, answering the opposition's charge that Marx and Engels, were they alive, would be alarmed at what was happening in Russia under an allegedly socialist regime, Stalin maintained that Marx and Engels would say: "May the devil take the old formulas; long live victorious socialism in the U.S.S.R." Quite apart from the administrative and personal intrigues of the Stalinists,[24] the program thus presented and thus stated would always gain some popularity, especially in a country still recovering from the ravages of war, and still mainly peasant in its population.

The struggle for succession reached its peak at the Fourteenth Party Congress, held in December 1925. It repays the effort to examine the proceedings of the Congress, for it was the culminating point in Stalin's rise to power, the most opportune moment when his rise could have been checked by a determined, skillful and united opposition to him within the Party. For the first and, up to the present day the last, time the division within the Communist ranks spilled out from the Central Committee into the larger body, and, to an extent not approximated in the days of the Workers' Opposition nor in the feeble last movements of opposition of the next few years, threatened to split the victorious Communist Party. The Fourteenth Congress was the last one about which there was still some of the air of a gathering of revolutionaries. Debates were heated, and yet there was some remnant of the free and comradely spirit of the underground and the Revolution. Future Congresses were to prostrate themselves before the dictator, and, like gatherings of Oriental satraps, respond to his slightest whim.

[The Communist Party and the world Communist movement were treated to the spectacle of the Central Committee split into two factions. Thus in place of a single report of the Central Committee, traditionally the token of united leadership of the movement delivered by its leading figure, two reports were presented: the majority's by Stalin, and the minority's by Zinoviev] All the negotiations in advance had not been able to prevent the split's becoming public and violent. Zinoviev and Kamenev felt that it was now or never: organizationally and politically they were being surrounded. Their frantic attempts to garner and convert delegates before and during the Congress were not successful. Stalin's machine now assured him of a strong majority. It was only in Leningrad, where Zinoviev had been the Party boss, that the Opposition, through methods similar to those used by Stalin in the Party at large, had secured very strong support —hence its name, the "Leningrad Opposition." Moscow, the other capital, where Kamenev's influence had been strong in the Party organization, at first gravitated somewhat to the Opposition, but just before the Congress

[24] For example, the fact that at the lower Party echelons the followers of the Secretary-General, profiting by the fact that Kamenev and Zinoviev as well as Trotsky were Jewish, were buttressing their propaganda with anti-Semitic hints.

the Stalinists obtained the adherence of the Moscow Party boss, Uglanov, and with him went the majority of his delegation. It was thus a struggle of Party bosses, of Party "machines," in which what had once been the Social-Democratic Party of Russia finally surrendered the last vestige of its democracy.

The substance of the debate has already been presented. Ranged with Stalin against the Left or Leningrad Opposition were the Party leaders whom in a few years he would denounce as "right-wing opportunists"— Chairman of the Council of Commissars, Alexei Rykov; leader of the trade unions, Tomsky; and an outstanding Communist writer and theoretician, Bukharin. They joined Stalin, seeing in him the advocate of moderate policy and a believer in collective leadership. Silent throughout the Congress remained Leon Trotsky, who, still a man of influence in the Party, refused to join Kamenev and Zinoviev, his persecutors of only a few months before. The Opposition's fire, at first, was directed mainly at Bukharin, in whom they saw the author of the lenient policy toward the peasant. It was only toward the end that an open attack was made upon the already fearsome figure of the Secretary-General. It was related how the Party's control organs abused their powers in persecuting and ejecting partisans of the Opposition. And the essence of the struggle was revealed when Kamenev proclaimed that the Secretariat of the Party had become *a political organ* and its head had raised himself to a position unheard of in a free revolutionary movement, that of a totalitarian leader. We believe, stated Kamenev, that the Party should be run by its senior officials (i.e., the Politburo) and we are against the theory of a Leader. An oligarchy rather than a personal dictatorship was the best that the Opposition could prescribe for the Party, and it was brought out by the Stalinists, not without justification, that Kamenev and Zinoviev were piqued at having had their personal ambitions thwarted, and that Stalin's ascendancy in the Party's councils was largely the product of their own organizational ineptitude and indolence. Stalin himself modestly denied any intention or possibility of dictatorship within the Party.

Five years later, at the Sixteenth Party Congress, the effect of the Fourteenth was fully demonstrated. The old Left Opposition had been fully shattered, its leaders had been stripped of their posts and many of its followers imprisoned. Trotsky was in exile. Russia was in the midst of forced collectivization, which was to lead to a famine in the Ukraine and the deportation of hundreds of thousands, if not millions, of peasant families. No longer the genial compromiser, the middle-of-the-road man who eschewed all extremism, Stalin now appeared as a resolute dictator, a man who would brook no opposition. Throughout his speech lashing out at his recent allies, Rykov, Tomsky, Bukharin, and Uglanov, he kept repeating with terrible intensity the phrase: "If you don't press those people, you don't get anywhere." The obedient delegates responded with jeers and abuse directed at the culprits, all of them at one time trusted lieutenants of Lenin and men of great popularity and influence within the Party.

It is instructive to compare Stalin's destruction of the Left Opposition with another great crisis in the Party, the crisis that took place before and after Stalin's death, and that is, as this is being written, still unresolved. The details of the latest crisis are largely a matter of conjecture. We do not possess, as we do for the period of the twenties, Party Congress speeches, minutes of the Central Committee, and even of the Politburo, with the position of contestants for power and their political moves clearly delineated. The struggle of the late forties and the fifties has been taking place in secrecy, illuminated only occasionally by a public announcement of the removal and execution of a high official. Yet it is possible to reconstruct the general outlines of the struggle for power within the Communist Party during the last years of Stalin and the current period of collective leadership. Like the preceding crisis, the current one has had the ingredients of personal rivalry, political and administrative maneuvering, and an ideological debate.

In the background of the crisis lay the absolute dictatorship of Stalin, which, since 1934, had liquidated physically not only all the members of opposing factions but many of Stalin's closest collaborators, who, for one reason or another, incurred the dictator's distrust or displeasure. To be specific and to list only those leaders who at one time or another had occupied the highest positions in the Party: to their deaths, after trials in which they had to confess to the most improbable crimes, went Zinoviev, Kamenev, as well as Rykov and Bukharin. Liquidated without a trial and in secrecy were Stalin's erstwhile closest collaborators and members of the Politburo: S. V. Kossior, Rudzutak, and Chubar. If we add to the list Kuibyshev and Ordzhonikidze, who assertedly died of natural causes but actually under suspicious circumstances, we get an impressive picture of the decimation of Lenin's and the post-Lenin Politburo.[25] It is superfluous to list all the other high officials of the army, Party and government who were purged, or to elaborate on what has now been admitted by the Soviets themselves, that the purge not only attacked the big people, but spread to all layers of Soviet society. Terror, as a regular philosophy of government, and the secret police and an elaborate system of spying and denunciation as the means of controlling the Party and the state, became the routine features of Soviet society. Even after the massive purge that ended

---

[25] Leon Trotsky died in exile, murdered by a hired assassin; Sergei Kirov, whom Stalin had delegated to clean up the Leningrad organization after Zinoviev's deposal, was assassinated allegedly by an anti-Stalinist in 1934.

in 1939, the dictator continued these practices on a more moderate scale, and indeed they are the essential ingredients of Soviet totalitarianism.

But apart from terror and concentration camps, and the frightening reality of the power structure, Soviet society underwent profound changes during the Stalin era. Social changes continued to exert a mounting pressure on the Communist Party of the U.S.S.R. To use a favorite Marxist term, an "inherent contradiction" developed between Russian society and the system of government. As society was modernized and industrialized, a new pattern of interests emerged. The Russian people, including the mass of members of the Communist Party, obviously longed to enjoy the fruits of progress: to acquire a higher standard of living, to achieve a modicum at least of personal security, of "normalcy," and a release from the continuous dread of terror. Yet this social pressure—which is merely another name for the needs and aspirations of Soviet citizens of all walks of life—was simply unavailing against what appeared then as a cast-iron system of dictatorship, buttressed by the secret police and fortified by the people's fear and downright inability to conceive of an alternative to Stalin's personal rule. In the eyes of the dictator and the ruling hierarchy, the situation, though secure, had two grave contradictions in it. There was, first of all and quite understandably, a decline of the *esprit de corps* of the Communist Party, a loss of vitality in the organization almost synonymous with Soviet power. And how could it be otherwise? The Party was terrorized. Its leading organs almost stopped functioning. In defiance of the Party statute no Party Congress took place between 1939 and 1952. If the Central Committee met between the end of the War and Stalin's death, we have no record of it. Even the Politburo functioned irregularly, with some members sometimes forbidden to attend because of the dictator's whim. The most crucial decisions were often taken by Stalin himself with whoever at the moment was closest to him. The day-to-day task of running the country was evidently in the hands of the secret police, the two ministries comprising it, the M.V.D. (the Ministry of Internal Affairs), and the M.B.G. (the Ministry of State Security) rapidly becoming a state within a state. If the situation bothered Stalin and some of his lieutenants, it was not because of democratic scruples. It was because of the simple realization that the economic growth of the country and the development of stability of Soviet society could not be assured by bayonets, prisons, and concentration camps, and that somehow the role of the Communist Party would have to be revived.

Closely connected with the preceding problem was that of leadership of the Party and succession to the despot. At the close of World War II Stalin was sixty-six. Whatever his health, his age would no longer allow him to exercise a continuous and detailed supervision of the many departments of the Party and the state. Authority had to be delegated, and at the same time Stalin, with a true dictator's instinct, lived in constant apprehension of a subordinate's becoming too powerful. His technique had always been to liquidate or demote those closest to him as soon as they became too influential. Thus, the period immediately after the Great Purge, 1939-41, saw reduction in status of those who in the thirties had been closest to him—Kaganovich, Molotov, and Voroshilov—and the emergence of new men in the leading positions; Zhdanov, Malenkov, Beria, and Khrushchev. At the same time, the logic of the situation and the tyrant's advanced age tended necessarily to enable his lieutenants to build strong personal followings. In the immediate postwar years, Lavrenti Beria obtained a powerful hold on the vast machinery of the security forces, as well as on the Party organizations in Transcaucasia, while the Party apparatus was the scene of an undercover struggle between Zhdanov and Malenkov. The competing factions vied for strategic positions as well as for the despot's favor. The latter was always distributed with the object of keeping any one of the powerful aides from becoming too powerful. Thus after Zhdanov's death in 1948 (under circumstances that have not been fully clarified) Malenkov appeared for a while in sole control of the Party apparatus. But not for long, for he was soon joined in the Party Secretariat by Nikita Khrushchev. Beginning in 1949-50, if not before, steps were taken to weaken Lavrenti Beria's hold on the security apparatus, and purges were carried out in his special preserve, the Georgian Communist Party.

The picture of the Party situation in conjunction with social and economic developments in the country at large may have inclined Stalin and whoever were the people who had his ear at the time to give yet another drastic turn to the development of the Communist regime. The reform was to conform to the usual recipes of Stalin's reforms: in part terror, in part an ideological offensive. In 1950-51 we have the reopening of the discussion of the future of Soviet agriculture. Amalgamation of the collective farms was designed to weaken elements of private property that still lingered in agriculture.[26]

At the same time the leadership of the Party was to be changed, and a new wave of terror perhaps on the scale of the Great Purge was to shake the Party. There are several solid pieces of evidence that this was what Stalin had in mind. The Nineteenth Party Congress, convened in the fall of 1952, doubled the size of the top organ, the Politburo, now renamed

---

[26] The rulers were casting about for a solution of a most pressing problem of the Soviet economy *and at the same time were seeking something that would restore the sense of ideological mission and purpose to the Party.* Stalin's *Economic Problems of Socialism in the U.S.S.R.*, a pamphlet written in 1952, was designed to inspire new ideological fervor into the rank and file of the Party.

Presidium of the Central Committee. The old leaders were still there but they were swamped by "new men," mostly younger bureaucrats and regional Party secretaries; the latter were obviously to be given on-the-job training and then to replace the old guard, whose scheming and intrigues may have wearied Stalin.[27] But the purge was not only to be political. In January 1953 a group of leading Soviet medical specialists was "unmasked" and promptly confessed to some successful and some planned assassinations of various leading figures in the Party, army, etc. Judged by the sad precedent of the thirties, the investigation would undoubtedly link the "criminal doctors" to some other currently leading figures. On the eve of Stalin's death in March 1953 a new purge was in the offing, and it was to be accompanied by a redirection of the Party's efforts and leadership.

Stalin's death at one blow cut short both processes. Its immediate consequence was a veritable coup d'état, in which the old leaders, some of them probably intended victims of the purge, proceeded to rearrange the highest state and Party positions. The Presidium was cut down to its old size, most of the newcomers from the Nineteenth Congress being ejected. From the bargaining that must have followed, Malenkov emerged as the head of the government but had to relinquish his seat on the Party Secretariat. Beria once again assumed what appeared to be full control of the security forces; even the position of the titular head of the state, unimportant in a stable totalitarian system, but potentially important in an unstable situation, changed hands and was entrusted to the senior member of the Presidium, Voroshilov. It was clear on the morrow of Stalin's death that none of his successors inherited all or even most of the tyrant's powers. None of them was in a position, as Stalin had been, to consign the majority of his colleagues to political obscurity or liquidation. None of them could, alone and at will, chart the future of the Communist Party and Soviet society. It was obvious that in public the leaders would strive to preserve the appearance of solidarity and unanimity, but at the same time sparring for position and political maneuvering would go on.

It is sometimes assumed in the West that political power in the Soviet Union is like a concrete object locked in the offices of the Presidium of the Communist Party of the U.S.S.R., and that anybody who seizes it becomes the absolute dictator. But the first effect of Stalin's death was that the arena of political maneuvering in Russia was considerably enlarged.

---

[27] From Khrushchev's indictment of Stalin at the Twentieth Congress: "Stalin evidently had plans to finish off the old members of the Political Bureau. He often stated that Political Bureau members should be replaced by new ones. His proposal, after the Nineteenth Congress, concerning the election of twenty-five persons to the Central Committee Presidium, was aimed at the removal of the old Political Bureau members and the bringing in of less experienced persons so that these would extol him in all sorts of ways."

Previously the struggle for influence had gone on in the closest entourage of the dictator. It was relatively unimportant what a Party secretary in Odessa may have felt about the relative virtues of policies advocated by Khrushchev and Malenkov. For one thing, any public disagreement among the Bolshevik leaders on policies reflected only a temporary hesitation on the given issue by the dictator. His closest collaborators had no identifiable ideological personalities. After his death the picture became different. With the situation fluid at the top, it *does* become important to the aspirants for power not only to have their men in the strategic positions in the Party and state apparatus but also to woo the whole mass of officialdom by appealing to their interests and convictions.

The classical case of a "political campaign" in a totalitarian system is the career of Beria between March and the summer of 1953. Like any politician in any country, the Minister of the Interior knew the requirement for success was twofold: strengthen your organization and have an attractive political platform. The widespread agencies of the Ministry of the Interior and the security forces were cleansed (though, as it turned out later, not completely) of the anti-Beria or neutral elements. But, in addition, Beria became both in his public pronouncements and official acts an advocate of "socialist legality" and national equality. He appeared desirous of taking to himself most of the credit for the curbing of the worst abuses of official terrorism—as shown by his repudiation of the doctors' case—and for the greater opportunities offered to non-Russian officials in the state and Party. It is not far-fetched to suggest that he realized the political appeal of measures that held out to the middle ranks of the Soviet hierarchy the promise of a modicum of security for their lives and their positions. And against the background of frantic Russian chauvinism of Stalin's last years, Beria's policies must likewise have suggested greater opportunities for advancement and more freedom from Great-Russian supervision for the non-Russian elements of the officialdom. The dramatic fall of Beria and his associates in June 1953 indicates, paradoxically, the success of those policies. Rehabilitation of the victims of Stalinist terror and greater latitude on the nationality issue have continued under the "collective leadership." It is unnecessary to postulate an attempted coup by Beria as an explanation for his liquidation. He was becoming too well entrenched in his administrative machinery, and was courting popularity too strenuously not to arouse the deepest apprehension of his colleagues. It does not matter that the propaganda machine has managed to picture him as an exponent of terror and the author of the plan to dismember the Soviet Union. The measures he had advocated have proved appealing and have been endorsed as their own by the rest of the leadership.

The elimination of Beria did not bring harmony to the ruling elite.

The vacuum created by Stalin's death continues down to our own day, and the impression of harmony that the ruling hierarchy attempts to convey conceals considerable strains.[28] Beria's personal empire was dismantled and his partisans throughout Russia purged.[29] The realization that the leadership of the vast security apparatus conferred enormous power upon an individual, and that the secret police was abhorred by the population, and—what in the context of Russia's politics is much more important—by influential Party and army leaders, has led the regime to weaken the principal arm of terror, to disband some of its armed forces and to make sure that no single person or organization should have exclusive control over the security apparatus.

If terror is weakened as the principal lever of totalitarian power, then other instrumentalities must take its place. The leaders must have realized that a mixed policy of concessions to the population and the strengthening of the Communist Party was the most fruitful approach. Concessions included a modest attempt to raise the standard of living, the attempt with which Malenkov especially identified himself, and the general relaxation of the most obnoxious features of the police state, including abolition of special police courts which meted out penalties in secret, reduction of the drastic labor discipline and partial disbanding of forced labor camps. We cannot tell how far those decisions were the result of a united decision of the Politburo-Presidium and how far they reflected maneuvering among the rulers and pressure of outside elements, such as the army. It is characteristic that Malenkov's degradation in February 1955, when he stepped down as chairman of the Council of Ministers though remaining in the government and the Presidium, was justified on the grounds of his alleged preference for the development of consumers' goods over heavy industries. As Stalin's favorite during his last years, and conceivably as the only member of the late dictator's entourage not slated for the purge he had been preparing, Malenkov must have been eyed suspiciously by his colleagues in the "collective leadership." Perhaps in his identification with the masses'

[28] It is interesting to list several instances of both the confusion produced by the lack of a single absolute leader and of the oligarchy's frantic attempts to conceal discords. On the morrow of Stalin's death the official communiqué spoke of the changes in Party and government leadership as having been executed so as to insure prevention of "disorder and panic." In the funeral orations over Stalin's bier delivered by the triumvirs Malenkov, Beria, and Molotov, it was Beria who made warm personal remarks about Malenkov, and it was on Beria's motions in the Supreme Soviet that Malenkov was confirmed as Chairman of the Council of Ministers. One is reminded of Stalin's warm eulogies of Bukharin in the twenties!

[29] The extent to which the secret police had penetrated all aspects of the governmental machinery is best indicated by the fact that among those tried and executed with Beria as his principal aides was one Dekanozov, Beria's personal appointee as Minister of the Interior in Georgia. Dekanozov's previous posts had included that of Ambassador to Germany and Deputy Commissar of Foreign Affairs. He had been, it is not too much to surmise, delegated to operate within the diplomatic corps.

desire for greater amenities of life his colleagues saw again a political campaign designed to secure absolute power, very much in the style of Stalin's
moderation and middle-of-the-road position of the early 1920's. The mildness of his "punishment" indicates that perhaps, unlike Beria, Malenkov
did not attempt to fight back. A wave of changes in Party posts followed
the change at the top. In their peregrinations throughout the Soviet Union, it has not been unusual for Khrushchev and Bulganin to meet with
the Party Committee of a republic or region, the result being very often
a new First Secretary of the given organization.

But the main effort of the new leadership, divided and fluctuating as
it is, has obviously been to infuse new spirit into the Party. The Twentieth
Congress, which met in February 1956, was to chart the new course. For
a long time prior to the Congress there had been a silent de-emphasis of
Stalin. During the dictator's absolute rule no public speech, no book on
any subject, no leading article, failed to refer to Comrade Stalin. Not long
after his death the references became scarcer and scarcer and even implied
criticism of the late dictator had been allowed. The Twentieth Congress
was to mark a definite break with this cautious de-emphasis and criticism
by implication. For reasons known only to themselves, the leaders decided
to attack Stalin's memory openly. Thus in the public speeches at the Congress Khrushchev and Mikoyan referred scathingly to the personality cult
and the atrophy of Party organs that prevailed during the last twenty years
of Stalin's reign. Mikoyan assailed Stalin's version of the Party's history,
History of the Communist Party, A Short Course, published under his
name, and filled with adulatory references to himself. Stalin's *Economic
Problems of Socialism in the U.S.S.R.*, hailed in 1952 by the same speakers
as a work of genius, was now described as containing serious theoretical
errors.

These speeches were only a prelude to a special address by Khrushchev
about Stalin. Though delivered before a closed session of the Congress, it
was circulated to all the Party organizations in the U.S.S.R. and thus became a public secret.[30] Khrushchev's speech was not an unqualified condemnation of Stalin. The great dictator was pictured as a man who, for
all his faults, until 1934 performed great services for socialism in the
U.S.S.R. But beginning with 1934 and the opening of the Great Purge,
Stalin is presented as a tyrant and sadist, dispatching people to death out
of whim and increasingly thirsty for adulation. In his last years the picture
is that of a psychologically sick man contemplating on the eve of his
death a wholesale liquidation of his associates.

Khrushchev's account cannot be entirely trusted. It should be borne in

[30] All the quotations from the speech are from the version published by the *New
Leader* under the title *The Crimes of the Stalin Era*, edited by Boris I. Nicolayevski.

mind that those who now denounced Stalin were coauthors, and at times probably instigators, of his purges. Nikita Khrushchev had himself been Stalin's chosen instrument of purge in the Ukraine; Georgi Malenkov, for many years an official of his personal secretariat. Many of the liquidations and executions of the period can be traced not only to Stalin's undoubted sadism, but also to the intense rivalry of those closest to him. Yet some of the facts cited by Khrushchev are supported by other evidence. Thus of the Central Committee elected in 1934 at the Seventeenth Party Congress 70 per cent of the membership was arrested or liquidated within the next five years. The same fate befell 1108 delegates out of 1966 who attended the same Congress. We have a confirmation of the fact that the Central Committee and even the Politburo practically ceased to function during Stalin's last years, and that the despot transacted the most important business by himself, or with whoever enjoyed his confidence at the moment. Thus in 1949 Nicolai Voznesensky, the head of Russia's economic planning and a member of the Politburo, was liquidated along with a number of other high officials at a period when Khrushchev asserts "Stalin became even more capricious, irritable and brutal; in particular his suspicion grew," and when "everything was decided by him alone without any consideration for anyone or anything." [31] In short, out of the mouth of the highest Party functionary, Soviet and foreign Communists heard the confirmation of the worst attacks of their enemies, and an avowal that for a long time the U.S.S.R. and world Communism had been ruled by a bloodthirsty tyrant who had thought nothing of ordering tortures for veteran Bolsheviks.

Some other details of Khrushchev's speech may or may not be confirmed by a future historian. There are two pertinent questions that belong in the study of the Soviet government. First, though we cannot know the exact reasons for the revelations, what lines of reasoning could have persuaded the leaders to admit so much, and thus, as they must have realized, to threaten their own positions as formerly the closest servants of Joseph Vissarionovich Stalin, not to mention the shock they must have imparted to millions of Party activists in telling them authoritatively that all they had been taught about the Party's history during the preceding twenty years was a big lie. As suggested before, the only reasonable explanation is twofold. First, in condemning the cult of the individual, the collective leadership may have thought that it was acquiring a collective insurance against any one of them trying to emulate the late dictator and to ascend the summit of power in Stalin's fashion. Secondly, the revival of the Party's

[31] The reason why Stalin's "suspicion grew" may have been a fairly rational feeling on his part that as he grew older his closest collaborators were maneuvering for power positions in the eventuality of his death.

spirit under conditions that would not allow one absolute dictator, would have indicated the necessity of a dramatic break with the past, a surgical operation on the Party's history, painful and dangerous, no doubt, but, in the long run, it was hoped, to prove salutary.

The other question turns on the hypothetical reasons and how far they have been and are likely to be justified by the events. There is no doubt that the regime gained in popularity through its new policies. The attempt to ascribe most of the repressive and unpleasant things of the preceding twenty years to Stalin's personal foibles has also been a qualified success. The deliberative organs of the Communist Party have revived. We hear of meetings of the Central Committee; there is more of the air of real discussion of issues in the Party press and less of the craven sycophancy that characterized Party speeches and writings in Stalin's time. The new developments have undoubtedly increased the administrative efficiency of the Party machinery and encouraged the development of more initiative and spirit at the lower levels. As a whole the Party is now a healthier organism, the average member less driven by mere compulsion, than was the case five or six years ago.

At the same time the fundamental problem has not been solved. Much has been said and written about a return to the Leninist principles and spirit. But the circumstances of today's Russia make the condition of the Party as it was in Lenin's time simply inapplicable and irrelevant to today's problems. By publicly confirming the terrible excesses of the past, the Party has not only shattered the incredible if not feigned innocence of many foreign Communists, but must have injured itself in the eyes of the younger and more credulous of Soviet Communists. Human gratitude for the removal of the worst type of repression is notoriously short-lived and succeeded by demands for more substantial freedoms.

The latest development in the evolution of Soviet leadership was the crisis of the summer of 1957, in which the erstwhile closest collaborators of Stalin, Molotov and Kaganovich as well as Stalin's intended successor Malenkov, were ejected both from the Presidium of the Communist Party and from its Central Committee. The outlines of the crisis are difficult to gauge either from the official account or from the "inside stories," some of them officially inspired and of doubtful authenticity. It is clear that the repercussions of the de-Stalinization campaign and the events of the fall of 1956 in the satellites (the Hungarian revolt, the loosening of the Soviet grip on Poland, etc.) alarmed some senior officials of the Communist Party. The solid front of collective leadership remained ostensibly unbroken, but Khrushchev's position was undoubtedly shaken toward the end of 1956, and it was probably only the inability of his opponents to agree on his successor that preserved the ebullient First Secretary in his post. Two events of the fall of that year and the early winter of 1957 indicated the threat to his position. In December of 1956 a reorganization of economic planning and management placed major direction of the economic life in the hands of Politburo member Mikhail Pervukhin, long considered a coming man in the Soviet hierarchy. In February 1957 Dimitri Shepilov resigned as Foreign Minister to devote himself completely to his functions as a secretary of the Central Committee. Both Pervukhin and Shepilov could have been logical successors of Khrushchev: younger than he and dynamic, they had been much less involved than the First Secretary in the inner councils of the Stalin regime, and while it would have been unimaginable that Molotov, Kaganovich, or for that matter Malenkov, could have resumed the active leadership of the Party, Pervukhin or Shepilov could have filled the bill. And then in the spring of 1957 the tide turned. A new reorganization of the economic apparatus was announced by Khrushchev. The new scheme emphasized decentralization in line with the previously announced ideas of the Party leader, and incidentally must have appealed to the local Party bosses as against the central hierarchy, where Khrushchev had lost ground.

And then in July 1957 a communiqué of the Central Committee disclosed the exclusion of Molotov, Malenkov, Kaganovich and Shepilov, and the demotion of Pervukhin from full to alternate member of the Presidium. The four excluded leaders were accused of "anti-Party" activities. They were pictured as opponents of the policy of raising the living standards in the U.S.S.R. Molotov was represented as the man who had attempted to sabotage the peaceful policies of the regime, opposed the normalization of relations between the U.S.S.R. and Tito's Yugoslavia—in fact, to use the word so long hurled by official propaganda at statesmen of the West, a warmonger. The official communiqué emphasized the prerogatives of the Central Committee. It promised new economic concessions to the population, e.g., the end of compulsory deliveries from the peasants' private plots. In brief, the condemned and defeated group were represented (and they had no opportunity to offer their version of the story) as the enemies of all the "liberal" policies since Stalin's death—the policies that brought a bit more comfort and less fear to the average Soviet citizen— while Khrushchev stood forth as the standard bearer of a better life and peaceful policies.

One is struck forcibly by the parallel between this episode of 1956-57 and the story of Stalin's maneuvers in 1923-27. The Khrushchev of 1957, like the Stalin of 1924, is the advocate of "normalcy," of concessions to the peasant, of better life for the citizen. Like his great predecessor, he eschews warlike policies; when his position is undermined in the Presidium he carries the struggle, as Stalin did, from the Politburo to the Central

Committee. He improvises freely to keep his grip on power. Stalin, to reinforce his position, established the practice of the Central Committee's meeting with the Control Commission, where his influence was even stronger. The meeting of June 1957 which chastised the dissidents was held by the Central Committee together with the Audit Commission, a body formerly of minor importance and with purely accounting duties but where evidently Khrushchev had additional support. And like Stalin's opponents so did Khrushchev's persist in their divisions until it was too late. Kamenev and Zinoviev, could they have joined with Trotsky in 1924 or 1925, might conceivably have unseated the General Secretary. Malenkov and his supporters did not join with the old guard of Molotov and Kaganovich until the First Secretary's position was too strong, and until "his" policies had gained the support of a majority of the Party bureaucrats and his moderation the support (probably) of the majority of Party members.

Is the parallel to be complete, and will Khrushchev, once his position is invulnerable, revert to terror and to the policies designed to increase production with scant thought for the consumer, as did Stalin once he no longer had to bother about popularity or votes in the Central Committee? This is most unlikely. For, in the first place, Khrushchev's position can never reach the pinnacle of personal dictatorship achieved by Stalin. His predecessor was a man in his forties when he became the absolute ruler; Khrushchev is in his sixties. But far more important than the biological factor is the new appearance of Soviet society, and the role of the Communist Party in it. The new and industrialized U.S.S.R. cannot be ruled by sheer despotism and terror, as was Russia in the thirties. Nor can the aspirations of the various newly born segments of Soviet society be trampled upon quite as ruthlessly as they were in the late twenties and thirties. This changed social picture in turn affects the role of the Party and of its leader.

Within the new Presidium, Khrushchev's position became stronger when the June 1957 Plenum appointed his supporters in place of his opponents. The Presidium now is heavily weighted with Party secretaries both of the central and of the major local organizations. If it is true that in the struggle against Molotov, Malenkov and Kaganovich, the First Secretary found himself in a minority on the Presidium and had to extricate himself by appealing to the Central Committee, then, as has been indicated since Stalin's death, the latter body will play a more important role than at any time since the twenties. On both the Presidium and the Central Committee Nikita Khrushchev's influence is now paramount but not absolute. The logic of the slogans propounded by the Party boss is in itself a threat to his position. If the Central Committee is to play a more important role, does it not encourage factions in the Party? And if the ejection of the old guard was also a repudiation of the bad old practices of Stalinism, is not Khrushchev one of the few close collaborators of Stalin still in a position of power? In brief, the parallel with Stalin's tactics cannot be complete and it must be assumed that the situation in the highest Party Councils is still fluid.

The Party's position as a whole must have been weakened by the series of events since March 1953. The gain in vitality resulting from de-Stalinization has been balanced by the loss in prestige due to the constant splits within its highest councils. Or rather, the internal weaknesses have now been exposed, for while there were purges and changes in personnel in Stalin's time, there was no question as to who was the boss and the ultimate source of power.

The weakening of the secret police has had the natural effect of strengthening the other source of armed power, namely, the Red Army. But it would be a gross exaggeration to speak of the Soviet Army as a homogeneous whole or of its officer corps as a united body of men with a definite viewpoint and a political philosophy of its own. The Red Army has been both a source of pride and an object of apprehension to the Communist leaders. From the very beginning the army has been honeycombed with political commissars, regular Party activists delegated for propaganda and political indoctrination work within the armed forces. Stalin's reign brought with it an increasing penetration of the armed forces by the security apparatus. The Great Purge decimated the officer corps. Three of the then five marshals of the Soviet Union were liquidated: the famous courtmartial of 1937 alone claimed the life of the Deputy Commissar of War, Marshal Tukhachevsky, and seven other leading commanders, executed for alleged treason. The regime took every care that the officer corps should be largely composed of Party members, that the rank and file should be strenuously educated in Communist ideology, and that, as in other upper segments of Soviet society, the higher officers should be compensated for their lack of freedom by all sorts of material and status amenities. Military figures were effectively barred from the highest Party councils, the only exceptions being political generals like Stalin's old-time collaborator and Commissar of War, Voroshilov, and Bulganin, who had been transferred from civil to military administration in the thirties. Military commanders who acquired too much national renown were either liquidated or thrust into obscurity, the former having been the fate of Marshals Tukhachevsky and Blucher before 1939, and the latter that of Zhukov after 1945. Thus within the mechanics of Stalin's dictatorship there could be no effective army pressure group either within or outside the Party.

In a divided rather than a united dictatorship, the army's role has changed. It was symptomatic that on the morrow of Stalin's death Marshal

Zhukov was brought out from the obscurity of a military district and named a First Deputy Minister of Defense. Military figures, and this time professional soldiers, began to appear in high Party posts. It has become something of a custom for military commanders of certain regions to become ex-officio members of the highest Party organs of the given regions. Thus the Presidium of the Central Committee of the Communist Party of the Ukraine, as of March 27, 1954, listed as its alternate members Marshals V. I. Chuikov and Ivan Konev; General Antonov, Commander of the Transcaucasian Military District, was in 1954 a full member of the Presidium of the Communist Party of Georgia, etc. It is rumored, though it cannot be ascertained, that the army took an active part in the downfall of Lavrenti Beria and in the partial suppression of the security forces that followed his arrest.[32]

On Malenkov's demotion in 1955 Zhukov became Minister of Defense. At the Twentieth Congress a rather large number of military figures, and this time primarily professional soldiers, airmen, and sailors, became members of the Central Committee. And for the first time in Soviet history a man primarily a soldier, Marshal Georgi Konstantinovich Zhukov, became a member of the highest policy-forming body as an alternate member of the Presidium. Neither Zhukov's subsequent advancement to full membership, supposedly for the help he rendered Khrushchev in the summer 1957 crisis, nor his later expulsion affect the fact that the army is now *politically* more important. It is inaccurate to speak of the army as competing with the Party or taking over the Party, but the enhanced status of the army leaders is at least a proof that realizing their weakened position the Party leaders are more and more constrained to bring into the inner councils of the regime professional military leaders, and are desirous of exploiting their prestige and ready to appease their ambitions. The enhanced status of the generals is emphasized by the small number of the Central Committee members and alternate members who are clearly identifiable with the security forces.

In brief, the post-Stalin reforms have introduced a new era of flux and, this time, more open maneuverings within the Communist Party of the U.S.S.R. Whether the intention of the authors of the reforms will be fulfilled or whether the apprehensions of those who feared too rapid a retreat from Stalinism will be justified will depend on several questions. Casting aside for the moment the international picture, and the turbulent state of the satellites, the principal equation in the answer will be the effect

[32] At the end of World War II, Beria was created a Marshal of the Soviet Union, a gesture that could not but grate upon even the thoroughly intimidated officer corps of the Red Army. A more substantial grievance must have been the penetration of the army by the security apparatus, which dominated the political administration of the defense forces.

TABLE 7   Formal Organization of the Communist Party at the Time of the 20th Congress—February 1956

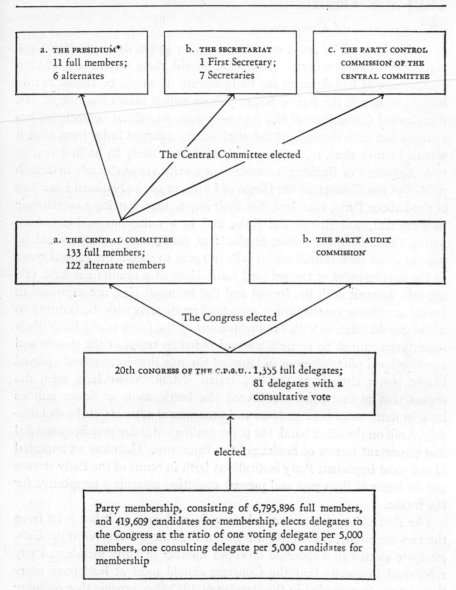

a. THE PRESIDIUM*
11 full members;
6 alternates

b. THE SECRETARIAT
1 First Secretary;
7 Secretaries

c. THE PARTY CONTROL
COMMISSION OF THE
CENTRAL COMMITTEE

The Central Committee elected

a. THE CENTRAL COMMITTEE
133 full members;
122 alternate members

b. THE PARTY AUDIT
COMMISSION

The Congress elected

20th CONGRESS OF THE C.P.O.U.. 1,355 full delegates;
81 delegates with a
consultative vote

elected

Party membership, consisting of 6,795,896 full members, and 419,609 candidates for membership, elects delegates to the Congress at the ratio of one voting delegate per 5,000 members, one consulting delegate per 5,000 candidates for membership

* As of March 1, 1958, 15 full members, 8 alternates.

of economic and social changes that within the last generation have transformed the life of the nations of the U.S.S.R.

The Formal Organization

Congresses and Conferences

Nothing would be more deceptive than to judge the importance and actual role of various organs of the Communist Party on the basis of their competence as laid down in the Party statute. It would be almost as misleading to ignore the flux of Soviet politics which makes the role of, say, the Central Committee of the Party—though its official competence has changed but little throughout the years—quite different today from what it was in Lenin's time, or, we may add, what it is likely to be in a year or two. A student of British government may write about the role in British politics of the Cabinet, or the House of Lords, or of the National Executive of the Labour Party, confident that their importance, barring a cataclysmic development, will change but little, and in a quite foreseeable fashion within the immediate future. Students of totalitarian systems would be wise to avoid such confidence. It falls to them to sketch the general *trend of the development* of the political institutions of a totalitarian state, taking into account both the formal and the informal (i.e., not expressed in formal statutes or constitutions) aspects of politics. As with the institutions of the Soviet state, so with the *institutions of the Communist Party*, their importance cannot be entirely assessed either in terms of the statute and constitutional phraseology or in terms of the role they have actually played in the power struggle of the totalitarian system. As we have seen, the organs that at one point constituted the battle scene of Soviet politics have in many cases become tame and ornamental adjuncts of the dictatorship. And, on the other hand, the paper realities of today may become vital and important factors of Soviet politics tomorrow. Therefore an appraisal of the most important Party institutions both in terms of the Party statute and in terms of their past and present evolution presents a perspective for the future.

[The Party Congress, as noted before, is in theory, as it has been from the very beginning, the sovereign organ of the Party. Delegates to the Congress are elected in a specified ratio per number of Party members. Party rules used to specify that the Congress should meet at least once every three years. As amended in the statutes of 1952 they provide that ordinary Congresses are to be convoked every four years. So much for the constitutional provisions. A student of Soviet politics will draw conclusions from the fact that following the Revolution Party Congresses met every year until 1925. Following the Fourteenth Congress, which marks a watershed

in the real importance of Congresses, there was a two-year hiatus before
the Fifteenth in 1927; then a three-year hiatus until 1930. In defiance of
the Party statute no Congress met for four years between the Sixteenth
and the Seventeenth, in 1934. Then came a five-year period, coinciding
with the Great Purge, until the Eighteenth in 1939, and after that thirteen
years until Stalin's last Congress in 1952!

[The lengthening and unstatutory interval has an eloquence of its own]
For the Congresses until 1925 still were fairly genuine representative assemblies. They had a life of their own, often a lively discussion, and at
times a clash of points of view: as between Lenin and the Workers' Opposition at the Ninth and Tenth Congresses (1920 and 1921); between
Trotsky's partisans and those of the ruling *troika* in 1923 and 1924; and the
decisive clash between Stalin and the Leningrad Opposition led by Zinoviev and Kamenev in 1925. Beginning with the Sixteenth Congress in 1927
the picture changes. Congresses are triumphant reviews by the Stalinist
rulers of their subordinates. There is no discussion in the sense of a controversy, but only obedient reports and unanimity on the theses presented
by the leader. Former opponents of Stalin as long as they are alive are
given the opportunity to recant and to crawl in the dirt to the revilings and
amusement of those assembled. At the Eighteenth Congress, held on the
morrow of the blood bath, no opposition voices are heard. Veteran Communist leaders, as if incredulous that they are still alive, recite little poems
in praise of Stalin, and a delegation of school children intones: "Thank
you Comrade Stalin for our happy childhood!"

The mechanics of the Congress stay the same. The Presidium and the
Secretariat (the former including the most prominent leaders) having been
elected, the central point of the proceedings is the report of the Central
Committee delivered by the acknowledged leader of the Party. Thus it was
Lenin who reported until his fatal illness; then in 1923 Zinoviev, followed
in succeeding Congresses by Stalin. At the Nineteenth Congress the report
was presented by Malenkov, Stalin contenting himself with a brief speech
at the end. Reasons for this may not be difficult to find. The report requires a not negligible physical effort, which in 1952 might have been
beyond the powers of the seventy-three-year-old despot. Thus for example
Khrushchev's report at the Twentieth Congress covers 116 pages in English translation. [The delivery usually occupies two separate sessions and the
speaker reviews both the world situation and domestic politics as well as
the state of the Party, usually in some detail and with elaborate statistical
data. Following the report a lengthy debate takes place, with scores of
delegates participating. Since 1925 the debate has increasingly consisted
in the speakers' agreeing with the report, praising Stalin, and actually
giving reports of their own on conditions in their particular organization

and part of the country. Another major speech might be delivered by a Party leader on, say, the directives for a new economic plan, and that in turn would be discussed, i.e., agreed to by numerous speakers. It used to be said of members of Hitler's Reichstag that they were the best paid male chorus in the world, for they met infrequently, heard the Fuehrer speak, sang the national anthem, and went home. The same claim cannot be made for members of the Party Congress, for when one reads the minutes of Stalin's Congresses, and even of the post-Stalin Twentieth Congress, one is struck by the massive monotony and tedium of the proceedings, which must have constituted hard work to the participants.

[The mechanics of the Congress include minor routine things such as the report of the Audit and Mandate Commissions, greetings from foreign Communist Parties, factories, army units, etc.] In the earlier and spontaneous days these indeed helped give an air of holiday and comradely meeting to the Congress; in Stalin's days they became a travesty. And at the end comes the concluding word of the leader or leaders and then a unanimous agreement on the reports, and unanimous election of the Central Committee and other organs of the Party. The Twentieth Congress, held in 1956, did not change the pattern. Here again was unanimity, which included a unanimous condemnation of the "cult of personality" and thus of Stalin. But though the speeches differed somewhat from the old monotonous pattern, it was still a propaganda show arranged and directed down to the smallest detail by the (this time collective) dictator, and not a congress, not a deliberation, in the proper sense of the word.

[Aside from the Party Congress, an assembly that has played an important role in Bolshevik history has been the *Party Conference*. The Conference was a less formal and smaller version of the Party Congress.] Instead of being elected by the body of the membership of the Party, it was a conclave of the Party hierarchy, i.e., its central organs and delegates of the committees and bureaus of regional and territorial organizations. In the twenties, the days of the struggle for power, the Conference was a more pliable and convenient assembly for the Party apparatus to manipulate than the Congress. The latter, as we have seen, still had some vestigial remnants of a democratic gathering, some delegates still could be swung by oratory, while the Party Conference, because of its character, could be relied upon to be more responsive and submissive to the *apparatus* headed by Stalin. That is how it worked at the Fifteenth Party Conference in 1926, when Zinoviev and Kamenev, previously crushed at the Fourteenth Congress, made one last effort at a defiance of Stalin. They were joined this time by Trotsky. But this combination, which two or three years before could have swung any Congress or Conference of the Party, was in 1926 impotent to break the hold that the Stalinist machine had on the majority of Party officials.

But with the dictatorial system fully grown, the Conference became something of a fifth wheel. It was abolished in 1934, restored by the Party Congress in 1939; and finally the Nineteenth Congress in 1952 abolished it again. It is interesting to speculate whether it will ever be restored. The Party Congress, which has thousands of delegates and meets infrequently, obviously cannot function as a deliberative assembly. There would appear to exist a place in the Party structure, assuming that "collective leadership" will prevail for some time, for a body that would bridge the gap between the Congress and the Central Committee. But the rulers of Russia are not bound to take the advice of foreign experts on their government!

The Central Committee

To the Central Committee belongs a more essential and continuous part in the history of the Party. Just as the constitutional fiction of the Party statutes proclaims that the Congress is the supreme body, so in theory the Central Committee is the executive arm of the Party, but in this case the theory has a more substantial link with the reality. The Secretariat, the Politburo, or the Presidium are thus in theory only organs and servants of the Central Committee. When Stalin between 1934 and 1939 imprisoned, dismissed, or sent to death two thirds of the Committee as elected by the Party in 1934, he was in the eyes of the law merely a Secretary of the Central Committee, "removable" by a simple majority of its members!

Again, the genealogy of the institution is an impressive reminder of change in history. The Central Committee of pre-World War I days was a handful of revolutionaries holding its meetings in a shabby room in London or somewhere else outside Russia. Today it is an assembly of potentates; of ministers, marshals and men who direct vast domains of power in the U.S.S.R. But the growth in splendor and numbers has not always coincided with the growth in real power. The few men who met in a shabby room abroad did really direct the activities of the Party, though their adherents may have been just a few thousands of clandestine revolutionaries. The assemblage of Party bigwigs, marshals, and directors of enterprises often surpassing (in size) the General Motors Corporation has been, at least for a generation, the servant of one man or a handful of men, officially just their colleagues and their executive officers but in truth their masters. That it should have become so will not surprise a student of government who remembers that the British Cabinet, officially the servant and executive committee of Parliament, is in fact the master of the House of Commons. But it is the extent and the character of subjugation of the Central Committee that require some comment.

[As organized originally the Committee was a relatively small group that met very frequently. Thus after the Seventh Congress in 1918 it consisted of twenty-three people; fifteen full members, eight alternates.] The earlier Party statutes required it to meet, at first twice a month then once every two months, etc. In fact in those early days it met usually more often than statutorily required. If, even in those early days, it was a bit too large to decide and execute really important decisions with speed and secrecy, it was still small enough to decide on most executive matters, and of an ideal size to debate and decide policy issues within the scope defined by the Congress. The Central Committee was then an active powerful body. Elected by the Congress it contained partisans of various viewpoints in the Party, though Lenin's views had almost always enjoyed a majority. Another factor of vital importance, in the years immediately after the Revolution, was that the personnel of the Central Committee was in its vast majority composed of persons domiciled in the capitals of Moscow and Leningrad. Many of its members, certainly more than after 1927, were people with no day-to-day administrative work.

The Stalinist period has profoundly altered the nature of the Central Committee and its work. It is best to look at the end result—the Central Committee of today—though there has already begun an evolution from the most extreme Stalinist pattern. For an executive body the Central Committee is enormous and unwieldy. Already in 1927 it was decreed that it should have seventy-one members and sixty-eight alternates. Since the Twentieth Congress it has 133 full members and 122 alternates. The rules adopted at the same time specify that it should meet ordinarily once every six months. But even this decrease over the earlier required frequency of meetings gives no idea of the decline of the Central Committee's meetings during the latter Stalin era. As a matter of fact for several years before 1952 there is no authenticated report of the Committee's meetings. It is not too much to say that from the end of World War II to 1952 it existed largely on paper and that various acts announced as having been done by the Committee were simply decrees issued by the dictator and his associates.] Stalin's death brought new life to the Central Committee. [It now undoubtedly exists and meets fairly frequently and in the era of *collective leadership* its importance is undoubtedly enhanced, though still not what it was in Lenin's time.]

This point is underlined if we look at the list of members whether at the time of Stalin's last Congress in 1952 or at the latest one in 1956. They are almost without an exception people who have at least one other full-time job, often at a great distance from Moscow. Once Stalin's rule was firmly planted, membership became a reward for faithful service, whether in the state, the Party or the armed forces. It was a recognition—though often a fleeting one, for the despot was whimsical and sadistic—that the man "had arrived." Thus a Party secretary six thousand miles away from Moscow, an ambassador to London, and an admiral of the Black Sea Fleet might sit on the Committee, though it is difficult to see how they could have performed their functions if the Committee had been a regularly meeting and active body.

Stalin's death has not changed the occupational pattern of the Committee. There are now perhaps more of military and naval personnel among its *full* members.[33] Also, in the Committee elected at the Twentieth Congress secret-service bureaucrats appear in much smaller numbers than before. But the character of the bulk of membership is still very much the same: bureaucrats from the central state and Party organs and most of the important local Party functionaries. While the will and choice of one man is no longer the key to all posts and honors, it is not too much to surmise that most of those on the Committee are there as protégés of one or another of the ruling group.

The Central Committee has undoubtedly gained in importance since Stalin's death. To repeat, as long as the ruling group in the Presidium is united, or dominated by one man, the Central Committee acts as a ratifying body and a sounding board of Soviet notables. Whenever there is factional strife in the Presidium the Central Committee may be called upon to decide. Thus, it is highly probable that the downfall of Beria and the demotion of Malenkov were preceded by discussion in the Committee. And the crisis of June 1957 was, it appears from all the available sources, actually decided in and by the Central Committee. It has been suggested that Khrushchev found himself isolated in the Presidium by the coalition of the Molotov-Kaganovich faction with Malenkov. Therefore, the struggle was referred to the Central Committee meeting jointly with the Central Audit Commission, and there the First Secretary gained a victory and ejected his enemies. If this is what happened, the Central Committee momentarily reverted to its role of the twenties, and Khrushchev imitated successfully Stalin's tactics of the early and middle twenties when, surrounded by rivals in the Politburo, he played against it the larger body, where the majority of the Party bureaucrats were his partisans.

While the June crisis was followed by the official admonition that the Central Committee is the parent body of and superior to the Presidium, it still remains true that the former is too large and too dispersed to function

---

[33] In Stalin's days an admiral or marshal of the Soviet Union, unless a special pet of the dictator, had to be content with the status of an alternate member.

TABLE 8 **Presidium of the Central Committee of the Communist Party of the U.S.S.R. as of March 1958**

(Asterisks indicate new members added since July 1, 1957)

Full members

A. B. Aristov*
Secretary of the C. C.

N. I. Belyayev*
Secretary of the C. C. Since Feb. 1958, First Secretary of the Communist Party of Kazakstan

L. I. Brezhnev*
Secretary of the C. C. (promoted from a candidate member)

N. A. Bulganin
Chairman of the Council of Ministers until March 1958

K. Y. Voroshilov
Chairman of the Supreme Soviet Presidium

N. G. Ignatov*
Secretary of the C. C. Until Feb. 1958, First Secretary of the Gorky Province Party Committee

A. I. Kirichenko
Secretary of the C. C. Until Feb. 1958, First Secretary of the Ukrainian Communist Party

F. R. Kozlov*
First Secretary of the Leningrad Province Party Committee

O. V. Kuusinen*
Secretary of the C. C.

A. I. Mikoyan
First Vice Chairman of the Council of Ministers

N. A. Mukhitdinov*
Secretary of the C. C. Until Feb. 1958, candidate member and First Secretary of the Uzbek Communist Party

M. A. Suslov
Secretary of the C. C.

Y. A. Furtseva*
Secretary of the C. C. Until Feb. 1958, First Secretary of the Moscow City Party Committee

N. S. Khrushchev
First Secretary of the C. C. of the Communist Party of the U.S.S.R. Chairman of the Council of Ministers since March 1958

N. M. Shvernik*
Chairman of the Party Control Commission of the C. C. (promoted from a candidate member)

[Marshal G. K. Zhukov, former Minister of Defense, was promoted to a full member in July 1957, dismissed from the Presidium and the Central Committee in October 1957.]

Candidate members

P. N. Pospelov*
Secretary of the C. C.

D. S. Korotchenko*
Chairman of the Presidium of the Ukraine Supreme Soviet

Y. E. Kalnberzin*
First Secretary of the Latvian Communist Party

A. P. Kirilenko*
First Secretary of the Sverdlovsk Party Committee

A. N. Kosygin*
Vice Chairman of the Council of Ministers of the U.S.S.R.

K. T. Mazurov*
First Secretary of the Byelorussian Party

V. P. Mzhavanadze*
First Secretary of the Georgian Party

M. G. Pervukhin
In Feb. 1958, appointed Soviet envoy to Eastern Germany; formerly Chairman of the State Commission for Foreign Economic Relations. (In July 1957, Pervukhin was demoted from a full member; since then he has probably been dismissed entirely from the Presidium, though no official announcement has been made as of this time.)

continually as the highest policy organ in the intricate Soviet structure. [If and when Khrushchev gets a Presidium entirely of his own choosing the Central Committee may revert to its ornamental function. But until then and at each occasion when there is factional strife within the ruling hierarchy, the Central Committee may be called upon to decide and thus become a decisive factor in a crisis of the Soviet system.]

The Politburo–Presidium

In justifying his decision in 1916 to run the British war effort with a war cabinet of five to seven members instead of the usual fifteen- to twenty-member Cabinet, Prime Minister Lloyd George stated that you cannot run a war "with a Sanhedrin." This assertion about the relations of arithmetic to the mechanics of a war is equally true of the mechanics of a totalitarian society. The latter, in a sense, lives in a continuous state of emergency. It cannot be "run" by a parliament nor by a many-member committee. It requires a unified direction by one person, or, at most, by a handful of people. Hence it is not suprising that it has been assumed that of all the organs of the Soviet government and the Communist Party of the U.S.S.R., it is in the Politburo-Presidium that the ultimate decision-making power has resided. This small group of people, usually of about ten full members, has been assumed to be the repository of all power, the kingpin of the political structure of the U.S.S.R. Like all generalizations, this one requires some elaboration and correction, though in the main it remains true.

The original Politburo, or, to give it its full name, the Political Bureau of the Central Committee, was set up for a specific purpose. On the eve of the November uprising in 1917 a special committee of seven members was set up by the Central Committee to provide guidance to the insurrection. [The Eighth Party Congress in 1919 sanctioned a permanent Politburo, as a subcommittee of the Central Committee, to which it would regularly report and of which it would remain a subordinate organ.] But the list of members already indicated then that the new organization could not be thought of as "subordinate" to any other. Elected as full members were Lenin, Kamenev, Trotsky, Stalin and Krestinsky; as alternates Zinoviev, Bukharin and Kalinin. All of them were persons of the highest importance, though Krestinsky, then the Party's Secretary, not long afterwards dropped from the most important political plane, and Kalinin, long the figurehead president of the Soviet Union, remained content to play a passive role, and received his reward by being the only member of the original group—in addition to Lenin and (probably) Stalin—to die a natural death in his old age.

The personnel of the organization assured it from the beginning of a decisive role in the structure of the Party and government organization.

Once united, the Politburo could settle everything, since other members of the Central Committee were for the most part either secondary figures or protégés and friends of the Politburo members. But by the same token, the Politburo could not initially assume absolute power over the Party, since most of its initial members were, except for Lenin, personal rivals and unlikely to agree on the most fundamental questions. The main arenas of struggle were the Party Congresses and the Central Committee meetings. In the struggle for succession after Lenin's stroke, Stalin could not use the Politburo as his instrument of rise, for every other member was his competitor! Hence his policy of working for power through the Secretariat and control organs of the Party. The Party leaders in the Politburo were increasingly "surrounded" as more and more of Stalin's partisans were put in the Central Committee. At the same time it was decreed that on certain important questions the Presidium of the Central Control Commission (then already filled with Stalin's partisans) would sit with the Politburo. At the Fourteenth Congress Kamenev in his attack upon Stalin demanded a "collective leadership" of the Party by the Politburo. Stalin piously denounced the proposal as smacking of oligarchical rule and not consonant with inner-Party democracy. The Politburo was the last of the power positions in the Party conquered by Stalin. It was only in 1925 and 1926, with the ejection from it of Zinoviev, Kamenev and Trotsky and the addition of Molotov, Voroshilov, Kalinin and Rudzutak, that he gained a majority on the Politburo, and it was not until 1930, when Bukharin, Rykov, and Tomsky were dismissed, that the Politburo, like everything else in the Party, became solidly Stalinist.

It was natural then that the Politburo would become the focus of all governmental action arrogating to itself most of the functions belonging to other Party organs such as the Central Committee and the Council of Commissars. The Politburo came to be composed of the leader and his principal lieutenants. We have very little to go on to illustrate the manner of its operation during Stalin's ascendancy. We know, however, that in the previous era in the twenties the Politburo already functioned as the supreme political and economic organ. It was the supreme decision-making body in political and economic matters; it required reports from the governmental and Party organs; and it supervised as a body or through subcommittees the most important spheres of action. It is natural to surmise that with the dictatorship firmly established after 1930, and with just one faction established in the Politburo, the supreme functions of that body were still further aggrandized. Even the most absolute despot needs advice and help in directing his government, and a small group of intimates, people who had been Stalin's main helps in his rise to power, was the best instrument of despotic government. Membership in the Politburo became the most exalted and powerful position in the Soviet hierarchy and those who achieved it became beings apart from the other, even the highest, Party and state officials. One thing even the highest office in a despotic system cannot bestow and that is physical security and safety from the tyrant's whim or wrath. And thus among the officials destroyed in the great purge of the thirties were Stalin's colleagues on the Politburo—people who had got there because they had been his most faithful and useful servants and creatures. Liquidated in secrecy were Stanislav V. Kossior, Vlas I. Chubar, and Ian E. Rudzutak among the full members. Two other full members, Valerian V. Kuibyshev and Georgi "Sergo" Ordzhonikidze, died in good graces but under suspicious circumstances. Among the alternate members of the Politburo who met their end suddenly, their name one day dropping out of the news and the well-informed simply forgetting that they ever existed, was the main instrument of terror and Commissar of the Interior, the unspeakable Nicolai Yezhov.

From Khrushchev's secret speech we get some occasional, though unverifiable, accounts of the functioning of the highest Party organ under Stalin. Thus, says Khrushchev, Stalin was in 1936 vacationing in the Caucasus with Andrei Zhdanov, then Stalin's favorite, head of the Leningrad Party organization and alternate member of the Politburo. From there they sent a telegram to the Politburo demanding the immediate dismissal of the then Commissar of the Interior, Yagoda, and his replacement by Yezhov. The Politburo complied, and terror was intensified under Yezhov until he, like his predecessor, was sent to his reward. Whether the other members of his Politburo were ever able to restrain or temper Stalin remains unclear, though there are unverified reports that the slackening of the terror in late 1938 and the liquidation of Yezhov were due to the intervention of Molotov and Kaganovich. But the incident, if true, illustrates what was undoubtedly the case most of the time: Stalin could dominate and overrule even the Politburo, and at times his closest advisers could be chosen from among others than full members of the Politburo. Thus in 1936 Zhdanov was only an alternate.

During the war the supreme function of the Politburo was largely superseded by the State Committee of Defense. As originally composed in June 1941 it comprised Stalin, Molotov, Voroshilov, Beria and Malenkov, the last two at the time alternate members of the Politburo. With victory, the committee was dissolved and the prewar structure of authority evidently restored. Of the postwar Politburo we know only scraps of information given by Khrushchev. Thus he informs us that the arrest and liquidation of Nikolai Voznesensky was not even brought before his colleagues on the supreme body but was a decision of the dictator himself. Khrushchev also confirms what could be suspected from other sources: a man nominally a member of the Politburo might still be forbidden by Stalin to attend its sessions, or simply ejected from it without any public notice. The latter was the fate of Andreyev in 1950. The former was the fate of Kliment Voroshilov, toward whom the dictator took a dislike just before his death.[34]

The Nineteenth Party Congress took measures that, had they survived Stalin's death, would have drastically changed the nature of the Politburo. [Renamed the Presidium, it was now composed of twenty-five full members and eleven alternates.]Co-opted into the supreme body were some veteran Communist Party functionaries but also a number of the younger and rising Party and state bureaucrats. As stated above and confirmed by Khrushchev, the warning must have been plain: the dictator contemplated a change of the guard, and most of the surviving members of the pre-1952 Politburo were going to be pushed out. [In the enlarged Presidium there was evidently a smaller directing body—the bureau of the Presidium.]Who its members were we do not know.[Before the new pattern could jell Stalin died, and on the morrow of his death the veteran members threw out most of the newcomers added at the Nineteenth Congress. The Presidium was restored to more or less its previous size: ten full members and four alternates.]

The Presidium after the Twentieth Congress remained of a mixed character. Of the Old Bolsheviks who helped Stalin in his rise to power, four remained: Vyacheslav Molotov, erstwhile premier and foreign minister; Lazar Kaganovich, long the chief economic planner and previously Stalin's chief helper in Party affairs; Marshal Kliment Voroshilov, formal head of the Soviet state, and Anastas Mikoyan, expert on trade. In the second group were those who rose to prominence when Stalin's dictatorship was already firmly established during the purges of the thirties: Georgi Malenkov, who had worked long in Stalin's personal secretariat and was probably his intended successor; Nikolai Bulganin, Premier until March 1958; and the head of the Party, Nikita Khrushchev. In the third group were pure products of the Stalin era who climbed the rungs of the Party and state hierarchy to merge into prominence after the war. Here were M. G. Pervukhin and Maxim Saburov, both of whom have been connected with industrial affairs, and Party bureaucrats Mikhail Suslov and Alexei Kirichenko.

The crisis of June 1957 changed the composition of the Presidium. The

---

[34] The career of A. A. Andreyev is one of the proverbial exceptions to the rule. An Old Bolshevik, involved in opposition activities in the early twenties, criticized for administrative incompetence in the thirties, Andreyev not only survived but continued in very important Party positions. Until 1950 he was in the Politburo and head of the Party Control Commission. He incurred disgrace in that year, allegedly for his views on agriculture (he was also the head of the Commission on the Kolkhoz Economy), yet he was merely demoted, and survived!

alleged leaders of the anti-Khrushchev faction, Molotov and Kaganovich, each of whom had served on the powerful council for over a generation, were ejected, as was Georgi Malenkov. Dropped, though without any charges, was Maxim Saburov. Mikhail Pervukhin was demoted to alternate member. Pervukhin and Dimitri Shepilov, who was dismissed as an alternate member, were presumably potential candidates for Khrushchev's job.

The present Presidium does not promise to be more stable than its predecessor. It reflects Khrushchev's increased dominance but also the kind of bargaining which must have gone on to compass the defeat of the Molotov-Kaganovich-Malenkov faction. It is not, then, like Stalin's Politburos, composed of the dictator and his most useful servants: it is composed of the leader of the Party and his protégés, but it also includes his potential rivals. Voroshilov and Bulganin are still in it, though their position was damaged by their reputed vacillation during the June crisis. A number of Party secretaries have been co-opted and most of them are personal protégés of the Party boss. Two veteran Soviet figures, neither of them of first-rank importance under Stalin, Nikolai Shvernik and Otto Kuusinen, have been added, perhaps as a symbol of continuity with Party history.[35] In a different category was the promotion of Marshal Zhukov to full membership from the status of alternate member. Zhukov had been "promoted" in every major Soviet shakeup since Stalin's death until his ejection in October 1957. His inclusion marked the first time that a man primarily a soldier had reached the highest body of the Communist Party As for other additions to the Presidium, it is noticeable that many of them are local party bosses and quite a few of non-Russian origin. In February 1958 an Uzbek, Mukhitdinov, was raised to full membership. Presumably, the preponderance of party secretaries reflects increased domination of the Presidium by Khrushchev. The increase in non-Russians on the supreme body is a testimony to the importance of the nationality problem and of the Soviet leaders' ideas of how to solve it.

The Presidium is now a large body though not as big as Stalin's short-lived Presidium "elected" by the Nineteenth Congress. After the period of collective leadership 1953-57, one man's influence is now paramount in the Presidium as it is in the Party. The manner of the operation of the highest organ remains obscure. Presumably it functions through subcommittees, and each member has a specific responsibility for an area of Party or state activity. In the current turbulent state of Soviet politics it is very

---

[35] Kuusinen, a Finn by birth, had been for a long time a high official of the Communist International. His election as well as his inclusion in the rank of the secretaries of the Central Committee may presage a new attempt at the consolidation of the world Communist movement, which has been shaken by the de-Stalinization campaign and the events of Fall 1956 in Poland and Hungary.

likely that both the personnel and the sphere of activity of the Presidium will not long remain unchanged.

The Party Control Organs

The Party Control Committee is a continuation in its ostensible function of the Central Control Commission, which existed until 1934. Insofar as its political powers and significance are concerned, it is but a feeble imitation of its predecessor, which in the twenties enjoyed a status almost equal to that of the Central Committee, and members of whose presidium were summoned to the sessions of the Politburo.

It would take too long to recite the full history of both Party and state control organs. But the moral of their evolution is very clear: no machinery of control, however elaborate, can substitute for the element of control that is provided by the multi-party system and by the give-and-take of democratic politics. The Party control organs were evolved originally to "guard the guardians," to save the Party from evils of bureaucratism, corruption and abuse of power. Yet operating within a totalitarian society the control organs did not prevent, but hastened, the shackling of the Party and the rise of absolute personal dictatorship.

The Central Control Commission was organized in 1920. It stood at the top of a control organization that paralleled the territorial organization of other Party organs. The personnel and the functions of the Commission soon expanded. It was given the additional duties of ferreting out anti-Party activities—in effect of probing into the lives of Party functionaries and even rank-and-file members in order to see if their behavior as well as politics were of a kind expected of a Bolshevik. The Commission was to be independent of other Party institutions. Thus a member of it could not simultaneously be a member of the Central Committee. The apparatus and the size of the Commission grew prodigiously. At the Sixteenth Party Congress in 1930 it reached the size of 187 members, some of them attached to the central organ, others delegated to tasks of local supervision. In its original concept as envisaged by Lenin, the control organs were to function so as to curtail and point out various abuses, to act as a check on the very considerable power of the "political" organs like the Central Committee. The Central Control Commission was to function as a restraint on political power, performing some of the role that an independent judiciary performs in democratic states. Lenin's last moments were occupied in thinking about the ways and means of controlling the inner Party strife and of erecting a bar both against fatal dissensions that would split the Party wide open, and against the seizure of power by one man.

Yet in a totalitarian system nothing can be apolitical. From its inception the Central Control Commission interpreted its task as that of enforcing the Party "line," i.e., rooting out various oppositionists, beginning with Lenin's opponents in the very early twenties and ending with Stalin's. From a censor of Communist morals and guardian of revolutionary morality, the control organs became almost from the beginning an instrument of political purges.

The Central Control Commission very early came to be dominated by Stalin's faction. It would be too simple to attribute this only to Stalin's personal machinations. In the control organs just as in the other branches of the Party's administration the dominant type became very soon the *apparatchik*, "man of the machine," with a bureaucratic mentality, seeing politics in terms of practical administrative problems and distrustful of intellectuals in the Party (and Trotsky, Zinoviev and Kamenev were *par excellence* revolutionary intellectuals). It was natural for such men to feel an affinity with Stalin and to see in him a man of practicality and moderation. In the struggle for power in the twenties the control organs regularly supported Stalin, chastised or expelled from the Party his opponents, and overlooked the transgressions of the Secretary-General's partisans. Quite apart from the "control" functions the Commission had an important political role. Certain important political decisions such as demotion of a Central Committee member could be transacted only at a joint meeting of the Central Committee and the Commission. Three members of the presidium of the Commission had the right to sit in with the Politburo. Thus the relative strength of Stalin's opponents in the Central Committee and the Politburo was effectively neutralized or overcome by his domination of the Control Commission.

With the end of all open opposition to dictatorship, the political function of the control organs became superfluous. The control organs could return to their administrative duties, without, however, abandoning the task of rooting out disloyal and would-be disloyal Party members. In connection with the latter, the personnel of the Central Control Commission was increasingly penetrated by high officials of the N.K.V.D. (the Commissariat of the Interior—the security forces). By 1934 the Commission was renamed the Committee of Party Control. The fiction of its independent status was abandoned, and though still elected by the Party Congress, it was now officially inferior to the Central Committee and charged with implementing its directives. The statutes of 1952 make the Party Control Committee fully a creature of the Central Committee. Unlike the Central Auditing Commission, a body of minor importance, the Party Control Committee is no longer elected by the Congress, but organized by the Central Committee of the Communist Party. In the structure of Soviet power the Control Committee no longer has any independent political role. It confines itself to its stated duties, i.e., the preservation of Party dis-

cipline and ethics,[36] supervises the fulfillment of the decrees of the central
organs, etc. It is not impossible, however, that any deep split within the
present leadership and factional strife could again awaken the political role
of the control organs, and that the dossiers and files of the Party Control
Committee could again become the instrument of factional strife.

The Secretariat

The nerve center of the Communist Party has been since the beginning
of the twenties the Secretariat of the Central Committee. Prior to the
Nineteenth Congress of 1952 there existed in addition to the Secretariat
the Organizational Bureau (Orgburo) of the Central Committee. But the
latter body, extremely important during the post-Revolutionary period and
again one of the avenues through which Stalin rose to power, was later increasingly superseded in its functions by both the Secretariat and the
Politburo, and at the time of its abolition was actually a fifth wheel.

The Secretariat, on the other hand, has preserved its crucial importance.
The First Secretary of the Communist Party is in the U.S.S.R. the leading
man in the country, whether he holds another office or not. The same pattern prevails in almost all Communist-ruled countries (except occasionally
as in China where there is the office of Chairman of the Party). The word
"secretary" evokes in our mind a rather clerical person occupied with shuf-
fling papers, etc. Actually the General or First Secretary of the Communist Party is not only the chief administrative officer, but also the man with
the dominant voice in formulating the policies of his Party, and, if it be in
power, of the country.

The pattern was set in 1922 when Joseph Stalin became the General
Secretary of the Central Committee of the Russian Communist Party. The
Party, which had inherited so much of the anarchistic contempt for problems of political organization, had given but little thought to its own administration prior to the Revolution. Following November 1917 the functions of the chief administrative officer of the Party were discharged by
Jacob Sverdlov, a close collaborator of Lenin. His death in 1919 left the
Party without a first-rate figure charged with administration. Lenin had all
the cares of the state and policies to be busy with. Trotsky was running
the Red Army, and other leading figures of the regime were much more
at home in making speeches, writing pamphlets, and preparing revolutions
abroad, than in day-to-day administrative routine. Yet the Party was no
longer a small conspiratorial organization that could be run informally.
One of the central problems was that of liaison between the center and
the local organizations. Another was the problem of admission of new

[36] A violation of Party ethics is defined as "dishonesty and insincerity in relation to
the Party, slander, bureaucracy, moral turpitude, etc."

members; of ideological education of Party members, their apportionment to the government apparatus, etc. To deal with the broader organizational problems the Eighth Congress created the Orgburo, one of whose original members was Stalin. To deal with immediate administrative problems, a Secretariat of the Central Committee was set up.

Under its first leaders the Secretariat remained very much what it had been intended to be: an administrative and liaison organ. The change came in 1921 when three secretaries were appointed (one of whom was Molotov) who were closely linked to Stalin. And in 1922 he himself became Secretary-General and the office underwent a transition.

The Secretariat rapidly arrogated to itself the function not only of administrative, but also of general, guidance of the Party. The tasks of agitation, propaganda, and ideological education were taken over by the rapidly expanding institution. From a modest office where unassuming secretaries sat ready to counsel and comfort visiting Party officials from the provinces, the Secretariat became a veritable command post, which transferred Party leaders from the Caucasus to the Ukraine, changed ideological instructors, and even disciplined and dismissed Party functionaries. A list of departments of the Secretariat between 1924 and 1930 gives a fair idea of this Frankenstein-like growth of an administrative department that came to engulf the whole Party. The departments included: organization—assignment one, village affairs, statistical, general administration, agitation and propaganda, information, etc.[37] From newspaper articles to the appointment of a Party secretary in a small town; all these affairs—the very lifeblood of a political organism—were regulated by the Secretariat. Complaints of the opposition, cries that the Secretariat should return to a purely administrative role and leave politics to political organs, went unheeded. The Secretariat more and more absorbed the real task of governing Russia as well as the Party.

With the effective elimination of opposition in the Party, the remnants of which task could now be handed over to the secret police, the Secretariat was adjusted largely to propelling the country toward industrialization. Thus the reorganization of 1930 split the organization–instruction section into two, one of which, the assignment department, had several sub-departments dealing with the assignment of Party workers to several major areas of the Russian economy, e.g., heavy industry, light industry, agriculture, sub-departments as well as sections devoted to Soviet administration, foreign Communist activities, etc.[38] Soviet government was thus reduced to the typical bureaucratic model. The main function of the Party organization became to select personnel, and this in turn would be

[37] After Fainsod, *op. cit.*, p. 167.

[38] Fainsod, *op. cit.*, p. 168.

decided in the offices of the Secretariat, which was now running not only
the Party, but also almost directly the whole country's administration and
economy. Even a more direct functional principle was introduced in 1934,
when this time special departments rather than sub-departments were
created in the Secretariat paralleling large areas of the Soviet economy,
i.e., agriculture, transport, industry, and finance and trade. The Secretariat
thus became not merely the power behind the throne, but a body *directly*
supervising and staffing all branches of the Soviet government, expanding
directly into industry, agriculture, etc. The resulting confusion of authority
led to the scheme's being temporarily abandoned in 1939, and most of
the departments again corresponded to purely Party affairs. But in 1948
the functional setup was restored, and among the departments there now
appeared a special one devoted to political administration of the armed
forces.[39]

＊ [The whole development since 1930 again demonstrates the dilemma of
a totalitarian regime, even at an administrative level. The regime feels the
need of checking and double-checking every sphere of activity. Everything
is controlled by the government apparatus, which in turn is supervised by
the Party apparatus—and then you have the secret police] It is likely that
during Stalin's last years there was a special personal secretariat surrounding the leader and independent of the Party apparatus. The result, however, when you come to concrete tasks of administration and economy, is
often inefficiency and confusion. So periodically the cry is raised that the
Party should not stick its fingers into the details of running the economic
machinery and just as periodically it is exclaimed that things are not going
well because the Party does not evidence enough care for economic problems. But the administrative history of the Secretariat shows how a modest
administrative office, in a system where there are no effective checks on
power, may grow into the kingpin of the whole political and economic
system of a vast country.

The actual work of the Secretariat, at the highest level, has been
shrouded in something of a mystery. Since the office has been the locus
of political power in the Soviet Union for at least thirty years, its inner-
most operations have been secret, and the only conjectures we can form
are on the basis of changes in its personnel. Stalin's ascendancy in the
Secretariat was immediate and unqualified. As Secretary-General in 1922
he was assisted by two secretaries, Molotov and V. V. Kuibyshev, both of
them members of his faction. From then on the pattern of Secretary-
General and two, three, or four "plain" secretaries of the Central Committee persisted. The latter were invariably the closest associates of the
dictator, though for reasons that are obvious none of them was allowed to

[39] Fainsod, *op. cit.*, pp. 173 and 195.

warm up his seat in the Secretariat for more than a few years before being transferred to other work. In the regional and republic party organizations there has often been the pattern of designating a hierarchy of secretaries, one of them being designated as first secretary, another as second, and sometimes there being even an official third secretary. In the central secretariat, except for Stalin, other secretaries were not differentiated in status. Yet with the dictatorship in full swing and Stalin occupied with other vast responsibilities it becomes possible to identify his chief deputy for organizational matters in the Party. In the early thirties that function was performed by Lazar M. Kaganovich. It was Kaganovich who first selected for higher Party posts many of the current leaders like Khrushchev and Malenkov. In the later thirties Andrei Zhdanov succeeded to the post of Stalin's main Party lieutenant. A Party secretary, since 1934 head of the Leningrad organization, he played a large but still unexplained role during the Great Purge of 1936-38 and in the immediate postwar era. During the latter period he was in open (insofar as anything in the Soviet system can be open) rivalry with Georgi Malenkov, Party secretary since 1939, but temporarily dropped from the Secretariat in 1946. Zhdanov died, assertedly of a heart attack, in the summer of 1948, and Malenkov, until Stalin's death, enjoyed the position of the main Party administrator, and presumably Stalin's intended successor. He was soon, however, joined on the Secretariat by another Party figure of importance, Nikita Khrushchev.

The story of the top personnel of the Secretariat preceding and immediately following Stalin's death has a little bit of the air of a mystery story. At the Nineteenth Congress the number of secretaries was raised to ten, all of them members of the Presidium. On the morrow of Stalin's death the communiqué about the changes in other branches of the government and the Party was quite explicit; but on the reconstruction of the secretariat its language was unclear and confused. Some secretaries were dropped, some were added, but it was impossible to tell whether anyone would occupy the chief position in the Secretariat, and whether Malenkov, just made Prime Minister, was retained on this body or not. The leaders who evidently agreed after Stalin's death and for the moment on the redistribution of other government and Party positions, were evidently unable to come to a full agreement on the redistribution of power in the most important office of all. Only one week later, on March 14, 1953, it was announced that Comrade Malenkov requested and was granted permission to resign from the Secretariat. One of the secretaries freshly appointed in March, S. D. Ignatiev, was dismissed on April 7.[40]

---

[40] S. D. Ignatiev was Minister of State Security at the time of the "Doctors' Plot," and made a member of the Presidium at the Nineteenth Congress. Chastised for political blindness on account of his role in the preparation of a new purge before Stalin's

The office of the General Secretary was not restored. As a matter of fact, for reasons that are difficult to divine, that title was not used by Stalin in the postwar era, he being referred to in his Party capacity as *a* secretary of the Central Committee. Among the secretaries appointed or confirmed after his death none was designated as the chief one. It was only after Beria's liquidation in the summer of 1953, and possibly as a part of another political bargain between the leaders, that Nikita Khrushchev was appointed as First Secretary. The personnel of the Secretariat following the Twentieth Congress confirms the impression that the other secretaries are mostly, but not entirely, Khrushchev's creatures, and that the same situation prevails in the regional and local Communist organizations. It is equally clear that the days of the greatest power of the Secretariat are over and that lacking a Stalin it cannot enjoy the absolute supremacy it had had in the thirties and forties vis-à-vis the Central Committee and the Presidium.

The sketch of the main organs of the Communist Party suggests forcibly the logic of both the development and the potential decline of a totalitarian state. Under one-Party government even the deliberative organs atrophy, and the control organs, instead of being checks on absolute despotism, become its tools. Power is withdrawn more and more into a tight administrative clique, and even this clique becomes subject to one man's rule. But the atrophy of the Party in turn weakens the very basis on which despotism rests, and the death of the despot reveals this weakness. For all its divisions and splits, for all of Russia's weaknesses, the Communist Party in the early twenties was a live, vigorous organism, which the powerful and monolithic Party of seven million members at the death of Stalin was not. Bureaucracy and terror have throttled what there was of the comradely spirit, of spontaneity and revolutionary enthusiasm and sense of mission among the Communists. The political and organizational future of the Communist Party is being shaped by its new masters so as to recapture some of the old spirit. This time, however, Russian society, vastly changed in the last thirty years, will have a potent voice in shaping that future.

---

death, he made a modest comeback after Beria's downfall. At the time of the Twentieth Congress he was head of the Party organization in Bashkiria.

SELECT BIBLIOGRAPHY

I: The Analysis of Political Systems

How political science can be made a more scientific discipline has been discussed a great deal in recent years. The student would do well to begin with Roy C. Macridis' essay, *The Study of Comparative Government*, in which he criticizes traditional approaches and suggests a general scheme for comparative analysis. Also highly critical of the present state of political science, David Easton, *The Political System*, like the present volume, takes the position that politics can best be studied as a system and explains the meaning of this approach in comparison with others. Harold Lasswell has probably done more than anyone else to develop the concept of power as a tool of analysis and the student will find his *Power and Society* (co-author, Abraham Kaplan) a rewarding, though difficult, book. Greater stress on the role of purpose will be found in R. M. MacIver, *The Web of Government*. A major work on interest groups in American politics, David Truman, *The Governmental Process*, is based on an explicit theoretical scheme that can also be used in the study of the politics of other countries.

The approach followed in the present volume owes a great deal to the sociological theory of Talcott Parsons. From him, for example, we have taken the three-fold division of culture into belief systems, values, and expressive symbols. Perhaps the best place to begin the study of his ideas is Part 2 ("Values, Motives, and Systems of Action") of *Toward a General Theory of Action*, a volume edited by Parsons and Edward A. Shils. For greater elaboration see Parsons, *The Social System*.

Almond, Gabriel, "Comparative Political Systems," *Journal of Politics*, Vol. 18 (1956).

Catlin, G. E. G., *Science and Methods of Politics*. New York, 1927.

————, A *Study of the Principles of Politics*. New York, 1930.

Duverger, Maurice, *Political Parties: Their Organization and Activity in the Modern State*, trans. by B. and R. North. New York, 1954.

Easton, David, *The Political System: An Inquiry into the State of Political Science*. New York, 1953.

Eulau, Heinz, Samuel J. Eldersveld, and Morris Janowitz (eds.), *Political Behavior: A Reader in Theory and Research*. Glencoe, 1956. Includes an extensive bibliography on methodology for political scientists.

Finer, Herman, *The Theory and Practice of Modern Government*, rev. edn. New York, 1949.

Friedrich, Carl J., *Constitutional Government and Democracy: Theory and Practice in Europe and America*, rev. edn. Boston, 1950.

Lasswell, Harold D., *Politics: Who Gets What, When, How*. New York, 1936.

———, and Abraham Kaplan, *Power and Society: A Framework for Political Inquiry*. New Haven, 1950.

MacIver, R. M., *The Web of Government*. New York, 1947.

Macridis, Roy C., *The Study of Comparative Government*. New York, 1955.

Merriam, Charles E., *Political Power*. New York, 1934.

———, *Systematic Politics*. Chicago, 1946.

Merton, Robert K., *Social Theory and Social Structure*. Glencoe, 1949. Ch. II, "The Bearing of Sociological Theory on Empirical Research."

Morgenthau, Hans J., *Scientific Man vs. Power Politics*. Chicago, 1946.

Neumann, Sigmund (ed.), *Modern Political Parties*. Chicago, 1955.

Parsons, Talcott, *Essays in Sociological Theory: Pure and Applied*. Glencoe, 1949. Ch. II, "The Present Position and Prospects of Systematic Theory in Sociology."

———, *The Social System*. Glencoe, 1951.

———, and Edward Shils (eds.), *Toward a General Theory of Social Action*. Cambridge, Massachusetts, 1951.

Russell, Bertrand, *Power: A New Social Analysis*. New York, 1938.

Truman, David B., *The Governmental Process: Political Interests and Public Opinion*. New York, 1951.

Weber, Max, *The Theory of Social and Economic Organization*, translated by A. M. Henderson and Talcott Parsons, with an introduction by Talcott Parsons. New York, 1947. Especially Part III, "The Types of Authority and Imperative Coordination."

II: The British Political System

SOURCES: The chief source material for the study of British government is found in the publications of Her Majesty's Stationery Office (especially the Reports of Parliamentary Debates—*Hansard*—annual reports of the administrative departments, and the reports of special committees), publications of the Conservative and Labour Parties, and certain newspapers and journals, notably (for reliability and thoroughness of coverage) *The Times* (of London) and *The Economist*. The standard work on parliamentary procedure is Sir Thomas Erskine May, *A Treatise on the Law, Privileges, Proceedings and Usage of Parliament*, but the beginner will find especially useful L. A. Abraham and S. C. Hawtrey, *A Parliamentary Dictionary* (1956).

IMPORTANT SECONDARY WORKS: The classic interpretation of British government, still valid in many ways, is Walter Bagehot, *The English Constitution*, first published in 1867. More recent interpretations include L. S. Amery's provocative *Thoughts on the Constitution* (2nd ed., 1953), H. R. G. Greaves's socialist interpretation in *The British Constitution* (1948) and Herbert Morrison's *Government and Parliament* (1954), the latter useful chiefly as a view of British government from the inside.

BACKGROUND: Dennis Brogan, *The English People* (1943), is a gay but highly informative work that should be read before such studies as Geoffrey Gorer, *Exploring English Character* (1956), and R. Lewis and A. Maude, *The English Middle Classes* (1949). The best introduction to constitutional history is S. B. Chrimes, *English Constitutional History* (1953), the best work for further study D. L. Keir, *Constitutional History of Modern Britain, 1485–1951*. K. G. Feiling, *History of England to 1918* (1950), is a useful general history.

BIOGRAPHIES AND MEMOIRS: An extensive bibliography of biographies and memoirs of British statesmen may be found in Sir Ivor Jennings, *Cabinet Government* (1951), Appendix V.

THE CABINET: The standard work is Jennings, *Cabinet Government* (2nd ed., 1951). A. B. Keith, *The British Cabinet System* (2nd ed., 1952), and Lord Hankey, *Diplomacy by Conference* (1947), are also widely used.

PARLIAMENT: Sir Ivor Jennings, *Parliament* (2nd ed., 1957), is a thorough and detailed study; A. P. Herbert, *The Ayes Have It* (1937), gives perhaps a more vivid picture of Parliament than any other book; J. F. S. Ross, *Parliamentary Representation* (1944), is an important analysis of the membership of the House. By far the best brief introduction to the subject is Eric Taylor, *The House of Commons at Work* (1951).

ADMINISTRATION: For the beginner, G. A. Campbell, *The Civil Service in Britain* (1955), is excellent. H. E. Dale, *The Higher Civil Service* (1941), is standard on the administrative class; H. R. G. Greaves, *The Civil Service in the Changing State* (1947), deals with problems of administration in the welfare state and E. W. Cohen, *The Growth of the Civil Service* (1941), is a useful historical account.

PARTIES: R. T. McKenzie, *British Political Parties* (1955), is a comprehensive empirical account, making other works on British parties almost superfluous. Students are referred, however, to the excellent studies of British general elections since 1945 published by the Oxford University Press.

ECONOMIC AND SOCIAL POLICY: Much of the British welfare state is based on *The Beveridge Report: Social Insurance and Allied Services* (1942) and Sir William Henry Beveridge, *Full Employment in a Free Society* (1944). R. Brady, *Crisis in Britain* (1950), remains the best general account of the Labour Government's policies. On the nationalized industries see D. N. Chester, *The Nationalized Industries* and the *Studies in National-*

ised Industry issued in pamphlet form by the Acton Society Trust. On national insurance services: D. C. Marsh, *National Insurance and Assistance in Great Britain* (1951). On the National Health Service: H. Eckstein, *The English Health Service* (1958). On Planning: S. H. Beer, *Treasury Control* (2nd ed., 1957). On Town and Country Planning: *Town and Country Planning 1943–1951*, H.M.S.O., Cmd. 8204.

III: The French Political System

The essential primary source of information about official acts of the French government is the *Journal Officiel de la République Française*. Laws and decrees, as well as the verbatim record of debates in all the parliamentary bodies, are to be found in various sections of this serial publication. Of even greater usefulness for most research is the annual series, *L'Année Politique*, which contains in each year's volume a chronological account of all phases of French public life and a selection of important documents, speeches, and statistics. The best current record of everyday politics, including a detailed description of party activities, is to be found in the Paris daily, *Le Monde*. Important, though purely descriptive, monographs on various parts of the governmental structure and on the content of government policy are published by the government publications service, *Documentation Française*. Their series of studies entitled *Notes et Etudes Documentaires* is especially useful. More analytical and scholarly studies are to be found regularly in the two leading journals of French political science: the *Revue Française de Science Politique*, published quarterly in Paris; and the *Revue du Droit Public et de la Science Politique*, published in Paris bi-monthly. Partisan, yet very suggestive, critical articles on French political and social matters are frequently found in the left-wing Catholic journal, *Esprit*, published monthly in Paris.

Any serious study of the French political system must begin with the three outstanding general works in English: dated, yet still very useful, is J. E. C. Bodley, *France* (New and Revised edition, London, 1902); for the Third Republic, Walter Rice Sharp, *The Government of France* (New York, 1938); and for the Fourth Republic, Philip Williams, *Politics in Postwar France* (Revised edition, London, 1958). Other interesting general essays and studies are: Michel Debré, *La Mort de l'Etat Républicain* (Paris, 1947); Maurice Duverger, *Droit Constitutionnel et Institutions Politiques* (Paris, 1955); François Goguel, *France Under the Republic* (Ithaca, New York, 1952), and his *Le Régime Politique Français* (Paris, 1955); Robert de Jouvenel, *La République des Camarades* (Paris, 1913); W. L. Middleton, *The French Political System* (New

York, 1933); André Tardieu, *La Révolution à Refaire* (2 vols. Paris, 1936, 1937).

The modern historical background can best be drawn from: D. W. Brogan, *The Development of Modern France 1870–1940* (London, 1939); J. P. T. Bury, *France 1814–1940* (Philadelphia, 1949); and Jean Jacques Chevallier, *Histoire des Institutions Politiques de la France* (Paris, 1952). For the history of the Third Republic there is: François Goguel, *Histoire des Partis Politiques sous la Troisième République* (Paris, 1946); David Thomson, *Democracy in France* (Revised edition, London, 1952); and Alexander Werth, *The Twilight of France* (New York, 1942). The history of France since 1940 is recounted and commented upon in: Herbert Luethy, *France Against Herself* (New York, 1955); Dorothy Pickles, *French Politics: The First Years of the Fourth Republic* (London, 1953), and her *France Between the Republics* (London, 1946); André Siegfried, *De la Troisième à la Quatrième République* (Paris, 1956); Alexander Werth, *France 1940–1956* (London, 1956).

The following are useful works on more specialized subjects:

Barthélemy, Joseph, *L'Introduction du Régime Parlementaire en France*. Paris, 1904.

Blum, Léon, *La Réforme Gouvernementale*. Paris, 1936.

Brayance, Alain, *Anatomie du Parti Communiste Français*. Paris, 1953.

Chapman, Brian, *Introduction to French Local Government*. London, 1953.

———, *The Prefects and Provincial France*. London, 1955.

Clough, Shepard, *France: A History of National Economics 1789–1939*. New York, 1939.

Curtius, Ernst, *The Civilization of France*. London, 1932.

Dansette, Adrien, *Les Présidents de la République de Louis Napoléon Bonaparte à Vincent Auriol*. Paris, 1953.

Earle, Edward M., editor, *Modern France: Problems of the Third and Fourth Republics*. Princeton, 1951.

Ehrmann, Henry W., *French Labor from Popular Front to Liberation*. New York, 1947.

Einaudi, Mario, et al., *Communism in Western Europe*. Ithaca, New York, 1951.

———, *Christian Democracy in France and Italy*. South Bend, Indiana, 1952.

———, *Nationalization in France and Italy*. Ithaca, New York, 1955.

Fauvet, Jacques, *Les Forces Politiques en France*. Paris, 1951.

Goguel, François, *Géographie des Elections Françaises de 1870 à 1951*. Paris, 1951.

Gooch, Robert K., *The French Parliamentary Committee System*. New York, 1935.

———, *Regionalism in France*. New York, 1931.

Howard, John E., *Parliament and Foreign Policy in France*. London, 1948.

Lidderdale, D. W. S., *The Parliament of France*. London, 1951.

Lorwin, Val R., *The French Labor Movement*. Cambridge, Massachusetts, 1954.

McKay, Donald C., *The United States and France*. Cambridge, Massachusetts, 1951.

Robson, William A., editor, *The Civil Service in Britain and France*. New York, 1956.

Sharp, Walter Rice, *The French Civil Service: Bureaucracy in Transition*. New York, 1931.

Siegfried, André, *France: A Study in Nationality*. New Haven, 1930.

Soulier, A., *L'Instabilité Ministérielle sous la Troisième République 1871–1938*. Paris, 1939.

Théry, Jacques, *Le Gouvernement de la Quatrième République*. Paris, 1949.

Wright, Gordon, *The Reshaping of French Democracy*. New York, 1948.

IV: The German Political System

No single up-to-date work on German government and politics, like Philip Williams's book on France, is available in English. Some of the comparative government textbooks listed in the General Bibliography do contain sections on Germany. There are a number of good general German histories, such as Valentin's, and others of more limited scope, such as Rosenberg's. Several fine studies have been written by political scientists. The best of these seem to have the narrowest focus, with regard to time and subject matter; e.g., the books by Watkins, Heberle, and Franz Neumann.

Among basic sources, reports of parliamentary debates are the most important, especially *Verhandlungen des deutschen Bundestages*, and its predecessor of the Weimar period and before, *Verhandlungen des deutschen Reichstages*. For the Bonn Republic, *Sitzungen des deutschen Bundesrates*, and *Entscheidungen des Bundesverfassungsgerichtes* are also useful. Many publications of the Office of the United States High Commissioner for Germany contain translations of German documents.

Deutschland-Jahrbuch, an annual edited by Mehnert and Schulte, is full of factual information. Among learned journals, the following are useful: *Archiv des öffentlichen Rechts, Süddeutsche Juristenzeitung, Zeitschrift für Politik, Politische Studien. Frankfurter Allgemeine Zeitung* is one of the best daily newspapers. *Das Parlament* is a weekly devoted to parliamentary affairs in particular and politics in general. *Der Wähler*, published by the German Voters' Association, concentrates on matters electoral. The Trade Union Federation publishes *Gewerkschaftliche Monatshefte. Der Spiegel* is Germany's equivalent of *Time* magazine. *Die Gegenwart* appeals to intellectuals. Among contemporary

German publications, the series of the Association for Political Science, edited by Dolf Sternberger, is of special interest. In this series, Breitling's work has been most helpful for our purposes.

I. GENERAL

Bergsträsser, Ludwig, *Geschichte der politischen Parteien in Deutschland*. 7th ed., Munich, 1952.

Bowen, Ralph H., *German Theories of the Corporative State*. New York, 1947.

Buchheim, Karl, *Geschichte der christlichen Parteien in Deutschland*. Munich, 1953.

Glum, Friedrich, *Das parlamentarische Regierungssystem in Deutschland, Grossbritannien und Frankreich*. Munich, 1950.

Meinecke, Friedrich, *The German Catastrophe*. Cambridge, Mass., 1950.

Neumann, Sigmund, *Die deutschen Parteien*. 2nd ed., Berlin, 1932.

Pollock, James K., and H. Thomas, *Germany in Power and Eclipse*. New York, 1952.

Schorske, Carl, *German Social Democracy*. Cambridge, Mass., 1950.

Taylor, A. J. P., *The Course of German History*. New York, 1946.

Treue, Wolfgang, *Deutsche Parteiprogramme, 1861–1954*. Göttingen, 1954.

Ullmann, R. K., and Sir Stephen King-Hall, *German Parliaments*. London, 1954.

Valentin, Veit, *The German People*. New York, 1946.

Wheeler-Bennett, John W., *The Nemesis of Power*. London, 1953.

II. THE WEIMAR PERIOD

Anschütz, Gerhard, and Richard Thoma, eds., *Handbuch des deutschen Staatsrechts*. 2 vols., Tübingen, 1930–32.

Bracher, Karl D., *Die Auflösung der Weimarer Republik*. Stuttgart, 1955.

Brecht, Arnold, *Federalism and Regionalism in Germany*. New York, 1945.

———, *Prelude to Silence*. New York, 1944.

Flechtheim, Ossip K., *Die Kommunistische Partei Deutschlands in der Weimarer Republik*. Offenbach, 1948.

Gatzke, Hans, *Stresemann and the Re-Armament of Germany*. Baltimore, 1954.

Halperin, S. William, *Germany Tried Democracy*. New York, 1946.

Heberle, Rudolf, *From Democracy to Nazism*. Baton Rouge, 1945.

Heiden, Konrad, *Der Fuehrer*. Boston, 1944.

Hermens, F. A., *Democracy or Anarchy*. Notre Dame, 1941.

Matthias, Erich, *Sozialdemokratie und Nation*. Stuttgart, 1952.

Rosenberg, Arthur, *The Birth of the German Republic*. London, 1931.

Scheele, Godfrey, *The Weimar Republic.* London, 1946.

Sturmthal, Adolf F., *The Tragedy of European Labor.* New York, 1943.

Watkins, F. M., *The Failure of Constitutional Emergency Powers under the German Republic.* Cambridge, Mass., 1939.

III. NATIONAL SOCIALISM

Bullock, Allan, *Hitler—A Study in Tyranny.* London, 1952.

Fraenkel, Ernst, *The Dual State.* New York, 1941.

Friedrich, Carl J., and Z. Brzezinski, *Totalitarian Dictatorship and Autocracy.* Cambridge, Mass., 1956.

Neumann, Franz, *Behemoth.* New York, 1944.

IV. 1945–1956

Breitling, Rupert, *Die Verbände in der Bundesrepublik*, Dolf Sternberger, ed. Meisenheim, 1955.

Clay, Lucius D., *Decision in Germany.* New York, 1950.

Dechamps, Bruno, *Macht und Arbeit der Ausschüsse*, Dolf Sternberger, ed. Meisenheim, 1954.

Eschenburg, Theodor, *Staat und Gesellschaft in Deutschland.* Stuttgart, 1956.

Flechtheim, Ossip K., *Die deutschen Parteien seit 1945.* Berlin, 1955.

Friedrich, Carl J., "Rebuilding the German Constitution," *American Political Science Review,* June, August, 1949.

Grosser, Alfred, *The Colossus Again.* New York, 1955.

Harbarth, Karl, *Das rechtliche Wesen des Fraktionsbeschlusses*, Dolf Sternberger, ed. Meisenheim, 1955.

Heydte, F. A. v. d., and K. Sacherl, *Soziologie der deutschen Parteien.* Munich, 1955.

Horne, Alistair, *Return to Power.* New York, 1956.

Hund, H., *Der BHE in Koalition und Opposition.* Heidelberg, 1953.

Institut für Staatslehre und Politik e.V. Mainz, *Der Kampf um den Südweststaat.* Munich, 1952.

Kirchheimer, Otto, "The Composition of the German Bundestag," *Western Political Quarterly,* 1950.

Litchfield, Edward H., ed., *Governing Postwar Germany.* Ithaca, 1953.

Markmann, Heinz, *Das Abstimmungsverhalten der Parteifraktionen in deutschen Parlamenten*, Dolf Sternberger, ed. Meisenheim, 1954.

Morgenthau, Hans J., ed., *Germany and the Future of Europe.* Chicago, 1950.

Pollock, James K., ed., *German Democracy at Work.* Ann Arbor, 1955.

Roth, Götz, *Fraktion und Regierungsbildung*, Dolf Sternberger, ed. Meisenheim, 1954.

Sänger, Fritz, *Handbuch des deutschen Bundestages.* Stuttgart, 1954.

Spiro, Herbert J., *The Politics of German Codetermination.* Cambridge, 1958.

Trossmann, Hans, *Der zweite deutsche Bundestag.* Bonn, 1954.

Wallenberg, Hans, *Report on Democratic Institutions in Germany.* New York, 1956.

Wallich, Henry C., *Mainsprings of German Revival.* New Haven, 1955.

V: The Russian Political System

The most essential materials toward the study of Soviet government are in Russian. Among them may be mentioned *Sbornik Zakonov S.S.S.R. I Ukazov Prezidiuma Verkhovnogo Soveta S.S.S.R. (Collection of the Laws of the U.S.S.R. and Decrees of the Supreme Soviet of the U.S.S.R.)*, Moscow, 1945; *Vsesoyuznaya Kommunisticheskaya Partiya V Rezolutsiyakh I Resheniyakh S'ezdov, Konferentsii, I Plenumov Tsk 1898–1939 (All-Union Communist Party (B) in Resolutions and Decrees of Congresses, Conferences, and Plenums of the Central Committee 1898– 1939)*, Moscow, 1941. Stenographic reports of Congresses and Conferences of the Communist Party of the U.S.S.R. are available in Russian, and they provide the most illuminating guide to the Soviet system.

Among many studies in English Merle Fainsod, *How Russia Is Ruled* and Barrington Moore, Jr., *Soviet Politics—The Dilemma of Power* are the most perceptive and comprehensive treatments of the Soviet government. The already existing volumes of E. H. Carr, *A History of Soviet Russia* provide the most detailed account of the development of Soviet power, though some of Mr. Carr's interpretations, especially in the first volume, are questioned by other authorities. Bertram Wolfe, *Three Who Made a Revolution* is an excellent treatment of the origins of Bolshevism. A valuable tool for the student who does not command Russian is the *Current Digest of the Soviet Press*, which translates the most important articles appearing in the Soviet press. Some of the bibliography available in English is indicated in the list below.

The Anti-Stalin Campaign and International Communism, Russian Institute, Columbia University. New York, 1956.

Arakelian, A., *Industrial Management in the U.S.S.R.* Washington, 1950.

Barghoorn, Frederick C., *The Soviet Image of the United States*. New York, 1950.

Bauer, Raymond A., *The New Man in Soviet Psychology*. Cambridge, 1952.

Berman, Harold J., *Justice in Russia*. Cambridge, 1950.

Bienstock, Gregory, Solomon M. Schwarz, and Aaron Yugow, *Management in Russian Industry and Agriculture*. London and New York, 1944.

Burns, Emile, *A Handbook of Marxism*. New York, 1935.

Carew Hunt, R. N., *The Theory and Practice of Communism*. New York, 1951.

Carr, E. H., *A History of Soviet Russia: The Bolshevik Revolution*, Vols. I–III. New York, 1951–53.

———, *A History of Soviet Russia: The Interregnum 1923–1924*. New York, 1955.

Chamberlin, W. H., *The Russian Revolution, 1917–1921*. 2 vols. New York, 1935.

Current Soviet Policies: *The Documentary Record of XIXth Communist Party Congress and the Reorganization After Stalin's Death*. New York, 1953.

Curtiss, J. W., *Church and State in Russia, 1900–1917*. New York, 1939.

Dallin, David J., *The Real Soviet Russia*. New Haven, 1944.

———, and Boris I. Nicolaevsky. *Forced Labor in Soviet Russia*. New Haven, 1947.

Deutscher, Isaac, *Soviet Trade Unions*. London and New York, 1950.

———, *Stalin: A Political Biography*. New York, 1949.

Fainsod, Merle, *How Russia Is Ruled*. Cambridge, 1953.

Fischer, Ruth, *Stalin and German Communism*. Cambridge, 1948.

Florinsky, Michael T., *The End of the Russian Empire*. New Haven, 1931.

Gsovski, Vladimir, *Soviet Civil Law*. 2 vols. Ann Arbor, 1948.

History of the Communist Party of the Soviet Union (Bolsheviks); Short Course. New York, 1939.

Holzman, Franklyn D., *Soviet Taxation*. Cambridge, 1955.

Inkeles, Alex, *Public Opinion in Soviet Russia*. Cambridge, 1950.

Kolarz, Walter, *Russia and Her Colonies*. New York, 1952.

Kursky, A., *The Planning of the National Economy of the U.S.S.R.* Moscow, 1949.

Lenin, V. I., *State and Revolution*. New York, 1935.

Lyashchenko, P. I., *History of the National Economy of Russia to the 1917 Revolution*. New York, 1949.

Marx, Karl, *Capital*. 3 vols. Chicago, 1908–09.

———, *The Civil War in France*. London, 1941.

———, *Critique of the Gotha Programme*. London, 1943.

Masaryk, Thomas G., *The Spirit of Russia*. 2 vols. London, 1919.

Mavor, James, *An Economic History of Russia*. 2 vols. London and Toronto, 1914.

Moore, Barrington, Jr., *Terror and Progress: the U.S.S.R.* Cambridge, 1955.

Radkey, Oliver H., *The Election to the Russian Constituent Assembly of 1917*. Cambridge, 1950.

Report of Court Proceedings in the Case of the Anti-Soviet "Bloc of Rights and Trotskyites." Moscow, 1938.

Report of Court Proceedings, the Case of the Trotskyite–Zinovievite Terrorist Centre, Heard before the Military Collegium of the Supreme Court of the USSR, August 19–24, 1936. Moscow, 1936.

Robinson, Geroid T., *Rural Russia under the Old Régime*. New York, 1949.

Schumpeter, Joseph, *Capitalism, Socialism and Democracy*. New York, 1942.

Schwartz, Harry, *Russia's Soviet Economy*. New York, 1950.

Seton-Watson, Hugh, *From Lenin to Malenkov*. New York, 1953.

Souvarine, Boris. *Staline: Aperçu historique du bolchévisme*. Paris, 1935.

Stalin, Joseph, *Foundations of Leninism*. New York, 1932.

———, *Problems of Leninism*. New York, 1934.

———, *Survey of Russian History*. 2nd ed. London, 1947.

Timasheff, Nicholas S., *The Great Retreat*. New York, 1946.

Towster, Julian, *Political Power in the USSR*. New York, 1948.

Treadgold, Donald W., *Lenin and His Rivals*. New York, 1955.

Trotsky, Leon, *The History of the Russian Revolution*. 3 vols. New York, 1932.

Vernadsky, George, *A History of Russia*. New York, 1944.

Webb, Sidney and Beatrice, *Soviet Communism: A New Civilisation?* 2 vols. London, 1936.

White, D. Fedotoff, *The Growth of the Red Army*. Princeton, 1944.

Wolfe, Bertram D., *Three Who Made a Revolution*. New York, 1948.

Wollenberg, Erich, *The Red Army*. London, 1938.

INDEX

THE AUTHORS

SAMUEL H. BEER, co-editor of *Patterns of Government* and author of *Part I: The Analysis of Political Systems*, has been the Chairman of the Department of Government of Harvard University since 1954. He holds an A.B. from the University of Michigan, a B.A. from Oxford University (where he attended Balliol College as a Rhodes Scholar), and a Ph.D. from Harvard University. Before joining the Harvard faculty in 1938, he worked for the Resettlement Administration as a writer, did some writing for the Democratic National Committee, was a reporter on the *New York Post* and, later, a researcher and writer on *Fortune*. He is the author of *The City of Reason*, of *Treasury Control*, of the section on Great Britain in *Modern Political Parties* (Sigmund Neumann, ed.), and of numerous articles in scholarly journals. He is an Associate Editor of the *American Political Science Review*.

ADAM B. ULAM, co-editor of *Patterns of Government* and author of *Part V: The Russian Political System*, received his B.A from Brown University and his Ph.D. from Harvard University. He began teaching at the University of Wisconsin and since 1947 has been on the faculty of Harvard University, where he was made an associate professor in 1953. He joined the Russian Research Center there in 1949 as a Research Associate and has since become a member of the Executive Committee and chairman of the Russian regional program. In 1953-54 he was a Research Associate of the Center for International Studies at the Massachusetts Institute of Technology and in 1956-57 he received the Rockefeller Fellowship in Political Theory. He was granted a Guggenheim Fellowship in 1956-57. He is the author of *Philosophical Foundations of English Socialism* and of *Titoism and the Cominform*. He has contributed to *Continuity and Change in Russian and Soviet Thought* (Ernest J. Simmons, ed.) and to *Constitutions and Constitutional Trends since World War II* (Arnold J. Zurcher, ed.). In addition, he has published many articles in professional journals.

HARRY H. ECKSTEIN, author of *Part II: The British Political System*, was granted his B.A., M.A., and Ph.D. by Harvard University, where he is now an Assistant Professor of Government and General Education. Two years of his graduate work were spent at the London School of Economics. He has contributed articles on British politics to academic journals and is the author of a book on the British Health Service, to be published shortly.

HERBERT J. SPIRO, author of *Part IV: The German Political System,* was graduated from Harvard College and holds a Ph.D. from Harvard University. He was in Europe in 1953-54 on a Sheldon Traveling Fellowship and a Fulbright Grant, doing research for his book on *The Politics of German Codetermination.* In 1955 he returned to Germany to gather material on some aspects of the Soviet occupation of East Germany. He has published many articles in American and foreign journals and has contributed to *Governing Postwar Germany* (E. H. Litchfield, ed.). He is currently completing a book on *Constitutional Government* to be published by Random House. He is an Assistant Professor of Government at Harvard University.

NICHOLAS WAHL, author of *Part III: The French Political System,* was awarded his bachelor's degree by the University of Wisconsin and his master's degree and doctorate by Harvard University, where he has been teaching since 1953. He has also studied at the University of Paris and the University of Geneva. He spent the academic year 1952-53 in France doing research on political parties as a Fellow of the Social Science Research Council. During the spring term of 1957 he was Visiting Lecturer in Political Science at the University of Saigon where he helped initiate a United States educational exchange program with Vietnam. He is currently in France on a grant from the Department of Government of Harvard University to complete research for a book on General de Gaulle and will spend a semester as Fulbright Lecturer at the University of Lyons.